Professional
Outlook 2000 Programming

Ken Slovak
Chris Burnham
Dwayne Gifford

Wrox Press Ltd. ®

Professional Outlook 2000 Programming

Published by Wrox Press Ltd, Arden House, 1102 Warwick Road, Acocks Green,
Birmingham, B27 9BH, UK
Printed in the USA
ISBN 1-861003-3-15

Trademark Acknowledgements

Wrox has endeavored to provide trademark information about all the companies and products mentioned in this book by the appropriate use of capitals. However, Wrox cannot guarantee the accuracy of this information.

Credits

Authors
Ken Slovak
Chris Burnham
Dwayne Gifford

Additional Material
Dennis Salguero
Nick Lewis
Karen Blomberg

Technical Editors
Louay Fatoohi
Dan Squier

Technical Reviewers
Vince Averello
Richard Bonneau
Matthew Borniker
Steve Danielson
Robin Dewson
Richard Harrison
Jessie Louise McLennan
Diane Poremsky
Helmut Watson

Managing Editor
Joanna Mason

Development Editor
Dominic Lowe

Project Manager
Tony Berry

Design/Layout
Tom Bartlett
Mark Burdett
William Fallon
Jonathan Jones
John McNulty

Cover
Chris Morris

Index
Nancy Humphreys
Martin Brooks
Alessandro Ansa

About the Authors

Ken Slovak is a consultant and developer specializing in Outlook, MS Office, VBA and VB programming. He is a Microsoft Outlook MVP (Most Valuable Professional), a designation conferred on him by Microsoft in recognition of his support work for the Outlook community. He has been a technical editor for a number of Outlook books, and is a technical reviewer for Exchange and Outlook magazine. Prior to becoming a consultant he was chief engineer of an industrial instrumentation manufacturing company for 14 years, and he has been working with computers for more than 20 years. He has designed integrated Outlook/Exchange/Office applications, numerous instrumentation systems, and has developed desktop applications and embedded system software in many computer languages, including Visual Basic, Access, C, Assembly languages, and FoxPro. He has written many technical and operating manuals, and has also developed technical and sales literature for numerous computerized systems. Ken currently resides in Central Florida.

Chris Burnham currently works as a Software Engineer for the Baan Company in Grand Rapids, MI. In addition to working for Baan, he also runs his own business, Burnham Development Solutions (*http://www.burnhamdev.com*) specializing in custom programming and database solutions using Microsoft technologies, such as Microsoft Access, Microsoft Outlook, Microsoft Visual Basic, and Microsoft Visual C++. He also serves as a Microsoft MVP (Most Valuable Professional) for Microsoft Outlook and is currently working toward a Masters of Computer Science at Grand Valley State University in Grand Rapids, MI.

Dwayne R. Gifford is a senior Engineer with remarkable database knowledge. His current position is Information Engineer Manager for Star Software Systems. He has been involved in designing, developing and architecting a number of very successful applications. His range of expertise includes MS Access, Visual Basic, MS SQL Server and Visual C++ to name a few. Computers have been a hobby that he has enjoyed since an early age. He began his professional career in Canada, working for Labatt Breweries; subsequently he consulted for Microsoft as a Lead Analyst for its Volume Licensing Operation. In addition, he is the author and co-author of several books on Microsoft Access, Visual Basic, Microsoft SQL Server and Microsoft Office. Throughout his career, he has delivered seminars, workshops and training courses to industry professionals worldwide.

Contributing Authors

Dennis Salguero currently runs his own consulting firm, Beridney Computer Services, which specializes in Microsoft Office, Visual Basic and Internet application development. A native of Los Angeles and a graduate of the George Washington University, he currently lives in the suburbs of Washington, DC. One of his career highlights includes teaching a computer class for agents of the Federal Bureau of Investigation. In his free time he enjoys reading and playing chess.

Nick Lewis is a senior partner with Inforward Technology in Chicago, IL. Providing project based consulting services, his primary areas of technical focus include VB, ASP, and Microsoft Office automation. He holds the Microsoft Certified Professional (MCP) certification, and spends evenings away from the computer earning an MBA at Northwestern University. He can be reached at nlewis@inforward.com.

Karen Blomberg is a senior software developer for a consumer goods company in Chicago, IL. Holding a MS in Computer Science from DePaul University, Karen's primary areas of focus include VB, MS Office automation, and SQL Server development.

Dedications & Acknowledgements

Ken Slovak

Dedication

This one is for the memory of my Dad, who would have loved to see me as an author; and as always, for my beloved Susie.

Acknowledgements

This is the fun part. My thanks go to my colleagues and friends in the Outlook and MVP communities. Their encouragement, helpfulness and friendship have made them a wonderful extended family. I especially want to thank the Outlook MVP's Sue Mosher, Randy Byrne, Vince Averello, Jessie Louise McClennan, Diane Poremsky, Russ Valentine, Jay Harlow, Hollis Paul, Chris Burnham, Milly Staples, Ben Schorr, Steve Moede, and Bill Rodgers for constantly teaching me new things about Outlook.

Sue Mosher, Randy Byrne and Siegfried Weber have contributed a lot to my knowledge of Outlook and CDO programming, and I owe them an extra debt of gratitude. I also want to thank Diane Poremsky for her work in reviewing this book, and in helping me whenever I need someone to test something.

Some of the many people at Microsoft I want to thank for their help, support and friendship are Abdias Ruiz, Ronna Pinkerton, and KC Lemson. Special thanks go to Sloan Crayton for his support of the Office MVP's. There are too many others to thank individually, but thanks to everyone else at Microsoft who has helped.

To all the people at Wrox Press who have helped develop this book, I am very thankful. Special thanks go to Dominic Lowe, Tony Berry, Louay Fatoohi, Daniel Squier, and to all the technical personnel, technical reviewers and others who have brought this book to life. Your professionalism has been an inspiration to me. It has been an enjoyable experience working with all of you, and I hope to do it again. Also, thanks go to my co-authors on this book. I hope that our efforts have produced a book that will teach you something about programming Outlook 2000.

Thanks and love go to the whole family; Mom and Ricky, Dad and Mom, Chris, Bobby and Donata, Sandie and Bruce. Finally, as always my gratitude goes to Susie, the love of my life and my best friend. And to Katie, my chief assistant and dog, who worked side by side with me through all the long hours writing this book.

Chris Burnham

Dedication

Dedicated to my late grandmothers Mary "Mom" Heltsley and Mabel Burnham. I miss them both more than words can express.

Acknowledgements

I'd like to thank first and foremost God for everything He's given me. Thanks to both of my mothers, Mary Burnham and Claudia Barrett, who I love very much, my father, Frank Burnham, and my aunt, Dovie Heltsley for moral support and always being there when I need them.

I also need to thank those that have taught me so much about programming - my colleagues at Baan: Santosh Menon, Tim Benner, Ajith Kumar, Tim Seeley and Paul Van Dyk; and my professors at Grand Valley State University: Dr. Yonglei Tao, Dr. Carl Erickson, and Dr. Greg Wolffe. Thanks to Sara for her always-cheerful disposition and outlook on life, and my friends Matt, Ray, Ken, Rick, and Dan for all the demented humor that keeps me laughing.

Finally, I'd be remiss if I didn't thank Ken Slovak and Sue Mosher for serving as mentors for Microsoft Outlook and Visual Basic, whether they realize it or not.

Dwayne Gifford

Dedication

This book is delightfully dedicated to a beautiful Angel:

There was never a question in my mind that you are the most beautiful angel I have ever met...

Mamita, you are such an adorable loving human being, an Angel out of this planet. You are always giving so much of yourself. You simply give the best that is in your spirit to others. Your love is manifested in so many dazzling, kind and peaceful ways. I realize how lucky we all are to have you in our lives. I often think of your remarkable kindness. Your spiritual charisma constantly brings happiness, harmony and serenity to others. You make miracles happen. Your intuition and integrity has transformed and touched the lives of so many people, including mine.

Whenever I reflect upon you, sweetly I realize why you are so important, so essential to our lives. My soul is filled with beautiful memories of your delightful presence in each of my days. Your loving and nurturing spiritual guidance, your extraordinary intuition lead me to find the most beautiful gift in my life "my adorable wife", how can I ever thank you for that, I guess I will always be in debt.

I thank God for blessing our beautiful family with an angel like you, whose mission in life is so inspiring, superior, and noble. Unquestionably you are the most beautiful kind human being I have ever meet, the one that thoughtfully and caringly keeps our beautiful family together. Your divine prayers keep us all safe.

You are that beautiful angel that I think about so much. You are that beautiful soul that is always in my thoughts and in my prayers, you are that beautiful person that holds the most distinctive place in my heart, a unique place that is there for just few very special people like you.

Acknowledgments

I would like to express great appreciation and recognition to many very special friends, relatives and business associates: Gonzalo Barrientos, Hernan Barrientos, Marco Peredo, William Rojas, Javier Revuelta, Hugo Barrientos, Juan Carlos Roman L., Celio Montaño, Bertha Anaya de Montaño, Tito Urquieta, Rosario Quiroga de Urquieta, Brian McDowell, Kim Spilker, Bruce Gillispie, Eric Borrows, Robert Atlinger, Lance Lindburg, Aaron Carta, Kwing Ng, Tom Buser, Jonathan Laughery, Mike Murphy, Steve Straiger, Larry Reed, Denise Gant and my Grandfather Stanley Boose. In particular I would like to thank Tom Eaves for his vast and unconditional support throughout my thrilling writing career.

Distinctive thanks and appreciation to Neil Charney.

My love to my parents, sister and brother; together we have shared wonderful times; unforgettable memories remain in my heart.

To my lovely sisters-in-law: Mirnita, Jimenita and Silvita, who are always in my heart.

To the beautiful memory of the greatest man I have ever met "Dr. Hernan Barrientos Urquieta", and to the memory of my adorable grandmother, Eva Elz.

To my precious children, for bringing peace, joy and gentle love to my heart, for making my days glow and shine even brighter. To our new addition of the family: Sammy. To my best friend "my wife", Sugarplum you are the reason my world is so beautiful, fabulous, and breathtaking.

Table of Contents

Chapter 2: Outlook 2000 Forms 37

Chapter 4: Office 2000 Automation   141

Chapter 5: Automating Outlook 2000 from Visual Basic   185

Chapter 6: Outlook 2000 Data Access   205

Chapter 7: COM Add-ins 247

Chapter 8: Retrieving External Data With Outlook 2000 291

Case Study : Asset Tracking Application 315

Case Study: Time and Billing Application **387**

Case Study: Customer Service Application **425**

Appendix A: Outlook 2000 Object Summary 455

Appendix B: CDO 1.21 Object Model Reference   575

Appendix C: Resources 607

Appendix D: Support and Errata 611

Index 619

Introduction

Microsoft Outlook has for several years been the most popular Windows-based e-mail and Personal Information Manager application in the world, managing e-mail, calendar information, contacts and tasks. Its latest incarnation, Outlook 2000, not only retains the power and flexibility of previous versions, but adds all the benefits of VBA programming, already familiar to generations of MS Office users. Using VBA, VB and VBScript, you can customize Outlook's functions to best serve your particular needs. You can also use its powerful programming environment to integrate Outlook with a whole host of other VBA-supporting applications.

This book is about the programming aspects of Outlook 2000 and how to use them with other applications. Among the areas we'll be covering are:

- ❑ The Outlook 2000 Object Model

- ❑ Programming Outlook using VB, VBA and VBScript

- ❑ Importing data into Outlook from Microsoft Word, Excel and Access

- ❑ Exporting data from Outlook into other VBA-supporting applications such as WinFax Pro

- ❑ CDO and Outlook

The discussion of Outlook built up through the book, and supported at every stage with sample code, is concluded with three case studies that demonstrate real-world application development. All of the source code for the examples and case studies in the book is provided online at the Wrox website, ready for you to use as is, or adapt to your own purposes.

In more detail, here's what you'll find in each chapter.

Chapter 1

This chapter gives a brief introduction to Visual Basic for Applications (VBA) and VBScript. Outlook 2000 is the first release of this Microsoft Office application to come with VBA, while VBScript is the underlying programming language of Outlook forms, and we discuss when to use each. This chapter also describes some of the limitations of the Outlook Object Model, and a comparison between the Outlook Object Model and the CDO (Collaboration Data Objects) Object Model is given. Finally, some of the differences between Outlook 2000's three installation modes are also discussed.

Chapter 2

This chapter studies in detail the unique development environment represented by Outlook forms. We look at Outlook's standard forms, how to create custom forms, and the various design options offered by VBA and VBScript. The last section deals with forms publishing and distribution, along with some of the issues involved in managing the forms cache and using the Forms Manager

Chapter 3

This chapter deals with Outlook projects and macros. We learn how to develop and distribute macros. The chapter discusses various Outlook events. New additions to Outlook, along with VBA, are Office UserForms. These are explained and you are shown how to work with them. Class modules in general (and the special class module `ThisOutlookSession`) are also discussed.

Chapter 4

This chapter concentrates on automation, which is a feature of **COM** (the Component Object Model). We learn how to make use of the automating of other Office applications from Outlook 2000. With illustratory examples, we look at ways of utilizing Word, Excel and Access and WinFax Pro as automation objects. Outlook data is passed to those applications and their features are used to handle it.

Chapter 5

In this chapter we use VB to automate Outlook . We see how to automate Outlook from standard EXE and ActiveX control projects. We then discuss how to respond to Outlook events from standard EXE and ActiveX DLL projects.

Chapter 6

In this chapter we delve further into the Outlook Object Model and CDO and see how they communicate with each other. We also learn how to retrieve data from the Windows Registry using Win32 API functions. We present a number of possible applications that cannot be implemented with pure Outlook, but can with the aid of CDO.

Chapter 7

This chapter covers COM add-ins, which are new to Office 2000 and offer significant opportunities for the integration of user-defined applications into the Outlook environment.

Chapter 8

In this chapter we learn how to retrieve external data with Outlook. We see how to get data into Outlook from four other object models/data access methods: Word, Excel, DAO and ADO.

Case Study: Asset Tracking Application

This case study profiles an Asset Tracking application, using Microsoft Outlook 2000, Microsoft SQL Server 6.5 (or later), and Microsoft Access 2000 to provide a robust mechanism for managing computer assets across a large, distributed organization.

Case Study: Time and Billing Application

This case study combines a number of Outlook capabilities: custom Outlook forms, A COM add-in, e-mail routing, interfacing output to a custom Word template, custom Outlook Bar group management, posting Office Document items to Outlook folders.

Case Study: Customer Service Application

This case study examines how you can make an application that extends far beyond your typical Outlook desktop programming, showing how the Collaboration Data Objects (CDO) components seen earlier in the book can be combined with other Microsoft technologies to create globally accessible applications complete with e-mail messaging.

Appendices

In the appendices you'll find a complete summary of the Outlook 2000 Object Model, covering all objects and collections and their methods and properties. You'll also find a similar reference for the CDO 1.21 Object Model.

Who is this book for?

This book is for professional developers who want to take full advantage of the Visual Basic for Application programming language that comes with Outlook 2000. If you are interested in developing sophisticated solutions that involve Outlook and other applications then this book is for you.

The basic requirement for this book is Outlook 2000. For examples in some of the chapters you will also need Microsoft Office 2000 Developer Edition and Visual Basic 6.0.

Conventions

We use font style and layout to distinguish the different types of information in the book; here are samples of these and an explanation of what each of them signifies:

❑ **Important words** are in a bold font.

❑ Words that appear onscreen, such as menu selections or options, appear in a similar font to that used onscreen (assuming a default Windows installation, that is), for instance the File | New menu. If you should select a submenu from a main menu, we use the vertical-bar (pipe) character to separate them (|).

❑ Code keywords appearing in the main body of text appear in `this font`, for instance we might say "A declaration of a module level Application variable in the Declarations section of a class module would look similar to the following declaration: `Dim WithEvents moOutlook As Outlook.Application`".

❑ Blocks of code to enter appear as follows:

```
' Create a session object we can log in to
    Dim s as MAPI.Session
    Set s = new MAPI.Session
```

❑ If we're altering existing bits of code, the new code appears as follows:

```
Dim n as Integer
    For n = 1 to 10
        Debug.Print n
        ' Now we actually do something
        DoSomething(n)
    Next
```

> **This sort of box is used to highlight important details that may crop up during discussion of something; anything in one of these boxes is vital information that you should be sure to take note of..**

Feedback

Please tell us what you think about this book – either return the reply card in the back of the book, or mail any comments to `feedback@wrox.com`.

All the source code files and project files for the examples are available for download at `http://www.wrox.com`.

We've made every effort to ensure that no typos or factual mistakes are in the book, but if one should have slipped through, you can find errata on our web site at `http://www.wrox.com` – if you find an error that isn't reported there, please let us know about it so we can update things appropriately.

Developing with Outlook 2000

With the advent of Visual Basic for Applications (VBA), the Microsoft Office suite was expanded from being the leading office software collection to serving as a development platform for completely customized applications. VBA allows developers to use the Office products and expand their use according to their own needs. Examples of this include customized databases with Access, mail merge programs with Word and expense reporting applications with Excel.

VBA is not just for use in Microsoft products. VBA has been licensed for use with WordPerfect and AutoCAD to name a few. There is also a VBA Software Development Kit (SDK) so that other developers can integrate the power of VBA into their programs, no matter the nature of the program or its native programming language.

As you might have guessed, VBA has its roots in Visual Basic (VB). The general concept behind VBA and VB remains the same: provide a standard programming interface that lets developers customize their programs with the individual application's object model. Each object model has its own objects, properties and methods. While VBA is not exactly like VB, it does let you use the knowledge you have of VB and use it in a host of other applications. If you have been programming for a while now, you will realize that this is quite a departure from the time that you had to know your own programming language, individual peripheral SDKs, and even some assembly code to get your program to display a few lines of text!

Microsoft initially launched VBA in its two most popular products, Word and Excel. It later introduced VBA into Access with Office 97. With Office 2000, Microsoft adds two more products with VBA functionality, FrontPage and Outlook.

If you already have experience working with Outlook, then you probably already know that VBA is not the first programming language for Outlook. Prior to packaging VBA with Access, developers used AccessScript. Likewise, Outlook developers have been using VBScript. You will notice that both of these languages share similarities since they are both rooted in VB. In fact, you could even argue that the main difference between VBA and VBScript in Outlook is the development environment. The VBA interface provides color-coding as well as the use of Microsoft's IntelliSense technology while the VBScript interface provides neither. Outlook 2000 provides both the VBA and VBScript development environment.

If you are familiar with AccessScript, then you might be wondering if there are plans to phase out VBScript, just like AccessScript. The long and short of it is: probably not. While AccessScript could only function from within the Access environment, VBScript has found another home on the Internet with developers of Active Server Pages (ASP). Judging by the legions of web sites that utilize the capabilities of ASP, VBScript is still worth exploring.

Since this book is written with developers in mind, you will find that the general programming concepts are not explained in detail. For example, instead of focusing on the use of For Loops, this book will focus on the syntax and proper usage of loops and then you can expand this into your own programs.

While this book will present code written in both the VBA and VBScript interface, the one you pick is up to you. Later on in the book you will also see some examples of how you can expand your usage of VBScript with an Internet messaging application.

Developing In Outlook

The most important thing to understand while developing with Outlook is when to use VBScript and when to use VBA.

The functionality and power of VBA are best understood when working with Outlook's global aspects, such as the look and feel of its environment and the Folders within it. Also, you should use VBA when creating functions that will be called from more than one element in your application.

If you are creating a completely new form, or customizing an existing one, it is best to use VBScript to handle the form events and control its other elements.

On the other hand, if you use a custom form that has to work with different folders (and possibly external data), you'll probably work with a combination of the two.

It should now be clear that there is no simple answer as to which language you should use. With some more programming experience in both VBScript and VBA environments, you will start to get a feel for the limitations of each language and begin to understand the complementary relationship that the two environments have within Outlook.

Using VBScript

Let's jump right in and start looking at how we can work with the VBScript environment. We must first choose a form to work with, so select Choose Form (in Tools | Forms) and select the form on which you wish to base the new one. The figure below illustrates this process:

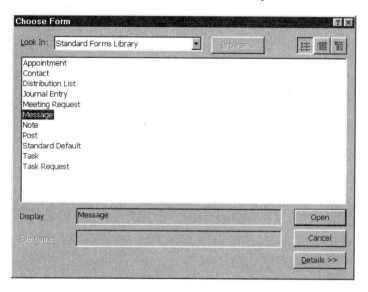

Once you have selected the appropriate form, open it and immediately enter design mode, by clicking on Tools | Forms | Design This Form. At this point, the form will look just like any other would in a VBA-enabled program:

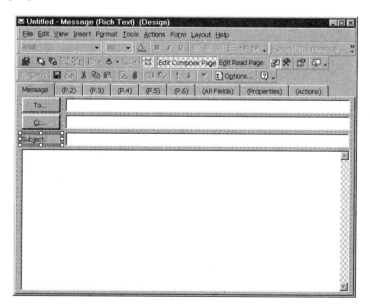

As you can see, Outlook forms have buttons and field boxes. This means that there are also some event procedures that can control these form elements. If you have programmed in VBA before, none of this so far should be new to you.

Next we will open the VBScript editor. This is where we begin to see the differences between the two environments. To open the editor, click Form | View Code on the form's menu bar (not the main menu bar). This will bring you to the Script Editor, shown below:

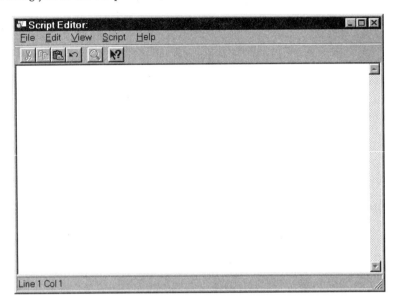

The first difference you should notice is that there are far fewer options on the toolbars and menu bars than in most VBA programming environments. In fact, many of the options available you will find in most other programs since these are just basic editing functions.

As mentioned earlier, the VBScript editor does not perform any automatic color-coding. In other programming languages, you must use tab-spacing diligently to separate your code. It is recommended that you follow this same method in the VBScript interface, to make your code easier to read. Also, try typing some code into this editor – you will soon realize that you no longer have the benefits of IntelliSense menus to help you with your coding. Needless to say, when using the VBScript environment it really pays to know your object model inside out.

Programming Forms

Being able to program your forms with some functionality is the first step to developing applications. In this section we will cover some main examples of programming event procedures with VBScript.

Working with Events

One way to add an event to the form is by clicking on Script | Event Handler, which will bring up the following dialog:

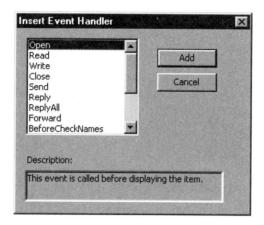

The dialog box lists all available events on the left, and a description of the highlighted event at the bottom. Notice that most of these events are based on program functions as opposed to user interaction. For example, an Access form would have On_Click and On_Current event procedures since these are functions that a user can trigger. In Outlook, the event procedures focus on program events that are carried out after the user has entered a command.

When you insert an event (by clicking on the Add button), you will find that the skeleton syntax is added for you in the scripting window. Note that there are several differences in events syntax between VBScript and VBA. The first is that all VBScript event procedures are written as functions (and not subs, as in VBA). This doesn't mean that you can't write sub functions for other utilities, just that the event procedures should always be functions.

The second difference is that these events have a Cancel parameter in VBA, but not VBScript – the question then arises: how do you stop an event from carrying on? The answer is simple but important – to cancel an event in VBScript, you must set its return value to False. The following examples illustrate these differences.

VBScript:

```
Function Item_Reply(ByVal Response)
   Item_Reply = False
End Function
```

VBA:

```
Private WithEvents m_omiMailItem As MailItem

Private Sub m_omiMailItem_Reply(ByVal Response As Object,_
                                Cancel As Boolean)
    Cancel = False
End Sub
```

The third difference between the two environments is that in order to work with events in VBA, you must declare a variable with the type of item that you are working with. You must also use the keyword `WithEvents` (for an example of syntax, refer to the example above). Declaring an object as a variable `WithEvents` makes it possible to attach code to any of that object's events.

Methods and Properties

There are two objects exposed for use in all VBScript, they are:

❏ **Item object:** exposes all of the methods and properties available in the Outlook object model.

❏ **Application object:** gives us access to all objects that are exposed by Outlook.

For a complete reference on these objects, refer to Appendix A.

To assist you in adding properties and methods to your code, you can use the Object Browser that is supplied with the Script Editor (accessed from View | Object Browser), also shown in the figure below. Note that these properties and methods are not exclusive to VBScript, but can also be called from VBA code.

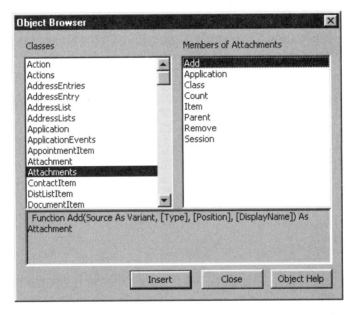

From this window we can locate the property or method that we want to use. Once it has been selected, clicking on Insert will place its name at the current cursor location.

A few things should be noted here. Firstly, the description window at the bottom of the browser displays the parameter list (for methods) or data type (for properties). Secondly, when you Insert a method, its parameters will not be carried with the insert – so you really need to know your objects! Finally, if you press the Object Help button, you will be taken directly to the appropriate help screen for whatever property or method is currently highlighted.

On a more aesthetic note, you will find that this object browser has far less information available to you than the object browser in VBA. While you could argue that the VBScript object browser is functional and quick, the VBA object browser provides links to code examples, and in some cases provides links to examples in the Microsoft Developers Network (MSDN) disc packs.

Error Handling

One of the problems you will run into with VBScript coding is its inability to catch errors being raised by the called methods. As a result, you must check for Return codes, or you will need to check the `Err` object. To make use of this, you will need to add the following line to your code:

```
On Error Resume Next
```

If you do not, then Outlook will handle all of your errors on its own, which means losing control of the program. (As a developer creating truly robust applications, this will be quite unacceptable to you.) This method of error handling is shown in the code below:

```
Function Item_Open()
  On Error Resume Next

  msgbox ActiveInspector.Name
  If Err.Number <> 0 then
    Msgbox "Err : " & Err.Number & vbcrlf & err.description
  End IF
End Function
```

As you can see in the example above, our code must check for an error each time we run it, in order to be notified of these errors. This code will generate an error, as we have not referenced the `Application` object or the `Item` object. Fortunately, it will generate an error in the format we want, and will provide information on the cause of that error. To make the code work we must add `Application` to the front of the `ActiveInspector` method.

Variables

VBScript has only one data type: Variant, so you don't need to mention it explicitly when you declare variables. To declare a variable called `lValue` we simply put:

```
Dim lValue
```

Once you assign a value to this variable it will take on one of thirteen subtypes:

Name	Description
Empty	Variable is uninitialized
Null	Variable has been set to Null
Boolean	`True` or `False`
Byte	Integer value between 0 and 255
Integer	Integer value between −32,768 and 32,767

Table Continued on Following Page

Name	Description
Currency	Value between –922,337,203,685,477.5808 and 922,337,203,685,477.5807
Long	Integer value between –2,147,483,648 and 2,147,483,647
Single	Single-precision floating-point number for negative numbers between –3.402823E38 and –1.401298E-45 and for positive numbers between 1.401298E-45 and 3.402823E38
Double	Double-precision floating-point number, for negative numbers between –1.79769313486232E308 and –4.94065645841247E-324 and for positive numbers between 4.94065645841247E-324 and 1.79769313486232E308
Date	Number that represents a Date between January 1, 100 and December 31, 9999
String	Variable length string up to 2 billion characters in length
Object	Object
Error	Error number

You can use the `VarType` function to check what subtype you are working with. Subtypes can be assigned to your variables when you are working with other applications or with Win32 API commands.

The fact that VBScript only accepts Variants becomes much more important when you start using VBScript in Active Server Pages and start to integrate ActiveX DLLs into your applications. Since VBScript can only handle Variants, all other code passing variables or parameters to your VBScript must also work with Variants, and no other variable types.

Using VBA

Now that we have looked briefly at VBScript, let's consider the VBA environment for working with the Outlook 2000 Object Model. If you have programmed in VBA before and have felt awkward working with VBScript so far, then this section is for you.

The Visual Basic Editor (VBE) gives us a common look and feel for developing VBA code. The code editor is the same one that you will find in all of the Office products and Visual Basic 5.0 and 6.0. The editor is where you will add code to describe events, properties, or methods. To get to the VBE we need to click on Tools | Macro | Visual Basic Editor (or use shortcut *Alt+F11*). Again, notice that you would use this same command to open the VBE in all VBA enabled programs.

> At this point it should be noted that the *Alt+F11* command is a popular key among VBA macro virus hackers. Many of these viruses disable the *Alt+F11* key to avoid the detection of their code in your programs or documents. Therefore, if you do not see the VBE appear after you press *Alt+F11*, you should scan your computer system for any possible viruses.

An example of the VBA editor is shown in the figure below:

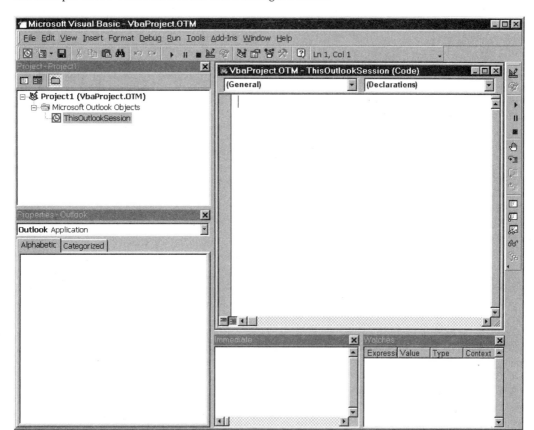

By default, the VBE presents us with four windows: Project, Properties, Immediate and Code. The Project window (shown top-left) gives us an overview of the Modules, User Forms, and Class Modules that make up the current project. In here you will see the `ThisOutlookSession` object, which is a Class Module. This is instantiated when Outlook is opened.

The big window (shown in the center) is the Code window. This is where we can add our own properties, methods, events, or variables. At the top of this window we have two combo boxes: the one on the left gives a list of all available objects, while the one on the right lists all Methods available on the selected object. If you change the selection in the Object Box then the Procedure box is automatically refreshed. This comes in very handy when you want to add an event procedure from the code window instead of adding it from the form.

The Properties window is shown to the bottom left, and this lists all available properties for the active object in the Project window. Shown along the bottom is the Immediate window, which is used to help in debugging our work. This window will become your best friend when you start debugging your VBA code.

There are two more windows we need to mention, first of which is the Locals window. Even though it is not shown by default, it is important to learn how to use it. You can open it by clicking on View | Locals Window.

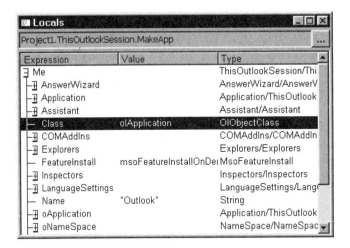

What you see in this window are all the variables that are presently in scope along with the value they presently have assigned to them. So instead of using the Immediate window to see what a Variable has in it, you can use the Locals window. This comes in handy when you are trying to locate type mismatches or calculation errors.

Equally important is the Watch window, in which you can name the variables in your code that you want to watch. Notice on the VBA toolbar, an icon with a pair of glasses on it – this is the Watch icon. To see the Watch window in action, first highlight the variable or expression that you want to watch. Then click on the Watch icon, and you will add this part of the code to the Watch window. When the code executes, all your watched variables will be shown in there. This also helps with finding errors in the code, and helps you to choose your variables' data types correctly.

Understand that this is a quick look at the VBE and in no way a complete study. The best way to learn about its ins and outs is through exploration and use. *For more information, see 'Outlook 2000 VBA Programmer's Reference', ISBN 1-861002-53-X, also from Wrox Press.*

Events

All VBA-enabled programs have a series of events that can trigger your VBA code. Understanding event procedures is a fundamental requirement for creating applications – at the same time they are very easy to understand. An event can occur before or after an action (such as a form load or the click of a button). We therefore have two types of events: those that occur after an action (triggered by the action) and those that occur before an action (triggered by other events).

One example of this would be when you create a new MailItem. By doing so you are adding an item, so the creation of the MailItem would trigger the `ItemAdd` event to be fired off, after you add the item to the form.

The way to tell the difference between events that occur before the action completes and those that occur after is to look for an argument called `Cancel`. An event with `Cancel` is a pre-action and the ones without are post-actions. This argument gives you a way to stop the action. If you set this argument to `True`, then the action will be cancelled.

An example is shown below:

```
Sub cmdOne_OnClick (Cancel as Boolean)
Msgbox "You have clicked on the first button"
End Sub
```

When calling this function, you have the option of setting the `Cancel` parameter to `False`, thus preventing the message box from appearing.

Creating Your Own Event

In order to create our own events we must be in a Class Module or a User Form.

```
Public Event FormMinimize(Cancel As Boolean)
```

Here, we create an event called `FormMinimize` with an argument of `Cancel`. As we shall see, this argument gives us the opportunity to stop the text from being changed.

RaiseEvent

Now that we have built the event, the next thing to do is to call or execute it. To do this we use the `RaiseEvent` method exposed to us by VBA.

```
RaiseEvent ChangeText(Cancel)
```

We pass an argument of `Cancel`, which will (by default) be passed in `ByRef`. This in turn allows us to update the `Cancel` argument and have the new value passed back to the user.

WithEvents

The last step in the event process involves being able to catch or handle the events as they are raised (by the Class Modules or User Forms). To do this, we use the `WithEvents` keyword when first declaring the variables for our function:

```
Private WithEvents varname As type
```

This variable will now appear in the Object box of the code window.

Keyword	Description
varname	Required. Name of the variable.
type	Required (in this case, as we cannot use WithEvents on a Variant data type). This will be the object from which we want to use the events.

There is more to variable declaration that we shall need to be aware of, but for now we need only concern ourselves with the `WithEvents` variable declaration.

```
Public WithEvents eText As text
Private Sub eText_ChangeText(Cancel As Boolean)
End Sub
```

In the example above, we declare a new variable called `eText` of type `text`. Next, notice below the declaration of `eText` that we have created the `ChangeText` event.

Error Trapping

If you are paying close attention, you will notice we have renamed the error-handling section in VBA as error *trapping*. That's because VBA handles errors in a fundamentally different way to VBScript. Remember that in VBScript you had to actively test for errors and then display them. In VBA you can actually set up commands to passively detect errors and have a standard format for displaying these errors. An example of the required code is shown below:

```
Function hello()

On Error GoTo Hello_Err
MsgBox "Hello World!", vbInformation, "Status"

Exit Function

Hello_Err:
MsgBox "Error: " & Err.Number & vbCrLf & "Description: " & Err.Description,
vbCritical, "Error"

End Function
```

In this snippet of code, there are a few important lines. First, let's look at the top of the code:

```
On Error GoTo Hello_Err
```

We first ask the code to passively check for errors. When one is detected, we direct it to a subcommand called `Hello_Err`.

```
Exit Function
```

We then tell the code to exit the function. Notice that this command is above the error display code. Without this, the function would still attempt to display the error message box. In other words, if the code executes without any errors, it will exit the function at this point. If an error did occur, then it would display the message box with the error and then end the function.

If you have worked with other object-oriented programming languages (like C++) you can see that the error-trapping code presented above can act as a quasi-object. In VB and VBA, this is also referred to as a wrapper. This snippet can be used to encase (or wrap) all of your functions and it allows you to have a consistent policy for displaying error messages. Obviously you can modify it to suit your taste, but setting up a wrapper with this error-trapping code can save you a lot of time in the long run.

Procedures

VBA supports three different types of procedure: Sub, Function, and Properties. We must also be aware of the Events statement, which is made up of a Sub or Function. When a user does something (or asks an object to do something), an event will occur and the corresponding event will be called.

Subs and Functions

Subs and Functions work the same way, except in one respect. They are both made up of a series of VBA statements terminated by an ending statement. However, a Function can return a value from its code, whereas a Sub cannot. This is not to say that you cannot return values back from Subs – you can do this by using arguments. However, for an argument to return a value it must be of type ByRef.

The other statement to be aware of here is Exit Sub/Function, which can be placed within Sub or Function procedures, allowing us to terminate execution at any point.

Properties

There are three types of procedures that let us to interact with each property available in VBA: Let, Get, and Set. Get allows us to retrieve the property value, Let allows us to update it (we use Let whenever the property does not reference an object data type), and Set allows us to update the value whenever the Property *does* reference an object data type.

```
Public Property Get FirstName() As String
   FirstName = m_sFirstName
End Property
```

In the example above, we retrieve the FirstName stored in m_sFirstName, a module level string variable.

```
Public Property Let FirstName(Value As String)
   m_sFirstName = Value
End Property
```

We have now updated m_sFirstName with the FirstName sent in as Value.

```
Public Property Get Application() As Application
   Set Application = m_oApplication
End Property

Public Property Set Application(Value As Application)
   Set m_oApplication = Value
End Property
```

Notice here the difference when we work with an object. We must now use the Set property to update the internal variable and the keyword Set in the Get property.

Properties therefore gives us a way to protect internal variables which other calling applications will need to update or retrieve. In the world of object-oriented programming, this is known as polymorphism.

```
Public Property Get IsDirty() As Boolean
   IsDirty = m_bIsDirty
End Property

Friend Property Let IsDirty(Value As Boolean)
   m_bIsDirty = True
End Property

Public Property Let FirstName(Value As String)
   If Value <> m_sFirstName Then
     m_sFirstName = Value
     IsDirty = True
   End If
End Property
```

In the example above we are setting a `Friend` property called `IsDirty`. This property is therefore only available to internal members of the object. If someone changes `FirstName`, we update `IsDirty` to tell us that the property has been changed.

Data Types

There are a total of 13 data types exposed to us in VBA:

Name	Range	Description
Byte	0 to 255	8-Bit unsigned integer value
Boolean	0 or 1	16-Bit number that will store True (1) or False (0)
Integer	−32,768 to 32,767	16-Bit signed integer value
Long	-2,147,483,648 to 2,147,483,647	32-Bit signed integer value
Single	±1.401298E-45 to ±3.402823E38	32-Bit signed floating-point real value
Double	-4.94065645841247E-324 to -1.79769313486231E308	64-Bit floating-point real value
	4.94065645841247E-324 to 1.79769313486232E308	
Currency	-922,337,203,685,477.5808 to 922,337,203,685,477.5807	64-Bit value having 15 integers to the left of the decimal point and 4 to the right

Name	Range	Description
Decimal	With 0 decimal places: 0 to ±79,228,162,514,264,337,593,543,950,335	96-Bit signed integer (scaled by power of 10) This gives us the ability to have as many as 28 digits to the right of the decimal point, or as few as 0
	With 28 decimal places: ±0.0000000000000000000000000001 to ±7.9228162514264337593543950335	You cannot declare a variable as type Decimal. See section on Variants (later in the chapter) for how to get a decimal value
String (variable-length)	0 to ~2 billion characters	10 bytes + 8-bits per char
String (fixed-length)	1 to ~65,400 characters	8-bits per char
Date	1 January 100 to 31 December 9999 0:00:00 to 23:59:59	64-Bit Floating-point number
Object	N/A	Holds an object's address
Variant	(various)	Holds any of the above types (except fixed-length strings)

One very important point to remember is that these types all have different memory requirements, so choosing the correct data type for each variable is critical to creating efficient applications. For example, while you can use the Variant type for any data type, it is very memory intensive. If you were to create a program that used only Variants, you would have a very slow and cumbersome application. Therefore, make sure that you accurately choose the data types you need throughout your code.

Arguments

Most procedures need external information to be passed to them in order to do any useful work – we can do this through use of arguments. To pass more than one argument to a procedure you must place a comma between each one:

```
Private Function NameCase(FirstName As String, ByVal LastName As String, Optional MiddleName)
```

In this example, we pass variables `FirstName`, `LastName` and `MiddleName` to the function `NameCase`.

Keyword	Description
`ByVal`	Indicates that the value is passed to the procedure and not the internal memory address. The benefit of this is that you can change the value in the procedure without affecting the variable in the calling routine.
`ByRef`	Indicates that you are passing in the address of the variable and not just the value.
`Optional`	Indicates that you do not need to supply this value when calling the procedure. Note that all optional parameters must be the last parameters in the argument list. You cannot use this in conjunction with `ParamArray`.
`ParamArray`	Allows you to pass in any number of arguments. This must be the last element in the argument list, and is of type `Variant`.

> If you do not supply an indicator to the Argument, **ByRef** is assumed.

Using VBA to test VBScript

Since VBScript does not offer us the IntelliSense menus or the color-coding that you might be accustomed to, we can make use of the VBA environment to develop the code for our forms. The trick is to use the `Application` and `Item` objects, since these are both exposed to us in VBScript. The first thing to do in VBA is create a new Class Module to work in. Note that we do not have an Item object in VBA as we do in the VBScript. We must therefore declare the `Item` object first, so as to make use of it as we would in the VBScript environment

```
Dim WithEvents Item As MailItem
```

We will assume for this example that we are working with a message form that is used to send e-mail. Note that this variable is defined as a `MailItem` type, since this form can use `MailItem` type variables. This means that the object will inherit all the `MailItem` properties and methods. We also use the keyword `WithEvents`, making sure we expose the same events that are exposed to us by the form we are building:

```
Function Item_Reply(ByVal Response)

  if Item.attachments.count <> 0 then
    iReply = Msgbox("Would you like to add the attachments?", vbyesno)

    if iReply = vbyes then
      for each iaAttachment in item.attachments
        stempname = "C:\Temp\" & iaAttachment.filename
        iaAttachment.SaveAsFile stempname
```

```
            Set iaNewAttachment = Response.Attachments.Add(stempname, _
                iaAttachment.Type, iaAttachment.Position, _
                iaAttachment.DisplayName)
            response.send
        next
      end if
   end if
End Function
```

The code above will work in VBScript, but notice that it isn't as easy to read as a VB or VBA code segment would be. If we now place the same code into the VBE, you can see how much easier it is to read and work with:

```
Private Sub Item_Reply(ByVal Response As Object, Cancel As Boolean)
   Dim iReply        As Integer
   Dim iaAttachments    As Attachments
   Dim iaAttachment  As Attachment
   Dim sTempName        As String
   Dim iaNewAttachment As Attachment

   If Item.Attachments.Count <> 0 Then
      iReply = MsgBox("Would you like to add the attachments?", vbYesNo)

      If iReply = vbYes Then
        For Each iaAttachment In Item.Attachments
          sTempName = "C:\Temp\" & iaAttachment.FileName
          iaAttachment.SaveAsFile sTempName
          Set iaNewAttachment = Response.Attachments.Add(sTempName, _
              iaAttachment.Type, iaAttachment.Position, _
              iaAttachment.DisplayName)
          Response.Send
        Next
      End If
   End If

End Sub
```

You will notice that this is effectively the same code as the VBScript, except that we are working with a Sub (not a Function) and that we now have a Cancel parameter. When you do this work, you must be sure not to forget that fact, or you will find that you need to do some cleaning up in the VBScript code. The other thing to note is that all our variables have been declared out to the objects or data types. This gives us early binding here, and then gives us the Auto List Member functionality (that VBA offers and VBScript does not).

```
Function Item_Reply(ByVal Response)

   Dim iReply
   Dim iaAttachments
   Dim iaAttachment
   Dim sTempName
   Dim iaNewAttachment
```

```
    If Item.Attachments.Count <> 0 Then
      iReply = MsgBox("Would you like to add the attachments?", vbYesNo)

    If iReply = vbYes Then
      For Each iaAttachment In Item.Attachments
        sTempName = "C:\Temp\" & iaAttachment.FileName
        iaAttachment.SaveAsFile sTempName
        Set iaNewAttachment = Response.Attachments.Add(sTempName, _
            iaAttachment.Type, iaAttachment.Position, _
            iaAttachment.DisplayName)
        Response.Send
      Next
    End If
  End If
End Function
```

Look at this function and you will notice that it is the same as the first, except that it is much easier to read. Furthermore, to place this code into the VBScript editor for the Form, I simply had to cut and paste the meat of the Sub from the VBA code. Once I had pasted it into the VBScript editor, I removed the variable declaration data types, removed the Cancel argument and the Method being set to True instead.

The Outlook Object Model

Now that we know the different programming environments available to us, we shift our attention to the object model available in Outlook. Remember that knowledge of this model is very important when programming Outlook with VBScript.

Understanding the Outlook 2000 Object Model is on fact essential for unlocking the application's true potential. Anyone with a basic knowledge of Visual Basic can create simple macros in Outlook 2000, but if you know the object model well, you can create very powerful macros, forms and add-ins.

> *Our focus in this chapter is on collections and objects only – for a detailed look at the methods, properties and events associated with each, please refer to the 'Outlook 2000 VBA Programmer's Reference' (ISBN 1-861002-53-X), also available from Wrox Press Ltd.*

A complete diagram of the Outlook 2000 Object Model appears below. There then follows an overview of each of the individual collections and objects.

> *A complete list of available objects can be found in Appendix A. All code samples that follow were written in Outlook Visual Basic for Applications (VBA), unless otherwise noted.*

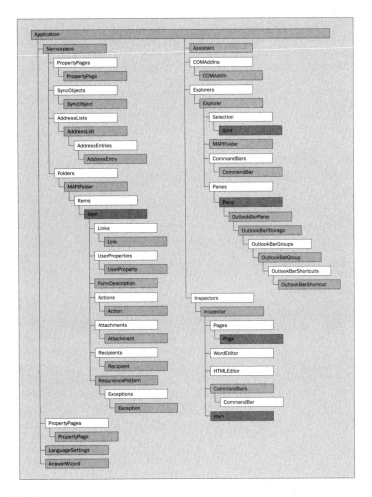

The Application Object

This is the object from which all other Outlook objects are derived and represents the entire Outlook application as a whole. The `Application` object serves two key purposes:

- ❏ It allows access to other objects in the Object Model
- ❏ It allows access to the interface objects – Explorers and Inspectors

Instantiating an instance of the `Application` object is only required when programming in VBA. It will also automatically start the Outlook application if it is not already running.

```
Dim oApplication As Outlook.Application
Dim oNameSpace As NameSpace

Set oApplication = CreateObject("Outlook.Application")
Set oNameSpace = oApplication.GetNameSpace("MAPI")
```

This snippet creates your `Application` and `NameSpace` variable, which you will be using throughout your functions. These lines of code will be used quite frequently in your programming solutions involving Outlook VBA, so you may want to copy them to your "code archive", or use the Code Librarian application, included with Microsoft Office 2000 Developer Edition.

> *Note that Outlook forms do not require you to declare the* `Application` *Object using NameSpace, as this is intrinsic to forms. The nuances of Outlook forms will be explored in depth in chapter 2.*

The first aspect of the Outlook 2000 Object Model we shall discuss is the difference between the User and Programming Interfaces. Simply put, the User Interface (UI) consists of two objects:

❑ The **Explorers** collection and object

❑ The **Inspectors** collection and object

The Programming Interface consists of just one object:

❑ The **NameSpace** object

Let's look at these collections and objects in more detail, with examples of each.

Explorers

Explorers are the forms that display folders such as Outlook's Folder View. They are equivalent to the Windows Explorer. Explorers are used primarily to navigate our folder structures, locate specific items and open them. The Explorers collection is a group of Explorer objects. The basic code to establish the current Explorer object in VBA is:

```
Dim oApplication As Outlook.Application
Dim oeExplorer As Explorer

Set oApplication = CreateObject("Outlook.Application")
Set oeExplorer = oApplication.ActiveExplorer
```

If there is not a current Explorer (for instance we have some code that is navigating the folder structure), this code returns a null value.

The Explorer object allows access to four collections and objects:

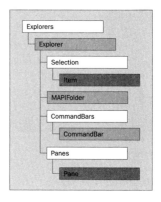

- ❏ **Selection** collection: contains all the currently selected items.

- ❏ **MAPIFolder** object: a folder in the current profile (for example, Inbox, Calendar, Tasks).

- ❏ **CommandBars** collection: contains **CommandBar** objects – each of these contains menus and toolbars objects for a given Explorer.

- ❏ **Panes** collection: contains a single **Pane** object – a Pane is one of the windows used to navigate the folder tree. In Outlook 2000, only one Pane is represented in the Object Model (and is thus accessible through coding), which is the Outlook Bar.

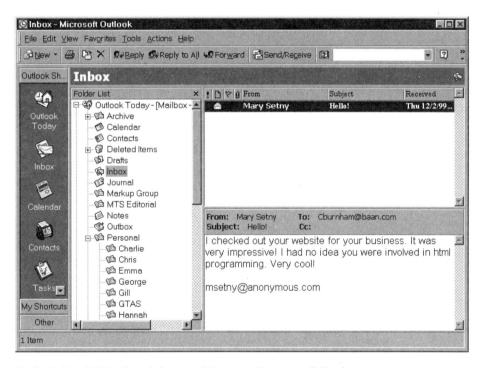

The Outlook Bar, Folder List, Inbox, and Preview Pane are all Explorers

Inspectors

Inspectors are the windows that display the contents of the *items* within a folder. The Task, Appointment, and Message forms are all examples of Inspectors. The basic code to establish the current `Inspector` object is:

```
Dim oApplication As Outlook.Application
Dim oInspector As Inspector

Set oApplication = CreateObject("Outlook.Application")
Set oInspector = oApplication.ActiveInspector
```

As with the code to determine the current Explorer, in the case that there is no current Inspector, a `Null` value is returned. A variation on this code is to use the `GetInspector` property instead of the `ActiveInspector` method. For this example, first insert this code into the VBA editor:

```
Sub ExampleOfGetInspector()
   Dim oApplication As New Outlook.Application
   Dim Item As ContactItem

   Set oApplication = CreateObject("Outlook.Application")
   Set Item = oApplication.ActiveInspector.CurrentItem
   Set txtBox1 = Item.GetInspector.ModifiedFormPages("P.3").Controls("TextBox1")
   Set currentForm = Item.GetInspector.ModifiedFormPages("P.3")
   txtBox1.Text = "Value of " & currentForm.ActiveControl.Name & _
            " is " & currentForm.ActiveControl.Value
End Sub
```

Next, open a standard Outlook form in design mode (**Tools I Forms I Design A Form**) and use the Control Toolbox to drop a TextBox control onto **P.3** of the form. The default name should be `TextBox1`, which is how we refer to it in this example. *If this is all new to you, don't worry. Form design is covered in more detail in the next chapter.*

Run the form you've just modified, and enter something simple, such as `Millions` in the textbox. From the **Tools** menu, select **Macro I Macros**, and the Macros dialog will open. Double-click on `ExampleOfGetInspector` and the code will execute, adding control-specific text to the `TextBox` contents.

The Inspector object allows access to five collections and objects:

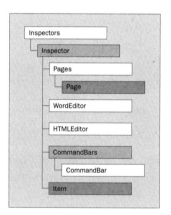

❑ **WordEditor** object: returns the Word Document Object Model if the `IsWordMail` method is `True`. Additional information on the WordMail object can be found in the *Word 2000 VBA Programmer's Reference*, ISBN 1-861002-55-6, also by Wrox Press.

❑ **HTMLEditor** object: returns the HTML Document Object Model if the `EditorType` property is `True`.

❑ **Pages** collection: contains **Page** objects – each Inspector item has several customizable pages on it. Open a form in Design mode and you can see five blank pages, marked **P.2** through **P.6**.

❏ **CommandBars** collection: contains `CommandBar` objects – these contain the menus and toolbars objects for a given Inspector.

❏ **Item** object: the basic elements that hold information, including TaskItem, MailItem, JournalItem.

The Message form is an example of an Inspector:

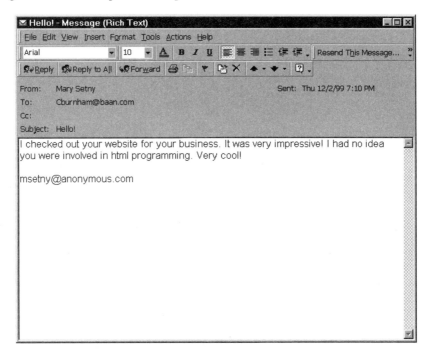

NameSpace

So far, we've presented an overview of the things you *see* while working in Outlook. Let's take a look 'under the hood' and check out the `NameSpace` object. This allows us to access the different data stores we've set up under individual Profiles in Outlook. Presently, there are only two ways to instantiate the `NameSpace` object in Outlook. The first is by using the `GetNameSpace` method:

```
Dim oApplication As Outlook.Application
Dim oNameSpace As NameSpace

Set oApplication = CreateObject("Outlook.Application")
Set oNameSpace = oApplication.GetNameSpace("MAPI")
```

The second way to retrieve the `NameSpace` is to use the `Session` property of any item that supports it:

```
Dim oApplication As Outlook.Application
Dim oItem As TaskItem
Dim oNameSpace As NameSpace

Set oApplication = CreateObject("Outlook.Application")
Set oItem = oApplication.CreateItem(olTaskItem)
Set oNameSpace = oItem.Session
```

The only NameSpace currently available to Outlook is MAPI (Messaging Application Programming Interface), which is why you often hear Outlook referred to as a MAPI-client. MAPI is an industry-standard API that allows Windows-based applications to interact with many different messaging services via a single, convenient interface. The exposed interface can be programmed using a development tool that allows you to create Component Object Model (COM) objects, such as Visual Basic and Visual C++.

The NameSpace object allows access to 4 collections and objects:

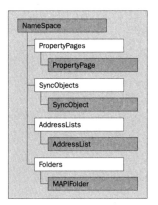

- ❑ **PropertyPages** collection: contains `PropertyPage` objects – these allow the addition of custom pages to Tools | Options, or to the Properties tag of an Outlook folder

- ❑ **SyncObjects** collection: contains `SyncObject` objects – settings that make a user's Profile available offline

- ❑ **AddressLists** collection: contains `AddressList` objects – each object holds a list of e-mail addresses (for example, a Personal Address Book)

- ❑ **Folders** collection: contains `Folder` objects – each Folder holds a group of specific items, such as Tasks or Appointments

Differences Between Outlook and CDO Object Models

When you program in Outlook 2000, you aren't limited to using just the Outlook Object Model. A very useful tool available to developers using Outlook 2000 is CDO (Collaboration Data Objects) – its Object Model is shown in the diagram below:

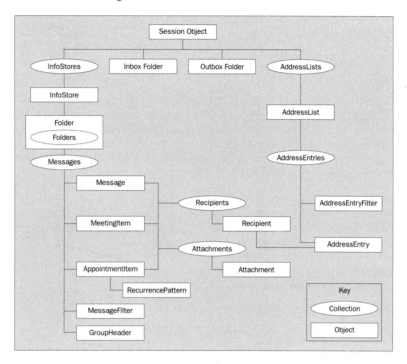

CDO is particularly useful for retrieving the sender's e-mail address on an incoming message, and allows greater manipulation of the Address Book than is possible with Outlook's own Object Model. Once familiarized with the inner workings of the CDO Object Model, you will find that it becomes quite easy to intermingle its use with that of the Outlook Object Model.

CDO functions primarily from the server side of things. In fact, it's a critical component in Microsoft Exchange and is used for Outlook Web Access (OWA) and the Exchange Server Scripting Agent, which manages server-side scripting. You can also use this server-side scripting for Active Server Pages for use on the Internet. However, bear in mind that, although CDO functions primarily from the server, it can still be a very useful tool when working with Outlook as a standalone application.

CDO lacks a direct link to the UI, so an Outlook folder or item must be passed to CDO by either its EntryID (item) or StoreID (folder). CDO also allows us to get at storage holds other than MAPI, such as Public Folders on Exchange.

We will look at CDO in more detail in Chapter 6 – additional information can also be found at `http://www.cdolive.com/` *and on MSDN.*

Differences Between Programming for Corporate Workgroup and Internet Mail Only

When Outlook 98 was released, Microsoft created a bit of confusion amongst users by introducing three separate and distinct modes from which to choose when installing:

- ❑ Internet Mail Only (IMO)
- ❑ Corporate or Workgroup (CW)
- ❑ No E-mail

A common misunderstanding about Outlook is that CW and IMO installations install the same basic program. The truth is that CW installs a program that is quite different from IMO. IMO offers some features many would like to see in the CW mode, such as progress bars for downloading mail, and a Send Using: option that allows the user to specify which mail account is used for outgoing mail (this would allow the use of different recipient addresses). The third, and infrequently used installation, No e-mail is based on the IMO mode, with e-mail features removed.

Most developers use CW mode, largely because this mode must be installed in order to interface with an Exchange Server. Much of Microsoft's documentation relating to programming Outlook was based on working in the CW mode, but there are some subtle differences between the two modes that developers need to keep in mind when creating custom solutions:

- ❑ IMO does not support multiple Profiles, except through multiple logins to Windows (if you share your PC with someone)
- ❑ IMO is not configurable to work with Microsoft Exchange
- ❑ IMO does not offer the Personal Address Book (PAB)
- ❑ Performance of IMO tends to become more sluggish as the Contacts folder grows in size
- ❑ IMO does not include the Manage Forms function, one of the biggest drawbacks for developers of custom forms
- ❑ IMO does not support Offline Folder Synchronization

The plain truth of the matter is, since the introduction of VBA in Outlook 2000, developers haven't had an opportunity to uncover all the potential differences that exist between these modes. Nevertheless, in the short time Outlook 2000 has been commercially available, a few specific programmatic limitations have been discovered:

- ❑ Adding a mail recipient during the `Application_ItemSend` event results in a **No Transport Provider** error in CW mode, but works fine in IMO. (The easiest workaround for the CW problem is to incorporate the `ResolveAll` method into the code – it will then work fine.)
- ❑ Setting a named argument as `True` in the `Session.AddressBook` method results in a runtime error when using IMO.
- ❑ IMO does not support the CDO method `DeliverNow`.

Most of the CDO objects, properties and methods will work with both of Outlook's modes, which are discussed in the next section. The `DeliverNow` method is a notable exception, only working in CW mode. This, and other mode-dependent limitations, will be discussed more specifically where appropriate.

What's Not Exposed in the Object Model

Most of Outlook's object model focuses on folders and the items contained within them. While this allows developers to do a great deal with custom solutions, it also limits the ability to program much of the user interface. The first thing many developers notice missing from Outlook is a macro recorder (which both Word and Excel offer). Outlook does not expose the entirety of its object model, so a macro recorder is not possible.

We've come up with a list of programming limitations of the Outlook Object Model, based on the most common needs of developers. Workarounds are indicated where applicable.

❑ You cannot access the drop-down calendar feature. You must therefore either use a third-party ActiveX controller or build the functionality yourself in Visual Basic or Visual C++.

❑ You cannot programmatically access portions of the Import/Export Wizard, making it difficult to create a 'backup utility' to easily move files between work and home.

❑ Most of the settings in Tools | Options cannot be set programmatically.

❑ There are only five available folder properties that *can* be modified programmatically: Application, Class, Count, Parent, and Session. Unfortunately, the rest are not accessible.

❑ Programmers commonly modify the text in an application's Status Bar to indicate when a file operation is in progress – Outlook does not expose it.

❑ Immediate sending is possible using CDO's `DeliverNow` method – as mentioned before, this can only be used in CW mode.

❑ Settings for an existing View can be modified using the `Explorer.CurrentView` property, but you cannot alter or create a new view programmatically.

❑ Digital signatures and encryption are not supported.

❑ When tracking for Deleted Items, there is no way to identify the originating folder.

❑ Information as to which mode is installed can be obtained through Registry key MailSupport. Later in this book, we see how to use a custom class that encapsulates the Win32 API Registry functions and how we can use it to detect which mode is installed.

❑ Runtime errors can arise from incorrect use of the `SyncObject` object.

❑ The `RemoteItem` object includes some methods and properties exposed by all Outlook items – however, these are not applicable to this object, as it is merely a representation of an item on the server. Keep in mind that the `RemoteItem` object is only intended to supply the user with enough information to make a decision whether or not to download the entire item.

Summary

This chapter has shown you some of the differences between VBScript and VBA, and has also given you an introduction to the Outlook and CDO object models. As you delve more and more into Outlook programming, you will perhaps find ways to extend your skills in each programming environment, and come to appreciate why it uses two environments. On the other hand, you may also want to use VBScript on a minimal basis, building your skills in VBA in order to carry them over to other Office products. Some developers 'cheat', creating all their functions in VBA and then just calling them from VBScript code.

In the end, the choice is really up to you. After all, you are the one that's going to spend long hours writing and debugging the code. You should choose the development environment that best suits your style and your needs for each particular project.

Think of this chapter as a foundation from which you can begin to customize your applications and come to benefit from the power and versatility of Outlook programming.

2

Outlook 2000 Forms

This chapter introduces a unique development environment – **Outlook forms**. At first glance, you might easily mistake an Outlook form for just another Visual Basic form, but you would be mistaken if you did. Outlook forms are exclusive to Outlook and cannot be directly used in other applications, or substituted for a more familiar form, such as those in Visual Basic. Once you understand the basic design environment, you'll discover great potential for creating custom programming solutions that utilize this unique tool.

The chapter will cover many of the basic elements of Outlook Forms development, including fields, controls, and VBScript. We will also take a look at the construction of two different forms, applying some of these concepts.

What Are Custom Forms and Why Use Them?

An expression you will see a great deal in this chapter is **custom forms**. A custom form in Outlook is any Outlook form that has been modified in some way. The modification can be the addition of a control or field, inserting VBScript code to extend a form's functionality, or simply changing the form's layout.

We mentioned that Outlook forms are different from the more familiar forms of Visual Basic – if this is the case, why use them? Quite simply, Outlook forms are much more portable than Visual Basic forms. You don't need to compile them, as any code behind a form executes at run-time. They are fully 32-bit, making them quite fast and generally very small (usually about 1KB in total).

Outlook forms allow you to expand an already rich information tool and customize it to your specific needs. A custom form can be used as a timesheet, expense report, or vacation request. You can use custom forms to easily distribute uniform data to others, without the need to use a fully-fledged database application like Microsoft Access. Outlook forms are most versatile and powerful when used for an enterprise-type solution using Microsoft Exchange, but they can also be used to better organize your personal data on a standalone machine.

Standard Form Types (a.k.a. Message Classes)

Let's get started by looking at the individual form types and discussing the types of data each form represents. Note that while Outlook has other forms that cannot be altered (such as the Distribution List form and the Net Folder Invitation form), we only examine those forms that are modifiable.

We provide this information to give you a broad overview of the modifiable forms, because all custom forms in Outlook are derived from the **standard** forms, or **message classes**, as Microsoft has dubbed them. The terms 'form types' and 'message class' are synonymous, but for the sake of clarity, we will use 'message class' throughout the rest of the chapter. Another important thing to note is the way in which Microsoft designates each form's internal name. All forms carry a prefix of IPM, which stands for **Interpersonal Message Class**. At the end of this section, we provide a convenient table detailing each form type, its IPM message class, whether page 1 is modifiable, and the default folder for each form type.

To follow our review of each of the standard forms, click the File menu, select New and then choose the appropriate form from the resulting submenu – Appointment, Meeting Request, etc. Once the form opens, enter design mode with Tools | Forms | Design This Form.

Message Form

The **Message** form is probably the most frequently used form in Outlook – after all, it's the form that's used to send e-mail.

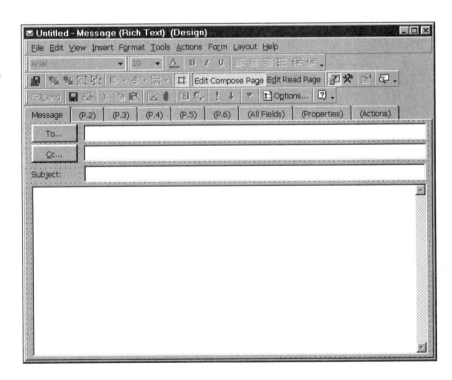

Appointment Form

The **Appointment** form is the default form for your Calendar. It allows you to schedule appointments by: Subject, Location, Start Time, and End Time. A nice addition to the Appointment form in Outlook 2000 is the Contacts field at the bottom of the form. This allows you to easily link an Appointment to a Contact.

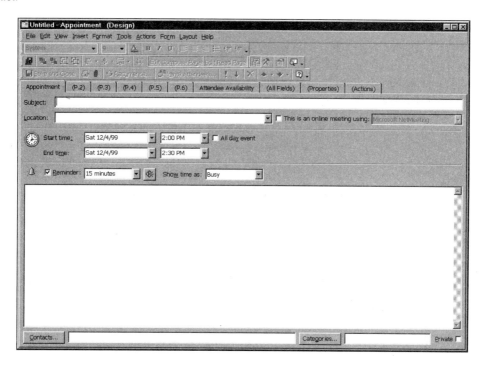

Contact Form

This is the default form of your Contacts folder. It allows you to store a great deal of information about a person or organization, such as name, address, phone numbers, e-mail addresses, Web page address, birthday, and anniversary. Outlook 2000 adds the Activities tab to the default Contact form. This allows you to see at a glance any Tasks, Appointments, E-mails, Journal Entries, and Notes relating to a specific Contact. Later in this chapter, we'll go over how to make sure your custom forms show up in the Contact Activities.

> *On the screenshot of the Contact form in design mode, notice the* Send plain text only: *checkbox. If you've installed Outlook in Corporate-Workgroup mode, you will probably not have seen this control before – it is an option that only appears in Internet Mail Only mode.*

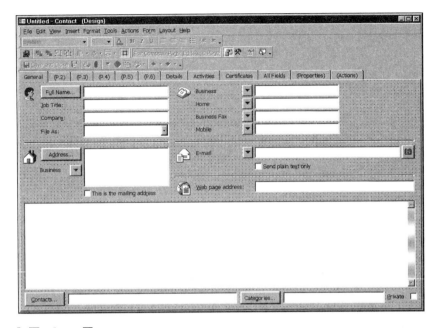

Journal Entry Form

Think of the **Journal Entry** as what ties Outlook to the rest of Office. If you've turned on the Journal to track documents from other Microsoft Office applications (such as Word, Excel, or Access), it will record an entry each time you open items within them. Journal Entries are also useful for tracking phone calls and other items that don't fit logically into the other form types. However, it is worth noting that this feature tends to slow down Outlook's performance – at certain times it keeps Outlook open as a background process (when tracking various types of Office documents for example), even when you think it is closed. Keep this in mind if you decide to customize a Journal form. Many users elect to turn off the Journal feature, particularly if they are not running a high-performance machine.

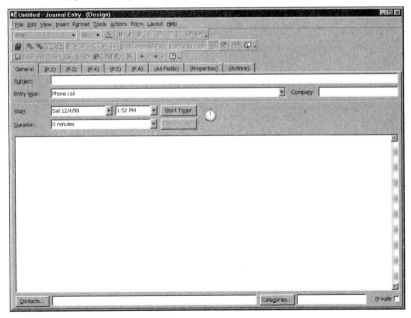

Meeting Request Form

A **Meeting Request** is sent as a mail message to others. Upon acceptance, it becomes an Appointment.

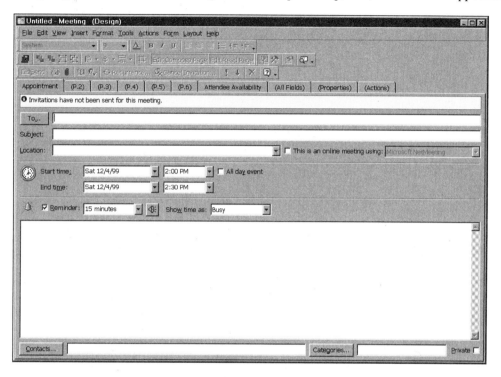

Post Form

This is a very useful, versatile form, even without custom modifications. It can be used in any Outlook folder for virtually any reason (posting general comments, for example). Its primary purpose is to facilitate communication and collaboration with others in the Public Folders environment of an Exchange Server.

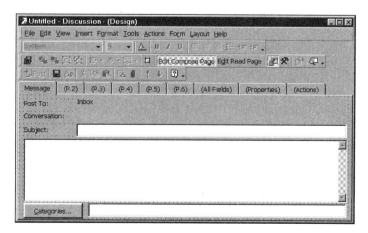

Task Form

The **Task form** functions as your 'to do' list in Outlook. Depending on how detailed an approach you want to take with managing your Tasks, you can:

- ❑ Use pop-up Reminders to help you remember important Tasks

- ❑ Set Start and Due Dates

- ❑ Track task progress through to completion

Outlook 2000 introduces the easy linking of Tasks directly to a Contact, using the Contacts field at the bottom of the form (the same functionality that was added to the Appointments form).

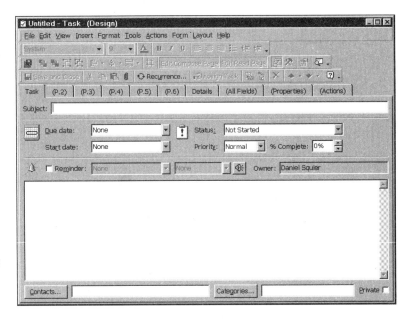

Task Request Form

The **Task Request form** is similar to the Meeting Request form – it is initially sent as a mail item, but upon acceptance, it becomes a Task.

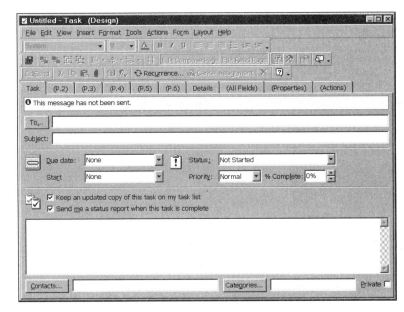

Office Document Form

Outlook 2000 offers a nifty variation on the forms concept by allowing you to embed a Microsoft Word, Excel or PowerPoint document directly into an Outlook form. Since Outlook is essentially placing a 'wrapper' around another Office application, you lose the ability to add custom tabs to the form. However, you can now take advantage of some of the specific functionality provided by Word, Excel or PowerPoint.

Another advantage of using an Office Document form is that you can use VBA in conjunction with the form. Using a standard Outlook form limits your programming capabilities to VBScript. Here's how you can create an Office Document form:

❑   Click New on Outlook's File menu, and then click Office Document.

❑   Double-click the type of document you want to use.

Select Post the document in this folder (to open the document as a post item) or Send the document to someone (to open the document as a mail item).

You can design and layout any type of form that meets your needs, using the features of the particular program used to create the document. For example, you could use Excel to create a simple custom form in which users enter data into an array of cells – think how useful this might be when requesting budget figures from another department. A summary of the standard form types, along with some of their key attributes is shown below:

Form Name	Message Class	Can PG.1 be modified?	Default Folder
Appointment	`IPM.Appointment`	No	Calendar
Contact	`IPM.Contact`	Yes	Contacts
Journal Entry	`IPM.Activity`	No	Journal
Meeting Request	`IPM.Schedule.Meeting.Request`	No	Calendar
Message	`IPM.Note`	Yes	Inbox, Outbox, Sent Items
Post	`IPM.POST`	Yes	Can be used in any folder
Task	`IPM.Task`	No	Tasks
Task Request	`IPM.TaskRequest`	No	Tasks

The Design Environment

In order to implement your Outlook forms design, you must first access a form in Design Mode. You do this by clicking the Tools, and selecting Forms. A submenu will open with two options: Choose Form and Design a Form. Select Design a Form and the relevant dialog will now open, allowing you to select the specific form type. Notice that the dropdown box labeled Look In: contains a listing of available libraries. Let's take a look at some of these libraries and explain a bit about them.

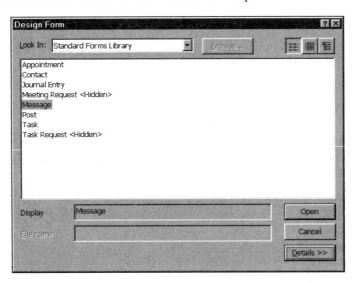

Outlook Forms Libraries

Outlook offers several forms libraries for use in designing, publishing and managing forms:

❑ **Standard Forms Library** – This is installed with every installation of Outlook. It includes all the basic form types, such as Tasks, Appointments, Posts, and Messages. The Standard Forms Library can reside on your local PC, or your Exchange Server mailbox.

❑ **Personal Forms Library** – This serves as a private library for custom forms not associated with any particular folder. The Personal Forms Library is user-specific, so each user may have different forms published in his or her Personal Forms Library.

❑ **Folder Forms Library** – Actually a series of libraries associated with specific folders. You don't view it in one central location (as with the Standard Forms Library and Personal Forms Library), but with each individual folder, such as Inbox, Tasks, or Appointments. Using this library makes the published form quickly accessible from the Actions menu as New <custom form name>.

The Personal Forms and Folder Forms Libraries are part of the user's default message store – either the Exchange mailbox, if connected to Exchange Server, or the **Personal Information Store** file (**PST**), if running Outlook as a standalone application. If you are connected to an Exchange Server, you may have access to two additional libraries:

❑ **Organizational Forms Library** – Most companies will use this as a central repository for all company forms. The Exchange Administrator controls access to this library, so you might need specific permissions in order to publish to it.

❑ **Web Forms Library** – A series of folders that resides on the company NT server running Microsoft Internet Information Server (IIS). Web Forms are generally custom Outlook forms that have been converted to HTML for use with **Outlook Web Access** (**OWA**). As with the Organizational Forms Library, the Exchange Administrator controls access to this library as well.

It is a good idea to adopt a publishing policy for all your forms development. For instance, if you are developing a form for your organization, you don't want it to be available to other users until it is complete. The Personal Forms Library is a perfect place to keep such 'in progress' forms. Upon completing the form, publish it to the Organizational Forms Library. Two suggestions on whatever policy you use:

❑ Back-up your files on a regular basis.

❑ Be sure to delete the incomplete copies from your Personal Forms Library – storing a form in more than one library can become very confusing if you do not have a definitive publishing policy in place.

Keep this information in mind when we look at publishing and distributing forms, and using the Outlook Forms Manager, later in the chapter.

Using the Field Chooser

When you open a form in design mode, on a page that can be modified, the Field Chooser appears automatically. For instance, if you've opened the Task form in design mode, selecting the first page (Task), you will not see the Field Chooser, but click on the tab for P.2 and it appears. Simply put, the Field Chooser allows you to create **User-Defined Fields** (hereby referred to as **UDF**s) and easily drag-and-drop fields onto Outlook forms. To create a new UDF, click the New button at the bottom of the Field Chooser:

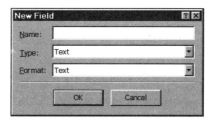

The New Field dialog will appear, allowing you to name the UDF, determine its type (Text, Formula, Number, etc.), and the formats available for that particular type.

Click OK, and your field will appear in the Field Chooser dropdown under User-defined fields in folder. If the field was created for a Message type form (e-mail), it defaults to User-defined fields in Inbox, regardless of the folder in which it is created.

Using Standard Controls

If you've used VBA, VB, or Visual C++, the Control Toolbox should look familiar to you – it's essentially the same tool you'll have seen in these other Microsoft development environments:

By simply dragging-and-dropping, you can place controls from the ToolBox onto the form you are designing. Outlook will automatically assign names to any controls you add to a form. For instance, the first new TextBox control added will be named `TextBox1`. You can of course rename these controls, and we advise using a standard naming scheme, to better describe your controls and what they do. One possible scheme is to denote the control type by inserting a 3-digit prefix in front of the name – for example, `txtTextbox1` for TextBox1.

To find other controls you can use, right-click anywhere inside the Toolbox and select Custom Controls. This will present you with the Additional Controls dialog, which displays all available ActiveX controls. You can add additional controls to the Control Toolbox by simply dragging them from Additional Controls and dropping them onto the Toolbox dialog.

Setting Control Properties

Control Properties are set using a different standard dialog than that which you might be used to seeing in other development environments. The Outlook dialog offers an intuitive interface for the most common properties of a control. Since you will probably be using this dialog a great deal in your forms development, let's go over some of its more interesting parts. (We won't cover properties like Font, Color and Position, as these are largely self-explanatory.)

Display Tab: The first tab you see when opening the Properties dialog. The properties here are self-explanatory and behave consistently with their usage in other development environments.

Value Tab: This becomes very important when we discuss binding. Controls are bound to UDFs by using the **Choose Field** command button. Clicking this button presents us with a dropdown menu of the same categories available in the Field Chooser, and allows you to select a specific field to bind to this particular control. If you haven't yet created a UDF to bind to the control, click the **New** button and it will present you with the New Field dialog. The **Initial Value** section of the tab comes into play if you need to set the value of the control or field to a specific value. You have two basic options for setting the initial value – calculate when composing a new form of this type, or calculate the formula automatically. Clicking the **Edit** button opens the formula dialog.

Validation Tab: Used for validating the field or control data before leaving the field or closing the form.

The specific properties available will vary with the selection of control or field type. Note that the screenshots included with this chapter are all taken from a TextBox field.

Outlook also offers the Advanced Properties dialog, which is the same as used in other Microsoft development environments. Properties such as Picture (which displays a picture in the background of the field or control) can only be set from the Advanced Properties dialog. Another useful property is ControlTipText. Any text entered into this property will appear when the user moves the cursor over the field.

Binding a Control to a Field

We've mentioned binding a few times in the sections above. If you've done any object-oriented programming, the chances are you've encountered it before. Binding is the process of matching the function calls written by the programmer to the actual code that implements the function when it runs (in this case, it refers to the Outlook application). Binding effectively pulls together the pieces of a program, either at compile time (early binding), or at run-time (late binding).

> *Microsoft has published a Knowledge Base article on the subject, Q245115, "INFO: Using Early Binding and Late Binding in Automation." You can find this at:*
>
> *http://support.microsoft.com/support/kb/articles/q245/1/15.asp*

Binding plays a part in Outlook forms development when you need to set or retrieve the underlying properties of a control or form. Note that Outlook forms can only use late binding, as all data types in VBScript are declared Variant, and all type checking is done at run-time, since Outlook forms are not compiled.

As shown above (in 'Setting Control Properties'), a control and a UDF are bound by using the Choose Field command button on the Value tab of the Properties dialog. After binding a control and field, any changes made to the control are also reflected in the field. All the values of a control are automatically reset to their default values every time a form is closed. If you need to set these values and have them 'stick', binding the control to a field allows the value to be established for the field – with a bit of coding, you can have the control 'remember' its previous value by retrieving the value of the field. These properties are set at the control level through the use of VBScript.

If you aren't familiar with binding, we'll cover it in more depth when we build the Task form with Subtasks. A thorough understanding of the concept and how it is used in Outlook forms is critical, since working without it can lead to frustrating design problems.

Controls vs. UDFs

UDFs automatically bind a control to the corresponding field. Controls do not automatically bind data – if you need to bind a control, you must do it manually by associating the control to a specific field. A simple rule of thumb to apply when deciding whether to use a control or UDF is "do I need to store a value?" If you do, use a UDF, otherwise use a control.

Adding Custom Controls

The Outlook forms environment can be expanded to include controls you make in Visual C++ or Visual Basic, as well as ActiveX controls. Once available, these custom controls can be used much like the standard toolbox controls, although additional coding is usually required in order to properly bind the control properties. How each control is bound varies widely, depending on the particular control and what you want to do with it.

> **It is very important to ensure that any custom controls you use in your forms are available to all computers that use your form. Outlook does not automatically distribute these controls as part of the form. If the control is not installed on a user's machine and the form is open, the user may see run-time errors, or portions of the form involving the control may be rendered inoperable.**

Creating Custom Actions

By default, Outlook offers four basic actions, exclusively for purposes of e-mailing:

- ❑ Reply
- ❑ Reply to All
- ❑ Forward
- ❑ Reply to Folder

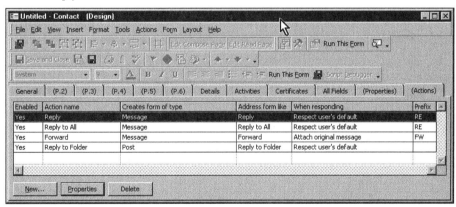

In many situations, these four are all you need – but what if you want more? Outlook allows you to create custom actions that behave according to your own specifications.

Timesheet — an Illustration of Custom Actions

One example of when a custom action might be appropriate is a timesheet form. After an employee completes his or her timesheet, it usually gets forwarded to one or more people for review. Processing the form could be greatly enhanced if we had two new actions – "approve" and "decline". For this illustration, we are going to use a pre-constructed custom form. We won't walk through the process of form creation, but will focus on how we might create the custom actions associated with the form.

When the employee creates his or her timesheet for the week, it is sent to the immediate supervisor with a standard subject line "Time Sheet for week ended <date>":

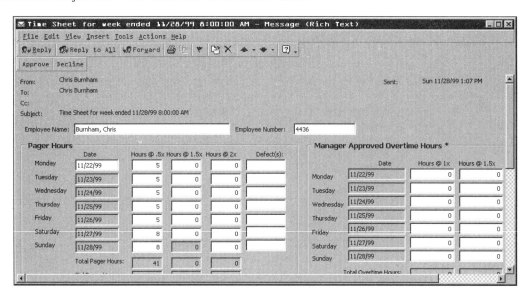

When the manager receives the timesheet, two options are given along the top of the form – Approve and Decline. Let's assume the manager chooses Approve, and follow the form through the rest of the process. As soon as the Approve button is clicked, the form is immediately replaced by another – the timesheet approval form:

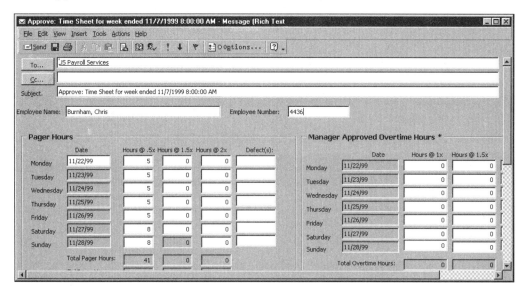

The manager clicks Send and the form is submitted to the appropriate department for processing. How did we replace the timesheet form with the timesheet approval form? The answer is simple: we created a custom action.

Implementing Custom Actions — Form Action Properties

Creating a custom action is quite simple – select the Actions tab of the form in design mode, and click the button marked New (at the bottom of the form). This brings up the Form Action Properties dialog, which has several important properties:

This action creates a form of the following type: — This allows you to specify an existing form, which will be instantiated when this action is executed. Note that this other form must also be installed on the user's machine (or in the Organizational Forms Library) in order for the action to open it.

Characteristics of the new form: — This features two drop-down fields.

When responding: – provides you with seven available actions:

❑ Do not include original message

❑ Attach original message

❑ Included original message text

❑ Include and indent original message text

❑ Prefix each line of the original message

❑ Attach link to original message

❑ Respect user's defaults

Address form like a: – provides five options for how to address the message:

❑ Reply

❑ Reply to All

❑ Forward

❑ Reply to Folder

❑ Response

Subject prefix: – This lets you define the default text appearing in the subject line upon executing this custom action. In our example, this is how we put **Approve:** in front of the subject on the original form.

When you create a custom action, Voting Buttons are automatically created for this form. Note though, that they will only be displayed on the received item, and you will not see them during form design. The button names correspond to the Action Name, so use of a descriptive action name becomes doubly important.

On viewing a received form, you can access the custom action from either the **Actions** menu or a toolbar icon, depending on the options selected in the **Show Action On:** checkbox when you created the action.

Implementing Custom Actions — VBScript

Custom actions can also be defined and used via VBScript. Creating a new object in code is easy, requiring just two lines:

```
Set myItem = Application.CreateItem(0)
Set myAction = myItem.Actions.Add
```

If we run this code, it will create a new instance of the Message form (`CreateItem(0)` is the `OlItemType` constant for `olMailItem`). The Outlook Help files list all the properties available for use in conjunction with the Actions method (under the subject 'Action Object').

Let's refer back to our timesheet example to illustrate how a custom action might be used in VBScript. The function `Item_CustomAction` passes two arguments:

❑ `CustomAction` – the action being executed by the user

❑ `NewItem` – the new item created by execution of the custom action

The `CustomAction` argument is passed as the `Case` test expression, while the `NewItem` argument is acted upon within the individual `Case` statements.

```
Function Item_CustomAction(ByVal CustomAction, ByVal NewItem)

  '********************************************************************************
  '**
  '** Subroutines run when manager Approves or Declines Time Sheet submission
  '** to 'US Payroll Services'
  '** **NOTE** this does NOT execute opening the second form for approval or
  '** decline. That function is executed in the Outlook form under "Actions"
  '**
  '********************************************************************************

  Select Case CustomAction.Name
    Case "Approve"
      If UserProperties.Find("MgrSign").Value = "" Then
        MsgBox "You must type in your name before Approval."
        Item_CustomAction = False
        Exit Function
      End If
```

```
        NewItem.Display
        Item.Close(1)
    Case "Decline"
        NewItem.Display
        Item.Close(1)
  End Select

End Function.
```

Notice how in both cases above (**Approve** or **Decline**) we execute `NewItem.Display` to open the form corresponding to the specific custom action, while closing the original form. Since we have already defined the new item as part of the custom action, `NewItem.Display` automatically displays the appropriate form, so we do not need to invoke the form explicitly.

Using VBScript to Enhance Functionality

VBScript, a subset of Visual Basic and Visual Basic for Applications (VBA), is the underlying programming language of Outlook forms. While VBScript is not as rich in features as VB or VBA, it is very lightweight and allows you to create forms that do not require compiling. In fact, all code in Outlook forms is run-time only. How do you enter VBScript to an Outlook form? By using the Outlook Script Editor, a bare-bones text editor. To open the Outlook Script Editor, open a form in design mode. Select **Form | View Code** and the editor will open.

The first time you use the script editor, you will realize the limitations. It offers no right-click context menus, and editing capabilities are limited to **Undo, Go To, Cut, Copy, Paste, Select All, Find, Find Next**, and **Replace**. Line numbers and column positions are displayed along the bottom of the window. Many developers choose to write the code using a fully-fledged script editor, or better yet, the Visual Basic editor. Using the Visual Basic Editor lends itself quite nicely to creating VBScript code, particularly since you can take advantage of the IntelliSense features integrated to VBA. Note that it may require you do some simple conversions in order that the code be compliant with VBScript. We'll point out some of the differences between VBA and VBScript as we continue reviewing how VBScript can be used to enhance functionality in Outlook forms.

Declarations and Variables

Using a variable in VBScript requires that either you explicitly declare the variable, or allow VBScript to implicitly do it for you. For example:

```
Option Explicit
'* declare my global variables
Dim taskObject
Dim  myStuff
Dim  yourStuff
```

Notice that we have not specified a data type (`int`, `bool`, `long`, `double`, etc.) for each of the above variables, as we would in C or C++. This is because VBScript only uses Variant data types – a generic data type. If you did not explicitly declare the above variables, VBScript would automatically do so at run-time. The danger of letting VBScript handle variable declarations is that if you incorrectly spell a variable name, VBScript will assume that it's a new variable and give it a default value, without raising an error. By requiring explicit declaration of variables through the `Option Explicit` statement, incorrectly spelled variables will at least return a run-time error. VBScript has several important restrictions relating to variable names:

❑   They must begin with an alphabetic character

❑   They cannot contain any embedded periods (periods in VBScript serve as separators between objects, methods, and properties)

❑   They cannot exceed 255 characters

❑   They must be unique in the scope in which they are declared

Scope and lifetime of VBScript variables is the same as with other programming languages – being either global or local. Global variables are generally declared at the top of the script, outside any specific function. This allows a global variable to be accessed (and modified) by any function within the script. The lifetime of a global variable is the lifetime of the script. In contrast, a local variable will be defined within a specific function and can then only be used in that function. The lifetime of a local variable is only as long as that of the procedure in which it is defined. Most programmers favor using local variables over global variables, as the variable's use of memory begins and ends with the function call. VBScript has two notable limitations relating to variable lifetimes, which may make this practice difficult for particularly large scripts:

❑   You are limited to 127 local variables (aggregate, not per procedure)

❑   You are limited to 127 global variables

If you stick to using just local variables, and you've reached your limit of 127, you must either use global variables or restructure your code into smaller procedures, each with their own local variables. Variables can be shared between procedures by passing parameters. If your code has grown this large, you will probably notice slow performance with your form, and may need to rethink the design.

Objects

This section doesn't cover every single object in the Outlook Object Model, but provides an overview of how objects are used in Outlook forms and VBScript. See Appendix A for more details. The Outlook Help files also offer a complete list of objects and their related methods, as does the Object Browser, accessible through the Outlook Script Editor. To use the Object Browser, open the Script Editor and select Script | Object Browser.

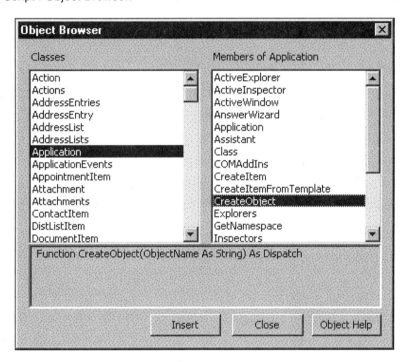

This is a very nice feature of the Outlook Script Editor, which allows you to quickly find objects and their related members (or methods, as they are generally referred to in VB). Note how the required usage of `Application.CreateObject` is displayed inside the gray text box in the lower portion of the Object Browser. Clicking Insert will only insert the text "CreateObject" into the Script Editor, and not the function prototype displayed in the gray text box. Clicking the button Object Help will open the Microsoft Visual Basic Help files and page to the selected method.

Working with objects is similar to working with variables, but with one important distinction – you use the Set statement with objects. Set has a very specific function in VBScript, allowing you to assign an object instance to an object variable declared by a Dim statement. For example:

```
Dim objApp As Object
Set objApp = CreateObject("Excel.Application")
```

To illustrate the need for the Set statement, run this code without using the Set statement. Outlook should return a run-time error, Object does not support this property or method, referencing a specific property or method and line number.

Sequence of Events

Events in VBScript occur in a specific sequence, depending on what action is taking place.

Action taken by user	Events
Opening an item	Open
An item is sent	Send, Write, Close
An item is posted	Write, Close
An item is saved	Write
An item is closed	Close
An item is opened	Read, Open
User replies to the sender of an item	Reply
User replies to the sender and all recipients of an item	ReplyAll
Newly-created item is passed to the procedure after Forward is clicked	Forward
One of an item's standard properties is changed	PropertyChange
One of an item's custom properties is changed	CustomPropertyChange
A user-defined action occurs	CustomAction
An attachment is added	AttachmentAdd
An attachment is opened for reading	AttachmentRead
Before an attachment is saved	BeforeAttachmentSaved
Before Outlook resolves recipient names	BeforeCheckNames

Unfortunately, this is the complete list of events available for VBScript. Noticeably absent from the list is a 'Delete' event.

Here's an example of how an event can be used in VBScript. Assume we have a custom form that includes a modified forms page named Updates. This page is used to record important announcements relating to the specific item. We want to make sure that everyone reads these announcements when they open the form. This can be accomplished using the following code:

```
Function Item_Open()
   Item.GetInspector.SetCurrentFormPage "Updates"
   Item_Open = True
End Function
```

In addition to the previously discussed Object Browser, the Outlook Script Editor also features the Event Handler (Script | Event Handler):

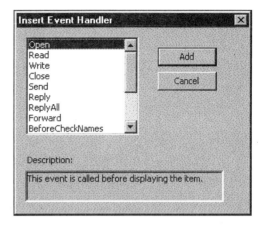

The Event Handler lets you quickly set up function prototypes for all the available events in VBScript. Double-clicking on **Open** in the selected window (or clicking the **Add** button) inserts the function prototype at the cursor:

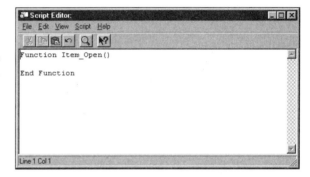

The Event Handler can be a bit of time saver when setting up your code in the Script Editor.

Error Handling

Error handling in Outlook forms is much the same as in any other development environment you may have used, though slightly more limited. Outlook offers a default error handler for any run-time errors that occur, but most developers choose to override these, as they are not intended for end users to see. Overriding the default error handler simply requires you to insert code along the lines of:

```
If Err.Number <> 0
    ' Tell Outlook what to do
    Exit Sub
End If
```

Errors in Outlook forms return a non-zero value, so (using standard logic) testing the error number against zero allows you to capture the error as simply (and quickly) as possible. Most error-handling code involves using a descriptive message explaining what went wrong in the process. An important difference between VBScript and VBA is that VBScript requires you to do all of the error handling within a specific procedure. VBA allows you to setup a generic error-handling function and lets you refer to it from any other function within the same script.

Make sure at least to include error-handling routines with all third-party and ActiveX controls you use.

Debugging Your VBScript

The debugger just might be the single most useful tool in any programmer's arsenal. Outlook uses the Microsoft Development Environment debugger, which is the same debugger used with Microsoft's Web Scripting, so it might appear familiar to you. It can be downloaded from Microsoft's Web site at:
http://www.microsoft.com/workshoop/prog/scriptie/scriptie.htm

There are two basic ways to invoke the debugger in VBScript: allow a run-time error to occur, or set a Stop statement in your code. Let's assume a run-time error has just occurred, when trying to test a new form we're developing. You should see a debug dialog appear that looks like this:

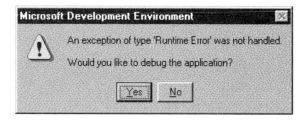

Since we want to open the debugger, click Yes. The Microsoft Development Environment will start to open, but you should receive another dialog prompting you with: Would you like to open a project for debugging? We don't, so click No. The debugger should open, displaying the code from the form that returned the error. The line where the debugger returned the error will be highlighted in yellow, and a yellow arrow will appear along the left-hand side of the debugger IDE.

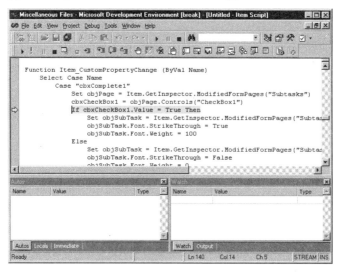

In the example above, note that the error actually occurred on the line above where the debugger stopped. Correct the code by inserting the Set statement at the beginning of line 139, closing the debugger and running the form again. There are times when you know a particular section of your code isn't quite right, but you aren't sure why. Setting a Stop statement at a specific point will invoke the debugger, allowing you to step through your code one line at a time (Debug I Step Into) and identify any errors.

Special Considerations Using Message and Post Forms

An interesting twist, and something that unexpectedly vexes many new Outlook forms developers – separate Read and Compose pages available on the Message and Post forms. The Read page of a message or Post form is the page that is going to be viewed by whoever is reading your mail or post item, while the Compose page is the page that *you* see when creating the mail or post item.

The option to separate the Read and Compose pages introduces an additional layer of power and flexibility to your forms development, but it can also bring an extra layer of complexity if you aren't careful. If you inadvertently separate the two pages, you might develop your entire form assuming that any modifications will appear on both pages, while you have in fact only made them on one. In many instances, the two pages will be identical, in which case you should make sure that Forms I Separate Read Layout is *not* selected before you start developing your form.

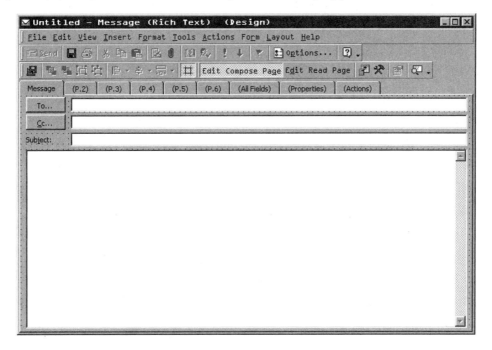

Creating a Custom Form

We've covered the basic concepts that allow you to create some very useful functionality in Outlook forms. Let's look at implementing some of these concepts with actual forms. We'll start with a relatively simple example – adding new fields to the Contact form, to store usernames for various Instant Message services.

Adding Instant Message Service Fields to the Contact Form

Our first custom form will be fairly straightforward and simple, but will illustrate how adding a few simple fields to your standard forms can expand the form's usefulness. It seems like everyone today uses at least one instant messenger service, be it America Online's AIM, ICQ, or MSN Messenger Service. It would be very useful if we could store someone's alias, or 'buddy name', with that person's Contact information. Since the aforementioned three services are the most commonly used, we'll add a new field for each of them on the standard Contact form.

Step 1: We begin by opening the standard Contact form in design mode (select Tools I Forms I Design a Form, then choose Contact in the Standard Forms Library).

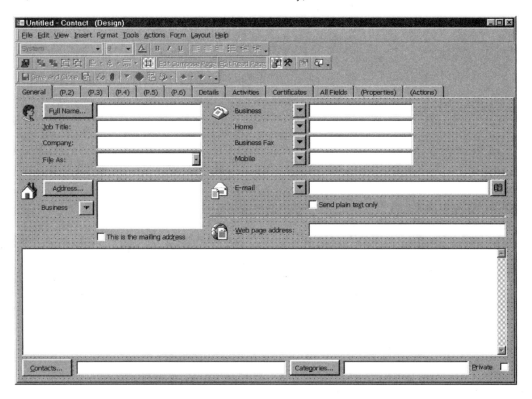

Step 2: Since we want to save the entries, we must create user-defined fields (UDFs) to store the aliases. Click **New** on the Field Chooser and create three new fields: 'AIM', 'ICQ', and 'MSNM'. All should be of **Type: Text** and **Format: Text.**

Step 3: The choice of where to place your new form fields is entirely your own. You can place them on another form page, but since we have the luxury of being able to adapt the first page of the Contact form, let's do that instead. A couple of spots on the standard form seem to have enough space to accommodate these relatively small fields. They could be placed along the right side of the phone numbers, or perhaps at the bottom of the form. By resizing the 'Notes' text box in the lower portion of the form, we can fit these three fields in quite nicely, just below the **Address** and **Web Page Address** fields.

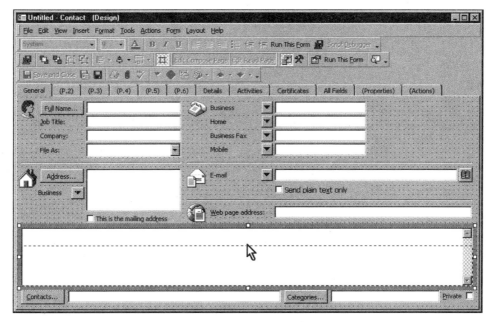

Step 4: Now that room has been made to accommodate the new fields, drag them to roughly where you want them on the form. Notice anything interesting about their behavior as they are dropped? They are automatically aligned for you. After you've dropped the fields, right-click on each one of them and open the Properties dialog. The Name: value in Properties should appear as something generic, like TextBox1. Modify this to something more descriptive, like AIM TextBox. You might also want to do this for the corresponding labels as well. You'll see why this is useful when we get to step 6.

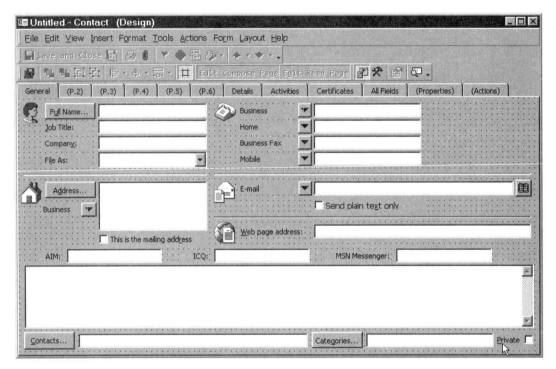

Step 5: When you create UDFs, you generally edit the labels to be more descriptive. In our case, we might want to right-justify the labels to make them a bit closer to the textbox field, and edit MSNM to read something like MSN Messenger. Resize any labels accordingly, and make sure the new fields are aligned to your liking.

Step 6: Adding any new fields or controls will alter the form's tab order (that is, the sequence in which the cursor moves through the form fields when pressing the *Tab* key). This can be modified by selecting Tab Order from the form's Layout menu. The tabs are ordered in sequence from left-to-right and top-to-bottom. Scroll down to the bottom of the Tab Order window. You should see your UDFs at the bottom. Assuming you dropped the UDFs in the sequential order, you won't need to reorder them, and you can take advantage of moving the tab order list up as a group, instead of an individual field at a time. Select the fields you want to move, and click Move Up or Move Down to position the fields where you want them.

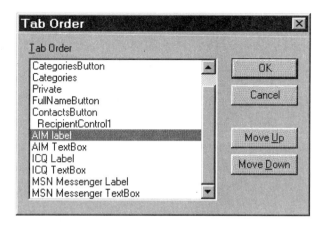

Step 7: Click the Properties tab on the form. It's a good idea to decide on a consistent method for how you want to document your custom − like commenting code, it's a good habit to develop. All the fields on this page are optional, but a few are particularly interesting, not to mention very useful:

- ❑ **Contact**: the name you enter in this field appears as the 'Contact' name in the Outlook Forms Manager, as well as in the 'About this form' dialog (accessible from the Help menu on your custom form).

- ❑ **Description**: this is a great place to briefly describe your form and what it does. As with Contact, this field also appears in the Outlook Forms Manager and the 'About this form' dialog.

- ❑ **Version**: you can assign a version number based on whatever numbering scheme you like. This field also appears in the Outlook Forms Manager and the 'About this form' dialog.

- ❑ **Change Large Icon/Change Small Icon**: clicking either button allows you to change the display icon for your custom form. Since this form is a Contact form, we have used Contact icons to represent it.

- ❑ **Protect Form Design**: checking this box allows you to prevent anyone from viewing your form in design mode, unless he or she has the password (which can be set by clicking the Set Password command button).

- ❑ **Send form definition**: checking this box allows you to send the form to recipients outside your organization (that is, not running on the same Exchange Server as you). If you are an individual user running Outlook standalone, or need to send this form outside your company, ensure you check this box − otherwise leave it empty. Bear in mind though, saving the form definition will increase the item size.

❑ **Category and Sub-Category**: using these enumerated fields allows you to define specific categories and sub-categories in which to organize your forms.

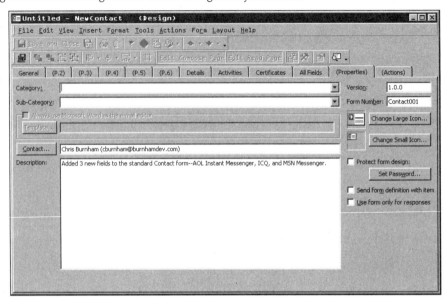

Step 8: The form looks like we want it to, and we've set all the Properties to our liking. Time to test it! On the Form menu, select Run This Form and your customized form will open an instance in regular mode. (Note that the form you've been designing remains in design mode.)

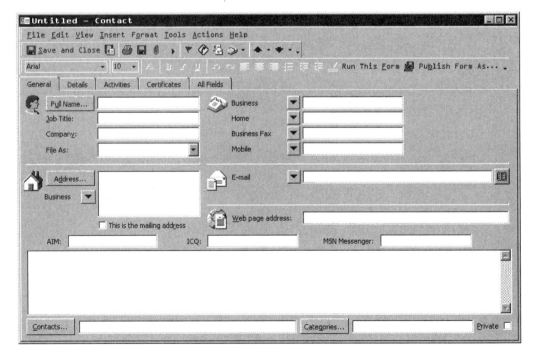

The process of testing a form varies with the form type, and exactly what it is you've modified. In this case, the changes have been relatively simple, so the logical test is to create a new Contact record and enter values into the three new fields. Save and close the form, then reopen it. Check that the values you entered still appear correctly in the appropriate fields. It's also a good idea to make sure your have the tab order in the correct sequence. The form is basically done, so set any additional properties that you'd like (such as a ControlTipText). Another nice touch might be to add small graphics (representing each of the three services) to make it easier to identify the fields and add some color to your form.

Step 9: Finally, we can publish the new form. If you recall our discussion about the various forms libraries, that information comes into play when we publish the form. If the form is intended for use by everyone in your company, publish it to the Organizational Forms Library, or a Public Folder (assuming you have adequate permissions from the Exchange Administrator). If the form is just for you, publish it to your Personal Forms Library, or to a Contacts folder. Publishing it to a specific folder offers you the advantage of being able to create a new instance of your form from the Actions menu.

To publish a form, click the Tools menu and select Forms. From the resulting submenu, select Publish Form As. The Publish Form As dialog will appear (looking very similar to the one used for opening a form in design mode). In the Look In: dropdown box, navigate to where you'd like to publish your form. Enter a Display Name for your form. Note that the Form Name is automatically completed as you name your form – feel free to modify it if you'd like to use something different. The Form Name determines the IPM Message class extension.

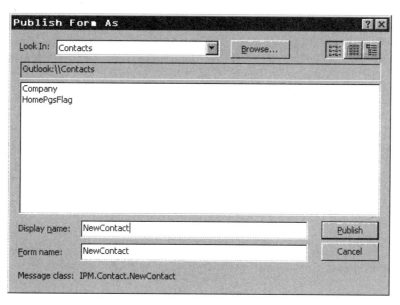

Creating a Task Form with Subtasks

Our first sample form was relatively simple and did not require any coding. The second is a bit more complex and requires code. It also provides a nice illustration of how to use binding, and why binding is important in Outlook forms development. A good approach to developing a complex form is:

- ❏ Plan the form design

- ❏ Create all the UDFs you need.

- ❏ Complete and polish the form layout to your liking, including changing any field and control names.

- ❏ Write the code to extend the functionality, and address binding where necessary.

We have already decided to create a new page on the standard Task form to keep track of subtasks. In this case, we will create three new fields to hold subtasks on P.2 of the Task form.

Step 1: We begin by opening the standard Task form in design mode (Tools | Forms | Design a Form) and locating the Task form in the Standard Forms Library.

Step 2: Since we are going to want to save the entries, we'll create user-defined fields (UDFs) to store the values entered. Click the New button on the Field Chooser and create three new fields – txtSubtask1, txtSubtask2, and txtSubtask3. All fields should be of Type: Text and Format: Text. The prefix txt has been included with each field to identify that it is a TextBox field. Similarly, cbx indicates a Checkbox field. We will use a similar three-character prefix to identify any other UDFs in this example. We've created the fields to hold the descriptions of each subtask, but how do we indicate if the task is complete or not? Go ahead and create three new UDFs by clicking New on the Field Chooser – cbxComplete1, cbxComplete2, and cbxComplete3.

> **Important note: if you were developing this form from scratch, you might very well overlook the creation the checkbox UDFs, assuming you could make use of the CheckBox control in the Control Toolbox. As our example progresses, we'll see why this approach would not work.**

Step 3: Rename the tab P.2 to Subtasks. Click the Form menu and select Rename This Page. As soon as you modify one of the tabs marked P.2 through P.6, the page will automatically show on the form when you run it. It's also possible to manually toggle which pages are displayed, through the use of the Display This Page option form (in the Forms menu).

Step 4: We've created our UDFs, and renamed the page where we want to create our subtasks, so the next step is to drag-and-drop the UDFs from the Field Chooser to the form layout. To minimize changes in the tab order, your best bet is to drop the UDFs in the sequence cbxComplete1, txtSubtask1, cbxComplete2, and so on.

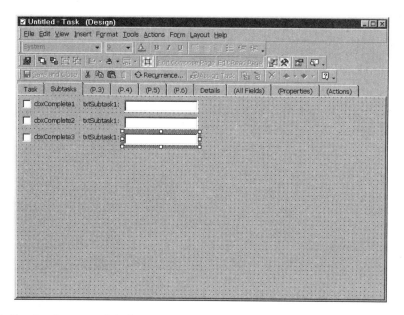

Step 5: For this form, our labels require a bit more editing than they did in the Contact form. We really don't need a label next to each checkbox, but when you click one of the checkbox UDFs, you'll notice that the label is part of the field. Right-click and select **Properties.** You should notice that the label text appears in the **Caption** field – delete this text and click **OK.** The checkboxes retain the same size they had with the captions, so let's resize those to more closely approximate the size of the checkbox.

> *There's a quick little shortcut for resizing multiple fields – click and drag one field to the size you'd like, then press SHIFT to select contiguous fields, or CTRL to select the non-contiguous fields. Notice how one of the fields is surrounded by white-filled squares, while the others are filled in black? The field that has the white squares is the field that will be used as the measure when we right-click on the group of fields, select Make Same Size from the context menu, and then Width from the submenu. This trick can be used to quickly and easily resize or align any fields on your form.*

Step 6: We've edited our checkboxes, so the next step is to modify the labels attached to the subtask fields. After modifying the label text, you may want to reposition your labels to the other side of the checkboxes. It's entirely up to you how you format the layout.

Step 7: Right-click on one of the fields and select **Advanced Properties.** We need to change all of the control names to something more descriptive to make the VBScript easier to code and read, as well as making it easy for us to set the tab order. Opening **Advanced Properties** instead of **Properties** lets you take advantage of a timesaving tip – you don't need to close the Advanced Properties dialog to move between forms. After opening the dialog, try clicking another field without closing it. You should note that the properties displayed in the dialog change as you move between the fields. The property we need to change is the **Name** property. If you click the label for Subtask1, the name of this field is probably something like `Label1`.

Let's change the name of each of these fields using the following scheme:

Control Type	Current Value of Name	Change Name to:
Label	Label1	lblSubtask1
CheckBox	CheckBox1	**no change required
TextBox	TextBox1	txtSubtask1

If you'd like to also change the captions that appear for the labels, feel free to do that while you are editing the name of the field.

Step 8: Modify the tab order to allow the user to tab through the fields in a logical sequence (as in the Contact form example, step 6). In most cases, 'logical sequence' flows from left-to-right and top-to-bottom.

Step 9: Update the tabs on your form's Properties page (again, as the Contact form).

Step 10: The layout is now complete, so go ahead and run the form to make sure it looks correct. While you are testing it, enter some values in the new fields you've added, just to see if they 'stick' after you close and open the form. Since we created them as UDFs, you should see any values you enter after closing and reopening the form.

Step 11: Have you ever noticed how when a Task is completed, Outlook lightens the font of the description and adds a strikethrough format to it? This is functionality we can build into our Subtask form, with a bit of coding.

VBScript has several notable differences from the VBA code you use in Outlook macros. In VBScript for Outlook forms:

- ❑ You do not need to instantiate the `Application` object with VBScript

- ❑ The `Application` object is intrinsic to Outlook forms – this also means you don't need to define the Namespace

- ❑ The `Item` object is also intrinsic to Outlook forms, so you do not need to specify which item is current

- ❑ VBScript only supports the Variant data type

- ❑ VBScript does not support the intrinsic Outlook constants – these must be declared, or you must use the numeric value representing the constant

How do we start coding the form? Well, since we already know that we don't need to instantiate the `Outlook` object, and we don't need to instantiate the `Item` object, we can start by setting the current Page of our object (the Task form) so Outlook knows this code only works with this form page:

```
Set objPage = Item.GetInspector.ModifiedFormPages("Subtasks")
```

Declaring the current page of our object allows us to create different code for each page in the Outlook form. Next, we need to create an object for our CheckBox control. Why? Isn't a CheckBox control already an object? Yes, it is, but Outlook forms do not allow us to perform operations in code directly upon a control object, so we need to access them using the 'Controls' property, either by name or index. Here's how we use this property to define our object:

```
Set cbxCheckBox1 = objPage.Controls("CheckBox1")
```

Using the same logic as with the CheckBox control, define an object for the TextBox Subtask1:

```
Set objSubTask = _
            Item.GetInspector.ModifiedFormPages("Subtasks").Controls("Subtask1")
```

We've defined our page and our control objects, so the next step is to code what we want to happen when we click our CheckBox control. Note that a CheckBox control has only two allowed values – True or False.

```
'*****************************************************************
'* If cbxCheckBox is checked (i.e., "True"), set font properties of
'* control Subtask1 to strikethrough and weight=100
'*****************************************************************
If cbxCheckBox1.Value = True Then
    objSubTask.Font.StrikeThrough = True
    objSubTask.Font.Weight = 100
Else
'*****************************************************************
' If cbxComplete1 is not checked (i.e. "False"), do nothing
'*****************************************************************
    objSubTask.Font.StrikeThrough = False
    objSubTask.Font.Weight = 0
End If
```

If you've done any coding before, the above syntax should be quite familiar. When looking for the available methods and properties, check your Outlook Help files. A complete list of every available method and property for each object appears there.

It appears that we've fully described the actions we want to take place when CheckBox1 is clicked. All that's left for this segment of code is to decide what function, or event we want to wrap it in. The logical choice would be to use Function Item_Click(). However, one of the quirks of Outlook forms programming is that you cannot use the Click event with a bound control (remember, when we created our UDFs, CheckBox1 was automatically bound to the field cbxComplete1). Instead, you must use a less direct approach, using the CustomPropertyChange method and case statements to accomplish the same thing:

```
Function Item_CustomPropertyChange (ByVal Name)
  Select Case Name
    Case "cbxComplete1"
  End Select
End Function
```

It would appear that our code is complete, so let's put it together and test our form to see how it works:

```
Function Item_CustomPropertyChange (ByVal Name)
  Select Case Name
    Case "cbxComplete1"
    '***********************************************************************
    '* Set the object objPage as the current form page, "Subtasks" and
    '* bind UDF cbxCheckBox1 to control CheckBox1
    '***********************************************************************
        Set objPage = Item.GetInspector.ModifiedFormPages("Subtasks")
        Set cbxCheckBox1 = objPage.Controls("CheckBox1")
        Set objSubTask = _
            Item.GetInspector.ModifiedFormPages("Subtasks").Controls("Subtask1")

    '***********************************************************************
    '* If cbxCheckBox is checked (i.e., "True"), set font properties of
    '* control Subtask1 to strikethrough and weight=100
    '***********************************************************************

        If cbxCheckBox1.Value = True Then
          objSubTask.Font.StrikeThrough = True
          objSubTask.Font.Weight = 100
        Else
    '***********************************************************************
    ' If cbxComplete1 is not checked (i.e. "False"), do nothing
    '***********************************************************************
          objSubTask.Font.StrikeThrough = False
          objSubTask.Font.Weight = 0
        End If
  End Select
End Function
```

Running the form doesn't return any run-time errors, so we know that we haven't made any syntax errors. Note that only code that is actually run will be checked for syntax errors, as it is not pre-compiled. The next test is to enter values in the Subtask1 field and click the checkbox to see if it works. Now, Save and close the form, then reopen it. You should notice that, while the checkbox is still checked, and the text still appears in the Subtask1 textbox, the strikethrough and weight formatting of the text has disappeared. Why?

This is the point where many forms developers can get confused or frustrated, trying to understand why properties do not persist, particularly since you made sure to use a UDF instead of an unbound control. The problem is that the objects we see on the form are the controls, *not* the UDFs. The special formatting applied to the UDF in the above code still exists – we just need to add some additional code to bring it back to the control level when the form is reopened.

Accomplishing this is actually quite easy, once you know that it needs to be done. We already know we want action to take place when the form opens, so we can use the Item_Open event. The first thing we need to do is find our UDF, cbxComplete1:

```
Set cbxChkBox1 = Item.UserProperties.Find("cbxComplete1")
```

If the value of the UDF is `True`, then we want to restore the properties set on `txtSubtask1` to the control, `Subtask1`:

```
If cbxChkBox1 = True Then
  Set txtSubTask1 = Item.UserProperties.Find("txtSubtask1")
  Set objSubTask =.
  Item.GetInspector.ModifiedFormPages("Subtasks").Controls("Subtask1")
  objSubTask.Font.StrikeThrough = True
  objSubTask.Font.Weight = 100
End If
```

Add the code we've just written above the previous code in the Outlook Script Editor and retest the form. You should see from the results that you were successful and the code works as we intended. All that's left with coding is to duplicate the code for the remaining fields:

```
'****************************************************************************
'* Code written by Chris Burnham
'* Original code date 08/15/1999
'*
'* Tools:
'* Outlook 2000 (v9.0)
'* VBScript 5.0
'*.
'****************************************************************************

Function Item_Open()
  '****************************************************************************
  '* Locate the value of cbxComplete1
  '****************************************************************************
  Set cbxChkBox1 = Item.UserProperties.Find("cbxComplete1")


  '****************************************************************************
  ' * If cbxComplete1 is checked (i.e., "True"), set font properties of
  ' * control Subtask1 to strikethrough and weight = 100 by binding the
  ' * control to UDF txtSubtask1, which holds these values
  '****************************************************************************
  If cbxChkBox1 = True Then
    Set txtSubTask1 = Item.UserProperties.Find("txtSubtask1")
    Set objSubTask = _
  Item.GetInspector.ModifiedFormPages("Subtasks").Controls("Subtask1")
    objSubTask.Font.StrikeThrough = True
    objSubTask.Font.Weight = 100
  End If
  Set cbxChkBox2 = Item.UserProperties.Find("cbxComplete2")
  If cbxChkBox2 = True Then
    Set txtSubTask2 = Item.UserProperties.Find("txtSubtask2")
    Set objSubTask = _
  Item.GetInspector.ModifiedFormPages("Subtasks").Controls("Subtask2")
    objSubTask.Font.StrikeThrough = True
    objSubTask.Font.Weight = 100
  Else
    Set txtSubTask2 = Item.UserProperties.Find("txtSubtask2")
```

```
      Set objSubTask = _
            Item.GetInspector.ModifiedFormPages("Subtasks").Controls("Subtask2")
      objSubTask.Font.StrikeThrough = False
      objSubTask.Font.Weight = 0
   End If
   Set cbxChkBox3 = Item.UserProperties.Find("cbxComplete3")
   If cbxChkBox3 = True Then
      Set txtSubTask3 = Item.UserProperties.Find("txtSubtask3")
      Set objSubTask = _
      Item.GetInspector.ModifiedFormPages("Subtasks").Controls("Subtask3")
      objSubTask.Font.StrikeThrough = True
      objSubTask.Font.Weight = 100
   Else
      Set txtSubTask3 = Item.UserProperties.Find("txtSubtask3")
      Set objSubTask = _
      Item.GetInspector.ModifiedFormPages("Subtasks").Controls("Subtask3")
      objSubTask.Font.StrikeThrough = False
      objSubTask.Font.Weight = 0
   End If
End Function

Function Item_CustomPropertyChange (ByVal Name)
   Select Case Name
     Case "cbxComplete1"
'*************************************************************************
'* Set the object objPage as the current form page, "Subtasks" and
'* bind UDF cbxCheckBox1 to control CheckBox1
'*************************************************************************
       Set objPage = Item.GetInspector.ModifiedFormPages("Subtasks")
       Set cbxCheckBox1 = objPage.Controls("CheckBox1")

'*************************************************************************
'* If cbxCheckBox is checked (i.e., "True"), set font properties of
'* control Subtask1 to strikethrough and weight=100
'*************************************************************************
       If cbxCheckBox1.Value = True Then
          Set objSubTask = _
             Item.GetInspector.ModifiedFormPages("Subtasks").Controls("Subtask1")
          objSubTask.Font.StrikeThrough = True
          objSubTask.Font.Weight = 100
       Else

'*************************************************************************
' If cbxComplete1 is not checked (i.e., "False"), do nothing
'*************************************************************************
          Set objSubTask = _
             Item.GetInspector.ModifiedFormPages("Subtasks").Controls("Subtask1")
          objSubTask.Font.StrikeThrough = False
          objSubTask.Font.Weight = 0
       End If
     Case "cbxComplete2"
        Set objPage = Item.GetInspector.ModifiedFormPages("Subtasks")
        Set cbxCheckBox2 = objPage.Controls("CheckBox2")
        If cbxCheckBox2.Value = True Then
```

```
              Set objSubTask = _
    Item.GetInspector.ModifiedFormPages("Subtasks").Controls("Subtask2")
              objSubTask.Font.StrikeThrough = True
              objSubTask.Font.Weight = 100
          Else
              Set objSubTask = _
    Item.GetInspector.ModifiedFormPages("Subtasks").Controls("Subtask2")
              objSubTask.Font.StrikeThrough = False
              objSubTask.Font.Weight = 0
          End If
       Case "cbxComplete3"
          Set objPage = Item.GetInspector.ModifiedFormPages("Subtasks")
          Set cbxCheckBox3 = objPage.Controls("CheckBox3")
          If cbxCheckBox3.Value = True Then
              Set objSubTask = _
    Item.GetInspector.ModifiedFormPages("Subtasks").Controls("Subtask3")
              objSubTask.Font.StrikeThrough = True
              objSubTask.Font.Weight = 100
          Else
              Set objSubTask = _
    Item.GetInspector.ModifiedFormPages("Subtasks").Controls("Subtask3")
              objSubTask.Font.StrikeThrough = False
              objSubTask.Font.Weight = 0
          End If
    End Select
End Function
```

Step 12: Publish the form.

Publishing and Distributing a Custom Form

To publish a form, click the Tools menu and select Forms. From the resulting submenu, select Publish Form As. The Publish Form As dialog will appear (it looks very similar to the dialog used to open a form in design mode). In the Look In: dropdown, navigate to where you'd like to publish your form. Enter a Display name for your form. Note that the Form name is automatically completed as you name your form. You can feel free to modify this if you'd like to use something different.

If you've published your completed form in your Personal Forms Library and need to roll it out to the rest of your organization, you can use the Outlook Forms Manager to simply copy the form over (only available in CW mode). See "Using the Outlook Forms Manager" topic in the 'Forms Management' section for an overview.

Sometimes, distributing a form as a file attachment could be an easy way for you to get the form to remote users. To do this, open an instance of your new form. On the File menu, select Save As. The Office file dialog opens and the Save as type: dropdown has an option to save as `Outlook Template (*.oft)` After you've saved the template file, you can attach it to a mail message like any other file.

Changing Default Form Types

Outlook 2000 makes changing the default form type very easy. On the Outlook Bar, or in Folder View, locate the folder for which you want to change the default form. Right-click on it and select Properties. On the General tab, you will see a dropdown box labeled, When posting to this folder, use: As long as the custom form has been published, and is based on the default form type for this folder, it should appear in the list of available forms. Simply select it and the next time you create a new item in that folder, it will use your custom form.

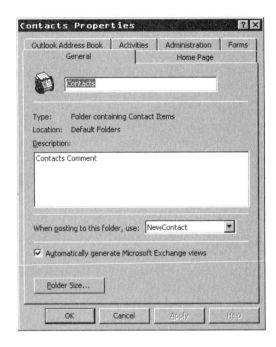

Changing Existing Items To a Custom Form

There are two common ways to change the default message class of an existing item to a custom form:

❑ Download and use the `omsgclas.exe` utility available from Microsoft's web site. The utility is a Word document with a built-in macro to automate the process of changing message classes. If you don't want to have to create a programmatic solution for changing existing items, this is a good alternative. The utility can be found at:
`http://support.microsoft.com/download/support/mslfiles/Omsgclas.exe`

❑ The Microsoft Knowledge Base article, Q201087, "OL2000: How to Update Existing Items to Use a New Custom Form" provides some sample code that can be modified and used as VBScript in a form to facilitate the process.

One-Off Forms

This is how we describe forms which have had their form definition saved along with them (rather than just a link to that definition, as is normally the case). The `FormDescription` object's Properties include the Boolean value `OneOff`. In the event that a custom form is to be used once and then discarded, this property can be set – the form and its definition are then saved (and can be subsequently discarded) together.

One-off forms are probably the single biggest point of confusion for anyone new to Outlook forms development. Understanding what the term means (and how one-off forms happen) can save you a great deal of frustration. How do forms become one-offed?

There are several common ways:

- ❑ Select the option "Send form definition with item", available on the Properties page of each custom form.

- ❑ Edit an existing custom form in design mode, then republish the custom form with the same name – all existing items will use the latest form design next time they are opened, but the form has become one-offed

Some VBScript methods and commands can change a form definition and cause it to one-off. Examples include, but are not limited to:

- ❑ `FormDescription` object methods

- ❑ Methods related to the properties of *controls*, usually for enabling / disabling controls or making them hidden / shown

- ❑ Any change to a form `Action` (using either the `Actions` collection or `Action` object methods)

It's quite easy to one-off a form, but what impact does this have on you and your users? Some common examples are:

- ❑ Macro virus warning every time the form is opened

- ❑ The file size of the form unexpectedly increases

- ❑ The icons displayed for your form changes

The Microsoft Knowledge Base article, Q207896, 'OL2000: Working with Form Definitions and One-Off Forms', offers sample code to verify if your form has become one-off, and code to prevent it.

Forms Management

The Final Section in this chapter is devoted to Forms Management. Let's look at some issues with managing the forms cache and using the Forms Manager.

Managing the Forms Cache

Managing the forms cache becomes extremely important when you update existing forms and republish them. In most organizations using Exchange, the form is published centrally in the Organizational Forms Library. When the user accesses the form from the library, the most current version is supposed to load locally in the user's cache (`frmcache.dat`). A common misconception among developers is that the version number assigned to a form in the Properties tab in design mode automatically supercedes any previous versions of the same form that might be stored in the cache. As we've recently learned from Microsoft, this is not so.

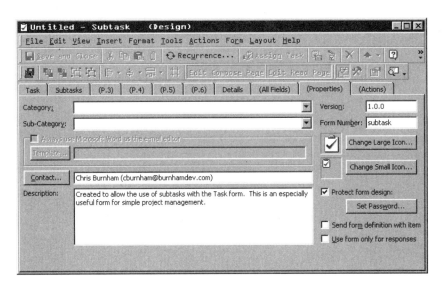

Microsoft has confirmed that the version property seems to be only for the personal tracking purposes of the form developer. Their recommendation to users, when rolling out a new version of the form, is to use a new form name. Keep in mind that this approach has a fundamental downside – you'll need to periodically purge the old forms from the users' forms cache, and may need to modify code in order to handle the new form name correctly.

Developers posting to the public newsgroup `microsoft.public.outlook.program_forms` have suggested a couple of workarounds:

❑ Have the users delete the file `frmcache.dat` (which holds the Outlook Forms Cache), each time the form is updated

❑ Add a version number to the end of the IPM class name, while leaving the form description the same.

Neither solution is terribly appealing to developers or Exchange Administrators. Deleting the forms cache on every machine in the company each time you update a form is terribly time-consuming, and may be unfeasible if you have many roaming users who do not reside in a central office. The latter method, while minimizing user confusion, has a huge drawback – by incrementing the version number in the IPM class, you end up creating a new form in the cache each time you update it. This is where the version number on the form's Properties tab *could* come nicely into play, but not if the caching algorithm built into the form's publishing mechanism simply doesn't use this number when determining which form is most current. Further confusing this situation is that all developers are not witnessing consistent problems with updating the organizational forms. In fact, some have had no problems at all.

Using the Outlook Forms Manager

The Forms Manager (only available in Corporate-Workgroup mode is a useful tool for managing all your forms libraries. It lets you easily move forms between two libraries or stores, and see the pertinent properties of each. Getting at the Forms Manager is a bit of a chore:

❑ First, select Tools | Options and select the Other tab.

❑ Select Advanced Options – the Advanced Options dialog will open.

❑ Then select Custom Forms – another Options dialog opens.

❑ Finally, click Manage Forms, and the Forms Manager will open.

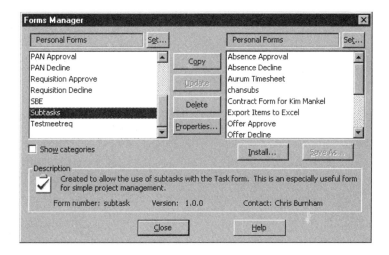

Note that custom forms must be sent in RTF format. Otherwise they may be received as standard items with no code or custom arrangement of the controls and tabs on the form pages. To set the address properties for a contact to be sent in RTF format in Corporate/Workgroup mode, right-click on the email address, select **Properties,** and check the box labeled **Always send to this recipient in Microsoft Outlook rich text format.** You can either do this when composing a message or in an open contact record. To do the same in Internet Only mode, open the contact record, and *uncheck* the **Send using plain text** checkbox.

Summary

This chapter has covered all the basics you'll need to get started in exploring Outlook forms. You've read about the different form types, the basic design environment, how to use fields and controls, and how to extend the functionality of a form with VBScript. Now that you have a foundation for learning, we encourage you to explore more on your own.

3

Outlook 2000 Projects and Macros

This chapter introduces the Outlook 2000 VBA Project and Outlook 2000 macros. These development features are new to Outlook 2000, the first member of the Outlook family of Outlook 97, Outlook 98, and Outlook 2000 to incorporate **VBA** (Visual Basic for Applications), Microsoft's development language for Office and other applications. The version of VBA installed with Office 2000 is VBA 6. The Outlook **Project** is where all the VBA code for Outlook is stored, and the **Macros** are VBA Sub procedures that are written to perform specific actions in Outlook. We will also cover using the new Outlook 2000 events, designing Office **UserForms** in Outlook, developing and using custom class modules and look at some ways of customizing Outlook to work the way we want it to work.

Outlook Projects

Unlike many of the other Office applications that include VBA, Outlook 2000 can only have one project open at a time (unless you have installed Microsoft Office 2000 Developer Edition), and the project is always named `Project1 (VbaProject.OTM)`. You can rename `Project1` with a more personalized name, but the project is always saved in the file system as `VbaProject.OTM`. Outlook will not automatically recognize or load projects with any other name. The `VbaProject.OTM` file is a special file that has a special class module named `ThisOutlookSession`. You cannot just rename a standard VBA project (`.VBA`) as `VbaProject.OTM` and have Outlook 2000 recognize it. Earlier members of the Outlook family, Outlook 97 and Outlook 98, cannot load or use the `VbaProject.OTM` file.

For users of Windows 95 and Windows 98 who do not use profiles, the `VbaProject.OTM` project file is usually located in `C:\Windows\Application Data\Microsoft\Outlook\`. Users of those operating systems who do use profiles have the project file located in `C:\Windows\<profile>\Application Data\Microsoft\Outlook\`, where `<profile>` is the profile name. Users of Windows NT usually have the project file located in `C:\Winnt\Profiles\<profile>\Application Data\Microsoft\Outlook\`.

The Outlook VBA Project

The Outlook VBA project organizes its contents into folders containing specific types of objects. It can contain folders for Modules, which contain code; Forms, which contain Office UserForms; and Class Modules, which contain user-defined classes. It always contains a folder named `Microsoft Outlook Objects`, which contains a special class module named `ThisOutlookSession`. The special uses of the `ThisOutlookSession` class module are discussed later in this chapter. The following screen shot shows the Project Explorer window with all the folders expanded.

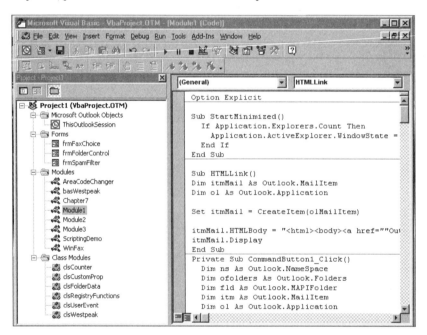

Unlike similar elements in a **VB** (Visual Basic) project, code modules, class modules, and Office UserForms in the Outlook project are internal to the VBA project. They have no existence in the file system unless they are exported by choosing File | Export File or by using the keyboard shortcut *Ctrl+E*. Once a module or UserForm is exported it can be imported into the Outlook project or into an Office .VBA project by choosing File | Import File. Items that are exported can be kept in a dedicated folder in the file system, enabling reuse of commonly used procedures, forms and classes. The following screen shot shows the File menu with the Microsoft Office 2000 Developer Edition installed.

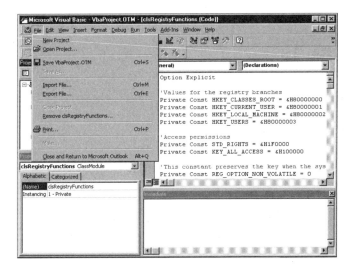

Modules and UserForms that are exported into the file system can be imported into a VB project by choosing Project | Add File or by using the keyboard shortcut *Ctrl+D*. VB code and class modules can also be imported into VBA projects, but VB forms are not compatible with VBA projects. If you import an Office UserForm into VB, be aware that all controls on the form are by default from the MS Forms 2.0 Library, and are not standard VB controls. MS Forms controls can be used in VB and VB forms by adding the MS Forms 2.0 Library to the controls on the VB control toolbox.

I recommend grouping procedures that are related in separate code modules. This keeps all related code together, and can make code maintenance easier. Each form and class in a project is always placed in its own module. To add new modules or forms to an Office VBA project use the Insert menu to add a UserForm, Module or Class Module to the project. To remove modules or UserForms from the project use the File | Remove command or right-click on the item to be removed and use the Remove command in the context menu. You will be given the choice of exporting the item before removing it. The following screen shot shows the Insert menu with the Microsoft Office 2000 Developer installed.

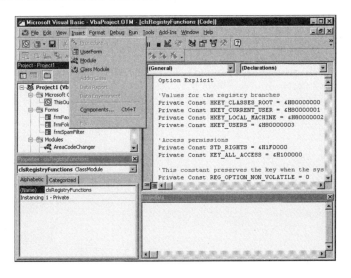

> **A module or UserForm that is removed from the project without being exported is gone forever. It has no existence in the file system unless it is exported, so be careful not to remove items that you may want to use later unless they are exported first.**

Since Outlook has only one project file, the only way to work with multiple Outlook projects is to rename them in the file system. You can give descriptive names to projects, such as `ContactManagement.OTM`. When you want to work with that project you can rename the existing `VbaProject.OTM` file with another name and rename `ContactManagement.OTM` as `VbaProject.OTM`. This process must be performed with Outlook closed so that the newly renamed project file is accessible to Outlook when it is opened again, and so the original `VbaProject.OTM` file is not locked while it is in use.

Projects With Microsoft Office 2000 Developer

Installing Microsoft Office 2000 Developer Edition enables you to have more than one project open at a time. These projects have a file extension of `.VBA` however, so they cannot be used as the intrinsic Outlook project. Since they have no `ThisOutlookSession` class module saving a `.VBA` project as an `.OTM` file won't work. Importing an exported `ThisOutlookSession` module into a VBA project file does not convert it into an OTM file. Code modules, class modules and forms from a VBA project can be exported to the file system and imported into the Outlook project..

Additions to the File menu are made when Microsoft Office 2000 Developer Edition is installed that enable working with multiple projects. The new File menu commands are New Project, Open Project and Save As. These commands do not apply to the Outlook project. The features, add-ins and extensions installed by Microsoft Office 2000 Developer Edition are not covered thoroughly in this book, but elements of Microsoft Office 2000 Developer Edition are discussed where they are appropriate. One of the most important enhancements that Microsoft Office 2000 Developer Edition provides is the capability of developing **COM Add-ins** in VBA, something that otherwise is only possible with VB, Delphi, or VC++. COM Add-ins are programs that are usually compiled as DLL files and are used to provide enhancements and add-ins for Outlook 2000. COM Add-ins are a new feature in Office 2000.

Distributing Outlook Projects

Distributing Outlook VBA projects is a problem. There are workarounds, but it still is a problem. Since Outlook can only have one project file, `VBAProject.OTM`, any project file with this name that you distribute will overwrite the user's version of this file. If the user has code in his project file that has been distributed by other developers, or that has been developed for macros or customizations they have written, that code will be lost when the current project file is replaced.

The only way to retain code that is currently in the project file is to merge new code with old code. When all code is maintained in separate modules the problem is not too bad. Where code has been written that has been placed in `ThisOutlookSession`, or that uses the intrinsic Application events that are available in `ThisOutlookSession`, the only solution is to manually merge the code that is placed in each event handler and procedure.

In situations where the contents of the project must be maintained, I recommend developing separate code modules and UserForms and then directing an import of those modules into the existing project. Event handling code should be placed in class modules to separate that code from `ThisOutlookSession`. In that case only initialization code must be placed in the `Application_Startup` procedure to instantiate the class module. This initialization code has to be merged with the existing `Application_Startup` procedure, if any.

> **The Profile Wizard from the Office 2000 Resource Kit can be used to distribute the current user's `VBAProject.OTM` file since it includes that file in the settings it builds for a rollout. However, this can be dangerous if done unwittingly. If you do use the Profile Wizard from the Office 2000 Resource Kit, and you do not want to distribute any custom code with it, make sure to run the Profile Wizard on a machine with a clean `VBAProject.OTM` file.**

By far the best solution is to distribute your code as a COM add-in if you have Microsoft Office 2000 Developer Edition or VB 6 once the code is fully developed and tested. Development of COM add-ins is covered in Chapter 7.

Outlook Macros

Outlook 2000 is the first version of Outlook that enables you to create and run macros. Macros in Outlook are created using VBA and are called from the User Interface by choosing Tools | Macro | Macros..., and selecting the desired macro. Macros also can be selected by using the keyboard shortcut *Alt+F8*. Unfortunately, this version of Outlook does not have a macro recorder facility for developing macros like the other Office applications. A macro in Outlook 2000 can be added as a command button to a toolbar, or it can be added as a menu item to any Outlook menu to make it easy to find and run.

What Are Outlook Macros?

Outlook macros are VBA Public Sub procedures that have no arguments passed to them. They are stored in code modules in the Outlook VBA Project, and can be tested and run from the VBA environment. Function procedures, Private Sub procedures and Sub procedures that have calling arguments can not be used as macros. Macros cannot be stored in class modules or in the code page (special class module) of a UserForm.

To add a macro to an Outlook toolbar or menu, first close the **VBE** (Visual Basic Editor) if it is open. You cannot customize the Outlook environment if the VBE is open, because it is considered an Outlook dialog box and you cannot have more than one dialog box open at a time. Right-click on a toolbar or the menu bar, and choose Customize. In the Customize dialog box, on the Commands tab, select Macros from the listbox on the left. The listbox on the right will show the macros that are available. Drag the macro you want to add to the toolbar to its desired position in the toolbar and drop it there. To add a macro to a menu, open the menu while in Customize mode and drag and drop the macro where you want it on the menu. If you want the macro to be available in certain Inspector or Explorer windows, open an instance of those windows and customize the toolbar or menu in that open Inspector or Explorer window.

After the macro is placed on the toolbar or menu, it is displayed as `Project1.MacroName`. The macro name can be changed by right-clicking on the macro button in the toolbar or menu in Customize mode and changing it in the **Name** textbox. Other customizations can be made such as changing the button image, how it is displayed and whether it begins a group of buttons.

Developing Outlook Macros

To develop our first sample macro, open the VBE by pressing *Alt+F11* and choose **Insert | Module**. The module will be inserted in the Outlook VBA Project as `Module1` in the Modules folder. The first macro that we will develop prints the currently open Outlook item to the default system printer.

> *The material in this chapter assumes that the VBE window displays the Project Explorer, the Properties Window and the Code Window. If any of these windows are not visible, open them from the **View** menu. These windows may be placed wherever you want within the VBE window and may be docked in position. If the Project Explorer does not show the folders then expand the Project tree to see them. You can also toggle the Project Explorer's display between folders and individual components by pressing the **Toggle Folders** button at the top of the Project Explorer.*

Rename the module by clicking in the **Name** box for the module when `Module1` is selected in the Project Explorer. It is a good idea to name the modules that you create with descriptive names that also indicate that the module is a VBA code module. I recommend using a naming convention of preceding the module name with `bas` to indicate this. A good choice for a name for the new module is `basMacros`.

> **Always give different names to code modules and the Sub procedures that they contain. If a module and a Sub procedure within that module are both named `CurrentUser` then you will be able to run the macro from within the VBE but Outlook will not be able to find the macro within the module to run it from the User Interface.**

Type the following code into the module that has been named `basMacros`.

```
Public Sub PrintItem()
  Dim oItem As Object 'Allow any type of Outlook item

  'The ActiveInspector object is the current open item
  Set oItem = Application.ActiveInspector.CurrentItem
  oItem.PrintOut

  Set oItem = Nothing
End Sub
```

> **All the code in this chapter will require that a reference is set to the Microsoft Outlook 9.0 Object Library. Some of the code samples will require references to other object libraries. To set a reference to the Outlook object library, choose **Tools | References** in the VBE window and scroll down the list of available object libraries. Check the Microsoft Outlook 9.0 Object Library.**

The following screen shot shows the **References** dialog box.

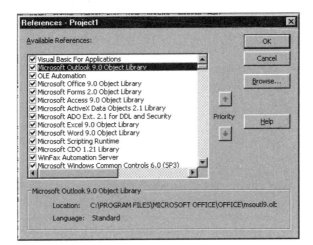

The `PrintItem` macro should now appear in the list of macros that appears when you press *Alt+F8* after closing the VBE. To close the VBE you can click on the close box at the top right hand corner of the VBE window. This macro will run only on an open Outlook item, so open any Outlook item in an Inspector window and run the macro by pressing *Alt+F8*, selecting the **PrintItems** Macro and then pressing **Run**. Whatever Outlook item is open is then printed on the default system printer.

> **The code for the sample macros in this section is contained in a code module named `basMacros.bas`.**

The next two sample macros show how to open a customized Outlook form from VBA code. These macros can be placed on a toolbar or menu for easy access to customized Outlook forms. Normally, if a custom form is published in an Outlook folder it is available in the **Actions** menu in that folder. Opening the form from a macro makes it possible to easily open the form from any menu or toolbar even if the form is not published in a folder or resides in the file system as an `.OFT` file.

The first of these macros opens a custom Contact form that is placed in the `C:\My Documents` folder. It uses the `CreateItemFromTemplate` method to open an instance of the form and the `Display` method of the item to display it. If code is present in the form then opening the form will trigger the **Macro Security** dialog box. See 'Code Security', later in this chapter, for ways of preventing the **Macro Security** dialog box from appearing.

The custom form in this example can be any custom form that is saved as a `.OFT` file. To create a sample `.OFT` file for this example, choose **Tools | Forms | Design a Form** in Outlook and choose any of the basic Outlook **IPM** (Interpersonal Message) forms. For this example, choose a Contact form. Save the form as a `.OFT` file by choosing **File | Save As** and save it in the `C:\My Documents` folder as `CustomContact.OFT`. If you change the file name or location, be sure to change the code sample.

```
Sub CustomContact()
  Dim myForm As Outlook.ContactItem

  Set myForm = Application.CreateItemFromTemplate("C:\My " _
    & "Documents\CustomContact.oft")
  myForm.Display

  Set myForm = Nothing
End Sub
```

The `CreateItemFromTemplate` method is used when the form has been saved to the file system as a .OFT file, and the `Add` method of the `Items` collection is used when the form has been published.

The next macro opens a custom Contact form that has been published in the default Contacts folder. It uses the `Add` method of the `Items` collection of the default Contacts folder to add a new item of the specified `MessageClass`, in this case `IPM.Contact.CustomContact`. Open a Contact form in design mode, as in the previous example, and choose **Tools | Forms | Publish Form**. Choose to save the form in the Contacts folder by selecting that folder in the **Look In** textbox. Enter `CustomContact` in the **Display Name** textbox and click on the **Publish** command button.

```
Sub OpenForm()
  Dim ns As Outlook.NameSpace
  Dim fld As Outlook.MAPIFolder
  Dim myForm As Outlook.ContactItem
  Dim itms As Outlook.Items

  Set ns = Application.GetNamespace("MAPI")
  Set fld = ns.GetDefaultFolder(olFolderContacts)
  Set itms = fld.Items
  Set myForm = itms.Add("IPM.Contact.CustomContact")
  myForm.Display

  Set ns = Nothing
  Set fld = Nothing
  Set itms = Nothing
  Set myForm = Nothing
End Sub
```

Our final macro example is a macro to display a message box with an email sender's name and email address. In many cases, Outlook displays only the "friendly name" of the sender in the **From** field of an email message. This macro gets the sender's email address using **CDO** (Collaboration Data Objects). CDO is covered in more depth in Chapter 6.

CDO is optionally installed when you install Outlook 2000, unlike earlier versions of Outlook which installed CDO automatically. Fully expand the Outlook item tree on the Office 2000 installation CD and install the CDO 1.21 object library to be able to run the code examples in this book that utilize CDO. To add a reference to the CDO library, open the **References** dialog box and check the **Microsoft CDO 1.21 Library**.

```vba
Sub FromAddress()
  Dim oNS As Outlook.NameSpace
  Dim oItm As Outlook.MailItem
  Dim obj As Object
  Dim oSession As MAPI.session
  Dim oMsg As MAPI.Message
  Dim oSndr As MAPI.AddressEntry
  Dim sAddress As String
  Dim sName As String
  Dim sEntry As String
  Dim sTitle As String

  sTitle = "Professional Programming Outlook 2000"

  'MAPI is the only NameSpace available to Outlook
  Set oNS = Application.GetNamespace("MAPI")
  'The ActiveInspector window is the currently active window
  'That is displaying individual Outlook items. Outlook folders
  'are displayed in Explorer windows.
  Set oItm = Application.ActiveInspector.CurrentItem
  'Sendername is the friendly name
  sName = oItm.SenderName
  'We need the EntryID of the item to locate it with CDO
  sEntry = oItm.EntryID

  'Establish a CDO (MAPI) Session object and logon to it
  Set oSession = CreateObject("MAPI.Session")
  oSession.Logon , , False, False

  'Locate the current message with the EntryID using CDO
  Set oMsg = oSession.GetMessage(sEntry)
  'Get the sender's name
  Set oSndr = oMsg.Sender
  'Get the actual email address
  sAddress = oSndr.Address
  'Display the information in a MsgBox
  MsgBox "Name: " & sName & vbCrLf & "Email Address: " _
    & sAddress, vbOKOnly, sTitle

  Set oNS = Nothing
  Set oItm = Nothing
  Set obj = Nothing
  Set oSession = Nothing
  Set oMsg = Nothing
  Set oSndr = Nothing
End Sub
```

The combination of macros and VBA give you the capability of creating custom actions in Outlook 2000 that can be executed on demand. This is a major step forward in enabling us to make Outlook work the way we want it to work. The next section, 'Outlook Events', covers the creation of event handlers that work automatically to customize Outlook to work the way we want it to work and enable us to respond to events that happen in the course of using Outlook.

The macro examples here are all fairly short, but there is no reason why we can't create macros that are extremely complex, and that call other Sub and Function procedures, open Outlook Forms and even use other object models. Object models such as the ones for other Office applications, CDO, ADO, DAO, RDO, the Win32 API can also be used in our Macros. You will see many examples of macros that use other object models throughout the book.

Distributing Outlook Macros

The best way to distribute Outlook macros is to place them in code modules that are exported to the file system. To export a code module to the file system, right-click on the module in the Project Explorer and select **Export File**, or use the keyboard shortcut *Ctrl+E* when that module is the current module. Give the module a descriptive file name (don't confuse the module's file name with the module name in VBA) and save it as a file of type .BAS. The module can then be imported by choosing **File | Import File** or by using the keyboard shortcut *Ctrl+M*. After the module is imported into the user's project file the macros it contains are immediately available. All module imports and exports are done from within the VBE.

Outlook Events

Previous versions of Outlook did not expose Outlook application and item level events. Form events were the only events available in previous versions of Outlook. Unlike the Form events and Item events that occur only in an open Outlook Form, Outlook 2000 has a rich and varied selection of events available for us to use in our programs.

Working With Outlook Events

Some of the application events are intrinsically available in the Application section of the Object listbox in the Code Window of the `ThisOutlookSession` class module. These events are available in `ThisOutlookSession` without having to declare an event handler using a `WithEvents` statement. These events can be added to any class module by declaring an Application variable that responds to those events in the class module, and then writing code to handle the event. Responding to events in class modules is discussed in 'Class Modules' later in this chapter. A declaration of a module level Application variable in the Declarations section of a class module would look similar to the following declaration:

```
Dim WithEvents moOutlook As Outlook.Application
```

The importance of these events is that they enable us to control the Outlook environment and how the user interacts with that environment. You can process data, save data to permanent storage, prevent the user from changing the environment, control the interface and do many other things. Some events, such as a reliable `Delete` event, are missing but the current list of events is a big advance over what was available in Outlook 97 and Outlook 98.

I make some suggestions about possible uses for some of the following events. There are many other uses that you can find for the events that Outlook provides. The key thing is to see what events your application needs to respond to or to prevent from happening. No list in a book can ever be comprehensive.

The following screen shot shows the Application level events intrinsically available in the Object listbox of the code window for `ThisOutlookSession`.

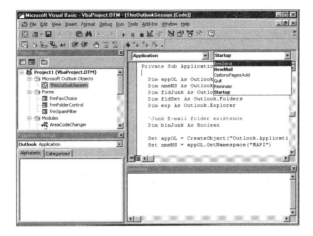

Application Level Events

The following events are the Application level events in Outlook 2000 that are intrinsic to the `ThisOutlookSession` class module. Event handlers for these events can also be added to other class modules. Events that can be canceled can be used to prevent the user from taking some action or making some change. If an event, such as `ItemSend`, is canceled the action or change does not occur. In the case of `ItemSend`, if `Cancel` is set to `True` the item is not sent. This can be useful in many situations where you want to limit what the user can do, or to verify certain things about an item or program state before you allow a change.

Event	Event Occurs
ItemSend	When an item is sent by the user. This event can be canceled in the event handler. Use this event to trap outgoing items for processing.
NewMail	When new items arrive in the Inbox. This event cannot be canceled in the event handler. This event fires for each item that is delivered into the Inbox. It does not fire when items are moved or copied into the Inbox.
OptionsPagesAdd	When either the **Options** dialog box is opened from the **Tools** menu, or the **Properties** page of an Outlook folder is accessed. This event enables you to add custom tabs to the **Options** or the **Properties** dialog boxes. Using property pages helps give your application the Outlook look and feel. This event cannot be canceled.

Table Continued on Following Page

Event	Event Occurs
Quit	When Outlook is terminated, after all Explorer and Inspector windows are closed. This event cannot be canceled. Most of Outlook is already closed when this event fires. Do not attempt to use any user interface features in this event. Use this event to dereference event variables and other global variables for your application.
Reminder	When a reminder fires for a Task, Appointment or Mail item, before the reminder is displayed. If the reminder is for a recurring appointment, the specific instance of the appointment is made available. This event cannot be canceled. This event will not fire on reminders that are not in the default Outlook folders. Task reminders will only fire for Task items that are in the default Tasks folder. Appointment reminders will only fire for Appointments that are in the default Calendar. Mail item reminders will only fire for items that are in the Inbox.
Startup	When Outlook initializes, after all add-in programs have been loaded. This event cannot be canceled. Use this event to initialize items and variables that your programs and Macros need. This event cannot be used in a COM add-in because Outlook has already started when the COM add-in is connected.

The previous events appear in the ThisOutlookSession module without having to be declared using the WithEvents statement. When you respond to these events in any other class module, they must be declared using the WithEvents statement.

Event handlers for the following Application level events can be added to any class module, including ThisOutlookSession. They are not intrinsic to the ThisOutlookSession module. You must declare variables with the WithEvents statement to be able to respond to them.

Event	Event Occurs
Activate	When the Explorer or Inspector becomes the active window. This event cannot be canceled. This event can be used to do things such as disabling menu or toolbar items based on the newly opened Explorer or Inspector.
BeforeFolderSwitch	Before the Explorer changes to a new folder. This event can be canceled in the event handler. Use this event to prevent the user from switching folders until certain conditions are true, or folder dependent actions are completed. This event can also be used for things such as writing data to storage before the active Explorer changes.
BeforeGroupAdd	Before a new group is added to the Outlook Bar. This event can be canceled in the event handler. This and the following Outlook Bar group and shortcut events can be used to prevent the user from making changes, or doing your own processing before the action takes place.

Event	Event Occurs
BeforeGroupRemove	Before a new group is removed from the Outlook Bar. This event can be canceled in the event handler.
BeforeGroupSwitch	Before a new group is opened in the Outlook Bar. This event can be canceled in the event handler.
BeforeShortcutAdd	Before a new shortcut is added to an Outlook Bar Group. This event can be canceled in the event handler.
BeforeShortcutRemove	Before a new shortcut is removed from an Outlook Bar Group. This event can be canceled in the event handler.
BeforeViewSwitch	Before the Explorer changes to a new view. This event can be canceled in the event handler. This event can be used to show specific views as conditions dictate, or to show mandatory views for certain folders.
Close	When the Explorer or Inspector is being closed. This event can be canceled in the event handler. Use this event to prevent the user from closing an Explorer or Inspector window until certain conditions are met.
Deactivate	When the Explorer or Inspector is no longer the active window. This event cannot be canceled.
FolderAdd	When a folder is added to the specified Folders collection. This event cannot be canceled.
FolderChange	When a folder is changed in the specified Folders collection. This event cannot be canceled.
FolderRemove	When a folder is removed from the specified Folders collection. This event cannot be canceled.
FolderSwitch	When the Explorer changes to a new folder. This event cannot be canceled.
GroupAdd	When a new group has been added to the Outlook Bar. This event cannot be canceled. When this event occurs the action has already taken place.
NewExplorer	When a new Explorer window has been opened, after it has been created but before it is visible. This event cannot be canceled.
NewInspector	When a new Inspector window has been opened, after it has been created but before it is visible. This event cannot be canceled.
OnError	When an error occurs while synchronizing folders using the specified synchronization profile. This event cannot be canceled.

Table Continued on Following Page

Event	Event Occurs
Progress	Occurs periodically while synchronizing folders. This event cannot be canceled.
SelectionChange	Only when the selection of the current view changes. Other selection changes do not cause this event to occur. This event does not occur if the current folder is a file system folder or if Outlook Today is displayed. This event cannot be canceled.
ShortcutAdd	When a new shortcut has been added to an Outlook Bar Group. This event cannot be canceled. When this event occurs, the action has already taken place.
SyncEnd	When synchronization is finished. This event cannot be canceled.
SyncStarth	When synchronization begins. This event cannot be canceled.
ViewSwitch	When the view in the current Explorer changes. This event cannot be canceled.

Item Level Events

The following events are all Item level events. Event handlers for these Item level events can be added to any class module, including `ThisOutlookSession`:

Event	Event Occurs
AttachmentAdd	When an attachment has been added to an item. This event cannot be canceled.
AttachmentRead	When an attachment in an item has been opened for reading. This event cannot be canceled.
BeforeAttachmentSave	Just before an attachment is saved. The syntax for this event is different than in VBScript. In VBA, the proper usage is `Sub objectBeforeAttachmentSave(Attachment As Attachment, Cancel As Boolean)`. This event can be canceled in the event handler.
BeforeCheckNames	Just before Outlook starts resolving names in the recipient collection for an item. The syntax for this event is different than in VBScript. In VBA, the proper usage is `Sub objectBeforeCheckNames(Cancel as Boolean)`. This event can be canceled in the event handler.
Close	When the Inspector for an Outlook item is being closed. The syntax for this event is different than in VBScript. In VBA, the proper usage is `Sub objectClose(Cancel as Boolean)`. This event can be canceled in the event handler.

Event	Event Occurs
CustomAction	When a custom action is executed. The syntax for this event is different than in VBScript. In VBA, the proper usage is `Sub objectCustomAction(Cancel as Boolean)`. This event can be canceled in the event handler.
CustomPropertyChange	When a custom property is changed. This event cannot be canceled.
Forward	When the Forward action is selected or performed. The syntax for this event is different than in VBScript. In VBA, the proper usage is `Sub objectForward(ByVal Forward as Object, Cancel as Boolean)`. This event can be canceled in the event handler.
ItemAdd	When an item is added to the specified collection. This event cannot be canceled. The `ItemAdd`, `ItemChange` and `ItemRemove` events are not available in VBScript.
ItemChange	When an item is changed in the specified collection. This event cannot be canceled.
ItemRemove	When an item is removed for the specified collection. This event cannot be canceled.
Open	When an Outlook item is being opened in an Inspector. When this event occurs, the Inspector object is initialized but not yet displayed. The syntax for this event is different than in VBScript. In VBA, the proper usage is `Sub objectOpen(Cancel as Boolean)`. This event can be canceled in the event handler.
PropertyChange	When a standard property of an Outlook item is changed. This event cannot be canceled.
Read	When an existing Outlook item is opened in an Inspector for editing. It also occurs whenever the user selects the item in a view that supports in-cell editing. This event cannot be canceled.
Reply	When the Reply action is selected or performed. The syntax for this event is different than in VBScript. In VBA, the proper usage is `Sub objectReply(ByVal Response as Object, Cancel as Boolean)`. The Response argument is the new item being sent in response to the original message. This event can be canceled in the event handler.
ReplyAll	When the Reply to All action is selected or the ReplyAll action is performed by program code. The syntax for this event is different than in VBScript. In VBA, the proper usage is `Sub objectReplyAll(ByVal Response as Object, Cancel as Boolean)`. The Response argument is the new item being sent in response to the original message. This event can be canceled in the event handler.

Table Continued on Following Page

Event	Event Occurs
Send	When an item is sent. The syntax for this event is different than in VBScript. In VBA, the proper usage is `Sub objectSend(Cancel as Boolean)`. This event can be canceled in the event handler.
Write	When an item is saved. The syntax for this event is different than in VBScript. In VBA, the proper usage is `Sub objectWrite(Cancel as Boolean)`. This event can be canceled in the event handler.

Outlook 2000 has added 30 new events in all, greatly enhancing the exposed object model and the programmability of Outlook. These events give us far greater control over Outlook 2000 than was possible with previous versions of Outlook, and enable easier and more comprehensive customization of Outlook than was previously possible.

Using Events to Extend Outlook

The easiest way to add event handling routines to Outlook 2000 is to add them to the `ThisOutlookSession` class module. They can be added to any class module however, and event handlers in custom class modules are discussed later in this chapter, in 'Responding to Events in Class Modules'. In this section we will create event handlers for some of the Outlook events at different levels of the object model.

> Although it is very easy to add event handlers to the `ThisOutlookSession` class module, in general this module should be reserved mainly for initializations and cleanup in the `Application_Startup` and `Application_Quit` events. Code for distribution should usually be distributed in COM add-ins, or in separate class modules. The best rule of thumb is to make minimal or no use of the `ThisOutlookSession` class module, and leave that module for the end user's customizations and macros.

The first event handler we will create automatically adds the current Outlook user to the BCC field of all MailItems when they are sent. This example uses the Application level `ItemSend` event. The `ItemSend` event is made available in `ThisOutlookSession` without needing any special `WithEvents` declarations.

To place this event handler in `ThisOutlookSession`, open `ThisOutlookSession` by expanding the Microsoft Outlook Objects folder in the Project Explorer and double-click on `ThisOutlookSession`. In the Object listbox at the top left of the Code window for `ThisOutlookSession` select the Application object. Then in the Procedure listbox at the top left of the Code Window select the `ItemSend` event. A template for the procedure is inserted in the class module. Enter the code for the event handler in the procedure framework.

```
Private Sub Application_ItemSend(ByVal Item As Object, Cancel As Boolean)
  Dim sUser As String
  Dim oRcp As Outlook.Recipient

  sUser = Application.GetNamespace("MAPI").CurrentUser
  If Item.Class = olMail Then
    Set oRcp = Item.Recipients.Add(sUser)
    oRcp.Type = olBCC
    oRcp.Resolve
  End If

  Set oRcp = Nothing
End Sub
```

> **If you are only responding to Mail items in the `ItemSend` event it is more efficient to use the `Send` event for Mail items. It is usually best to respond only to those events that are needed. Making an event handler as granular as possible will make your code run faster and be more efficient. See the sections below for examples of setting up event handlers for Item level events.**

When any new item that is a `MailItem` is sent, the name of the current user is added to the `Recipients` collection for the item. The `Type` of the new `Recipient` is then set to be a BCC entry, using the constant `olBCC`. This code requires that the current user has a resolved entry in an Outlook Address Book. If no resolved entry is present, or there is more than one entry and they are not resolved then the code will fail.

> **The use of the `Resolve` method is not required in the Internet only mode of Outlook but does no harm. If the new `Recipient` is not resolved in Corporate/Workgroup mode though, an error can result. This is a result of the order of events that fire on the item. The form level `BeforeCheckNames` event fires before the `ItemSend` event, so all the names are already resolved by the time the `ItemSend` event fires. This is one example of the differences in the Outlook operating modes that you have to watch out for when programming Outlook.**

The next example of working with Outlook events is an Item level event. This example copies any new items that are added to the Journal folder to a Public Journal folder located on an Exchange Server. Since events that aren't Application events are not automatically provided in `ThisOutlookSession`, a `WithEvents` statement is required to set up the event handler. Place the following declaration in the Declarations section of `ThisOutlookSession`.

```
Private WithEvents oJournal As Outlook.Items
```

This statement establishes the object variable `oJournal` as a variable used to respond to events, in this case events that are related to `Items`. The `Private` statement limits the visibility of the variable to the `ThisOutlookSession` class module. Variables declared `WithEvents` also can use `Dim` and `Public` statements to set the visibility that you need for the variable. Next, the code that initializes the event handler for `Items` in the Journal folder is placed in the `Application_Startup` procedure.

```
Private Sub Application_Startup()
  Dim oNS As Outlook.NameSpace

  Set oNS = Application.GetNameSpace("MAPI")
  Set oJournal = oNS.GetDefaultFolder(olFolderJournal).Items

  Set oNS = Nothing
End Sub
```

The NameSpace object is always required for accessing the items in the Outlook data store. The only NameSpace object currently supported is the MAPI namespace. Finally, the actual event handler is created.

```
Private Sub oJournal_ItemAdd(ByVal Item As Object)
  Dim oNS As Outlook.NameSpace
  Dim oPublic As Outlook.MAPIFolder
  Dim oItem As Outlook.JournalItem

  Set oNS = Application.GetNameSpace("MAPI")
  Set oPublic = oNS.Folders("Public Folders"). _
    Folders("All Public Folders").Folders("Public Journal")
  Set oItem = Item.Copy
  oItem.Move oPublic

  Set oNS = Nothing
  Set oPublic = Nothing
  Set oItem = Nothing
End Sub
```

The Public Journal folder is located under the Public Folders and All Public Folders branches of the Personal Folder hierarchy. The Copy method of the Item that is passed to the event handler is used to make a copy of the item, and then the Move method is used to move the copy to the Public Journal folder. Other Item level procedures can be created for the oJournal object variable once it is initialized in Application_Startup.

> The code that is placed in the ThisOutlookSession class module in this chapter is contained in a class module named clsThisOutlookSession.cls.

To establish event handlers for Folder level events, declarations can be made for each folder you want to monitor, using the following syntax to declare variables in the Declarations section of ThisOutlookSession.

```
Private WithEvents oFolder As Outlook.Folders
```

These Folder object variables are then initialized in the Application_Startup procedure the same way that Item level event variables are initialized.

```
Set oFolder = oNS.GetDefaultFolder(olFolderInbox).Folders
```

Establish separate object variables that are declared `WithEvents` for each set of `Folder` and `Item` level events that you want to respond to. Similarly, event variables can be declared for the events for specific types of Outlook items, such as ContactItems. Event variables can also be declared for the Explorers and Inspectors collections and for individual Explorer and Inspector objects. Most of the interactions with individual Outlook items occur through Inspector windows.

```
Private WithEvents oExplorers As Outlook.Explorers
Private WithEvents oExplorer As Outlook.Explorer
Private WithEvents oInspectors As Outlook.Inspectors
Private WithEvents oInspector As Outlook.Inspector
Private WithEvents oContact As Outlook.ContactItem
```

The preceding declarations all were placed in the Declarations section of `ThisOutlookSession`. Initialization of the event handler variables are placed in the `Application_Startup` procedure, which ensures that the event handlers initialized there run on every occurrence of the event. You can also be more selective about when the event handlers run by placing their initialization code in the `Class_Initialize` procedure of custom class modules. The declarations for event handler variables are placed in the Declarations section of the custom class module.

Event handlers placed in custom classes will run while the class is instantiated and in scope, and when the class gets destroyed they will stop running. This is discussed further in 'Responding to Events in Class Modules' later in this chapter. An event handler that is placed in a class module is created when the class is instantiated, and is no longer in existence when the class is terminated. The scope of such event handlers (when they are in effect) is only during the lifetime of the class.

When you work with event handlers for Explorer objects and the Explorers collection you should check for the active window being an Explorer object. Outlook can open without an active Explorer window when a shortcut is used to create an Outlook item. The `TypeName` Function procedure is used to check for the Outlook active window type.

```
Private Sub Application_Startup()
  Set oExplorers = Application.Explorers
  If TypeName(Application.ActiveWindow) = "Explorer" Then
    Set oExplorer = Application.ActiveWindow
  End If
  Set oInspectors = Application.Inspectors
End Sub
```

The previous code snippet also initialized an `Inspectors` collection object that can be used to set up an event handler for new Inspector windows. In this case, the event handler set up for the new Inspector window is only active when the item in the Inspector window is a `ContactItem`. This is done so that any Contact item in any Contacts folder will trigger the event. Then, an event handler is created for responding to the `Write` event of a `ContactItem`. This can be used to check the validity of data in the item, or you can add or edit data in the item before it is saved. If the `Cancel` variable is set to `True`, the `Write` is canceled. Any available event for the item can be responded to in this fashion.

```
Private Sub oInspectors_NewInspector(ByVal Inspector As Inspector)
  Set oInspector = Inspector
  'only respond to ContactItem events
  If oInspector.CurrentItem.Class = olContact Then
```

```
        Set oContact = oInspector.CurrentItem
    End If
End Sub

Private Sub oContact_Write(Cancel As Boolean)
    'Code to check data validity or perform other actions here
End Sub
```

The capability of writing event handlers for all the events available in the Outlook object model gives us the ability to extend Outlook's functionality in many different ways. A few of the things you can add to Outlook are incoming and outgoing mail filters; automatic creation of new Journal entries for items that aren't supported by the standard Journal categories; performing actions when Reminders fire; automatic forwarding of items based on content, subject or recipient; and performing actions when new items or folders are created. There are some Outlook events that are not exposed in this version of the object model, but Outlook 2000 is far more extensible than previous versions.

Office UserForms

Office UserForms are new to Outlook, along with VBA. They have been included in past versions of Office, but offer a new feature in Office 2000: modeless UserForms. Previously all UserForms were modal forms only. The addition of modeless forms enables the creation of display and informational windows that don't need an immediate response from the user, and that allow the program to continue executing.

Modal forms force the user to respond before anything else can be done in your application, and program execution halts until the form is closed. A typical use for a modal UserForm is for the creation of dialog boxes and message windows that require acknowledgement from the user.

Outlook forms are derived from the IPM message class, and have various controls already inserted in the forms and bound to Outlook item properties. They are associated with specific Outlook folders based on the IPM message class. You cannot create new Outlook forms from UserForms.

New UserForms have no controls and are not associated with any Outlook folders or items. UserForms run in the Application, not in specific folders. UserForms have more form events than Outlook forms, and have a richer object model. You can insert any available controls in a UserForm by adding them to the Controls Toolbox, but the default controls are the ones from the Microsoft Forms 2.0 library. If you are familiar with VB forms take some time to familiarize yourself with these controls, which have somewhat different properties than the controls that are available by default in the VB Controls Toolbox. The following screen shot shows a new UserForm and the Control Toolbox. Notice the similarity to VB forms and controls.

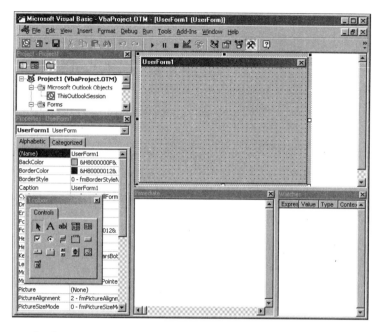

UserForms have no built-in connection to any Outlook items, although you can display information from Outlook items on UserForms. UserForms are primarily used for dialog boxes and informational displays although you can design any form based solution from a UserForm. You can design a UserForm to provide a means of inputting data into an Outlook item, but you probably will end up replicating the Outlook form designed for that purpose. Outlook forms have been created for that purpose and can be customized to fit your needs, so use them unless you need to respond to events that aren't available in Outlook forms. Working with Outlook forms was covered in Chapter 2.

Creating Dialog Boxes and Message Windows With UserForms

There are no rigid differences between dialog boxes and message windows, I make those classifications for convenience. Usually the main difference is whether the UserForm is opened modally or non-modally. If you need to get input from the user or have the user acknowledge a message then open the UserForm modally.

Open the UserForm non-modally when you are providing an informational window that can be allowed to remain open while the user works, or when the information that the form provides can be acquired asynchronously in your program. The controls that are placed on the form determine its usage and functions, not any arbitrary classifications.

Dialog Boxes

Dialog boxes are opened modally, to force the user to provide information or acknowledge a message before he can continue to work in Outlook. UserForms are opened modally by default, so you do not have to use the vbModal argument of the Show method except for clarity. The same form can be opened modally in one place in your program and non-modally in another. The only difference is the argument used (or not used) with the call to the Show method. Using the same form both modally and non-modally isn't good programming practice though, since it can confuse the user.

Insert a new UserForm from the Insert menu. Set the Font for the form to MS Sans Serif or some other nonproportional font. Nonproportional fonts often display more uniformly than proportional fonts and are easier to substitute if the user doesn't have your font installed. In addition, lining up text is done more easily with nonproportional fonts. Change the form Name to frmDialogBox and change the Caption to Programming Outlook 2000 in the Properties window for the form.

Add a listbox and two command buttons to the form. Name the listbox lstContacts. Name the first command button cmdOK, change its Caption to OK and set its Accelerator key to O. Name the other command button cmdCancel, change its Caption to Cancel and set its Accelerator key to C. Set the tab order for the controls by right-clicking on the form when no controls are selected and choosing **Tab Order**. Set the order to lstContacts, cmdOK and cmdCancel. The form should look similar to the screen shot shown below.

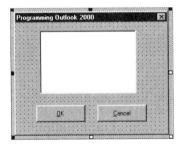

Right-click on the form and choose **View Code** and insert the following procedures. The cmdCancel procedure runs when the **Cancel** command button is clicked and unloads the UserForm.

```
Private Sub cmdCancel_Click()
  Unload Me
End Sub
```

The cmdOK procedure runs when the **OK** command button is clicked. It sets the global variable gsContact to the selection in the listbox and then unloads the UserForm.

```
Private Sub cmdOK_Click()
  'Set a global String variable to the
  'selected contact name.
  gsContact = lstContacts.Value
  Unload Me
End Sub
```

When a selection is made in the listbox the `Click` event fires and the **OK** command button is enabled.

```
Private Sub lstContacts_Click()
   cmdOK.Enabled = True
End Sub
```

The `Initialize` event is used to set the startup state of the **OK** button to disabled until a selection is made from the listbox. It also adds all the contacts in the default Contacts folder to the list in the listbox.

```
Private Sub UserForm_Initialize()
   Dim oNS As Outlook.NameSpace
   Dim oItems As Outlook.Items
   Dim oFolder As Outlook.MAPIFolder
   Dim oObj As Object

   cmdOK.Enabled = False

   Set oNS = Application.GetNamespace("MAPI")
   Set oFolder = oNS.GetDefaultFolder(olFolderContacts)
   Set oItems = oFolder.Items

   'Contacts folders can contain items other than
   'Contact items, for example DistributionList items,
   'so check each for Class = olContact. This can take a
   'while if you have a lot of contacts.
   For Each oObj In oItems
      If oObj.Class = olContact Then
         'Add each Contact name to the listbox
         lstContacts.AddItem oObj.FullName
      End If
   Next oObj

   Set oNS = Nothing
   Set oItems = Nothing
   Set oFolder = Nothing
   Set oObj = Nothing
End Sub
```

Testing each item in the Contacts folder ensures that only the items that are of the `olContact Class` are added to the listbox.

> Most Outlook 2000 folders can contain items of various classes, such as `DistributionListItems` in a Contacts folder or `PostItems` in a Mail folder. Checking for the item `Class` prevents runtime errors when assigning the item to a specific Outlook item type.

Add a new code module to the Outlook project and name it basUserForms. The form is initially loaded by a Sub procedure GetContact, that is contained in the module basUserForms. This module declares the global String variable gsContact, which is initialized to a Null string in GetContact. If a selection was made in the form, the name of the selected contact is displayed in a message box. The form is shown with the line frmDialogBox.Show vbModal, which explicitly uses the default vbModal argument. The result would be the same if that argument was simply omitted.

```
Public gsContact As String

Public Sub GetContact()
  gsContact = ""
  Load frmDialogBox
  frmDialogBox.Show vbModal
  'goContact now is set to either a selected
  'contact or to Nothing. Now you can do something
  'with the selected contact.
  If gsContact <> vbNullString Then
    MsgBox "You selected " & gsContact, , "Wrox"
  Else
    MsgBox "You canceled the selection process", , "Wrox"
  End If
End Sub
```

> **Although the preceding example showed interprocess communication by the use of global variables, it is often better practice to use a class module for this purpose. The properties of the class module can be used to set and read variables between different modules. The use of classes avoids problems in cases where multiple instances of a process are running, and keeps your variables limited in scope to the procedures where they are declared.**

Other, more complicated forms are developed throughout the book but they all follow the pattern laid out here. First set the properties of the new form, and then insert and adjust the desired controls. Set the control properties and tab order, and then add code to make the form do something useful.

Message Windows

Message windows don't have to display just text messages. They can display any information, even pictorial information in controls such as the Image control. Choose the controls best suited for displaying the information for that form. For text messages, the label control is often the best choice. You can update the message by changing the Caption of the control and it doesn't look grayed out like a disabled textbox. If you use a textbox to display the message it must be locked or disabled to prevent the user from tabbing to the textbox and altering its information.

Insert a UserForm, change its Name to frmMessageWindow and its Caption to Message Window. Set the form's font to MS Sans Serif. Insert a label control and a command button. Name the label control lblMessage. Name the command button cmdOK, set its Accelerator key to O and set its Caption to OK. Insert the following code in the form's code page.

```
Private Sub cmdOK_Click()
   Unload Me
End Sub

Private Sub UserForm_Initialize()
   lblMessage.Caption = gsContact
End Sub
```

The form should look similar to the screen shot shown below.

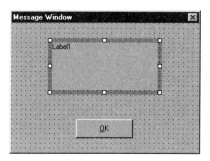

Insert the following code in the `basUserForms` module.

```
Public Sub ShowMessage()
   gsContact = "This listbox will display any message"
   Load frmMessageWindow
   frmMessageWindow.Show vbModeless
End Sub
```

This form can remain open while you continue working in Outlook because it was opened using the vbModeless argument of the Show method.

Interfacing With UserForms

To launch a UserForm from your code use the Load statement. This loads the form but doesn't show it to the user. The Initialize event for the form fires after the Load is completed to enable you to initialize the controls on the form and set its initial state. After the UserForm is loaded it can be shown modally or non-modally with the Show property of the UserForm. The code fragment to load and show the frmUser dialog box modally follows.

```
Load frmUser
'Showing modally is the default
'so this works the same
'FrmUser.Show
FrmUser.Show vbModal
```

The code fragment to load and show the `frmMsgWindow` message window non-modally follows.

```
Load frmMsgWindow
frmMsgWindow.Show vbModeless
```

UserForms can load Outlook forms in response to an action taken on the form, such as pressing a command button. The code used is the same as the code shown earlier in this chapter. The following code opens an Outlook form stored in the computer's file system.

```
Sub CustomContact()
   Dim myform As Outlook.ContactItem

   Set myform = Application.CreateItemFromTemplate("c:\My " _
      & "Documents\CustomContact.oft")
   myform.Display

   Set myform = Nothing
End Sub
```

The following code opens an Outlook form that has been published in the Contacts folder.

```
Sub OpenForm()
   Dim ns As Outlook.NameSpace
   Dim fld As Outlook.MAPIFolder
   Dim myform As Outlook.ContactItem
   Dim itms As Outlook.Items

   Set ns = Application.GetNamespace("MAPI")
   Set fld = ns.GetDefaultFolder(olFolderContacts)
   Set itms = fld.Items
   Set myform = itms.Add("IPM.Contact.CustomContact")
   myform.Display

   Set ns = Nothing
   Set fld = Nothing
   Set myform = Nothing
   Set itms = Nothing
End Sub
```

The easiest way to get information from a UserForm is to use a global variable for the information. Global variables are often frowned on because they can be changed from anywhere in your project, and can cause problems if multiple instances of forms are running, but they are often the easiest method of exchanging information with modal UserForms. The problem with accessing form data from outside the form is that modal forms are already closed by the time other code begins running again. Another method of passing information to and from UserForms is to encapsulate the required information as properties of a custom class module. Creating and using custom class modules is discussed in the next section.

Class Modules

You can create custom classes using VBA, and define properties, methods and events for those classes. Why do you want to create custom classes? Custom classes enable you to hide all the details of the implementation of your data and procedures. Only the exposed interface of the class is visible to users of the class. This creates a "black box" where the class has clearly defined inputs and outputs but the details of how you work with those inputs and outputs are hidden. The `Public` Sub and Function procedures of the class are its methods, and any procedures that are not `Public` are not exposed outside the class. The code that is within the methods is also hidden from the outside world.

Another reason to create custom classes is to simplify things. An example of this is function calls to the Win32 API. Many of the Win32 API functions are complex, with complicated calling syntax and arguments. You can package the calls to the Win32 API functions you need to use in a class object, and use simple more understandable arguments with the class's properties. Reading and writing the class properties invisibly hides the complexity of the Win32 API function calls.

Reusability of components is another reason to use custom classes. Class modules that you define serve as templates for creating new instances of the class objects with the `New` keyword. The class has already been debugged and can be treated as a program building block without worrying about variable or procedure naming conflicts.

Hiding the details of what is going on inside the class is called **encapsulation**. Encapsulation enables you to change the internal workings of the class and not affect users of the class. Only changing the definitions of the methods and properties of the class will affect class users. Another advantage of creating class modules and custom classes is that unlike global data in a code module, which exists once in the entire project, class data is created independently for each instance of the class that is created. This helps to isolate interactions in your code that can be created by using shared, global variables in different places. Class data is created when the class is created, and exists only during the lifetime of the class. Classes can be thought of as user defined types that hide their details from the outside world, although classes can do much more than user defined types, since they also can encapsulate methods and handle events.

Class modules and forms are the only containers that can respond to events. You can use a class module to respond to events that belong to the class, or to respond to events that Outlook raises. Outlook events that are responded to in a class module are only responded to during the lifetime of the class. `ThisOutlookSession` is a class module that has a lifetime that corresponds to the time that an Outlook session is open. This is one of the reasons that responding to Outlook events in `ThisOutlookSession` is the easiest way to respond to Outlook events.

Creating New Classes

To insert a new class module choose **Insert | Class Module**. Each new class that you create should be created in its own class module because the name for the class module is used as the class name.

Each class module provides two `Private` events when it is created, an `Initialize` event and a `Terminate` event. Once a class is designed, it is created in your program by referencing it with the `New` keyword. The class is destroyed when no further references to it remain in your code or when it is explicitly set to `Nothing`.

The `Initialize` event is used to initialize class variables, initial property settings for the class and error handlers for the class. The `Terminate` event is used to place error handling code, to release `Public` and module level variables and to destroy objects created in the class. Objects are destroyed by being set to `Nothing`. Any variables or objects that are created in the class, and remain in memory after the class is destroyed, will cause memory leaks. The `Initialize` and `Terminate` events should not normally be used to interact with the user interface.

Each class has two intrinsic properties, `Name` and `Instancing`. The `Instancing` property merits some explanation. The `Instancing` property for a class determines whether you can create instances of the class outside of the project that it is defined in. VB allows six settings for this property but only the first two, `Private` and `PublicNotCreatable`, are allowed in VBA. `SingleUse`, `GlobalSingleUse`, `MultiUse` and `GlobalMultiUse` are not allowed in VBA.

`Private Instancing` means that other applications aren't allowed access to type library information about the class, and cannot create instances of it. `Private` objects are only for use within your project and are visible only within the Outlook project. `PublicNotCreatable Instancing` means that other applications can use objects of your class only if your project creates those objects first. The `CreateObject` function and the `New` keyword cannot be used by other applications to create new objects from your class

Adding Properties to a Class

Properties are added to a custom class by using the `Property Let`, `Property Get` and `Property Set` procedure statements. `Property Let` sets the value of a property, `Property Get` returns the value of a property, and `Property Set` sets a reference to an object. Declaring only the `Property Get` procedure for a property creates a read-only property. Declaring only the `Property Let` procedure for a property creates a write-only property. Declaring both procedures creates a read/write property.

These procedures have `Public` scope by default. Using the `Private` keyword sets the visibility of the property to only the other procedures in the class module. Using the `Friend` keyword sets the visibility to any procedure in the project, like `Public`, but the property is not visible to controllers of an instance of the class if they are not in the same project as the class. `Friend` Property procedures cannot be used with late binding, and do not appear in the type library for the class. `Friend` procedures are new to VBA in Office 2000.

Property procedures can retain the values of their local variables between calls by using the `Static` keyword. If the `Static` keyword is not used, local variables in the Property procedure do not retain their values between procedure calls.

`Property Let` procedures must define at least one argument and if there is more than one argument defined then the last argument becomes the value of the property. `Property Get` procedures must define their arguments (if any) in the same order and with the same data types as the arguments in the corresponding `Property Let` procedure. There is always one less argument for a `Property Get` procedure than for a `Property Let` procedure. The return value for the `Property Get` procedure must be the same type as the last argument of the `Property Let` procedure.

Since `Property Get` procedures return a value, they can be used on the right side of the equal sign in an equation, the same way that Function procedures are used. `Property Get` procedures can be assigned a default return value.

Property procedures can use the `Optional`, `ParamArray`, `ByRef` and `ByVal` keywords to modify their argument lists. Procedure arguments in VBA are passed by reference (`ByRef`) unless the `ByVal` modifier is explicitly used, unlike VBScript arguments which are passed as the value of the arguments (`ByVal`). The `Optional` keyword is used to indicate that all arguments that follow are optional arguments for the procedure. If `Optional` is used then all succeeding arguments must also be `Optional`. `ParamArray` is used only for the last argument in an argument list and indicates that the argument is an optional array of Variants. An argument that is declared as `ParamArray` cannot use the `Optional`, `ByVal` or `ByRef` keywords.

You should avoid declaring `Public` variables in a class module, since that makes the variables visible throughout the project. Use module level variables when you need to have a variable visible throughout the class module. Use `Public` or `Friend` properties for the class data that needs to be visible outside the class module. The reason for avoiding declaring `Public` variables is that they can be changed anywhere in your project, and there is no way to control or validate such changes. Using properties instead is preferable since any changes to the properties are controlled and validated by the `Property Let` procedure for that property. Properties are also specific to a specific instance of a class, and are not shared when multiple instances of a class are running.

Adding Methods to a Class

The Sub and Function procedures that are declared in the class module are the methods of your class. They usually are declared as `Public` procedures, but they can also be declared as having `Friend` scope. `Public` procedures can be used anywhere your class is visible. `Friend` procedures can only be used within your project. You can also declare `Private` procedures, which become private methods of your class, not visible outside the class. Methods that are Function procedures return a value and can be used on the right side of an equation, or anywhere else a Function procedure is used.

Adding Events to a Class

You have already seen one of the statements that is associated with event handling, the `WithEvents` statement, in the section on Outlook Events earlier in this chapter. `WithEvents` was used to define an object that was used as an event handler for various intrinsic Outlook events. `WithEvents` is also used to define event handlers for user defined events in your class module or form. `WithEvents` must appear in the same class module or form where the event handler code appears.

The other two statements associated with user defined event handling are `Event` and `RaiseEvent`. These statements are used only with user defined events, they are not needed or permitted for intrinsic Outlook events. `Event` and `RaiseEvent` are paired to declare and fire user defined events. Both statements must appear in the same class module or form. Intrinsic events in Outlook or other applications are raised by the application itself, you don't have to do anything to cause the events to fire. Events in user defined classes only fire when your code causes them to fire by using the `RaiseEvent` statement. Outlook, VBA or VB don't know when your events need to be fired. That is where the `Event` and `RaiseEvent` statement pair come in.

> **A class or form that raises an event is called an event source. Classes or forms that implement the event handler are called event sinks. There can be more than one event sink for any one event. If there is more than one event sink for an event, the event will fire in every class or form that implements an event handler for that instance of the object. The order in which the event sinks fire the event is not guaranteed.**

The Event and RaiseEvent statement pair cannot be placed in the same class module or form that declares that it handles the event by using the WithEvents statement. The trick is to use one class module or form to instantiate a second class module that defines the event with the Event and RaiseEvent statement pair. Then the first class module or form can itself be instantiated or opened from anywhere in your project.

Using Custom Classes

In this section we will create a custom class module. This class will have two read-only properties, two read/write properties and one method. The two read-only properties are HowMany and WhatType. HowMany returns the number of items in the current folder in the active Explorer. WhatType returns the default item type for the current folder in the active Explorer. They are both implemented as Property Get procedures.

The first read/write property is Describe, implemented as paired Property Get and Property Let procedures. This property returns or sets the description of the current folder. The description of the current folder is visible in the user interface on the folder Property sheet. To view the folder Property sheet, right-click on the folder in the Folder List or the Outlook Bar and select Properties in the context menu.

The second read/write property is ThisFolder, which returns or sets the current folder in the active Explorer. It is implemented as paired Property Get and Property Set procedures. The write portion of the property, the Property Set procedure, has one MAPIFolder object argument in its call. The Property Set procedure takes the MAPIFolder object argument and uses it to set a new current folder. The read portion of the property, the Property Get procedure, has no arguments. All the Property Get procedures are declared with specific return data types.

First, create a new class module by choosing Insert | Class Module in the VBE. Change the Name of the class module from the default name Class1 to clsFolderData. Leave the Instancing property set to Private for this example. Creating and working with events in custom classes is covered later in this section.

The method is DefaultView which sets a default view for the current folder in the active Explorer depending on the type of the current folder. It is implemented as a Public Sub procedure with no calling arguments.

In the Outlook object model, objects are separated by the classes and collections to which they belong. These classes and collections cannot be mixed. To access members of the Folders, Items or Explorers collections you need different variable types. The custom class clsFolderData encapsulates the internal operations and data types that are needed to access these different collections. It makes objects from different collections available in one unified interface. This class example is a simple one, but it shows how the inner complexity and workings of the Outlook object model can be concealed and presented as a unified interface to other programs, procedures or objects.

Insert the following procedures in the clsFolderData class module. The read-only property HowMany reads the count of items in the current folder.

```
Public Property Get HowMany() As Long
   'Read-only Property
   'Number of individual items in this folder
   HowMany = Application.ActiveExplorer.CurrentFolder.Items.Count
End Property
```

The read-only property `WhatType` uses the default item type for the current folder to decide which type of folder is the current folder.

```
Public Property Get WhatType() As String
   'Read-only Property
   'The default item type for the folder
   Dim lType As Long

   lType = Application.ActiveExplorer.CurrentFolder.DefaultItemType
   Select Case lType
   Case olAppointmentItem
      WhatType = "Appointment"
   Case olContactItem
      WhatType = "Contact"
   Case olJournalItem
      WhatType = "Journal"
   Case olMailItem
      WhatType = "Mail"
   Case olNoteItem
      WhatType = "Note"
   Case olPostItem
      WhatType = "Post"
   Case olTaskItem
      WhatType = "Task"
   End Select
End Property
```

The read/write `Describe` property is implemented as a pair of `Property Let` and `Property Get` procedures. The `Description` property of the current folder is set or read by these procedures.

```
Public Property Let Describe(sName As String)
   'Write portion of read/write Property
   'Change the description of the current folder
   Dim oFld As Outlook.MAPIFolder

   Set oFld = Application.ActiveExplorer.CurrentFolder
   oFld.Description = sName

   Set oFld = Nothing
End Property

Public Property Get Describe() As String
   'Read portion of read/write Property
   'Get the description of the current folder as a string
   Describe = Application.ActiveExplorer.CurrentFolder.Description
End Property
```

The read/write `ThisFolder` property is implemented as a pair of `Property Set` and `Property Get` procedures. The `Property Set` procedure uses an object reference to set the new current folder, and the `Property Get` procedure returns the name of the current folder.

```
Public Property Set ThisFolder(oFld As Outlook.MAPIFolder)
    'Write portion of read/write Property
    'Implemented as a Property Set procedure, using an object
    'Set a new current folder

    If Not oFld Is Nothing Then
        Set Application.ActiveExplorer.CurrentFolder = oFld
    End If
End Property

Public Property Get ThisFolder() As String
    'Read portion of read/write Property
    'Get the name of the current folder as a string
    ThisFolder = Application.ActiveExplorer.CurrentFolder.Name
End Property
```

The `DefaultView` method switches to a default view for any folder. A standard Outlook view is used as the default view for each type of Outlook folder.

```
Public Sub DefaultView()
    'Method
    Dim lType As Long
    Dim sView As String

    'Set the view for the current folder to a default setting
    lType = Application.ActiveExplorer.CurrentFolder.DefaultItemType
    Select Case lType
    Case olAppointmentItem
        sView = "Day/Week/Month"
    Case olContactItem
        sView = "Address Cards"
    Case olJournalItem
        sView = "Last Seven Days"
    Case olMailItem
        sView = "Messages"
    Case olNoteItem
        sView = "Notes List"
    Case olPostItem
        sView = "Messages"
    Case olTaskItem
        sView = "Simple List"
    End Select

    Application.ActiveExplorer.CurrentView = sView
End Sub
```

To instantiate a new instance of the `clsFolderData` class for this example we will create a modeless UserForm to control the class and a macro to launch the UserForm. Choose Insert | UserForm to create a new, blank UserForm. Change the form's name to `frmFolderControl` and the caption to `Folder Control`.

Place a label at the top left of the form, with a command button to the right of the label. Below that row of controls place two more labels. Below those labels place a textbox at the left side of the form, with a command button to its right. Below that place two more command buttons. Set the name and properties of the labels, text box and command buttons as follows.

Control	Name	Property
Label 1	lblFolder	Caption = Current folder:
Button 1	cmdFolder	Caption = Change Folder
Label 2	lblItems	Caption = # of Items
Label 3	lblType	Caption = Folder type:
Label 4	lblDescribe	Caption = Description
Text box	txtDescribe	Multiline = True
Button 2	cmdDescribe	Caption = Change Description
Button 3	cmdView	Caption = Default View
Button 4	cmdQuit	Caption = Quit

The UserForm `frmFolderControl` should look similar to the following screen shot.

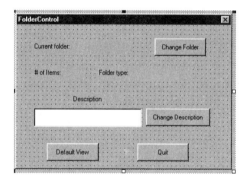

Place the following code in the code page of the form. A module level variable is declared in the Declarations section of the form code to declare the custom class module. The `Click` event for the `cmdDescribe` command button is used to alternately enable and disable the description textbox, and to set a property of the class module when new descriptive text has been entered.

```
Private m_class As clsFolderData

Private Sub cmdDescribe_Click()
  If txtDescribe.Enabled = True Then
    m_class.Describe = txtDescribe.Value
    txtDescribe.Enabled = False
  Else
```

111

```
            txtDescribe.Enabled = True
            txtDescribe.SetFocus
        End If
    End Sub
```

The `Click` event for the `cmdFolder` command button performs a number of functions. It brings up the `PickFolder` dialog box, which is a standard Outlook dialog box, to allow the user to choose a new folder. Then, it updates the class `ThisFolder` property to the new folder, and updates the labels and textbox with the information from the new folder.

```
    Private Sub cmdFolder_Click()
        Dim oNS As Outlook.NameSpace
        Dim oFld As Outlook.MAPIFolder

        Set oNS = Application.GetNamespace("MAPI")
        'Let the user pick a folder
        Set oFld = oNS.PickFolder

        'Set the new folder
        Set m_class.ThisFolder = oFld
        lblItems.Caption = "# of Items: " & CStr(m_class.HowMany)
        lblType.Caption = "Folder type: " & m_class.WhatType
        lblFolder.Caption = "Current folder: " & m_class.ThisFolder
        txtDescribe.Value = m_class.Describe

        Set oNS = Nothing
        Set oFld = Nothing
    End Sub
```

The next two procedures unload the form when the **Quit** command button is clicked and set the default view for the current folder. The default view is set by the `DefaultView` method of the custom class.

```
    Private Sub cmdQuit_Click()
        Unload Me
    End Sub

    Private Sub cmdView_Click()
        m_class.DefaultView
    End Sub
```

The `Initialize` event for the form creates a new instance of the custom class and sets the initial state of the labels and textbox. The `Terminate` event is used to destroy the instance of the custom class by setting it to `Nothing`.

```
    Private Sub UserForm_Initialize()
        Set m_class = New clsFolderData
        lblItems.Caption = "# of Items: " & CStr(m_class.HowMany)
        lblType.Caption = "Folder type: " & m_class.WhatType
        lblFolder.Caption = "Current folder: " & m_class.ThisFolder
        txtDescribe.Value = m_class.Describe
        txtDescribe.Enabled = False
```

```
End Sub

Private Sub UserForm_Terminate()
   Set m_class = Nothing
End Sub
```

A module level variable `m_class` is declared as `clsFolderData` (the name of our class) type. Once a class module is created, its data type is available for use in declarations. The `Form_Initialize` event is used to instantiate the class module with the line `Set m_class = New clsFolderData`. The captions of the label controls and the value of the text box are then updated with the class's current properties.

The Change Folder button executes the `cmdFolder_Click` procedure, which uses the `PickFolder` method of the `NameSpace` object to let the user choose a new folder. The `PickFolder` method returns the selected folder as a `MAPIFolder` object. If the user has canceled the selection the value `Nothing` is returned. If the `MAPIFolder` object is `Nothing`, the `Property Set` procedure is exited without changing anything. If it is `Not Nothing`, the `MAPIFolder` object is used to set the new current folder in the `ThisFolder Property Set` procedure. Since the write portion of the property takes an object as an argument, a `Set` statement is required in the line `Set m_class.ThisFolder = oFld`. The following screen shot shows the UserForm displaying information from the class about the Inbox.

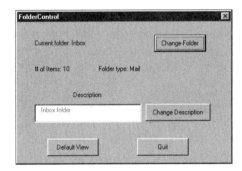

We could also retrieve the `EntryID` and `StoreID` of that folder if we wanted. We then could use the `EntryID` and `StoreID` properties of the folder to connect to that folder in CDO if necessary, although this custom class doesn't use CDO. An alternative method of changing the folder uses the `GetFolderFromID` method of the `NameSpace` object in conjunction with the `EntryID` and `StoreID` properties. This method can retrieve any folder in the current data store, not only default folders, as shown in the code snippet below.

```
Dim oNS As Outlook.NameSpace
Dim sFID As String 'EntryID for the folder
Dim sSID As String 'StoreID for the folder

   Set oNS = Application.GetNamespace("MAPI")
   Set Application.ActiveExplorer.CurrentFolder = _
        oNS.GetFolderFromID(sFID, sSID)
```

The code that changes the current folder leads an interesting "feature" of the `CurrentFolder` property of the `ActiveExplorer` object.

```
If Not oFld Is Nothing Then
   Set Application.ActiveExplorer.CurrentFolder = oFld
End If
```

If the `CurrentFolder` property is changed in a code statement that doesn't use the `Set` keyword then the result is that the current folder is renamed. The line `Application.ActiveExplorer.CurrentFolder = oFld` will rename the current folder with the name of the selected folder returned by the `PickFolder` method. `Application.ActiveExplorer.CurrentFolder = olFolderInbox` would result in the current folder being renamed "6", the value of `olFolderInbox`. Be very careful when setting object properties to use the `Set` keyword, so that you don't inadvertently run into problems.

Finally, create the Macro `ClassDemo` with the following code to load and show the `frmFolderControl` UserForm. The UserForm is shown non-modally so that other work in Outlook can continue while the form is open. The `ClassDemo` Macro is stored in the `basMacros` code module.

```
Sub ClassDemo()
   Load frmFolderControl
   frmFolderControl.Show vbModeless
End Sub
```

The class we created in the previous example shows some of the uses and features of custom classes. It shows how to create and use the three `Property` procedures `Property Let`, `Property Get` and `Property Set` and how to create and use class methods. The creation of read-only and two different types of read/write properties was also shown, as was the instantiation of a new instance of the class.

Read/write-once and Write-once only properties can also be created by setting a module level Boolean variable `Written` to `True` when the first write occurs to a property. Checking the state of the Boolean variable in the `Property Let` or `Property Set` procedure for that property enables you to decide when or if the write to the property should occur.

The next section demonstrates the handling of intrinsic Outlook events and user defined events in class modules.

Responding to Events in Class Modules

Two types of events can be handled in class modules, intrinsic events and user defined events. Most of the intrinsic events will usually be handled in the `ThisOutlookSession` module since it is always instantiated when Outlook is running, and Outlook events that are being handled require less setup and code when they are handled there. When Outlook is being controlled as an Automation object by another application, the techniques discussed in this section will be needed to handle Outlook events. In addition, if you want certain Outlook events to be handled only at certain times then the event handling can be performed in a class module or form, and when the class module or form is closed, the event handler will no longer be active.

Outlook Events in Class Modules

We have already looked at responding to some Outlook events in `ThisOutlookSession`, a special class module that is part of the Outlook Project. In this section we will look at responding to Outlook events in a custom class module. Insert a new class module and change its `Name` to `clsCounter`. Insert the following code in the `clsCounter` class module.

The event variables are declared in the Declarations section of the class module, and the `Initialize` event of the class is used to instantiate an `Application` event variable and an event variable for items in the Journal folder.

```
Private WithEvents oApp As Outlook.Application
Private WithEvents oJournal As Outlook.Items

Private Sub Class_Initialize()
  Dim oNS As Outlook.NameSpace

  Set oApp = CreateObject("Outlook.Application")
  Set oNS = Outlook.GetNamespace("MAPI")
  Set oJournal = oNS.GetDefaultFolder(olFolderJournal).Items

  Set oNS = Nothing
End Sub
```

The `NewMail` event can be handled here since the `Application` variable was declared `WithEvents`. This is not necessary if this event is handled in the `ThisOutlookSession` class module, since it is one of the intrinsic events in that module. In this case, `NewMail` is used to update a message about the number of unread items in the Inbox.

```
Private Sub oApp_NewMail()
  Dim oNS As Outlook.NameSpace
  Dim oFolder As Outlook.MAPIFolder
  Dim obj As Object
  Dim lCount As Long

  lCount = 0
  Set oNS = Outlook.GetNamespace("MAPI")
  Set oFolder = oNS.GetDefaultFolder(olFolderInbox)
  For Each obj In oFolder.Items
    If obj.Class = olMail And obj.UnRead Then
      lCount = lCount + 1
    End If
  Next
  MsgBox "There are " & lCount & "unread items"

  Set oNS = Nothing
  Set oFolder = Nothing
  Set obj = Nothing
End Sub
```

The `ItemAdd` event for items in the default Journal folder is used here to present a message about how many items are in the Journal.

```
Private Sub oJournal_ItemAdd(ByVal Item As Object)
  Dim oNS As Outlook.NameSpace
  Dim oFolder As Outlook.MAPIFolder
  Dim lCount As Long

  Set oNS = Outlook.GetNamespace("MAPI")
```

```
    Set oFolder = oNS.GetDefaultFolder(olFolderJournal)
    lCount = oFolder.Items.Count

    MsgBox "There are now " & lCount & _
        " items in the Journal folder"

    Set oNS = Nothing
    Set oFolder = Nothing
End Sub
```

The `Terminate` event for the class is used to destroy the class's module level object variables by setting them to `Nothing`.

```
Private Sub Class_Terminate()
    Set oJournal = Nothing
    Set oApp = Nothing
End Sub
```

The statement `Private WithEvents oApp As Outlook.Application` indicates that we want to handle Outlook events in our class module. The statement adds all the Outlook `Application` events that are shown in `ThisOutlookSession` to the Procedure box in the class module (`ItemSend`, `NewMail`, `OptionPagesAdd`, `Quit`, `Reminder` and `Startup`). The following statement, `Private WithEvents oJournal As Outlook.Items` enables handling Outlook `Items` events and adds the `Items` events `Add`, `Change` and `Remove` to the Procedure box.

The `Application` event `NewMail` is exposed when the `Class_Initialize` event uses the `CreateObject` procedure to create an instance of the Outlook `Application` event. When this statement is executed in the `Class_Initialize` event the class is ready to handle `Application` events, since the variable that the `Application` event is assigned to was declared `WithEvents`. The `NewMail` event is used to count the number of `UnRead MailItems` in the Inbox folder when any new item is received in the Inbox.

The `Class_Initialize` event is used to instantiate `oJournal` to handle the `Items` events that occur in the Journal folder. The `oJournal_ItemAdd` procedure is the only event handler for `Items` events in the class, and uses the `Count` property of the folder `Items` as data for a message box that displays the number of items in the Journal folder. The `Class_Terminate` procedure is used to set the class module level objects to `Nothing` and release the memory and resources they are using.

Insert the following code in the `basMacros` code module. If you have Auto List Members enabled in the **Options** dialog box in the **Tools** menu, when you press the spacebar after the `As` clause a list of possible items to complete the statement pops up. The class `clsCounter` is one of those items after the class module is created.

```
Private m_counter As clsCounter 'Note: insert this in the Declarations section

Public Sub InitItemCounter()
    Set m_counter = New clsCounter
End Sub
```

Since the event handling code is not in `ThisOutlookSession`, which automatically runs the `Application_Startup` event code when Outlook is started, the Sub procedure `InitItemCounter` must be run either manually, as a macro or as part of some other code. If the `m_counter` object variable was declared in the `InitItemCounter` procedure then it would go out of scope when `InitItemCounter` ended. That would stop the event handler from continuing to run, because the class is destroyed when the procedure that created it and is the only reference to it ends. By making `m_counter` a module level variable it remains in scope until Outlook is exited. The next time Outlook is started, the code in the class module won't run until `InitItemCounter` is executed.

Another way to handle events when you want to limit when the events are handled is to place the code that instantiates the class and contains the class variable in a UserForm. The Sub procedure `InitItemCounter` can be placed in the `Initialize` event of the form and the `m_counter` would be declared at the module level of the form's code. Loading the form will then activate the class and the event handlers and closing it will destroy the class and stop the event handlers from running. If the form is not made visible by using its `Show` method then the user will never know that the form has been loaded.

These techniques enable you to have precise control of when the Outlook events are handled by specific event handlers. You can even have multiple event handlers for the same events that run at different times depending on the current state of the Outlook application. Remember that if you have multiple event handlers for the same events there is no guaranteed order in which the event handlers will receive the events.

> If you want a class module to be ready to handle Outlook events throughout an Outlook session, you can create an instance of the class in the `Application_Startup` event in the `ThisOutlookSession` module. That way the `ThisOutlookSession` module does not contain a lot of code, only as much as is necessary to create the instance of the class module.

Custom Events in Class Modules

To demonstrate how to work with user defined events in class modules we will modify the `clsFolderData` class module we created earlier in this chapter and add an event to it. Insert a new class module and name it `clsUserEvent`. Copy the code from the `clsFolderData` class module and paste it into the `clsUserEvent` class module. We will add a declaration for the event and modify the code in the `Property Set ThisFolder` procedure to raise the event. The event declaration takes the following form.

```
Public Event NothingError(sErr As String)
```

The remaining sections of code are the same as in the `clsFolderData` class module, except for the `ThisFolder` procedure.

```
Public Property Get HowMany() As Long
    'Read-only Property
    'Number of individual items in this folder
    HowMany = Application.ActiveExplorer.CurrentFolder.Items.Count
```

```
      End Property

      Public Property Get WhatType() As String
        'Read-only Property
        'The default item·type for the folder
        Dim lType As Long

        lType = Application.ActiveExplorer.CurrentFolder.DefaultItemType
        Select Case lType
        Case olAppointmentItem
          WhatType = "Appointment"
        Case olContactItem
          WhatType = "Contact"
        Case olJournalItem
          WhatType = "Journal"
        Case olMailItem
          WhatType = "Mail"
        Case olNoteItem
          WhatType = "Note"
        Case olPostItem
          WhatType = "Post"
        Case olTaskItem
          WhatType = "Task"
        End Select
      End Property

      Public Property Let Describe(sName As String)
        'Write portion of read/write Property
        'Change the description of the current folder
        Dim oFld As Outlook.MAPIFolder

        Set oFld = Application.ActiveExplorer.CurrentFolder
        oFld.Description = sName

        Set oFld = Nothing
      End Property

      Public Property Get Describe() As String
        'Read portion of read/write Property
        'Get the description of the current folder as a string
        Describe = Application.ActiveExplorer.CurrentFolder.Description
      End Property
```

The ThisFolder property now has a RaiseEvent statement in it. The user defined event NothingError is raised (fired) by this statement. The event is not handled within the class, but is handled by a class or form that creates the class.

```
      Public Property Set ThisFolder(oFld As Outlook.MAPIFolder)
        'Write portion of read/write Property
        'Implemented as a Property Set procedure, using an object
        'Set a new current folder
```

```
      If oFld Is Nothing Then
        RaiseEvent NothingError("You canceled the selection")
      Else
        Set Application.ActiveExplorer.CurrentFolder = oFld
      End If
  End Property


  Public Property Get ThisFolder() As String
    'Read portion of read/write Property
    'Get the name of the current folder as a string
    ThisFolder = Application.ActiveExplorer.CurrentFolder.Name
  End Property

  Public Sub DefaultView()
    'Method
    Dim lType As Long
    Dim sView As String

    'Set the view for the current folder to a default setting
    lType = Application.ActiveExplorer.CurrentFolder.DefaultItemType
    Select Case lType
    Case olAppointmentItem
      sView = "Day/Week/Month"
    Case olContactItem
      sView = "Address Cards"
    Case olJournalItem
      sView = "Last Seven Days"
    Case olMailItem
      sView = "Messages"
    Case olNoteItem
      sView = "Notes List"
    Case olPostItem
      sView = "Messages"
    Case olTaskItem
      sView = "Simple List"
    End Select

    Application.ActiveExplorer.CurrentView = sView
  End Sub
```

The `RaiseEvent` statement is used in the `ThisFolder` procedure when the user cancels the selection of a folder in the `PickFolder` method and passes a string describing the error to the class (in this case a UserForm) that implements the error handler and serves as the event sink. The following code snippet shows the use of the `RaiseEvent` statement.

```
    If oFld Is Nothing Then
      RaiseEvent NothingError("You canceled the selection")
```

To implement the error handler and serve as the event sink we will copy and then modify the frmFolderControl UserForm. Insert a new UserForm and change its Name to frmUserEventDemo. Change the Caption to User Event, and change the Font to MS Sans Serif. Double-click on the frmFolderControl UserForm in the Project Explorer and choose **Select All** from the **Edit** menu. Then choose **Copy** from the **Edit** menu and select the frmUserEventDemo UserForm. Choose **Paste** from the edit menu to paste all the controls from frmFolderControl into frmUserEventDemo. Adjust the size of frmUserEventDemo and the placement of the controls until they are satisfactory.

Copy the code from the frmFolderControl UserForm into frmUserEventDemo.

Modify the statement declaring the module level variable instance of the class m_class as follows:

```
Private WithEvents m_class As clsUserEvent
```

The remaining code in the UserForm will remain the same as before, except for adding a new event handling procedure m_class_NothingError, and changing one line in the initialization event. After the WithEvents statement for the m_class declaration, the event is available as a prototype in the Procedure listbox for the m_class object.

```
Private Sub cmdDescribe_Click()
  If txtDescribe.Enabled = True Then
    m_class.Describe = txtDescribe.Value
    txtDescribe.Enabled = False
  Else
    txtDescribe.Enabled = True
    txtDescribe.SetFocus
  End If
End Sub

Private Sub cmdFolder_Click()
  Dim oNS As Outlook.NameSpace
  Dim oFld As Outlook.MAPIFolder

  Set oNS = Application.GetNamespace("MAPI")
  'Let the user pick a folder
  Set oFld = oNS.PickFolder

  'Set the new folder
  Set m_class.ThisFolder = oFld
  lblItems.Caption = "# of Items: " & CStr(m_class.HowMany)
  lblType.Caption = "Folder type: " & m_class.WhatType
  lblFolder.Caption = "Current folder: " & m_class.ThisFolder
  txtDescribe.Value = m_class.Describe

  Set oNS = Nothing
  Set oFld = Nothing
End Sub

Private Sub cmdQuit_Click()
  Unload Me
End Sub
```

```
Private Sub cmdView_Click()
  m_class.DefaultView
End Sub
```

In this case the event handler for the user defined error is displaying a message box describing the error that was raised.

```
Private Sub m_class_NothingError(sErr As String)
  MsgBox sErr, , "Wrox"
End Sub
```

Change the first code line that creates a new instance of the class so that it creates the correct class. Otherwise you will get a runtime error because `clsUserEvent` fires our user defined event, which `clsFolderData` knows nothing about.

```
Private Sub UserForm_Initialize()
  Set m_class = New clsUserEvent
  lblItems.Caption = "# of Items: " & CStr(m_class.HowMany)
  lblType.Caption = "Folder type: " & m_class.WhatType
  lblFolder.Caption = "Current folder: " & m_class.ThisFolder
  txtDescribe.Value = m_class.Describe
  txtDescribe.Enabled = False
End Sub

Private Sub UserForm_Terminate()
  Set m_class = Nothing
End Sub
```

The following code is placed in the `basMacros` code module to open the `frmUsrEvent` UserForm.

```
Sub EventDemo()
  Load frmUserEventDemo
  frmUserEventDemo.Show vbModeless
End Sub
```

This example shows how you can add user defined events to your custom classes and how to handle the events. The main limitation of user defined events is that you have to fire them, Outlook will not know when to fire the events for you.

Extending Outlook Functionality Using ThisOutlookSession

There are four main ways to extend Outlook 2000's functionality and change its user interface. The first is through the user interface, using the Options dialog box and the Property sheets for the folders. Customizing Outlook's menus, toolbars and the Outlook Bar also can be done in the user interface. Since this is a programming book we won't cover those methods here. The second way is to use customized Outlook forms, which is limited to folders that have those forms published in them or when those forms are explicitly opened. This only changes the specific forms that Outlook uses for various functions. The third way, and perhaps the best way, is to develop COM add-ins, which are discussed in Chapter 7. Finally, we can develop VBA code in `ThisOutlookSession`.

The limitations of distributing code in `VbaProject.OTM` were discussed earlier in this chapter. However, if you are developing code for yourself these limitations are minimal. Code developed and tested in `ThisOutlookSession` can later be ported to an Add-in Project in Office Developer or VB, so using `ThisOutlookSession` makes sense even if you will later distribute the code. The major advantage of developing code in `ThisOutlookSession` is that it is always present and running in Outlook, and it provides a class module that makes the Outlook `Application` events easily accessible. This section demonstrates a number of enhancements to Outlook that can make it work more the way you want it to work.

Adding Features to Outlook

Code that is placed in the `Application_Startup` Sub procedure in `ThisOutlookSession` runs each time Outlook starts. It is the best place to put not only initialization code for Outlook event handlers but also code that changes the way Outlook looks and functions. Any changes that you make to Outlook in `Application_Startup` will be initialized automatically when Outlook starts up.

A question that is often asked is how to make Outlook start up in a minimized state, rather than in an open window. The following code causes Outlook to be minimized after it is initialized. It sets the window state for the active Explorer to `olMinimized`, which minimizes Outlook and leaves an icon in the Taskbar. The part of the code that is interesting is the check for `Application.Explorers.Count`. If Outlook is started from a standard shortcut, or is started directly by executing the `Outlook.exe` file, then an Explorer window is always opened. If Outlook is opened from an item shortcut, such as this one that opens a new mail item Outlook /c ipm.note, then no Explorer window is opened or active. In these cases the line `Application.ActiveExplorer.WindowState = olMinimized` will cause a runtime error since there is no active Explorer. The test for `Explorers.Count` will only succeed if one or more Explorer windows is open, preventing the runtime error. This technique is also used for COM add-ins to prevent errors from occurring in the add-in's startup and shutdown routines. This code is integrated in the `clsThisOutlookSession` class module.

```
Private Sub Application_Startup()
  If Application.Explorers.Count Then
    Application.ActiveExplorer.WindowState = olMinimized
  End If
End Sub
```

Another feature that is often requested is a way of sending items immediately. In Internet only mode and some configurations of Corporate/Workgroup mode, items that are sent using the **Send** toolbar button in an open item just go to the Outbox. They are not actually sent until a Send/Receive action is manually performed. If the user is in Corporate/Workgroup mode a `SendReceiveNow` command can be performed using the CDO `DeliverNow` method. Place the following code in the `basMacros` code module to implement a Send/Receive now Macro for Corporate/Workgroup mode. Set a reference to the Microsoft CDO 1.21 Library before you run this code.

```
Sub SendReceiveNowCorpMode()
   'Only works in Corporate/Workgroup mode
   Dim oCDO As MAPI.session

   Set oCDO = CreateObject("MAPI.Session")
   oCDO.Logon "", "", False, False
   oCDO.DeliverNow

   Set oCDO = Nothing
End Sub
```

However, the `DeliverNow` method is one of the CDO functions that does not work in Internet only mode. A method that does work in both modes is pressing the **Send/Receive** toolbar button. This can be performed in code, and illustrates using methods that are present as menu or toolbar actions. The Office `CommandBars` collection contains all the Outlook toolbars and menus, as well as toolbars and menus from other Office applications. More information about the `CommandBars` collection is presented later in this chapter in the 'Menu and Toolbar Customizations' section.

The `Execute` method of a menu or toolbar item can be used to perform the built-in or user defined `Action` assigned to that item. If the item is a user defined item, the `OnAction` property is used to define the `Action` that is performed. The `OnAction` property can also be used to change the `Action` that is assigned to a built-in menu or toolbar command, by defining a new `Action` for that command. The code for the macro listed below uses the `Execute` method of the **All Accounts** menu item, located in the **Send/Receive** `CommandBarPopup` in the **Tools** menu to perform a send immediate action. First, the current item in the `ActiveInsepctor` window is found and sent to the Outbox, using the item's `Send` method. Once the item is placed in the Outbox, the `Execute` method of the **All Accounts** menu item is performed to send the item immediately. The macro executes a receive action as well as a send action, so using it may tie up the computer while both actions are performed. Place the following code in the `basMacros` code module.

```
Public Sub SendReceiveNow()
   Dim oCtl As Office.CommandBarControl
   Dim oPop As Office.CommandBarPopup
   Dim oCB As Office.CommandBar
   Dim oNS As Outlook.NameSpace
   Dim oItem As Object

   'First find and send the current item to the Outbox
   Set oNS = Application.GetNamespace("MAPI")
   Set oItem = Application.ActiveInspector.CurrentItem
   oItem.Send

   'Then use the Send/Receive on All Accounts action in the Tools
```

```
       'menu to send the item from the Outbox, and receive new items
       Set oCB = Application.ActiveExplorer.CommandBars("Menu Bar")
       Set oPop = oCB.Controls("Tools")
       Set oPop = oPop.Controls("Send/Receive")
       Set oCtl = oPop.Controls("All Accounts")
       oCtl.Execute

       Set oCtl = Nothing
       Set oPop = Nothing
       Set oCB = Nothing
       Set oNS = Nothing
       Set oItem = Nothing
   End Sub
```

To execute a send only action for the default mail account with no receive action, use the **Send** action from the **Tools** menu. The following listing shows the code for the `SendNow` macro. Place the following code in the `basMacros` code module.

```
   Public Sub SendNow()
       Dim oCtl As Office.CommandBarControl
       Dim oPop As Office.CommandBarPopup
       Dim oCB As Office.CommandBar
       Dim oNS As Outlook.NameSpace
       Dim oItem As Object

       'First find and send the current item to the Outbox
       Set oNS = Application.GetNamespace("MAPI")
       Set oItem = Application.ActiveInspector.CurrentItem
       oItem.Send

       'Then use the Send action in the Tools menu
       'to send the item from the Outbox
       Set oCB = Application.ActiveExplorer.CommandBars("Menu Bar")
       Set oPop = oCB.Controls("Tools")
       Set oCtl = oPop.Controls("Send")
       oCtl.Execute

       Set oCtl = Nothing
       Set oPop = Nothing
       Set oCB = Nothing
       Set oNS = Nothing
       Set oItem = Nothing
   End Sub
```

To integrate any Outlook feature enhancement you create as a macro into the Outlook user interface, place the macro in a toolbar or a menu or both. 'Menu and Toolbar Customizations', later in this chapter, shows how to add new items to the Outlook menus and toolbars from your code.

Changing the User Interface

Outlook can be customized from the user interface to have customized menus and toolbars, Outlook Bar Groups and Views. All of these customizations can be done from your programs except for Views. Creating custom views from code is not supported in Outlook 2000. One other item that is often asked about is the context menu that appears when you right-click the mouse. The context menus are not customizable either from the user interface or code. Outlook 2000 is the first member of the Outlook family to support these customizations in code.

The collections that you deal with in customizing Outlook are the `OutlookBarGroups`, `OutlookBarShortcuts`, `Panes`, `PropertyPages` and `CommandBars` collections. All of these are members of the Outlook object model except for the `CommandBars` collection, which is a member of the Office object model. The `PropertyPages` collection enables you to add your own tabs to the folder Property pages and to the Options dialog box that is available in the Tools menu.

Storing Customized Settings in the VBA Windows Registry

There are two main ways to store the settings for your customizations. You can store them in text files and read the settings from the text files. The System and Windows INI files are examples of system wide text files, with sections for individual applications and settings. Storing information in text files was the method used in earlier versions of Windows, prior to Windows 95. For Windows 95, Windows 98 and Windows NT the preferred method of storing program specific information and settings is in the Windows Registry. The Registry provides a standardized, centralized place to put data and Windows provides utilities to clean and validate the contents of the Registry. We will only cover storing data in the Registry in this section.

VBA and VB provide intrinsic standard statements to read, write and delete Registry data. These statements are `GetSetting`, `SaveSetting` and `DeleteSetting`. They use a default registry key where the application settings are kept. That registry key is `HKEY_CURRENT_USER\Software\VB and VBA Program Settings`. If you want to store your settings in other locations in the Registry you cannot use these statements. We will cover using other sections in the Registry in Chapter 6.

To create a new Registry key for your application use the `SaveSetting` statement. This statement has four arguments, which can be named `arguments`; `appname`, `section`, `key` and `setting`. `Setting` is an argument that always saves a string value. The VBA and VB Registry statements do not support the use of binary or DWORD values. The following statement creates a new Registry string key named `Size` at `HKEY_CURRENT_USER\Software\VB and VBA Program Settings\AppName\Init` and sets its value to 0. Substitute the name of your application for `AppName`, and your `section` and `key` names for `Init` and `Size`. If the `appname`, `section` or `key` do not exist they are created by this statement.

```
SaveSetting appname:="AppName", section:="Init", key:="Size", setting:=0
```

To retrieve the value of this Registry key use the `GetSetting` statement. If the optional `Default` argument is used a value is guaranteed to be returned even if the Registry key or section do not exist. If `Default` is not used and the key does not exist or has not been set, a `Null` string will be returned.

```
sString = GetSetting appname:="AppName", section:="Init", _
key:="Size", default:="0"
```

To remove sections of the Registry that were created by your application, use the `DeleteSetting` statement. You can be as specific as you want in the deletion, deleting only the `key` or the `section` with all the keys it contains, or the entire application set of keys and sections.

```
DeleteSetting appname:="AppName", section:="Init", key:="Size"
```

> The Help file says that the `section` argument is required, but that is not true. You can omit the `section` and `key` arguments. If the area of the Registry specified does not exist, an error is returned.

These statements provide a complete set of functions for Registry manipulations. For standalone programs they provide read, write, create and delete functionality. In many cases this is sufficient. However, you might need to work with other areas of the Registry, interface with Registry keys that were created by other application or use binary or DWORD values for Registry keys. To do that you need to work with the Win32 API functions, which are covered in Chapter 6.

Outlook Bar Customizations

Outlook 2000 makes it possible to customize the Outlook Bar by adding new Outlook Bar groups and by adding or modifying the shortcuts within those groups. The capability of doing this in code is new to Outlook 2000. The `OutlookBars` collection is referenced through the `Panes` collection, which is also new to Outlook 2000. At the present time the only member of the `Panes` collection is "OutlookBar", which is assigned to an `OutlookBarPane` object. The `Contents` property of the `OutlookBarPane` object returns an `OutlookBarStorage` object that contains the current Outlook Bar groups.

The following listing contains a complete set of procedures to check for the existence of an Outlook Bar group; create an Outlook Bar group; check for the existence of an Outlook Bar group shortcut; and create Outlook Bar group shortcuts for Outlook folders, system folder paths, and HTTP (Hypertext Transfer Protocol) URLs (Universal Resource Locators). Any system or network folder path can be added as a shortcut by using the full UNC (Universal Naming Convention) path to that folder. Any HTTP URL can be added as a shortcut by providing the full HTTP path. Any shortcuts that point to URL's will open the Web page in an Outlook Explorer window within Outlook.

The procedure to create a system folder shortcut is the same one used for creating a URL shortcut. Both sets of path specifications are treated the same in creating a shortcut in an Outlook Bar group. The procedure that creates the path shortcuts uses the `Split` function to separate the elements of the path into a string array, using \ as a delimiter. The final element of the path, which is the `UBound` of the array, is used to name the shortcut.

Insert a new code module in the Outlook project and name it `basOutlookBars`. Insert the following code in the `basOutlookBars` module.

The `GroupExist` function checks to see if a specific Outlook bar group exists, and if it does it returns `True`.

```
Public Function GroupExist(sGroup As String) As Boolean
    Dim oGroup As Outlook.OutlookBarGroup
    Dim oPane As Outlook.OutlookBarPane
```

```
        GroupExist = False
        'Get the Pane object
        Set oPane = Application.ActiveExplorer.Panes.Item("OutlookBar")

        'See if any Group has the specified name in the Groups collection
        For Each oGroup In oPane.Contents.Groups
          If oGroup.Name = sGroup Then
            GroupExist = True
          End If
        Next oGroup

        Set oGroup = Nothing
        Set oPane = Nothing
    End Function
```

The `GroupCreate` function creates a new Outlook Bar group and places it at the specified position in the Outlook Bar. If the `lPosition` argument is passed as a `0`, the new group is placed at the last position in the Outlook Bar. Any other value will place it in the specified position, where `1` is the first position.

```
    Public Sub GroupCreate(sGroup As String, lPosition As Long)
        Dim oPane As Outlook.OutlookBarPane
        Dim oGroup As Outlook.OutlookBarGroup
        Dim lGroups As Long
        Dim lInsertAt As Long

        'Get the Pane object
        Set oPane = Application.ActiveExplorer.Panes.Item("OutlookBar")

        If lPosition = 0 Then
          'Insert at last position
          lGroups = oPane.Contents.Groups.Count
          lInsertAt = lGroups + 1
        Else
          'Insert at specified position
          lInsertAt = lPosition
        End If

        'Add the new group using the Add method. The groups are stored
        'in the Contents object. Use the Index argument to set the
        'position of the new group to the specified position in the Outlook Bar
        oPane.Contents.Groups.Add sGroup, lInsertAt

        Set oGroup = oPane.Contents.Groups.Item(sGroup)
        'Set the group to use small icons
        oGroup.ViewType = olSmallIcon

        Set oPane = Nothing
        Set oGroup = Nothing
    End Sub
```

The `ShortcutExist` function returns `True` if the specified Outlook Bar group contains the specified shortcut.

```
Public Function ShortcutExist(sShortcut As String, sGroup As String) As Boolean
   Dim oShortcuts As Outlook.OutlookBarShortcuts
   Dim oShortcut As Outlook.OutlookBarShortcut
   Dim oGroup As Outlook.OutlookBarGroup
   Dim oPane As Outlook.OutlookBarPane

   ShortcutExist = False
   'First see if the group exists, if not, the shortcut cannot exist
   If GroupExist(sGroup) Then
      'Find the Shortcuts collection for that group
      Set oPane = Outlook.ActiveExplorer.Panes.Item("OutlookBar")
      Set oGroup = oPane.Contents.Groups.Item(sGroup)
      Set oShortcuts = oGroup.Shortcuts

      'See if any shortcut has the specified name in the Shortcuts collection
      For Each oShortcut In oShortcuts
         If oShortcut.Name = sShortcut Then
            ShortcutExist = True
         End If
      Next oShortcut
   End If

   Set oShortcuts = Nothing
   Set oShortcut = Nothing
   Set oGroup = Nothing
   Set oPane = Nothing
End Function
```

The `FolderShortcutCreate` function creates a shortcut to an Outlook folder in a specified Outlook Bar group.

```
Public Sub FolderShortcutCreate(sGroup As String, oFolder _
            As Outlook.MAPIFolder)
   Dim oShortcuts As Outlook.OutlookBarShortcuts
   Dim oPane As Outlook.OutlookBarPane
   Dim oGroup As Outlook.OutlookBarGroup

   'Find the Shortcuts collection for the group
   Set oPane = Outlook.ActiveExplorer.Panes.Item("OutlookBar")
   Set oGroup = oPane.Contents.Groups.Item(sGroup)
   Set oShortcuts = oGroup.Shortcuts

   'Use the Add method to add the specified folder to the Shortcuts collection
   oShortcuts.Add oFolder, oFolder.Name

   Set oShortcuts = Nothing
   Set oPane = Nothing
   Set oGroup = Nothing
End Sub
```

The `PathShortcutCreate` function creates a shortcut to a path in a specified Outlook Bar group. The path can be to a system or network folder, and it can also be an HTTP URL.

```
Public Sub PathShortcutCreate(sGroup As String, sPath As String)
   Dim oShortcuts As Outlook.OutlookBarShortcuts
   Dim oPane As Outlook.OutlookBarPane
   Dim oGroup As Outlook.OutlookBarGroup
   Dim sArray() As String
   Dim sName As String
   Dim lTop As Long

   'Find the Shortcuts collection for the group
   Set oPane = Outlook.ActiveExplorer.Panes.Item("OutlookBar")
   Set oGroup = oPane.Contents.Groups.Item(sGroup)
   Set oShortcuts = oGroup.Shortcuts

   'Split the path using "\" as the delimiter. Collect the split elements
   'into a string array, the final element is used for the name of the
   'shortcut. Use the UBound function to find the final element.
   sArray = Split(sPath, "\")
   lTop = UBound(sArray)
   sName = sArray(lTop)
   'Use the Add method to add either a system folder, network folder or
   'HTTP URL as a shortcut in the specified group.
   oShortcuts.Add sPath, sName

   Set oShortcuts = Nothing
   Set oPane = Nothing
   Set oGroup = Nothing
End Sub
```

The following listing demonstrates using the Outlook Bar procedures. It first checks for the existence of a group named `Wrox`, and if the group doesn't exist it is created. Then, shortcuts to the Outlook Inbox folder, the `C:\My Documents` folder and the Wrox web site at http:\\www.wrox.com are created in the `Wrox` group. All the shortcuts are checked for their prior existence before being created. Place the following code in the `basOutlookBars` module.

```
Sub testOLB()
   Dim oFld As Outlook.MAPIFolder
   Dim ns As Outlook.NameSpace

   If Not GroupExist("Wrox") Then
     GroupCreate "Wrox", 0
     Set ns = GetNamespace("MAPI")
     If Not ShortcutExist("Inbox", "Wrox") Then
       Set oFld = ns.GetDefaultFolder(olFolderInbox)
       FolderShortcutCreate "Wrox", oFld
     End If
     If Not ShortcutExist("My Documents", "Wrox") Then
       PathShortcutCreate "Wrox", "C:\My Documents"
     End If
     If Not ShortcutExist("www.wrox.com", "Wrox") Then
```

```
            PathShortcutCreate "Wrox", "http:\\www.wrox.com"
        End If
    End If

    Set oFld = Nothing
    Set ns = Nothing
End Sub
```

The `OutlookBarGroups` and the `OutlookBarShortcuts` collections each have three events. These events enable you to respond to the addition of items to the collections before and during the addition and to the removal of items from the collections. The `OutlookBarPane` object has two events, `BeforeGroupSwitch` which occurs before a new group is opened in the Outlook Bar, and `BeforeNavigate` which occurs before the switch to a new Explorer window to view the selected shortcut item. These events were described earlier in this chapter, in 'Outlook Events'.

> The **Remove method of the `OutlookBarGroups` and the `OutlookBarShortcuts`
> collections enables us to remove any of the Outlook Bar groups or shortcuts, even the
> default ones. The `Target` property of the `OutlookBarShortcut` object returns the
> target of the shortcut. For an Outlook folder it returns a `MAPIFolder` object, and for
> file system paths and URLs it returns a string. It returns an object for the special
> system folders such as `My Documents`.**

I like to use the capability of customizing the Outlook Bar to create a group that gathers together all the elements of an Outlook application. Any Outlook folders, web pages, Office documents or file system folders containing elements related to the project can all be placed in one easy to find Outlook Bar group. Combining custom Outlook Bar groups with custom menus, toolbars and Options dialog box tabs enables seamless integration of your programs with the Outlook environment.

Menu and Toolbar Customizations

Menus and toolbars are not part of the Outlook object model, they are members of the Office `CommandBars` collection. To add new menu or toolbar items you first have to add a reference to the Microsoft Office 9.0 object library in the **References** dialog box in the **Tools** menu. Adding or modifying a menu or toolbar is handled the same in your program, since they are regarded as the same type of objects. The set of menus and toolbars that are available for a particular Explorer or Inspector window are available in the Outlook object model as the `CommandBars` property of that Explorer or Inspector as an `Office.CommandBars` object.

The following listing provides procedures for checking for the existence of a particular menu or toolbar, creating a new menu or toolbar, and adding controls to the new menu or toolbar. You can add buttons, edit textboxes, dropdown listboxes, comboboxes and popups to a menu or toolbar. Creating a procedure that uses the `Delete` method of the `Controls` collection for a menu or toolbar enables you to remove items from that menu or toolbar. Code that adds or removes menu and toolbar items enables you to customize the Outlook user interface to the requirements of your programs and business organization.

Menus, toolbars and the controls associated with them have `Enabled` and `Visible` properties that enable you to customize the available choices based on the state of your program and the current Explorer or Inspector window. Checking the type of folder or item visible in the current Explorer or Inspector window enables you to enable or disable menu or toolbar items, and make them visible or invisible based on the current context the same way the Outlook user interface does.

Insert a new code module in the Outlook project and name it `basMenus`. Insert the following code in the `basMenus` module.

The `IsMenuThere` function returns `True` if a specified menu exists in any menu bar. It iterates through the `Controls` collection of a menu looking for a specific `Control` name.

```
Private Function IsMenuThere(sMenu As String, _
           sName As String) As Boolean
  'Returns True if menu sName exists in sMenu.
  Dim oCB As Office.CommandBar
  Dim oControl As Office.CommandBarControl

  IsMenuThere = False
  Set oCB = ActiveExplorer.CommandBars(sMenu)
  For Each oControl In oCB.Controls
    If oControl.Caption = sName Then
      IsMenuThere = True
      Exit For
    End If
  Next

  Set oCB = Nothing
  Set oControl = Nothing
End Function
```

The `AddMenu` function adds a new menu to a menu bar. New menus are popup controls and you can add and access menu items on them as controls in a popup control's `Controls` collection.

```
Private Function AddMenu(sCBName As String, _
    sName As String, sTag As String) As CommandBarControl
  'Add the menu named in sName to the
  'Outlook command bar named in sCBName.

  Dim oBar As Office.CommandBar
  Dim oControl As Office.CommandBarControl
  Dim lCount As Long

  Set oBar = ActiveExplorer.CommandBars(sCBName)
  lCount = oBar.Controls.Count
  With oBar
    'A new menu is a popup control
    'Add it before the Help menu, which is last
    Set oControl = .Controls.Add(msoControlPopup, _
      , , lCount - 1)

    oControl.Caption = sName
```

```
      'Any Tag must be unique
      oControl.Tag = sTag
   End With
   Set AddMenu = oControl

   Set oBar = Nothing
   Set oControl = Nothing
End Function
```

The `AddControl` function adds a control of the specified type to a menu. A menu is a popup control and can contain controls of five different types. A control may be a command button, text edit control, dropdown control, combobox, or popup control.

```
Private Sub AddControl(oCtrl As CommandBarPopup, lType As Long, _
   sCaption As String, sTag As String, sOnAction As String)

   'Add a control to the menu specified in oCtrl and set
   'its Caption, Tag and OnAction properties to the values specified in
   'the sCaption, sType and sOnAction arguments.
   'The type of control added is specified in lType. It must be one
   'of the following:
   'msoControlButton (1)
   'msoControlEdit (2)
   'msoControlDropdown (3)
   'msoControlComboBox (4)
   'msoControlPopup (10)
   'Always make sure that any Tag supplied is unique

   Dim oNewCtrl As Office.CommandBarControl

   With oCtrl
      Set oNewCtrl = .Controls.Add(lType)
      With oNewCtrl
         .Caption = sCaption
         .OnAction = sOnAction
         .Tag = sTag
      End With
   End With

   Set oNewCtrl = Nothing
End Sub
```

The following listing shows how to use the previous procedures to check for the existence of a menu bar item named `Wrox`. If the menu bar item does not exist then it is created and a button control is added that is named `Item Count`. The ampersand (`&`) character before the `W` in `Wrox` and before the `C` in `Count` provide shortcuts for these items. Setting the `OnAction` property of the `Item Count` menu button to `NewAction` executes the `NewAction` Sub procedure when the button is pressed. This is the procedure that you use to create items that execute your procedures when the menu or toolbar item is activated. In addition to executing your own procedures you can use the built-in procedures provided by the standard menu and toolbar items themselves as actions that are executed by your custom menu and toolbar items. Insert the following code in the `basMenus` module.

```
Public Sub TestMenus()
  Dim oCB As Office.CommandBarPopup
  Dim bResult As Boolean

  bResult = IsMenuThere("Menu Bar", "&Wrox")
  If bResult = False Then
    Set oCB = AddMenu("Menu Bar", "&Wrox", "WroxTag")
    AddControl oCB, msoControlButton, "Item &Count", _
      "WroxCount", "NewAction"
  End If

  Set oCB = Nothing
End Sub
```

The NewAction Sub is executed when the Item Count menu button is pressed.

```
Private Sub NewAction()
  Dim lCount As Long
  Dim oNS As Outlook.NameSpace
  Dim oExp As Outlook.Explorer

  Set oExp = Application.ActiveExplorer
  lCount = oExp.CurrentFolder.Items.Count
  MsgBox lCount & " items", , "Wrox"

  Set oNS = Nothing
  Set oExp = Nothing
End Sub
```

It is important that any tags you create for your custom menu and toolbar items use unique strings. If you add a menu item and a toolbar item that link to the same procedure and they have the same tag, that procedure will be executed once for each instance of the tag.

Another thing to be aware of is that Outlook has different Actions menus. Which one is active depends on the context of the current Explorer or Inspector. Correctly modifying or accessing the Actions menu depends on knowing the correct context and the correct ID property for that context. The following table lists the Actions menu ID properties for the different folder types.

Folder Type	Actions menu ID
Calendar	30142
Contacts	30141
Journal	30081
Mail	30131
Tasks	30149

Explore the properties of the controls that you can use for menus and toolbars in the Object Browser to see how you can change the look of the controls, add icons to the face of the controls and otherwise control how your custom controls appear in the user interface. Some of the properties that can be useful are AdaptiveMenu which controls whether the new adaptive menus are enabled for that menu or toolbar, the previously mentioned Enabled and Visible properties, Position which sets the position and floating properties of the command bar or control, Protection which controls whether the placement and content of the menu or toolbar can be changed from the user interface. BeginGroup, BuiltInFace, Caption, the PasteFace method, State, Style and TooltipText control the appearance of a command bar control. HelpContextId and HelpFile enable you to provide help for your custom items that is integrated into the Outlook Help system.

The OnAction property enables you to set a custom or built-in action that is performed when the command bar button is pressed. The Parameter property enables you to pass arguments to both custom and built-in actions.

The following listing shows one way of using the Parameter property to pass an argument to a procedure. Executing the Sub procedure TestParameter creates a Wrox menu item in the menu bar with a button named Test Parameter that creates another button named Item Count when it is pressed. The name for the Item Count button is stored in the Parameter property of the Test Parameter button. The OnAction property of the Test Parameter button executes the UseParameter Sub procedure, which recovers the Parameter property string from the Test Parameter button control and uses that to name the new control. You can get user input that is stored as the argument for a user defined or built-in procedure from a dialog box in this way.

Insert the following code in the basMenus module.

```
Public Sub TestParameter()
    Dim oButton As Office.CommandBarButton
    Dim oCB As Office.CommandBarPopup
    Dim oBar As Office.CommandBar
    Dim bResult As Boolean

    bResult = IsMenuThere("Menu Bar", "&Wrox")
    If bResult = False Then
        Set oCB = AddMenu("Menu Bar", "&Wrox", "WroxTag")
    Else
        Set oBar = ActiveExplorer.CommandBars("Menu Bar")
        Set oCB = oBar.FindControl(, , "WroxTag")
    End If

    With oCB
        Set oButton = .CommandBar.FindControl(msoControlButton, , "WroxTestParameter")
        If oButton Is Nothing Then
            Set oButton = .Controls.Add(msoControlButton)
            With oButton
                .Caption = "Test &Parameter"
                .Tag = "WroxTestParameter"
                .OnAction = "UseParameter"
                .Parameter = "&Item Count2"
            End With
        End If
    End With
```

```
      Set oButton = Nothing
      Set oCB = Nothing
      Set oBar = Nothing
   End Sub
```

The UseParameter Sub uses the Parameter property of a menu button to create a new menu button.

```
   Private Sub UseParameter()
      Dim oCB As Office.CommandBarPopup
      Dim oBar As Office.CommandBar
      Dim oButton As Office.CommandBarButton
      Dim sArgument As String

      Set oBar = Application.ActiveExplorer.CommandBars("Menu Bar")
      Set oCB = oBar.FindControl(Tag:="WroxTag")
      Set oButton = oCB.CommandBar.FindControl(msoControlButton, , "WroxCount2")
      If oButton Is Nothing Then
         Set oButton = oCB.Controls.Item("Test Parameter")
         sArgument = oButton.Parameter
         AddControl oCB, msoControlButton, sArgument, _
            "WroxCount2", "NewAction"
      End If

      Set oCB = Nothing
      Set oBar = Nothing
      Set oButton = Nothing
   End Sub
```

One additional thing that you can do with a custom button control in a menu or toolbar is to use it to open a HTTP URL. The following listing shows a new menu button created in a menu item named Wrox that when pressed opens the Wrox Web site home page in an instance of the default web browser. Depending on the web browser brand and version installed you might have to use a fully qualified URL, in the form http://www.wrox.com. To set a URL as the action that a hyperlink enabled CommandBar button performs, set the Tooltip property of the button to the path of the URL. Place the following code in the basMenus module.

```
   Public Sub AddHyperlink()
      Dim oButton As Office.CommandBarButton
      Dim oCB As Office.CommandBarPopup
      Dim oBar As Office.CommandBar
      Dim bResult As Boolean

      bResult = IsMenuThere("Menu Bar", "&Wrox")
      If bResult = False Then
         Set oCB = AddMenu("Menu Bar", "&Wrox", "WroxTag")
      Else
         Set oBar = ActiveExplorer.CommandBars("Menu Bar")
         Set oCB = oBar.FindControl(, , "WroxTag")
      End If

      With oCB
         Set oButton = .Controls.Add(msoControlButton)
```

```
      With oButton
         .Caption = "Wrox Web &Site"
         .Tag = "WroxwebSite"
         .HyperlinkType = msoCommandBarButtonHyperlinkOpen
         .TooltipText = "www.wrox.com"
      End With
   End With

   Set oButton = Nothing
   Set oCB = Nothing
   Set oBar = Nothing
End Sub
```

Customizing the menus, toolbars and Outlook Bar create a user interface that integrates your programs into Outlook, and can make Outlook much easier to work with.

Using the PropertyPages Collection

The `PropertyPages` collection, which is new to Outlook 2000, enables you to add new tabs to the Property pages for Outlook folders, and to the Options dialog box available in the Tools menu. These new tabs are added to the `PropertyPages` collection by your event handler for the `OptionsPagesAdd` event of either the Outlook `Application` or `NameSpace` objects. Each time the Options dialog box or the Property pages for a folder are opened the `OptionsPagesAdd` event occurs. Your event handler, placed in a class module or `ThisOutlookSession` module (which is a special type of class module) adds your custom property pages to the `Pages` object passed as an argument to the `OptionsPagesAdd` event.

For Outlook 2000 these custom property pages are usually implemented as ActiveX controls, or as COM add-ins. The actual property page that is displayed can be implemented as a User Control or Form with supporting code in VB, or as a UserForm if you use VBA to develop the property page as a COM add-in. A property page uses the `Implements` keyword as a declaration for a property page to tell Outlook that you are providing a custom property page. When we use this declaration Outlook exposes the properties and methods of a property page. When an interface is implemented you must provide code for all the methods, properties and events of that interface, even if the code is only a comment line.

You can use the `Implements` keyword to add code to an interface and then add new properties, events or methods to the class that implements the interface. The `Implements` keyword can only appear in a class module. Interfaces can only appear in classes or type libraries.

An interface contains only the declarations for the `Public` methods and properties of a class. No code appears in the interface itself. It serves only as a template that is inserted in a class when the `Implements` keyword is used. All classes implement at least one interface, if none is specifically implemented then the default interface is implemented. The class that implements the interface must provide code for all the `Public` methods and properties that are declared in the interface. In addition, the class can add other methods and properties that it implements.

The read-only `Dirty` property, and the `Apply` and `GetPageInfo` methods of the `PropertyPage` are templates with no implementation code that are provided by the Outlook object model. If you need to use `Dirty`, `Apply` or `GetPageInfo` you must implement the code for them in your own procedures. You use the `OnStatusChange` method of the `PropertyPageSite` object to notify Outlook that a custom property page has been changed. The `PropertyPageSite` object represents the container for a custom property page. You access the `PropertyPageSite` object by using the `Parent` property for the custom page provider.

The class module that implements the code for the `PropertyPage` object can also implement code for the controls on the Property page if it is the class module for a VB Form or User Control or a VBA UserForm. The code for each control calls a procedure to set the module level dirty flag when that control is changed, and the dirty flag procedure then uses the `OnStatusChange` method to notify Outlook that something has changed. The following code appears in the `clsCustomProp` module.

```vb
Dim mbDirty As Boolean
Dim moSite As Outlook.PropertyPageSite

Implements Outlook.PropertyPage

Private Sub SetDirty()
  mbDirty = True
  moSite.OnStatusChange
End Sub

Private Sub Class_Initialize()
  'Initializations for the page controls and variables
  mbDirty = False
  Set moSite = Parent
End Sub

Private Property Get PropertyPage_Dirty() As Boolean
  'Read-only Property that indicates a change in the page
  'gbDirty is a global Boolean that is maintained by
  PropertyPage_Dirty = gbDirty
End Property

Private Sub PropertyPage_Apply()
  'Read the settings from the page controls and set
  'application settings in this procedure.
End Sub

Private Sub PropertyPage_GetPageInfo(HelpFile As String, HelpContext As Long)
  'This procedure is for specifying a Help file and
  'context ID for context sensitive Help.
End Sub
```

The sample COM add-in that is developed in Chapter 7, 'COM Add-ins', creates a custom property page that uses this property page implementation framework.

Code Security

When code is present in the Outlook project you may get a security warning about enabling or disabling macros when Outlook is started. If you choose to disable macros then none of the code in the project will run. There is no way to disable this warning in code, but there are two methods of preventing it from appearing: changing the security settings and signing the code.

Outlook implements three levels of security. The security settings are accessed by choosing Tools | Macro | Security (see screen shot). The default Medium setting generates the warning for all unsigned code. Changing the security setting to Low permanently disables the warning but is very dangerous these days with macro viruses so common. I strongly recommend not using the Low setting. High security will only allow signed code to run. Outlook does not have the Trust all installed add-ins and templates checkbox that some of the other Office 2000 applications have that automatically disables the macro warning for items installed in certain trusted folders.

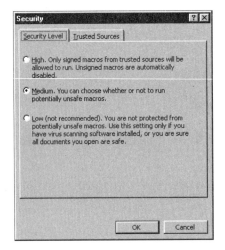

The best solution for preventing the macro warning from appearing is to sign the code. There are two methods of signing code, signing with a commercially obtained certificate and signing with the SelfCert.exe application. A commercial certificate can be obtained from a certifying authority such as Verisign or Thawte, or can be issued by your organization if it runs the Microsoft Certificate Server. Microsoft Certificate Server is included with the Microsoft Windows NT Option Pack, and may be used to sign files. If you also use Exchange Server, check to see whether Exchange Server has been configured to disable signing from Microsoft Certificate Server before you attempt to use it. Commercial certificates are relatively expensive and may require having incorporation papers, a domain name and a Dun and Bradstreet rating depending on the certifying authority and the type of certificate purchased.

SelfCert.exe is included in Office 2000 and Office Developer 2000. It is not installed with any of the standard installations and must be explicitly selected from the Office Tools section of the Office 2000 installation routines. If you have already installed Office 2000 and do not have SelfCert.exe on your computer, choose the Add/Remove Programs applet in the Control Panel and choose Add or Remove Features after selecting Office 2000 in the Install/Uninstall tab. SelfCert.exe is installed by choosing to install as Run from My Computer the Digital Signature for VBA projects item.

The `SelfCert.exe` program enables you to create your own certificate for your use. The certificate that you create is not authenticated by a certifying authority, but if you elect to trust it the macro warning won't be generated. These certificates aren't validated by an certifying authority, so other users will see a warning not to trust them. To create a certificate for use with your own programs, run the `SelfCert.exe` program and enter a name in the Your name box and click OK. A digital certificate will be created for the name you entered.

Summary

This chapter has covered a lot of ground. We covered the Outlook project, how to use and distribute them, and why COM add-ins are better distribution methods for your applications. We also covered macros, events and event handling, Office UserForms, and class modules. We then covered customizing the Outlook interface in your applications, and finished with a brief discussion of code security and signing code.

Office 2000 Automation

This chapter covers Automation, which was formerly called OLE Automation. Automation is a feature of **COM** (the Component Object Model), which is a standard which applications use to expose their object models to other applications. Automation is implemented in many programs, not only programs in the Office 2000 suite, but this chapter concentrates on making use of the automation of other Office applications from Outlook 2000. Controlling Outlook from other Office applications is also covered briefly.

The VBA programming language included in Outlook 2000 enables you to work with the methods and properties of other applications that support VBA or support COM in exposing their object models. The next chapter covers automating Outlook from Visual Basic, which is very similar to automating Outlook from VBA. To work with the exposed object models of other applications you use the `CreateObject` function, which creates a new object of the specified type, or the `GetObject` function, which retrieves an already existing object from a file or memory.

> **When we are using the automation models and object libraries for other applications we should always test to make sure that the automation objects can be instantiated without errors. We have to make sure the users of our automation programs have the correct object libraries installed to run our code. Setting a reference to an object library in the VBE is done from the References dialog box, accessed from the Tools menu. Be aware that in many cases you are not legally able to distribute the required libraries, they must be purchased or licensed for each user. When you use other object models in your programs, always make sure to set references to those object libraries to avoid automation errors at runtime.**

Many applications support automation, such as Internet Explorer, AutoCAD, WinFax Pro, Visio and Corel Draw, to name a few. By making use of the objects that are exposed by automation compatible applications you can utilize their functionality without having to reinvent all the functions they provide.

> **Some applications, such as Word and Excel, have macro recorders that capture the keystrokes for various actions and generate VBA code from those keystrokes. You can use such macro recorders to see how to work with the object models of those applications, and then copy and paste the resulting code into your VBA code. The code generated by the macro recorder can be modified as needed. This makes learning how to work with those object models easier than starting to write code from scratch.**

Working with Microsoft Word

In this section we will look at four ways of utilizing Word as an automation object. The first two of these examples use custom Word templates to create documents that simulate a mail merge. The third example uses Word to print all the selected Outlook items, and the fourth example uses a custom template to place data from all uncompleted Tasks into a dynamically resized Word table.

A *true* mail merge uses a master document that contains the fields that will be merged with data from the selected contact records. This has the advantages of not storing individual documents, and of being able to change the recipients of the merge by changing the file that contains the contact record information. A true mail merge, like those that are created in the user interface, also has certain disadvantages. It doesn't create documents that can later be edited, and it is overkill for creating a customized document for one or a few contacts. A *simulated* mail merge creates individual documents that are stored in the file system, enabling them to be edited later. It also is the easiest method for working with individual documents, such as letters, for a selected contact.

The two methods of simulating a mail merge that we will cover both require the creation of a custom Word template that contains the fields to merge from the Outlook contact record. These fields may be created as Bookmarks, and as Custom Document Properties. There are few real advantages in one method over the other, unless you need to use text fields that are longer than 255 characters. Long text fields should use Bookmarks to work around the limits of Custom Document Properties. First we will create a merge template using Bookmarks, then we will create a similar merge template using Custom Document Properties. Another method of creating merged documents that is covered later in this chapter is the use of Word FormFields.

One main difference between using Bookmarks and Custom Document Properties is that you can retrieve the information more reliably at any time from the CustomDocument Properties (assuming the user doesn't use File | Properties to delete or change them). Bookmarks are more *exposed* in the document text, unless you've happened to write the information to a document variable, at the same time.

Using Bookmarks to Merge Information to Word

Open Microsoft Word and choose File | New to create a new template. Choose the Blank Document selection in the General tab to create the template based on the Normal.dot template, and make sure that the Create New Template radio button is selected. Set the margins for the template in the Page Setup dialog box in the File menu. Set the Top, Bottom, Left and Right margins to 1" and the Gutter to 0". Set both the Header and Footer margins in the From edge section to 0.5".

The template will be easier to design if you set Bookmarks and Paragraph marks to be visible in the View tab of the Options dialog box in the Tools menu. This will make placement of the date field and Bookmarks easier to see. Bookmarks are inserted by using the Bookmark dialog box in the Insert menu, or by using the keyboard shortcut *Alt+I, K*. A toolbar button for inserting Bookmarks can also be placed on a toolbar to make inserting Bookmarks easier by customizing a toolbar. See the Word documentation for information about customizing menus and toolbars.

Choose Date and Time from the Insert menu to insert a date field in your preferred format, and then press the *Enter* key three times. Insert a Bookmark and name it FullName, then press the *Enter* key. Insert another Bookmark and name it StreetAddress, and press the *Enter* key again. Insert a Bookmark named City, then a comma, then a Bookmark named State, followed by a space. Then insert a Bookmark named PostalCode and press the *Enter* key twice. Finally, add the word Dear and then insert a Bookmark named FirstName. Add a colon and press the *Enter* key again. This completes the Word template.

The template should look similar to the screen shot opposite, when Field codes have been made visible in the View tab of the Options dialog box in the Tools menu. Save the template in your preferred user template file location as BookmarkMaster.dot.

For users of Windows 95 and Windows 98 who do not use profiles, the default user template file location is usually `C:\Windows\Application Data\Microsoft\Templates\`. Users of those operating systems who do use profiles usually have the project file located in `C:\Windows\<profile>\Application Data\Microsoft\Templates\`, where `<profile>` is the profile name. Users of Windows NT usually have the project file located in `C:\Winnt\Profiles\<profile>\Application Data\Microsoft\Templates\`. For reasons of simplicity, the template is assumed to have been stored in the `C:\My Documents` folder.

> When you use another object model in your Outlook programs there are two ways to approach coding that object model. You can set a reference in the **References** dialog box in the **Tools** menu of the VBE, or you can use late binding. Late binding does not make use of specific object type declarations such as `Dim oDoc As Word.Document`, but uses the declaration `Dim oDoc As Object`. Late binding is slower and can use more variable storage than early binding, but it has the advantage of enabling your code to run when the target computers may have older versions of the referenced object libraries. The code in these examples uses early binding, and requires that a reference is set to the Microsoft Word 9.0 Object Library.

Open the Outlook VBE, insert a code module and name it `basAutomation`. All the examples for this chapter will be inserted in this code module. Insert the code that follows in the `basAutomation` module. If you change the name of the Word template or its location in the file system make sure you change the reference to it in the code. This code, and all the following code, can be run from VBA or from VB 6. If you run the code from VB 6, adjust any directions that are VBA specific to the VB equivalents. This code requires that references are set to the Microsoft Word 9.0 and Microsoft Outlook 9.0 Object Libraries. The Sub `WordBookmark` is broken up for readability, but should be entered as one Sub in VBA or VB.

The lines that instantiate the `Application` object variables disable error handling and error messages, and then use the `GetObject` function to check for the prior existence of Outlook and Word `Application` object variables. If the `Application` objects don't already exist, the `Application` object variables are set to `Nothing` by the `GetObject` function. In these cases the `Application` objects are created with the `CreateObject` function. This method is used to prevent opening new `Application` objects if they exist already.

If the macro is run from within Outlook, the intrinsic `Application` object can be used instead of instantiating an Outlook `Application` object named `oOutlook`. In that case, references to `oOutlook` can be replaced by references to `Application`. If the macro is run from another application, instantiating the Outlook `Application` object is required. If the macro is run from Word the intrinsic Word `Application` object can be used instead of instantiating the Word `Application` object. To make the macros more universal, it is best to use automation to instantiate instances of both the Word and Outlook `Application` objects.

The existence of an open `ContactItem` is verified by checking for an open, active `Inspector` window that contains a `ContactItem` before the Word automation object is instantiated. If either of the tests for an open `Inspector` or an item of `ContactItem` type fails, a message box is displayed with an error message and the macro is exited.

```
Public Sub WordBookmark()
   Dim oOutlook As Outlook.Application
   Dim oInspector As Outlook.Inspector
   Dim oItem As Object
   Dim oContact As Outlook.ContactItem
   Dim oWord As Word.Application
   Dim oDoc As Word.Document
   Dim sBkmName As String
   Dim sTemplateName As String
   Dim blnFill As Boolean
   'Change this file name and location if necessary.
   sTemplateName = "C:\My Documents\BookmarkMaster.dot"

   'Get an Outlook Application object
   On Error Resume Next
   Set oOutlook = GetObject(, "Outlook.Application")
   If oOutlook Is Nothing Then
      Set oOutlook = CreateObject("Outlook.Application")
   End If
   On Error GoTo WordBookmarkError

   Set oInspector = oOutlook.ActiveInspector

   'Look for an open Inspector window.
   If oInspector Is Nothing Then
      MsgBox "There is no open item", , "Wrox"
   Else
      Set oItem = oInspector.CurrentItem
      'Make sure the open item is a ContactItem.
      If oItem.Class = olContact Then
         Set oContact = oItem
         'Get a Word Application object
         On Error Resume Next
         Set oWord = GetObject(, "Word.Application")
         If oWord Is Nothing Then
            Set oWord = CreateObject("Word.Application")
         End If
```

A `Private Function FillBookmark` is used to do the actual work. It is called once for each Bookmark that is to be filled with Outlook data. The function takes three arguments as input to make it as universal as possible. The first argument is the name of the Bookmark, the second is the string to insert in the Word document at the position of the Bookmark, and the third is the Word `Document` object where the Bookmarks are located. This function returns a Boolean value indicating the success or failure of filling the Bookmark. The return value isn't used in this example, but it can be used if you want to check for problems with any call to `FillBookmark`.

`FillBookmark` checks for the existence of each Bookmark, and if the Bookmark exists the Outlook Contact data is inserted at the Bookmark's location. Finally, the Bookmarks are made invisible and the cursor is placed at the end of the document. Word and the new document are made visible so the new document can be worked on.

The address that is inserted in the document is composed of individual address properties: `BusinessAddressStreet`, `BusinessAddressCity`, `BusinessAddressState`, and `BusinessAddressPostalCode`. The next example uses a different way of generating the address, the `MailingAddress` property. The `BusinessAddress`, `HomeAddress` and `OtherAddress` properties can also be used if you want to use a preassembled address.

```
On Error GoTo WordBookmarkError
'Add a document based on our template.
Set oDoc = oWord.Documents.Add(sTemplateName)
With oContact
  'Fill each bookmark in turn.
  sBkmName = "FullName"
  blnFill = FillBookmark(sBkmName, .FullName, oDoc)

  'Repeat the function call for each bookmark.
  sBkmName = "StreetAddress"
  blnFill = FillBookmark(sBkmName, .BusinessAddressStreet, oDoc)
  sBkmName = "City"
  blnFill = FillBookmark(sBkmName, .BusinessAddressCity, oDoc)

  sBkmName = "State"
  blnFill = FillBookmark(sBkmName, .BusinessAddressState, oDoc)

  sBkmName = "PostalCode"
  blnFill = FillBookmark(sBkmName, .BusinessAddressPostalCode, oDoc)

  sBkmName = "FirstName"
  blnFill = FillBookmark(sBkmName, .FirstName, oDoc)
End With
```

The next lines activate the newly created document, turn off the display of Bookmarks, and show the document. The cursor is placed at the end of the document, ready for the user to enter text in the letter. Finally, all the object variables are set to Nothing to release the resources that the variables are using.

```
  'Activate our new document.
  oDoc.Activate
  'Turn off the display of bookmarks.
  oDoc.ActiveWindow.View.ShowBookmarks = False
  'Move the cursor to the end of the document.
  oWord.Selection.EndKey Unit:=wdStory, Extend:=wdMove
  'Make the document visible.
  oWord.Visible = True
  oDoc.ActiveWindow.Visible = True
Else
  MsgBox "This is not a Contact item", , "Wrox"
End If
End If
```

```
WordBookmarkExit:
  'Set all objects to Nothing to prevent memory and
  'resource leaks. This still leaves the new document open.
  Set oItem = Nothing
  Set oContact = Nothing
  Set oInspector = Nothing
  Set oOutlook = Nothing
  Set oDoc = Nothing
  Set oWord = Nothing
  Exit Sub

WordBookmarkError:
  MsgBox "Error occurred: " & Err.Description, , "Wrox"
  GoTo WordBookmarkExit
End Sub
```

> All the examples in this chapter have a simple error handling routine that prints the
> text of the error using the `Err.Description` property. You can, and should,
> construct more complex error handlers as needed that save machine state, attempt to
> recover from errors or launch other programs when an error occurs. If no error
> handler is active when an error occurs, a runtime error occurs and your application is
> shut down. Make sure that you handle any error that can occur in your program to
> prevent this.

The code for the `FillBookmark` utility function follows. It checks for the existence of the specified
Bookmark and sets its `Text` property if it exists.

```
Private Function FillBookmark(sBookmark As String, sValue As String, _
      oDoc As Word.Document) As Boolean
  With oDoc
    If .Bookmarks.Exists(sBookmark) Then
      .Bookmarks(sBookmark).range.Text = sValue
      FillBookmark = True
    Else
      FillBookmark = False
    End If
  End With
End Function
```

You can also use automation to merge complex documents that combine data and the analytical
features from Outlook, Excel, Access and other VBA-enabled applications. You can use Excel to
analyze Outlook generated data, and then merge that data from Excel into a Word document. The
entire process can be managed from Outlook 2000. Automation enables you to use any parts of the
server program that are exposed in its object model. This powerful concept enables you to make use of
the features that are already provided by other programs, such as the members of the Office suite, as
features of your own program. I strongly encourage you to explore the object models of other VBA-
enabled programs to see which features might be useful in your own applications.

The newly created document with the data from the open Contact inserted into the Bookmarks should look similar to the following screen shot. You can create as many Bookmark fields as you need for information that you want to merge into the document, up to a maximum of 16,379 per document. You also can have up to 32,000 fields in any one document. Word templates and code macros can be created for custom documents such as invoices, memos, contracts, HelpDesk forms, and any other documents that don't require a full mail merge and aren't suitable for the built-in Outlook merging capabilities.

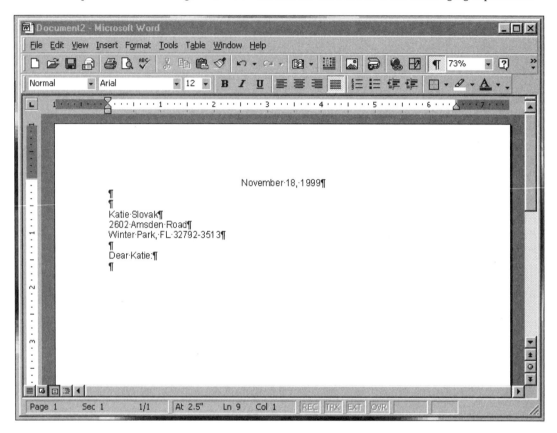

Many of the code examples use `Application` to refer to Outlook. These will work unchanged only in Outlook. Using automation to instantiate an Outlook `Application` object with the `CreateObject` or `GetObject` functions can be used within Outlook, and is required when other applications are used to control Outlook. The preceding example can be placed in a Word macro, or in the `AutoNew` macro in a Word template, to run automatically when the template is opened. It can also be placed in a macro in any other application that supports VBA, such as Excel, and it will run without change if an Outlook `ContactItem` is already opened in an Inspector window. The next chapter, Automating Outlook from Visual Basic, shows an example that uses the same `BookmarkMaster.dot` Word template, opens Outlook, and presents a list of Contacts. That example does not require Outlook to already be open with a selected Contact.

This example sets all declared objects to Nothing at the end of the procedure. This is a good idea, even though when all the objects go out of scope they are destroyed automatically. Setting the objects explicitly to Nothing enables you to control when these objects are destroyed, and guarantees that no objects can be left in memory to cause memory or resource leaks. Some of the code examples do not show explicitly setting all objects to Nothing for reasons of space and simplicity. However, you should always do so in your own code.

Using Custom Document Properties to Merge Information to Word

The next example uses Custom Document Properties to merge Outlook data into a Word document. Start with a new, blank template and choose Date and Time from the Insert menu to insert a date field in your preferred format, then press the *Enter* key three times. Set the margins for the template in the Page Setup dialog box in the File menu. Set the Top, Bottom, Left and Right margins to 1" and the Gutter to 0". Set both the Header and Footer margins in the From edge section to 0.5".

Creating and inserting Custom Document Properties is a more complicated process than creating and inserting Bookmarks. Open the Properties dialog from the File menu and select the Custom tab. To create a new Custom Document Property, type a name in the Name textbox and a blank string, "", in the Value textbox. Then press the Add button. Add Custom Document Properties named Full Name, First Name, and Address and then press the OK button. Custom Document Properties can have names that have spaces in them, unlike Bookmarks, which do not allow spaces in their names.

To insert a Custom Document Property, choose Insert | Field (or use the keyboard shortcut *Alt+I, F*) and choose the Document Information category. In the Field names listbox select DocProperty and press the Options button. Scroll down the Property listbox and select the desired Property. Then press the Add to Field button to insert the Custom Document Property at the cursor position. Insert the Full Name Property and press the *Enter* key. Repeat this process for the Address and First Name Document Properties.

The completed template with the Custom Document Properties inserted and toggled to show the field codes should look similar to the following screen shot. The easiest way to toggle the field code visibility is to use the keyboard shortcut *Alt+F9*. Save the completed template as C:\My Documents\DocPropsMaster.dot. If you use a different name or file path for the template, change the reference in the macro to reflect the new name or file path.

The code for the WordDocProperties macro is very similar to the code for the previous example. The difference is in how the Custom Document Properties are handled. All the Custom Document Properties are members of the `CustomDocumentProperties` collection. Individual items in the collection are set to the Outlook data by setting their `Value` properties as the following code fragment demonstrates:

```
Set oCustProps = oDoc.CustomDocumentProperties
With oCustProps
   .Item("Full Name").Value = oContact.FullName
   .Item("Address").Value = oContact.MailingAddress
   .Item("First Name").Value = oContact.FirstName
End With
```

Remember to set references to the Microsoft Outlook 9.0 and Microsoft Word 9.0 Object Libraries for this procedure. The code instantiates an Outlook automation object and then looks for an open Inspector window containing a Contact item. If the currently open item is a Contact item a Word automation object is then instantiated.

```
Public Sub WordDocProperties()
   Dim oOutlook As Outlook.Application
   Dim oInspector As Outlook.Inspector
   Dim oItem As Object
   Dim oContact As Outlook.ContactItem
   Dim oWord As Word.Application
   Dim oDoc As Word.Document
   Dim oCustProps As Object
   Dim sTemplateName As String

   'Change this file name and location if necessary.
   sTemplateName = "C:\My Documents\DocPropsMaster.dot"

   'Get an Outlook Application object
   On Error Resume Next
   Set oOutlook = GetObject(, "Outlook.Application")
   If oOutlook Is Nothing Then
      Set oOutlook = CreateObject("Outlook.Application")
   End If
   On Error GoTo WordDocPropertiesError

   Set oInspector = oOutlook.ActiveInspector

   'Look for an open Inspector window.
   If oInspector Is Nothing Then
      MsgBox "There is no open item", , "Wrox"
   Else
      Set oItem = oInspector.CurrentItem
      'Make sure the open item is a ContactItem.
      If oItem.Class = olContact Then
        Set oContact = oItem
        'Get a Word Application object
        On Error Resume Next
        Set oWord = GetObject(, "Word.Application")
        If oWord Is Nothing Then
           Set oWord = CreateObject("Word.Application")
        End If
        On Error GoTo WordDocPropertiesError
```

Once we have a Word object we can open a new Word document based on our custom template by using the Add method of the Documents collection. The CustomDocumentProperties collection of the document is used to access our Document Properties, and each custom property is set to the value of the corresponding property of the Contact item. The document is then activated and the entire document is then selected so that the Fields collection can be updated.

```
        'Add a document based on our template.
        Set oDoc = oWord.Documents.Add(sTemplateName)
        Set oCustProps = oDoc.CustomDocumentProperties
        With oCustProps
           .Item("Full Name").Value = oContact.FullName
           .Item("Address").Value = oContact.MailingAddress
           .Item("First Name").Value = oContact.FirstName
```

```
            End With
            'Activate our new document.
            oDoc.Activate
            'Select the entire document.
            With oWord.Selection
               .WholeStory
```

After the Custom Document Properties are set the `Fields` collection is updated, using the
`.Fields.Update` statement. The Custom Document Properties do not show the newly assigned values
until the `Update` method is used. Then the cursor is moved to the end of the document, ready for the
user to enter text in the letter, and the document is made visible. Finally, all object variables are set to
`Nothing`.

```
            'Update all the fields (Custom Document Properties).
               .Fields.Update
            'Move the cursor to the end of the document.
               .EndKey Unit:=wdStory, Extend:=wdMove
            End With
            'Make the document visible.
            oWord.Visible = True
            oDoc.ActiveWindow.Visible = True
         Else
            MsgBox "This is not a Contact item", , "Wrox"
         End If
      End If

WordDocPropertiesExit:
      'Set all objects to Nothing to prevent memory and
      'resource leaks. This still leaves the new document open.
      Set oItem = Nothing
      Set oContact = Nothing
      Set oInspector = Nothing
      Set oOutlook = Nothing
      Set oDoc = Nothing
      Set oCustProps = Nothing
      Set oWord = Nothing
      Exit Sub

WordDocPropertiesError:
      MsgBox "Error occurred: " & Err.Description, , "Wrox"
      GoTo WordDocPropertiesExit
End Sub
```

The newly created document with the data from the open Contact inserted into the Custom Document Properties should look similar to the following screen shot.

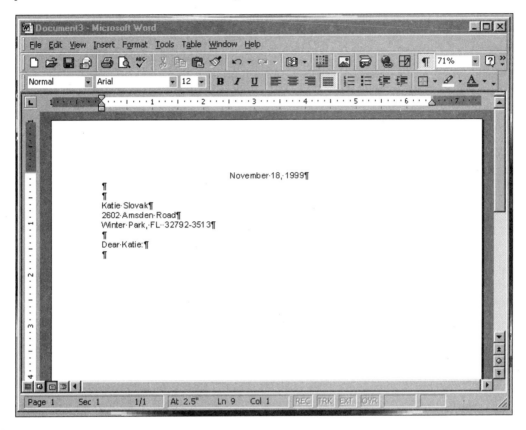

In addition to using Custom Document Properties, you can also use Custom Document Variables to store information from data sources external to Word. Word also provides many standard Document Properties that can provide information about such things as the author of the document, the document itself, and statistics about the document. Familiarize yourself with the various properties that are available by opening the Properties dialog box in the File menu. Another method of storing and retrieving information in a Word document is to use FormFields. FormFields are used to store data from Outlook in a Word table in the Tasks example later in this chapter.

Using Word to Print Outlook Information

Word can be used to print Outlook information from documents based on formatted templates. Outlook 2000 has more and better printing features and options than previous versions of Outlook, but printing from Outlook is still not as flexible and customizable as many user want. Microsoft has released an ActiveX control and COM add-in that does simulate **WYSIWYG** (What You See Is What You Get) printing of Outlook forms, but the control only works for Message and Post forms. For more information about XPrint, see http://www.slipstick.com/dev/customprint.htm#wysiwyg.

The following example shows how to use Word to print Outlook information. The only formatting that is performed in this example is setting the document margins, but you can construct complex templates that format things such as Outlook Calendars and custom forms for printing. Word templates can even have fields inserted that provide the look of various Outlook form controls to provide documents that can provide highly formatted printouts. If you select more than one message in the Inbox, the example prints them out all.

> When using Word to print from other applications, it is recommended that background printing be disabled and foreground printing be enabled. This ensures that the entire print job is sent to the system print spooler before Word is shut down. The following example shows how to set this in your code.

The following example uses the `TypeText` and `TypeParagraph` methods of the `Selection` object to insert the `Subject` and `Body` properties of all selected Outlook items into Word documents. This example uses Boolean variables to store whether the macro started Word or Outlook, or if they were already running. If the macro started either or both applications, they are terminated using the `Quit` method. If Word or Outlook were already running when the procedure was entered, they are left running. The new document is added to Word's `Documents` collection without being based on a custom template, so the new document is based on the `Normal.dot` template. Remember to set references to the Microsoft Outlook 9.0 and Microsoft Word 9.0 Object Libraries for this example.

```
Public Sub PrintItemsToWord()
   Dim oOutlook As Outlook.Application
   Dim oItems As Outlook.Selection
   Dim oItem As Object
   Dim oWord As Word.Application
   Dim oDoc As Word.Document
   Dim oPageSetup As Object
   Dim blnBackground As Boolean
   Dim blnWordExists As Boolean
   Dim blnOutlookExists As Boolean
```

The three Boolean variables above are used to store the existing background printing setting and whether Word and Outlook sessions existed before the code was run. This method can be used to track if we had to open the sessions and whether they need to be closed when the code finishes.

```
'Get an Outlook Application object
On Error Resume Next
blnOutlookExists = True
Set oOutlook = GetObject(, "Outlook.Application")
If oOutlook Is Nothing Then
   Set oOutlook = CreateObject("Outlook.Application")
   blnOutlookExists = False
End If
On Error GoTo PrintItemsToWordError
```

```
    If oOutlook Is Nothing Then
      MsgBox "Couldn't start Outlook.", , "Wrox"
    Else
      Set oItems = oOutlook.ActiveExplorer.Selection

      'Get a Word Application object
      On Error Resume Next
      blnWordExists = True
      Set oWord = GetObject(, "Word.Application")
      If oWord Is Nothing Then
        Set oWord = CreateObject("Word.Application")
        blnWordExists = False
      End If
      On Error GoTo PrintItemsToWordError

      If oWord Is Nothing Then
        MsgBox "Couldn't start Word.", , "Wrox"
      Else
```

The current background printing setting is captured from the Options collection, using the PrintBackground Boolean property. The Options settings are application wide, not specific to one document, so it is important to save the original settings of any that you change so they can be restored when you are finished using them.

```
        For Each oItem In oItems
          'Open a new document
          With oWord
            Set oDoc = .Documents.Add
            'Save the current Word setting for background printing
            blnBackground = .Options.PrintBackground
            'Turn background printing off
            .Options.PrintBackground = False
          End With
```

The PageSetup property collection is used to set the margins and printout orientation. This collection corresponds to the settings available from the File | Page Setup menu.

```
          'Set a page setup object variable
          Set oPageSetup = oDoc.PageSetup
          With oPageSetup
            'Set the margins to .75" (54 points)
            .TopMargin = 54
            .BottomMargin = 54
            .LeftMargin = 54
            .RightMargin = 54
            'Portrait orientation
            .Orientation = wdOrientPortrait
          End With
```

The `TypeText` method is used to insert the `Subject` and `Body` from the Outlook item into the Word document, and the `TypeParagraph` method is used to insert paragraph marks into the document. Then the `PrintOut` method of the document is used to do the actual printing. Finally, the document is closed without saving it, the Outlook and Word sessions are closed if we opened them, and the object variables are set to `Nothing`.

```
            'Type in the Subject and Body.
            With oWord.Selection
               .TypeText oItem.Subject
               .TypeParagraph
               .TypeText oItem.Body
               .TypeParagraph
            End With
            'Print the word document
            oDoc.PrintOut
            'Restore background printing setting
            oWord.Options.PrintBackground = blnBackground
            'Close document without saving
            oDoc.Close wdDoNotSaveChanges
         Next oItem

         'Close the Word instance if we created it
         If blnWordExists = False Then
            oWord.Quit
         End If
      End If

      'Close the Outlook instance if we created it
      If blnOutlookExists = False Then
         oOutlook.Quit
      End If
   End If

PrintItemsToWordExit:
   'Clean up objects
   Set oItem = Nothing
   Set oItems = Nothing
   Set oOutlook = Nothing
   Set oPageSetup = Nothing
   Set oDoc = Nothing
   Set oWord = Nothing
   Exit Sub

PrintItemsToWordError:
   MsgBox "Error occurred: " & Err.Description, , "Wrox"
   GoTo PrintItemsToWordExit
End Sub
```

Highly formatted output can be generated by using different fonts, font colors, font sizes and font weights. You can insert backgrounds or themes in your custom templates and use any of the formatting tools and features that Word offers. Templates can be formatted when they are designed, or they can be formatted in your code. Image files can be inserted in your custom documents based on criteria that your code establishes. You can even save the final output as HTML files for use on Web pages, instead of printing it as hard copy output.

Using Word Tables From Outlook

You can use all the formatting features in Word from your code to format a document. You can use standard and custom Word document fields to insert information into your documents. You also can use Word tables to organize your data in documents based on custom templates. The data can be dynamic, it is not limited to a fixed number of rows or columns. Word tables can be expanded and reformatted in your code. Tables themselves can be created in your code and inserted in blank documents.

The following example uses a template that has a skeleton Word table inserted. This table has two rows, one for headings and the other for data. Five columns of data are provided, in this case to place information from uncompleted Outlook Tasks. To create this template create a new Word template based on `Normal.dot`. Use the Options dialog box to make paragraph marks and field codes visible to help in placing the elements of the template. Paragraph mark visibility can also be controlled by using the `Show Paragraphs` toolbar button, and you also can make field codes visible by using the keyboard shortcut *Alt+F9*.

Type Outstanding Tasks and then press the *Enter* key to provide a title for the document. Choose Date and Time from the Insert menu to insert a date field in your preferred format and then press the *Enter* key three times. Place the cursor before the last paragraph mark and choose Insert | Table from the Table menu. Choose to create the table with two rows and five columns. In the first row insert the column titles Subject, Due Date, Start Date, Status and % Complete. This example uses Text FormFields for the Outlook data, which are inserted from the Forms toolbar. To make the Forms toolbar visible, choose Toolbars from the View menu and select the Forms toolbar. Move the cursor into each cell in the second row of the table in turn, and click on the Text Form Field icon to insert a Text Form Field in each cell.

> **Outlook uses the date 1/1/4501 when a date field is blank or set to None. You can add code to test for this condition if there is a possibility that any Outlook date fields you work with may be blank.**

Right-click in each Text Form Field in turn, and select Properties from the context menu. In the Bookmark textbox of the Field settings group, enter the name for that Text Form Field. The names should be Subject, DueDate, StartDate, Status, and PercentComplete. The finished template should look similar to the screen shot below. Save the new template as `C:\My Documents\OutstandingTasks.dot`. If you use a different name or file path for the template, change the reference in the macro to reflect the new name or file path. Remember to set references to the Microsoft Outlook 9.0 and Microsoft Word 9.0 Object Libraries for this example.

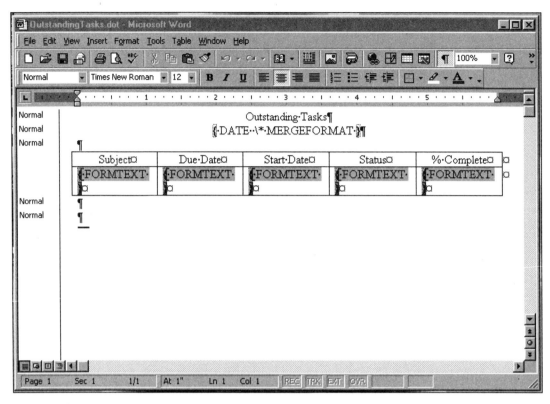

The code first performs the now familiar steps of opening Outlook and Word sessions and adding a document based on our custom template.

```
Public Sub WordTable()
    Dim oOutlook As Outlook.Application
    Dim oNS As Outlook.NameSpace
    Dim oFolder As Outlook.MAPIFolder
    Dim oTask As Outlook.TaskItem
    Dim oItems As Outlook.Items
    Dim oWord As Word.Application
    Dim oDoc As Word.Document
    Dim sStatus As String
    Dim sDueDate As String
    Dim sPercentComplete As String
    Dim sStartDate As String
    Dim sTemplateName As String
    Dim lRowCount As Long

    'Change this file name and location if necessary.
    sTemplateName = "C:\My Documents\OutstandingTasks.dot"

    'Get an Outlook Application object
    On Error Resume Next
```

```
Set oOutlook = GetObject(, "Outlook.Application")
If oOutlook Is Nothing Then
  Set oOutlook = CreateObject("Outlook.Application")
End If
On Error GoTo WordTableError

Set oNS = oOutlook.GetNamespace("MAPI")
Set oFolder = oNS.GetDefaultFolder(olFolderTasks)
Set oItems = oFolder.Items

'Get a Word Application object
On Error Resume Next
Set oWord = GetObject(, "Word.Application")
If oWord Is Nothing Then
  Set oWord = CreateObject("Word.Application")
End If
On Error GoTo WordTableError
'Add a document based on our template.
Set oDoc = oWord.Documents.Add(sTemplateName)
```

The code uses a Long variable to keep track of the rows in the table. The variable is initialized to 2, the initial row count after the title row. The row count is incremented after each unfinished Task is processed, and a new row is inserted before the last row if there are more unfinished Tasks. New rows, columns and cells are always inserted before the referenced row, column or cell. The data is moved from each Text Form Field's Result property to the Text property of the newly inserted cell in the row above the Text Form Fields.

```
lRowCount = 2
For Each oTask In oItems
  If oTask.Status <> olTaskComplete Then
    If lRowCount > 2 Then
      oDoc.Tables(1).Rows.Add _
        BeforeRow:=oDoc.Tables(1).Rows(lRowCount - 1)
      With oDoc.Tables(1).Rows(lRowCount - 1)
        .Cells(1).range.Text = oDoc.FormFields("Subject").Result
        .Cells(2).range.Text = oDoc.FormFields("DueDate").Result
        .Cells(3).range.Text = oDoc.FormFields("StartDate").Result
        .Cells(4).range.Text = oDoc.FormFields("Status").Result
        .Cells(5).range.Text = oDoc.FormFields("PercentComplete").Result
      End With
    End If
  End If
```

A Select Case block is used to translate the Task's Status property, which is a Long, to a meaningful text string.

```
With oTask
  sPercentComplete = CStr(.PercentComplete) & "%"
  sDueDate = CStr(.DueDate)
  sStartDate = CStr(.StartDate)
```

```
      Select Case .Status
      Case olTaskNotStarted '0
        sStatus = "Not Started"
      Case olTaskInProgress '1
        sStatus = "In Progress"
      'No check for olTaskComplete (2)
      Case olTaskWaiting '3
        sStatus = "Waiting"
      Case olTaskDeferred '4
        sStatus = "Deferred"
      End Select
    End With
```

The Task data is then inserted in the `Result` property of the appropriate Text Form Field.

```
    With oDoc
      .FormFields("Subject").Result = oTask.Subject
      .FormFields("DueDate").Result = sDueDate
      .FormFields("StartDate").Result = sStartDate
      .FormFields("Status").Result = sStatus
      .FormFields("PercentComplete").Result = sPercentComplete
    End With
    lRowCount = lRowCount + 1
  End If
Next oTask
```

After all the unfinished Tasks are processed the `Text` property of the final row, which is still the row containing the Text Form Fields, is updated with the final data placed in the Text Form Fields. The table is then sorted on the second column (**Due Date**), excluding the row containing the headers from the sort. The sort is performed chronologically based on the text derived from dates using a `wdSortFieldDate` parameter for the `SortFieldType` argument of the `Sort` method.

```
  'Update the text in the final row.
  With oDoc.Tables(1).Rows(lRowCount - 1)
    .Cells(1).range.Text = oDoc.FormFields("Subject").Result
    .Cells(2).range.Text = oDoc.FormFields("DueDate").Result
    .Cells(3).range.Text = oDoc.FormFields("StartDate").Result
    .Cells(4).range.Text = oDoc.FormFields("Status").Result
    .Cells(5).range.Text = oDoc.FormFields("PercentComplete").Result
  End With

  'Sort the table by column 2 (DueDate),
  'exclude the title row from the sort, sort as dates
  oDoc.Tables(1).Sort ExcludeHeader:=True, _
      FieldNumber:=2, SortFieldType:=wdSortFieldDate
```

Finally, the cursor is moved to the start of the document, the document is made visible and activated, and the object variables are set to `Nothing`.

```
'Move the cursor to the start of the document.
oWord.Selection.HomeKey Unit:=wdStory, Extend:=wdMove
'Make the document visible.
oWord.Visible = True
oDoc.Activate
oDoc.ActiveWindow.Visible = True

WordTableExit:
  Set oTask = Nothing
  Set oItems = Nothing
  Set oFolder = Nothing
  Set oNS = Nothing
  Set oOutlook = Nothing
  Set oDoc = Nothing
  Set oWord = Nothing
  Exit Sub

WordTableError:
  MsgBox "Error occurred: " & Err.Description, , "Wrox"
  GoTo WordTableExit
End Sub
```

The document that results from running this macro should look similar to the following screen shot.

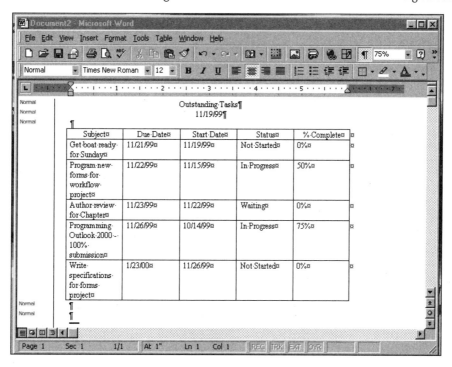

This section has shown some of the ways that you can use Word to provide formatted output for Outlook data, to print Outlook data with formatting not available when printing from Outlook, and three ways of generating custom documents based on Outlook contact data. Word provides such a rich object model, with so many properties and methods that this only scratches the surface of what you can do with automation and the Word object model.

Working with Microsoft Excel

You can use Excel to provide formatted output for Outlook data just as you can with Word. Word has more options for formatting data than Excel does, but both applications are more flexible in their output options than Outlook. However, the main reasons to use Excel as a container for Outlook data are to make use of Excel's data analysis and charting features, and to use Excel as a database for data storage. This section provides two examples of using automation from Outlook to control Excel. As with the Word examples, these Excel examples barely scratch the surface of what you can do with your Outlook data in Excel. For these examples make sure to set references to the Microsoft Outlook 9.0 and Microsoft Excel 9.0 Object Libraries.

Exporting Outlook Contacts to Excel

This example exports the contacts in the default Outlook Contacts folder into an Excel Worksheet. The Worksheet is created on the fly, so no custom template is used. After the Outlook and Excel automation objects are instantiated the old setting for SheetsInNewWorkbook in Excel is saved and SheetsInNewWorkbook is set to 1, creating only one Worksheet for the new Workbook. The new Worksheet is then created and made the active Worksheet.

```
Public Sub OutlookContactsToExcel()
    'Excel definitions
    Dim oExcel As Excel.Application
    Dim oRange As Excel.range
    Dim oSheet As Excel.Worksheet
    'Number of sheets in new WorkBook
    Dim lSheets As Long

    'Outlook definitions
    Dim oOutlook As Outlook.Application
    Dim oNS As Outlook.NameSpace
    Dim oFolder As Outlook.MAPIFolder
    Dim oItems As Outlook.Items
    Dim oContact As Outlook.ContactItem
    Dim oItem As Object

    Dim sRange As String
    Dim sCol As String
    Dim iRow As Integer

    'Get an Outlook Application object
    On Error Resume Next
    Set oOutlook = GetObject(, "Outlook.Application")
    If oOutlook Is Nothing Then
      Set oOutlook = CreateObject("Outlook.Application")
```

```
End If
On Error GoTo OutlookContactsToExcelError

'Initialize Outlook items
Set oNS = oOutlook.GetNamespace("MAPI")
Set oFolder = oNS.GetDefaultFolder(olFolderContacts)
Set oItems = oFolder.Items

'Get an Excel Application object
On Error Resume Next
Set oExcel = GetObject(, "Excel.Application")
If oExcel Is Nothing Then
   Set oExcel = CreateObject("Excel.Application")
End If
On Error GoTo OutlookContactsToExcelError

'Initialize Excel items
'Save the previous setting for the number of Sheets
'in a new WorkBook
lSheets = oExcel.SheetsInNewWorkbook
'Only 1 sheet in this WorkBook
oExcel.SheetsInNewWorkbook = 1
'Create a new WorkBook and make it active
oExcel.Workbooks.Add
'Activate Sheet 1
Set oSheet = oExcel.ActiveWorkbook.Sheets(1)
oSheet.Activate
oExcel.Visible = True
```

The Worksheet title and column headings are then created by calling a `Private` procedure `SetSheetHeadings`. This Sub procedure uses seven arguments to define the range, name, font, font size and weight, and border styles of the heading and column titles.

```
'Column A, Row 1 Sheet Title - Bold, 14 pt, underlined
Set oRange = oSheet.range("A1")
SetSheetHeadings oRange, "Outlook Contacts", True, 14, _
   xlHairline, xlLineStyleNone, xlUnderlineStyleSingle

'Column headings - Bold, 12 pt, thick bottom border
'Column A heading
Set oRange = oSheet.range("A2")
SetSheetHeadings oRange, "Last Name", True, 12, xlThick, _
   xlContinuous, xlUnderlineStyleNone

'Column B heading
Set oRange = oSheet.range("B2")
SetSheetHeadings oRange, "First Name", True, 12, xlThick, _
   xlContinuous, xlUnderlineStyleNone

'Column C heading
Set oRange = oSheet.range("C2")
SetSheetHeadings oRange, "Mailing Address", True, 12, xlThick, _
   xlContinuous, xlUnderlineStyleNone
```

```
'Column D heading
Set oRange = oSheet.range("D2")
SetSheetHeadings oRange, "Phone", True, 12, xlThick, _
  xlContinuous, xlUnderlineStyleNone

'Column E heading
Set oRange = oSheet.range("E2")
SetSheetHeadings oRange, "Fax", True, 12, xlThick, _
  xlContinuous, xlUnderlineStyleNone

'Start adding data at Column A, Row 3
iRow = 2 'this number will be incremented in the For Each loop
```

Another `Private` Sub procedure, `SetRangeData`, is called with four arguments that define the Worksheet, row, column, and data to insert into the cell. This procedure calculates a range setting in Excel format from the row and column arguments and inserts the data into that range.

```
For Each oItem In oItems
   If oItem.Class = olContact Then
      Set oContact = oItem
      With oContact
         'Each call to SetRangeData increments the Column,
         'so we have to start out at A - 1
         sCol = "A"
         sCol = Chr(Asc(sCol) - 1)
         'Start a new data Row
         iRow = iRow + 1

         SetRangeData oSheet, sCol, iRow, .LastName
         SetRangeData oSheet, sCol, iRow, .FirstName

         'Get the MailingAddress property
         'If there is a newline in MailingAddress, it
         'will appear as a box shape in Excel.
         SetRangeData oSheet, sCol, iRow, .MailingAddress

         SetRangeData oSheet, sCol, iRow, .BusinessTelephoneNumber
         SetRangeData oSheet, sCol, iRow, .BusinessFaxNumber
      End With
   End If
Next oItem
```

After all the data has been inserted into the Excel table the table is sorted on Last Name, and First Name. Then the entire table is AutoFitted, first by column and then by row, to produce a neatly formatted Worksheet. If any of the address entries include a newline (carriage return and line feed), the newline is displayed in Excel as a square box character. Finally, the original setting for `SheetsInNewWorkbook` is restored. The usual cleanup code sets the object variables to `Nothing`.

```
        'Set up a string variable for the last cell
        sCol = "E"
        sRange = sCol & CStr(iRow)

        'Set a Range covering all the data in the Sheet
        Set oRange = oSheet.range("A3", sRange)

        'Sort the Sheet by Last Name, then First Name
        oRange.Sort Key1:=oSheet.range("A3"), _
                Key2:=oSheet.range("B3")

        'Set a Range covering all the headings and data in the Sheet
        sRange = "A2:" & sRange

        'AutoFit the Columns
        oSheet.range(sRange).Columns.AutoFit
        'AutoFit the Rows
        oSheet.range(sRange).Rows.AutoFit

        'Restore the old setting for number of Sheets
        'in a new WorkBook
        oExcel.SheetsInNewWorkbook = lSheets

OutlookContactsToExcelExit:
    Set oSheet = Nothing
    Set oRange = Nothing
    Set oExcel = Nothing
    Set oContact = Nothing
    Set oItem = Nothing
    Set oItems = Nothing
    Set oFolder = Nothing
    Set oNS = Nothing
    Set oOutlook = Nothing
    Exit Sub

OutlookContactsToExcelError:
    MsgBox "Error occurred: " & Err.Description, , "Wrox"
    GoTo OutlookContactsToExcelExit
End Sub
```

The `SetSheetHeadings` procedure sets the `Value` property of the range, in this case the title and column headings, and uses some of the `Font` and `Border` properties to format the text in the range. There are many more properties that can be used to format the look of the Excel Worksheet. Experiment with the different properties, and use the Object Browser to see what properties and settings are available.

```
    Private Sub SetSheetHeadings(oRange As Excel.range, _
            sValue As String, blnBold As Boolean, lFontSize As Long, _
            lBorderWeight As Long, lLineStyle As Long, _
            lUnderLine As Long)
      With oRange
        .Value = sValue
        .Font.Bold = blnBold
        .Font.Size = lFontSize
        .Font.Underline = lUnderLine
        .Borders(xlEdgeBottom).LineStyle = lLineStyle
        .Borders(xlEdgeBottom).Weight = lBorderWeight
      End With
    End Sub
```

The `SetRangeData` procedure does no formatting of the data inserted into the specified range, it just sets the `Value` property of the range after deriving a range variable from the supplied arguments for the column and row.

```
Private Sub SetRangeData(oSheet As Excel.Worksheet, sCol As String, _
        iRow As Integer, sValue As String)
    Dim oRange As Excel.range
    Dim sRange As String

    sCol = Chr(Asc(sCol) + 1)
    sRange = sCol & CStr(iRow)
    Set oRange = oSheet.range(sRange)
    oRange.Value = sValue

    Set oRange = Nothing
End Sub
```

The Excel Worksheet created by running this macro should look similar to the screen shot below.

Using Excel to Analyze Outlook Data

Excel provides extremely powerful data analysis functions that can be controlled with automation. Almost any formula, function or formatting that can be used from the Excel user interface can be used by an automation controller. The following example does not use any formulas or complex data functions, using only the Subtotal method on the **Duration** column of the Worksheet. The techniques used are the same as with more complex analytical functions though, and this example can serve as a model for working with any analytical function. Make sure your references are set to the Microsoft Outlook 9.0 and Microsoft Excel 9.0 Object Libraries.

This example illustrates one of the incompatibilities between Outlook 2000 and previous versions of Outlook. Items that were created in previous versions of Outlook that had contacts linked into the Contacts field in the Outlook form will have those contacts in the ContactNames *read-only string property. These names are also the members of the* Recipients *collection for the item, separated by semicolons in the* ContactNames *string property. Contacts placed in the Contacts field in an item created in Outlook 2000 are not placed in the* ContactNames *property or the* Recipients *collection, they are placed only in the* Links *collection. The* Links *collection is new to Outlook 2000, and does not exist in previous versions of Outlook.*

The workaround for this problem depends on the compatibility you need to preserve for the Journal entries. If you need to maintain compatibility with previous versions of Outlook, add the members of the Links *collection to the* ContactNames *property. Use the* Add *method of the* Recipients *collection for each member of the* Links *collection. To update older items for full Outlook 2000 compatibility, use the* Add *method of the* Links *collection for each member of the* Recipients *collection. To maintain compatibility with all versions of Outlook, use both methods.*

> **The Links collection is one of the biggest differences that can cause problems in Outlook 2000 programming that has to maintain backward compatibility. Other new properties, methods and events can just not be used if backward compatibility has to be maintained. But the Links collection affects the data in Outlook forms, and how the forms can be used.**

The example uses the Outlook Journal, and looks for Journal items that are of Type Phone Call that have been created in the previous thirty days. This code can be modified to look for Journal items that are of Type Phone Call that have been created in the prior week, month, quarter, or year to provide a phone log.

```
Public Sub AnalyzePhoneCalls()
  'Excel definitions
  Dim oExcel As Excel.Application
  Dim oRange As Excel.range
  Dim oSheet As Excel.Worksheet
  'Number of sheets in new WorkBook
  Dim lSheets As Long

  'Outlook definitions
  Dim oOutlook As Outlook.Application
  Dim oNS As Outlook.NameSpace
  Dim oFolder As Outlook.MAPIFolder
  Dim oItems As Outlook.Items
  Dim oJournal As Outlook.JournalItem

  Dim sContact As String
  Dim sRange As String
  Dim sCol As String
  Dim iRow As Integer
  Dim lTotal As Long
  Dim lAvg As Long
  Dim lCount As Long
  Dim lPeriod As Long

  'In this case 30 days is the time period to look at
  lPeriod = 30

  'Get an Outlook Application object
  On Error Resume Next
  Set oOutlook = GetObject(, "Outlook.Application")
  If oOutlook Is Nothing Then
    Set oOutlook = CreateObject("Outlook.Application")
  End If
  On Error GoTo AnalyzePhoneCallsError

  'Initialize Outlook items
  Set oNS = oOutlook.GetNamespace("MAPI")
  Set oFolder = oNS.GetDefaultFolder(olFolderJournal)
  Set oItems = oFolder.Items

  'Get an Excel Application object
  On Error Resume Next
  Set oExcel = GetObject(, "Excel.Application")
  If oExcel Is Nothing Then
    Set oExcel = CreateObject("Excel.Application")
  End If
  On Error GoTo AnalyzePhoneCallsError

  'Initialize Excel items
  'Save the previous setting for the number of Sheets
  'in a new WorkBook
  lSheets = oExcel.SheetsInNewWorkbook
  'Only 1 sheet in this WorkBook
```

```
oExcel.SheetsInNewWorkbook = 1
'Create a new WorkBook and make it active
oExcel.Workbooks.Add
'Activate Sheet 1
Set oSheet = oExcel.ActiveWorkbook.Sheets(1)
oSheet.Activate
oExcel.Visible = True
```

The basic design of the code and the Worksheet are the same as in the previous example. The same
SetSheetHeadings and SetRangeData utility Sub procedures are called to set the title, headings,
and data.

```
'Column A, Row 1 Sheet Title - Bold, 14 pt, underlined
Set oRange = oSheet.range("A1")
SetSheetHeadings oRange, "Phone Calls", True, 14, _
   xlHairline, xlLineStyleNone, xlUnderlineStyleSingle

'Column headings - Bold, 12 pt, thick bottom border
'Column A heading
Set oRange = oSheet.range("A2")
SetSheetHeadings oRange, "Company", True, 12, xlThick, _
   xlContinuous, xlUnderlineStyleNone

'Column B heading
Set oRange = oSheet.range("B2")
SetSheetHeadings oRange, "Contact", True, 12, xlThick, _
   xlContinuous, xlUnderlineStyleNone

'Column C heading
Set oRange = oSheet.range("C2")
SetSheetHeadings oRange, "Started", True, 12, xlThick, _
   xlContinuous, xlUnderlineStyleNone

'Column D heading
Set oRange = oSheet.range("D2")
SetSheetHeadings oRange, "Duration (minutes)", True, 12, xlThick, _
   xlContinuous, xlUnderlineStyleNone

'Column E heading
Set oRange = oSheet.range("E2")
SetSheetHeadings oRange, "Subject", True, 12, xlThick, _
   xlContinuous, xlUnderlineStyleNone

'Start adding data at Column A, Row 3
iRow = 2 'this number will be incremented in the For Each loop
```

The period of time to use is set with a Long variable lPeriod. The function call to the DateDiff
function, DateDiff("d", oJournal.CreationTime, Date), does this by looking for the
difference in days between the CreationTime property of the Journal item and the present system
date.

```
For Each oJournal In oItems
   If oJournal.Type = "Phone Call" And _
   DateDiff("d", oJournal.CreationTime, Date) <= lPeriod Then
      With oJournal
         'Each call to SetRangeData increments the Column,
         'so we have to start out at A - 1
         sCol = "A"
         sCol = Chr(Asc(sCol) - 1)
         'Start a new data Row
         iRow = iRow + 1
```

Full version compatibility is maintained for the Outlook form data by using the ContactNames property if it isn't a Null string, and using the Links collection if the ContactNames is a Null string.

```
         'Items created in Outlook 2000 will have any
         'associated contacts in the Links collection.
         'If the items were created in older versions of
         'Outlook the associated contacts will be in the
         'ContactNames read-only string property as well
         'as the Recipients and Links collections.
         'This code segment checks for the contents of the
         'ContactNames property and uses it if it is not blank.
         'You can update the ContactNames property from the
         'members of the Links collection so that items can
         'be compatible with older versions of Outlook.
         sContact = ""
         If .ContactNames <> "" Then
            sContact = .ContactNames
         ElseIf .Links.Count <> 0 Then
            sContact = .Links(1).Name
            For lCount = 2 To .Links.Count
               sContact = sContact & "; " & .Links(lCount).Name
            Next lCount
         End If

         SetRangeData oSheet, sCol, iRow, .Companies
         SetRangeData oSheet, sCol, iRow, sContact
         SetRangeData oSheet, sCol, iRow, .CreationTime
         SetRangeData oSheet, sCol, iRow, .Duration
         SetRangeData oSheet, sCol, iRow, .Subject
      End With
   End If
Next oJournal
```

The resulting Excel Worksheet is sorted on three fields: **Company**, then **Contact**, then **Started**. The Worksheet.Subtotal method is used to calculate the total time spent on phone calls, and the Worksheet.Average method is used to calculate the average phone call length. Both methods are used with the range set to all the data cells in the **Duration** column for the programmed period of time. The time period can also be used as an argument to the procedure if you want. The results of these calculations is then pasted in the **Duration** column below the last data cell.

```
'Set up a string variable for the last cell
sCol = "E"
sRange = sCol & CStr(iRow)
'Set a Range covering all the data in the Sheet
Set oRange = oSheet.range("A3", sRange)
'Sort the Sheet by Company, Contact and Start
oRange.Sort Key1:=oSheet.range("A3"), _
            Key2:=oSheet.range("B3"), _
            Key3:=oSheet.range("C3")

sCol = "D"
'Set up for column D and the last data row
sRange = sCol & CStr(iRow)
'Set up range for chart
sRange = "D3:" & sRange
```

Excel's charting functions are used to graph the inserted data on a Scatter chart through automation. The X-axis of the chart is given the legend **Calls** and the Y-axis of the chart is given the legend **Minutes**. The chart is given the title **Phone Time**. The range of data cells in the duration column is used as the data source for the chart. The chart is embedded in the Worksheet as an embedded object. It also can be placed as a separate sheet in the Workbook if you want, or you can let Excel decide where to place it.

```
With oExcel
    'Add a scatter chart
    .Charts.Add
    .ActiveChart.ChartType = xlXYScatter
    'Source data is all phone call durations
    .ActiveChart.SetSourceData _
        Source:=Sheets("Sheet1").range(sRange), PlotBy:=xlColumns
    'Embed the chart as an object in the sheet
    .ActiveChart.Location xlLocationAsObject, Name:="Sheet1"
End With

With oExcel.ActiveChart
    'Set chart title to "Phone Time"
    .HasTitle = True
    .ChartTitle.Characters.Text = "Phone Time"
    'X axis legend is "Calls"
    .Axes(xlCategory, xlPrimary).HasTitle = True
    .Axes(xlCategory, xlPrimary).AxisTitle.Characters.Text = "Calls"
    'Y axis legend is "Minutes"
    .Axes(xlValue, xlPrimary).HasTitle = True
    .Axes(xlValue, xlPrimary).AxisTitle.Characters.Text = "Minutes"
End With

'Set up a string variable for the summation data cell
sCol = "D"
sRange = sCol & CStr(iRow)
Set oRange = oSheet.range("D3", sRange)
'Sum the minutes spent on Phone Calls
lTotal = oExcel.WorksheetFunction.Subtotal(9, oRange)
'Average minutes per call
lAvg = oExcel.WorksheetFunction.Average(oRange)
```

```
'Paste the total after the last data cell in column D
   iRow = iRow + 1
   sRange = sCol & CStr(iRow)
   Set oRange = oSheet.range(sRange)
   oRange.Value = "Total time : " & lTotal
   oRange.Font.Bold = True
   oRange.Font.Size = 12

   'Paste the average after the total in Column D
   iRow = iRow + 1
   sRange = sCol & CStr(iRow)
   Set oRange = oSheet.range(sRange)
   oRange.Value = "Average time : " & lAvg
   oRange.Font.Bold = True
   oRange.Font.Size = 12

   'Set a Range covering all the headings and data in the Sheet
   sCol = "E"
   sRange = sCol & CStr(iRow)
   sRange = "A2:" & sRange
   'AutoFit the Columns
   oSheet.range(sRange).Columns.AutoFit
   'AutoFit the Rows
   oSheet.range(sRange).Rows.AutoFit

   'Restore the old setting for number of Sheets
   'in a new WorkBook
   oExcel.SheetsInNewWorkbook = lSheets

AnalyzePhoneCallsExit:
   Set oSheet = Nothing
   Set oRange = Nothing
   Set oExcel = Nothing
   Set oJournal = Nothing
   Set oItems = Nothing
   Set oFolder = Nothing
   Set oNS = Nothing
   Set oOutlook = Nothing
   Exit Sub

AnalyzePhoneCallsError:
   MsgBox "Error occurred: " & Err.Description, , "Wrox"
   GoTo AnalyzePhoneCallsExit
End Sub
```

The Excel Worksheet created by running the `AnalyzePhoneCalls` macro should look similar to the following screen shot. This example just scratches the surface of the data analysis that you can use Excel to perform. You can use complex formulas or any of the available mathematical, financial or statistical functions for analysis. The full power of Excel for data analysis, charting, and data formatting is available for you to use in your automation code.

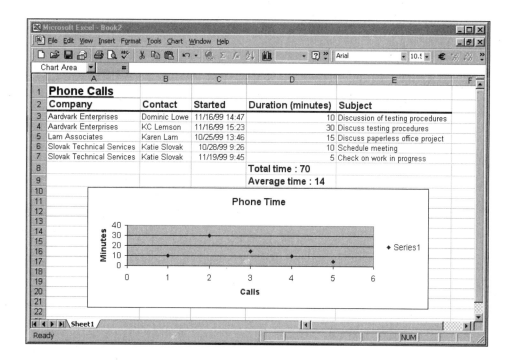

Working With Microsoft Access

Most of the work we do with Access in automation code will involve Access tables and records. That automation code usually uses either the **ADO** (ActiveX Data Objects) or **DAO** (Data Access Objects) object libraries. Those libraries are covered in Chapter 6, 'Outlook Data Access', and Chapter 8, 'Retrieving External Data with Outlook 2000'. This section covers using automation code to work with other Access objects.

Running an Access Report From Outlook

Although you can create new Access reports using the Access and DAO object models it is far easier to create them with the Access Report Designer. The Report Designer enables you to design the placement of controls on the form visually, and the initial properties of the controls and the report itself can be set with property sheets. However, it is easy to run existing reports using automation code, as the following example demonstrates.

This example uses the sample Contact database that can be installed with Access 2000. This sample database is an Access database, it does not use the Outlook Contacts. The sample is usually installed as `C:\Program Files\Microsoft Office\Office\Samples\Contact.mdb`. If your installation path is different, change the string in the code to match your installation path. If you did not install the sample databases when you installed Access 2000, rerun the Office installation program from the Office CD and choose to install both the `Contact` and `Northwind` sample databases (the `Northwind` sample database is used in one of the other Access examples in this chapter).

If you expect to run the same reports on a regular basis it's a good idea to design the report using the facilities of the Access Report designer and then reuse the report each time you need it. You can use the method shown in this example to make use of a predefined Access report when needed. Examples of working with Outlook and Access data together are shown in Chapter 8. Access data is not worked with directly from the Access object model, instead you use ADO or DAO for that. This particular example only needs a reference set to the Microsoft Access 9.0 Object Library.

```
Public Sub RunAccessReport()
   Dim oAccess As Access.Application

   Dim sDBPath As String
   Dim sReport As String

   'Get an Access Application object
   On Error Resume Next
   Set oAccess = GetObject(, "Access.Application")
   If oAccess Is Nothing Then
      Set oAccess = CreateObject("Access.Application")
   End If
   On Error GoTo RunAccessReportError

   sReport = "Alphabetical Contact Listing"
   sDBPath = "C:\Program Files\Microsoft Office\Office\Samples\Contact.mdb"

   'Set a new current database
   oAccess.OpenCurrentDatabase (sDBPath)
   oAccess.Visible = True
   'Run an existing report in Preview mode
   oAccess.DoCmd.OpenReport sReport, acViewPreview

RunAccessReportExit:
   'Clean up
   Set oAccess = Nothing
   Exit Sub

RunAccessReportError:
   MsgBox "Error occurred: " & Err.Description, , "Wrox"
   GoTo RunAccessReportExit
End Sub
```

The Alphabetical Contact Listing report is opened in preview mode, and should look similar to the following screen shot. When you are done viewing this report, close the Access application.

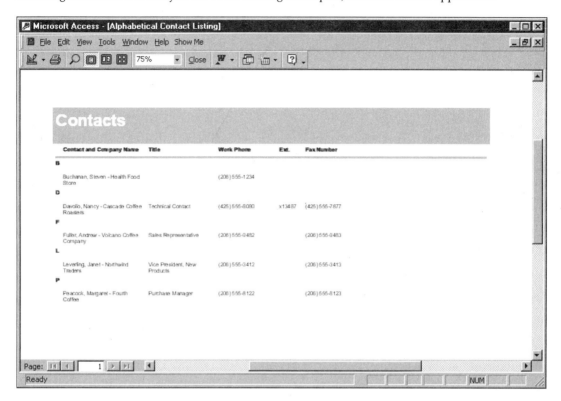

Running a Filtered Access Report From Outlook

The previous example displayed the Alphabetical Contact Listing report, based on all the data in the Contacts table in the Contact sample database. Close the report and the Access application after you are finished with it. The next example also only requires a reference to the Microsoft Access 9.0 Object Library.

The next example uses the same database and report, but filters the output with a **SQL** (Structured Query Language) WHERE clause. The SQL WHERE clause is stored in a string, and only selects data for the report where the contact's last name begins with the letter D. The SQL WHERE statement is implicit and is not used as part of the syntax in this case. The filter clause used is Left([LastName],1)='D'. In large databases, with many records, using the appropriate SQL filters and queries can selectively reduce the size of the returned datasets. The performance of filters is improved when the field or fields that are being used for the filter are indexed fields. In this case the LastName field is one of the indexed fields in the table.

```
Public Sub RunSQLWhereReport()
   Dim oAccess As Access.Application

   Dim sDBPath As String
   Dim sReport As String
   Dim sSQL As String

   'Get an Access Application object
   On Error Resume Next
   Set oAccess = GetObject(, "Access.Application")
   If oAccess Is Nothing Then
      Set oAccess = CreateObject("Access.Application")
   End If
   On Error GoTo RunSQLWhereReportError

   sReport = "Alphabetical Contact Listing"
   sDBPath = "C:\Program Files\Microsoft Office\Office\Samples\Contact.mdb"
   'Set up an SQL Where clause looking for Last Names
   'beginning with the letter "D"
   sSQL = "Left([LastName],1)='D'"

   'Set a new current database
   oAccess.OpenCurrentDatabase (sDBPath)
   oAccess.Visible = True
   'Run an existing report in Preview mode,
   'only report on items meeting the SQL Where criteria
   oAccess.DoCmd.OpenReport sReport, acViewPreview, , sSQL

RunSQLWhereReportExit:
   'Clean up
   Set oAccess = Nothing
   Exit Sub

RunSQLWhereReportError:
   MsgBox "Error occurred: " & Err.Description, , "Wrox"
   GoTo RunSQLWhereReportExit
End Sub
```

The preview report should produce output showing only one entry, the only contact record with a last name that begins with the letter D. It should look similar to the following screen shot.

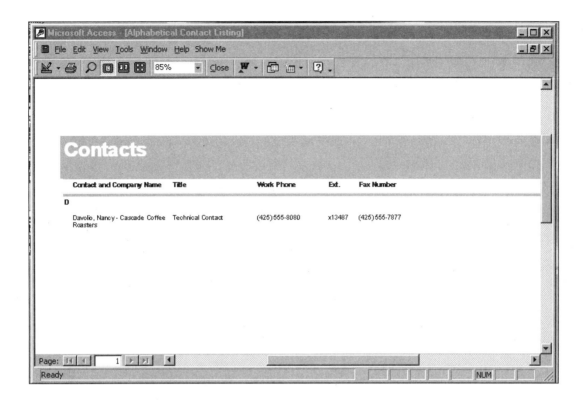

Opening an Access Form From Outlook

Access forms, like Access reports, can be designed using the Access and DAO object models in your programs. However, like reports, forms are much easier to design in the forms design mode where you can see the controls and the layout of the form. The following example shows how to open a pre-existing form from the Northwind sample database using automation. The example filters the output to the form by limiting the dataset to records in the Employees table whose job titles are Sales Representative. Filtering the dataset is again performed by an SQL WHERE clause, [Title]='Sales Representative'. Working with both forms and reports in automation code is generally performed using different methods of the DoCmd object.

```
Public Sub ShowFilteredForm()
  Dim oAccess As Access.Application
  Dim sDBPath As String

  'Get an Access Application object
  On Error Resume Next
  Set oAccess = GetObject(, "Access.Application")
  If oAccess Is Nothing Then
    Set oAccess = CreateObject("Access.Application")
  End If
  On Error GoTo ShowFilteredFormError
```

```
    sDBPath = "C:\Program Files\Microsoft Office\Office\Samples\Northwind.mdb"

    'Set a new current database
    oAccess.OpenCurrentDatabase (sDBPath)
    oAccess.Visible = True
    'Open an existing Form with an SQL WHERE clause,
    'only show rows that are [Title]='Sales Representative'
    oAccess.Visible = True
    oAccess.DoCmd.OpenForm "Employees", , , "[Title]='Sales Representative'"

ShowFilteredFormExit:
    'Clean up
    Set oAccess = Nothing
    Exit Sub

ShowFilteredFormError:
    MsgBox "Error occurred: " & Err.Description, , "Wrox"
    GoTo ShowFilteredFormExit
End Sub
```

The form should show that six records of the nine in the `Employees` table were selected, and should show that the view is filtered. It should look similar to the following screen shot.

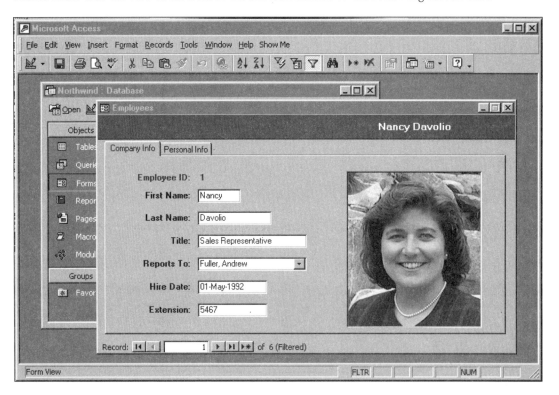

Printing Filtered Access Data From Outlook

This next example uses the RunSQL method of the DoCmd object to generate a read-only temporary table that is used as the source for a hard copy printout. The SQL statement that creates the temporary table is stored in a string variable and is used as the argument for the RunSQL method. The SQL statement creates a new table named tblSales using a SELECT INTO statement on the Employees table for all employees that have a job title of Sales Representative: SELECT [FirstName],[LastName],[Title],[Region] INTO tblSales FROM [Employees] WHERE [Title]='Sales Representative'. Any SQL statement that is supported by Access can be used in our automation code. The RunCommand method of the DoCmd object is used to open the Print dialog box.

```
Public Sub PrintFilteredTable()
  Dim oAccess As Access.Application
  Dim sDBPath As String
  Dim sSQL As String

  'Get an Access Application object.
  On Error Resume Next
  Set oAccess = GetObject(, "Access.Application")
  If oAccess Is Nothing Then
    Set oAccess = CreateObject("Access.Application")
  End If
  On Error GoTo PrintFilteredTableError

  sDBPath = "C:\Program Files\Microsoft Office\Office\Samples\Northwind.mdb"
  'Set a new current database.
  oAccess.OpenCurrentDatabase (sDBPath)
  oAccess.Visible = True

  'Store an SQL MakeTable Query in the string.
  sSQL = "SELECT [FirstName],[LastName],[Title],[Region] " _
  & "INTO tblSales FROM [Employees] WHERE [Title]='Sales Representative'"

  'Create the new temporary table using the SQL
  'statement to limit records.
  oAccess.DoCmd.RunSQL sSQL

  'Open the new table.
  oAccess.DoCmd.OpenTable "tblSales", acViewNormal, acReadOnly

  'Print out the table.
  oAccess.DoCmd.RunCommand acCmdPrint

PrintFilteredTableExit:
  'Clean up. This will also close Access,
  'since no forms or reports are open.
  Set oAccess = Nothing
  Exit Sub

PrintFilteredTableError:
  MsgBox "Error occurred: " & Err.Description, , "Wrox"
  GoTo PrintFilteredTableExit
End Sub
```

Although most Access data access is performed with the objects from the DAO or ADO libraries, the Access object model can be used for working with Access objects such as forms and reports. You can also combine Access automation code with code that utilizes the DAO or ADO object models when working with Access as an automation object. For more information about working with SQL, see *Instant SQL Programming*, ISBN 1874416508, from Wrox Press.

Other Programs With VBA

Many other applications incorporate VBA, which Microsoft licenses to developers. In Office 2000 you can program PowerPoint 2000 and FrontPage 2000, as well as the Office Binder and some of the shared Office utilities. Some of the other applications that incorporate VBA or are accessible to automation programming are Corel Draw, Corel Photo-Paint, AutoCAD R14, the WordPerfect Office Suite, and WinFax Pro. You can work with the exposed object models for these and many other programs in the same way you work with Word, Excel and Access.

The following example uses automation to work with WinFax Pro, a fax program from Symantec. One of the features that is lacking in the integration that WinFax Pro provides with Outlook is a way of sending a fax to a Contact that is selected in Outlook. When WinFax Pro is started from Outlook either the Send New Fax window or the Send Fax Wizard is started. The addressee of the fax has to be selected from WinFax Pro, using the Contacts folder from Outlook.

Many people have requested the capability of selecting a Contact in Outlook and starting WinFax Pro with the information for that Contact already filled in on the fax form. The following macro does exactly that. It looks for a `ContactItem` in an open Inspector window and sends the information from that Contact to WinFax Pro. It uses the first non-blank fax number in the contact record, starting with the Business Fax number, then the Other Fax number and finally the Home Fax number.

The example makes no attempt to examine and use the stored Dialing Properties and Location settings, so it works best if WinFax Pro is set to use the WinFax Dialer rather than the Windows Dialer. Because of a bug in the display routines in WinFax Pro if the number is in canonical format (preceded by a "+" sign and the country code) the "+" and country code appear to be duplicated in the beginning of the fax number when viewed from the Send New Fax window. This display bug does not affect the actual fax number or how it is dialed by WinFax Pro. The dialing and location properties are kept in the registry, in the `HKEY_LOCAL_MACHINE\SOFTWARE\Microsoft\Windows\CurrentVersion\Telephony\Locations\Location0` key.

If you want to use the dialing and location properties in your code, you can use the registry class module that is shown in Chapter 6 to read the telephony settings from that key.

This example requires that a reference is set to WinFax Automation Server, which is a library named `WFXCTL32.TLB`. This file is installed when you install WinFax Pro. Once the contact information has been acquired from the selected contact, WinFax Pro is opened as an automation object with the line `Set oWinFaxSend = New wfxctl32.CSDKSend`. The automation object is then tested to see if it is `Nothing`, in which case the instantiation of the object failed. The remainder of the code block uses WinFax Send properties and methods to fill in the fax information and launch the **Send New Fax** window. The **Send New Fax** window is left open for the user to actually send the fax so they can add attachments and additional recipients to the fax.

```
Public Sub ContactToWinFax()
  Dim oWinFaxSend As Object
  Dim oOutlook As Outlook.Application
  Dim oInspector As Outlook.Inspector
  Dim oContact As Outlook.ContactItem
  Dim oItem As Object
  Dim sRecipient As String
  Dim sFaxNumber As String
  Dim sCompany As String

  'Get an Outlook Application object
  On Error Resume Next
  Set oOutlook = GetObject(, "Outlook.Application")
  If oOutlook Is Nothing Then
    Set oOutlook = CreateObject("Outlook.Application")
  End If
  On Error GoTo ContactToWinFaxError

  Set oInspector = oOutlook.ActiveInspector
  'Look for an open Inspector window.
  If oInspector Is Nothing Then
    MsgBox "There is no open item", , "Wrox"
  Else
    Set oItem = oInspector.CurrentItem
    'Make sure the open item is a ContactItem.
    If oItem.Class = olContact Then
      Set oContact = oItem
      With oContact
        'Name
        sRecipient = .FullName
        'Company
        sCompany = .CompanyName
```

This section of the code looks first for a Business Fax number, and if that is not present, it tries to use the Other Fax number. If that is not present it attempts to use the Home Fax number.

```
        'Try the Business Fax number first
        sFaxNumber = .BusinessFaxNumber
        If sFaxNumber = "" Then
          'If Business Fax is blank use Other Fax
          sFaxNumber = .OtherFaxNumber
          If sFaxNumber = "" Then
          'If Other Fax is blank use Home Fax
            sFaxNumber = .HomeFaxNumber
          End If
        End If
      End With
```

This next section contains the WinFax automation code.

```
            If sFaxNumber <> "" Then
              'Open the WinFax automation object
              On Error Resume Next
              Set oWinFaxSend = New wfxct132.CSDKSend
              If oWinFaxSend Is Nothing Then
                MsgBox "Could not start WinFax Pro", , "Wrox"
              Else
                On Error GoTo ContactToWinFaxError
                With oWinFaxSend
                  'This is the WinFax automation code
                  'Leave WinFax running after the code ends
                  .LeaveRunning
                  'No Call Progress Window
                  .ShowCallProgess 0
                  'Set the To name
                  .SetTo sRecipient
                  'Set the Fax number
                  .SetNumber sFaxNumber
                  'Set the Company name
                  .SetCompany sCompany
                  'Resolve and add this recipient
                  .AddRecipient
                  'No automatic preview
                  .SetPreviewFax 0
                  'Show the Send New Fax Window
                  .ShowSendScreen 1
                  'Initiate the Send New Fax Window
                  .Send 0
                End With
              End If
            Else
              MsgBox "No Fax numbers", , "Wrox"
            End If
          Else
            MsgBox "Not a Contact item", , "Wrox"
          End If
        End If
```

Finally, the clean up code sets all the object variables to Nothing. The Send New Fax window is left open for the user to edit or modify the fax before sending it out.

```
ContactToWinFaxExit:
  'Clean up
  Set oContact = Nothing
  Set oItem = Nothing
  Set oInspector = Nothing
  Set oOutlook = Nothing
  Set oWinFaxSend = Nothing
  Exit Sub

ContactToWinFaxError:
  MsgBox "Error occurred: " & Err.Description, , "Wrox"
  GoTo ContactToWinFaxExit
End Sub
```

Summary

The examples in this chapter have shown a number of ways of working with other programs using automation. Each program that supports automation has an exposed object model that can be viewed in the Object Browser. Each application and its object model is different, and has to be approached differently, but automation and the incorporation of VBA in Outlook 2000 makes Outlook a wonderful automation controller. The main limits now are the object models that are available to you, and your imagination.

5

Automating Outlook 2000 from Visual Basic

Programming and automating Outlook from Visual Basic is very similar to programming and automating Outlook from VBA. In fact, this whole book can be viewed as being about automating Outlook from Visual Basic. Specifically, it is similar to automating Outlook from any other applications that include VBA. The main thing to remember is to set a reference to the Outlook object library in each VB project that you start. With VB you can create a number of different types of projects, while with VBA you can only create standard VBA projects. An exception to this is with the Office 2000 Developer Edition, where you can create COM Add-ins.

In this chapter we will show examples of VB projects that create standard .exe files, an ActiveX .dll file and an ActiveX Control (.ocx file). The creation of COM Add-ins using VBA and VB is covered in Chapter 7, 'COM Add-ins'. Each type of project creates a program that is opened and utilized differently. You select the type of project to create based on how the program will be used and your own preferences. All the examples were developed and tested using VB 6.

Using the Outlook Object Model

To set a reference to the Outlook object model for a VB project choose Project | References after the project is created. In the References dialog box select the Outlook 9.0 object library. Once the reference to the Outlook object library is set you can use the various objects and classes exposed by the Outlook object model just as you would in Outlook 2000 VBA code.

An exception to this is if you need to write code that will be run with different versions of Outlook. In this case, do not set a reference to the Outlook object library and do not declare your variables as specific Outlook data types. Declare all of your object variables as `Object`, to enable late binding of the objects with the user's version of the Outlook object library. For example, don't declare `Dim oMailItem As Outlook.MailItem`, declare it with `Dim oMailItem As Object`. If you write code that must be able to run on different versions of Outlook, make sure that you use only classes, properties, methods and events that are present in the oldest version of Outlook on which the code will be run, or write code that takes these differences into account..

The version of VBA included with Office 2000, VBA 6, has matured from earlier versions of VBA. VBA 6 has almost all of the language features that VB 6 has, so your code is very interchangeable between your VB and VBA code. After a reference is set to the Outlook 9.0 object library in your VB project the use of the Outlook object model is identical to the way you use it in VBA. You do have to instantiate an instance of the Outlook `Application` object, unlike VBA code that is only running within Outlook, but that is the same as you have to do in VBA code that will be run from other VBA enabled applications.

Automating Outlook From a Standard .exe Project

This first example is developed using a standard EXE project. A standard EXE project developed in VB normally interacts with the user from one or more VB forms. These forms are similar to the Office UserForms that are used in VBA, but with some differences in the default control set in the Control Toolbox. The VB control set includes these controls that are not included in the MS Forms controls that constitute the default VBA control set: Timer, FileList, DriveList, Horizontal Scrollbar, DirList, Shape, Line, PictureBox, Data and OLE controls. The MS Forms controls include these controls that are not in the default VB Toolbox: TabStrip, MultiPage and SpinButton. Many other controls are also available in addition to the default controls, and they can be added to the Control Toolbox. Additional controls are available in the Microsoft Common Controls that are included with Windows, and third-party vendors also sell custom controls that you can use in your projects.

You can add the MS Forms controls to the VB Control Toolbox, just as you can add the VB controls and others to VBA, if you have those forms libraries. Some of the controls in the MS Forms and VB control sets have similar names and functions, but differ in some of their properties and methods. One example is the ListBox control, which handles multicolumn lists differently in the VB and the MS Forms controls. It also is a form that is oriented more toward data binding in VB, where it is often used to display lists from Access or other data sources.

If you are more familiar with the controls from one set or the other, don't assume that just because they are similar and share the same names that they are identical. Take the time to familiarize yourself with the differences in similar controls so that you get the most out of the ones you are using. You can add the MS Forms controls to the VB Control Toolbox if you want to use the same controls in VB as in VBA, but some potential conflicts have been reported when using the MS Forms controls in VB. I have used many of the ones from the MS Forms library in VB without problems, but take extra time to check and debug your forms if you do use the MS Forms controls in your VB project. If you do want to add those or other controls to the VB Control Toolbox, right-click on a blank area of the Toolbox and choose **Components**, and add the desired libraries from the **Controls** tab. The MS Forms controls are listed as **Microsoft Forms 2.0 Object Library**. You can also add new tabs to the Toolbox to keep your controls organized.

Start a new VB Standard EXE project and name it `WordMerge`. Choose **Project | References** and make sure that references are selected for the **Microsoft Outlook 9.0 Object Library, Microsoft Word 9.0 Object Library, and Microsoft CDO 1.21 Library**.

The Microsoft CDO 1.21 Library is not installed as a default when you install Outlook 2000. Earlier versions of Outlook did install CDO by default. If CDO is not installed on your system, start the Office 2000 installation routines by choosing Microsoft Office 2000 in the Add/Remove Programs applet in the Control Panel and pressing the Add/Remove command button. Choose Add or Remove Features, open the installation tree and navigate to the Microsoft Outlook for Windows group. Install CDO by choosing to install Collaboration Data Objects in Run from My Computer mode. Chapter 6 shows a code procedure that can be used to demand install CDO if it is not present on the computer running an application.

Name the default form `frmContExitactPicker` and add a Module from the Projects menu. Name the Module `basMergeCode`. Click on the form and change its Caption to `Merge to Word`. Place two command buttons on the form, and name them `cmdMerge` and `cmdExit`. Change the Caption for `cmdMerge` to `Merge` and the Caption for `cmdExit` to `Exit`. The project and form should look similar to the screen shot below.

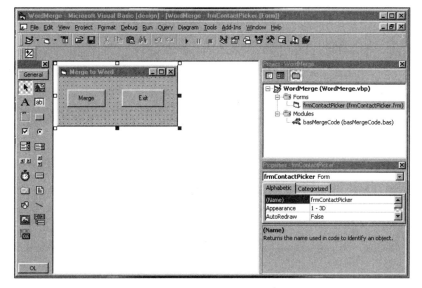

Add the following code to unload the form and terminate the program to the `cmdExit_Click` procedure.

```
Private Sub cmdExit_Click()
   Unload Me
End Sub
```

Add the following code to call the main code procedure to the `cmdMerge_Click` procedure.

```
Private Sub cmdMerge_Click()
   WordBookmark
End Sub
```

The Word template `C:\My Documents\BookmarkMaster.dot` used in this example is the same one used for the VBA automation example in the previous chapter. If you have moved or renamed this template be sure to change the reference to the template in the `WordBookmark` procedure.

Add the following code to the code module `basMergeCode`. This code is very similar to the procedure from the last chapter that used Word Bookmarks to merge the currently selected Contact's data into a document based on a custom Word template. The major difference is that instead of depending on an open Contact item in an Inspector window, this example displays the familiar Outlook AddressBook dialog box. A new procedure, `GetContact`, is used to display this dialog box and return the selected contact to `WordBookmark`.

```
Public Sub WordBookmark()
   Dim oOutlook As Outlook.Application
   Dim oContact As Outlook.ContactItem
   Dim oWord As Word.Application
   Dim oDoc As Word.Document
   Dim sBkmName As String
   Dim sTemplateName As String
   Dim blnFill As Boolean

   'Change this file name and location if necessary.
   sTemplateName = "C:\My Documents\BookmarkMaster.dot"

   'Get an Outlook Application object
   On Error Resume Next
   Set oOutlook = GetObject(, "Outlook.Application")
   If oOutlook Is Nothing Then
      Set oOutlook = CreateObject("Outlook.Application")
   End If
   On Error GoTo WordBookmarkError

   Set oContact = GetContact

   'Look for the Recipients to not be Nothing.
   If oContact Is Nothing Then
      MsgBox "No item selected", , "Wrox"
```

```
      Else
        'Get a Word Application object
        On Error Resume Next
        Set oWord = GetObject(, "Word.Application")
        If oWord Is Nothing Then
           Set oWord = CreateObject("Word.Application")
        End If
        On Error GoTo WordBookmarkError
        'Add a document based on our template.
        Set oDoc = oWord.Documents.Add(sTemplateName)
        With oContact
           'Fill each bookmark in turn.
           sBkmName = "FullName"
           blnFill = FillBookmark(sBkmName, .FullName, oDoc)

           'Repeat the function call for each bookmark.
           sBkmName = "StreetAddress"
           blnFill = FillBookmark(sBkmName, .BusinessAddressStreet, _
              oDoc)
           sBkmName = "City"
           blnFill = FillBookmark(sBkmName, .BusinessAddressCity, _
              oDoc)

           sBkmName = "State"
           blnFill = FillBookmark(sBkmName, .BusinessAddressState, _
              oDoc)

           sBkmName = "PostalCode"
           blnFill = FillBookmark(sBkmName, .BusinessAddressPostalCode, _
              oDoc)

           sBkmName = "FirstName"
           blnFill = FillBookmark(sBkmName, .FirstName, _
              oDoc)
        End With
        'Activate our new document.
        oDoc.Activate
        'Turn off the display of bookmarks.
        oDoc.ActiveWindow.View.ShowBookmarks = False
        'Move the cursor to the end of the document.
        oWord.Selection.EndKey Unit:=wdStory, Extend:=wdMove
        'Make the document visible.
        oWord.Visible = True
        oDoc.ActiveWindow.Visible = True
      End If

WordBookmarkExit:
   'Set all objects to Nothing to prevent memory and
   'resource leaks. This still leaves the new document open.
   Set oContact = Nothing
   Set oOutlook = Nothing
   Set oDoc = Nothing
   Set oWord = Nothing
   Exit Sub
```

```
WordBookmarkError:
  MsgBox "Error occurred: " & Err.Description, , "Wrox"
  GoTo WordBookmarkExit
End Sub
```

The following utility procedure is identical to the one written in VBA from the last chapter. Place this code in the `basMergeCode` module. We are using Bookmarks here in this example, but we also could have used Word Custom Document Properties for the same purpose. One difference between the two is that you can paste more text into a Bookmark than into a Custom Document Property, although that difference is not exploited in this example.

```
Private Function FillBookmark(sBookmark As String, sValue As String, _
      oDoc As Word.Document) As Boolean
  With oDoc
    If .Bookmarks.Exists(sBookmark) Then
      .Bookmarks(sBookmark).Range.Text = sValue
      FillBookmark = True
    Else
      FillBookmark = False
    End If
  End With
End Function
```

The following procedure, also placed in the `basMergeCode` module, does the work of displaying the AddressBook dialog box and returning a contact to `WordBookmark`. The AddressBook dialog box cannot be displayed by using any of the methods in the Outlook object model. Instead, it is displayed using the `Session.AddressBook` method of CDO. CDO is covered more fully in Chapter 6, 'Outlook 2000 Data Access'.

A CDO `Session` object is established and logged onto. Then the `Session.AddressBook` method is used to display the Contacts list and enable the user to select a contact for the merge to Word. The `OneAddress` restriction argument causes an error in the Internet only mode of Outlook if it is set as True, so only the first contact selected is used if more than one contact was selected. The `AddressBook` method returns a CDO `Recipients` collection, and the first item in the collection is the only one used in this procedure.

```
Private Function GetContact() As Outlook.ContactItem
  Dim oSession As MAPI.Session 'CDO declaration
  Dim oRecips As MAPI.Recipients 'CDO declaration
  Dim oRecip As MAPI.Recipient 'CDO declaration
  Dim oOutlook As Outlook.Application
  Dim oNS As Outlook.NameSpace
  Dim oFolder As Outlook.MAPIFolder
  Dim oItem As Object
  Dim sName As String
  Dim sFilter$

  'Create or get a MAPI (CDO) session object and log on.
  On Error Resume Next
  Set oSession = GetObject(, "MAPI.Session")
```

```
If oSession Is Nothing Then
   Set oSession = CreateObject("MAPI.Session")
End If
On Error GoTo GetContactError

oSession.Logon "", "", False, False

'Get an Outlook Application object
On Error Resume Next
Set oOutlook = GetObject(, "Outlook.Application")
If oOutlook Is Nothing Then
   Set oOutlook = CreateObject("Outlook.Application")
End If
On Error GoTo GetContactError

'Get NameSpace and Contacts folder objects
Set oNS = oOutlook.GetNamespace("MAPI")
Set oFolder = oNS.GetDefaultFolder(olFolderContacts)

'The OneAddress argument allows forcing the choice
'of only one Recipient, but setting it to True
'causes an error in Outlook Internet only mode. The
'argument works in corporate/workgroup mode.
On Error Resume Next
Set oRecips = oSession.AddressBook( _
Title:="Wrox", _
OneAddress:=False, _
ForceResolution:=True, _
RecipLists:=1, _
ToLabel:="&Merge to Word")
```

The Id (EntryID) of the selected contact is used as the argument for the GetRecipientFromID method of the NameSpace object. The Recipient.AddressEntry property gives us the name of the Recipient, which is used as a filter to find the selected contact in the Contacts folder. The selected contact is then returned as the function result, since the function was declared to have a return type of Outlook.ContactItem.

```
'Const CdoE_USER_CANCEL = -2147221229 (&H80040113)
'CdoE_USER_CANCEL is returned if the user cancels
'the AddressBook dialog box. Check for Nothing to
'see if the user cancelled.
If oRecips Is Nothing Then
   MsgBox "Selection cancelled", , "Wrox"
ElseIf oRecips.Count > 1 Then
   MsgBox "Only select 1 contact", , "Wrox"
Else
   'Only 1 selection allowed, so always #1
   Set oRecip = oRecips(1)
   'Get the item's MAPI Entry ID
   Set oItem = oNS.GetRecipientFromID(oRecip.Id)
   'Get the items's full name
   sName = oItem.AddressEntry
   'Set up a filter string
```

```
      sFilter$ = "[FullName] = """ & sName & """"
      'find the item in the Contacts folder
      Set oItem = oFolder.Items.Find(sFilter$)
      If oItem Is Nothing Then
        MsgBox "Item not found in Contacts", , "Wrox"
        Set GetContact = Nothing
      ElseIf oItem.Class = olContact Then
        Set GetContact = oItem
      Else
        MsgBox "Selected item not a contact", , "Wrox"
        Set GetContact = Nothing
      End If
    End If

GetContactExit:
    oSession.Logoff 'Log off MAPI session

    'Clean up
    Set oItem = Nothing
    Set oRecip = Nothing
    Set oRecips = Nothing
    Set oSession = Nothing
    Set oFolder = Nothing
    Set oNS = Nothing
    Set oOutlook = Nothing
    Exit Function

GetContactError:
    MsgBox "Error occurred: " & Err.Description, , "Wrox"
    Set GetContact = Nothing
    GoTo GetContactExit
End Function
```

The AddressBook dialog box that is displayed as a result of calling the CDO `Session.AddressBook` method should look similar to the following screen shot.

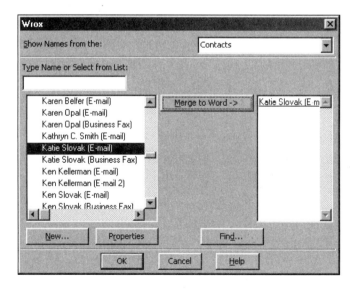

This example produced identical results to the automation example in the previous chapter and demonstrates that you can automate Outlook 2000 (as well as Word 2000) the same from VB as from VBA. In fact, the CDO `AddressBook` method could also have been used in the VBA example in the previous chapter.

Automating Outlook From an ActiveX Control Project

This example shows how to create a new ActiveX control (`.ocx` file) that automates Outlook. Create a new VB project that is an ActiveX control project. Name the project `CreateJournalEntry`, and name the default control that is added to the project `ctlNewJournalEntry`. Make sure that a reference is set to the Microsoft Outlook 9.0 Object Library. Add a command button to the control's form and name it `cmdNew`. Change the Caption of the command button to `Create Journal Entry`. Add the following code to the `cmdNew_Click` event procedure and compile it by choosing **File | Make CreateJournalEntry.ocx**.... The code creates a new Journal entry, copying the `Subject` and `Body` of the item into the new Journal entry. It also sets the Journal item's entry type depending on the `Class` of the Outlook item.

```
Private Sub cmdNew_Click()
   Dim oJournal As Outlook.JournalItem
   Dim oOutlook As Outlook.Application
   Dim oInspector As Outlook.Inspector
   Dim oItem As Object
   Dim sType As String

   On Error Resume Next
   'Only using GetObject since Outlook has
   'to be running.
   Set oOutlook = GetObject(, "Outlook.Application")
   'If Outlook was running
   If Not oOutlook Is Nothing Then
      'Find the current item in the active Inspector.
      Set oInspector = oOutlook.ActiveInspector
      Set oItem = oInspector.CurrentItem

      'Create a new Journal entry.
      Set oJournal = CreateItem(olJournalItem)
      'Copy the subject and body of the active
      'item to the new Journal entry.
      oJournal.Subject = oItem.Subject
      oJournal.Body = oItem.Body

      'Set a Journal entry type based on the
      'class of the current item.
      Select Case oItem.Class
      Case olAppointment
         sType = "Appointment"
      Case olMail
         sType = "E-mail Message"
      Case olTask
         sType = "Task"
```

```
      Case olTaskRequest
        sType = "Task Request"
    End Select

      'Set the type and save the Journal entry.
      oJournal.Type = sType
      oJournal.Save
    End If

      'Clean up
    Set oJournal = Nothing
    Set oItem = Nothing
    Set oInspector = Nothing
    Set oOutlook = Nothing
  End Sub
```

The procedure itself is nothing special, what makes it useful is the type of project it is. When the code is compiled the resulting file is an OCX, an ActiveX control. This control can be used not only on forms created in VB and VBA, but it can also be placed in Outlook forms. The automation code doesn't use the intrinsic `Application` or `Item` objects that are available for use in the VBScript that is used in Outlook forms, since it is running in an ActiveX control that was created in VB.

This procedure does not attempt to create an Outlook `Application` object, it assumes that an instance of Outlook is running since it will be placed in a form that is designed to run either in Outlook or when an Outlook `Application` object is already instantiated. Adding the control to the Control Toolbox for VB, VBA or Outlook Forms Design mode makes the control available for use in any of those design environments.

To test the new ActiveX control, go to Outlook, open a Task form in design mode by choosing Tools | Forms | Design a Form and choose a Task form from the Standard Forms Library. Select the (P.2) tab and rename it Create Journal Entry by choosing Form | Rename page.

Add our new custom control to the Control Toolbox by right-clicking on a blank area of the Control Toolbox and choosing Custom Controls. If the Control Toolbox is not visible, open it by choosing the Toolbox in the Standard toolbar or by right-clicking on a blank area of the Outlook form. A dialog box similar to the following screen shot should be displayed.

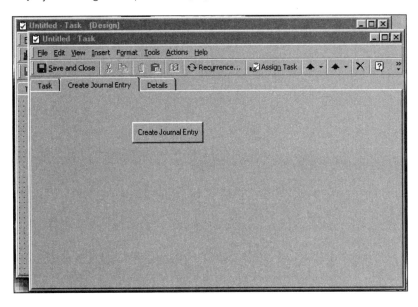

Select the **Create Journal Entry** tab in the custom Outlook Task form. Place the custom `ctlNewJournalEntry` control anywhere in the **Create Journal Entry** tab. Choose **Form | Run This Form** in the custom Outlook Task form to place the form into run mode. Enter a `Subject` for the Task, and add some text to the Note (`Body`) field in the **Task** tab of the form. Switch to the **Create Journal Entry** tab, and press the **Create Journal Entry** command button. A new Journal entry will be created from the automation code in the ActiveX control.

Creating ActiveX controls using VB is an excellent way to extend the control set available for your designs in VB, VBA or Outlook Forms. When you create ActiveX controls that you need to distribute with your projects make sure to distribute not only the `.ocx` file but also the `.oca` file if one exists.

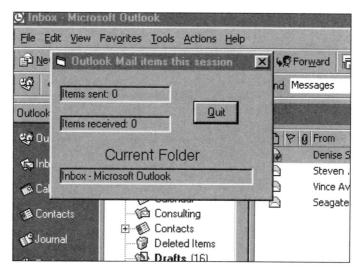

The automation code in this example can create new Journal entries for Appointment and Task entry types. These entry types do not exist in Outlook without customizing the Journal entry types in the Windows Registry. The types of entries that can be created in the Journal are determined by the contents of subkeys of the Windows Registry key `HKEY_Current_User\Software\Microsoft\ Shared Tools\Outlook\Journaling`. Each type of Journal entry has its own subkey under that key.

A valid Journal entry has at least 5 values. The string values `Large Icon` and `Small Icon`, and the DWORD values `AutoJournaled` and `JournalByContact`, are always present. If the entry type is an Outlook item that Outlook can automatically Journal, then there is an additional DWORD value `DescriptionID`. If it is not, there is an additional string value `Description`.

The DWORD values `AutoJournaled` and `JournalByContact` determine where an item is listed in the Journal Options dialog box when the item can be automatically journaled by Outlook. If `AutoJournaled` is 0, the item does not appear in the Journal Options dialog box. If it is 1, it does. If it appears in the Journal Options dialog box, `JournalByContact` determines where it appears. If `JournalByContact` is 0, it appears in the lower listbox, if it is 1 it appears in the upper listbox with the Outlook items. If an item is checked for Journaling in the Journal Options dialog box another DWORD value, `Enabled`, is created and set to 1.

> If you decide to create these custom Journal entry types, make sure to back up your Windows Registry first. Always do that whenever you modify Registry entries, since an invalid Registry can prevent your computer from functioning correctly.

First open the Registry editor, `Regedit.exe`, and navigate to the `HKEY_Current_User\Software\Microsoft\Shared Tools\Outlook\Journaling` key. Then choose Edit | New | Key and create an Appointment key. Open the Appointment key and choose Edit | New | DWORD Value. Change the name of the value to `JournalByContact`. Select the Appointment key in the tree list and repeat the process to create a DWORD value named `AutoJournaled`. Next, create three string values named `Large Icon`, `Small Icon`, and `Description`. Repeat the entire process to create a Journal type for Tasks.

Since Outlook cannot automatically Journal Tasks and Appointments, we need to set the DWORD values `AutoJournaled` and `JournalByContact` to 0. The following tables list the necessary settings for the Appointment and Tasks Journal types.

Appointment entries	Value
AutoJournaled	0
JournalByContact	0
Description	"Appointment"
Large Icon	"[19]"
Small Icon	"[19]"

Task entries	Value
AutoJournaled	0
JournalByContact	0
Description	"Task"
Large Icon	"[11]"
Small Icon	"[11]"

After this process is finished, any Journal item will have entry types of Appointment and Task added to the list of possible entry types.

Responding to Events From Outlook

Just as you can respond to Outlook events in a class module or UserForm in VBA, you can respond to Outlook events in a class module or the intrinsic class module of a form in VB. The procedure is very similar, using the `WithEvents` statement to signal that you will be responding to events for that object.

Responding to Events From a Standard EXE Project

Since a form in a VB project contains an intrinsic class module where the code for the form is placed, it can be used to respond to Outlook events. Create a new VB Standard EXE project and name the project `OutlookMailEvents`. Make sure that a reference is set to the Microsoft Outlook 9.0 Object Library in the References dialog in the **Project** menu. Save the project with the file system name `OutlookAppEvents.vbp`.

Change the name of the default form to `frmOutlookItems` and set the Border Style to Fixed Dialog, the Caption to `Outlook Mail items this session`, and the Shown in Taskbar property to True. Add three labels and name them `lblSent`, `lblReceived` and `lblFolder`. Set the `BorderStyle` property to Fixed Single for all three. Add another label just above the `lblFolder` label and name it `lblCurrent`. Change its Caption to `Current Folder` and set the font size to 12 point. Add a command button, change its Name to `cmdQuit` and its Caption to `&Quit`. The form should look similar to the following screen shot.

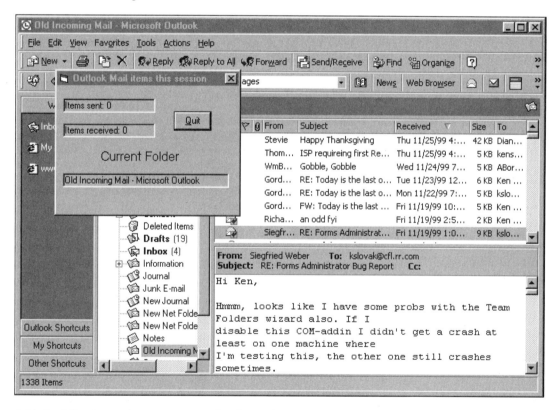

Add the following code statements to the General section of the code module, placing them at the module level. These statements declare two module level `Long` variables, and two module level `Boolean` variables. They also declare `WithEvents Outlook.Application` and `Outlook.Explorer` objects.

```
'Respond to Outlook events.
Private WithEvents moOL As Outlook.Application
'Respond to Explorer events.
Private WithEvents moExplorer As Outlook.Explorer

'Module level variables for items sent and received
'during the session.
Private mlItemsSent As Long
Private mlItemsReceived As Long

'Outlook was open previously.
Private mblnOutlookExists As Boolean
'An Outlook object was created.
Private mblnOutlookCreated As Boolean
```

The code for the `cmdQuit_Click` event procedure unloads the form and triggers the
`Form_Terminate` event procedure.

```
Private Sub cmdQuit_Click()
   Unload Me
End Sub
```

The `Form_Load` event procedure first instantiates the module level `Outlook.Application` object. If
the `Outlook.Application` object can't be instantiated the code unloads the form, terminating the
program. The line `Set moExplorer = moOL.ActiveExplorer` instantiates the module level
`Explorer` object and assigns it to the `ActiveExplorer` object. The remainder of the `Form_Load`
event procedure sets the initial display of the label controls. The module level `Boolean` variables are
used to keep track of whether the `Outlook.Application` object was successfully instantiated and
whether our code created the object. These variables are used to decide whether to close the Outlook
application when the program is exited.

```
Private Sub Form_Load()
   mblnOutlookCreated = True
   mblnOutlookExists = True

   'Get an Outlook Application object.
   On Error Resume Next
   Set moOL = GetObject(, "Outlook.Application")
   If moOL Is Nothing Then
     Set moOL = CreateObject("Outlook.Application")
     mblnOutlookExists = False
   End If

   If moOL Is Nothing Then
     MsgBox "Couldn't start Outlook.", , "Wrox"
     mblnOutlookCreated = False
     Unload Me
   Else
     'Instantiate the event handler for Explorer events.
     Set moExplorer = moOL.ActiveExplorer
     'Show initial display of the current Explorer window.
     lblFolder.Caption = moExplorer.Caption
   End If
```

```
      'Initial display of items sent.
      mlItemsSent = 0
      lblSent.Caption = "Items sent: " & mlItemsSent

      'Initial display of items received.
      mlItemsReceived = 0
      lblReceived.Caption = "Items received: " & mlItemsReceived
   End Sub
```

The `Form_Terminate` event procedure checks to see whether the `Outlook.Application` object was instantiated. If it was, and we created it, a message box is shown asking the user if he wants to close Outlook. Then the module level object variables are destroyed. This is especially important in an independent program that uses automation to prevent memory and resource leaks.

```
   Private Sub Form_Terminate()
     Dim lResponse As Long

     'If the Outlook object was instantiated,
     If mblnOutlookCreated Then
       'And we created it,
       If mblnOutlookExists = False Then
         'See if the user wants to close it.
         lResponse = MsgBox("Close Outlook?", vbYesNo + vbQuestion, "Wrox")
         If lResponse = vbYes Then
           moOL.Quit
         End If
       End If
     End If

     'Clean up
     Set moExplorer = Nothing
     Set moOL = Nothing
   End Sub
```

The next event procedure responds to the `Explorer.FolderSwitch` event. This Outlook event can be responded to after the `moExplorer` object is instantiated in the `Form_Load` procedure. This example updates the caption for the `lblFolder` label control with the value of the `Caption` property of the `ActiveExplorer` object.

```
   Private Sub moExplorer_FolderSwitch()
     'Update the display of the current Explorer.
     lblFolder.Caption = moOL.ActiveExplorer.Caption
   End Sub
```

Any `Explorer` event can be responded to by writing the code for an event handler for that event. Events for the other collections and objects of Outlook can be handled in the same way. Declaring a module level object variable using the `WithEvents` statement enables us to handle the Outlook events in the following manner:

```
'Declare a variable for Explorer and Inspector objects
'and collections whose events you want to handle.
Private WithEvents moExplorer As Outlook.Explorer
Private WithEvents moExplorers As Outlook.Explorers
Private WithEvents moInspector As Outlook.Inspector
Private WithEvents moInspectors As Outlook.Inspectors

'Declare one Folders variable for events in each Outlook
'folder (MAPIFolder) whose events you want to handle.
Private WithEvents moCalendar As Outlook.Folders

'Declare a specific Outlook item type variable for each Outlook
'item type whose events you want to handle.
Private WithEvents moAppointment As Outlook.AppointmentItem

'Declare one Items variable for the events for the Items in Folders
'that you want to handle.
Private WithEvents moItems As Outlook.Items
```

For more information about handling Outlook events, see 'Using Events to Extend Outlook' in Chapter 3, 'Outlook 2000 Projects and Macros'. The next example shows an event handler for the `Forward` event for an Outlook `MailItem`.

The next two Outlook event handlers use the events that are provided in the `Outlook.Application` object. The `ItemSend` event is handled by updating the count of items sent in this session and updating the display in the `lblSent` control. Processing of the outgoing item can be performed here in this procedure.

```
Private Sub moOL_ItemSend(ByVal Item As Object, Cancel As Boolean)
   'Update the count of sent items.
   mlItemsSent = mlItemsSent + 1
   'Display the count in the label control.
   lblSent.Caption = "Items sent: " & mlItemsSent
End Sub
```

The `NewMail` event is handled by updating the count of items received in this session and updating the display in the `lblReceived` control. Processing of the incoming item can be performed here in this procedure.

```
Private Sub moOL_NewMail()
   'Update the count of received items.
   mlItemsReceived = mlItemsReceived + 1
   'Display the count in the label control.
   lblReceived.Caption = "Items received: " & mlItemsReceived
End Sub
```

Responding to Events From an ActiveX DLL Project

An ActiveX DLL project can also be used to respond to Outlook events. Unlike an ActiveX control, the class module for the ActiveX DLL has no user interface, so we will instantiate it and use it in a form to provide a way to terminate the DLL. Create a new ActiveX DLL project and name it OutlookItemEvent. Name the class module clsItemEvent. Choose **File | Add Project** and choose to add a Standard EXE project. Name it TestOutlookItemEvent and name the form that is provided frmOutlookitemEvent. Save the projects and save the project group as Group1.

Add the following declarations to the General section, at the module level:

```
Private WithEvents moOutlook As Outlook.Application
Private WithEvents moInspectors As Outlook.Inspectors
Private WithEvents moInspector As Outlook.Inspector
Private WithEvents moMail As Outlook.MailItem
```

The MailItem variable will be used to respond to MailItem events that occur in Inspector windows. Most interactions with Outlook items occur in Inspector windows, so this is a good approach to dealing with item events.

However, if an item is selected in an Explorer window then the user can cause events to fire on that item without opening an Inspector window. Explorer objects do not provide item-specific events, so handling other item events that might occur in those cases is a problem.

You can use the Selection collection of Items for the active Explorer, but that only provides a SelectionChange event. The Items collection for a folder only provides Add, Change and Remove events. The only workaround is to use the Selection collection to retrieve an Items collection and then assign an item variable for each selected item that belongs to a specific class that you are interested in. This solution has one major problem, you don't know beforehand how many items will be selected and therefore you don't know how many item variables you need to declare WithEvents. This example handles only events that occur in Inspector windows.

The Class_Initialize procedure instantiates the module level Outlook.Application and Inspectors collection variables. The Inspectors variable is used so that we can have a NewInspector event handler.

```
Private Sub Class_Initialize()
  'Get an Outlook Application object
  On Error Resume Next
  Set moOutlook = GetObject(, "Outlook.Application")
  If moOutlook Is Nothing Then
    Set moOutlook = CreateObject("Outlook.Application")
  End If
  If moOutlook Is Nothing Then
    MsgBox "Could not start Outlook", , "Wrox"
  Else
    Set moInspectors = moOutlook.Inspectors
  End If
End Sub
```

The `Class_Terminate` procedure sets all the module level object variables to `Nothing`, destroying them.

```
Private Sub Class_Terminate()
   Set moMail = Nothing
   Set moInspector = Nothing
   Set moInspectors = Nothing
   Set moOutlook = Nothing
End Sub
```

The `NewInspector` event procedure is used to check the `CurrentItem.Class` property to see if the new current item is a mail item. If it is, it is assigned to the module level `MailItem` variable.

```
Private Sub moInspectors_NewInspector(ByVal Inspector As Outlook.Inspector)
   'When a new Inspector is opened
   Set moInspector = Inspector
   If moInspector.CurrentItem.Class = olMail Then 'only Mail items
      Set moMail = moInspector.CurrentItem
   End If
End Sub
```

Any of the item events can be handled in this way when the item is in an open `Inspector` window. In this example only the `Forward` event is handled. A new Journal item is created, with an entry type of `E-mail Message` and the `Subject` and `Body` properties of the `MailItem` are copied to the new Journal entry.

```
Private Sub moMail_Forward(ByVal Forward As Object, Cancel As Boolean)
   Dim oJournal As Outlook.JournalItem
   Dim oMail As Outlook.MailItem

   Set oMail = Forward
   Set oJournal = CreateItem(olJournalItem)
   oJournal.Subject = oMail.Subject
   oJournal.Body = oMail.Body
   oJournal.Type = "E-mail Message"
   oJournal.Save

   Set oJournal = Nothing
   Set oMail = Nothing
End Sub
```

When the class is finished and tested, compile it into a `.dll` file. Remember to set a reference to the Microsoft Outlook 9.0 Object Library. This class has no user interface, and no methods, properties or events of its own. You can add your own methods, properties and events to an ActiveX DLL class if you need to extend the interface that the Outlook events provide. In this case the only control over the class is provided by the form that instantiates the class and provides a command button to destroy the class.

Add a command button to the form `frmOutlookitemEvent` in the `TestOutlookItemEvent` project. Name the command button `cmdQuit` and change its Caption to `&Quit`. In the General section at the module level of the code for the form declare a variable that is of the ActiveX DLL class's type. To be able to declare this variable type you have to set a reference to the `OutlookItemEvent` class module in the `TestOutlookItemEvent` project.

```
Private mClass As clsItemEvent
```

The `cmdQuit_Click` procedure unloads the form and fires the `Form_Terminate` procedure, where the class is destroyed.

```
Private Sub cmdQuit_Click()
  Unload Me
End Sub
```

The `Form_Load` procedure instantiates the class using the `New` keyword. This class is self-sufficient, only handling certain Outlook events, and does not have any methods, properties or events. If there were any properties to the class, this procedure could be used to initialize them.

```
Private Sub Form_Load()
  Set mClass = New clsItemEvent
End Sub
```

The `Form_Terminate` procedure sets the instance of the class to `Nothing`, thereby destroying the class.

```
Private Sub Form_Terminate()
  Set mClass = Nothing
End Sub
```

Summary

This chapter covered the use of Visual Basic with Outlook 2000. In a way, this whole book can be viewed as being about automating Outlook from Visual Basic, so if you are a VB developer you can use the information about working with Outlook in VBA in the other chapters to control Outlook from VB.

6

Outlook 2000 Data Access

In previous chapters we've introduced working with Outlook data using the Outlook object model and **CDO** (Collaboration Data Objects). This chapter will go more deeply into those areas.

> *CDO is a big topic, too big to cover completely in this book. For more complete coverage of CDO see*
> Professional CDO Programming *from Wrox Press, ISBN 1861002068.*

ADO (ActiveX Data Objects) is presently used mostly for accessing databases, such as Access, SQL Server, and Oracle. ADO can be used to access Outlook data also, through **ADSI** (Active Directory Services Interface), and ADO's role will become more important when Exchange 2000 is released. ADO will be a primary way to work with the Exchange 2000 data store, running on top of CDO. Exchange 2000 will have a native interface to and drivers for ADO. However, at the moment, most usage of ADO is related to either database or ADSI access.

CDO is used by Outlook developers to access properties of Outlook items that are not available in the Outlook object model, to perform certain functions that you cannot perform using the Outlook object model, to run Exchange Server scripts, and to work with Outlook data from Outlook Web Access and **ASP** (Active Server Pages) scripts. For resources of information on CDO, ADO, ADSI and ASP see Appendix C.

Using the Outlook Object Model

The Outlook object model is what you will use for most of your Outlook client side development. It has the advantage of being more accessible and "user-friendly" than CDO, although that is relative. There are some things that are not accessible to the Outlook object model that are accessible to the CDO object model, so often you will have to work with both. For a complete reference to the Outlook object model, see Appendix A. This section will cover Outlook data access and point out oddities of the Outlook object model and things to watch out for when using it.

Outlook Object Model Organization

Outlook separates its object model into what can be considered user interface and data models under the `Application` object. The user interface model is comprised of `Explorers` and `Inspectors`.

User Interface Objects

We've worked with `Explorers` and `Inspectors` in previous chapters, but they are somewhat hard to grasp and very important to working with Outlook. `Explorers` are the windows that Outlook shows to display various folders. `Inspectors` are the windows that open to display specific Outlook items when they are selected in an `Explorer` window. The exception to this rule is when an Outlook window is opened using the Send to Mail facility. In that case, an item is opened in an `Inspector` and no `Explorer` is present. To get access to the current `Explorer` object, use code similar to the following code snippet. If no Explorer is present the Explorer variable object is set to `Nothing`.

```
Dim oOL As Outlook.Application
Dim oExplorer As Outlook.Explorer

Set oOL = CreateObject("Outlook.Application")
Set oExplorer = oOL.ActiveExplorer
```

To access the current Inspector window, use code similar to the following.

```
Dim oInspector As Outlook.Inspector

Set oInspector = oOL.ActiveInspector
```

To get the current item in an Inspector, use code similar to the following.

```
Dim oItem As Object

Set oItem = oInspector.CurrentItem
```

The code referencing the current item may look strange, since it uses an `Object`, rather than a `MailItem`, `ContactItem`, or other specific type of Outlook item. The reason for this is that Outlook folders can hold items of different object classes. If you know what class of object is open in an Inspector window then you should use the specific Outlook item. If you don't know, you have to test the item to see what class the item is. Generally, the Outlook items you will find in different folders are one of the following `OlObjectClass` enumerated constants.

Item Class	Value
OlAppointment	26
OlContact	40
OlDistributionList	69
OlDocument	41
OlJournal	42

Item Class	Value
OlMail	43
OlNote	44
OlPost	45
OlTask	48

To test for the Class of the item that is open in the current Inspector window, use the following code.

```
Dim oOL As Outlook.Application
Dim oInspector As Outlook.Inspector
Dim oItem As Object
Dim oExplorer As Outlook.Explorer

Set oOL = CreateObject("Outlook.Application")
Set oInspector = oOL.ActiveInspector
If oInspector.CurrentItem.Class = olMail Then
  'your code
End If
```

The selected items in the current Explorer window (a Selection collection) would be referenced by the following code.

```
Dim oOL As Outlook.Application
Dim oExplorer As Outlook.Explorer
Dim oSelected As Outlook.Selection

Set oOL = CreateObject("Outlook.Application")
Set oExplorer = oOL.ActiveExplorer

Set oSelected = oExplorer.Selection
```

The number and type of the items in the Selection collection can be checked by the following code. Either type of For loop can be used, although the For…Each loop is faster.

```
Dim oOL As Outlook.Application
Dim oExplorer As Outlook.Explorer
Dim oSelected As Outlook.Selection
Dim oItem As Object
Dim lCount As Long
Dim lIndex As Long

Set oOL = CreateObject("Outlook.Application")
Set oExplorer = oOL.ActiveExplorer

Set oSelected = oExplorer.Selection
For Each oItem In oSelected
  If oItem.Class = olMail Then
```

```
        'your code
    End If
  Next

  'Or you can use this type of loop
  For lIndex = 1 To oSelected.Count
    If oSelected.Item(lIndex).Class = olMail Then
      'your code
    End If
  Next
```

Data Objects

The root object of the data model is the NameSpace object. All folders in Outlook (and Exchange Server), AddressLists, Items and other data objects are children of the NameSpace object. The LanguageSettings and AnswerWizard objects are exceptions to this, they can be accessed even if no Application object is open.

Folders in Outlook or Exchange are accessed by calling the GetDefaultFolder method with an argument that is a member of the olDefaultFolders enum if the folders are default folders in a user's Personal Folders or Mailbox data stores. If the folders are not default folders, or are folders in Exchange Server that are shared by another user or are in the Public Folders hierarchy, the methods are different. However, all the different methods first establish the NameSpace object. The following code shows how to access folders using these different methods. To start with we dimension the necessary variables:

```
  Dim oOL As Outlook.Application
  Dim oNS As Outlook.NameSpace
  Dim oFolder As Outlook.MAPIFolder
  Dim oRecipient As Outlook.Recipient

  Set oOL = CreateObject("Outlook.Application")
  Set oNS = oOL.GetnameSpace("MAPI")
```

The next few lines show how to access a default folder in a Personal Folders or Mailbox data store.

```
  'Accessing a default folder
  'or olFolderCalendar, olFolderJournal, olFolderContacts, etc.
  Set oFolder = oNS.GetDefaultFolder(olFolderInbox) 'Personal Folders or Mailbox
```

The following lines show how to access a shared folder in an Exchange environment.

```
  'Accessing a shared default folder
  'You must create and resolve a recipient to get to a shared folder
  Set oRecipient = oNS.CreateRecipient("Diane Poremsky")
  oRecipient.Resolve
  'You can only access the folder if the recipient was resolved
  If oRecipient.Resolved Then
    Set oFolder = oNS.GetSharedDefaultFolder(oRecipient, olFolderInbox)
  End If
```

The next lines show how to access a Public Folder in an Exchange environment.

```
'Accessing a Public Journal folder in the Public Folders tree
Set oFolder = oNS.Folders("Public Folders"). _
Folders("All Public Folders").Folders("Public Journal")
```

The following lines show how to access a subfolder in a Personal Folders data store.

```
'Business Contacts folder under the default Contacts
'folder in a Personal Folders file
Set oFolder = oNS.Folders("Personal Folders"). _
Folders("Contacts").Folders("Business Contacts")
```

The following is an alternate method of accessing the same subfolder in a Personal Folders data store.

```
'Alternate method of accessing the same folder
Set oFolder = oNS.GetDefaultFolder(olFolderContacts).Folders("Business Contacts")
```

The following table lists the `olDefaultFolders` enumeration constants. This constant enum is available only in VBA and VB. If you are using VBScript, you must use the numeric values of the constants or declare your own constants for this enum.

Named Constant	Numeric Value
olFolderCalendar	9
olFolderContacts	10
olFolderDeletedItems	3
olFolderDrafts	16
olFolderInbox	6
olFolderJournal	11
olFolderNotes	12
olFolderOutbox	4
olFolderSentMail	5
olFolderTasks	13

The root folder of the user's Mailbox folder in an Exchange environment is accessed as follows:

```
Dim oOL As Outlook.Application
Dim oNS As Outlook.NameSpace
Dim oFolder As Outlook.MAPIFolder
Dim sUser As String

Set oOL = CreateObject("Outlook.Application")
```

```
Set oNS = oOL.GetnameSpace("MAPI")
sUser = oNS.CurrentUser
sUser = "Mailbox - " & sUser
'Accessing the Mailbox folder
'This folder has the name "Mailbox - " followed by the user name
Set oFolder = oNS.Folders(sUser)
```

The corresponding list of default folder constants for CDO is listed in the CDO section of this chapter.

> In some cases, the `CreateRecipient` method may not work reliably. When this happens, no resolved recipient is created. If you experience this problem there is a workaround that many Outlook developers use. This workaround is also useful if the `Recipient` you are trying to create is not in any of the available Address Books, but you have an email address for them. The workaround is to create a dummy `MailItem` and add the name or email address to that item. The `Recipient` can then be extracted from the dummy `MailItem` and the `MailItem` can then be discarded.

The following code snippet uses an email address to produce a resolved `Recipient`.

```
Set oMail = oOL.CreateItem(olMailItem)
Set oRecipient = oMail.Recipients.Add("anyone@anywhere.com")
If Not oRecipient.Resolve Then
   Debug.Print "error"
Else
   Debug.Print oRecipient.Address
End If
```

This snippet uses a name that is resolved to an entry in an Address Book.

```
Set oMail = oOL.CreateItem(olMailItem)
Set oRecipient = oMail.Recipients.Add("Diane Poremsky")
If Not oRecipient.Resolve Then
   Debug.Print "error"
Else
   Debug.Print oRecipient.Address
End If

'Once you have created the Recipient, discard the MailItem
oMail.Close olDiscard
```

Collections and Objects

The Outlook object model is organized into objects and collections. Collections can consist of groups of objects or groups of properties of objects. One thing to be careful of when you are working with the Outlook object model is that many collections have similar names, in plural, as the objects or properties that are incorporated in the collection. Examples of this are:

Collection	Object
Recipients	Recipient
Attachments	Attachment
Actions	Action
Explorers	Explorer
Inspectors	Inspector
Items	Item

Some of these, Recipients, Attachments, and Actions, are collections that are associated with individual Outlook items. Some are not usually thought of as being part of items, such as Explorers and Inspectors, but they are really parts of the Application object. The top level object for all Outlook object model programming is the Application object. See Chapter 1 for an illustration of the Outlook object model hierarchy.

Collections can contain other collections, as well as individual items. The example of accessing a subfolder that was previously shown illustrates this. That example showed a collection that is contained in another collection, which is contained in another collection.

```
Set oFolder = oNS.Folders("Personal Folders"). _
    Folders("Contacts").Folders("Business Contacts")
```

One limitation of the present Outlook object model has been mentioned previously, the absence of some desired collections. For example, the nineteen different phone and fax number type properties of a contact item are not organized into a collection, but must be referenced by the specific names of the properties. The same limitation applies to the address and email address properties available in a contact item, they must be accessed by using the actual property names. If collections existed for those properties we could access them in code using For...Next or For...Each loops, or by using syntax similar to oContactItem.PhoneNumbers.Items.Item(i).

> One thing to be aware of is that when you delete items from collections you should use For...Next loops that count down. The problem is inconsistent, but sometimes when you use standard For...Next or For...Each loops only every other item in the collection is deleted. The problem is particularly evident on For...Next loops based on the count of items in the collection. This occurs because you are deleting items using the count as the index counter for the loop, and the count is being changed by the deletions. This changes the internal loop counter as well. Use count down loops to always avoid this problem.

Use the following procedure as an example of the safest method of deleting items from various collections. This code will delete all attachments from the currently open item.

> All the code samples for this chapter should be installed in a code module named basOutlookDataAccess unless stated otherwise. To create this module, insert a code module in your project and name it basOutlookDataAccess.

```
Sub DeleteAttachments()
    Dim oOL As Outlook.Application
    Dim oInspector As Outlook.Inspector
    Dim oAttachments As Outlook.Attachments
    Dim lIndex As Long

    Set oOL = CreateObject("Outlook.Application")
    Set oInspector = oOL.ActiveInspector
    If oInspector.CurrentItem.Class = olMail Then
        Set oAttachments = oInspector.CurrentItem.Attachments
        For lIndex = oAttachments.Count To 1 Step -1
            oAttachments(lIndex).Delete
        Next
    End If

    Set oAttachments = Nothing
    Set oInspector = Nothing
    Set oOL = Nothing
End Sub
```

Accessing individual Outlook items is also a matter of drilling down into the object hierarchy. The previous example used the `CurrentItem` property of the currently active Inspector window to access the `Attachments` collection of the item. Explorer windows have a corresponding `CurrentFolder` property that you can use to access the `Items` in the folder that currently has focus.

```
Dim oOL As Outlook.Application
Dim oExplorer As Outlook.Explorer
Dim oItems As Outlook.Items

Set oOL = CreateObject("Outlook.Application")
Set oExplorer = oOL.ActiveExplorer
Set oItems = oExplorer.CurrentFolder.Items
```

Working with Outlook's Different Modes

We have mentioned many times in this book that Outlook has different operating modes. The differences in these operating modes often makes it necessary for your code to know in what mode the user has installed Outlook. This information is available in the Windows Registry.

If you want to store and retrieve data from the Windows Registry in registry keys that are not supported by the intrinsic VB and VBA `GetSetting`, `GetAllSettings`, `SaveSetting` and `DeleteSetting` statements you must use Win32 API functions to access the registry data. The following section shows how to do that.

Storing Customized Settings Anywhere in the Windows Registry

To work with the Win32 API functions you have to `Declare` them in the Declarations section of a module. A `Declare` statement for the Win32 API function to open a Registry key takes the following form.

```
'RegOpenKeyExA is the internal name of the function
'It opens a registry key which can be of any type
'You can give it a more meaningful name by using the Alias keyword
Declare Function OpenKey Lib "advapi32.dll" Alias "RegOpenKeyExA" _
(ByVal hKey As Long, ByVal lpSubKey As String, ByVal ulOptions As Long, _
ByVal samDesired As Long, phkResult As Long) As Long
```

Using the `Alias` keyword enables you to give the function a more meaningful name that you choose. There are standard functions for creating, opening, closing, reading and writing Registry keys. The syntax of the Win32 API Registry functions is fairly obscure, and the library entry point names are case sensitive. In addition, the arguments used for the functions are similar no matter what type of key is being accessed. Creating a class that encapsulates and simplifies the syntax makes working with these functions much simpler than calling them directly.

❑ The functions for reading and writing Registry keys are the same whether the keys are string, binary or DWORD, but the arguments have different values depending on what type of key is being accessed.

❑ The Win32 API functions are C++ based, so all string keys that are stored in the Registry are Null terminated strings.

❑ The strings that are used are fixed length strings that must be long enough for the data that is received or data corruption may result from string overflow.

The following class module, `clsRegistryFunctions`, encapsulates some of the Win32 API Registry functions and hides their complexity. The class has two read/write properties, `LongKey` and `StringKey`, which set and return DWORD and string Registry values. It has one read-only property, `ErrorFlag`, which returns the error code for the last Registry access. It also has three methods, `CreateKey`, `OpenKey` and `CloseKey`. Using this class to work with the Registry functions makes it possible to use only a few simple arguments for the class properties and methods, instead of the complex and mistake prone syntax required for direct usage of the Win32 API Registry functions.

The class does not implement an error handler for the Win32 API Registry functions, it only sets a `Long` property corresponding to the error code returned by the last Registry access. Registry accesses that are error free return an error code of 0, `ERROR_NONE`. The `Constant` declarations include the most common errors returned by the Registry functions, which can be handled externally to the class, or the class can be extended to handle the errors in the class.

Insert a new class module in your project and name it `clsRegistryFunctions`. The following constant declarations in the Declarations section of the class show the values used to access the different Windows Registry branches.

```
'Values for the registry branches
Private Const HKEY_CLASSES_ROOT = &H80000000
Private Const HKEY_CURRENT_USER = &H80000001
Private Const HKEY_LOCAL_MACHINE = &H80000002
Private Const HKEY_USERS = &H80000003
```

The following constants are used for the most common access permissions for the Windows Registry, and provide a constant for ensuring that any values we create are permanent entries.

```
'Access permissions
Private Const STD_RIGHTS = &H1F0000
Private Const KEY_ALL_ACCESS = &H100000

'This constant preserves the key when the system is rebooted.
Private Const REG_OPTION_NON_VOLATILE = 0
```

The following constants are used for the different registry values we will be working with.

```
'Null-terminated registry string value
Private Const REG_STRINGZ = 1
'registry 32-bit number (DWORD)
Private Const REG_DWORD = 4
'0 value for DWORD
Private Const ZERO_DWORD = &H0
```

The following constants are the most common errors that are returned when using the Win32 API functions to access the Windows Registry.

```
'Error return codes
Private Const ERROR_NONE = 0
Private Const ERROR_BADDB = 1
Private Const ERROR_BADKEY = 2
Private Const ERROR_CANTOPEN = 3
Private Const ERROR_CANTREAD = 4
Private Const ERROR_CANTWRITE = 5
Private Const ERROR_OUTOFMEMORY = 6
Private Const ERROR_INVALID_PARAMETER = 7
Private Const ERROR_ACCESS_DENIED = 8
Private Const ERROR_INVALID_PARAMETERS = 87
Private Const ERROR_NO_MORE_ITEMS = 259
```

The following function declaration is used for the function that opens a registry key.

```
'RegOpenKeyExA opens a registry key
Private Declare Function RegOpenKeyExA Lib "advapi32.dll" _
(ByVal hKey As Long, ByVal lpSubKey As String, _
ByVal ulOptions As Long, ByVal samDesired As Long, _
phkResult As Long) As Long
```

The following function declaration is used for the function that closes a registry key.

```
'Closes an open registry key
Private Declare Function RegCloseKey Lib "advapi32.dll" _
(ByVal hKey As Long) As Long
```

The following function declaration is used for the function that creates a new registry key.

```
'Create a new registry key
Private Declare Function RegCreateKeyExA Lib "advapi32.dll" _
(ByVal hKey As Long, ByVal lpSubKey As String, _
ByVal Reserved As Long, ByVal lpClass As String, _
ByVal dwOptions As Long, ByVal samDesired As Long, _
ByVal lpSecurityAttributes As Long, phkResult As Long, _
lpdwDisposition As Long) As Long
```

The following function declaration is used for the function that gets a Long (DWORD) value from the registry.

```
'Get a Long value from a registry key
Private Declare Function RegQueryValueExA Lib "advapi32.dll" _
(ByVal hKey As Long, ByVal lpValueName As String, _
ByVal lpReserved As Long, lpType As Long, _
lpData As Long, lpcbData As Long) As Long
```

The following function declaration is used for the function that gets a string value from the registry.

```
'Get a String value from a registry key
'This is the same function as the one that gets
'a Long value. For a String the declaration of
'lpData is As String and is passed ByVal
Private Declare Function RegGetString Lib "advapi32.dll" _
Alias "RegQueryValueExA" (ByVal hKey As Long, _
ByVal lpValueName As String, ByVal lpReserved As Long, _
lpType As Long, ByVal lpData As String, _
lpcbData As Long) As Long
```

The following function declaration is used for the function that sets a string value in the registry.

```
'Set a registry String value
'This is the same function as the one that sets
'a Long value. For a String the declaration of
'lpData is As String and is passed ByVal
Private Declare Function RegSetString Lib "advapi32.dll" _
Alias "RegSetValueExA" (ByVal hKey As Long, ByVal _
lpValueName As String, ByVal Reserved As Long, ByVal _
dwType As Long, ByVal lpValue As String, ByVal cbData _
As Long) As Long
```

The following function declaration is used for the function that sets a Long (DWORD) value in the registry.

```
'Set a registry DWORD value
Private Declare Function RegSetValueExA Lib "advapi32.dll" _
(ByVal hKey As Long, ByVal lpValueName As String, _
ByVal Reserved As Long, ByVal dwType As Long, _
lpValue As Long, ByVal cbData As Long) As Long
```

The following module level variables are used for the handle that is used to access a registry key, and for an error indicator.

```
'Handle to the registry key
Private hKey As Long

'Error number of last registry access
Private mlErr As Long
```

The OpenKey method of the clsRegistry class uses the registry branch constants and the name of the registry key to open that key and return a handle to it.

```
Public Sub OpenKey(lSection As Long, sPath As String)
    Dim lReturn As Long

    lReturn = RegOpenKeyExA(lSection, sPath, 0&, STD_RIGHTS, hKey)

    'Set the error flag
    RegError lReturn
End Sub
```

The CloseKey method closes the registry key referenced by the existing registry key handle.

```
Public Sub CloseKey()
    Dim lReturn As Long

    lReturn = RegCloseKey(hKey)

    'Set the error flag
    RegError lReturn
End Sub
```

The CreateKey method creates a new, permanent key in the desired branch of the registry.

```
Public Sub CreateKey(lSection As Long, sPath As String)
    Dim lReturn As Long
    Dim lDisposition As Long

    lReturn = RegCreateKeyExA(lSection, sPath, 0&, _
    "", REG_OPTION_NON_VOLATILE, KEY_ALL_ACCESS, 0&, _
    hKey, lDisposition)

    'Set the error flag
    RegError lReturn
End Sub
```

The `Property Let StringKey` function is used to set the value of a string type registry key. Note that the string is a `Null` terminated string.

```
Public Property Let StringKey(sKey As String, sValue As String)
   Dim sKeyVal As String
   Dim lLen As Long
   Dim lReturn As Long

   'sValue is the value of the string, must be 0 terminated
   If Right(sValue, 1) <> Chr(0) Then
     sKeyVal = sValue & Chr(0)
   Else
     sKeyVal = sValue
   End If

   lLen = Len(sKeyVal)
   'hkey is the previously acquired key handle
   'sKey is the name of the key
   'sKeyVal sets the value
   lReturn = RegSetString(hKey, sKey, 0&, REG_STRINGZ, _
   sKeyVal, lLen)

   'Set the error flag
   RegError lReturn
End Property
```

The `Property Get StringKey` function is used to return the value of a string key in the registry. The length of the return string is first initialized to 256 Null characters. This prepares the string for receiving the actual registry key. Then the actual Win32 API function call is made.

```
Public Property Get StringKey(sKey As String) As String
   Dim sKeyVal As String
   Dim lLen As Long
   Dim lReturn As Long

   'hkey is the previously acquired key handle
   'sKey is the name of the string key
   'sKeyVal is the value of the string, 0 terminated

   lLen = 256
   sKeyVal = String(lLen, 0)
   lReturn = RegGetString(hKey, sKey, 0&, REG_STRINGZ, _
     sKeyVal, lLen)
   lLen = InStr(1, sKeyVal, Chr(0), vbBinaryCompare)
   sKeyVal = Left(sKeyVal, lLen - 1)

   'Set the error flag
   RegError lReturn

   StringKey = sKeyVal
End Property
```

The `Property Let LongKey` function is used to set the value of a DWORD registry key.

```
Public Property Let LongKey(sKey As String, lValue As Long)
    Dim lLen As Long
    Dim lType As Long
    Dim lReturn As Long

    lType = REG_DWORD 'value is DWORD type
    lLen = REG_DWORD 'length of the value is 4 bytes

    'hkey is the previously acquired key handle
    'sKey is the name of the key
    'lValue sets the value
    lReturn = RegSetValueExA(hKey, sKey, 0&, _
    lType, lValue, lLen)

    'Set the error flag
    RegError lReturn
End Property
```

The `Property Get LongKey` function is used to return the value of a DWORD registry key. Both `lType` and `lLen` are always set to 4 for this Win32 API call.

```
Public Property Get LongKey(sKey As String) As Long
    Dim lLen As Long
    Dim lReturn As Long
    Dim lType As Long
    Dim lValue As Long

    lType = REG_DWORD 'value is DWORD type
    lLen = REG_DWORD 'length of the value is 4 bytes

    'hkey is the previously acquired key handle
    'sKey is the name of the key
    'lValue returns the value
    lReturn = RegQueryValueExA(hKey, sKey, 0&, _
      lType, lValue, lLen)

    'Set the error flag
    RegError lReturn

    LongKey = lValue
End Property
```

The `RegError` Sub is called to set the module level error variable that is used to set the read-only `ErrorFlag` property, which returns the error number of any error that occurs when using the `clsRegistry` class. The class Initialize event is used to set the starting value of the module level error variable `mlErr`.

```
Private Sub RegError(lError As Long)
 'Set the error flag to the last return value
 mlErr = lError
End Sub

Public Property Get ErrorFlag() As Long
  'Refresh the property from the module level variable
  ErrorFlag = mlErr
End Property

Private Sub Class_Initialize()
  'Initialize the error flag to no error
  mlErr = 0
End Sub
```

The syntax for the methods of the class that open or create a registry key use the `lSection` argument for the registry branch desired, `HKEY_CURRENT_USER` for example. The `sPath` argument establishes the registry path within the specified registry branch, `Software\Microsoft\Office\9.0\Outlook\Setup` for example. Both of these methods set a `Private` module level `Long` variable `hKey` to the handle returned by the Win32 API Registry function. One of these two methods must be used before any of the properties are read or written. The `CloseKey` method uses the previously established handle to the registry and requires no calling arguments.

```
OpenKey(lSection As Long, sPath As String)
CreateKey(lSection As Long, sPath As String)
CloseKey()
```

The syntax to write the properties of the class is very similar, which is not surprising since the two `Property Let` procedures are calling different aliased versions of the same Win32 API function, `RegSetValueExA`. Both use the argument `sKey` to set the registry key to be written using the previously established registry path. The property that writes a `Long` value to the registry uses the argument `lValue` to pass the `Long` value to the property, and the property that writes a `String` value to the registry uses the argument `sValue`, which is actually passed by value to the Win32 API function.

```
Property Let LongKey(sKey As String, lValue As Long)
Property Let StringKey(sKey As String, sValue As String)
```

Both property procedures that read a value from the registry use the argument `sKey` to set the registry key to be read using the previously established registry path. The only external difference in the two property procedures is the type of the values returned by the procedures, one a `Long` value and the other a `String` value.

```
Property Get LongKey(sKey As String) As Long
Property Get StringKey(sKey As String) As String
```

To use this class, first use either the method to open or create a registry key. If the open method is used the return code, which is available in the property ErrorFlag, should be checked for the value ERROR_BADKEY which is returned when the registry key does not already exist. If this return code is set when the property ErrorFlag is read then the method to create the key should be used. Once the registry key is opened or created a handle to that key is stored internally in the class. That handle is used by the other properties and method of the class to access the registry key. After any accesses to the registry key are finished, use the method to close the key. The FindInstalledMode function in the next section uses the clsRegistry class to find out what mode of Outlook is installed.

Once the CloseKey method is used to dereference the registry key handle then no further use of that key should be made without a new call to either the method OpenKey or CreateKey.

Finding the Installed Outlook Mode

Outlook has three modes of operation: Corporate/Workgroup mode, Internet only mode, and No Email (PIM only) mode. Corporate/Workgroup mode is the mode that you will use if you are working with Exchange Server, and it is also used for standalone users. It contains the full MAPI libraries. Internet only mode can only work with POP3 email services, and contains a "light" version of the MAPI libraries. No Email mode is the same as Internet only mode, except that no email accounts are configured.

It is important to know what mode the user is in if your program makes use of features that are not available in the user's mode. For example, if the user is running Internet only mode you cannot make use of different profiles, since Internet only mode only supports one profile. If your program attempts to access the Public Folders tree or a user's Mailbox, an Internet only mode user will have a runtime error. Also, some CDO functions do not work in Internet only mode

The InstalledMode function uses the clsRegistry class developed in the previous section to read the Windows Registry to find out Outlook's mode of operation. Insert the following code in the code module basOutlookDataAccess.

```
Public Function InstalledMode() As String
    Const HKEY_CURRENT_USER = &H80000001
    Const ERROR_NONE = 0

    Dim lBranch As Long
    Dim sPath As String
    Dim sKey As String
    Dim lReturn As Long
    Dim bErr As Boolean

    Dim oClass As clsRegistryFunctions

    Set oClass = New clsRegistryFunctions

    bErr = False 'Initialize error flag
    lBranch = HKEY_CURRENT_USER
    sPath = "Software\Microsoft\Office\9.0\Outlook\Setup"
    sKey = "MailSupport" 'installed Outlook mode

    oClass.OpenKey lBranch, sPath
    If oClass.ErrorFlag = ERROR_NONE Then
       lReturn = oClass.LongKey(sKey)
```

```
      If oClass.ErrorFlag = ERROR_NONE Then
        Select Case lReturn
        Case 0
          InstalledMode = "Internet Only"
        Case 1
          InstalledMode = "Corporate/Workgroup"
        Case 2
          InstalledMode = "PIM Only"
        End Select
      Else
        bErr = True
      End If
    Else
      bErr = True
    End If
    oClass.CloseKey

    If bErr = True Then
      InstalledMode = "Error"
    End If

    Set oClass = Nothing
  End Function
```

The `TestForMode` macro will display the user's operating mode in a message box dialog.

```
  Sub TestForMode()
    Dim sMode As String

    sMode = InstalledMode
    MsgBox "Installed mode is " & sMode
  End Sub
```

Exchange server data that you will make use of through the Outlook object model is mostly stored in the user's Mailbox folders, the Exchange Server Public Folders tree, and various shared folders. The methods of accessing those folders was shown earlier in this chapter. Other properties that involve Exchange Server are usually accessed using CDO, as the next section will demonstrate.

Things to Watch Out For

There are a number of documented problems and bugs in the Outlook programming model. Problems with deleting items from collections, creating recipients, and working with Outlook's different operating modes have been mentioned previously in this chapter. This section discusses some other problems, and shows you workarounds for them.

One nasty bug that is present in Outlook 2000 is that if you access the `Body` property of a `MailItem` it is converted to **RTF** (Rich Text Format). You cannot convert it to, or back to, plain text. The Outlook online Help documents a behavior in this respect that is not what really happens. With any luck, this bug will be corrected when the first service release for Office 2000 is released.

Why is this bug so nasty? If you are working only in an Exchange Server environment, there is no problem. Everyone will be running mail clients that understand how to interpret RTF formatted messages. However, if the messages are being sent to people who are using mail clients that cannot understand RTF, such as UNIX email clients, Outlook Express, and Internet based email clients, all formatting will be stripped off and an attachment called `Winmail.dat` will be generated.

The following screen shot shows a plain text message, before the `Body` property is accessed in code. The title bar shows that the message is indeed plain text.

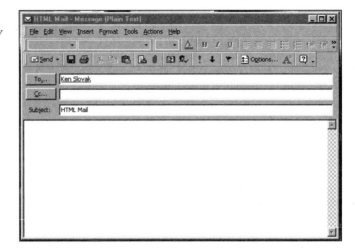

The following screen shot shows that the message has become RTF after text was inserted in the `Body` of the message. The conversion to RTF format occurs as soon as the `Body` property of the item is written to in any way.

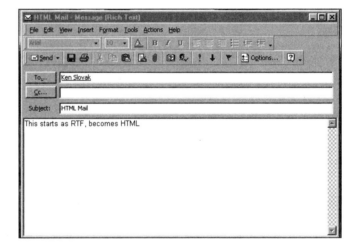

There are two ways you can change the message to another, more compatible format. If your correspondent email clients can read **HTML** (Hypertext Markup Language) formatted email, you can use the workaround that is shown in the next procedure. If you have to send messages in plain text format, you can use the workaround that is shown in the CDO section of this chapter.

The following procedure converts the RTF text to HTML text.

```
Sub HTMLMail()
   Dim oOL As Outlook.Application
   Dim oInspector As Outlook.Inspector
   Dim oMail As Outlook.MailItem

   Set oOL = CreateObject("Outlook.Application")
   Set oMail = oOL.CreateItem(olMailItem)
   oMail.Subject = "HTML Mail"
   oMail.To = "Ken Slovak"
   oMail.Recipients.ResolveAll
   oMail.Display
   'At this point the message is plain text format
   oMail.Body = "This starts as RTF, becomes HTML"
   'At this point the message is RTF format
   oMail.HTMLBody = "<html><body>" & oMail.Body & _
   "</body></html>"
   'At this point the message is HTML format

   Set oOL = Nothing
   Set oInspector = Nothing
   Set oMail = Nothing
End Sub
```

The next screen shot shows that the message has now been converted into an HTML message, avoiding sending an RTF message to non-compatible email clients.

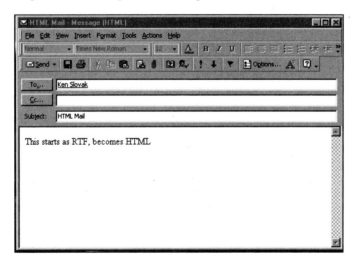

Using CDO

CDO is an object oriented wrapper for **MAPI** (Messaging Application Programming Interface). It makes working with the MAPI interface easier for the programmer, and makes MAPI functionality available to programmers using VB, VBA and VBScript. The use of CDO in programming ASP pages is covered in the Customer Service Application Case Study, later in this book. This section will cover mainly the use of CDO to work with Outlook and Exchange properties and methods that are not available in the Outlook object model.

> **Some of the information and undocumented property tags used in this section are courtesy of Siegfried Weber, of CDOLive.com. The use of undocumented property tags is not documented or supported by Microsoft, and those tags may change in the future. All information presented in this book is as accurate as possible at the time this was written.**

Installing CDO

One major difference in developing with CDO in Outlook 2000, is that the developer cannot assume that the CDO libraries are loaded on the user's computer.

The main CDO library, CDO.DLL, was installed automatically when previous versions of Outlook were installed. That is not the case with Outlook 2000, where the CDO library installation is optional. The other CDO libraries, the CDO rendering library (CDOHTML.DLL), a server side library, and CDONTS.DLL, a subset of CDOHTML.DLL for Windows NT, are not of concern in this context.

Until recently, the only alternative for a developer was to check to see whether CDO was installed on the user's computer, and to display a message to the user to install CDO if it was not. However, Randy Byrne, a prominent Outlook developer and author has discovered a way to demand installation of CDO if it is not installed on the user's computer. The CDO library is not redistributable, so the user must install it from the Office installation CD.

The following code example, originally credited to Micro Eye, Inc. Items Command Bar Example at http://www.microeye.com/outlook/ItemsCB.zip, and used with permission, shows how to demand installation of CDO on a user's computer if it is not installed already. This code requires that references are set to the Microsoft Outlook 9.0 Object Library, the Microsoft CDO 1.21 Library, and the Microsoft Windows Installer Object Library. The original code has been made into a class module and modified to make it easier to use from any Outlook program.

```
'****************************************************************************
'Items Command Bar
'Module: modInstaller
'Sample Outlook 2000 COM Add-in application
'Provided by Micro Eye, Inc.
'http://www.microeye.com
'You can modify this COM Add-in project to suit your own requirements
'No support is provided for this sample COM Add-in project
'Purpose: Install CDO for correct functioning of Items Command Bar
```

```
'
'Modified for Professional Outlook 2000 Programming, Wrox Press.
'
'*********************************************************************

'These routines can be adapted to other Office 2000 Features
```

To use this code, insert a new class module in your project and name it `clsCDOInstaller`. Declare a module level Boolean variable in the Declarations section of the class module.

```
Private m_blnIsCDOInstalled As Boolean
```

The `InstallFeature` method of the class checks to see whether CDO is already installed, and attempts to install CDO if it is not. This function should be called from your code before you attempt to use the CDO object model. The computer that is running the code must have the Windows Installer (`MSI.EXE`) installed. Demanding installation of CDO will also require that the Office 2000 Installation CD is available. If CDO is installed when `InstallFeature` terminates it returns a value of `True`.

```
'*********************************************************************
'Use MSI Object Library to install CDO
'Return the success or failure of the installation.
'*********************************************************************
Public Function InstallFeature() As Boolean
  Dim Installer As Object
  'The GUID for the app which you are installing the feature on
  Dim strProduct As String
  Dim strErr As String
  Dim strCDO As String
  Dim blnSuccess As Boolean

  On Error Resume Next

  'Office 2000 Premium MSI GUID
  'strProduct = "{00000409-78E1-11D2-B60F-006097C998E7}"
  'The following approach using the ProductCode
  'works with any version of Office
  'Office 2000 MSI GUID
  strProduct = Application.ProductCode
  'This is the feature name that we want MS Installer to install
  strCDO = "OutlookCDO"

  'Requires Microsoft Windows Installer Object Library is referenced
  'It should be in your \Windows\system\msi.dll in your VB project
  Set Installer = CreateObject("WindowsInstaller.Installer")
  If Err = 0 Then
    m_blnIsCDOInstalled = Install(Installer, strProduct, strCDO)
  Else
    m_blnIsCDOInstalled = False
  End If
```

```
      If (m_blnIsCDOInstalled = False) Then
        m_blnIsCDOInstalled = IsCDOInstalled()
        InstallFeature = False
      Else
        InstallFeature = True
      End If

      Set Installer = Nothing
    End Function
```

The `Install` private function first checks to see if CDO is installed on the hard drive of the user's computer. If CDO is not locally installed then `Install` attempts to install it. CDO is installed by using a call to the MSI object library.

```
'**********************************************************************
'Install Feature if not installed using FeatureState method
'**********************************************************************
Private Function Install(objInstaller, _
    strProductID As String, strFeatureName As String)
  Dim blnSuccess As Boolean

  On Error Resume Next

  If objInstaller.FeatureState(strProductID, _
    strFeatureName) <> msiInstallStateLocal Then
    objInstaller.ConfigureFeature strProductID, _
      strFeatureName, msiInstallStateLocal
    If Err.Number <> 0 Then
      blnSuccess = False 'Unable to install feature
    Else
      blnSuccess = True
    End If
  Else
    blnSuccess = True
  End If

  Install = blnSuccess
End Function
```

The `IsCDOInstalled` private function tests to see whether CDO is installed on the user's computer by attempting to create a new MAPI `Session` object.

```
'**********************************************************************
' Test if CDO is installed:
'**********************************************************************
Private Function IsCDOInstalled() As Boolean
  Dim testCDOObj As Object

  On Error GoTo errorCDOInstalled

  Set testCDOObj = New MAPI.session

  IsCDOInstalled = True
```

```
        Set testCDOObj = Nothing
        Exit Function

    errorCDOInstalled:
        IsCDOInstalled = False
        If Not testCDOObj Is Nothing Then
            Set testCDOObj = Nothing
        End If
End Function
```

Using this class module in your own code enables you to work around the fact that the installation of Outlook 2000 on a computer does not automatically install CDO on that computer. To test the installation of CDO, run the `TestCDODemandInstall` macro.

```
Sub TestCDODemandInstall()
    Dim oClass As clsCDOInstaller

    Set oClass = New clsCDOInstaller
    If oClass.InstallFeature Then
        MsgBox "CDO is installed"
    Else
        MsgBox "CDO is not installed"
    End If

    Set oClass = Nothing
End Sub
```

CDO Logons

Although Outlook only supports logging into one profile for each Outlook session, CDO supports a number of different logon methods. You can use the logon that was established by an existing Outlook session, logon to any existing profile, or use an anonymous logon. Within Outlook code, a CDO logon to an existing Outlook session is established as follows.

```
Dim oSession As MAPI.Session

Set oSession = CreateObject("MAPI.Session")
oSession.Logon "", "", False, False
```

The arguments to the `Logon` method are `Logon([ProfileName], [ProfilePassword], [ShowDialog], [NewSession], [ParentWindow], [NoMail], [ProfileInfo])`. When using an existing Outlook session to piggyback into a CDO session the preceding method is the most commonly used way. To have the user select from an existing profile, use the following code.

```
Dim oSession As MAPI.Session

Set oSession = CreateObject("MAPI.Session")
oSession.Logon "", "", True, False
```

The following screen shot shows the profile logon dialog box that is displayed.

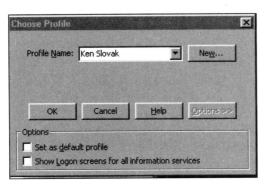

The last argument shown would be changed to `True` if you want to establish a new session during the CDO logon. Since Outlook in Internet only mode supports only one profile, the arguments that relate to choosing profiles don't work in this mode. No errors are generated, but you cannot choose profiles in Internet only mode.

> **CDO is intended for use with Outlook running in Corporate/Workgroup mode. Microsoft does not support or document CDO usage with Outlook running in Internet only mode. Despite this, I have discovered that many of the CDO properties and methods work with Outlook Internet only mode. Some obvious things do not work, such as the use of different profiles, since Outlook in Internet only mode only has one profile. Other obvious things that do not work are properties that relate to Exchange Server data stores, public folders, offline and Remote Mail use, and shared folders.**

You can also use the `ProfileInfo` argument to logon to CDO without having the user choose a profile. The `ProfileInfo` argument can be used to generate a randomly named profile logon or an anonymous profile logon. Either type of logon profile is used to create a temporary profile for that session. For an authenticated profile, the format of the `ProfileInfo` string is `<server name> & vbLf & <mailbox name>` where the server name and mailbox name can be unresolved. The mailbox name is not the user's display name, but the alias or account name used internally by the user's Exchange Server. This information must be available ahead of time.

For an anonymous profile, the format used is `<server distinguished name> & vbLf & vbLf & "anon"`, where the distinguished name of the server takes the form: `/o=<enterprise>/ou=<site>/cn=Configuration/cn=Servers/cn=<server>`, as shown in this code:

```
Dim sProfileInfo As String
Dim sEnterprise As String
Dim sSite As String
Dim sServer As String

'Set the strings for the Enterprise, Site and Server
' Construct CDO profile
sProfileInfo = "/o=" & sEnterprise & "/ou=" & sSite & _
"/cn=Configuration/cn=Servers/cn=" & sServer & vbLF & vbLF + "anon"
```

Another way to logon to a CDO session is to supply the user's default profile as an argument for the logon method. The following code assumes no password is needed to logon to the default profile.

```
Sub DefaultProfileLogon()
  Dim oSession As MAPI.session
  Dim sDefaultProfile As String

  sDefaultProfile = DefaultProfile()
  Set oSession = CreateObject("MAPI.Session")
  oSession.Logon ProfileName:=sDefaultProfile, _
            ShowDialog:=False
  'session code here
  Set oSession = Nothing
End Sub
```

The default profile is stored in the Windows registry, in the HKEY_CURRENT_USER branch. Depending on whether the user is running Windows NT or Windows 95/98 the location of the key is different. Users running Windows NT have the key located at Software\Microsoft\Windows NT\CurrentVersion\Windows Messaging Subsystem\Profiles. Users running Windows 95 or Windows 98 have the key located at Software\Microsoft\Windows Messaging Subsystem\Profiles.

The DefaultProfile function used in DefaultProfileLogon reads the Windows Registry and attempts to find the key at the location for Windows 95 or Windows 98. If that key is not found, it attempts to find the key at the location for Windows NT. If the key is found, the DefaultProfile value is read and used to supply the default profile name. This function uses the clsRegistry class module that was shown earlier in this chapter. Calling the DefaultProfile function in your code will return the user's default profile or a null string if the call failed.

```
Public Function DefaultProfile() As String
  Const HKEY_CURRENT_USER = &H80000001
  Const ERROR_NONE = 0
  Const ERROR_BADKEY = 2

  Dim lBranch As Long
  Dim sPathWin As String
  Dim sPathNT As String
  Dim sKey As String
  Dim sReturn As String
  Dim bErr As Boolean

  Dim oClass As clsRegistryFunctions

  Set oClass = New clsRegistryFunctions

  bErr = False 'Initialize error flag
  lBranch = HKEY_CURRENT_USER

  sPathWin = "Software\Microsoft\Windows Messaging" _
  & " Subsystem\Profiles"
```

```
      sPathNT = "Software\Microsoft\Windows NT\CurrentVersion\" _
              & "Windows Messaging Subsystem\Profiles"

   sKey = "DefaultProfile"

   oClass.OpenKey lBranch, sPathWin
   If oClass.ErrorFlag = ERROR_NONE Then
     sReturn = oClass.StringKey(sKey)
     If oClass.ErrorFlag <> ERROR_NONE Then
       bErr = True
     End If
   ElseIf oClass.ErrorFlag = ERROR_BADKEY Then
     oClass.OpenKey lBranch, sPathNT
     If oClass.ErrorFlag = ERROR_NONE Then
       sReturn = oClass.StringKey(sKey)
       If oClass.ErrorFlag <> ERROR_NONE Then
         bErr = True
       End If
     Else
       bErr = True
     End If
   Else
     bErr = True
   End If
   oClass.CloseKey

   If bErr = True Then
     DefaultProfile = ""
   Else
     DefaultProfile = sReturn
   End If

   Set oClass = Nothing
End Function
```

Using CDO

Once you are logged into a CDO session, you can use CDO to work with properties and methods that you can't use or find in the Outlook object model. We've used CDO in previous chapters to display the AddressBook dialog box, find the actual email address of the sender of an email, and send items immediately. Now we'll see how to use CDO for some other things. Before we do, one important thing is how we communicate between the Outlook and CDO object models.

Although CDO and the Outlook object model share some objects that have the same names, those objects are not compatible with each other. Objects such as Recipients, AddressLists, AddressEntries, Folders and others may have the same name in CDO as in Outlook, but they are not the same objects. This leads to two things, the importance of explicit object declaration references, and the question of how to transfer information from one object model to the other.

When you declare object variables in your VBA or VB code, make sure to be specific as to which library the object is using if you use early binding. If you don't, the object library that is listed first in the references for the project is what will be used to supply the objects.

```
'Ambiguous reference
Dim oRecipients As Recipients
'Specific references
Dim oRecipients As Outlook.Recipients
Dim oRecipients As MAPI.Recipients
```

Transferring information from one object model to the other is done by using the `EntryID` and `StoreID` properties. There are methods in both object libraries that make use of those properties, as the following code snippets demonstrate. `GetFolderFromID` and `GetItemFromID` are methods of the Outlook `NameSpace` object that enable you to get `MAPIFolder` and `Item` objects from the `EntryID` and `StoreID` strings. The corresponding CDO methods are `GetFolder` and `GetMessage`. These methods are demonstrated later in this section.

Displaying the AddressBook Dialog Box

The `AddressBook` dialog box that is displayed as a method of the CDO `Session` object is the same familiar dialog box that is displayed when you are asked to select names from an address list, or when you press the To, CC or BCC command buttons in an item. The following screen shot displays the standard `AddressBook` dialog box.

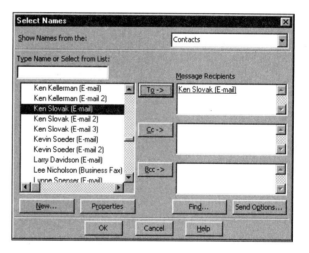

This dialog box can be customized in a number of different ways. You can choose to not display any of the To, Cc or Bcc panels, display custom names for them, permit only one recipient to be selected (only in Corporate/Workgroup mode), display a customized title, not force resolution of the selected recipients, or preload a list of names to the To panel as selected recipients.

> If the AddressBook dialog box is displayed using the `OneAddress:=True` argument to enable selecting only one recipient, an error will be generated if the user is running Outlook in Internet only mode. Setting the argument to the default value of `False`, or not using it, will not cause an error.

The following screen shot shows a customized AddressBook dialog box, with a custom title and custom names for the To and Cc panels. The Bcc panel is not displayed in this example.

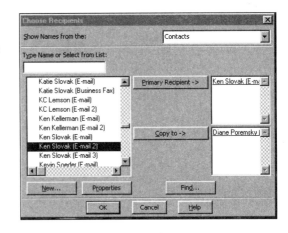

The function that displayed this customized AddressBook dialog box is shown in the next example:

```
Function GetRecipientsFromAddressBook() As MAPI.Recipients
   Dim oSession As MAPI.session
   Dim oRecips As MAPI.Recipients

   Set oSession = Application.CreateObject("MAPI.Session")
   oSession.Logon "", "", False, False

   On Error Resume Next
   Set oRecips = oSession.AddressBook( _
   Title:="Choose Recipients", _
   OneAddress:=False, _
   ForceResolution:=True, _
   RecipLists:=2, _
   ToLabel:="&Primary Recipient", _
   CcLabel:="&Copy to")

   If Err = 0 Then
      Set GetRecipientsFromAddressBook = oRecips
   Else
      MsgBox "Selection cancelled"
      Set GetRecipientsFromAddressBook = Nothing
   End If

   oSession.Logoff

   Set oSession = Nothing
   Set oRecips = Nothing
End Function
```

The `Title`, `ToLabel`, and `CcLabel` named arguments are used to customize the dialog box with personalized captions. The `RecipLists` named argument is set to 2, showing only the To and Cc panels. The `RecipLists` named argument can have the following values:

RecipLists Setting	Action
-1	Displays the To, Cc and Bcc panels with default captions and without forced resolution.
0	Displays no list boxes. No recipients are returned with this setting.
1	Displays the To panel (the default if no RecipLists argument is used).
2	Displays the To and Cc panels.
3	Displays all three panels (To, Cc, and Bcc).

The function uses the `On Error Resume Next` statement to prevent an error message from occurring if the user cancels the `AddressBook` dialog box. Canceling the `AddressBook` dialog box will generate a `MAPI_E_USER_CANCEL` error if no error trapping is used. The `Err` object is checked to see whether an error occurred, and if not, the returned `Recipients` collection is assigned to the function return value. If an error occurred, the function return value is set to `Nothing`.

CDO Folders

The `GetFolder` method uses the `FolderID`, and optionally the `StoreID`, to locate the desired folder. The folder IDs for the default folders are listed in the following table, with the CDO property tag names for those folders. All of these folders are child folders to the Inbox folder in the CDO schema.

CDO Folder Property Tag for CDO	FolderID
CdoDefaultFolderCalendar	0
CdoDefaultFolderContacts	5
CdoDefaultFolderDeletedItems	4
CdoDefaultFolderInbox	1
CdoDefaultFolderJournal	6
CdoDefaultFolderNotes	7
CdoDefaultFolderOutbox	2
CdoDefaultFolderSentItems	3
CdoDefaultFolderTasks	8

To instantiate a `Folder` object as one of these default folders use code similar to the following.

```
'Get the default Calendar folder
Set oFolder = oSession.GetDefaultFolder(CdoDefaultFolderCalendar)
'Get the default Journal folder
Set oFolder = oSession.GetDefaultFolder(CdoDefaultFolderJournal)
'Get the default Deleted Items folder
Set oFolder = oSession.GetDefaultFolder(CdoDefaultFolderDeletedItems)
```

You may have noticed that the list of default folders does not include the Drafts folder. To instantiate a `Folder` object as the Drafts folder you have to use an alternate method of folder access. All the default folders are subsidiary to the Inbox, so in CDO terms they are members of the `Fields` collection of the Inbox folder. To access any of the `Items` in that collection, you use the property tag for that `Item`.

The following table lists the default folders and their property tags as `Items` of the `Fields` collection of the Inbox folder. Note that all property tags are `Long` numbers in hexadecimal notation.

Folder	Property Tag
Calendar	&H36D00102
Contacts	&H36D10102
Drafts	&H36D70102
Journal	&H36D20102
Notes	&H36D30102
Tasks	&H36D40102

The following procedure finds the Drafts folder by using the Drafts property tag of the `Fields` collection of the Inbox to find the `FolderID` of the Drafts folder. It then uses the `GetFolder` method to instantiate a Drafts folder object. It then gets the `Messages` collection of the Inbox folder and finds the first message in the Inbox, using the `GetFirst` method. That message is then copied to the Drafts folder using the message's `CopyTo` method to create a copy of the message in the Inbox. The `Update` method is then used to post the copy to the Drafts folder.

```
Sub AlternateFoldersMethod()
  Const PR_DRAFTS_FOLDER = &H36D70102

  Dim oSession As MAPI.session
  Dim oMessage As MAPI.Message
  Dim oMessages As MAPI.Messages
  Dim oCopy As MAPI.Message
  Dim oFolder As MAPI.Folder
  Dim oInbox As MAPI.Folder
  Dim sDraftsFolderID As String

  Set oSession = CreateObject("MAPI.Session")
  oSession.Logon "", "", False, False
  'Use property tags of the Fields of the Inbox access the drafts folder
  'First get inbox folder
  Set oInbox = oSession.Inbox
  'Get the FolderID of the Drafts folder
  sDraftsFolderID = oInbox.Fields.Item(PR_DRAFTS_FOLDER)
  'Now we can get drafts folder
  Set oFolder = oSession.GetFolder(sDraftsFolderID)
  'Get message collection of the inbox
  Set oMessages = oInbox.Messages
  'Get first message from the Inbox
  Set oMessage = oMessages.GetFirst()
  'Copy it to the Drafts folder
```

```
    Set oCopy = oMessage.CopyTo(oFolder.ID)
    OCopy.Update

    OSession.Logoff

    Set oSession = Nothing
    Set oMessage = Nothing
    Set oCopy = Nothing
    Set oMessages = Nothing
    Set oFolder = Nothing
    Set oInbox = Nothing
End Sub
```

The previous procedure also illustrates working with what are known as "large collections" using CDO. CDO maintains large and small collections of objects. Small collections can be worked with using the Count property to determine the number of objects in the collection. Large collections are not guaranteed to have an accurate Count property. The method of working with items in large collections is to use the provided "Get" methods. There are GetFirst, GetLast, GetNext, and GetPrevious methods that are used for these large collections. The following are the types of collections maintained by CDO.

Collection	Type
AddressEntries	Large
AddressLists	Small
Attachments	Small
Columns	Small
Fields	Small
Folders	Large
Formats	Small
InfoStores	Small
Messages	Large
Patterns	Small
Recipients	Small
Views	Small

Communicating Between Outlook and CDO

The following `CDOandOutlook` procedure shows how items and folders can be passed between the Outlook and CDO object models, using the `EntryID` and `StoreID` properties of the items and folders. First, the Calendar folder object is instantiated in Outlook, and the `EntryID` and `StoreID` properties are assigned to string variables.

```
Sub CDOandOutlook()
    Dim oSession As MAPI.session
    Dim oMessage As MAPI.Message
    Dim oCDOFolder As MAPI.Folder
    Dim oMail As Outlook.MailItem
    Dim oNS As Outlook.NameSpace
    Dim oFolder As Outlook.MAPIFolder
    Dim sEntry As String
    Dim sStore As String
    Dim oOL As Outlook.Application

    'Create an Outlook session
    Set oOL = CreateObject("Outlook.Application")

    'Create a MAPI session
    Set oSession = CreateObject("MAPI.Session")
    'logon using a shared session
    oSession.Logon "", "", False, False

    Set oNS = oOL.GetNamespace("MAPI")
    'Get the Outlook Calendar folder
    Set oFolder = oNS.GetDefaultFolder(olFolderCalendar)
    'Get the EntryID and StoreID of the Calendar
    sEntry = oFolder.EntryID
    sStore = oFolder.StoreID
```

Next, the same folder is instantiated in CDO and the name of the folder is displayed. This shows that the `EntryID` and `StoreID` properties are the same in both Outlook and CDO.

```
    'Now get the same folder in CDO using the IDs passed from Outlook
    Set oCDOFolder = oSession.GetFolder(sEntry, sStore)
    sEntry = oCDOFolder.ID
    MsgBox "Folder is named: " & oCDOFolder.Name
```

Next, a message is created in the Inbox, using CDO. The message is posted in the Inbox using the `Update` method. It is important to remember that a newly created item has no valid `EntryID` and `StoreID` properties until it is updated or saved. The same message is then displayed using the Outlook object model with the `Display` method.

```
    'Now add a message to the Inbox
    Set oMessage = oSession.Inbox.Messages.Add
    oMessage.Subject = "This is a test"
    oMessage.Update
    'Get the message EntryID and StoreID
    sEntry = oMessage.ID
    sStore = oMessage.StoreID
    'Now display the message in Outlook, using the IDs passed from CDO
    Set oMail = oNS.GetItemFromID(sEntry, sStore)
    oMail.Display
```

Finally, another message is created and saved using the Outlook object model. The `Save` method posts the item to the Drafts folder. That message is then retrieved using CDO and the subject of the message is then displayed.

```
'Now create a message using Outlook
Set oMail = oOL.CreateItem(olMailItem)
oMail.Subject = "This is another test"
'Note that the Save method saves this item to the Drafts folder
oMail.Save
'And now get the message using CDO
sEntry = oMail.EntryID
Set oMessage = oSession.GetMessage(sEntry)
MsgBox "Message subject: " & oMessage.Subject

oSession.Logoff

Set oMessage = Nothing
Set oCDOFolder = Nothing
Set oMail = Nothing
Set oNS = Nothing
Set oFolder = Nothing
Set oOL = Nothing
Set oSession = Nothing
End Sub
```

Address Lists in CDO

When you work with the `AddressBook` method of the `Session` object all enabled address books are available in the dialog box. There is no way to specify which address book to use with this method. To work with either **GAL** (Global Address List) or **PAB** (Personal Address Book) `AddressEntries` collections in Corporate/Workgroup mode, a different method is used, the `GetAddressList` method. Note that there is no display method for the returned `AddressList` or its `AddressEntries`. If you want to display the entries in one of these address books you have to design a form and write code to populate the form with the entries from that address book. CDO provides predefined constants for both the GAL and PAB.

❑ `CdoAddressListGAL` = 0

❑ `CdoAddressListPAB` = 1

This next procedure shows how to access the PAB using CDO. It instantiates an `AddressList` object for the PAB, gets the first entry in the PAB, and displays the name of the person associated with that entry.

```
Sub GetFirstPABEntry()
  Dim oSession As MAPI.session
  Dim oAddressEntry As MAPI.AddressEntry
  Dim oAddressEntries As MAPI.AddressEntries
  Dim oAddressList As MAPI.AddressList

  Set oSession = CreateObject("MAPI.Session")
  oSession.Logon "", "", False, False
  Set oAddressList = oSession.AddressLists.Item("Personal Address Book")
```

```
      Set oAddressEntries = oAddressList.AddressEntries
      Set oAddressEntry = oAddressEntries.GetFirst()
      oAddressEntry.Details
      oSession.Logoff

      Set oSession = Nothing
      Set oAddressEntry = Nothing
      Set oAddressEntries = Nothing
      Set oAddressList = Nothing
   End Sub
```

The `Details` method of the `AddressEntry` object shows the same dialog box that is shown by the Properties command button in an address book dialog box. The following screen shot shows the dialog box that is displayed by the `Details` method. Different tabs will be shown depending on what types of services are installed. If no Internet Email service was installed, the SMTP - Internet tab would not be shown. Additional installed services will add tabs.

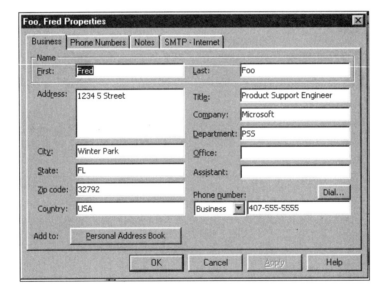

The CDO documentation shows that you can use the `GetAddressList` method with an argument of `CdoAddressListPAB` to access the PAB. However, in Outlook 2000, this can result in returning the default Contacts folder rather than the PAB as the selected `AddressList` object. I have found that using `oSession.AddressLists.Item("Personal Address Book")` is a method that works more reliably.

This next procedure gets the last entry in the GAL and displays its email address.

```
   Sub GetLastGALEntry()
     Dim oSession As MAPI.session
     Dim oAddressEntry As MAPI.AddressEntry
     Dim oAddressEntries As MAPI.AddressEntries
     Dim oAddressList As MAPI.AddressList

     Set oSession = CreateObject("MAPI.Session")
```

```
    oSession.Logon "", "", False, False
    Set oAddressList = oSession.GetAddressList(CdoAddressListGAL)
    Set oAddressEntries = oAddressList.AddressEntries
    Set oAddressEntry = oAddressEntries.GetLast()
    MsgBox "Last GAL entry: " & oAddressEntry.Address

    oSession.Logoff

    Set oSession = Nothing
    Set oAddressEntry = Nothing
    Set oAddressEntries = Nothing
    Set oAddressList = Nothing
End Sub
```

AddressList objects contain AddressEntries collections, which in turn contain AddressEntry objects. Once you have obtained an AddressEntry object you can extract the details about that person by using the Details method, as shown above.

Some Things You Can't Do With Outlook But Can With CDO

You can use CDO to do some things that you can't do with the Outlook object model. We have previously shown displaying the AddressBook dialog box, finding the email address of the sender of a message, and using the DeliverNow method to send items immediately for users of Corporate/Workgroup mode. The following procedures illustrate some other things that you can do with CDO. There are many other things that you can do with CDO that you cannot do with the Outlook object model that aren't covered in this book. See the references in Appendix C to find out more about working with CDO.

Detecting and Setting Offline Synchronization State of a Folder

This only works with Corporate/Workgroup mode, offline synchronization is not available for Internet only mode.

```
Function OfflineFolder() As Boolean
   Const PR_OFFLINE_FLAGS = &H6632000B

   Dim oSession As MAPI.session
   Dim oFolder As MAPI.Folder
   Dim oFields As MAPI.Field
   Dim oTag As Object

   On Error Resume Next
   Set oSession = CreateObject("MAPI.Session")
   oSession.Logon "", "", False, False
   'Check the status of the Public Folders offline state
   Set oFolder = oSession.GetDefaultFolder(CdoDefaultFolderCalendar)
   Set oFields = oFolder.Fields
   'Property tag is 1 if offline, 0 if not
   Set oTag = oFields.Item(PR_OFFLINE_FLAGS)
   If oTag Is Nothing Then
     OfflineFolder = False
     'If you want to make it available offline
     Set oTag = oFields.Add(PR_OFFLINE_FLAGS, 1)
```

```
      oTag.Value = 1
      oFolder.Update
   ElseIf oTag.Value = 0 Then
      OfflineFolder = False
   Else
      OfflineFolder = True
   End If

   oSession.Logoff

   Set oFolder = Nothing
   Set oFields = Nothing
   Set oTag = Nothing
   Set oSession = Nothing
End Function
```

Working with the Text of an Email Message Without Changing its Format to RTF

One nasty bug that is present in Outlook 2000 is that if you touch the `Body` property of a `MailItem` it is converted to **RTF** (Rich Text Format). You can work around this bug by using CDO. If you have to send messages in plain text format, you can to use the following workaround. You can avoid the problem entirely by only changing the `Body` property using CDO, which will not convert the item to RTF. The next procedure shows how to do that.

The procedure creates an email message using the Outlook object model. It sets the `To` and `Subject` properties of the mail item, and gets the `EntryID` of the item. A CDO session is then started and the `EntryID` of the Outlook mail item is used to open it as a CDO `Message` object. The Outlook `Body` property is called the `Text` property in CDO, and is plain text only. The text of the message is inserted in CDO and the item is updated. Finally, the item is moved to the user's Inbox. If the item is not moved, it will be located in the drafts folder. The screen shot shown below shows the message when it is displayed by Outlook, using the `Display` method. It is a plain text message.

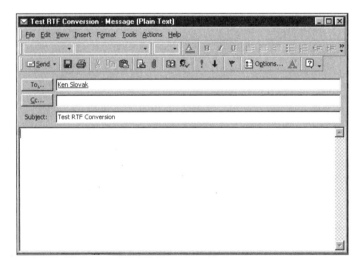

```
Sub cdoAvoidRTF()
  Dim oSession As MAPI.session
  Dim oMsg As MAPI.Message
  Dim oOL As Outlook.Application
  Dim oNS As Outlook.NameSpace
  Dim oMail As Outlook.MailItem
  Dim oInbox As Outlook.MAPIFolder
  Dim sEntry As String
  Dim sFolder As String
  Dim sStore As String

  Set oOL = CreateObject("Outlook.Application")
  Set oNS = oOL.GetNamespace("MAPI")
  Set oMail = oOL.CreateItem(olMailItem)
  oMail.To = "Ken Slovak"
  oMail.Subject = "Test RTF Conversion"
  oMail.Save
  oMail.Display
  Set oInbox = oNS.GetDefaultFolder(olFolderInbox)
  sStore = oInbox.StoreID
  sFolder = oInbox.EntryID
  'We need the EntryID of the item to locate it with CDO
  sEntry = oMail.EntryID
  oMail.Close olDiscard

  'Establish a CDO (MAPI) Session object and logon to it
  Set oSession = CreateObject("MAPI.Session")
  oSession.Logon , , False, False

  'Locate the current message with the EntryID using CDO
  Set oMsg = oSession.GetMessage(sEntry)
  oMsg.Text = "This is not RTF, even though the Body was touched"
  oMsg.Update
  oMsg.MoveTo sFolder, sStore

  oSession.Logoff

  Set oSession = Nothing
  Set oMsg = Nothing
  Set oOL = Nothing
  Set oNS = Nothing
  Set oMail = Nothing
  Set oInbox = Nothing
End Sub
```

The following screen shot shows the message after the `Body` text has been inserted using CDO. The message is still in plain text format.

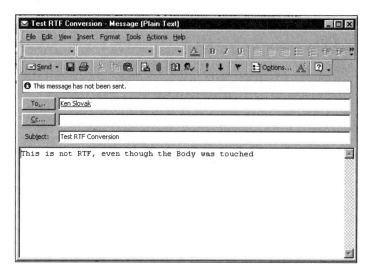

Getting the Internet Headers of an Email Message

The Outlook object model does not give you access to the Internet headers of email messages. Those headers are available with CDO however. The following procedure gets the `EntryID` of an email message that is open in the current Inspector window. It then passes the `EntryID` to the CDO `GetMessage` method to open a CDO `Message` object. The `CdoPR_TRANSPORT_MESSAGE_HEADERS` property tag is used to access the Internet headers. The value of the property tag is then assigned to a string variable.

```
Sub GetHeaders()
   Const CdoPR_TRANSPORT_MESSAGE_HEADERS = &H7D001E

   Dim oSession As MAPI.session
   Dim oMessage As MAPI.Message
   Dim oOL As Outlook.Application
   Dim oInspector As Outlook.Inspector
   Dim oMail As Outlook.MailItem
   Dim sHeaders As String
   Dim sEntry As String

   Set oOL = CreateObject("Outlook.Application")
   Set oInspector = oOL.ActiveInspector
   If oInspector.CurrentItem.Class = olMail Then
     Set oMail = oInspector.CurrentItem
     sEntry = oMail.EntryID

     Set oSession = CreateObject("MAPI.Session")
     oSession.Logon "", "", False, False

     'Get the open email message
     Set oMessage = oSession.GetMessage(sEntry)
```

```
        'Use the CdoPR_TRANSPORT_MESSAGE_HEADERS
        '(&H7D001E) property tag to retrieve the
        'Internet headers. If the message is not
        'an Internet email message the property
        'will not exist.
        'This will generate a MAPI_E_NOT_FOUND error.
        sHeaders = oMessage.Fields(CdoPR_TRANSPORT_MESSAGE_HEADERS)
        'Now you can do something with the headers.
        MsgBox sHeaders
        oSession.Logoff
    End If

    Set oSession = Nothing
    Set oMessage = Nothing
    Set oOL = Nothing
    Set oInspector = Nothing
    Set oMail = Nothing
End Sub
```

The following screen shot shows a message box displaying an example of some typical Internet headers captured by this procedure.

CDO Property Tags

CDO has some default properties available for different types of items, such as the `Sender` property of the `Message` object. However, many of the properties are only accessible using property tags. In fact, CDO only provides default `Message`, `AppointmentItem` and `MeetingItem` objects. All other item types that you are familiar with in Outlook, such as Contacts, Tasks, and Journal items, are considered CDO `Message` objects. The special properties of those items can only be accessed using property tags.

There are hundreds of documented property tags for CDO, which are listed in the CDO Help file. There are also many undocumented property tags, some of which are listed at the www.cdolive.com web site. Usage of these undocumented property tags is also described at the CDOLive web site. The following procedure shows how to access some of the properties of a `Message` object. In this case, the `Message` object is a contact item. The first two properties that are accessed are intrinsic properties, and can be accessed directly using the property tag. If the property is an Outlook property, in this case a contact property, you must use the second method by using the property tag and the property set ID. The item that is accessed is the first item that was created in the Contacts folder, not the first item of the current sort order of the folder.

```
Sub CDOPropertyTags()
    Const CdoPR_DISPLAY_NAME = &H3001001E
    Const CdoPR_STREET_ADDRESS = &H3A29001E
    Const CdoPropSetID3 = "0420060000000000C000000000000046"
    Const CdoContact_EmailAddrType = "0x8082"

    Dim oSession As MAPI.session
    Dim oFolder As MAPI.Folder
    Dim oMessage As MAPI.Message
    Dim oFields As MAPI.Fields
    Dim oField As MAPI.Field

    Set oSession = Application.CreateObject("MAPI.Session")
    oSession.Logon "", "", False, False
    'Get the contacts folder
    Set oFolder = oSession.GetDefaultFolder(CdoDefaultFolderContacts)
    'Get the first message of the contacts folder
    'Note that it is still a message object,
    'So the class property will always return a value of CdoMsg
    Set oMessage = oFolder.Messages.GetFirst

    Set oFields = oMessage.Fields

    'Get a single field using the MAPI property tag
    Set oField = oFields.Item(CdoPR_DISPLAY_NAME)
    MsgBox oField
    Set oField = oFields.Item(CdoPR_STREET_ADDRESS)
    MsgBox oField

    Set oField = oFields.Item(CdoContact_EmailAddrType, CdoPropSetID3)
    MsgBox oField

    Set oSession = Nothing
    Set oFolder = Nothing
    Set oMessage = Nothing
    Set oFields = Nothing
    Set oField = Nothing
End Sub
```

This brief introduction into using CDO with Outlook should be considered a jumping-off point for working with CDO. There are many other properties and methods of Outlook items that are not available to the Outlook object model that you can access from CDO.

Summary

In this chapter we looked at some details and oddities of the Outlook object model, and covered using CDO to supplement the things that we can do using only the Outlook object model. Class modules were developed to read and write Windows Registry keys, and to demand installation of CDO if it is not already installed.

7

COM Add-ins

COM add-ins are new to Office 2000, and provide a secure and easy way to develop and distribute your Outlook applications. Since COM add-ins are compiled into .dll or .exe files their code is more secure than VBA code, which is distributed as source code. COM add-ins are usually compiled into .dll files rather than .exe files, because .dll files usually provide better performance. This chapter will only cover developing COM add-ins as .dll files.

Although VBA code can be compiled, and can be locked for viewing with a password (in the Protection tab of the project Properties sheet), the result is less secure than a compiled .dll file. Also, since only one Outlook VBA project can be loaded by Outlook, any changes made to a distributed VBA project will overwrite the previous project. This will destroy any macros or customizations that the user has made. Some workarounds for the VBA project distribution problem have been discussed previously, but COM add-ins do not overwrite the user's customizations and Outlook can load many COM add-ins, with little or no unwanted interaction between them.

COM add-ins for Outlook 2000 can be created and compiled using a number of different development environments; such as Delphi, VC++, VB5, VB6 and Microsoft Office 2000 Developer Edition (MOD). This chapter will cover developing COM add-ins using VB6 and MOD, with a primary focus on VB6. The primary differences in developing COM add-ins using VB5 will be mentioned where they apply.

The COM add-in developed in this chapter was developed using VB6, but the development cycle for developing COM add-ins using MOD is very similar. Both VB6 and MOD provide development features for COM add-ins that are missing in VB5. These include self-registration of the COM add-ins in the Windows Registry, and the provision of Designers.

Designers are special class modules that provide a user interface for setting the properties of COM add-ins along with an intrinsic code module that serves as a repository for the implementation code for the IDTExtensibility2 object library. This object library enables a COM add-in to connect with its host application. The user interface consists of two property pages, General and Advanced. The properties that you set in these two pages provide the data that VB or MOD need to create the add-in and make it self-registers in the Windows Registry when it is installed. This saves a lot of the extra work that is needed when a COM add-in is created in VB5, VC++ or other development languages.

The COM Add-in Project

The COM add-in project created in this chapter is not only a demonstration of how to create a COM add-in for Outlook 2000, but it also answers the need for a feature that is often requested by users. Phone numbers are being changed at ever-increasing frequencies, driven by the explosion of new cell phone, fax and Internet numbers being assigned. There is no way to globally change the numbers in a Contacts folder, except by going through every contact record and changing them manually. The COM add-in presented here addresses that need, and can be modified for more specific requirements. It also serves as an example of how the features that Outlook makes available can be extended by you, the programmer.

The COM add-in, `PhoneChanger`, can globally change country codes, area codes, exchanges and numbers within a Contacts folder. The default formatting characters "(", ")" and "-" can be changed to account for the formatting characters used for phone numbers in different countries. All numbers can be made to have a "+" in front of them, in compliance with the canonical phone number format, recommended for use with the **TAPI** (Telephony API) library. Each phone number sub-field can have an exception list of numbers to restrict the changes.

While this COM add-in utility doesn't address all possible changes that might occur internationally, it can serve as the basis of an even more extended utility. In many cases, it will provide all the functionality you desire. Use it as an example of how you can enhance Outlook 2000 with features that Outlook's developers left out, or implemented in a way you don't like. COM add-ins let you make Outlook 2000 work the way you, or your users, want Outlook to work.

Creating COM Add-ins with Designers

To create a new COM add-in project in VB6, choose File | New Project | Add-in from the list of available projects. If you are using MOD, choose File | New Project | Add-In Project. In both cases, a new project with an Add-in Designer will be created. There is a checkbox at the bottom of the designer's General tab that is used if the add-in is command-line safe and does not put up a user interface. This checkbox will disappear when Outlook is selected as the Application, since it does not apply to Outlook COM add-ins. The user interface of the designer in both VB6 and MOD looks like the following screenshot:

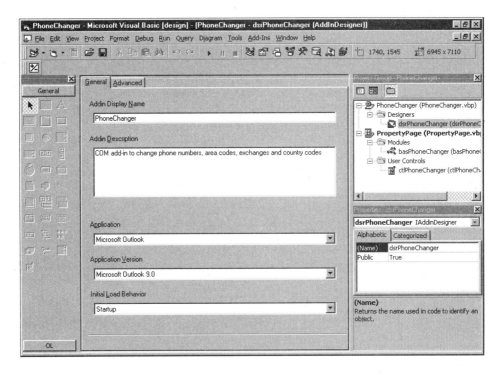

The settings in the General and Advanced tabs create a registry key that is automatically added to the Windows Registry when the COM add-in is installed. If you create the COM add-in using VB5, you must manually create this registry key and move the files to the required locations, or write code that does so.

A COM add-in created in VB5 would be installed with a registry key for the settings shown in the previous screenshot of the user interface presented by the VB6 Designer. The registry key would be similar to the following: [HKEY_CURRENT_USER\Software\Microsoft\Office\Outlook\Addins\PhoneChanger.dsrPhoneChanger]

"CommandLineSafe"=dword:00000000

"Description"="COM add-in to change phone numbers, area codes, exchanges and country codes"

"FriendlyName"="PhoneChanger"

"LoadBehavior"=dword:00000002

LoadBehavior can be set to 0 (None), 2 (Startup), 8 (Load on Demand) or 16 (Load on Next Startup).

The display name and add-in description fields set the name and description that appears in the Property sheet for the COM add-in file. Some Office 2000 applications can share COM add-ins, such as Word and Excel. However, Outlook COM add-ins must be specifically compiled for Outlook only. The application version is always Microsoft Outlook 9.0 in Office 2000. COM add-ins cannot be used with versions of Outlook prior to Outlook 2000.

The initial load behavior selected in the designer's Initial Load Behavior listbox can be set to None, Startup, Load on Demand and Load on Next Startup Only. None will leave the COM add-in unloaded but available for loading in the Tools | Options | Other | Advanced Options | COM add-ins dialog box. Startup is the most commonly used setting – it loads the COM add-in when Outlook starts, as long as the user hasn't disabled the add-in. Load on Demand is used when the add-in is loaded only when called from a menu or toolbar button. Load on Next Startup Only is used to provide initialization for an add-in on its first run. After the first run, the setting is automatically changed to Load on Demand. COM add-ins can also be enabled and disabled in code by using the Boolean `Connect` property of the `COMAddIn` object of the Microsoft Office 9.0 Object library.

The Designer's Advanced tab provides user interface settings for a satellite `.dll` that the COM add-in uses, and an additional registry key for data storage. A satellite `.dll` is one that is automatically loaded by the add-in when the add-in is connected. The initial data values of this registry key can be set in the Add-in Specific Data field. This COM add-in does not use the Windows Registry for data storage, since it has no persistent data. If you do store data in the registry you can use the inherent `GetSetting`, `SaveSetting` and `DeleteSetting` functions to save the data in the default registry location. You can also use the Win32 API registry functions to save the data anywhere in the registry. The `clsRegistryFunctions` class module that we created in Chapter 6 can be included in a COM add-in project and instantiated in the add-in code to support using the registry. The following screenshot shows the Designer's Advanced tab. This tab is identical in a MOD Designer.

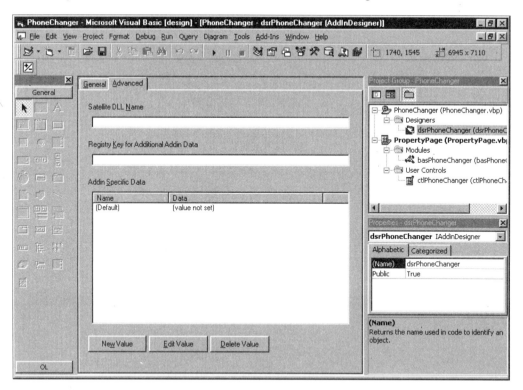

If you do use a class module in your COM add-in project then make sure that you set its `Instancing` property to `PublicNotCreatable` if you are using MOD, or to `PublicNotCreatable` or `MultiUse` if you are using VB6. Otherwise the class will not be visible to the add-in when the COM add-in is run. Procedures within the class would be set to `Friend` or `Public` if you want them to be visible to other modules in the project.

The IDTExtensibility2 Interface

The IDTExtensibility2 Interface is a set of five events that provides functionality for a COM add-in. These events are provided as an interface only – no code is provided for them, only procedure stubs. All five events must be present in the compiled code, or compilation will fail – any events that you don't use in your add-in should have at least a comment line in their procedures, to prevent the compiler from removing them. The following table summarizes the Interface events.

IDTExtensibility2 Event	When It Occurs
OnAddInsUpdate	When any add-in is connected or disconnected in the COMAddIns collection.
OnBeginShutdown	When Outlook begins its shutdown routines, if the add-in is connected.
OnConnection	When the add-in is connected to Outlook.
OnDisconnection	When the add-in is disconnected from Outlook.
OnStartupComplete	When Outlook completes its startup routines. Only if the add-in connects at startup.

Explanations of the arguments for the IDTExtensibility2 events are given when each event is encountered in the add-in sample code.

After the designer is inserted in the project, change the project's name to your desired project name and access the designer's intrinsic code module by right clicking on the designer's property sheet (or the name of the designer in the Project Explorer) and choosing **View Code**.

Make sure that the references for the project include Microsoft Add-In Designer, Microsoft Outlook 9.0 Object Library and Microsoft Office 9.0 Object Library. If your COM add-in uses objects from any other object libraries, make sure that you set references to those object libraries in your project. In VB6, references are set by choosing **Project | References**. In VBA, select **Tools | References**.

There are two schools of thought about where to place the supporting code for the COM add-in. You can place only the required event handling code in the Designer's code module, and create a class module to provide the `InitHandler` and `UnInitHandler` procedures and any other implementation code. This has the advantage of separating the supporting code and the implementation code, which may make for easier code maintenance and more standardization amongst any further COM add-ins you develop. If you follow this methodology, make sure that the supporting class is instanced as `PublicNotCreatable` or `MultiUse` so that it is visible to the Designer at run-time. The other possibility is to place all the code in the Designer's code module – this is the method followed in this project, having the advantage of simplicity and a minimum number of components in the add-in project.

The following general section of the Designer's code module declares the implementation of IDTExtensibility2, and declares module-level variables for the Outlook events to which the project responds. Notice that these event variables are declared WithEvents to enable the add-in to handle Outlook events. You can declare variables for any Outlook events to which your project needs to respond.

```
Option Explicit
'Outlook COM add-ins require references to the
'following object libraries:
'Microsoft Add-In Designer
'Microsoft Outlook 9.0 Object Library
'Microsoft Office 9.0 Object Library
'Add other references as required for your COM add-in.

'IDTExtensibility2 is the implementation
'interface required for COM Add-ins.
Implements IDTExtensibility2

'Module-level object variables for Event procedures.
Private WithEvents moOL As Outlook.Application
Private WithEvents moNS As Outlook.NameSpace
Private WithEvents moActiveExplorer As Outlook.Explorer

'Use msProgID to set the OnAction property of CommandBar buttons.
'CommandBar buttons are normally responded to using
'a variable declared WithEvents to respond to the Click
'event of the button. If Outlook was started from
'SendTo Mail Recipient then the button click event may not fire.
'In that case, the OnAction property of the button is used.
Private msProgID As String
```

This project does not create any toolbar or menu buttons, all the settings and activation for the add-in are performed from a custom Property Page. If you do need to create toolbar or menu buttons, the procedure is the same as the procedure shown in the basMenus module in Chapter 3.

If your add-in creates menu or toolbar buttons, the Click events of the buttons are normally used to respond to the user pressing the buttons. However, when Outlook is started from the Send To Mail Recipient action it is opened with no active Explorer windows, only an Inspector window. In those cases the button's Click event may not fire. The workaround for this is to use a module-level declaration similar to Private msProgID As String to make the unique ProgramID for the add-in available to the OnAction property of the button. The required syntax for the OnAction property setting is OnAction = "<!" & msProgID & ">".

The OnAddInsUpdate event occurs when the set of loaded COM add-ins in Outlook changes. When any add-in is loaded or unloaded, this event occurs in all the other loaded add-ins. The custom Variant array is empty, and is ignored by Office 2000 COM add-ins. If your COM add-in depends on another add-in being loaded (or unloaded), use this event in conjunction with the Application.COMAddIns property, which returns a collection of the loaded COMAddIn objects. This collection can be checked to see whether any necessary dependencies are satisfied.

```
Private Sub IDTExtensibility2_OnAddInsUpdate(custom() As Variant)
'All of the implementation procedures must have a
'comment or code to not be removed by the compiler.
'All implementation procedures must be present to
'compile without errors.
End Sub
```

The `OnBeginShutdown` event occurs when Outlook begins its shutdown routines, when Outlook closes while the COM add-in is still loaded. If the add-in is not loaded when Outlook closes, the event does not occur. The `custom Variant` array is empty and is ignored in Office 2000 COM add-ins. This event occurs before the `OnDisconnection` event. Outlook's objects won't have been destroyed when this event occurs, so it is a good place to put code that saves data contained inside them.

```
Private Sub IDTExtensibility2_OnBeginShutdown(custom() As Variant)
'All of the implementation procedures must have a
'comment or code to not be removed by the compiler.
'All implementation procedures must be present to
'compile without errors.
End Sub
```

The `OnConnection` event occurs when the add-in is loaded. This event is where any initialization code (or calls to initialization procedures) is placed. The `custom Variant` array provides additional data about how Outlook was started. The first element of the array provides a numeric value indicating how Outlook was started. If the value is 1, Outlook was started from the user interface. If the value is 2, it was started by embedding an Outlook item in another application. If the value is 3, Outlook was started by automation.

The name of the host application is provided, though since Outlook COM add-ins cannot be shared with other Office 2000 applications, the name is always "Outlook". The `ConnectMode` argument provides a value for which connect mode caused the add-in to load. Only two connect modes are valid for Office 2000 applications, `ext_cm_Startup` and `ext_cm_AfterStartup`. A connection mode of `ext_cm_Startup` indicates that the add-in was loaded at Outlook's startup. A connection mode of `ext_cm_AfterStartup` indicates that the add-in was loaded after startup or in code, by setting the add-in's `Connect` property to True. The `AddInInst` argument provides a `ProgId` property that provides the add-in's unique ProgramID. This property was mentioned previously in the discussion of adding toolbar and menu buttons.

```
Private Sub IDTExtensibility2_OnConnection(ByVal Application As Object, _
   ByVal ConnectMode As AddInDesignerObjects.ext_ConnectMode, _
   ByVal AddInInst As Object, custom() As Variant)
   On Error Resume Next
   'Evaluate ConnectMode if required here.
   Select Case ConnectMode
     Case ext_cm_Startup
     Case ext_cm_AfterStartup
     Case ext_cm_CommandLine 'Not used in Office 2000 COM add-ins
     Case ext_cm_External 'Not used in Office 2000 COM add-ins
   End Select
```

```
        'You can also place the InitHandler procedure in a separate
        'class module to separate the implementation and
        'interface portions of the COM add-in. That can
        'help in maintenance.
        Call InitHandler(Application, AddInInst.ProgId)
    End Sub
```

The OnDisconnection event occurs when the COM add-in is unloaded. This event is usually used to clean up any objects created by the add-in, and to restore Outlook's state to what it was before the add-in was connected. Make sure that you destroy any objects that the add-in created. Failing to do so can cause Outlook to fail to shut down and can cause memory and resource leaks. The OnDisconnection event will not fire when the disconnect mode is ext_dm_HostShutdown. It only fires when the disconnect mode is ext_dm_UserClosed, when the user disables the COM add-in or the Connect property is set to False. The custom Variant array provides the same information as in the OnConnection event.

```
    Private Sub IDTExtensibility2_OnDisconnection(ByVal RemoveMode As _
        AddInDesignerObjects.ext_DisconnectMode, custom() As Variant)
        On Error Resume Next
        'This event will not fire when
        'RemoveMode = ext_dm_HostShutdown.
        'It will fire when RemoveMode = ext_dm_UserClosed
        If RemoveMode = ext_dm_UserClosed Then
            'If UserClosed, then remove any added buttons.
        End If

        'You can also place the UnInitHandler procedure in a separate
        'class module to separate the implementation and
        'interface portions of the COM add-in. That can
        'help in maintenance.
        Call UnInitHandler
    End Sub
```

The OnStartupComplete event occurs after Outlook completes its startup routines. All Outlook objects and interface components are available when this event fires. If you need to interact with the user when Outlook starts, place your code for that in this procedure. The custom Variant array is empty and is ignored in Office 2000 COM add-ins.

```
    Private Sub IDTExtensibility2_OnStartupComplete(custom() As Variant)
    'All of the implementation procedures must have a
    'comment or code to not be removed by the compiler.
    'All implementation procedures must be present to
    'compile without errors.
    End Sub
```

The code for the InitHandler procedure can be placed in the designer class, or it can be placed in a separate class module. In this case the code is placed in the same module as the designer. The InitHandler procedure instantiates object variables that were declared WithEvents, and assigns the ProgramID to a module-level variable. Try to keep the amount of code that is run directly or indirectly from the OnConnection event to a minimum, since your COM add-in may not be the only one loaded in Outlook. Large amounts of code in the OnConnection event can lead to Outlook's starting slowly.

```
'This procedure may be placed in a separate Class module
'that is instanced as multiuse to separate the implementation
'code from other procedures. Such procedures should be declared
'as Friend to limit their visibility to the project.
Private Sub InitHandler(oApp As Outlook.Application, sProgID As String)
  On Error Resume Next
  'Declared WithEvents
  Set moOL = oApp
  Set moNS = oApp.GetNamespace("MAPI")
  Set moActiveExplorer = moOL.ActiveExplorer

  'Instantiate a public global-level Outlook application variable.
  'Use the ProgID when you add toolbars and buttons.
  'Even if a button click event is handled by an event
  'handler, it will not fire if Outlook is opened
  'from SendTo Mail Recipient. The ProgID is used for the OnAction
  'property of the button.
  msProgID = sProgID
End Sub
```

The code in the following `UnInitHandler` procedure dereferences all the global and module-level objects that are declared in the COM add-in. You should handle all errors that occur in the COM add-in, either with error handling routines or by using the `On Error Resume Next` statement. Unhandled errors in your COM add-in will cause the add-in to terminate and may cause problems with the error stack.

```
'This procedure may be placed in a separate Class module
'that is instanced as multiuse to separate the implementation
'code from other procedures. Such procedures should be declared
'as Friend to limit their visibility to the project.
Private Sub UnInitHandler()
  'You must dereference all objects in this procedure
  'or Outlook will remain in memory
  On Error Resume Next
  Set moActiveExplorer = Nothing
  Set moNS = Nothing
  Set moOL = Nothing
End Sub
```

In certain cases the `OnDisconnection` event may not fire. You can trap these cases by utilizing the `Close` event for the `ActiveExplorer` object. If one (or fewer) Explorer objects remains when the `Close` event fires, you should process the event in the same way as you would process the `OnDisconnection` event. This is normally done by calling the `UnInitHandler` procedure.

```
'Due to MAPI issues, OnDisconnection might not fire during Outlook shutdown.
'Call UnInitHandler in moActiveExplorer_Close event.
Private Sub moActiveExplorer_Close()
  On Error Resume Next
  'If 1 or fewer Explorer windows are present
  'then the close event indicates Outlook shutdown.
  If moOL.Explorers.Count <= 1 Then
      Call UnInitHandler
  End If
End Sub
```

Adding Custom Property Pages

Custom Property Pages are one way to display the data and settings for your COM add-in. The **Apply** or **OK** buttons on the Properties sheet can be one way to initiate the actions that the add-in performs. You can also display a VB form or a VBA UserForm instead of a Property Page. This COM add-in doesn't use any persistent data storage for its settings, so no use is made of the Windows Registry or of `.ini` files for data storage.

> *One thing to keep in mind when you utilize Property Pages is that when more than one add-in responds to the* `OptionsPagesAdd` *event, there is no way to guarantee which add-in will handle the event first. The order in which Pages are added to the collection is also not guaranteed.*

You can display a Property Page that is constructed from a form object, but the preferred method is to create an ActiveX control that serves as the Property Page. That is the method that is used in this chapter. Custom Property Pages can be displayed in the **Options** dialog box of the **Tools** menu, or can reside in the Properties sheets for each folder, or both. Analyze your add-in's requirements to see which place is the most logical place to display your Property Page.

The `NameSpace` level `OptionsPagesAdd` event is used to add pages to the Properties sheet for individual Outlook folders. The folder Properties dialog box is activated by right-clicking on a folder in the Folder List (or the Outlook Bar) and choosing **Properties** in the context menu. In the `OptionsPagesAdd` event handler for our COM add-in, the page is added only when the newly active folder is a Contacts type folder. You can use any tests you wish to define a complex tree of Property Pages activate, according to the current Outlook state. The first argument of the `Pages.Add` method is the name of the page, and the second argument is the title of the new tab in the Properties sheet.

```
Private Sub moNS_OptionsPagesAdd(ByVal Pages As PropertyPages, _
   ByVal Folder As MAPIFolder)
   On Error Resume Next
   'For all contact folders load the custom Property Page.
   If Folder.DefaultItemType = olContactItem Then
      Pages.Add "PropertyPage.ctlPhoneChanger", "Wrox Phone Number Changer"
   End If
End Sub
```

Code that adds a Property Page in the `Application` level `OptionsPagesAdd` event will add a new tab to the Options dialog box in the Tools menu. This type of page is usually added for application wide settings. These settings can be kept in the Windows Registry and loaded quickly into the page when it becomes active. The method of adding this type of page, and for responding to changes in its controls, is exactly the same as for folder-specific pages, except that no folder argument is passed to the event handler.

```
Private Sub moOL_OptionsPagesAdd(ByVal Pages As PropertyPages)
'If a Property Page is being added to the Options dialog box
'in the Tools menu then the Pages.Add code goes here.
End Sub
```

ActiveX Controls as Property Pages

Property Pages can be ActiveX controls, standalone `.exe` files, in-process `DLLs` or VBA programs. In this chapter we will implement the Property Page as an ActiveX control. This control is designed in VB6 and looks like the following screenshot.

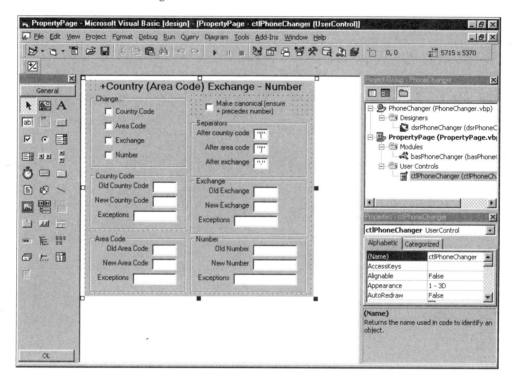

To design this control, choose File | Add Project | ActiveX control to add a control project to the COM add-in project. Name the control `ctlPhoneChanger`. Save the ActiveX control project as `ctlPhoneChanger.ctl`. Choose File | Save Project Group As to save both projects as a group. Name the group `PhoneChanger.vbg`. Having related projects saved in a group enables you to load all the projects in the group in one operation and to keep the projects open together to enable working on all elements of the group. It will also make it easier later when it comes time to deploy the COM add-in to produce one package for deployment.

> *Property Pages can be resized by Outlook when they are opened. If the size of the design is too large, some of the controls on your form may be clipped from view, and thus unavailable. Two of the many possible solutions are to place code that dynamically resizes the controls in the UserControl_Initialize event (based on the run-time size of the Page), or to restrict the form height to less than 5400 Twips.*

Insert six frame controls in the form. Arrange them as shown in the previous screenshot. Place four checkbox controls in the first frame, name and caption them as shown in the following table. We will make extensive use of ToolTips in the controls in this form to provide help text when the user hovers the mouse pointer over the controls, so add `ToolTipText` help information for each control. Set the `Width` of each control to 1575 Twips and the `Height` to 375 Twips:

Name	Caption	ToolTipText
chkCountry	Country	Change the country code
chkArea	Area Code	Change the area code
chkExchange	Exchange	Change the exchange
chkNumber	Number	Change the number

Add three textbox controls to each of the remaining frame controls and add corresponding label controls for each textbox control. Use the following settings for the textbox controls:

Name	Label Caption	ToolTipText	Height	Width
txtOldCountry	Old Country	Country code to be changed	285	615
txtNewCountry	New Country	Replacement country code	285	615
txtCountry Exceptions	Exceptions	Enter exceptions separated by commas	285	1095
txtOldArea	Old Area Code	Area code to be changed	285	615
txtNewArea	New Area Code	Replacement area code	285	615
txtArea Exceptions	Exceptions	Enter exceptions separated by commas	285	1095
txtSeparator1	After country code	Enter character surrounded by quotes	285	375
txtSeparator2	After area code	Enter character surrounded by quotes	285	375
txtSeparator3	After exchange	Enter character surrounded by quotes	285	375
txtOldExchange	Old Exchange	Exchange to be changed	285	615
txtNewExchange	New Exchange	Replacement exchange	285	615
txtExchange Exceptions	Exceptions	Enter exceptions separated by commas	285	1095

Name	Label Caption	ToolTipText	Height	Width
txtOldNumber	Old Number	Number to be changed	285	1100
txtNewNumber	New Number	Replacement number	285	1100
txtNumber Exceptions	Exceptions	Enter exceptions separated by commas	285	1575

Set MultiLine to True for all four Exceptions textboxes. Set the alignment for the Separator textboxes to Center. Add one final checkbox above the separators e and name it chkCanonical, caption it 'Make canonical (ensure + precedes number)', and set its height to 375 Twips and its width to 2055 Twips. Add a label to the top of the control, caption it '+Country (Area Code) Exchange – Number', and set its font to Bold 12. The resulting form should look like the previous screenshot.

To function as a Property Page, the control must implement the Outlook.PropertyPage interface. This interface provides three procedures: PropertyPage_Apply, PropertyPage_GetPageInfo, and PropertyPage_Dirty (which is a Property Get procedure). All three procedures must be present in your control to avoid compiler errors. PropertyPage_GetPageInfo is used to provide a help file for the Property Page. This example does not have a separate help file – all help information is provided by the ToolTipText help.

The module-level declarations listed below declare the Outlook.PropertyPage implementation, declare Boolean variables to track whether the form is dirty, and declare a PropertyPageSite object that is used to notify Outlook that the page is dirty. This notification is what enables the Apply and OK command buttons on the Property sheet.

Note that when you declare the Outlook.PropertyPage implementation, the PropertyPage implementation procedures are automatically inserted in the module.

```
'******************************************
'This module provides the code for the ActiveX
'control that is used as a custom Property
'Page for Outlook Contacts folders.
'******************************************
'The control should be less than 5400 Twips
'in Height to avoid clipping it in the
'Property Pages Sheet.
'******************************************
Option Explicit

'Required declaration for Property Pages
Implements Outlook.PropertyPage

'Module-level flag for a dirty property page
Private mblnDirty As Boolean
'Module-level flag used when loading fields
'in code.
Private mblnLoadField As Boolean

'Variable set to Parent and used with the
'OnStatusChange method to notify Outlook
'that the page has changed.
Dim oSite As Outlook.PropertyPageSite
```

The `PropertyPage_Apply` event is called when the user presses the **Apply** or **OK** command buttons. It copies the information from the controls on the form to global variables that are used by the code module to process the phone numbers. It then calls the `ChangeNumbers` procedure, located in the `basPhoneChanger` module. When execution of the event handler resumes, the `UserControl_InitProperties` procedure is called, to reinitialize the controls for another use of the Property Page.

```
Private Sub PropertyPage_Apply()
   'This is called when the user presses the Apply
   'or OK buttons.
   On Error Resume Next
   gblnCanonical = chkCanonical 'make canonical

   'change country code
   gblnCountry = chkCountry
   gsOldCountry = txtOldCountry.Text
   gsNewCountry = txtNewCountry.Text
   gsCountryExceptions = txtCountryExceptions.Text

   'change area code
   gblnCode = chkArea
   gsOldCode = txtOldArea.Text
   gsNewCode = txtNewArea.Text
   gsCodeExceptions = txtAreaExceptions.Text

   'change exchange
   gblnExchange = chkExchange
   gsOldExchange = txtOldExchange.Text
   gsNewExchange = txtNewExchange.Text
   gsExchangeExceptions = txtExchangeExceptions.Text


   'change number
   gblnNumber = chkNumber
   gsOldNumber = txtOldNumber.Text
   gsNewNumber = txtNewNumber.Text
   gsNumberExceptions = txtNumberExceptions.Text

   'Use these separators
   'Separator #1
   If Left(txtSeparator1, 1) = Chr(34) And _
   Right(txtSeparator1, 1) = Chr(34) Then
      gsSeparator1 = Mid(txtSeparator1, 2, 1)
   End If

   'Separator #2
   If Left(txtSeparator2, 1) = Chr(34) And _
   Right(txtSeparator2, 1) = Chr(34) Then
      gsSeparator2 = Mid(txtSeparator2, 2, 1)
   End If

   'Separator #3
   If Left(txtSeparator3, 1) = Chr(34) And _
   Right(txtSeparator3, 1) = Chr(34) Then
```

```
        gsSeparator3 = Mid(txtSeparator3, 2, 1)
    End If

    'This is located in the basPhoneChanger code module.
    Call ChangeNumbers

    'Now reset the page to the initial state.
    Call UserControl_InitProperties
End Sub
```

The `PropertyPage_Dirty Property Get` procedure sets the dirty property of the page. This is set from the module-level Boolean variable that is updated when the `Change` event fires for any of the textbox controls on the form. Since the intializations of the textboxes will cause these events to fire, there is an interlocking set of semaphore flags that are used to tell whether the events fired due to the controls being changed by the user or by code. When the `OnStatusChange` method of the `PropertyPageSite` object is called Outlook reads the `Dirty` property to determine whether to enable the **Apply** and **OK** command buttons.

```
Private Property Get PropertyPage_Dirty() As Boolean
    On Error Resume Next
    'mirror the state of the module-level flag.
    'If True then the Apply button is enabled.
    PropertyPage_Dirty = mblnDirty
End Property
```

The `GetPageInfo` event is not used to provide a help file for this COM add-in, but it must be present to enable the control to compile without errors. Any procedure that is not used for an implementation you are providing must still be present in your code. To prevent such procedures from being removed from the code by the compiler, place comment lines in the unused procedures.

```
Private Sub PropertyPage_GetPageInfo(HelpFile As String, HelpContext As Long)
'If you provide Help for the Property Page it goes here.
'All of the implementation procedures must have a
'comment or code to not be removed by the compiler.
'All implementation procedures must be present to
'compile without errors.
End Sub
```

The `Click` events for the checkboxes are used to enable and disable the textboxes in the related frames. The module-level Boolean variable `mblnLoadField` is used to notify the `Change` events for the controls that the changes are being made by code and that the Apply and OK command buttons should not be enabled.

When a sub-field of the number is enabled for changing, the textboxes for the old and new contents of the sub-field are enabled in the appropriate `Click` event. The Exceptions textbox for that sub-field is then disabled. This is done so that the exceptions list only applies when that particular sub-field is not being changed. (Since only one value in the sub-field is being changed at a time it would make no sense to have exceptions to that value.)

Once the updating of the controls is finished, the `mblnLoadField` flag is reset to enable the user to make changes and have the page be marked as dirty.

The following procedure is the `Click` event for the **Area Code** checkbox.

```
Private Sub chkArea_Click()
  On Error Resume Next
  mblnLoadField = True

  If (chkArea.Value) Then
    'Enable the text and label fields.
    'Since area code is enabled, disable
    'exceptions for area codes.
    lblOldArea.Enabled = True
    lblNewArea.Enabled = True
    txtOldArea.Enabled = True
    txtNewArea.Enabled = True
    lblAreaExceptions.Enabled = False
    txtAreaExceptions.Enabled = False
  Else
    'Disable the text and label fields.
    'Since area code is disabled, enable
    'exceptions for area codes.
    lblOldArea.Enabled = False
    lblNewArea.Enabled = False
    txtOldArea.Enabled = False
    txtOldArea.Text = ""
    txtNewArea.Enabled = False
    txtNewArea.Text = ""
    lblAreaExceptions.Enabled = True
    txtAreaExceptions.Enabled = True
  End If

  mblnLoadField = False
End Sub
```

The following procedure is the `Click` event for the **Country Code** checkbox.

```
Private Sub chkCountry_Click()
  On Error Resume Next
  mblnLoadField = True

  If (chkCountry.Value) Then
    'Enable the text and label fields.
    'Since country is enabled, disable
    'exceptions for country codes.
    lblOldCountry.Enabled = True
    lblNewCountry.Enabled = True
    txtOldCountry.Enabled = True
    txtNewCountry.Enabled = True
    lblCountryExceptions.Enabled = False
    txtCountryExceptions.Enabled = False
  Else
```

```
                    'Disable the text and label fields.
                    'Since country is disabled, enable
                    'exceptions for country codes.
                    lblOldCountry.Enabled = False
                    lblNewCountry.Enabled = False
                    txtOldCountry.Enabled = False
                    txtOldCountry.Text = ""
                    txtNewCountry.Enabled = False
                    txtNewCountry.Text = ""
                    lblCountryExceptions.Enabled = True
                    txtCountryExceptions.Enabled = True
                End If

            mblnLoadField = False
        End Sub
```

The following procedure is the `Click` event for the **Exchange** checkbox.

```
        Private Sub chkExchange_Click()
            On Error Resume Next
            mblnLoadField = True

            If (chkExchange.Value) Then
                'Enable the text and label fields.
                'Since exchange is enabled, disable
                'exceptions for exchanges.
                lblOldExchange.Enabled = True
                lblNewExchange.Enabled = True
                txtOldExchange.Enabled = True
                txtNewExchange.Enabled = True
                lblExchangeExceptions.Enabled = False
                txtExchangeExceptions.Enabled = False
            Else
                'Disable the text and label fields.
                'Since exchange is disabled, enable
                'exceptions for exchanges.
                lblOldExchange.Enabled = False
                lblNewExchange.Enabled = False
                txtOldExchange.Enabled = False
                txtOldExchange.Text = ""
                txtNewExchange.Enabled = False
                txtNewExchange.Text = ""
                lblExchangeExceptions.Enabled = True
                txtExchangeExceptions.Enabled = True
            End If

            mblnLoadField = False
        End Sub
```

The following procedure is the `Click` event for the **Number** checkbox.

```
Private Sub chkNumber_Click()
  On Error Resume Next
  mblnLoadField = True

  If (chkNumber.Value) Then
      'Enable the text and label fields.
      'Since number is enabled, disable
      'exceptions for numbers.
      lblOldNumber.Enabled = True
      lblNewNumber.Enabled = True
      txtOldNumber.Enabled = True
      txtNewNumber.Enabled = True
      lblNumberExceptions.Enabled = False
      txtNumberExceptions.Enabled = False
  Else
      'Disable the text and label fields.
      'Since number is disabled, enable
      'exceptions for numbers.
      lblOldNumber.Enabled = False
      lblNewNumber.Enabled = False
      txtOldNumber.Enabled = False
      txtOldNumber.Text = ""
      txtNewNumber.Enabled = False
      txtNewNumber.Text = ""
      lblNumberExceptions.Enabled = True
      txtNumberExceptions.Enabled = True
  End If

  mblnLoadField = False
End Sub
```

All the `Change` events for the controls call the `CheckForDirty` procedure to determine if the changes were made in-code or by the user. Change events are not processed for the checkboxes or by the **Separator** textboxes, enabling the user to change configuration settings for the page without enabling the **Apply** and **OK** command buttons.

The default separators are the correct separators for phone number fields for the United States. They can be changed to reflect the separators used for phone numbers in other countries. No size is used to determine where each sub-field begins and ends, since the sizes of each of these sub-fields may vary from country to country. Some of the sub-fields may not be present in phone numbers for other countries, and the sizes may vary even within a country. The sub-field sizes may also be altered within countries as the demand for new numbers continues to grow. The add-in was written to be as flexible as possible for a working example that is not meant to be a comprehensive, universal solution or commercial application.

```
'The next set of procedures check whether
'the field is dirty (changed by the user) or
'was changed in code (not dirty).
Private Sub txtCodeExceptions_Change()
  Call CheckForDirty
End Sub
```

```
    Private Sub txtCountryExceptions_Change()
      Call CheckForDirty
    End Sub

    Private Sub txtExchangeExceptions_Change()
      Call CheckForDirty
    End Sub

    Private Sub txtNewArea_Change()
      Call CheckForDirty
    End Sub

    Private Sub txtNewCountry_Change()
      Call CheckForDirty
    End Sub

    Private Sub txtNewExchange_Change()
      Call CheckForDirty
    End Sub

    Private Sub txtNewNumber_Change()
      Call CheckForDirty
    End Sub

    Private Sub txtNumberExceptions_Change()
      Call CheckForDirty
    End Sub

    Private Sub txtOldArea_Change()
      Call CheckForDirty
    End Sub

    Private Sub txtOldCountry_Change()
      Call CheckForDirty
    End Sub

    Private Sub txtOldExchange_Change()
      Call CheckForDirty
    End Sub

    Private Sub txtOldNumber_Change()
      Call CheckForDirty
    End Sub
```

When any control is being initialized or changed in code, the mblnLoadField flag is set. This flag is cleared once the procedure changing the control has finished its changes. It tells the CheckForDirty procedure not to call SetDirtyFlag when set as True. If it is False, the SetDirtyFlag procedure first checks that the PropertyPageSite object variable is set properly, and then sets the module-level dirty flag if PropertyPageSite is not Nothing. The OnStatusChange method of the PropertyPageSite object is called, to alert Outlook that the page has changed and that the Apply and OK buttons should be enabled.

```
Private Sub CheckForDirty()
  'If loading data then do not set dirty
  On Error Resume Next
  If (mblnLoadField = True) Then
    Exit Sub
  Else
    'Not loading data so dirty = True
    SetDirtyFlag
  End If
End Sub

Private Sub SetDirtyFlag()
  On Error Resume Next
  'Check for Parent = Nothing
  If Not oSite Is Nothing Then
    If (mblnLoadField) Then
      Exit Sub
    Else
      'Set the module-level dirty flag.
      mblnDirty = True
      'Notify Outlook that the page has changed
      oSite.OnStatusChange
    End If
  End If
End Sub
```

The UserControl_Initialize and InitProperties events are used to initialize the controls to their default states (which for all textboxes is a null string). The mblnLoadField flag is used to signal that the control changes are being done in-code, rather than by the user. The PropertyPageSite object is instantiated to the name of the ActiveX control, which is the container object for the PropertyPage object.

```
Private Sub UserControl_Initialize()
  On Error Resume Next
  mblnDirty = False
End Sub

Private Sub UserControl_InitProperties()
  'Use this procedure for all property initializations.
  On Error Resume Next
  'Init the PropertyPageSite variable
  Set oSite = Parent

  mblnDirty = False

  'Set the change flags to False
  gblnCanonical = False
  gblnCountry = False
  gblnCode = False
  gblnExchange = False
  gblnNumber = False
```

```
            'This prevents the Apply button from
            'being activated while initializing data.
            mblnLoadField = True

            'Set the default number part separators.
            'These default to the U.S. separators -
            ' "(", ")", and "-" to make a number like
            '(555)111-9999
            txtSeparator1.Text = Chr(34) & "(" & Chr(34)
            txtSeparator2.Text = Chr(34) & ")" & Chr(34)
            txtSeparator3.Text = Chr(34) & "-" & Chr(34)
            gsSeparator1 = "("
            gsSeparator2 = ")"
            gsSeparator3 = "-"

            'Set all the textbox fields to vbNullString
            txtOldCountry.Text = ""
            txtNewCountry.Text = ""
            txtCountryExceptions.Text = ""

            txtOldExchange.Text = ""
            txtNewExchange.Text = ""
            txtExchangeExceptions.Text = ""

            txtOldArea.Text = ""
            txtNewArea.Text = ""
            txtAreaExceptions.Text = ""

            txtOldNumber.Text = ""
            txtNewNumber.Text = ""
            txtNumberExceptions.Text = ""

            'Enable all the Exceptions textboxes
            txtCountryExceptions.Enabled = True
            lblCountryExceptions.Enabled = True

            txtAreaExceptions.Enabled = True
            lblAreaExceptions.Enabled = True

            txtExchangeExceptions.Enabled = True
            lblExchangeExceptions.Enabled = True

            txtNumberExceptions.Enabled = True
            lblNumberExceptions.Enabled = True

            'Disable all the other textboxes
            'until the checkboxes are enabled.
            txtOldCountry.Enabled = False
            txtNewCountry.Enabled = False
            lblOldCountry.Enabled = False
            lblNewCountry.Enabled = False
```

```
            txtOldArea.Enabled = False
            txtNewArea.Enabled = False
            lblOldArea.Enabled = False
            lblNewArea.Enabled = False

            txtOldExchange.Enabled = False
            txtNewExchange.Enabled = False
            lblOldExchange.Enabled = False
            lblNewExchange.Enabled = False

            txtOldNumber.Enabled = False
            txtNewNumber.Enabled = False
            lblOldNumber.Enabled = False
            lblNewNumber.Enabled = False

            'Clear checkboxes
            chkNumber.Value = False
            chkExchange.Value = False
            chkCountry.Value = False
            chkArea.Value = False

            mblnLoadField = False
        End Sub
```

The `Terminate` event for the control is used to clean up any changes made by the control, and to dereference any objects that it declared. You can also use this event handler to write any persistent data storage objects to the Windows Registry or to an `.ini` file.

```
        Private Sub UserControl_Terminate()
        'Any code you need at the control termination
        'goes here.
          'clean up the module-level object variable.
          Set oSite = Nothing
        End Sub
```

The basPhoneChanger Module

The basPhoneChanger module is used as a repository for the code that performs the actual changes to the Outlook Contact items. The global variables declared here are used for inter-process communication between the code module and the ActiveX control. Module-level string arrays are also declared to hold the exception elements for the phone number sub-fields.

The use of global variables in COM add-ins does not produce many of the problems that globals in a standard Outlook project can. Each instance of a COM add-in will have its own pool of globals, so there is no interaction between instances of a COM add-in. Additionally, globals in a COM add-in are not visible outside of the COM add-in, so they cannot interact with code outside the COM add-in. An alternate method of inter-process communication is the use of properties of a class module to replace the use of global variables.

```
'Global variables for the data from
'the fields in the ActiveX control that
'provides the custom Property Page.

'Flags for changing parts of the number
Public gblnCanonical As Boolean
Public gblnCountry As Boolean
Public gblnCode As Boolean
Public gblnExchange As Boolean
Public gblnNumber As Boolean

'Strings for Country codes
Public gsOldCountry As String
Public gsNewCountry As String
Public gsCountryExceptions As String

'Strings for Area codes
Public gsOldCode As String
Public gsNewCode As String
Public gsCodeExceptions As String

'Strings for exchanges
Public gsOldExchange As String
Public gsNewExchange As String
Public gsExchangeExceptions As String

'Strings for the number part
Public gsOldNumber As String
Public gsNewNumber As String
Public gsNumberExceptions As String

'Strings to hold the separators of the parts
Public gsSeparator1 As String
Public gsSeparator2 As String
Public gsSeparator3 As String

'String arrays to hold the separated exceptions.
'These are used only in this module so are Private.
Private msCodeExceptions() As String
Private msCountryExceptions() As String
Private msNumberExceptions() As String
Private msExchangeExceptions() As String
```

This general error handler procedure displays the number and description of any error that occurs in the `ChangeNumbers` procedure. No errors should be left unhandled in any COM add-in, so error handling is highly recommended, even if it is only a message about the error, or an `On Error Resume Next` statement. Your applications may require more complex error handlers with logic to take different actions based on the error number and application state, but this is a working example and is not meant to be comprehensive.

```
Private Sub AddInErr(oErr As ErrObject)
    'Display a message box with error information.
    Dim sMsg As String

    sMsg = "An error occurred " & vbCrLf & "Error #:" & oErr.Number _
        & vbCrLf & oErr.Description
    MsgBox sMsg, vbCritical, "Error!"
End Sub
```

The ChangeNumbers procedure instantiates an Outlook Application object and verifies that the current folder is a Contacts folder. Since this code is only called from Property Pages for Contacts folders, this test can be omitted, but is provided nevertheless (serving as it does as a double-check to prevent run-time errors).

```
Public Sub ChangeNumbers()
    Dim oApp As Outlook.Application
    Dim oContact As Outlook.ContactItem
    Dim oItems As Outlook.Items
    Dim oCurrentFolder As Outlook.MAPIFolder
    Dim oItem As Object
    Dim sNewNum As String
    Dim Flag As Boolean
    Dim lCount As Long

    'All errors should be handled in some way or
    'other in a COM add-in. Unhandled errors can
    'cause all kinds of problems.
    On Error GoTo ChangeNumbersError

    'Instantiate an Outlook object and get the current folder.
    Set oApp = GetObject(, "Outlook.Application")
    Set oCurrentFolder = oApp.ActiveExplorer.CurrentFolder

    'This should only be called when a Contacts folder
    'is the current folder, but double-checking is a good idea.
    If oCurrentFolder.DefaultItemType <> olContactItem Then
        MsgBox "This is not a Contacts folder", vbOKOnly, "Wrox"
        Exit Sub
    End If
```

Additionally, each item in the folder is checked to verify that it is a Contact item. Since a Contacts folder can hold Distribution Lists, this test is required. If this code were to be placed in the COM add-in rather than in the ActiveX control the instantiation of the Outlook Application object could be avoided by using the Application object that is passed to the COM add-in in the OnConnection event procedure for the COM add-in.

The Split function is used to break the four exception lists into separate string variables and assign them to arrays for each type of exception. A comma is used as the delimiting character for the Split function. Each of the possible phone number type properties for a Contact item are checked to see if they need to be changed. One of the difficulties in dealing with Outlook properties is that there is no way to use an index variable to iterate through the properties. Each property must be explicitly loaded and tested by name.

```
'Use Split to break the exceptions lists into arrays.
msCodeExceptions = Split(gsCodeExceptions, ",", -1, vbTextCompare)
msCountryExceptions = Split(gsCountryExceptions, ",", -1, vbTextCompare)
msNumberExceptions = Split(gsNumberExceptions, ",", -1, vbTextCompare)
msExchangeExceptions = Split(gsExchangeExceptions, ",", -1, vbTextCompare)

lCount = 0 'init count of changed items

Set oItems = oCurrentFolder.Items
For Each oItem In oItems
   'It could be a DistributionList item,
   'so it cannot be assigned directly to ContactItem.
   If oItem.Class = olContact Then
     Set oContact = oItem

     'Set the flag to False for each pass
     Flag = False
```

The `ChangeCodes` procedure changes the argument passed to it. The default method of passing arguments in VB and VBA is `ByRef`, meaning that the address of the argument is passed to the called procedure. This enables the called procedure to access and change the original argument.

The default method of passing arguments in VBScript is `ByVal`, meaning that only the argument's value is passed to the called procedure. Arguments passed `ByVal` cannot be changed in the called procedure, since it only has access to a copy of the argument. I make it a practice to note in a comment when one or more arguments are changed in the body of the procedure, and to explicitly declare that argument as being passed `ByRef` to further underline that fact.

If the number has been changed in the `ChangeCodes` procedure, the property corresponding to the number is also changed, and a flag is set to force the item to be saved after every phone number property for that item has been checked. This flag is used to save only items that have been changed, and is reset at the beginning of every pass through the folder for each item – saving only changed items makes the code run faster than if it were to save them all. After the procedure has finished running, a message box is displayed showing the number of items in the folder that were changed.

```
With oContact
    'Repeat for each of the 19 phone type properties.
    'Too bad Outlook doesn't provide a collection
    'of the properties that can be indexed.

    sNewNum = .Business2TelephoneNumber
    '(sNewNum) is changed in ChangeCodes if a
    'change is needed. The function returns a
    'boolean value indicating need for change.
    If (ChangeCodes(sNewNum) = True) Then
      .Business2TelephoneNumber = sNewNum
      Flag = True
    End If

    sNewNum = .AssistantTelephoneNumber
    If (ChangeCodes(sNewNum) = True) Then
      .AssistantTelephoneNumber = sNewNum
```

```
      Flag = True
   End If

   sNewNum = .BusinessFaxNumber
   If (ChangeCodes(sNewNum) = True) Then
     .BusinessFaxNumber = sNewNum
     Flag = True
   End If

   sNewNum = .BusinessTelephoneNumber
   If (ChangeCodes(sNewNum) = True) Then
     .BusinessTelephoneNumber = sNewNum
     Flag = True
   End If

   sNewNum = .CallbackTelephoneNumber
   If (ChangeCodes(sNewNum) = True) Then
     .CallbackTelephoneNumber = sNewNum
     Flag = True
   End If

   sNewNum = .CarTelephoneNumber
   If (ChangeCodes(sNewNum) = True) Then
     .CarTelephoneNumber = sNewNum
     Flag = True
   End If

   sNewNum = .CompanyMainTelephoneNumber
   If (ChangeCodes(sNewNum) = True) Then
     .CompanyMainTelephoneNumber = sNewNum
     Flag = True
   End If

   sNewNum = .Home2TelephoneNumber
   If (ChangeCodes(sNewNum) = True) Then
     .Home2TelephoneNumber = sNewNum
     Flag = True
   End If

   sNewNum = .HomeFaxNumber
   If (ChangeCodes(sNewNum) = True) Then
     .HomeFaxNumber = sNewNum
     Flag = True
   End If

   sNewNum = .HomeTelephoneNumber
   If (ChangeCodes(sNewNum) = True) Then
     .HomeTelephoneNumber = sNewNum
     Flag = True
   End If

   sNewNum = .ISDNNumber
   If (ChangeCodes(sNewNum) = True) Then
     .ISDNNumber = sNewNum
     Flag = True
   End If
```

```
            sNewNum = .MobileTelephoneNumber
            If (ChangeCodes(sNewNum) = True) Then
              .MobileTelephoneNumber = sNewNum
              Flag = True
            End If

            sNewNum = .OtherFaxNumber
            If (ChangeCodes(sNewNum) = True) Then
              .OtherFaxNumber = sNewNum
              Flag = True
            End If

            sNewNum = .OtherTelephoneNumber
            If (ChangeCodes(sNewNum) = True) Then
              .OtherTelephoneNumber = sNewNum
              Flag = True
            End If

            sNewNum = .PagerNumber
            If (ChangeCodes(sNewNum) = True) Then
              .PagerNumber = sNewNum
              Flag = True
            End If

            sNewNum = .PrimaryTelephoneNumber
            If (ChangeCodes(sNewNum) = True) Then
              .PrimaryTelephoneNumber = sNewNum
              Flag = True
            End If

            sNewNum = .RadioTelephoneNumber
            If (ChangeCodes(sNewNum) = True) Then
              .RadioTelephoneNumber = sNewNum
              Flag = True
            End If

            sNewNum = .TelexNumber
            If (ChangeCodes(sNewNum) = True) Then
              .TelexNumber = sNewNum
              Flag = True
            End If

            sNewNum = .TTYTDDTelephoneNumber
            If (ChangeCodes(sNewNum) = True) Then
              .TTYTDDTelephoneNumber = sNewNum
              Flag = True
            End If

            'If we changed a property then save the item.
            If (Flag = True) Then
              .Save 'save the changed item
              lCount = lCount + 1 'increment the changed count
            End If
          End With
        End If
    Next
```

```
MsgBox "Done!" & vbCrLf & lCount & " items changed in the " _
& oCurrentFolder.Name & " folder.", vbInformation, "Wrox PhoneChanger"

ChangeNumbersExit:
  'clean up all the object variables.
  Set oContact = Nothing
  Set oItem = Nothing
  Set oItems = Nothing
  Set oCurrentFolder = Nothing
  Set oApp = Nothing
  Exit Sub
ChangeNumbersError:
  Call AddInErr(Err)
  GoTo ChangeNumbersExit
End Sub
```

The `ChangeCodes` procedure, which changes the passed argument's value if the number needs to be changed, does most of the add-in's work. It first splits the phone number into its constituent parts: country code, area code, exchange and number. It looks to see if the checkbox was set to make all numbers canonical (preceded by a '+'). If it was, and the number has no '+', this is added to a working string variable. The number is split according to the user-specified delimiters, so it is not specific to any one country's telephone number formatting conventions.

> **Outlook automatically formats country codes inserted in a phone number field. This is a problem if you want to change a country code beginning with a '1'. You can enter a country code of '11' in the user interface, but entering the same value in code results in the country code becoming '1'. (The same thing happens with any country code that begins with a '1', such as '19'.) The only current workaround for this is to enter such country codes with a preceding '0'. So enter '19' as '019'.**

```
'sParm is explicitly declared ByRef to serve as a reminder
'that the value may be changed in the Function.
Private Function ChangeCodes(ByRef sParm As String) As Boolean
  Dim sCountry As String
  Dim sCode As String
  Dim sExchange As String
  Dim sNumber As String
  Dim sTest As String
  Dim sNew As String
  Dim lStart As Long
  Dim lEnd As Long
  Dim blnChange As Boolean

  On Error GoTo ChangeCodesError
  'Start out assuming no change needed.
  blnChange = False
  ChangeCodes = False
  'Work with a copy of the argument.
  sTest = sParm
```

```
'If the existing property is vbNullString
'then exit.
If sTest = "" Then
  Exit Function
End If

'Get the starting position of the number
'and test for an existing "+" or the need
'to add one.
lStart = 1
If Left(sTest, 1) = "+" Then
  lStart = 2
  sNew = "+"
ElseIf (gblnCanonical) Then
  sNew = "+"
Else
  sNew = ""
End If

'Break out the country code portion.
sCountry = GetPhonePart(lStart, sTest, gsSeparator1)
If sCountry = "" Then
  'If no country code then back up 1 place.
  lStart = lStart - 1
End If

'Break out the area code portion.
'Find the beginning of the area code.
lStart = lStart + Len(sCountry) + 1
sCode = GetPhonePart(lStart, sTest, gsSeparator2)
If sCode = "" Then
  'If no area code then back up 1 place.
  lStart = lStart - 1
End If

'Break out the exchange portion.
'Find the beginning of the exchange.
lStart = lStart + Len(sCode) + 1
sExchange = GetPhonePart(lStart, sTest, gsSeparator3)
If sExchange = "" Then
  'If no exchange then not a valid number.
  Exit Function
End If

'Break out the number portion.
'Find the beginning of the number.
lStart = lStart + Len(sExchange) + 1
'Find the number of characters in the number.
lEnd = (Len(sTest) - lStart) + 1
sNumber = Trim(Mid(sTest, lStart, lEnd))
If sNumber = "" Then
  'If no number then exit.
  Exit Function
End If
```

The resulting string parts are trimmed of leading and following spaces, using the `Trim` function. Each sub-field is checked to see if it was selected for changing, and the `TestForChange` procedure is called to see if there is a match with any specified change. If so, the replacement sub-field is substituted for the original sub-field, and a flag is set to indicate that the change was made. If any changes were made, the replacement phone number string is then built up from the sub-fields, and formatted, placing appropriate delimiters between the sub-fields.

```
'Get rid of leading and trailing spaces.
sCountry = Trim(sCountry)
sCode = Trim(sCode)
sExchange = Trim(sExchange)

'Now test all 4 portions of the number to
'see if we have a match with no exceptions.
'Only do portions that are enabled for change.
If (gblnCountry = True) And _
(TestForChange(gsOldCountry, sCountry, _
sCountry, sCode, sExchange, sNumber) = True) Then
    'Set a flag so we know to construct a new number.
  blnChange = True
    'New country code.
  sCountry = gsNewCountry
End If

If (gblnCode = True) And _
(TestForChange(gsOldCode, sCode, _
sCountry, sCode, sExchange, sNumber) = True) Then
  blnChange = True
    'New area code.
  sCode = gsNewCode
End If

If (gblnExchange = True) And _
(TestForChange(gsOldExchange, sExchange, _
sCountry, sCode, sExchange, sNumber) = True) Then
  blnChange = True
    'New exchange.
  sExchange = gsNewExchange
End If

If (gblnNumber = True) And _
(TestForChange(gsOldNumber, sNumber, _
sCountry, sCode, sExchange, sNumber) = True) Then
  blnChange = True
    'New number.
  sNumber = gsNewNumber
End If

If (blnChange = True) Then
    'If we need to change something then construct
    'a new number string and format it.
  sNew = sNew & sCountry
  If sCountry <> "" Then
```

```
            sNew = sNew & " "
      End If
      If sCode <> "" Then
         sNew = sNew & gsSeparator1 & sCode & _
         gsSeparator2 & " "
      End If
      sNew = sNew & sExchange & gsSeparator3 & sNumber
      'Change the function argument to return
      'the new number.
      sParm = sNew
      'Set the change flag = True
      ChangeCodes = True
   End If

ChangeCodesExit:
   Exit Function
ChangeCodesError:
   Call AddInErr(Err)
   ChangeCodes = False
   GoTo ChangeCodesExit
End Function
```

The `GetPhonePart` utility procedure returns the sub-field of the phone number string starting at the indicated place in the string and ending at the first occurrence of the specified delimiter. This procedure will work properly even if the delimiter occurs more than once in the phone number string. Since the user selects the delimiters to use in the different sub-fields the number can be formatted according to the conventions of different countries.

```
Private Function GetPhonePart(lBegin As Long, _
   sPhone As String, sDelimiter As String) As String

   Dim lPlace As Long

   On Error Resume Next

   'Make sure we don't find a zero length string
   'if the delimiter and the start of the string
   'are the same character (such as a space).
   If Mid(sPhone, lBegin, 1) = sDelimiter Then
      lBegin = lBegin + 1
   End If

   'Return the indicated portion of the number.
   lPlace = InStr(lBegin, sPhone, sDelimiter, vbTextCompare)
   If lPlace <> 0 Then
      GetPhonePart = Mid(sPhone, lBegin, (lPlace - lBegin))
   Else
      GetPhonePart = ""
   End If
End Function
```

The `TestForChange` procedure tests for a match between the phone number sub-field and the user-defined sub-field that is to be replaced. The exception lists are checked for each of the sub-fields, with the current sub-field not used for exceptions. Since only one string is specified for replacement it would make no sense to have an exception list for that sub-field. The function returns a Boolean value, based on the matches it found for the sub-field and the exceptions lists.

```
Private Function TestForChange(sOldValue As String, _
   sCurrentValue As String, sCountryC As String, sCodeC As String, _
   sExchangeC As String, sNumberC As String) As Boolean

   Dim lCount As Long

   On Error Resume Next
   TestForChange = False

   'First check for a match on the current number segment
   'and the number segment that is to be changed.
   If (sOldValue = sCurrentValue) Then
     TestForChange = True

     'Check each of the exception lists in turn.
     'Only use the exception list for a segment
     'if it is not the current segment being changed.
     If sCurrentValue <> sCountryC Then
       For lCount = 0 To UBound(msCountryExceptions)
         If sCountryC = msCountryExceptions(lCount) Then
           TestForChange = False
         End If
       Next lCount
     End If

     If sCurrentValue <> sCodeC Then
       For lCount = 0 To UBound(msCodeExceptions)
         If sCodeC = msCodeExceptions(lCount) Then
           TestForChange = False
         End If
       Next lCount
     End If

     If sCurrentValue <> sExchangeC Then
       For lCount = 0 To UBound(msExchangeExceptions)
         If sExchangeC = msExchangeExceptions(lCount) Then
           TestForChange = False
         End If
       Next lCount
     End If

     If sCurrentValue <> sNumberC Then
       For lCount = 0 To UBound(msNumberExceptions)
         If sNumberC = msNumberExceptions(lCount) Then
           TestForChange = False
```

```
        End If
    Next lCount
  End If

  End If
End Function
```

This COM add-in makes no use of custom toolbar or menu buttons, or custom Outlook Bar groups or shortcuts. Its user-interface and execution are both controlled by the Property Page we created (and added to the Properties sheet for Contacts folders). However, adding these elements is not hard, and can be done in a COM add-in in just the same way as they are added to a VBA application. The basMenus and basOutlookBars modules that we created in Chapter 3 can serve as a guide to creating these elements if your COM add-in needs them.

Data storage in the Windows Registry can be used for the persistent data and settings for your COM add-in. You can also save data in an .ini file, but Microsoft recommends that you use the registry for data storage. To save and restore data and settings in the Windows Registry you can instantiate the clsRegistryFunctions class module that we created in Chapter 6 and use the properties that it provides to read and write registry keys. If you do use this or any other class module in your COM add-ins, make sure that they are instanced as Public so that they are visible to the other elements of your add-in.

Compiling the COM Add-in

When you have finished developing your COM add-in it must be compiled in order to run. If more than one project is being used in a Project Group, as we are doing, choose File | Make Project Group to compile the source into a COM add-in .dll file. Otherwise, choose File | Make <projectname> (where <projectname> is the name of your project) to compile it.

If you compile the COM add-in in either VB6 or MOD, it will be automatically installed and registered on your computer. However, to distribute it to other users you must consider deploying it.

Deploying the COM Add-in

Deploying, installing and registering your COM add-in is very easy if you are using VB6 or MOD. You can use the Package and Deployment Wizard to create a Setup program, a list of files to install and the location of the file installations, along with a compressed file (.cab file) containing all the add-in's components. The .dll files that contain your COM add-in are self-registering files.

If you are using VB5 or some other development system that does not create self-registering .dll files, you will have to create a .reg file similar to the one shown earlier in this chapter and install the necessary keys in the registry.

To create a deployment package for this COM add-in, select the Package and Deployment Wizard from the Add-Ins menu. In the event that it is not installed, use the Add-In Manager to install it – if you are using MOD, you will need to do this from the installation CD.

When the Package and Deployment Wizard opens, you may, if necessary, be prompted to save it. If the compiled code is out of date with respect to the source, you will be asked whether you want to use the compiled code or have the source recompiled. You will then be presented with the window shown below.

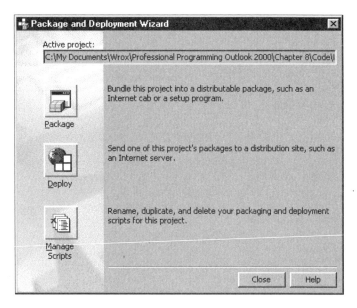

In this case we are packaging the COM add-in, so click on the Package button. After some background work by the Wizard, a dialog box appears from which you choose your package type. Your choices are: to create a package that will be installed by running a Setup program; to create a package that will be installed by being downloaded from the Internet; or to create a dependency file that lists all the runtime components that the project requires. The Package Type dialog box is shown in the following screenshot.

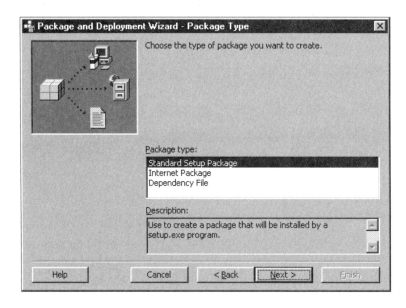

Choose **Standard Setup Package** and click the **Next** button. The next dialog box lets you choose where the package is to be assembled. A package consists of the application itself (along with all dependent files), stored in a .cab file, a `Setup.lst` file (which lists the contents of the .cab file) and a `Setup.exe` file to actually install the application. A subfolder is created containing all the files that are compressed in the .cab file. (A package script is also generated, so that in the event that you package an application more than once, you can shorten the process by using a scripted process). The following screenshot shows the Package Folder dialog box.

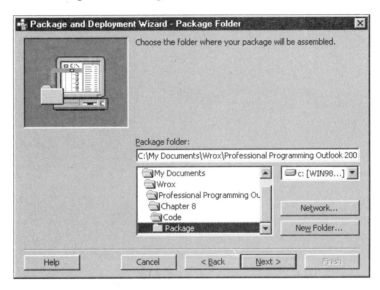

Select where you want to assemble the package (which can be on a network drive), and click the **Next** button. The next dialog box shows the files that will be included in the package. I do not usually include `MSCOMCTL.dll`, `MS09.dll` or `MSOUTL9.OLB`, which will be installed on the user's system along with Outlook 2000. The following screenshot shows the Included Files dialog box.

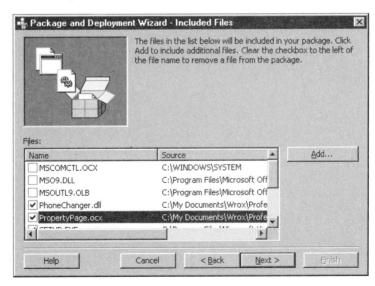

> **If your application uses ActiveX controls, .dll files, or other objects that must be included in the package for distribution, always make sure that they are listed in this dialog box or a dependency file. If not, add them by clicking on the Add button and browsing to their location.**

Click on Next and select whether to create a single .cab file, or multiple .cab files sized for floppy disk formats. This screenshot shows the Cab Options dialog box:

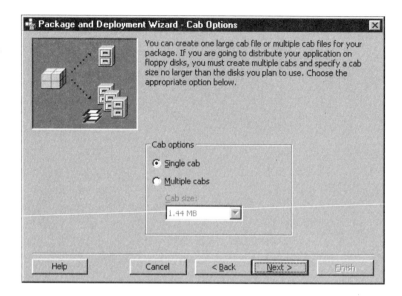

Click on the Next button and the Installation Title dialog box comes up. Here you can enter a title for the installer to display when the package is installed.

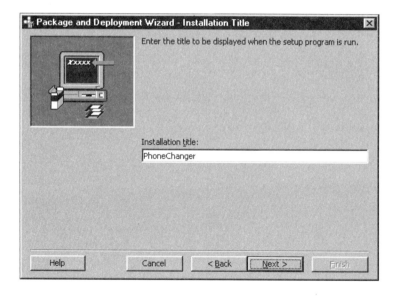

Click on the Next button, and a dialog box comes up that enables you to create Start Menu groups and shortcuts, which will be created when the package is installed. This feature (along with the uninstaller that is also included) gives a nice professional touch to such installations. The following screenshot shows the Start Menu Items dialog box:

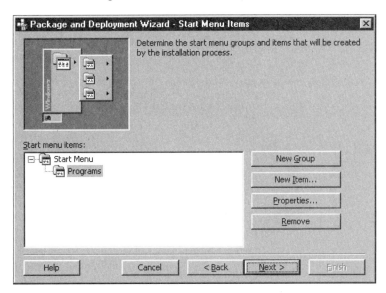

Once you have created the program groups and shortcuts to items that you want, and have placed your groups and items in the Start Menu, click on the Next button. This takes you to the Install Locations dialog box, which enables you to decide where the objects making up your COM add-in will be installed. The normal locations will be the `<Windir>\System` folder for any ActiveX controls, and `C:\Program Files\<InstallationTitle>` for the COM add-in itself. (These locations will have been selected by using the $(WinSysPath) variable for ActiveX controls, and the $(AppPath) variable for the COM add-in.) The Install Locations dialog box is shown in the following screenshot.

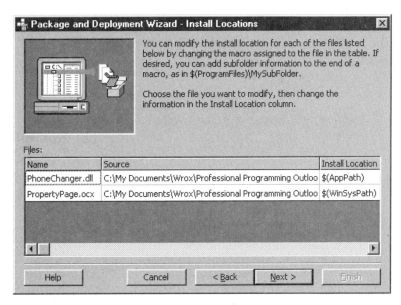

After you have decided where to install the package files, click on the Next button. The Shared Files dialog box enables you to install files in your package as shared files. You should never share the COM add-in, because Outlook 2000 COM add-ins are compiled only for connection to Outlook. ActiveX controls that you have created (or have distribution licenses for) can be shared if you want. The following screenshot shows the Shared Files dialog box:

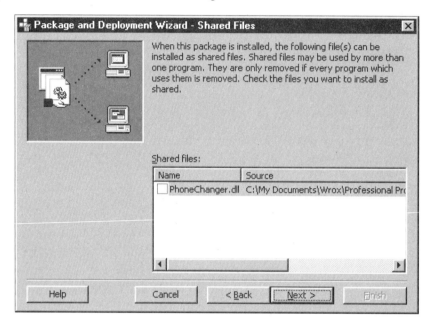

Click on the Next button and enter a name for the packaging script that will be created for the settings for this package. Every package variation that you create can be saved as a package script. The following screenshot shows the final dialog box for the Package and Deployment Wizard:

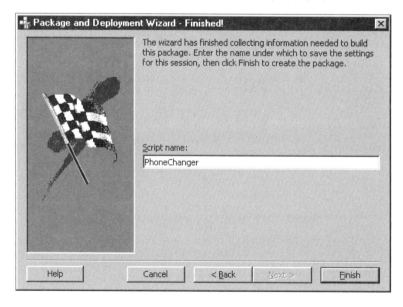

Click on the Finish button and the Wizard will produce your deployment package. After the package is created, a report is created that can either be saved or discarded. The following screenshot shows the packaging report for the package created for the PhoneChanger COM add-in:

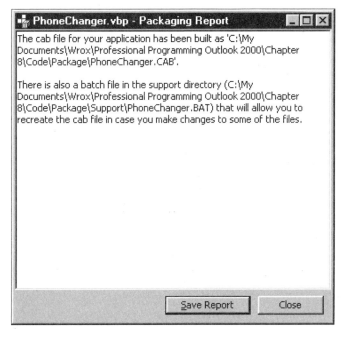

If you've used the settings I described, the final result will be three files (stored in the folder you chose for the deployment package location). These will be named Setup.exe, Setup.1st and PhoneChanger.cab. They can be distributed as the deployment package or compressed into one file (by a program such as WinZip).

> *The* .cab *file will not be compressed, as it is already a compressed file, but this enables you to distribute your complete deployment package as one file.*

Whichever method is used, the deployment package should be loaded to a temporary folder. (If the package was zipped into one file it must be unzipped into its constituent files.) When the Setup program is executed, the COM add-in will be installed and registered. The next time Outlook is started, the new COM add-in will be available for use.

Use of the Package and Deployment Wizard also creates an uninstall program (available in the Add/Remove programs applet of the Control Panel) in case you decide to uninstall the COM add-in. For more information on using the Package and Deployment Wizard, see the relevant topics in the MSDN Library (included with VB6 and MOD).

The Finished COM Add-in

Once you have finished and deployed the `PhoneChanger` COM add-in, it will automatically load the next time Outlook is started. Right-clicking on a Contacts folder in the Folder List (or the Outlook Bar) and choosing Properties should show the Properties sheet with a brand new tab. This will be named Wrox Phone Number Changer and is the custom Property Page created by our COM add-in. The Properties sheet should look similar to the following screenshot.

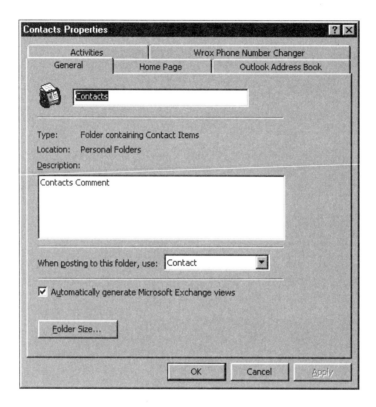

Selecting this tab will show us the custom Property Page, which should look similar to the following screenshot.

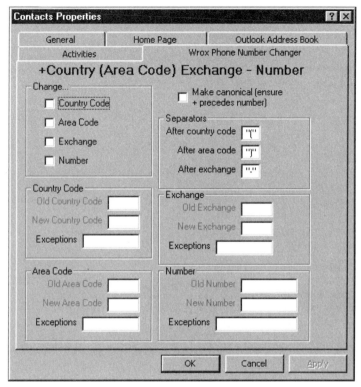

The process of creating COM add-ins is complicated and a little difficult to understand at first, but once you understand the mechanics required, creating COM add-ins is no more difficult than creating any other program. The process of creating a COM add-in in VBA (assuming you have Microsoft Office 2000 Developer Edition installed) is the same as that of creating a COM add-in using VB6. Remember though, that the COM add-in is compiled as a `.dll`, so a reference to the Microsoft Outlook 9.0 object library is required whether you develop it using VB6 or MOD.

Debugging COM Add-ins

Precisely how you set up for debugging a COM add-in will depend on whether it was developed in VB6 or MOD. If your add-in was developed in MOD (in the Outlook VBE interface), it cannot be debugged in Outlook, since the COM add-in is also running in Outlook.

In either case, first disable the COM add-in, by deselecting it in the COM add-ins dialog box, assuming that it's already installed. (This dialog box is well hidden, but is accessible by selecting Tools | Options | Other | Advanced Options | COM Add-ins from Outlook.) Then exit Outlook.

The best way to debug a VBA COM add-in is to load the add-in project into Word or Excel VBA and set breakpoints there. Start the COM add-in project, and then start Outlook. When the add-in reaches the breakpoints it will break in the Word or Excel VBA, ready for the standard debugging techniques.

COM add-ins developed in VB6 can be debugged in VB6. Disable the COM add-in (as described above) and exit Outlook. Then load the add-in project into VB6 and run the project in VB6 before you start Outlook or enable the COM add-in in Outlook.

Set your breakpoints in the project before you run it. You can also create a debug procedure in a debug module that is similar to the following code and set a debug variable such as argDebug = -1 in the conditional compilation textbox in the Make tab of the project's Properties sheet in the Project menu. If you use this method make sure that the module is removed and the conditional compilation argument is removed before you distribute your COM add-in.

```
Sub DebugWrite(sDebug)
    #If argDebug Then
        Debug.Print sDebug
    #End If
End Sub
```

ActiveX controls cannot be debugged by these methods. For information about debugging ActiveX controls, look in the MSDN library that comes with VB6 and MOD.

Removing COM Add-ins

COM add-ins can be prevented from running in Outlook by clicking the **Remove** command button in the Outlook COM add-ins dialog box. Note though that this does not uninstall the COM add-in, or remove it from the Windows Registry.

To uninstall and deregister a COM add-in that was installed with a Package and Deployment Wizard deployment package, go to the **Add/Remove Programs** applet in the Control Panel and choose the appropriate COM add-in from the programs list. Clicking on the **Add/Remove** command button will automatically take care of all necessary steps to remove the add-in from your system.

If the COM add-in was not installed from a Package and Deployment Wizard deployment package, you must delete the .dll file manually, but only after deregistering it from the registry. To deregister it, open the Windows **Start | Run** dialog box and type Regserver /u, followed by the name of the .dll (or ActiveX control) to be deregistered.

Summary

In this chapter we developed an Outlook 2000 COM add-in and examined the events of the IDTExtensibility2 Interface. We also saw how to develop and use a custom Property Page by implementing the Outlook.PropertyPage interface. Deploying and debugging COM add-ins was also covered.

COM add-ins are the preferred method of distributing customized Outlook code, so an understanding is critical to us as Outlook developers. Although the COM add-in developed in this chapter was developed in VB6, the information in this chapter can be applied to whatever development system you use to develop COM add-ins.

8

Retrieving External Data With Outlook 2000

In this chapter we are going to work with getting data into Outlook from four different object models and data access methods; Word, Excel, DAO and ADO. There are many times that we need to get information for our Outlook applications, and this information often already exists somewhere else. So instead of making the user re-enter information again, we can make use of the different object models listed above and use this existing data. You can also use other object models that expose the data contained in their applications.

This chapter is designed to show you how to work with the different object models, but not to give you detailed information on the methods, properties and events that are exposed by the object models. To get that type of information I suggest that you take a look at the Wrox *Excel 2000 VBA Programmer's Reference*, ISBN 1861002548, *Word 2000 VBA Programmer's Reference*, ISBN 1861002556, *ADO 2.1 Programmer's Reference*, ISBN 1861002688, *Beginning Access 2000 VBA*, ISBN 1861001762, and *Outlook 2000 VBA Programmer's Reference*, ISBN 186100253X.

We covered putting Outlook data into Word and Excel in Chapter 4. Getting data from Word and Excel is very similar to putting data into them. Even though we don't usually think of Word as a container for data, any finished document has data in it that can be retrieved using automation. In Chapter 4 we also worked with the Access object model, but that is not used to get data that is in an Access database. Instead, to get data that is stored in an Access database we would use DAO or ADO.

In previous chapters we used procedures in code modules to put data into different object models and data access models. In this chapter we will use class modules to get data from various object models and data access methods. Both are valid methods of working with other object models and data access methods. Your personal preferences, working habits and the circumstances of each project will determine whether you use procedural code or classes in different cases.

Getting Data From Word

We can get more data from Word than just the actual content of a document. We can get data from form fields, built-in and custom document properties, properties of the `LetterContent` object, and from other objects that Word maintains. In this section we will look at some of the ways that we can get data from Word into Outlook.

The following screen shot shows a Word document that has a number of form fields in it. Word form fields retain the data that is inserted in them, unlike bookmarks, which merely point to places in the document. This document also contains data in fields that aren't visible in the document, the built-in document properties of the document. This Word document is available for download on the Wrox web site.

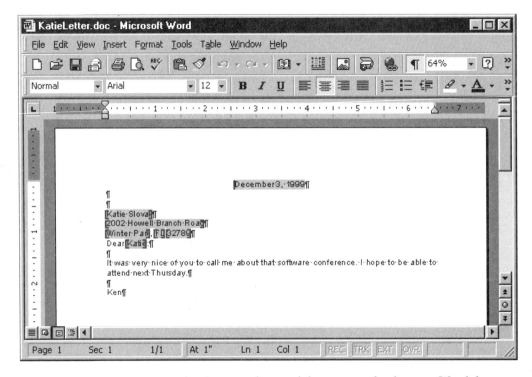

The code in this section is an example of using a class module to access the data in a Word document. To run the code in this section, make sure that you have references set to the Microsoft Word 9.0 and Microsoft Outlook 9.0 Object Libraries.

Insert a new class module in the Outlook VBA project, or in a VB project, and name it `clsWord`. We will instantiate a Word `Application` object and a Word `Document` object and use them in various places in the class, so declare these variables in the declarations section of the class module so they are available throughout the class. We will also set up a module level Boolean variable to store whether we opened Word, or it was already open.

```
Private m_oWord As Word.Application
Private m_oDoc As Word.Document
Private m_blnOurWord As Boolean
```

The `Initialize` procedure for the class, which is called when a new instance of the class is created, instantiates a Word `Application` object and sets the module level Boolean variable `m_blnOurWord` depending on whether we opened Word. The class `Terminate` procedure, which is called when the class is destroyed, sets the module level object variables to `Nothing` and closes Word if our code opened it.

```
Private Sub Class_Initialize()
  On Error Resume Next

  m_blnOurWord = False
  'Get a Word Application object.
  Set m_oWord = GetObject(, "Word.Application")
  If m_oWord Is Nothing Then
    m_blnOurWord = True
    Set m_oWord = CreateObject("Word.Application")
  End If
End Sub

Private Sub Class_Terminate()
  If m_blnOurWord = True Then
    'Close Word
    m_oWord.Quit
  End If

  Set m_oDoc = Nothing
  Set m_oWord = Nothing
End Sub
```

The only exposed method of the `clsWord` class is the `GetWordData` function. This function is called with the name of the document from which we want to pull data as an argument of the function, and returns a Boolean result indicating the success or failure of the function call. The `GetWordData` method creates a new contact if one does not already exist for the person the document is addressed to, and a Journal entry containing a link to the contact and a copy of the Word document embedded in the Journal entry. The information for the contact is acquired from data that is stored in the Word document.

```
Public Function GetWordData(sFileName As String) As Boolean
  Dim oOL As Outlook.Application
  Dim oNS As Outlook.NameSpace
  Dim oFolder As Outlook.MAPIFolder
  Dim oItems As Outlook.Items
  Dim oRestricted As Outlook.Items
  Dim oRecip As Outlook.Recipient
  Dim oJournal As Outlook.JournalItem
  Dim oContact As Outlook.ContactItem
  Dim oLetterContent As Word.LetterContent
```

```
Dim sFieldName As String
Dim sManager As String
Dim sAuthor As String
Dim sTitle As String
Dim sSubject As String
Dim sCompany As String
Dim sCreated As String
Dim sBody As String
Dim sInstructions As String
Dim sRecipAddress As String
Dim sRecipName As String
Dim sConferenceDate As String
Dim sRestrict$

Dim blnMAPI As Boolean
```

After instantiating an Outlook `Application` object, we create objects for the new contact and Journal entry. We also create an Outlook `Items` object that we will use to make sure that the new contact is not a duplicate of an existing contact. If the new contact is a duplicate of an existing contact it will be discarded.

```
'Get an Outlook Application object.
On Error Resume Next
Set oOL = GetObject(, "Outlook.Application")
If oOL Is Nothing Then
    Set oOL = CreateObject("Outlook.Application")
End If

'Set up the variables for the new contact, journal
'item and an Items collection for a duplicate
'contact check.
'If the new contact is a duplicate it will be discarded.
Set oNS = oOL.GetNamespace("MAPI")
Set oContact = oOL.CreateItem(olContactItem)
Set oFolder = oNS.GetDefaultFolder(olFolderContacts)
Set oItems = oFolder.Items
```

The document specified in the argument passed to the `GetWordData` method is added to the Word `Documents` collection and activated. First some data is acquired from the document from properties that are available as `Application` properties, or are available in the document's `LetterContent` property. We will get an `Application` property that is a Boolean variable indicating whether MAPI is available to Word, and `LetterContent` properties for mailing instructions, the recipient name and address. Some of the `LetterContent` properties are automatically set by Word, others have to be set by code. Study the Word object model in the Object Browser to become familiar with the many properties that Word makes available.

```
On Error GoTo GetWordDataError

'Add a document.
Set m_oDoc = m_oWord.Documents.Add(sFileName)

With m_oDoc
    'Activate the new document.
```

```
    .Activate

    'Although this information is not being
    'used at this time, it is an example of
    'types of information available in a
    'Word document.
    blnMAPI = m_oWord.MAPIAvailable
    Set oLetterContent = .GetLetterContent
    With oLetterContent
        sInstructions = oLetterContent.MailingInstructions
        sRecipAddress = oLetterContent.RecipientAddress
        sRecipName = oLetterContent.RecipientName
    End With
```

Word maintains built-in document properties that you can set in the Property sheet for the document. The Property sheet is available in Word's File menu. In this case, we are going to acquire the data for the document author, title, subject and the date and time the document was created. We will also acquire the manager and company of the document's author. The current user's name is also available as the `UserName` property of the `Application` object.

```
    'Now get the data from the Word document
    'built-in document properties.
    sManager = _
        .BuiltinDocumentProperties(wdPropertyManager)

    sAuthor = _
        .BuiltinDocumentProperties(wdPropertyAuthor)

    'You can also get information such as the
    'current user's name.
    'sAuthor = m_oWord.UserName

    sTitle = _
        .BuiltinDocumentProperties(wdPropertyTitle)
    sSubject = _
        .BuiltinDocumentProperties(wdPropertySubject)
    sCompany = _
        .BuiltinDocumentProperties(wdPropertyCompany)
    sCreated = _
        .BuiltinDocumentProperties(wdPropertyTimeCreated)
    End With
```

We can check to see whether the manager listed in the document's properties will resolve to a valid contact.

```
    'Check to see if the Manager listed in the
    'built-in document properties resolves to
    'a valid contact.
    Set oRecip = oNS.CreateRecipient(sManager)
    oRecip.Resolve
    If Not oRecip.Resolved Then
        MsgBox sManager & " not resolved"
    End If
```

The parts of the address block of this document are inserted as form fields. We will get that data and use it for information for the new contact entry we are creating. The form field data is read by a utility function GetFormFieldData. We will use it to get the contact's name, street address, city, state, and postal code. Then the mailing address of the contact is assigned to the business address, which was populated with information from the document. The contact's company name and manager's name are populated with data acquired from the built-in document properties.

```
With oContact
    'Get data from each form field in turn.
    sFieldName = "FullName"
    .FullName = GetFormFieldData(sFieldName, m_oDoc)

    'Repeat the function call for each form field.
    sFieldName = "StreetAddress"
    .BusinessAddressStreet = _
        GetFormFieldData(sFieldName, m_oDoc)

    sFieldName = "City"
    .BusinessAddressCity = GetFormFieldData(sFieldName, m_oDoc)

    sFieldName = "State"
    .BusinessAddressState = GetFormFieldData(sFieldName, m_oDoc)

    sFieldName = "PostalCode"
    .BusinessAddressPostalCode = _
        GetFormFieldData(sFieldName, m_oDoc)

    sFieldName = "FirstName"
    .FirstName = GetFormFieldData(sFieldName, m_oDoc)

    'Set the mailing address, company and manager
    'in the contact item.
    .MailingAddress = .BusinessAddress
    .CompanyName = sCompany
    .ManagerName = sManager
```

The memo field of the new contact entry is filled with the author's name, title, and subject of the document, the document file name, and the time and date the document were created.

```
'Add details from the letter to the contact Body.
sBody = "Created from letter written by: " & sAuthor
.Body = sBody & vbCrLf

sBody = "Letter title: " & sTitle
.Body = .Body & sBody & vbCrLf

sBody = "Letter Subject: " & sSubject
.Body = .Body & sBody & vbCrLf

sBody = "Letter filename: " & sFileName
.Body = .Body & sBody & vbCrLf

sBody = "Letter created: " & sCreated
.Body = .Body & sBody & vbCrLf
```

The default Contacts folder is checked to see whether the new contact is a duplicate of an existing contact. This is done very quickly by setting a restriction on the Contacts folder matching the new contact's `FullName` field with the `FullName` field of the existing contacts. If no matching contact is found, the new contact is saved and a Journal entry is created. The Journal entry is set to a Microsoft Word entry type and the original document is embedded in the Journal entry.

The newly saved contact is added to the Links collection of the Journal entry, enabling the Journal entry to be seen in the **Activities** tab of the contact. Double-clicking on the contact entry in the Links collection will open the contact record.

```
      'Now make sure this is not a duplicate contact.
      'Check for duplicate FullName.
      sRestrict$ = "[FullName] = """ & .FullName & """"
      Set oRestricted = oItems.Restrict(sRestrict$)
      If oRestricted.Count = 0 Then
        .Save 'save contact.

        'Create a journal entry related to the contact.
        Set oJournal = oOL.CreateItem(olJournalItem)
        oJournal.Companies = .CompanyName
        oJournal.Subject = sSubject
        oJournal.Type = "Microsoft Word"
        oJournal.Links.Add oContact 'Add a link to the contact.
        'oJournal.Save
        oJournal.Attachments.Add sFileName 'attach letter.
        oJournal.Save
        GetWordData = True
      Else
        MsgBox "This is a duplicate contact", , "Wrox"
        .Close (olDiscard)
        GetWordData = False
      End If
   End With
```

Finally, the Word document is closed, with an argument of `wdDoNotSaveChanges` to not save any changes to the document, and the object variables for the method are destroyed by setting them to `Nothing`.

```
   GetWordDataExit:
      If Not m_oWord Is Nothing Then
        'Close document, do not save.
        m_oDoc.Close wdDoNotSaveChanges
      End If

      Set oLetterContent = Nothing
      Set oOL = Nothing
      Set oNS = Nothing
      Set oRecip = Nothing
      Set oFolder = Nothing
      Set oItems = Nothing
      Set oRestricted = Nothing
      Set oJournal = Nothing
      Set oContact = Nothing
      Exit Function
```

```
GetWordDataError:
   MsgBox "Error occurred: " & Err.Description, , "Wrox"
   GetWordData = False
   GoTo GetWordDataExit
End Function
```

The utility function `GetFormFieldData` is used to read the data from the specified form field and document.

```
Private Function GetFormFieldData(sFormField As String, _
   m_oDoc As Word.Document) As String

   GetFormFieldData = m_oDoc.FormFields(sFormField).Result
End Function
```

All of the wrapper procedures for this chapter will be placed in one code module. Insert a new code module and name it `basDataImport`. The `GetDataFromWord` procedure is used to create a new instance of the `clsWord` class module, and to call the class to extract data from the document. The document in this case is named `KatieLetter.doc`, and is stored in the `C:\My Documents` folder. If you use a different document or location make sure to change the `sLetter` variable.

```
Private Sub GetDataFromWord()
   Dim oClass As clsWord
   Dim sLetter As String
   Dim blnSuccess As Boolean

   Set oClass = New clsWord

   'Change this file name and location if necessary.
   sLetter = "C:\My Documents\KatieLetter.doc"

   'Call the Word class module
   blnSuccess = oClass.GetWordData(sLetter)

   If blnSuccess Then
     MsgBox "Contact creation succeeded", , "Wrox"
   Else
     MsgBox "Contact creation failed", , "Wrox"
   End If

   Set oClass = Nothing
End Sub
```

The contact record created from the Word document is shown in the following screenshot. Notice how the data that we just got from the document has supplied all the information needed to create a new contact record.

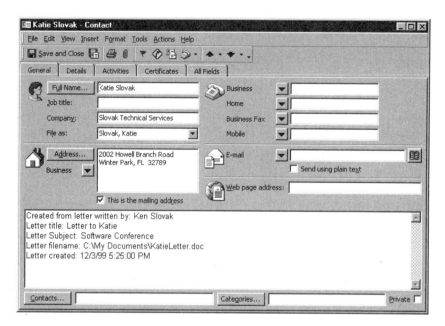

The Journal entry that we created is shown in the following screen shot. Notice how a copy of the Word document is embedded in the Journal entry. Also notice how the newly created contact is shown in the Contacts field of the Journal entry, which shows the Links collection in Outlook 2000. As discussed in earlier chapters, the Links collection is new to Outlook 2000.

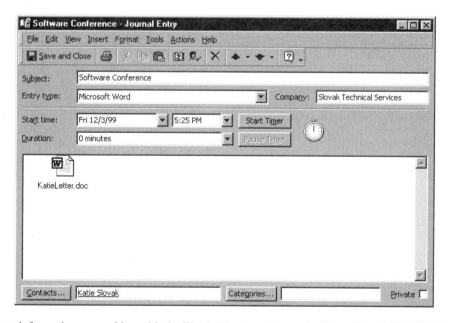

For more information on working with the Word object model, see the Wrox *Word 2000 VBA Programmer's Reference*, ISBN 1861002556.

Getting Data From Excel

The example in this section requires that references are set to the Microsoft Excel 9.0 and Microsoft Outlook 9.0 Object Libraries in your project. In this section we are going to be looking at how to extract data stored in an Excel spreadsheet, and use this data in Outlook. This Excel spreadsheet is available for download on the Wrox web site. To get to this data we need to open a spreadsheet. To open a spreadsheet we need to use the `Workbooks` collection that is exposed by the Excel `Application` object. The `Workbooks` collection gives us the ability to work with the `Workbook` object that holds the data that we need.

When you are opening workbooks that contain an `Auto_Open` macro, the macro will not be run automatically for you. To run the macro you need to use the `RunAutoMacros` method. The `RunAutoMacros` method has one argument that specifies which macro to run. The parameter can be anyone of the `xlRunAutoMacro` constants. The following table lists the `xlRunAutoMacro` constants.

Name	Description
XlAutoOpen	runs the `Auto_Open` macro.
xlAutoClose	runs the `Auto_Close` macro
xlAutoActive	runs the `Auto_Activate` macro
xlAutoDeactivate	runs the `Auto_Deactivate` macro.

The following code snippet shows an example of using the `RunAutoMacros` method to run the `Auto_Open` macro.

```
m_owbFinancialBook.RunAutoMacros xlAutoOpen
```

This section uses a class module to work with Excel, so insert a new class module and name it `clsExcel`. We will be working with a spreadsheet named `Sales by Rep.xls`, located in the `C:\My Documents` folder. The spreadsheet can be downloaded from the Wrox web site. The `Sales by Rep` spreadsheet looks like the following screen shot.

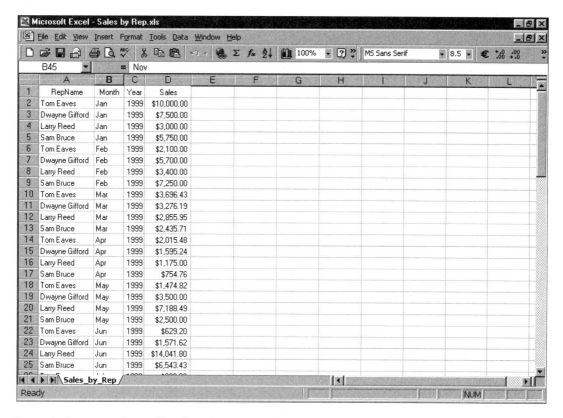

Instead of opening the workbook and getting a reference to the `Sales by Rep` Worksheet object each time we need it, we will create the reference when the class module is instantiated and use it throughout the class. We will do the same for Excel `Application` and `Workbook` objects. Place these module level variable declarations in the Declarations section of the class.

```
Private m_owbFinancialBook As Excel.Workbook
Private m_oaExcel As Excel.Application
Private m_owsSales As Excel.Worksheet
```

The class `Initialize` event is used to instantiate the module level Excel `Application` object, and the `Terminate` event is used to destroy the module level objects. The instance of Excel we created is also closed in the `Terminate` event.

```
Private Sub Class_Initialize()
  Set m_oaExcel = New Excel.Application
  OpenWorkbook
End Sub

Private Sub Class_Terminate()
  If Not m_owsSales Is Nothing Then
    Set m_owsSales = Nothing
  End If
```

```
      If Not m_owbFinancialBook Is Nothing Then
        m_owbFinancialBook.Close False
        Set m_owbFinancialBook = Nothing
      End If

      If Not m_oaExcel Is Nothing Then
        m_oaExcel.Quit
        Set m_oaExcel = Nothing
      End If
   End Sub
```

The private `OpenWorkbook` method is used to set the instance of Excel to be visible for debugging purposes. It also opens the worksheet and runs the worksheet's `Auto_Open` macro.

```
   Private Sub OpenWorkbook()
      On Error GoTo ErrorHandler

      m_oaExcel.Visible = True
      Set m_owbFinancialBook = m_oaExcel.Workbooks.Open _
        ("C:\My documents\Sales by Rep.XLS")
      m_owbFinancialBook.RunAutoMacros xlAutoOpen
      Set m_owsSales = m_owbFinancialBook.Worksheets _
        ("Sales_by_Rep")
      Exit Sub


   ErrorHandler:
      Err.Raise Err.Number, "OpenWorkBook", Err.Description
   End Sub
```

We also have set up an error handler to raise any error that has occurred in the `OpenWorkbook` method back to the calling routine. If we cannot open the `Sales by Rep` workbook we will raise the error back to notify the calling routine of the problem.

The `GetSalesReprFigures` method of the class does all the work of extracting the data from Excel and putting it in an Outlook e-mail item that the method creates. First, the year that the data is for is extracted from the Year column of the spreadsheet. Next, an Outlook `Application` object and a new email item are created.

```
   Public Sub GetSalesReprFigures()
      Dim oOL As Outlook.Application
      Dim oMail As Outlook.MailItem

      Dim iRow As Integer
      Dim i As Integer
      Dim iNewRow As Integer
      Dim sYear As String
      Dim sTab As String

      iNewRow = 2
      sTab = vbTab & vbTab
      sYear = m_owsSales.Cells(2, 3).Text
      Set oOL = CreateObject("Outlook.Application")
      Set oMail = oOL.CreateItem(olMailItem)
```

The `Subject` for the email message is set using the year acquired from the spreadsheet data. Then the `Body` of the email message is created by using the column headings from the spreadsheet as the column titles for the email message.

```
oMail.Subject = "Sales Figure for - " & sYear

oMail.Body = oMail.Body & m_owsSales.Cells(1, 1).Text & sTab

oMail.Body = oMail.Body & m_owsSales.Cells(1, 2).Text & sTab

oMail.Body = oMail.Body & m_owsSales.Cells(1, 4).Text
```

Next, the spreadsheet is activated and the worksheet selection area is set to the last entry in column A of the spreadsheet. This row is assigned to a variable that is used as the upper limit for the loop that gets the Excel data.

```
m_owsSales.Activate
m_owsSales.range("A1").Select
m_oaExcel.Selection.End(xlDown).Select

iRow = m_oaExcel.ActiveCell.Cells.Row

oMail.Body = oMail.Body & vbCrLf & vbCrLf
```

The sales rep name, sales month and monthly sales total is then extracted from the spreadsheet, row by row. This data is added to the e-mail message's `Body`, with tab characters that align the text in the email message.

```
'Add the Information from the master spreadsheet
'to the mail message.
For i = 2 To iRow
   oMail.Body = oMail.Body & m_owsSales.Cells(i, 1).Text & sTab

   oMail.Body = oMail.Body & m_owsSales.Cells(i, 2).Text & sTab

   oMail.Body = oMail.Body & m_owsSales.Cells(i, 4).Text

   iNewRow = iNewRow + 1
   oMail.Body = oMail.Body & vbCrLf
Next

oMail.Body = oMail.Body & vbCrLf
```

The intrinsic SUM function is used to total the sales figures and the overall sales total is then inserted in the email message.

```
m_owsSales.Cells(iNewRow, 4).FormulaR1C1 = "=SUM(R1C:R" & iNewRow - 1 & "C)"

m_owsSales.Cells(iNewRow, 2).FormulaR1C1 = "Total Sales"

oMail.Body = oMail.Body & "Total Sales" & sTab

oMail.Body = oMail.Body & sTab & m_owsSales.Cells(iNewRow, 4).Text

oMail.Body = oMail.Body & vbCrLf & vbCrLf
```

Finally, the original spreadsheet is attached to the email message as an embedded item, and the email message is displayed, ready to be addressed to a recipient.

```
oMail.Attachments.Add "C:\My Documents\Sales by Rep.XLS", olEmbeddeditem

oMail.Display

Set oOL = Nothing
Set oMail = Nothing
End Sub
```

> **Items may also be attached as a link to the original item, using the olByReference parameter instead of the olEmbeddedItem parameter. However, in another example of the differences in Outlook operating modes, the olByReference parameter is not supported by Outlook in Internet only mode.**

The clsExcel class module is instantiated and used by the GetExcelData wrapper procedure. Place the code for this procedure in the basDataImport code module.

```
Private Sub GetExcelData()
    Dim oClass As clsExcel

    Set oClass = New clsExcel

    'Call the Excel class module
    oClass.GetSalesReprFigures

    Set oClass = Nothing
End Sub
```

The email message that is created is shown in the following screen shot. Note the attached spreadsheet, as indicated by the Excel shortcut icon shown at the bottom of the spreadsheet. Also, note that the message is in RTF format because the `Body` of the email message was accessed in code.

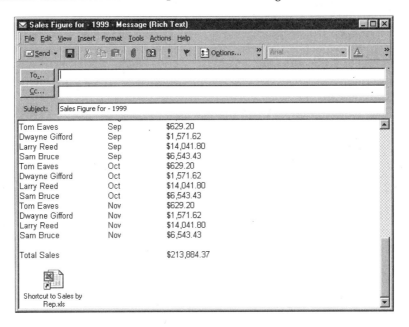

Getting Data From Access Using DAO

In this case we are working with the data stored in Access, and not with the objects exposed by the Access object model. So this time we need to get a Reference to DAO (Data Access Objects), and not the Access object model. To do this we need to set a reference to the Microsoft DAO 3.6 Object Library. We will also need a reference to the Microsoft Outlook 9.0 Object Library.

You might ask why we would use DAO, when ADO (ActiveX Data Objects) is touted as the successor technology to DAO. While ADO is part of Microsoft's UDA (Universal Data Access) strategy, DAO still has some advantages when it comes to working with Access data. DAO is optimized for use with the Jet database engine that Access uses. It also natively supports the use of data definition language (DDL), users, and groups. ADO supports those things only with an extension library, ADOX (ActiveX Data Objects Extensions for DDL and Security). Even with the ADOX extensions, DAO still works better for certain types of Access data creation, access and modification than ADO does.

We will work with DAO from a class module, so insert a new class module in your project and name it `clsDAO`. The first step in retrieving data from an Access data source with DAO is to declare a variable for a `Database`. Place this declaration for a module level `Database` variable in the Declarations sections of the `clsDAO` module.

```
Private m_odbSales As DAO.Database
```

If your projects have a reference set only to DAO, then you can declare variable types such as Database and Recordset. If you also have a reference set to ADO in your projects, then you should qualify your variable types. Both DAO and ADO have Database and Recordset types that are incompatible with each other. If you use unqualified references and have both the DAO and ADO libraries referenced, the object library that is listed first in the references list will supply the data type. This can produce runtime errors if the variable is assigned to an object type that you do not expect. I recommend always using fully qualified data types to avoid confusion as to what data types are being referenced, as the following code snippet shows.

```
'Example code only, not to be placed in clsDAO
'Qualified DAO references
Private m_odbSales As DAO.Database
Dim oRecipients As DAO.Recordset

'Unqualified references, could be DAO or ADO
Private m_odbSales As Database
Dim oRecipients As Recordset
```

The next step is to open a data source. To do this we use the OpenDatabase method. This method will return to us a Database object. If you have not installed the sample Northwind Access database, you will need to do so for the example in this section. You can install this database from the Office CD using the Office installation program. If you install it to a path other than the default path, adjust the statement below where it appears in the Initialize event for the clsDAO class.

```
Private Sub Class_Initialize()
  On Error Resume Next
  Set m_odbSales = OpenDatabase _
    ("C:\Program Files\Microsoft " _
    & "Office\Office\Samples\Northwind.mdb")
End Sub
```

With the OpenDatabase method you can also open other databases for which you have ODBC (Open Database Connectivity) drivers. To do this you would make use of the Connect parameter of the OpenDatabase method. This parameter will take a connection string including username, password and DSN (Data Source Name). The creation of a DSN can make connecting to databases simpler to code than having to provide all the parameters in your code. Creation of a DSN is discussed in the following section on using ADO. The following code snippet shows how to use a DSN to open a database.

```
'Example only, not to be placed in clsDAO
Set m_odsales = OpenDatabase("Northwind", _
  Connect:="ODBC;DATABASE=Northwind;UID=sa;PWD=;DSN=Northwind")
```

The Terminate event of the class is used to destroy the module level Database variable.

```
Private Sub Class_Terminate()
    If Not m_odbSales Is Nothing Then
        Set m_odbSales = Nothing
    End If
End Sub
```

So with the reference to the database created, the next step is to get the data. The data we will be working with in this example are the Sales Representative records in the Employees table of the Northwind sample database. To get at this data we need to make use of the Recordset object. This object gives us the ability to open a table, and to limit the returned table by using a query or a SQL statement. In our case we will make use of a SQL statement because we want to limit the number of columns returned in the Recordset. All of the external interaction with the class module takes place through the DAOSendMail method of the class.

```
Public Sub DAOSendMail()
  Dim oRecipients As DAO.Recordset
  Dim oOL As Outlook.Application
  Dim oMail As Outlook.MailItem

  On Error Resume Next
  Set oRecipients = m_odbSales.OpenRecordset _
    ("SELECT FirstName, LastName FROM Employees " _
    & "WHERE Title = 'Sales Representative';")
```

In the code above we are using a SQL statement that will return the FirstName and LastName columns from the Employees table. The last piece of the SQL statement is the WHERE clause, and in this case we are specifying that we want to return only records that have a Title of Sales Representatives. If we have any employees meeting our criteria we will now be able to access them through our Recordset object.

In the code below we will use the Recordset.RecordCount property to see if we have any Employees meeting the criteria set in the SQL statement. The Recordset that was opened was the default table type Recordset. If we had opened a Recordset that returned a dynaset, a snapshot, or a forward-only Recordset object, the Recordset.RecordCount property would not be guaranteed to be accurate until all the records in the Recordset had been accessed. This can be done by using the Recordset.MoveLast method.

The Recordset.EOF (End of File) property is used to terminate the loop that accesses the records returned in our Recordset, and the Recordset.MoveNext method is used to navigate through the Recordset. Each name of a returned employee that is a Sales Representative is added to the Recipients collection of a newly created email.

```
    If oRecipients.RecordCount <> 0 Then
      oRecipients.MoveFirst
      Set oOL = CreateObject("Outlook.Application")
      Set oMail = oOL.CreateItem(olMailItem)

      Do While Not oRecipients.EOF
        oMail.Recipients.Add oRecipients("FirstName") _
          & " " & oRecipients("LastName")

        oRecipients.MoveNext
      Loop
```

The email item is then given a `Subject` and the `Body` of the e-mail is created. Finally, the e-mail item is displayed and the method's object variables are destroyed.

```
    'Setup the other Mail information
    oMail.Subject = "Sales Information for " & Format(Now, "YYYY")

    oMail.Body = "We had a good year."
    oMail.Display
  End If

  Set oMail = Nothing
  Set oRecipients = Nothing
End Sub
```

The wrapper procedure `GetDAOData` is used to instantiate and call the `clsDAO` class, and should be placed in the `basDataImport` code module we created earlier in this chapter.

```
Private Sub GetDAOData()
  Dim oClass As clsDAO

  Set oClass = New clsDAO
  oClass.DAOSendMail

  Set oClass = Nothing
End Sub
```

The following screen shot shows the email message that is created, with the names of the Sales Representatives in the To field. Note that creating the Body of the message in code has converted the e-mail message to RTF format, as discussed earlier in this book.

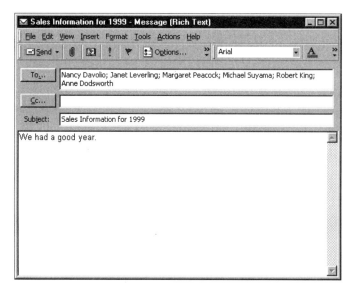

DAO can also be used to create new databases, database tables, queries on tables, and to update data in tables. Consider using DAO mainly when you are working with Access databases, for which it is optimized.

Getting Data From Access and SQL Server Using ADO

For this section. we need to set a reference to ActiveX Data Objects(ADO). Once in the references dialog, we are looking for the Microsoft ActiveX Data Objects 2.1 Library. Once we have the reference set we are going to look up employees in the Employees table of the `Northwind` sample database in Microsoft SQL Server 7.0. A reference to the Microsoft Outlook 9.0 Object Library is also required.

This section refers to using ADO with SQL Server and with Access. Another database that is provided by Microsoft, MSDE (Microsoft Data Engine), was introduced with Office 2000. This database is code compatible with SQL Server databases. It provides a transaction based client/server database that can be run on Windows 95 and Windows 98, in addition to running on Windows NT.

MSDE has a 2-gigabyte database size limit, and is optimized for small workgroups and individual users. MSDE is optimized for 5 users, although it can have more than this number. MSDE provides scalability to SQL Server, and supports logging transactions and most of the Transact-SQL statements.

The first step in using ADO with the `Northwind` database is to get a reference to the database. To do this we need to create a `Connection` variable that can hold the reference to it. The following code snippet shows the declaration of a `Connection` variable.

```
Private m_ocCon As ADODB.Connection
```

Once we have created the variable we have to connect to the database. To do this we use the `Open` method that is exposed to us by the `Connection` object. To make use of the `Open` method, we need to first set the `ConnectionString` so that the `Open` method knows what database we want to work with. In the example here the only difference to make it work with SQL Server or MS Access is the connection strings, so we have placed them in their own section.

ConnectionString for MS Access

Although this section will primarily show the use of ADO with SQL Server, the same methods are applicable to using ADO with Access. In this case to get the data from Access we can create a DSN (Data Source Name), so in the `ConnectionString` we would reference the DSN.

```
m_ocCon.ConnectionString = "DSN=Employee"
```

The code snippet above will connect us to the DSN called Employee. In this case we create Employee to point to the `Northwind` sample database that came with Access 2000. To create the DSN use the ODBC Data Sources (32bit) applet in the Control Panel. Once in the ODBC Data Source Administrator Dialog you need to click on **Add**, select an Access database driver, and click on **Finish**.

This will bring up a dialog box that is similar to the following screen shot.

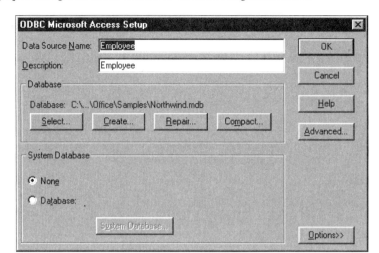

Enter Employee in both the Data Source Name and Description fields. Click on the Select command button and navigate to the Northwind sample database in the C:\Program Files\Microsoft Office\Office\Samples folder. Select it and click on OK to finish the creation of the DSN.

ConnectionString for SQL Server

To connect to a SQL Server database we could use a DSN as we did with Access, or we could provide the same information a DSN does in our code, as the following code snippet shows.

```
m_ocCon.ConnectionString = "driver={SQL Server};" & _
    "server=gifforddr;uid=sa;pwd=;database=NorthWind"
```

In this ConnectionString we need to define which driver we are going to use. To find this name out check the ODBC Data Sources (32bit) applet in the Control Panel, select the Drivers tab and see the names that are listed for the drivers that are installed. You should see the SQL Server driver. The next part of the ConnectionString is the name of the server where the database is located. Change the server name to the name of your SQL Server. The next is the uid which stands for the User ID, in this case we will use sa. The last part of the ConnectionString is the name of the database.

Retrieving Data through ADO

This section uses a class module to perform all the ADO functions, so insert a new class module in your project and name it clsADO. Declare a module level Connection variable in the Declarations section of the class.

```
Private m_ocCon As ADODB.Connection
```

The class's `Initialize` event is used to connect to the database, and the class's `Terminate` event is used to destroy the module level class variable.

```
Private Sub Class_Initialize()
   Set m_ocCon = New ADODB.Connection

   'Set the ConnectionString
   m_ocCon.ConnectionString = "driver={SQL Server};" & _
      "server=gifforddr;uid=sa;pwd=;database=NorthWind"

   'Open a Connection to the Database
   m_ocCon.Open
End Sub

Private Sub Class_Terminate()
   If Not m_ocCon Is Nothing Then
      Set m_ocCon = Nothing
   End If
End Sub
```

Once we have opened the connection to the database, the next step is to retrieve the data from the data source. To do this we need to make use of the `Recordset` object. Note that the ADO `Recordset` object is not compatible with the DAO `Recordset` object. All data operations of the class are performed by the `ADOSendMail` method of the class. The criteria for the `Recordset` will be that the `Title` for a record is set to `Sales Representative`.

```
Public Sub ADOSendMail()
   Dim oRec As ADODB.Recordset
   Dim oOL As Outlook.Application
   Dim oMail As Outlook.MailItem

   Dim sSql As String

   Set oRec = New ADODB.Recordset
   'Build the Select Statement
   sSql = "SELECT FirstName, LastName FROM Employees " _
      & "WHERE Title = 'Sales Representative';"
```

Once we have created a SQL statement to use to retrieve records from the database, we then pass the SQL statement into the `Recordset` object with the `Connection` variable. For us to retrieve data from a data source we must have an active `Connection` to use with the `Recordset` object. The other parameter we can pass to the `Open` method is a `CursorType`. The default `CursorType` is `adOpenForwardOnly`. By using the `adOpenForwardOnly`, you are specifying that you will only move forward inside the recordset. With this type of `CursorType`, once you have moved past a record you cannot go back to it unless you reopen the recordset. The other available types of `CursorType` settings are `adOpenKeyset`, `adOpenDynamic`, and `adOpenStatic`.

```
'Open the Recordset
oRec.Open sSql, m_ocCon, adOpenForwardOnly
```

The remainder of the code is similar to the code used in the DAO data access example.

```
Set oOL = CreateObject("Outlook.Application")
Set oMail = oOL.CreateItem(olMailItem)

Do While Not oRec.EOF
  'If we locate the Sales Recipient
  'then Add them to the mail item.
  oMail.Recipients.Add oRec("FirstName") & _
    " " & oRec("LastName")
  oRec.MoveNext
Loop

'Setup the other Mail information
oMail.Subject = "Sales Information for " _
  & Format(Now, "YYYY")

oMail.Body = "We had a good year."
oMail.Display

Set oMail = Nothing
Set oOL = Nothing
Set oRec = Nothing
End Sub
```

The wrapper procedure GetADOData is used to instantiate the clsADO class and to call the ADOSendMail method of the class. Place this wrapper procedure in the basDataImport module.

```
Private Sub GetADOData()
  Dim oClass As clsADO

  Set oClass = New clsADO
  oClass.ADOSendMail

  Set oClass = Nothing
End Sub
```

The e-mail that is produced as the output of the class module should look the same as the email that is produced by the DAO example earlier in this chapter.

Updating Data with ADO

To update SQL Server data by using ADO we need to first get the connection to the data source. This connection is the same as the connection that was just used in the preceding section. Once we have a connection, we can make use of the Execute method that is exposed by the Command object to run a stored procedure in the SQL Server database. This method gives us a way to update the data directly, instead of having to pull the data into a Recordset object and then updating it in the Recordset. The Command object needs the text it is to run, what type of text it is, and any parameters appended to the command object before the Execute method is called.

```
Dim oCon As ADODB.Connection
Dim oCom As ADODB.Command
Dim oParam As ADODB.Parameter

Set oCon = New ADODB.Connection

'Set the ConnectionString
oCon.ConnectionString = "driver={SQL Server};" & _
  "server=gifforddr;uid=sa;pwd=;database=NorthWind"
'Open a Connection to the Database
oCon.Open
```

To add a `Parameter` to the `Command` object we use the `CreateParameter` method exposed by the `Command` object. Once we have set the value of the `Parameter`, we use the `Append` method to add it to the `Command` object. The `CreateParameter` method takes 5 parameters; these are the name of parameter, the data type of the data, the type of `Parameter` it is (Input or Output), the data size, and the value for the `Parameter`.

```
'Load the Parameters for the CustomerObject
Set oParam = oCom.CreateParameter _
  ("Title", adVarChar, adParamInput, 30, "Sales Representative")
oCom.Parameters.Append oParam
```

The next piece of information that the `Command` object needs is the `Text` to be executed. This can be the name of a stored procedure, or it can be a SQL Statement. After we have set the `Text` for the `Command`, we have to specify what type of `Text` it is. This parameter can be any one of the `CommandTypeEnum` constants, in this case we are using `adCmdStoredProc`, which specifies that we are using a stored procedure in the `CommandText` property. After we have set the `CommandText`, `Parameters` and `CommandType` for the `Command` object we can use the `Execute` method. In our case this will run the stored procedure that was passed into the `CommandText` property.

```
'Set which Stored Procedure to use
oCom.CommandText = SPU_UPDATEEMPLOYEE
oCom.CommandType = adCmdStoredProc
'Execute the Stored Procedure
oCom.Execute
```

This method enables us to work with stored procedures in a SQL Server database from our code.

For more information on ADO check out the Wrox *ADO 2.1 Programmer's Reference*, ISBN 1861002688.

Summary

In this chapter we saw how to get data from the Word, Excel, DAO and ADO object models and data access methods. That data was then used in Outlook to create new Outlook items, address e-mail, and fill an email message with data. Just as you can export Outlook data into other applications using automation, you can use automation to get data from other applications and use that data in Outlook.

Using ADO, and the examples of using ADO with Access and SQL Server as a model, we can also synchronize Outlook databases with relational databases. Any application that exposes its data through its object model, such as Word or Excel, can be used to supply data for Outlook. Any database or file that can be used with ADO or ODBC drivers can also supply Outlook with data.

Case Study: Asset Tracking Application

For many organizations, keeping track of computer hardware is an incredibly difficult proposition. Employee turnover, inter-office transfers, and highly distributed operations all contribute to the problem of mixed up, inaccurate, and out-of-date equipment records. In fact, large organizations often employ Asset Tracking teams to manage the distribution, upgrade, and management of computer hardware.

These teams typically maintain a database of employees and the computer hardware and peripherals that each uses. This database might be as crude as a paper-based property ledger, or as sophisticated as an enterprise, ERP-like package that manages the distribution of *all* corporate assets.

However, no matter how Asset Tracking teams go about maintaining equipment records, they all face the same problem: how to ensure that those records stay as accurate as possible. Most commonly, assets are tracked when first deployed – additionally, some organizations will conduct hardware audits to re-establish positive control of computer hardware or send inventory surveys to employees. Of course, these approaches to updating the inventory are impractical when working with a geographically distributed workforce – employees may not return surveys, audits may be incomplete, any number of possible problems that can't easily be dealt with from a distance.

Unlike other methods of collecting information, e-mail has established itself as a reliable conduit within distributed workforces. For most, checking and responding to e-mail is as routine as returning a phone call. Moreover, most large corporations have sophisticated and standardized e-mail infrastructures. It is relatively straightforward to use Microsoft's Outlook and Exchange programs to deliver hardware inventory surveys to employees. Collecting data via e-mail avoids the introduction of a new workflow process, while providing a more structured response mechanism than pen and paper. The benefits of e-mail-based inventory surveying include:

- increased response numbers
- lower asset management costs
- quicker responses

Since corporate users tend to standardize on a common e-mail platform (to reduce costs, risks, etc.), deployment of an Outlook 2000 Asset Tracking application requires little or no modification to employees' computers. You can therefore deploy 'thin', e-mail-based forms, which make use of the Outlook 2000 development/execution environment.

Because an asset inventory will be used to support decisions such as hardware purchases and upgrade strategy, Asset Managers need a clear picture of users' equipment status. With accurate inventory status, managers are far more likely to make high-impact, cost-effective hardware acquisition decisions.

Asset Tracking Forms in Outlook 2000

This case study profiles an Asset Tracking application, using Microsoft Outlook 2000, Microsoft SQL Server 6.5 (or later), and Microsoft Access 2000 to provide a robust mechanism for managing computer assets across a large, distributed organization. The application will operate as follows:

- ❑ Asset Managers use the Access-based administration tool to generate lists of employees who need to update their computer inventory profile.

- ❑ Using these employee lists, Access builds Outlook forms to e-mail to each employee on the list. Each form includes a personalized hardware inventory for the e-mail recipient, as well as personal and professional profile information.

- ❑ Employees who receive an e-mail from the Asset Tracking team use a simple Outlook form interface to submit any relevant changes or updates to their own inventory.

- ❑ Users mail their updated Asset Tracking form back to the management team.

- ❑ Asset Managers review changes and use the administrative tab of the Outlook form to update the central database.

Because the query/update process is so simple, Asset Management teams can afford to update their records on a frequent basis. Although we've already touched on the general benefits of deploying an Asset Tracking application using an e-mail-based solution such as Outlook 2000, we can now look specifically at how this application can help us:

- ❑ Inter-office mail and hardware audits are slow – using Outlook forms, even a large organization can audit their hardware inventory in a few days.

- ❑ Paper consumption, mailing costs, etc. are reduced

- ❑ The time that Asset Management staff spend on administrative tasks (such as managing the database) is reduced. Since the hardware owners provide direct feedback (which Outlook writes directly to the master database), the Asset Management team can spend more time making upgrade/enhancement decisions.

- ❑ Distributing the Asset Tracking software is as simple as publishing a new form to the Organizational Forms Library. There is no client component other than the Outlook 2000 e-mail client, so support and upgrade costs are minimized.

Environment Assumptions

In order to actively follow this case study, you will need a development environment in place, capable of hosting the necessary software components. Minimum requirements are:

- ❑ Windows 95,98SR2, or NT 4.0 SP5 (Client)
- ❑ Windows NT Server 4.0SP5 (SQL Server)
- ❑ MS Exchange Server (if you wish to publish forms to an organizational library)
- ❑ Microsoft Outlook 2000 (Client)
- ❑ Microsoft SQL Server 6.5 or later (SQL Server)
- ❑ Microsoft Access 2000 (Client)
- ❑ MDAC 2.1 (Microsoft Data Access Components) (Client)
- ❑ ODBC Manager (Client - Asset Manager)

Architectural Overview of Asset Tracker Application

Although the relationship between them is not entirely distinct, we can identify three layers in the proposed Asset Tracking application. As the figure below illustrates, the **Data Services** layer provides the physical store of employee and asset information. The **Middle-Tier** is often considered to consist of standalone business objects or server side components. However, stored procedures will often handle information flow between the data and presentation layers adequately, as is the case in our application. Finally, the **Presentation** layer consists of two sets of Outlook forms: one for end users, and the other for Asset Tracking Administrators.

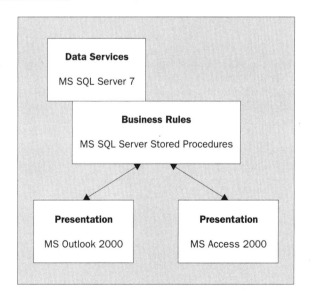

Physical Diagram

The diagram below illustrates the physical layout of the Asset Tracking software system.

❑ **End Users** are those employees with assets that require tracking. They simply require Outlook 2000 and access to an Exchange Server with an Organizational Forms Library containing the necessary Asset Tracking forms.

❑ **Administrators** are the members of the Asset Tracking staff who manage hardware deployment, upgrades, etc. They require administrative software components (in addition to Outlook 2000) – specifically, these will be Access 2000, a configured ODBC connection, and MDAC (Microsoft Data Access Components) 2.0 or later.

❑ To automatically deploy Outlook forms to End Users, Exchange must to be configured to support an Organizational Forms library. Otherwise, End Users must store the Asset Tracking forms in their Personal Forms Library.

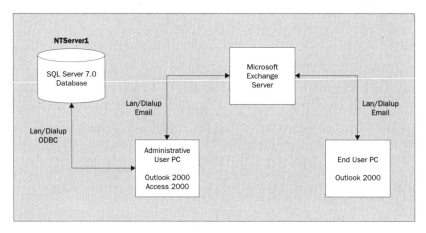

Data Flow View

One of the great advantages of implementing a software system using Outlook 2000 is that it supports a logical and sequential flow of information. Outlook forms flow from Inbox to Inbox, so work flows as users respond to their e-mail. This makes it very easy for End Users and Asset Tracking Administrators to build up a picture of what tasks need to be completed. The diagram below shows the flow of Asset Tracking information.

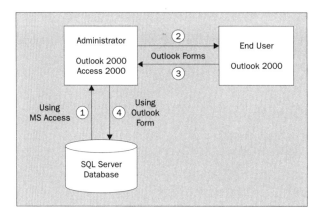

As you can see, there are four distinct steps involved in updating the Asset Tracking database with new information:

❑ First, the Administrator uses the Access application to generate a list of End Users to survey.

❑ Once selected, Access generates appropriate Outlook forms and e-mails them to the relevant End Users.

❑ End Users then update the Asset Tracking information by opening their e-mail, modifying fields on the Outlook forms, and e-mailing the response page back to the Administrator.

❑ Finally, the Administrator uses the **Administrative** tab on the Outlook form to review changes that the user has made and to send updates back to the SQL Server database.

Building the Asset Tracking Application

This case study will walk you through the creation of one part of a robust Asset Tracking application, which large organizations might use to maintain accurate inventories of PC hardware and peripherals. We will focus on building the components that leverage Outlook 2000, and show how Outlook forms can be used to automate workflow. To construct this application, we shall build up project components in the following order:

❑ Create the SQL Server database, views, and stored procedures

❑ Populate the SQL Server database with dummy data (to support testing and demonstration)

❑ Construct the Outlook 2000 form(s) and place form controls

❑ Write the Outlook 2000 form code necessary to populate fields, validate entries, and update the SQL Server

❑ Configure the ODBC connection (necessary for the Asset Manager to use the Access-based administrative tool)

❑ Construct the Access database tables, queries, and form for the Asset Manager tool

❑ Write the Access VBA code necessary to build a list of End Users, generate the populated Outlook 2000 Asset Survey forms, and e-mail the completed form

> Note that fully-fledged Asset Tracking tools will generally also include features such as reporting and database management — while these are necessary for a complete solution, they are outside the scope of this case study and will not be implemented here.

Creating SQL Server 7.0 Database, Views, and Stored Procedures

As we've already noted, SQL Server provides a number of clear advantages over personal database environments such as Access – however, its setup and development can be a bit trickier. Significantly, most developers don't have a Windows NT Server with SQL Server sitting around at their disposal. We overlook this limitation for the purposes of our case study, assuming that you have administrative privileges on a SQL Server machine and can create tables, stored procedures, and views. If this is not the case, most of the following code can be executed in an Access 2000 environment without modification. While the database you create using Access won't be able to handle a large, distributed user base, it will provide a perfectly adequate environment in which to solidify your understanding of Outlook 2000 development techniques.

Database Setup

Before we can begin executing SQL scripts to build our database, we must create a new database in the SQL Server Enterprise Manager.

> *We assume you are reasonably familiar with the SQL Server 6.5 or 7.0 administrative tools Enterprise Manager and Query Analyzer. If not, you may wish to refer to 'Professional SQL Server 7 Programming', ISBN 1861002319, from Wrox Press.*

❑ First, on your SQL Server machine, open up Enterprise Manager and click on the **Server** group.

❑ Right-click on the appropriate SQL Server (**NTSERVER1** in the accompanying screenshot), and select **New Database**.

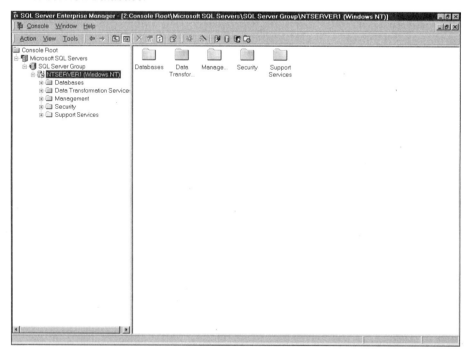

❑ This opens a database creation dialog box that you use to specify database details.

❑ Enter the database name as "KAT" and click OK.

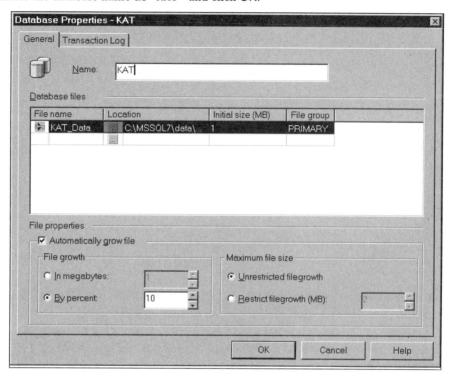

❑ Depending on how fast your SQL Server performs, you will soon return to the Enterprise Manager control panel. You should be able to click on your SQL Server database and view the automatically created elements for the KAT database. At this point you are ready to begin building tables, views, and stored procedures for the KAT database.

The steps described above deliberately omit any discussion of database security, performance optimization, transaction logging, or database management. Practices vary significantly from organization to organization, so we leave it up to you to implement any necessary customizations for production implementation of the KAT database.

Data Model & Table

The diagram below shows the data model of the database we are going to create, and was generated with MS SQL Server 7.0 Enterprise Manager. After executing the following creation scripts for tables, views, and stored procedures, you can choose to auto-create a database model from the existing data structures. As you will see, the EMPLOYEE table serves as the root table, while most of the others contain information regarding specific equipment, lease information, or details of equipment location. The two free-standing tables are used for data lookups, and are used to maintain data integrity from record to record.

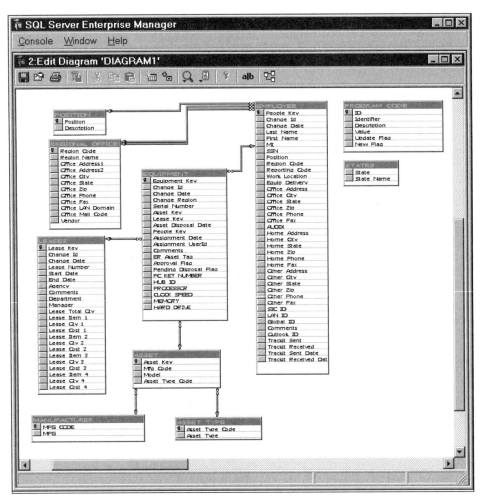

Rather than spend time describing the data elements for each of these tables, I'll let the table creation scripts do the talking. If specific data elements are unique or critical to program execution, I'll make note in the appropriate section.

Creating the Database Elements

To build the structure of the Asset Tracking (KAT) database, we will execute SQL scripts that can be invoked from the SQL Server 7.0 Query Analyzer. The scripts below will build the tables, relationships, indices, and foreign keys necessary to replicate the entity relationship diagram above. Once we have created the necessary tables, we will build views and stored procedures that we will call from the MS Access Administration Tool and from our Outlook 2000 forms.

For those of you not interested in building the database enviornment manually, you can download the database creation scripts from the Wrox Press website, at www.wrox.com. Loading and executing the file KAT.SQL will build ALL the database elements necessary to complete this case study.

In either case, you must first open the Query Analyzer application and select the KAT database from the dropdown list box.

> **You must be sure to select the KAT database in this way before executing any of the scripts below. Otherwise everything will be created in SQL Server's "master" database.**

Next, enter the necessary SQL from the code blocks below (or by loading the KAT.SQL file). Once you complete typing each block of SQL, click the green arrow to run the script – if errors arise, it will consequently be easier to debug.

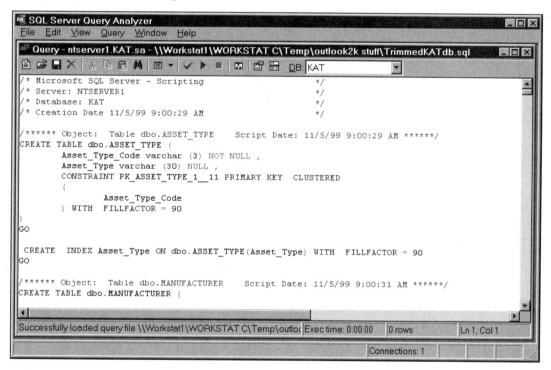

Table Creation Scripts

ASSET_TYPE

This table will hold definitions of the various types of assets to track (such as printers, laptops, fax/modems, etc.). These item types will be used to enforce validation when users modify or add new pieces of equipment to their inventory.

```
CREATE TABLE dbo.ASSET_TYPE (
  Asset_Type_Code varchar (3) NOT NULL ,
  Asset_Type varchar (30) NULL ,
  CONSTRAINT PK_ASSET_TYPE_1__11 PRIMARY KEY  CLUSTERED
```

```
   (
     Asset_Type_Code
   )
 )
 GO


   CREATE   INDEX Asset_Type ON dbo.ASSET_TYPE(Asset_Type)
 GO
```

MANUFACTURER

This table holds equipment manufacturer descriptions and abbreviations for standard PC and peripheral suppliers such as HP, IBM, COMPAQ, etc. Again, information in this table is used to enforce manufacturer validation when users add or modify their equipment inventory.

```
 CREATE TABLE dbo.MANUFACTURER (
   MFG_CODE varchar (3) NOT NULL ,
   MFG varchar (30) NOT NULL ,
   CONSTRAINT PK_MANUFACTURER_1__11 PRIMARY KEY   CLUSTERED
   (
     MFG_CODE
   )
 )
 GO

   CREATE   INDEX MFG ON dbo.MANUFACTURER(MFG)
 GO
```

ASSET

This table will hold the specific asset nomenclature of items that are being tracked. In a large corporation, it is important to view or classify equipment together. Often, specific types of equipment (such as a particular laptop model) are distributed at the same time. It is therefore useful for Asset Managers to view a list of equipment aggregated by type, in order to make decisions about replacement, upgrades, etc.

```
 CREATE TABLE dbo.ASSET (
   Asset_Key int IDENTITY (1, 1) NOT NULL ,
   Mfg_Code varchar (3) NOT NULL ,
   Model varchar (50) NOT NULL ,
   Asset_Type_Code varchar (3) NOT NULL ,
   CONSTRAINT PK_ASSET_1__11 PRIMARY KEY   CLUSTERED
   (
     Asset_Key
   ) ,
   CONSTRAINT Asset_Type_Code FOREIGN KEY
   (
     Asset_Type_Code
   ) REFERENCES dbo.ASSET_TYPE (
     Asset_Type_Code
   ),
```

```
   CONSTRAINT Mfg_Code FOREIGN KEY
   (
     Mfg_Code
   ) REFERENCES dbo.MANUFACTURER (
     MFG_CODE
   )
)
GO

 CREATE   INDEX Asset_Type_Code ON dbo.ASSET(Asset_Type_Code)
GO
```

POSITION

This table holds the position descriptions and abbreviations for the company employees who maintain physical possession of tracked assets. They include Sales Rep, Administrative Assistant, etc.

```
CREATE TABLE dbo.POSITION (
  Position varchar (10) NOT NULL ,
  Description varchar (35) NOT NULL ,
  CONSTRAINT PK_POSITION_1__11 PRIMARY KEY  CLUSTERED
  (
    Position
  )
)
GO
```

REGIONAL_OFFICE

This table holds the names and details of operating offices that a large company might use. These offices, usually geographically dispersed, include Chicago, Los Angeles, etc. As we've already seen, Asset Managers need to view assets using various aggregation techniques. The advantage of looking at equipment by regional office is that it allows managers to strategically execute hardware and software rollout plans. To save money and personnel, many large companies send Asset Management teams to regional offices to upgrade/replace all PC equipment at the same time.

```
CREATE TABLE dbo.REGIONAL_OFFICE (
  Region_Code int NOT NULL ,
  Region_Name varchar (50) NOT NULL ,
  Office_Address1 varchar (50) NULL ,
  Office_Address2 varchar (50) NULL ,
  Office_City varchar (30) NULL ,
  Office_State varchar (15) NULL ,
  Office_Zip varchar (9) NULL ,
  Office_Phone varchar (10) NULL ,
  Office_Fax varchar (10) NULL ,
  Office_LAN_Domain varchar (7) NULL ,
  Office_Mail_Code varchar (10) NULL ,
  Vendor int NULL ,
  CONSTRAINT PK_REGIONAL_OFFICE_1__11 PRIMARY KEY  CLUSTERED
```

```
  (
     Region_Code
  )
)
GO

  CREATE   INDEX Region_Name ON dbo.REGIONAL_OFFICE(Region_Name)
GO
```

EMPLOYEE

As you can probably tell from the model, this table is central to the data structure of the Asset Tracking application. It holds detailed information on each employee maintaining possession of tracked equipment. Even if you didn't have a graphical representation of the database to confirm your suspicions, the FOREIGN KEY constraints below should be a dead giveaway. Notice that there are four indices for this table, including a compound INDEX for employee name and a unique INDEX for SSN.

You do see a lot of replication of field types in this database including addresses, phone number, etc. While the database structure would have been much more elegant if these replications were removed into a 1-N related table, this would have necessarily increased the complexity of the Outlook form code used to populate and extract these values.

```
CREATE TABLE dbo.EMPLOYEE (
   People_Key int IDENTITY (1, 1) NOT NULL ,
   Change_Id varchar (20) NULL ,
   Change_Date datetime NULL ,
   Last_Name varchar (25) NOT NULL ,
   First_Name varchar (25) NULL ,
   MI varchar (1) NULL ,
   SSN varchar (9) NULL ,
   Position varchar (10) NULL ,
   Region_Code int NOT NULL ,
   Reporting_Code varchar (3) NULL ,
   Work_Location varchar (10) NULL ,
   Equip_Delivery varchar (10) NULL ,
   Office_Address varchar (100) NULL ,
   Office_City varchar (30) NULL ,
   Office_State varchar (15) NULL ,
   Office_Zip varchar (9) NULL ,
   Office_Phone varchar (11) NULL ,
   Office_Fax varchar (11) NULL ,
   AUDIX varchar (5) NULL ,
   Home_Address varchar (100) NULL ,
   Home_City varchar (30) NULL ,
   Home_State varchar (15) NULL ,
   Home_Zip varchar (9) NULL ,
   Home_Phone varchar (11) NULL ,
   Home_Fax varchar (11) NULL ,
   Other_Address varchar (100) NULL ,
   Other_City varchar (30) NULL ,
```

```
      Other_State varchar (15) NULL ,
      Other_Zip varchar (9) NULL ,
      Other_Phone varchar (11) NULL ,
      Other_Fax varchar (11) NULL ,
      SIC_ID varchar (5) NULL ,
      LAN_ID varchar (8) NULL ,
      Global_ID varchar (50) NULL ,
      Comments varchar (255) NULL ,
      Outlook_ID varchar (100) NULL ,
      Trackit_Sent varchar (1) NULL ,
      Trackit_Received varchar (1) NULL ,
      Trackit_Sent_Date datetime NULL ,
      Trackit_Received_Date datetime NULL ,
      CONSTRAINT PK_EMPLOYEE_1__11 PRIMARY KEY  CLUSTERED
      (
        People_Key
      ),
      CONSTRAINT Employee_Position FOREIGN KEY
      (
        Position
      ) REFERENCES dbo.POSITION (
        Position
      ),
      CONSTRAINT FK_EMPLOYEE_1__10 FOREIGN KEY
      (
        Region_Code
      ) REFERENCES dbo.REGIONAL_OFFICE (
        Region_Code
      ),
      CONSTRAINT Region_Code FOREIGN KEY
      (
        Region_Code
      ) REFERENCES dbo.REGIONAL_OFFICE (
        Region_Code
      )
)
GO

 CREATE  INDEX Name ON dbo.EMPLOYEE(Last_Name, First_Name, MI)
GO

 CREATE  INDEX Position ON dbo.EMPLOYEE(Position)
GO

 CREATE  INDEX Region_Code ON dbo.EMPLOYEE(Region_Code)
GO

 CREATE  UNIQUE  INDEX SSN ON dbo.EMPLOYEE(SSN)
GO
```

LEASES

This table contains lease information for equipment that is leased. Since many organizations hold a combination of owned and leased PC equipment, it is important for Asset Managers to know the lease status of all property. As you can see from the data digram, LEASES is related to the EQUIPMENT table. However, not all EQUIPMENT requires an associated LEASE. That's why Lease_Key can be NULL in the EQUIPMENT table.

```
CREATE TABLE dbo.LEASES (
  Lease_Key int IDENTITY (1, 1) NOT NULL ,
  Change_Id varchar (20) NULL ,
  Change_Date datetime NULL ,
  Lease_Number varchar (25) NOT NULL ,
  Start_Date datetime NULL ,
  End_Date datetime NULL ,
  Agency varchar (35) NULL ,
  Comments varchar (255) NULL ,
  Department varchar (10) NULL ,
  Manager varchar (20) NULL ,
  Lease_Total_Qty int NULL ,
  Lease_Item_1 int NULL ,
  Lease_Qty_1 int NULL ,
  Lease_Cost_1 money NULL ,
  Lease_Item_2 int NULL ,
  Lease_Qty_2 int NULL ,
  Lease_Cost_2 money NULL ,
  Lease_Item_3 int NULL ,
  Lease_Qty_3 int NULL ,
  Lease_Cost_3 money NULL ,
  Lease_Item_4 int NULL ,
  Lease_Qty_4 int NULL ,
  Lease_Cost_4 money NULL ,
  CONSTRAINT PK_LEASES_1__11 PRIMARY KEY  CLUSTERED
  (
    Lease_Key
  )
)
GO

  CREATE  INDEX Lease_Number ON dbo.LEASES(Lease_Number)
GO
```

EQUIPMENT

This table holds detailed information for each piece of tracked equipment. While no piece of equipment can exist outside the possession of an EMPLOYEE, this table clearly holds the most critical information in the database. As you can see, there is a FOREIGN_KEY constraint with the ASSET table. This ensures that equipment entered into this table is classified into aproved ASSETS, ASSET_TYPES, and MANUFACTURER. Moreover, EQUIPMENT serves as the link between employees and their associated equipment leases.

```
CREATE TABLE dbo.EQUIPMENT (
  Equipment_Key int IDENTITY (1, 1) NOT NULL ,
  Change_Id varchar (20) NULL ,
```

```
    Change_Date datetime NULL ,
    Change_Region varchar (60) NULL ,
    Serial_Number varchar (20) NULL ,
    Asset_Key int NOT NULL ,
    Lease_Key int NULL ,
    Asset_Disposal_Date datetime NULL ,
    People_Key int NOT NULL ,
    Assignment_Date datetime NULL ,
    Assignment_UserId varchar (20) NULL ,
    Comments varchar (255) NULL ,
    ER_Asset_Tag varchar (20) NULL ,
    Approval_Flag int NULL ,
    Pending_Disposal_Flag int NULL ,
    PC_KEY_NUMBER varchar (20) NULL ,
    HUB_ID varchar (20) NULL ,
    PROCESSOR varchar (20) NULL ,
    CLOCK_SPEED varchar (20) NULL ,
    MEMORY varchar (20) NULL ,
    HARD_DRIVE varchar (20) NULL ,
    CONSTRAINT PK_EQUIPMENT_1__11 PRIMARY KEY  CLUSTERED
    (
        Equipment_Key
    ) ,
    CONSTRAINT Equipment_Asset_Key FOREIGN KEY
    (
        Asset_Key
    ) REFERENCES dbo.ASSET (
        Asset_Key
    ),
    CONSTRAINT Equipment_Lease_Key FOREIGN KEY
    (
        Lease_Key
    ) REFERENCES dbo.LEASES (
        Lease_Key
    ),
    CONSTRAINT Equipment_People_Key FOREIGN KEY
    (
        People_Key
    ) REFERENCES dbo.EMPLOYEE (
        People_Key
    )
)
GO

CREATE  INDEX Asset_Key ON dbo.EQUIPMENT(Asset_Key)
GO

CREATE  INDEX Lease_Key ON dbo.EQUIPMENT(Lease_Key)
GO

CREATE  INDEX People_Key ON dbo.EQUIPMENT(People_Key)
GO

CREATE  UNIQUE  INDEX Serial_Number ON dbo.EQUIPMENT(Serial_Number)
GO
```

329

PROGRAM_CODE

This table contains lookup values that will be used by the Outlook Form to build the form, validate entries, and store temporary data. This table serves as a utility scratchpad, and as you will see later, most of the fields that this data populates on the Outlook 2000 form are not visible.

```
CREATE TABLE dbo.PROGRAM_CODE (
   ID int IDENTITY (1, 1) NOT NULL ,
   Identifier varchar (7) NULL ,
   Description varchar (255) NULL ,
   Value varchar (100) NULL ,
   Update_Flag int NULL ,
   New_Flag int NULL ,
   CONSTRAINT PK___1__13 PRIMARY KEY  CLUSTERED
   (
      ID
   )
)
GO
```

STATES

This table speaks for itself – a simple lookup table containing state names and descriptions. Tables such as this are necessary to ensure that data entry errors don't cause your database to be full of erroneous state designations. This table is used to populate appropriate dropdown list boxes.

```
CREATE TABLE dbo.STATES (
   State varchar (2) NULL ,
   State_Name varchar (50) NULL
)
GO
```

View creation Scripts

ASSET_VIEW

This view is often required to present details about specific assets to the end-user in an easy to read and understandable format. It does not require the user to understand the table relationships to extract details about equipment. It is also used to populate selection boxes on the outlook form and ensure data integrity.

```
CREATE VIEW ASSET_VIEW AS
SELECT      ASSET.Asset_Key,MANUFACTURER.MFG + '' + ASSET.Model
                                    + '' + ASSET_TYPE.Asset_Type AS Asset
FROM        ASSET INNER JOIN ASSET_TYPE ON
                    ASSET.Asset_Type_Code
                    = ASSET_TYPE.Asset_Type_Code INNER JOIN
                    MANUFACTURER ON ASSET.Mfg_Code
                    = MANUFACTURER.MFG_CODE

GO
```

EMPLOYEE_FULL_VIEW

This view connects the employee and their equipment, clearly the most common way that Asset Managers will wish to look at equipment. Normally, managers wish to see employee details and their equipment grouped together. The Outlook 2000 forms used for equipment list changes depend on this view to populate controls with default or startup values. The WHERE clause at the end of the SELECT block ensures that only approved equipment can be associated with a user. Until Asset Managers approve new additions to an employee's equipment list, Approval_Flag is FALSE, ensuring that employees can't just add and subtract equipment to and from their own inventory.

```
CREATE VIEW EMPLOYEE_FULL_VIEW AS
SELECT          EQUIPMENT.Equipment_Key, EMPLOYEE.*, ASSET.Model,
                MANUFACTURER.MFG, ASSET_TYPE.Asset_Type,
  EQUIPMENT.Serial_Number, EQUIPMENT.Asset_Key,
  EQUIPMENT.Pending_Disposal_Flag, EQUIPMENT.Lease_Key,
                LEASES.Lease_Number, POSITION.Description AS PosDescription,
          EQUIPMENT.PC_KEY_NUMBER, EQUIPMENT.HUB_ID, EQUIPMENT.PROCESSOR,
          EQUIPMENT.CLOCK_SPEED, EQUIPMENT.MEMORY, EQUIPMENT.HARD_DRIVE,
                EQUIPMENT.Comments AS EquipmentComments,
  REGIONAL_OFFICE.Region_Name, REGIONAL_OFFICE.Vendor,
  REPORTING_OFFICE.Region_Name As Reporting_Region_Name
FROM    POSITION RIGHT OUTER JOIN REGIONAL_OFFICE
        RIGHT OUTER JOIN EMPLOYEE ON REGIONAL_OFFICE.Region_Code =
EMPLOYEE.Region_Code
          AND REGIONAL_OFFICE.Region_Code = EMPLOYEE.Region_Code
          ON POSITION.Position = EMPLOYEE.Position
  FULL OUTER JOIN LEASES RIGHT OUTER JOIN EQUIPMENT INNER JOIN ASSET ON
EQUIPMENT.Asset_Key =
  ASSET.Asset_Key
  INNER JOIN ASSET_TYPE ON ASSET.Asset_Type_Code = ASSET_TYPE.Asset_Type_Code
  INNER JOIN MANUFACTURER ON ASSET.Mfg_Code = MANUFACTURER.MFG_CODE ON
LEASES.Lease_Key = \
  EQUIPMENT.Lease_Key ON EMPLOYEE.People_Key = EQUIPMENT.People_Key
  WHERE EQUIPMENT.Approval_Flag <>0 or EQUIPMENT.Approval_Flag IS NULL

GO
```

EMPLOYEE_FULLNAME_VIEW

This view is used to populate list boxes so the End User may easily select the specific person they would like. As you can see from the SQL, this view builds LastName, FirstName, and MiddleInitial views of EMPLOYEE names.

```
CREATE VIEW EMPLOYEE_FULLNAME_VIEW AS
  SELECT    Last_Name + ', ' + First_Name + ' ' + MI AS Name,
    People_Key,Last_Name,First_Name,MI,Region_Code
  FROM EMPLOYEE
GO
```

Stored Procedure Creation Scripts

sp_CheckUpdatePermission

This stored procedure checks that changed fields on an updated Asset Tracking form are OK to upload to the central database. This stored procedure is executed when an Administrator receives an updated Asset Tracking form from an employee, and wishes to approve changes and write them to the central database. The PROGRAM_CODE table contains a list of approved fields, which can be updated from the Asset Tracking form.

```
CREATE PROCEDURE sp_CheckUpdatePermission
(
@updateFlag int OUTPUT,
@fieldName varchar(50)
)
AS
SELECT @updateFlag = UPDATE_FLAG
FROM PROGRAM_CODE
WHERE Value = @fieldName
AND Identifier = "EQ" /*Equipment*/
GO
```

sp_SelectEmployeeFullView

This stored procedure builds a formatted view of all equipment for a particular individual by SERIAL_NUMBER. It converts position and region information into more understandable equivalents and it uses the PEOPLE_KEY identifier as a passed-in parameter.

```
CREATE PROCEDURE sp_SelectEmployeeFullView
(
@peopleKey int
)
AS
SELECT Last_Name, First_Name, MI, Position_Desc =
        CASE
            WHEN Position IS NULL THEN NULL
            ELSE PosDescription + " {" + Position + "}"
        END,
    Work_Location, Region_Code_Desc =
        CASE
            WHEN Region_Code IS NULL THEN NULL
            ELSE Region_Name + " {" + RTRIM(CONVERT(CHAR,Region_Code)) + "}"
        END,
    Equip_Delivery,
    Office_Address, Office_City, Office_State, Office_Zip,
    Office_Phone, Office_Fax, AUDIX,
    Home_Address, Home_City, Home_State,
    Home_Zip, Home_Phone, Home_Fax,
    Other_Address, Other_City, Other_State,
    Other_Zip, Other_Phone, Other_Fax,LAN_ID,
    SIC_ID, Global_ID, Outlook_ID, Comments, Serial_Number,
    MFG, Model, Asset_Type, Lease_Number
FROM EMPLOYEE_FULL_VIEW
WHERE People_Key = @peopleKey
ORDER BY Serial_Number
GO
```

UpdateEmployeeInfo

This stored procedure represents part of the great value of the Outlook form solution! Once called, this stored procedure updates the SQL Server tables with values from the Outlook form. It uses the `fieldName` and `peopleKey` identifiers, to perform an UPDATE operation on records. The code inside the BEGIN...END block extracts the region_id from the region description before it writes to the database.

```
CREATE PROCEDURE sp_UpdateEmployeeInfo
(
@fieldName varchar(50),
@value varchar(100),
@peopleKey int
)
AS
DECLARE
@@intEnd int,
@@intStart int

If Right(@fieldName,4) = "Desc"
BEGIN
  SELECT @@intEnd = PATINDEX("%_DESC%",@fieldName)
  SELECT @fieldName = SUBSTRING(@fieldName,1,@@intEnd-1)
  /* PRINT @fieldName */
  SELECT @@intStart = PATINDEX("%{%",@value)
  SELECT @@intEnd = PATINDEX("%}%",@value)
  SELECT @value = SUBSTRING(@value,@@intStart+1,@@intEnd-(@@intStart+1))
  /* PRINT @value */

END
IF @fieldName = "Last_Name"

  UPDATE EMPLOYEE
  SET Last_Name = @value
  WHERE People_Key = @peopleKey
ELSE IF @fieldName = "First_Name"
  UPDATE EMPLOYEE
  SET First_Name = @value
  WHERE People_Key = @peopleKey
ELSE IF @fieldName = "MI"
  UPDATE EMPLOYEE
  SET MI = @value
  WHERE People_Key = @peopleKey
ELSE IF @fieldName = "Position"
  UPDATE EMPLOYEE
  SET Position = @value
  WHERE People_Key = @peopleKey
ELSE IF @fieldName = "Region_Code"
  UPDATE EMPLOYEE
  SET Region_Code = CONVERT(int,@value)
  WHERE People_Key = @peopleKey
ELSE IF @fieldName = "Work_Location"
  UPDATE EMPLOYEE
  SET Work_Location = @value
  WHERE People_Key = @peopleKey
```

333

```
ELSE IF @fieldName = "Equip_Delivery"
  UPDATE EMPLOYEE
  SET Equip_Delivery = @value
  WHERE People_Key = @peopleKey
ELSE IF @fieldName = "Office_Address"
  UPDATE EMPLOYEE
  SET Office_Address = @value
  WHERE People_Key = @peopleKey
ELSE IF @fieldName = "Office_City"
  UPDATE EMPLOYEE
  SET Office_City = @value
  WHERE People_Key = @peopleKey

ELSE IF @fieldName = "Office_State"
  UPDATE EMPLOYEE
  SET Office_State = @value
  WHERE People_Key = @peopleKey
ELSE IF @fieldName = "Office_Zip"
  UPDATE EMPLOYEE
  SET Office_Zip = @value
  WHERE People_Key = @peopleKey
ELSE IF @fieldName = "Office_Phone"
  UPDATE EMPLOYEE
  SET Office_Phone = @value
  WHERE People_Key = @peopleKey
ELSE IF @fieldName = "Office_Fax"
  UPDATE EMPLOYEE
  SET Office_Fax = @value
  WHERE People_Key = @peopleKey
ELSE IF @fieldName = "AUDIX"
  UPDATE EMPLOYEE
  SET AUDIX = @value

  WHERE People_Key = @peopleKey
ELSE IF @fieldName = "Home_Address"
  UPDATE EMPLOYEE
  SET Home_Address = @value
  WHERE People_Key = @peopleKey
ELSE IF @fieldName = "Home_City"
  UPDATE EMPLOYEE

  SET Home_City = @value

  WHERE People_Key = @peopleKey
ELSE IF @fieldName = "Home_State"
  UPDATE EMPLOYEE
  SET Home_State = @value
  WHERE People_Key = @peopleKey
ELSE IF @fieldName = "Home_Zip"
  UPDATE EMPLOYEE
  SET Home_Zip = @value
  WHERE People_Key = @peopleKey
```

```
ELSE IF @fieldName = "Home_Phone"
   UPDATE EMPLOYEE
   SET Home_Phone = @value
   WHERE People_Key = @peopleKey
ELSE IF @fieldName = "Home_Fax"
   UPDATE EMPLOYEE
   SET Home_Fax = @value
   WHERE People_Key = @peopleKey
ELSE IF @fieldName = "Other_Address"
   UPDATE EMPLOYEE
   SET Other_Address = @value
   WHERE People_Key = @peopleKey
ELSE IF @fieldName = "Other_City"
   UPDATE EMPLOYEE
   SET Other_City = @value
   WHERE People_Key = @peopleKey
ELSE IF @fieldName = "Other_State"
   UPDATE EMPLOYEE
   SET Other_State = @value
   WHERE People_Key = @peopleKey
ELSE IF @fieldName = "Other_Zip"
   UPDATE EMPLOYEE
   SET Other_Zip = @value
   WHERE People_Key = @peopleKey
ELSE IF @fieldName = "Other_Phone"
   UPDATE EMPLOYEE
   SET Other_Phone = @value
   WHERE People_Key = @peopleKey
ELSE IF @fieldName = "Other_Fax"
   UPDATE EMPLOYEE
   SET Other_Fax = @value
   WHERE People_Key = @peopleKey
ELSE IF @fieldName = "SIC_ID"
   UPDATE EMPLOYEE
   SET SIC_ID = @value
   WHERE People_Key = @peopleKey
ELSE IF @fieldName = "LAN_ID"
   UPDATE EMPLOYEE
   SET LAN_ID = @value
   WHERE People_Key = @peopleKey
ELSE IF @fieldName = "Global_ID"
   UPDATE EMPLOYEE
   SET Global_ID = @value
   WHERE People_Key = @peopleKey
ELSE IF @fieldName = "Comments"
   UPDATE EMPLOYEE
   SET Comments = @value
   WHERE People_Key = @peopleKey
ELSE IF @fieldName = "Outlook_ID"
   UPDATE EMPLOYEE
   SET Outlook_ID = @value
   WHERE People_Key = @peopleKey
GO
```

UpdateEquipmentInfo

This stored procedure is used to update the date and change control 'tags' for pieces of equipment, as they are added or modified in the database. This routine uses the GetDate() function to timestamp changes to the EQUIPMENT table.

> *While the administrative tool required to use this data is beyond the scope of this case study, note that Administrators can use date information to track equipment status changes across location, designation, etc.*

```
CREATE PROCEDURE sp_UpdateEquipmentInfo
(
@newPeopleKey int,
@userName varchar(20),
@peopleKey int,
@serialNumber varchar(25)
)
AS

UPDATE EQUIPMENT
SET   Serial_Number = @serialNumber,
      Assignment_Date = GetDate(),
      Assignment_Userid = @userName,
      Change_Date = GetDate(),
      Change_Id = @userName
WHERE People_Key = @peopleKey

GO
```

Populating Tables for Testing and Demonstration

The scripts above create empty tables that would normally be populated through a robust administration tool. Since we're only covering the part of the administration tool that generates Outlook forms, we don't have a way to *create* lookup table data, employee information, etc. Since you'll want to test and experiment with this application, I've included some dummy data to prevent processing errors, populate list boxes on the Outlook forms, etc. Simply copy this code into Query Analyzer and run it. You can edit tables through the Enterprise Manager, but you'll have to ensure that you manually add data that maintains referential integrity. Don't worry about violating referential integrity, as SQL Server will not let you. Instead, it will generate ODBC errors and complain.

```
insert into PROGRAM_CODE (IDENTIFIER, DESCRIPTION, Value, Update_Flag, New_Flag)
values ("EQ","","MFG",1,1)
go
insert into PROGRAM_CODE (IDENTIFIER, DESCRIPTION, Value, Update_Flag, New_Flag)
values ("EQ","","Model",1,1)
go
insert into PROGRAM_CODE (IDENTIFIER, DESCRIPTION, Value, Update_Flag, New_Flag)
values ("EQ","","Asset_Type",1,1)
go
insert into PROGRAM_CODE (IDENTIFIER, DESCRIPTION, Value, Update_Flag, New_Flag)
values ("EQ","","Serial_Number",0,1)
go
insert into PROGRAM_CODE (IDENTIFIER, DESCRIPTION, Value, Update_Flag, New_Flag)
values ("EQ","","Lease_Number",2,0)
go
```

```
insert into PROGRAM_CODE (IDENTIFIER, DESCRIPTION, Value, Update_Flag)
values ("EQ","","Deleted Serial_Number",0)
go
insert into ASSET_TYPE(Asset_Type_Code, Asset_Type) values("PRT", "Printer")
go
insert into MANUFACTURER(MFG_Code, MFG) values("HP", "HP")
go
insert into ASSET(Mfg_Code, Model, Asset_Type_Code)
        values("HP", "LaserJet 4 Plus", "PRT")
go
insert into POSITION(Position, Description) values("SR", "Sales Representative")
go
insert into LEASES(Lease_Number) values("11121999HP4")
 go
insert into STATES(State, State_Name) values("IL", "Illinois")
go
insert into REGIONAL_OFFICE(Region_Code, Region_Name) values(1000, "Chicago")
go
insert into EMPLOYEE(Last_Name, First_Name, MI, SSN, Region_Code)
        values("Jones", "Jane", "S", "666889999", 1000)
go
insert into EQUIPMENT(Asset_Key, People_Key, Serial_Number) values(1, 1, "123455")
go
```

Creating the Outlook 2000 Forms

Now that the database is completely assembled and we've inserted some test data, we can shift our focus to developing the Outlook 2000 forms that will transport Asset Tracking data between the SQL Database and End Users. We now construct the forms, controls, and support code that will bring our application to life.

❑ First, enter design mode in a Message form (we won't actually be using the fields, but it is the least cluttered of the default types.)

❑ Publish it in your Personal Forms library as TrackitForm2 (so that it operates properly with the included code).

❑ Next, we eliminate controls that we won't be using, so go ahead and delete the large message box field that would typically be used to hold the body of an e-mail message.

As you've already seen, there are two parts to every Outlook form: a Compose page and a Read page. Since we want our Read and Compose pages need to look identical, we must clear out the message box on the Read page as well.

The following steps will be performed for each of five tabs. Three primary tabs should be renamed as: **Employee Message**, **Employee Equipment**, and **Admin Approval**. Two others (**Modify Equipment** and **Add Equipment**) will be invisible under normal circumstances, but will appear when users choose to **Modify** or **Add Equipment** to their inventory listing.

❑ Using the Control Toolbox, add custom controls and fields to the form as indicated in the following tables. Take care to name them accurately, as supporting code assumes all controls are named exactly as indicated below.

❑ Once you've added a field, right-click on it and select the **Properties** option from the context menu.

❑ On the **Display** tab in the Properties dialog box, enter the Field Name and Caption (where necessary), and ensure that checkboxes are checked appropriately.

Note that some controls do not use associated Outlook fields. If the tables don't indicate a value in the Choose Field column, you can ignore the next two steps and move on to the next control.

❑ On the Values tab, click the New button to create a new field for the `TrackitForm2` form.

❑ Type in the field name (e.g. `Last_Name`) and click OK. Note that this will generally match the name of the control – we do this intentionally, to reduce complexity by allowing Access to populate the Outlook form using field value names.

Of course, you must repeat the previous five steps for the Read page. However, do not attempt to create a New field for controls on this page. Instead, choose the same field you created on the Compose page. This will ensure that values are transferred to the response page when users send the tracking form back to the Asset Management team.

❑ Once you've repeated these steps for all five tabs on both pages, save and publish the form (by choosing Tools | Forms | Publish Form).

We're now ready to begin entering code to make the form do some work.

Tab 1: Employee Message Form

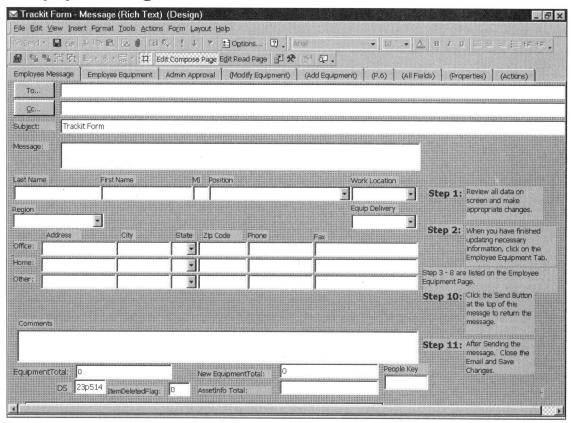

Fields for Employee Message Form

Control Type	Control Name	Caption	Visible	Enabled	ReadOnly	Locked	Field Name	Type	Prop. Used	List Type	Possible Values
TextBox	txtMessage		TRUE	TRUE	FALSE	FALSE	txtMessage	text	value		
TextBox	Last_Name		TRUE	TRUE	FALSE	FALSE	LastName	text	value		
TextBox	First_Name		TRUE	TRUE	FALSE	FALSE	FirstName	text	value		
TextBox	MI		TRUE	TRUE	FALSE	FALSE	MI	text	value		
Combo Box	Position_Desc		TRUE	TRUE	FALSE	FALSE	Position	text	value	Dropdown	
Combo Box	Work_Location		TRUE	TRUE	FALSE	FALSE	WorkLocation	text	value	Dropdown	Office; Home
Combo Box	Region_Code_Desc		TRUE	TRUE	FALSE	FALSE	RegionName	text	value	Dropdown	
Combo Box	Equip_Delivery		TRUE	TRUE	FALSE	FALSE	EquipDelivery	text	value	Dropdown	Office; Home; Other
TextBox	Office_Address		TRUE	TRUE	FALSE	FALSE	OfficeAddress	text	value		
TextBox	Office_City		TRUE	TRUE	FALSE	FALSE	OfficeCity	text	value		
TextBox	Office_State		TRUE	TRUE	FALSE	FALSE	OfficeState	text	value	Dropdown	US States
TextBox	Office_Zip		TRUE	TRUE	FALSE	FALSE	OfficeZip	text	value		
TextBox	Office_Phone		TRUE	TRUE	FALSE	FALSE	OfficePhone	text	value		
TextBox	Office_Fax		TRUE	TRUE	FALSE	FALSE	OfficeFax	text	value		
TextBox	Home_Address		TRUE	TRUE	FALSE	FALSE	HomeAddress	text	value		
TextBox	Home_City		TRUE	TRUE	FALSE	FALSE	HomeCity	text	value		
TextBox	Home_State		TRUE	TRUE	FALSE	FALSE	HomeState	text	value	Dropdown	US States
TextBox	Home_Zip		TRUE	TRUE	FALSE	FALSE	HomeZip	text	value		
TextBox	Home_Phone		TRUE	TRUE	FALSE	FALSE	HomePhone	text	value		
TextBox	Home_Fax		TRUE	TRUE	FALSE	FALSE	HomeFax	text	value		
TextBox	Other_Address		TRUE	TRUE	FALSE	FALSE	OtherAddress	text	value		
TextBox	Other_City		TRUE	TRUE	FALSE	FALSE	OtherCity	text	value		
TextBox	Other_State		TRUE	TRUE	FALSE	FALSE	OtherState	text	value	Dropdown	US States
TextBox	Other_Zip		TRUE	TRUE	FALSE	FALSE	OtherZip	text	value		
TextBox	Other_Phone		TRUE	TRUE	FALSE	FALSE	OtherPhone	text	value		
TextBox	Other_Fax		TRUE	TRUE	FALSE	FALSE	OtherFax	text	value		
TextBox	Comments		TRUE	TRUE	FALSE	FALSE	TrackitComments	text	value		
Label	lblLastName	Last Name	TRUE	TRUE	FALSE	FALSE					
Label	lblFirstName	First Name	TRUE	TRUE	FALSE	FALSE					
Label	lblMI	MI	TRUE	TRUE	FALSE	FALSE					
Label	lblPosition	Position	TRUE	TRUE	FALSE	FALSE					
Label	lblWorkLocation	Work Location	TRUE	TRUE	FALSE	FALSE					

Table Continued on Following Page

Control Type	Control Name	Caption	Visible	Enabled	ReadOnly	Locked	Field Name	Type	Prop. Used	List Type	Possible Values
Label	lblRegion	Region	TRUE	TRUE	FALSE	FALSE					
Label	lblEquipDelivery	Equipment Delivery	TRUE	TRUE	FALSE	FALSE					
Label	lblOffice	Office	TRUE	TRUE	FALSE	FALSE					
Label	lblHome	Home	TRUE	TRUE	FALSE	FALSE					
Label	lblOther	Other	TRUE	TRUE	FALSE	FALSE					
Label	lblAddress	Address	TRUE	TRUE	FALSE	FALSE					
Label	lblCity	City	TRUE	TRUE	FALSE	FALSE					
Label	lblState	State	TRUE	TRUE	FALSE	FALSE					
Label	lblZip	Zip Code	TRUE	TRUE	FALSE	FALSE					
Label	lblPhone	Phone	TRUE	TRUE	FALSE	FALSE					
Label	lblFax	Fax	TRUE	TRUE	FALSE	FALSE					
Label	lblComments	Comments	TRUE	TRUE	FALSE	FALSE					
TextBox	Equip_Total		FALSE	TRUE	FALSE	FALSE	EquipmentTotal	number	value		
TextBox	New_Equip_Total		FALSE	TRUE	FALSE	FALSE	NewEquipmentTotal	number	value		
TextBox	People_key		FALSE	TRUE	FALSE	FALSE	Peoplekey	text	value		
TextBox	DSN		FALSE	TRUE	FALSE	FALSE	DSN	text	value		
TextBox	ItmeDeletedFlag		FALSE	TRUE	FALSE	FALSE	ItemDeletedFlag	number	value		
TextBox	Asset_Info_Total		FALSE	TRUE	FALSE	FALSE	AssetInfoTotal	text	value		
TextBox	Message		FALSE		FALSE	FALSE					

Tab 2: Employee Equipment Form

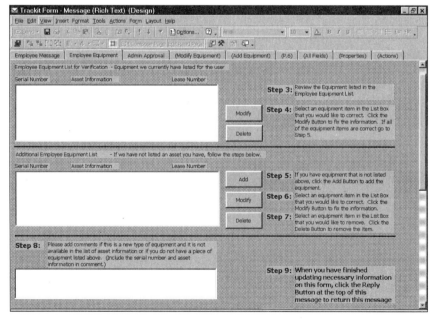

Fields for Employee Equipment Form

Control Type	Control Name	Caption	Visible	Enabled	ReadOnly	Locked	Field Name	Type	Prop. Used	Possible List Type Values
ListBox	lstEquipment		TRUE	TRUE	FALSE	FALSE				
Button	cmdModify	Modify	TRUE	TRUE	FALSE	FALSE				
Button	cmdDelete	Delete	TRUE	TRUE	FALSE	FALSE				
ListBox	lstAddEquipment		TRUE	TRUE	FALSE	FALSE				
Button	cmdAdd	Add	TRUE	TRUE	FALSE	FALSE				
Button	cmdModifyNew	Modify	TRUE	TRUE	FALSE	FALSE				
Button	cmdDeleteNew	Delete	TRUE	TRUE	FALSE	FALSE				
TextBox	NewEquipment Comments		TRUE	TRUE	FALSE	FALSE	NewEquipment Comments	text	value	

Tab 3: Admin Approval Form

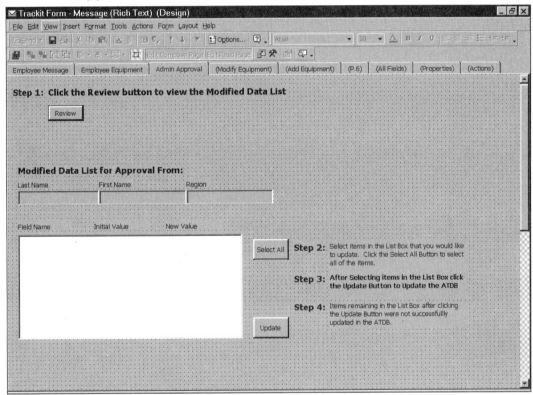

Fields for Admin Approval Form

Control Type	Control Name	Caption	Visible	Enabled	ReadOnly	Locked	Field Name	Type	Prop. Used	List Type	Possible Values
Button	cmdReview	Review	TRUE	TRUE	FALSE	FALSE					
TextBox	Display_Last _Name		TRUE	TRUE	TRUE	FALSE	LastName	text	value		
TextBox	Display_First _Name		TRUE	TRUE	TRUE	FALSE	FirstName	text	value		
TextBox	Display_Region _Name		TRUE	TRUE	TRUE	FALSE	RegionName	text	value		
ListBox	lstModifiedData		FALSE	TRUE	FALSE	FALSE					
Button	cmdSelectAll	Select All	FALSE	TRUE	FALSE	FALSE					
Button	cmdUpdate	Update	FALSE	TRUE	FALSE	FALSE					
Label	lblInstructions3		FALSE	TRUE	FALSE	FALSE					
Label	lblInstructions4		FALSE	TRUE	FALSE	FALSE					
Label	lblInstructions1		FALSE	TRUE	FALSE	FALSE					

Tab 4: Modify Equipment Form

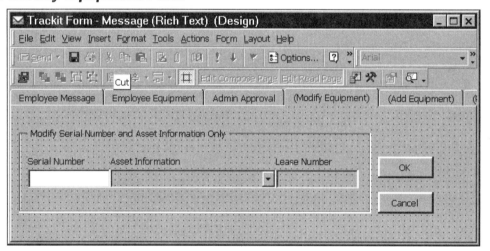

Fields for Modify Equipment Form

Control Type	Control Name	Caption	Visible	Enabled	Read Only	Locked	Field Name	Type	Prop. Used	List Type	Possible Values
TextBox	Serial_Number		TRUE	TRUE	FALSE	FALSE	SerialNumber				
ComboBox	Asset_Info		TRUE	TRUE	FALSE	TRUE	AssetInfo			Dropdown	
TextBox	Lease_Number		TRUE	TRUE	FALSE	TRUE	LeaseNumber				
Button	cmdChangeEquipment	OK	TRUE	TRUE	FALSE	FALSE					
Button	cmdCancelEquipment	Cancel	TRUE	TRUE	FALSE	FALSE					

Tab 5 Add Equipment Form

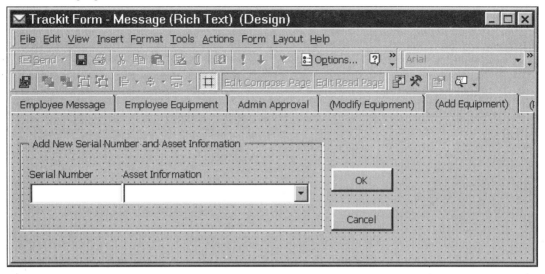

Fields for Add Equipment Form

Control Type	Control Name	Caption	Visible	Enabled	Read Only	Locked	Field Name	Type	Prop. Used	List Type	Possible Values
TextBox	New_Serial_Number		TRUE	TRUE	FALSE	FALSE	NewSerial Number				
ComboBox	NewAsset_Info		TRUE	TRUE	FALSE	FALSE	NewAssetInfo			Dropdown	
Button	cmdAddEquipment	OK	TRUE	TRUE	FALSE	FALSE					
Button	cmdCancelAdd Equipment	Cancel	TRUE	TRUE	FALSE	FALSE					

Support Code for Outlook Forms

Now that we've completed development of the Outlook Form pages, we can shift focus to developing the support code to populate controls, validate entries, and update the SQL Server database. This would be more fun if Microsoft included the same editor for Outlook forms as they did for macro development. As it stands, however, we are forced to use VBScript and a fairly crude editing tool, so the only way we can test form code is to publish and run it.

To begin adding code to the form, open the `TrackitForm2` Form in design mode and open the Script Editor. Add the following code to the Script Editor, and save/publish when you're done. You probably want to test publish and execute the code from time to time, so as to verify syntax. *Note that the* Admin Approval *tab assumes you'll have configured the ODBC connection to the SQL Server database – we'll be doing that in the next section: 'Configuring the ODBC connection', so this tab won't work until then.*

cmdUpdate_Click()

This code executes the Database Update routines when Administrators click the **Update** button on the **Admin Approval** tab.

First, we must declare constants to be used when executing stored procedures using ADO (ActiveX Data Objects) throughout the code. We must also declare an unbound global array, `AssetInformation()` that will hold Asset descriptions. These descriptions will be used to populate the Asset Information combo boxes on the **Modify** and **Add Equipment** tabs of the Asset Tracking Form. The rest of the declarations are for `Variants` that will be used to pass parameters to stored procedures, hold `RecordSet` information, etc.

```
Const adInteger = 3
Const adVarchar = 200
Const adCmdStoredProc = 4
Const adParamOutput = 2
Const adParamInput = 1
Const olFolderInbox = 6
Const olPersonalRegistry = 2
Dim Conn
Dim AssetInformation()
Dim strUserPrivileges


'************************************************
'* Procedure:  cmdUpdate_Click()
'* Description:  This procedures updates
'*        information in the ATDB
'*
'************************************************
Sub cmdUpdate_Click()
'On Error Resume Next

Dim objModifiedData
Dim Rs
Dim lngRC
Dim cmdStoredProcedure
Dim paramFlag
Dim paramFieldName
Dim paramValue
Dim paramPeopleKey
Dim paramSerialNumber
Dim DisplayedMessageFlag
Dim strTemp
```

For each item to be updated in the SQL server database from the user's Tracking form, we need to perform a check. This identifies whether the change request involves personal information or equipment serial number information. We conduct this check by passing the field name to the `sp_CheckUpdatePermission` procedure. This stored procedure identifies the field and where it should be updated. (Changes to the serial number need to be updated in the `Equipment` table, while changes to personal information need to be updated in the `Employee` table.) Once we've identified the type of information that needs to be modified (or added), we call either the `UpdateEquipment` function (to update equipment information), or the `sp_UpdateEmployeeInfo` stored procedure (to update personal information).

```
DisplayedMessageFlag = 0
Set objModifiedData= Item.GetInspector.ModifiedFormPages("Admin Approval") _
                                  .Controls("lstModifiedData")
Redim arrItemsToRemove(objModifiedData.ListCount)
intCounter = 0

Set cmdUpdateDatabase= CreateObject("ADODB.Command")
cmdUpdateDatabase.ActiveConnection = Conn
If objModifiedData.ListCount > 0 then
      For intIndex = 0 To objModifiedData.ListCount - 1
    If objModifiedData.Selected(intIndex) = True Then
        Set cmdStoredProcedure= CreateObject("ADODB.Command")
        cmdStoredProcedure.ActiveConnection = Conn
        cmdStoredProcedure.CommandText = "sp_CheckUpdatePermission"
        cmdStoredProcedure.CommandType = adCmdStoredProc
        set paramFlag= cmdStoredProcedure.CreateParameter("updateflag", _
                                        adInteger, adParamOutput)
        cmdStoredProcedure.Parameters.Append paramFlag
        set paramFieldName= cmdStoredProcedure.CreateParameter("fieldName", _
                                        adVarchar, adParamInput, 25)
        cmdStoredProcedure.Parameters.Append paramFieldName
        paramFieldName.value = objModifiedData.List(intIndex,0)
        cmdStoredProcedure.Execute

        If cmdStoredProcedure(0) = 0 Then 'Serial_Number changed
           msgbox("serial number changed")
           If Len(objModifiedData.List(intIndex,1))= 0 Then
              MsgBox("Please forward this Trackit Form to the Asset Tracking " & _
                     "Admin for new equipment approval." & Chr(10) & _
                     "New Serial Number - '" & _
                     objModifiedData.List(intIndex,2) & "'")
           ElseIf Instr(objModifiedData.List(intIndex,0),"Deleted") _
                                        Then 'Serial_Number deleted
              'Assign removed serial number to unassigned
              lngRC = UpdateEquipment(1, Item.UserProperties.Find("UserName") _
                      .Value, Item.UserProperties.Find("PeopleKey").Value, _
                            objModifiedData.List(intIndex,1))
           Else
              msgbox("updated serial number of existing equipment")
              lngRC = UpdateEquipment(Item.UserProperties.Find("PeopleKey").Value, _
                            Item.UserProperties.Find("UserName").Value, _
                            Item.UserProperties.Find("PeopleKey").Value, _
                            objModifiedData.List(intIndex,2))
              'Update equipment list
              Set objEquipment = Item.GetInspector.ModifiedFormPages _
                            .Item("Employee Equipment") _
                            .Controls("lstEquipment")
              For intCounter = 0 to Item.UserProperties.Find("EquipmentTotal")-1
                If objModifiedData.List(intIndex,2) = _
                                  objEquipment.List(intCounter, 0) Then
                   objEquipment.List(intCounter, 3) = ""
                   Exit For
                End If
```

```
                Next
            End If
        Else
            Set cmdStoredProcedure= CreateObject("ADODB.Command")
            cmdStoredProcedure.ActiveConnection = Conn
            cmdStoredProcedure.CommandText = "sp_UpdateEmployeeInfo"
            cmdStoredProcedure.CommandType = adCmdStoredProc
            set paramFieldName= cmdStoredProcedure.CreateParameter("fieldName", _
                                                    adVarChar, _
                                                    adParamInput, 50)
            cmdStoredProcedure.Parameters.Append paramFieldName
            paramFieldName.value = objModifiedData.List(intIndex,0)
            set paramValue= cmdStoredProcedure.CreateParameter("value", adVarchar, _
                                                    adParamInput, 100)
            cmdStoredProcedure.Parameters.Append paramValue
            paramValue.value = objModifiedData.List(intIndex,2)
            set paramPeopleKey= cmdStoredProcedure.CreateParameter("peopleKey", _
                                                    adInteger, _
                                                    adParamInput)
            cmdStoredProcedure.Parameters.Append paramPeopleKey
            paramPeopleKey.value = Item.UserProperties.Find("PeopleKey").Value
            cmdStoredProcedure.Execute
        End If
      End If
      Next
   End If

   lngRC = FillModifiedDataList

End Sub
```

cmdSelectAll_Click()

This procedure loops through each item in the lstModifiedData list on the **Admin Approval** form, and sets the selected property to True. Typically, Asset Administrators want to approve user-identified changes to asset records, and the **Select All** button speeds up the record selection process.

```
'***********************************************
'* Procedure:  cmdSelectAll_Click()
'* Description:
'*
'***********************************************
Sub cmdSelectAll_Click()
'On Error Resume Next
Dim objModifiedData
Dim intIndex

  Set objModifiedData= Item.GetInspector.ModifiedFormPages("Admin Approval") _
                                        .Controls("lstModifiedData")
  If objModifiedData.ListCount > 0 then
       For intIndex = 0 To objModifiedData.ListCount - 1
       objModifiedData.Selected(intIndex) = True
       Next
  End If

End Sub
```

UpdateEquipment

This function executes the `sp_UpdateEquipmentInfo` stored procedure, to update equipment information in the SQL Server database. As noted above, it is called from the `cmd_Update` procedure, after determining that the selected item on the update list is equipment information (rather than personal information).

```
Function UpdateEquipment(intNewPeopleKey, strUserName, _
                         intPeopleKey, strSerialNumber)
Dim cmdStoredProcedure
Dim paramNewPeopleKey
Dim paramUserName
Dim paramPeopleKey
Dim paramSerialNumber

  Set cmdStoredProcedure= CreateObject("ADODB.Command")
  cmdStoredProcedure.ActiveConnection = Conn
  cmdStoredProcedure.CommandText = "sp_UpdateEquipmentInfo"
  cmdStoredProcedure.CommandType = adCmdStoredProc
  set paramNewPeopleKey= cmdStoredProcedure.CreateParameter("newPeopleKey", _
                                                adInteger, adParamInput)
  cmdStoredProcedure.Parameters.Append paramNewPeopleKey
  paramNewPeopleKey.value = intNewPeopleKey
  set paramUserName= cmdStoredProcedure.CreateParameter("UserName", _
                                                adVarchar, adParamInput, 20)
  cmdStoredProcedure.Parameters.Append paramUserName
  paramUserName.value = strUserName
  set paramPeopleKey= cmdStoredProcedure.CreateParameter("peopleKey", _
                                                adInteger, adParamInput)
  cmdStoredProcedure.Parameters.Append paramPeopleKey
  paramPeopleKey.value = intPeopleKey
  set paramSerialNumber= cmdStoredProcedure.CreateParameter("serialNumber", _
                                                adVarChar, adParamInput, 25)
  cmdStoredProcedure.Parameters.Append paramSerialNumber
  paramSerialNumber.value = strSerialNumber
  cmdStoredProcedure.Execute

  Set cmdStoredProcedure = Nothing
End Function
```

cmdReview_Click()

This procedure works in conjunction with the `FillModifiedDataList` function below, to build a list of modified information for the Administrative User to approve. It connects to the SQL Server database, looks up stored values for all the Outlook form fields, and compares them to the values currently stored in the form. If the values differ, we add the relevant item to the list of modified data on the Admin Approval form. This facilitates review and approval/rejection processing by Asset Tracking staff members.

When the Outlook form is first created and populated by Access (see the following sections on the Access 2000 Administrator Tool), the DSN user property is assigned the DSN value. This procedure gets the value stored in the DSN user property and connects to the database. It then calls the function `FillModifiedDataList` to populate the modified data list box on the Admin Approval tab of the form. Finally, it sets the lstModifiedData listbox, cmdSelectAll button, and cmdUpdate button visible.

```
'************************************************
'* Procedure:  cmdReview_Click()
'* Description:
'*
'************************************************
Sub cmdReview_Click()

Dim Rs
Dim objControl
Dim objQueryField
Dim RowNumber
Dim strOldValue
Dim objEquipment
Dim cmdStoredProcedure
Dim paramUserName
Dim paramPassword
Dim paramPeopleKey

    On Error Resume Next
        Conn = " DSN=" & Item.UserProperties.Find("DSN")
    If Err <> 0 Then
      MsgBox("Find DSN: Error #" & Err.Number & ": " & Err.Description)
      Err.Clear
    End If
        lngRC = FillModifiedDataList

        Set objControl= Item.GetInspector.ModifiedFormPages.Item("Admin Approval") _
                                            .Controls("cmdUpdate")
        objControl.Visible = True
        Set objControl= nothing

        Set objControl= Item.GetInspector.ModifiedFormPages.Item("Admin Approval") _
                                            .Controls("cmdSelectAll")
            objControl.Visible = True
        Set objControl= nothing

        Set objControl= Item.GetInspector.ModifiedFormPages.Item("Admin Approval") _
                                .Controls("lstModifiedData")
            objControl.Visible = True
        Set objControl= nothing

        Set objControl= Item.GetInspector.ModifiedFormPages.Item("Admin Approval") _
                                .Controls("lblModifiedData")
            objControl.Visible = True
        Set objControl= nothing

        Set objControl= Item.GetInspector.ModifiedFormPages.Item("Admin Approval") _
                                .Controls("lblInstructions1")
            objControl.Visible = True
        Set objControl= nothing

        Set objControl= Item.GetInspector.ModifiedFormPages.Item("Admin Approval") _
                                .Controls("lblInstructions3")
            objControl.Visible = True
        Set objControl= nothing
```

```
            Set objControl= Item.GetInspector.ModifiedFormPages.Item("Admin Approval") _
                                            .Controls("lblInstructions4")
                objControl.Visible = True
            Set objControl= nothing

    End Sub
```

FillModifiedDataList()

This function completes the process of examining field values on the Employee and Equipment tabs, comparing them to values in the SQL Server database, and adding changes to the list of modified information on the **Admin Approval** tab. First, it executes the `sp_SelectEmployeeFullView` stored procedure to get a recordset of the current personal information for the employee. It then loops through each control on the Employee Message page and compares its value to the value of the matching fieldname in the recordset. If the items are different then it adds the field name, initial value, and new value to the Modified Data List box on the **Admin Approval** tab.

```
    Function FillModifiedDataList()

    Dim Rs
    Dim rstIsItEquipment
    Dim objControl
    Dim objQueryField
    Dim cmdStoredProcedure
    Dim paramPeopleKey
    Dim paramFieldName
    Dim lngRC

        Set cmdStoredProcedure= CreateObject("ADODB.Command")
        cmdStoredProcedure.ActiveConnection = Conn
        cmdStoredProcedure.CommandText = "sp_SelectEmployeeFullView"
        cmdStoredProcedure.CommandType = adCmdStoredProc
        set paramPeopleKey = cmdStoredProcedure.CreateParameter("peopleKey", _
                                                    adInteger, adParamInput)
        cmdStoredProcedure.Parameters.Append paramPeopleKey
        paramPeopleKey.value = Item.UserProperties.Find("PeopleKey")

        Set Rs = CreateObject("ADODB.Recordset")
        Set Rs = cmdStoredProcedure.Execute

        Set objModifiedData= Item.GetInspector.ModifiedFormPages _
                                    .Item("Admin Approval") _
                                    .Controls("lstModifiedData")
        objModifiedData.MultiSelect = 2 'Extended Select

        'Look for changed values on the message page
        objModifiedData.Clear
        Set objControlCollection = Item.GetInspector.ModifiedFormPages _
                                            .Item("Employee Message").Controls
        For each objControl in objControlCollection
            if objControl.visible = True then
                on error resume next
                If IsNull(Rs.Fields(objControl.Name)) Then
                    strOldValue = ""
```

```
        Else
          strOldValue = Rs.Fields(objControl.Name).Value
      End If
      If Err.Number = 0 then 'The field is in the query
              If Trim(strOldValue) <> Trim(objControl.Text) Then
          'Add Changed item information to the lstModifiedData list box
          RowNumber = objModifiedData.ListCount
          objModifiedData.AddItem objControl.Name
          objModifiedData.List(RowNumber, 1) = strOldValue
          objModifiedData.List(RowNumber, 2) = objControl.Text
          'msgBox(strOldValue)
          'msgBox(objControl.Text)
        End If
      End If
      Err.Clear
    End If
    Next
```

Next, it loops through each value in the lstEquipment listbox on the **Employee Equipment** tab. If the value in the hidden column 3 (containing the original serial number) does not match the serial number in column 0, then the serial number must have been changed. If this is the case then the function adds the field name, initial value, and new value to the lstModifiedData List box on the **Admin Approval** tab. Moreover, if the value in the hidden column 4 (containing asset info description) does not match the asset info in column 1, the asset information must have been changed. Likewise, we must add the field name, initial value, and new value to the lstModifiedData List box for review and approval/rejection.

```
'Look for changed values in the equipment list
Set objEquipment = Item.GetInspector.ModifiedFormPages _
                                .Item("Employee Equipment") _
                                .Controls("lstEquipment")
If Err <> 0 Then
  MsgBox "lstEquipment: " & Err.Number & ": " & Err.Description
  Err.Clear
End If
For intCounter = 0 to Item.UserProperties.Find("EquipmentTotal")-1
  If len(trim(objEquipment.List(intCounter, 3))) > 0 Then
    'msgbox("sn changed: " & objEquipment.List(intCounter, 3))
    If objEquipment.List(intCounter, 3) <> objEquipment.List(intCounter, 0) Then
      lngRC = AddToList("Serial_Number", objEquipment.List(intCounter, 3), _
                                objEquipment, intCounter, 0)
    End If
  End If
  If len(trim(objEquipment.List(intCounter, 4))) > 0 Then
    'msgbox("asset info changed: " & objEquipment.List(intCounter, 4))
    If objEquipment.List(intCounter, 4) <> objEquipment.List(intCounter, 1) Then
    lngRC = AddToList("Asset_Info", objEquipment.List(intCounter, 4), _
                                objEquipment, intCounter, 1)
    End If
  End If
Next
```

350

Next, the function checks the `ItemDeletedFlag` user property on the form to see if the user deleted any equipment from their equipment list. If the `ItemDeletedFlag` is 1, then an item has been deleted. For each serial number in the recordset returned by the `sp_SelectEmployeeFullView` stored procedure, the function loops through all the items in the lstEquipment list box until it finds a match. If the function can't find a match then the serial number has been deleted from the equipment list. The function then adds the Deleted Asset values to the lstModifiedData list box to inform the Administrative User that the user has deleted a piece of equipment from their inventory.

```
'Look for items that were removed from equipment list
blFound = "False"
If Item.UserProperties.Find("ItemDeletedFlag") = 1 Then
  If Err <> 0 Then
     MsgBox "ItemDeletedFlag: " & Err.Number & ": " & Err.Description
     Err.Clear
  End If
  'msgbox("item deleted: " & Item.UserProperties.Find("ItemDeletedFlag"))
  Do Until Rs.EOF
     For intCounter = 0 to Item.UserProperties.Find("EquipmentTotal")-1
        If Rs.Fields("Serial_Number") = objEquipment.List(intCounter, 0) Then
           blFound = "True"
           Exit For
        End If
     Next
     If blFound = "False" Then
        lngRC = AddToList("Deleted Serial_Number", Rs.Fields("Serial_Number"), _
                                       objEquipment, intCounter, 0)
        strAssetInfo = Rs.Fields("MFG")& " " & _
                    Rs.Fields("Model")& " " & Rs.Fields("Asset_Type")
        lngRC = AddToList("Deleted Asset_Info", strAssetInfo, _
                                       objEquipment, intCounter, 0)
     End If
     blFound = "False" 'reinitialize for next round

     Rs.MoveNext
  Loop
End If

Rs.Close
Set Rs = Nothing

If Err <> 0 Then
  MsgBox "Rs.close " & Err.Number & ": " & Err.Description
  Err.Clear
End If
```

Finally, the function loops through each item in the lstAddEquipment list box, and adds each to the lstModifiedData list box. This ensures that the Asset Tracking manager sees *all* new items added to the user's inventory.

```
'Add new equipment list
Set objEquipment = Item.GetInspector.ModifiedFormPages _
                      .Item("Employee Equipment").Controls("lstAddEquipment")
intCounter = 0
'MsgBox(objEquipment.ListCount)
For intCounter = 0 to Item.UserProperties.Find("NewEquipmentTotal")-1
'objEquipment.ListCount-1
   lngRC = AddToList("Serial_Number", "", objEquipment, intCounter, 0)
   lngRC = AddToList("Asset_Info", "", objEquipment, intCounter, 1)
      Next

   Set objControl = Nothing
   Set objQueryField = Nothing

End Function
```

AddToList

This function adds an item to the lstModifiedData list box.

```
Function AddToList(strFieldName, strFieldValue, objEquipment, intRow, intColumn)
Dim RowNumber

   Set objModifiedData= Item.GetInspector.ModifiedFormPages.Item("Admin Approval") _
                                  .Controls("lstModifiedData")
   'Add Changed item information to the lstModifiedData list box
   RowNumber = objModifiedData.ListCount
   objModifiedData.AddItem strFieldName
   objModifiedData.List(RowNumber, 1) = strFieldValue
   If Not InStr(strFieldName, "Deleted") Then
      objModifiedData.List(RowNumber, 2) = objEquipment.List(intRow, intColumn)
   End If
End Function
```

cmdModify_Click()

When a user decides to modify information about a particular piece of equipment, we need a way to give them a parameterized view of available fields and options. The hidden Modify Equipment tab provides this service. Once a user selects a row of data from the equipment listbox on the Employee Equipment tab and clicks modify, this procedure builds a dialog box that allows the user to modify information about that piece of equipment. It sets the serialnumber, leasenumber, and assetinfo user properties to the values of the row selected in the lstEquipment listbox. It then shows the Modify Equipment page and populates the AssetInfo combo box with valid asset descriptions. Then, it hides the Employee Message form and sets the focus to the serialnumber field on the newly populated Modify Equipment page.

```
'***************************************************
'* Procedure:   cmdModify_Click()
'* Description:  This procedure is used to modify
'*       equipment information
'*
'***************************************************
Sub cmdModify_Click()
On Error Resume Next

Dim strEquipment
Dim objInspector
Dim Serial_Number
dim intIndex
dim Selected_Item

    Set objInspector = Item.GetInspector
  If Err <> 0 Then
      MsgBox Err & " :GetInspector: " & Err.Description
      Err.Clear
    End If

    Set Selected_Item = objInspector.ModifiedFormPages.Item("Employee Equipment") _
                                        .Controls("lstEquipment")
    If Selected_Item.ListCount > 0 then
      For intIndex = 0 To Selected_Item.ListCount
          If Selected_Item.Selected(intIndex) = True Then
      Item.UserProperties.Find("SerialNumber").Value = _
                                        Selected_Item.List(intIndex,0)
      Item.UserProperties.Find("LeaseNumber").Value = _
                                        Selected_Item.List(intIndex,2)
      Item.UserProperties.Find("AssetInfo").Value = Selected_Item.List(intIndex,1)
          End If
      Next

  If Len(Trim(Item.UserProperties.Find("SerialNumber").Value)) > 0 Then
    objInspector.ShowFormPage("Modify Equipment")
        Set AssetInfo = objInspector.ModifiedFormPages.Item("Modify Equipment") _
                                        .Controls("Asset_Info")

      AssetInfo.List() = AssetInformation
      If Err <> 0 Then
        MsgBox Err & " :ShowFormPage: " & Err.Description
        Err.Clear
      End If

      objInspector.SetCurrentFormPage("Modify Equipment")
       If Err <> 0 Then
        MsgBox Err & " :SetCurrentFormPage: " & Err.Description
        Err.Clear
      End If
```

```
               'objInspector.HideFormPage("Employee Message")
            If Err <> 0 Then
               MsgBox Err & " :HideFormPage:Employee Message: " & Err.Description
               Err.Clear
            End If

            Set Serial_Number = objInspector.ModifiedFormPages.Item("Modify Equipment") _
                             .Controls("Serial_Number")
            If Err <> 0 Then
               MsgBox Err & " :Controls: " & Err.Description
               Err.Clear
            End If

      If Err <> 0 Then
               MsgBox Err & " :Get List Info: " & Err.Description
               Err.Clear
            End If

            Serial_Number.SetFocus
            If Err <> 0 Then
               MsgBox Err & " :SetFocus: " & Err.Description
               Err.Clear
            End If
      Else
         MsgBox("Please select an item in the list to modify.")
      End If
         End If

   End Sub
```

cmdChangeEquipment_Click()

This procedure is initiated when the user clicks OK on the Modify equipment form. It first checks to see if the equipment information was modified. If so, it stores the original values for the equipment in hidden fields. This helps the Asset Manager understand the changes that the End User made to their equipment listing. Finally, it re-populates the Equipment list box on the Employee Equipment tab to reflect changes, and it closes the Modify Equipment tab.

```
'*************************************************
'* Procedure:  cmdChangeEquipment_Click()
'* Description:  This procedure is used to modify
'*      equipment information
'*
'*************************************************
Sub cmdChangeEquipment_Click()
dim objInspector
Dim objControl
Dim objEquipment
Dim Serial_Number
```

If the serial number and/or asset information has changed, then the procedure stores it in the hidden columns 3 and/or 4 for later review when the Asset Tracking Manger views modifications on the **Admin Approval** tab. Finally, it hides the Modify Equipment page and shows the Employee Message, Employee Equipment, and Admin Approval pages.

```
If Instr(Item.UserProperties.Find("SerialNumber").Value, ",") <> 0 Then
   MsgBox("Please remove commas from the Serial Number.")
   Set Serial_Number = Item.GetInspector.ModifiedFormPages. _
                       Item("Modify Equipment").Controls("Serial_Number")
   Serial_Number.SetFocus
Else
   Set objControl= Item.GetInspector.ModifiedFormPages.Item("Employee Equipment") _
                                        .Controls("lstEquipment")

   'MsgBox(objControl.ListIndex)
   If Len(Item.UserProperties.Find("SerialNumber")) = 0 Or _
     Len(Item.UserProperties.Find("AssetInfo")) = 0 Then
      MsgBox("Serial Number and Asset Information are required fields. " & _
            "Please enter information or click Cancel.")
      Set Serial_Number = Item.GetInspector.ModifiedFormPages.Item("Modify Equipment") _
                          .Controls("Serial_Number")
   Serial_Number.SetFocus
Else
   If len(trim(objControl.List(objControl.ListIndex, 3))) = 0 Then 'previous
                                                    'sn not saved
      objControl.List(objControl.ListIndex, 3) = _
                    objControl.List(objControl.ListIndex, 0)
      objControl.List(objControl.ListIndex, 4) = _
                    objControl.List(objControl.ListIndex, 1)
   End If
   objControl.List(objControl.ListIndex, 0) = _
                 Item.UserProperties.Find("SerialNumber").Value
   objControl.List(objControl.ListIndex, 1) = _
                 Item.UserProperties.Find("AssetInfo").Value


   Set objInspector = Item.GetInspector
If Err <> 0 Then
      MsgBox Err & " :GetInspector: " & Err.Description
      Err.Clear
   End If


   objInspector.ShowFormPage("Employee Message")
   If Err <> 0 Then
      MsgBox Err & " :ShowFormPage:Employee Message: " & Err.Description
      Err.Clear
   End If


   objInspector.ShowFormPage("Employee Equipment")
   If Err <> 0 Then
      MsgBox Err & " :ShowFormPage:Employee Equipment: " & Err.Description
      Err.Clear
   End If
```

```
            objInspector.ModifiedFormPages("Employee Equipment").Enabled = True
          If Err <> 0 Then
             MsgBox Err & " :Enabled:Employee Equipment: " & Err.Description
             Err.Clear
          End If

          objInspector.ShowFormPage("Admin Approval")
          If Err <> 0 Then
             MsgBox Err & " :ShowFormPage:Admin Approval: " & Err.Description
             Err.Clear
          End If

          objInspector.SetCurrentFormPage("Employee Equipment")
          If Err <> 0 Then
             MsgBox Err & " :ShowFormPage:Employee Equipment: " & Err.Description
             Err.Clear
          End If

          objInspector.HideFormPage("Modify Equipment")
          If Err <> 0 Then
             MsgBox Err & " :HideFormPage:Modify Equipment: " & Err.Description
             Err.Clear
          End If

      Set objControl = Nothing
     End If
   End If

End Sub
```

cmdCancelEquipment_Click()

This procedure executes when the user clicks the Cancel button on the Modify Equipment page. It discards any change, hides the Modify Equipment tab, and re-displays the Employee Message, Employee Equipment, and Admin Approval tabs.

```
'*************************************************
'* Procedure:  cmdCancelEquipment_Click()
'* Description:  This procedure is used to modify
'*        equipment information
'*
'*************************************************
Sub cmdCancelEquipment_Click()
dim objInspector

    Set objInspector = Item.GetInspector
  If Err <> 0 Then
      MsgBox Err & " :GetInspector: " & Err.Description
      Err.Clear
    End If
```

```
          objInspector.ShowFormPage("Employee Message")
          If Err <> 0 Then
             MsgBox Err & " :ShowFormPage:Employee Message: " & Err.Description
             Err.Clear
          End If

          objInspector.ShowFormPage("Employee Equipment")
          If Err <> 0 Then
             MsgBox Err & " :ShowFormPage:Employee Equipment: " & Err.Description
             Err.Clear
          End If

          objInspector.ModifiedFormPages("Employee Equipment").Enabled = True
          If Err <> 0 Then
             MsgBox Err & " :Enabled:Employee Equipment: " & Err.Description
             Err.Clear
          End If

          objInspector.ShowFormPage("Admin Approval")
          If Err <> 0 Then
             MsgBox Err & " :ShowFormPage:Admin Approval: " & Err.Description
             Err.Clear
          End If

          objInspector.SetCurrentFormPage("Employee Equipment")
          If Err <> 0 Then
             MsgBox Err & " :ShowFormPage:Employee Equipment: " & Err.Description
             Err.Clear
          End If

          objInspector.HideFormPage("Modify Equipment")
          If Err <> 0 Then
             MsgBox Err & " :HideFormPage:Modify Equipment: " & Err.Description
             Err.Clear
          End If

       End Sub
```

cmdDelete_Click()

This procedure executes when the user clicks the Delete button next to the Equipment list on the Employee Equipment page. It removes the selected item from the list and updates the ItemDeletedFlag and EquipmentTotal user properties.

```
'***********************************************
'* Procedure:  cmdDelete_Click()
'* Description:  This procedure is used to remove
'*      equipment information from the
'*      current equipment list.
'***********************************************
Sub cmdDelete_Click()
On Error Resume Next
```

```
      Set Selected_Item = Item.GetInspector.ModifiedFormPages _
                      .Item("Employee Equipment").Controls("lstEquipment")
   If Err<>0 Then
     Msgbox "cmdDelete: set selected_item " & Err.Number & ": " & Err.Description
     Err.Clear
   End If
       If Selected_Item.ListIndex <> -1 Then
     If Err<>0 Then
       Msgbox "cmdDelete: if selected_item " & Err.Number & ": " & Err.Description
       Err.Clear
     End If
     Selected_Item.RemoveItem (Selected_Item.ListIndex)
     If Err<>0 Then
       Msgbox "cmdDelete: remove selected_item " & _
                         Err.Number & ": " & Err.Description
       Err.Clear
     End If
       End If

   Item.UserProperties.Find("ItemDeletedFlag") = 1
   If Err<>0 Then
     Msgbox "cmdDelete: find itemdeletedflag" & Err.Number & ": " & Err.Description
     Err.Clear
   End If
   Item.UserProperties.Find("EquipmentTotal") =
 Item.UserProperties.Find("EquipmentTotal")-1
   If Err<>0 Then
     Msgbox "cmdDelete: find equipmenttotal" & Err.Number & ": " & Err.Description
     Err.Clear
   End If

 End Sub
```

cmdAddEquipment_Click()

This procedure executes when the user clicks the Add button on the Add Equipment page. It adds the newly entered information to the lstAddEquipment list box on the Employee Equipment page, updates the NewEquipmentTotal property, hides the Add Equipment page, and shows the Employee Equipment, Employee Message, and Admin Approval pages.

```
'*************************************************
'* Procedure:  cmdAddEquipment_Click()
'* Description:  This procedure is used to modify
'*      equipment information
'*
'*************************************************
Sub cmdAddEquipment_Click()
dim objInspector
Dim objControl
Dim RowNumber

  If Instr(Item.UserProperties.Find("NewSerialNumber").Value, ",") <> 0 Then
    MsgBox("Please remove commas from the Serial Number.")
    Set Serial_Number = Item.GetInspector.ModifiedFormPages.Item("Add Equipment") _
                                .Controls("txtSerialNumber")
```

```
        Serial_Number.SetFocus
    Else

      Set objControl= Item.GetInspector.ModifiedFormPages.Item("Employee Equipment") _
                            .Controls("lstAddEquipment")

    If Len(Item.UserProperties.Find("NewSerialNumber")) = 0 Or _
      Len(Item.UserProperties.Find("NewAssetInfo")) = 0 Then
      MsgBox("Serial Number and Asset Information are required fields." & _
            "Please enter information or click Cancel.")
      Set Serial_Number = Item.GetInspector.ModifiedFormPages.Item("Add Equipment") _
                            .Controls("New_Serial_Number")
    Serial_Number.SetFocus
    Else
      If objControl.ListIndex <> -1 Then
        objControl.List(objControl.ListIndex, 0) = Item.UserProperties. _
                                          Find("NewSerialNumber").Value
        objControl.List(objControl.ListIndex, 1) = Item.UserProperties. _
                                          Find("NewAssetInfo").Value
      Else
        RowNumber = objControl.ListCount
        If Len(Item.UserProperties.Find("NewSerialNumber").Value) > 0 Then
          objControl.AddItem Item.UserProperties.Find("NewSerialNumber").Value
          objControl.List(RowNumber, 1) = Item.UserProperties _
                                      .Find("NewAssetInfo").Value
          Item.UserProperties.Find("NewEquipmentTotal").Value = objControl.ListCount
      End If
          Set objControl = Nothing
      End If


        Set objInspector = Item.GetInspector
    If Err <> 0 Then
          MsgBox Err & " :GetInspector: " & Err.Description
          Err.Clear
      End If

      objInspector.ShowFormPage("Employee Message")
      If Err <> 0 Then
          MsgBox Err & " :ShowFormPage:Employee Message: " & Err.Description
          Err.Clear
      End If

      objInspector.ShowFormPage("Employee Equipment")
      If Err <> 0 Then
          MsgBox Err & " :ShowFormPage:Employee Equipment: " & Err.Description
          Err.Clear
      End If
```

```
                objInspector.ShowFormPage("Admin Approval")
                If Err <> 0 Then
                   MsgBox Err & " :ShowFormPage:Admin Approval: " & Err.Description
                   Err.Clear
                End If


                objInspector.SetCurrentFormPage("Employee Equipment")
                If Err <> 0 Then
                   MsgBox Err & " :ShowFormPage:Employee Equipment: " & Err.Description
                   Err.Clear
                End If

                objInspector.HideFormPage("Add Equipment")
                If Err <> 0 Then
                   MsgBox Err & " :HideFormPage:Add Equipment: " & Err.Description
                   Err.Clear
                End If
          End If
       End If

    End Sub
```

cmdCancelAddEquipment_Click()

This procedure executes when the user clicks the Cancel button on the Add Equipment page. It discards all changes, hides the Add Equipment page and displays the Employee Equipment, Employee Message, and Admin Approval tabs.

```
'*************************************************
'* Procedure:  cmdCancelAddEquipment_Click()
'* Description:  This procedure is used to modify
'*       equipment information
'*
'*************************************************
Sub cmdCancelAddEquipment_Click()
dim objInspector

    Set objInspector = Item.GetInspector
    If Err <> 0 Then
       MsgBox Err & " :GetInspector: " & Err.Description
       Err.Clear
    End If

    objInspector.ShowFormPage("Employee Message")
    If Err <> 0 Then
       MsgBox Err & " :ShowFormPage:Employee Message: " & Err.Description
       Err.Clear
    End If

    objInspector.ShowFormPage("Employee Equipment")
    If Err <> 0 Then
       MsgBox Err & " :ShowFormPage:Employee Equipment: " & Err.Description
       Err.Clear
    End If
```

```
       objInspector.ShowFormPage("Admin Approval")
       If Err <> 0 Then
          MsgBox Err & " :ShowFormPage:Admin Approval: " & Err.Description
          Err.Clear
       End If

       objInspector.SetCurrentFormPage("Employee Equipment")
       If Err <> 0 Then
          MsgBox Err & " :ShowFormPage:Employee Equipment: " & Err.Description
          Err.Clear
       End If

       objInspector.HideFormPage("Add Equipment")
       If Err <> 0 Then
          MsgBox Err & " :HideFormPage:Add Equipment: " & Err.Description
          Err.Clear
       End If

    End Sub
```

cmdAdd_Click()

This procedure executes when the user clicks the Add button next to the New Equipment list on the Employee Equipment form. It displays the hidden Add Equipment form, and hides the Employee Equipment form.

```
'************************************************
'* Procedure:  cmdAdd_Click()
'* Description:  This procedure is used to add
'*       new equipment.
'*
'************************************************
Sub cmdAdd_Click()
On Error Resume Next

Dim strEquipment
Dim objInspector
Dim txtSerialNumber

'Reset Values
Set objControl= Item.GetInspector.ModifiedFormPages.Item("Employee Equipment") _
                                          .Controls("lstAddEquipment")
   objControl.ListIndex = -1

   Item.UserProperties.Find("NewSerialNumber").Value = ""
   Item.UserProperties.Find("NewAssetInfo").Value = ""

   Set objInspector = Item.GetInspector
   If Err <> 0 Then
      MsgBox Err & " :GetInspector: " & Err.Description
      Err.Clear
   End If
```

```
      objInspector.ShowFormPage("Add Equipment")
      Set AssetInfo = objInspector.ModifiedFormPages.Item("Add Equipment") _
                                          .Controls("NewAsset_Info")
      AssetInfo.List() = AssetInformation
      If Err <> 0 Then
         MsgBox Err & " :ShowFormPage: " & Err.Description
         Err.Clear
      End If

      objInspector.SetCurrentFormPage("Add Equipment")
      If Err <> 0 Then
         MsgBox Err & " :SetCurrentFormPage: " & Err.Description
         Err.Clear
      End If

      'objInspector.HideFormPage("Employee Message")
      If Err <> 0 Then
         MsgBox Err & " :HideFormPage:Employee Message: " & Err.Description
         Err.Clear
      End If

      Set txtSerialNumber = objInspector.ModifiedFormPages.Item("Add Equipment") _
                              .Controls("New_Serial_Number")
      If Err <> 0 Then
         MsgBox Err & " :Controls: " & Err.Description
         Err.Clear
      End If

      txtSerialNumber.SetFocus
      If Err <> 0 Then
         MsgBox Err & " :SetFocus: " & Err.Description
         Err.Clear
      End If

   End Sub
```

cmdModifyNew_Click()

This procedure executes when the user clicks the Modify button next to the lstAddEquipment list box on the Employee Equipment page. It functions similarly to the cmdModify_Click() procedure, however, this procedure is used to change newly entered equipment before it is sent to the Asset Tracking team to be added to the database. First, the procedure sets the values of the serial number and asset information of the selected item to the NewSerialNumber and NewAssetInfo user properties. Then it shows the normal Add Equipment form and hides the Employee Equipment form.

```
'*************************************************
'* Procedure:  cmdModifyNew_Click()
'* Description:  This procedure is used to modify
'*       new equipment information
'*
'*************************************************
```

```
Sub cmdModifyNew_Click()
Dim strEquipment
Dim objInspector
Dim txtSerialNumber


    Set objInspector = Item.GetInspector
    If Err <> 0 Then
       MsgBox Err & " :GetInspector: " & Err.Description
       Err.Clear
    End If

    'Set Values
    Set Selected_Item = objInspector.ModifiedFormPages.Item("Employee Equipment") _
                                              .Controls("lstAddEquipment")

    If Selected_Item.ListCount > 0 then
       For intIndex = 0 To Selected_Item.ListCount
          If Selected_Item.Selected(intIndex) = True Then
            Item.UserProperties.Find("NewSerialNumber").Value = _
                                     Selected_Item.List(intIndex,0)
            Item.UserProperties.Find("NewAssetInfo").Value = _
                                     Selected_Item.List(intIndex,1)
          End If
       Next

       objInspector.ShowFormPage("Add Equipment")
       Set AssetInfo = objInspector.ModifiedFormPages.Item("Add Equipment")
                                       .Controls("NewAsset_Info")
       AssetInfo.List() = AssetInformation
       If Err <> 0 Then
          MsgBox Err & " :ShowFormPage: " & Err.Description
          Err.Clear
       End If

       objInspector.SetCurrentFormPage("Add Equipment")
       If Err <> 0 Then
          MsgBox Err & " :SetCurrentFormPage: " & Err.Description
          Err.Clear
       End If

       'objInspector.HideFormPage("Employee Message")
       If Err <> 0 Then
          MsgBox Err & " :HideFormPage:Employee Message: " & Err.Description
          Err.Clear
       End If

       Set txtSerialNumber = objInspector.ModifiedFormPages.Item("Add Equipment")
                                 .Controls("New_Serial_Number")
       If Err <> 0 Then
          MsgBox Err & " :Controls: " & Err.Description
          Err.Clear
       End If
```

```
         txtSerialNumber.SetFocus
         If Err <> 0 Then
            MsgBox Err & " :SetFocus: " & Err.Description
            Err.Clear
         End If
      End If


End Sub
```

cmdDeleteNew_Click()

This procedure executes when the user clicks the Delete button next to the lstAddEquipment list box on the Employee Equipment form. It removes the selected row from the lstAddEquipment list box. Again this functions similarly to the cmdDelete_Click() procedure, but it deletes newly added equipment instead of existing equipment. It is important to note that this procedure doesn't modify the value of the ItemDeletedFlag since the database never had the new piece of equipment anyway.

```
'**********************************************
'* Procedure:  cmdDeleteNew_Click()
'* Description:  This procedure is used to delete
'*      new equipment information
'*
'**********************************************
Sub cmdDeleteNew_Click()
Dim strEquipment
Dim objInspector
Dim txtSerialNumber

    Set objInspector = Item.GetInspector
    If Err <> 0 Then
       MsgBox Err & " :GetInspector: " & Err.Description
       Err.Clear
    End If

    Set Selected_Item = objInspector.ModifiedFormPages.Item("Employee Equipment")
                                      .Controls("lstAddEquipment")
    If Selected_Item.ListIndex <> -1 Then
    Selected_Item.RemoveItem (Selected_Item.ListIndex)
    End If

    Item.UserProperties.Find("NewEquipmentTotal") = Item.UserProperties _
                                    .Find("NewEquipmentTotal")-1

  If Err<>0 Then
    Msgbox "cmdDeleteNew: find Newequipmenttotal" & Err.Number & _
                                      ": " & Err.Description

    Err.Clear
  End If

End Sub
```

364

Item_Open()

Check to see if the Outlook form has an attachment – if so, save the attached file to the C:\ drive for later use. We'll come back to the attached file later, but it is important to note that this function fires when the form is first opened.

```
Function Item_Open()
Dim cmdUpdate
Dim objInspector
Dim objControl
Dim lngRC
Dim olTrackit
Dim olFolder

  On Error Resume Next

  If Item.Attachments.Count > 0 then
    If Err <> 0 Then
          MsgBox  "Item.Attachments.Count: Error# " & Err.Number & _
                                          ": " & Err.Description
          Err.Clear
       End If

    If Len(Item.UserProperties.Find("PeopleKey")) > 0 Then
       Item.Attachments(1) _
          .SaveAsFile("c:\" & Item.UserProperties.Find("PeopleKey") & ".txt")
    End If
    If Err <> 0 Then
          MsgBox  "Find PeopleKey: Error# " & Err.Number & ": " & Err.Description
          Err.Clear
       End If
  Else
    If Len(Item.UserProperties.Find("PeopleKey")) > 0 Then
      Item.Attachments.Add "c:\" & Item.UserProperties.Find("PeopleKey") & ".txt"
    End If
    If Err <> 0 Then
          MsgBox  "Find PeopleKey: Error# " & Err.Number & ": " & Err.Description
          Err.Clear
       End If
  End If
```

The following code handles an error that can occur when a user has an Outlook Tracking form in their Inbox. When they delete the mail item above the Tracking form mailitem, Outlook will automatically try to open the Tracking form mailitem. Unfortunately, it doesn't seem to run the full item_open routine, and it can't find objects on the form. If the function receives an error 424, then it cancels the item_open event. If it doesn't receive an error, it continues opening up the form and calls the FillEquipmentList function.

```
Set objControl= Item.GetInspector.ModifiedFormPages.Item("Employee Equipment") _
                                      .Controls("lstEquipment")
  If Err <> 424 Then
' The Trackit Form is not fully loaded.  Object required error message.
    If Err <> 0 Then
```

```
            MsgBox  "Get EquipmentPage: Error# " & Err.Number & _
                              ": " & Err.Description
         Err.Clear
    End If

   Set objEquipment = Item.UserProperties.Find("EquipmentTotal")
   If Err <> 0 Then
         MsgBox  "Find EquipmentTotal: Error# " & Err.Number & _
                              ": " & Err.Description
         Err.Clear
    End If

   lngRC = FillEquipmentList(objControl, objEquipment.Value)
        Set objControl = Nothing
   Set objEquipment = Nothing

      Set objControl= Item.GetInspector.ModifiedFormPages.Item("Admin Approval") _
                                           .Controls("cmdUpdate")
   If Err <> 0 Then
         MsgBox  "Get cmdUpdate: Error# " & Err.Number & _
                           ": " & Err.Description
         Err.Clear
    End If
      objControl.Visible = False
   Set objControl= nothing

   Set objControl= Item.GetInspector.ModifiedFormPages.Item("Admin Approval") _
                                       .Controls("cmdSelectAll")
   If Err <> 0 Then
         MsgBox  "Get cmdSelectAll: Error# " & Err.Number & _
                              ": " & Err.Description
         Err.Clear
    End If
      objControl.Visible = False
   Set objControl= nothing

   Set objControl= Item.GetInspector.ModifiedFormPages.Item("Admin Approval") _
                              .Controls("lstModifiedData")
   If Err <> 0 Then
         MsgBox  "Get lstModifiedData: Error# " & Err.Number & _
                              ": " & Err.Description
         Err.Clear
    End If
      objControl.Visible = False
   Set objControl= nothing

   Set objControl= Item.GetInspector.ModifiedFormPages.Item("Admin Approval") _
                              .Controls("lblModifiedData")
   If Err <> 0 Then
         MsgBox  "Get lblModifiedData: Error# " & Err.Number & _
                              ": " & Err.Description
         Err.Clear
```

```
         End If
          objControl.Visible = False
     Set objControl= nothing

     Set objControl= Item.GetInspector.ModifiedFormPages.Item("Admin Approval") _
                              .Controls("lblInstructions1")
     If Err <> 0 Then
          MsgBox  "Get lblInstructions1: Error# " & Err.Number & _
                              ": " & Err.Description
          Err.Clear
       End If
        'objControl.Visible = False
     Set objControl= nothing

     Set objControl= Item.GetInspector.ModifiedFormPages.Item("Admin Approval") _
                              .Controls("lblInstructions3")
     If Err <> 0 Then
          MsgBox  "Get lblInstructions3: Error# " & Err.Number & _
                              ": " & Err.Description
          Err.Clear
       End If
        'objControl.Visible = False
     Set objControl= nothing

     Set objControl= Item.GetInspector.ModifiedFormPages.Item("Admin Approval") _
                              .Controls("lblInstructions4")
     If Err <> 0 Then
          MsgBox  "Get lblInstructions4: Error# " & Err.Number & _
                              ": " & Err.Description
          Err.Clear
       End If
        'objControl.Visible = False
     Set objControl= nothing

        Set objInspector = Item.GetInspector
        If Err <> 0 Then
          MsgBox  "GetInspector: Error# " & Err.Number & ": " & Err.Description
          Err.Clear
        End If

        objInspector.HideFormPage("Modify Equipment")
        If Err <> 0 Then
          MsgBox Err & " :HideFormPage:Modify Equipment: " & Err.Description
          Err.Clear
        End If

        objInspector.HideFormPage("Add Equipment")
       If Err <> 0 Then
          MsgBox Err & " :HideFormPage:Add Equipment: " & Err.Description
          Err.Clear
        End If
     Else
     Item_Open = False
       End If

End Function
```

FillEquipmentList()

This function opens the attached file that was saved to the C:\ drive in the item_open event, reads the file, and populates the controls on the Outlook form. The rationale for storing EquipmentList information in an attached text file instead of the Outlook form is discussed below.

```
Function FillEquipmentList(objEquipmentList, intEquipmentTotal)

Const ForReading = 1
Dim arrEquipment()
Dim intCounter
Dim objFileSystemObject
Dim objTextFile
Dim strPath
Dim strEquipmentInfo
Dim strDetail
Dim varPosition

  Set objFileSystemObject = CreateObject("Scripting.FileSystemObject")
  On error Resume Next
      Set objTextFile = objFileSystemObject _
                  .OpenTextFile("c:\" & Item.UserProperties _
                                  .Find("PeopleKey") & _
                                  ".txt", ForReading)
  If Err = 0 then
    strRead = objTextFile.ReadLine

    strRead = objTextFile.ReadLine
    Item.UserProperties.Find("DSN") = strRead
    strRead = objTextFile.ReadLine

    Set objControl = Item.GetInspector.ModifiedFormPages.Item("Employee Message") _
                                  .Controls("Position_Desc")
    strRead = objTextFile.ReadLine
    Do until strRead = "[Region]"
      objControl.AddItem strRead
      strRead = objTextFile.ReadLine
    Loop
    Set objControl = Item.GetInspector.ModifiedFormPages.Item("Employee Message") _
                                  .Controls("Region_Code_Desc")
    strRead = objTextFile.ReadLine
    Do until strRead = "[Asset]"
      objControl.AddItem strRead
      strRead = objTextFile.ReadLine
    Loop
    Item.GetInspector.ShowFormPage("Modify Equipment")
    Item.GetInspector.ShowFormPage("Add Equipment")
    Set objControl = Item.GetInspector.ModifiedFormPages.Item("Modify Equipment") _
                                  .Controls("Asset_Info")
      Set objControl2 = Item.GetInspector.ModifiedFormPages.Item("Add Equipment") _
                                  .Controls("NewAsset_Info")
```

```
strRead = objTextFile.ReadLine
Do until strRead = "[Equipment]"
  objControl.AddItem strRead
  objControl2.AddItem strRead
  strRead = objTextFile.ReadLine
Loop
Item.GetInspector.HideFormPage("Modify Equipment")
Item.GetInspector.HideFormPage("Add Equipment")
Redim AssetInformation(objControl.ListCount)
For Index = 0 to objControl.ListCount-1
  AssetInformation(Index)=objControl.List(Index)
Next
Item.UserProperties.Find("AssetInfoTotal") = objControl.ListCount

ReDim arrEquipment(intEquipmentTotal, 5)


objEquipmentList.clear
For intCounter=0 to intEquipmentTotal-1
  'Add equipment to the list
  'Serial Number
  strEquipmentInfo = objTextFile.ReadLine
  varPosition = InStr(strEquipmentInfo, ",")
  strDetail= Left(strEquipmentInfo,varPosition-1)
  arrEquipment(intCounter, 0) = strDetail

  'Asset Information
  strEquipmentInfo = Right(strEquipmentInfo, _
                        Len(strEquipmentInfo) - varPosition)
  varPosition = InStr(strEquipmentInfo,",")
  strDetail = Left(strEquipmentInfo,varPosition-1)
  arrEquipment(intCounter, 1) = strDetail

  'Lease Number
  strEquipmentInfo = Right(strEquipmentInfo, _
                        Len(strEquipmentInfo) - varPosition)
  varPosition = InStr(strEquipmentInfo,",")
  strDetail = Left(strEquipmentInfo,varPosition-1)
  arrEquipment(intCounter, 2) = strDetail

  varLastPosition = varPosition
  'Old Serial Number
  strEquipmentInfo = Right(strEquipmentInfo, _
                        Len(strEquipmentInfo) - varPosition)
  varPosition = InStr(strEquipmentInfo,",")
  If varPostion <> varLastPosition Then
  strDetail = Left(strEquipmentInfo,varPosition-1)
  arrEquipment(intCounter, 3) = strDetail

    'Old Asset Information
  strDetail = Right(strEquipmentInfo, _
                  Len(strEquipmentInfo) - varPosition)
  arrEquipment(intCounter, 4) = strDetail
  Else 'person with ATDB ver3.00.00
```

```
                arrEquipment(intCounter, 3) = ""
                arrEquipment(intCounter, 4) = ""
           End If
        Next

            'Load data into the lstEquipment list box
            objEquipmentList.List() = arrEquipment

        'MsgBox(objEquipmentList.ListCount)

        Set objControl = Nothing
        Set objEquipment = Nothing

        Set objControl= Item.GetInspector.ModifiedFormPages.Item("Employee Equipment") _
                                     .Controls("lstAddEquipment")
        Set objEquipment = Item.UserProperties.Find("NewEquipmentTotal")

        ReDim arrEquipment(objEquipment.Value, 5)

        For intCounter=0 to objEquipment.Value-1
           'Add equipment to the list
           strEquipmentInfo = objTextFile.ReadLine
           varPosition = InStr(strEquipmentInfo, ",")
           strDetail= Left(strEquipmentInfo,varPosition-1)
           arrEquipment(intCounter, 0) = strDetail
           strEquipmentInfo = Right(strEquipmentInfo, _
                                    Len(strEquipmentInfo) - varPosition)
           varPosition = InStr(strEquipmentInfo,",")
           strDetail = Left(strEquipmentInfo,varPosition-1)
           arrEquipment(intCounter, 1) = strDetail
           strDetail = Right(strEquipmentInfo,Len(strEquipmentInfo) - varPosition)
           arrEquipment(intCounter, 2) = strDetail
        Next

        If objEquipment.Value > 0 Then
              'Load data into the lstEquipment list box
             objControl.List() = arrEquipment
        End If

        Set objControl = Nothing
        Set objEquipment = Nothing

        objTextFile.Close
           Set objFileSystemObject = Nothing
     Else
        Err.Clear
     End If
  End Function
```

Item_Reply

This function creates a new text file, and writes values of the Database DSN information, position list, region list, asset Information list, lstEquipment list box, and lstNewEquipment list box to the file. This file will be attached to the e-mail when sent and it will be read later by the `FillEquipmentList` fuction to populate the tracking form.

This file is necessary because the values in the list boxes will not be saved on the form if there are multiple columns or if there are more than 200 rows. Position lists, region lists, and list box values may exceed 200 rows and/or contain multiple columns, ensuring that data passes from user to administrator. Moreover, storing the postion codes and asset information descriptions in a file rather than on the form makes changes to these lists easier to manage. If the list values were stored on the form, then the form would need to be updated and republished everytime a value changed.

```
Function Item_Reply(ByVal Response)
Dim objFileSystemObject
Dim objTextFile
Dim objEquipmentList
Dim objInspector


  Set objInspector = Item.GetInspector

  Set objFileSystemObject = CreateObject("Scripting.FileSystemObject")
  Set objTextFile = objFileSystemObject _
                 .CreateTextFile("c:\" & Item.UserProperties _
                              .Find("PeopleKey") & ".txt", True)

  objTextFile.WriteLine "[Database]"
  objTextFile.WriteLine Item.UserProperties.Find("DSN")

  set objControl = objInspector.ModifiedFormPages.Item("Employee Message") _
                            .Controls("Position_Desc")
  objTextFile.WriteLine "[Position]"
  If objControl.ListCount > 0 then
       For intIndex = 0 To objControl.ListCount -1
     objTextFile.WriteLine objControl.List(intIndex)
      Next
      End If

  set objControl = objInspector.ModifiedFormPages.Item("Employee Message") _
                            .Controls("Region_Code_Desc")
  objTextFile.WriteLine "[Region]"
  If objControl.ListCount > 0 then
       For intIndex = 0 To objControl.ListCount -1
     objTextFile.WriteLine objControl.List(intIndex)
      Next
      End If

  objTextFile.WriteLine "[Asset]"
  If Item.UserProperties.Find("AssetInfoTotal") > 0 then
       For intIndex = 0 To Item.UserProperties.Find("AssetInfoTotal") -1
     objTextFile.WriteLine AssetInformation(intIndex)
```

```
            Next
        End If

objTextFile.WriteLine "[Equipment]"
        Set objEquipmentList= objInspector.ModifiedFormPages _
                                    .Item("Employee Equipment") _
                                    .Controls("lstEquipment")
        If objEquipmentList.ListCount > 0 then
        For intIndex = 0 To Item.UserProperties.Find("EquipmentTotal")-1
'objEquipmentList.ListCount-1
            objTextFile.Write (objEquipmentList.List(intIndex,0))
            objTextFile.Write ("," & objEquipmentList.List(intIndex,1))
            objTextFile.Write ("," & objEquipmentList.List(intIndex,2))
            objTextFile.Write ("," & objEquipmentList.List(intIndex,3))
            objTextFile.WriteLine ("," & objEquipmentList.List(intIndex,4))
        Next
        End If

    Set objEquipmentList= objInspector.ModifiedFormPages.Item("Employee Equipment") _
                                .Controls("lstAddEquipment")
        If objEquipmentList.ListCount > 0 then
            For intIndex = 0 To Item.UserProperties.Find("NewEquipmentTotal")-1
        objTextFile.Write (objEquipmentList.List(intIndex,0))
        objTextFile.Write ("," & objEquipmentList.List(intIndex,1))
        objTextFile.WriteLine ("," & objEquipmentList.List(intIndex,2))
            Next
        End If

        objTextFile.Close
        Set objFileSystemObject = Nothing

    While Item.Attachments.Count > 0
            Item.Attachments.Remove 1
    Wend

    Item.Attachments.Add "c:\" & Item.UserProperties.Find("PeopleKey") & ".txt"

End Function
```

Item_Send()

Before sending the form to the Asset Tracking manager, this function verifies that the unique Employee identifier `PeopleKey` is non-zero. This ensures that the update procedure on the **Admin Approval** tab will work properly when executed.

```
Function Item_Send()
  If Len(Item.UserProperties.Find("PeopleKey")) = 0 Then
    MsgBox("You do not have permission to send this form.")
    Item_Send = False
  End If
End Function
```

ODBC Setup for Administrative Tool Users

Before Administrators can use MS Access to manage Asset Tracking information, they must create an ODBC connection to the SQL Server database. Large organizations would normally handle ODBC setup for Administrative Users by distributing a standard software image to the Asset Tracking staff, which included all necessary ODBC configurations. Alternatively, you could use RegisterServer API calls to automatically register a new ODBC connection. For this case study however, we will manually configure the ODBC connection to allow you to use the Access administration application.

NOTE: These setup steps assume that users have ODBC Manager and SQL Server database types installed.

❑   Open the ODBC Data Source Administrator from the Control Panel, and click on Add.

❑   From the Create New Data Source dialog, select **SQL Server** and click on Finish to return to the Administrator window.

❑   Now select KAT_SQL from the **User Data Sources** list on the **User DSN** tab, and click on **Add**.

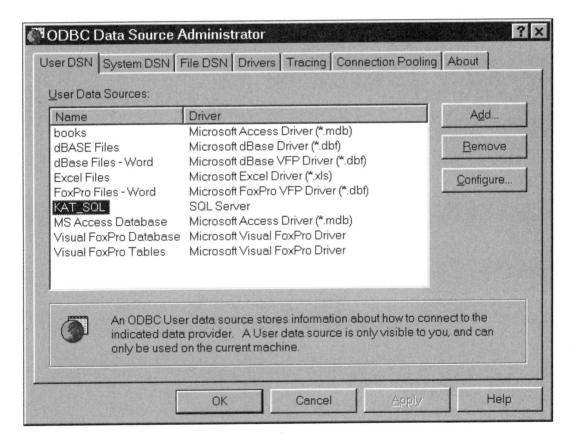

❑ This will open a DSN Configuration wizard that will walk you through most of the setup steps. The code for the MS Access Application and the Outlook Administration features assume that Administrative Users have a DSN named KAT_SQL. Use this for your Name. You can type any meaningful description into the second text field, and the final field should be the name of your SQL Server machine (ntserver1 in this example).

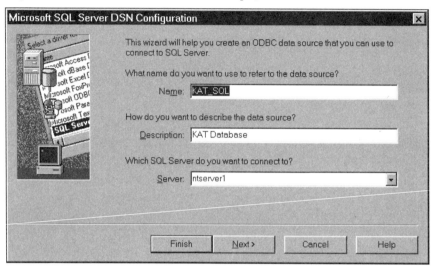

❑ Click on Next, and accept all defaults unless otherwise noted. When asked to change the default database, select KAT from the dropdown list.

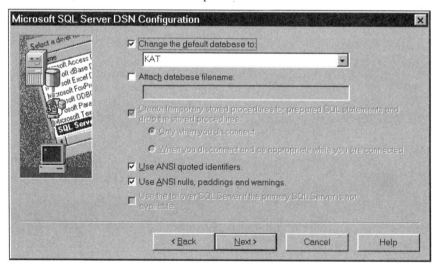

❑ Click Finish when complete. You should see your new DSN appear in the User DSN list. You can also test the connection to verify connectivity to the SQL Server database using the final screen of the DSN setup wizard.

Creating the MS Access 2000 Administration Tool

The final component necessary to make our Asset Tracking application work is the Administration Tool. As mentioned before, this tool would typically contain many more features than we've included in this case study. However, because the focus of the study is to build Outlook components, we will include only the Outlook form generation features of the Administration application.

Administrators use the Administration tool to select user(s) that need to update their Asset Inventory information. After selecting users using the e-mail form, the the Access code will generate Outlook 2000 forms for each selected employee, populate the forms with data stored in the SQL Server database, and transmit the e-mailed package. Let's walk through the creation of the Administration Tool.

Steps

❏ Open up Access and create a new database. The name is unimportant, but we'll call ours KAT Admin

❏ Go to File | Get External Data | Link Tables

❏ Select ODBC Databases() from the Files of type: combo box, and click Import.

❏ You will be prompted to select a data source and the dialog below will appear:

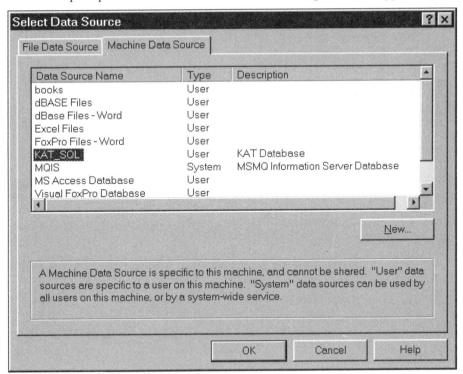

❏ Select the Data Source KAT_SQL from the Machine Data Source tab, and Click OK.

❑ Select the following tables:

    ❑ `dbo_ASSET_VIEW`

    ❑ `dbo_EMPLOYEE_FULL_VIEW`

    ❑ `dbo_EMPLOYEE_FULLNAME_VIEW`

    ❑ `dbo_POSITION`

    ❑ `dbo_REGIONAL_OFFICE`

❑ Click **OK**.

❑ Rename each linked table to remove the `dbo_` prefix. You can do this by right-clicking on a table name in the database view screen. Choose **Rename** and remove the prefix.

Populating the MS Access Administration Tool

At this point, you have completed the basic setup of the MS Access application. We must now:

❑ Create Access Queries to support the e-mail form

❑ Build the Access e-mail form

❑ Add code behind buttons on the e-mail form

❑ Add module `basTrackitFunctions`

❑ Save the completed solution

Create MS Access Queries

We won't go into detail discussing the features behind each of these queries. They are used simply to facilitate populating the Outlook 2000 forms when the e-mail form is used. Each of the queries gathers asset, position, region, and employee information from the SQL Server 7.0 database, and populates the newly created Outlook form fields.

To build each of these queries, select **Queries** from the main switchboard, and click on the **New** icon. When prompted, select **Design View** for the query (instead of using one of the Access wizards). Once the empty query is open in design mode, you can right-click on the upper portion of the window. This will let you open a SQL editor window (**SQL View**), into which you can then type in the query creation code. Alternatively, you can download the `KATAdmin.mdb` database from the Wrox website (www.wrox.com).

ASSET_DESC_Query

```
SELECT ASSET_VIEW.Asset AS Asset_Desc
FROM ASSET_VIEW
ORDER BY ASSET_VIEW.Asset;
```

POSITION_DESC_Query

```
SELECT [Description] & " {" & [Position] & "}" AS Position_Desc
FROM POSITION
ORDER BY POSITION.Description;
```

REGION_DESC_Query

```
SELECT [Region_Name] & " {" & [Region_Code] & "}" AS Region_Desc
FROM REGIONAL_OFFICE
ORDER BY REGIONAL_OFFICE.Region_Name;
```

TrackitEMPLOYEE_FULL_VIEW_Query

```
PARAMETERS PeopleKey Short;
SELECT EMPLOYEE_FULL_VIEW.Last_Name, EMPLOYEE_FULL_VIEW.First_Name,
EMPLOYEE_FULL_VIEW.MI, [PosDescription] & " {" & [Position] & "}" AS
Position_Desc, EMPLOYEE_FULL_VIEW.Work_Location, [Region_Name] & " {" &
[Region_Code] & "}" AS Region_Code_Desc, EMPLOYEE_FULL_VIEW.Equip_Delivery,
EMPLOYEE_FULL_VIEW.Office_Address, EMPLOYEE_FULL_VIEW.Office_City,
EMPLOYEE_FULL_VIEW.Office_State, EMPLOYEE_FULL_VIEW.Office_Zip,
EMPLOYEE_FULL_VIEW.Office_Phone, EMPLOYEE_FULL_VIEW.Office_Fax,
EMPLOYEE_FULL_VIEW.Home_Address, EMPLOYEE_FULL_VIEW.Home_City,
EMPLOYEE_FULL_VIEW.Home_State, EMPLOYEE_FULL_VIEW.Home_Zip,
EMPLOYEE_FULL_VIEW.Home_Phone, EMPLOYEE_FULL_VIEW.Home_Fax,
EMPLOYEE_FULL_VIEW.Other_Address, EMPLOYEE_FULL_VIEW.Other_City,
EMPLOYEE_FULL_VIEW.Other_State, EMPLOYEE_FULL_VIEW.Other_Zip,
EMPLOYEE_FULL_VIEW.Other_Phone, EMPLOYEE_FULL_VIEW.Other_Fax,
EMPLOYEE_FULL_VIEW.Comments, EMPLOYEE_FULL_VIEW.People_Key,
EMPLOYEE_FULL_VIEW.Serial_Number, EMPLOYEE_FULL_VIEW.MFG, EMPLOYEE_FULL_VIEW.Model,
EMPLOYEE_FULL_VIEW.Asset_Type, EMPLOYEE_FULL_VIEW.Lease_Number
FROM EMPLOYEE_FULL_VIEW
WHERE (((EMPLOYEE_FULL_VIEW.People_Key)=[PeopleKey]))
ORDER BY EMPLOYEE_FULL_VIEW.Serial_Number;
```

Creating the E-Mail Form

Now that the queries are complete, let's focus on building a simple e-mail form to select Asset Tracking form recipients.

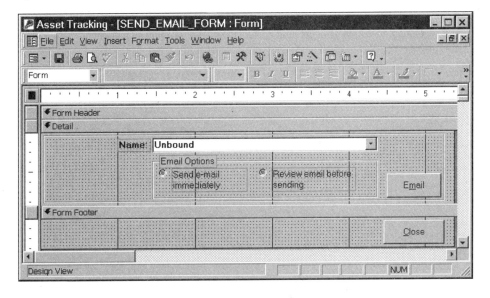

Steps

Follow these steps to build this simple Access form. Create a new form called SEND_E-MAIL_FORM, open it in design mode, and add the following controls and properties:

❑ Add a combo box control from the toolbox

Name	Field1
RowSourceType	Table/Query
RowSource	Select Name, People_Key from EMPLOYEE_FULLNAME_VIEW ORDER BY Name
ColumnCount	2
Column Widths	2, 0
Bound Column	1

❑ Add Label control from the toolbox with caption Name:

❑ Add Option Group control from the toolbox

Label Name 1	Send e-mail immediately
Label Name 2	Review e-mail before sending
Default Choice	1 - Send e-mail immediately
Control Type	Option buttons
Caption	E-mail Options

❑ Add button control from the toolbox called cmdE-mailTrackit with Caption e-mail

❑ Add button control from the toolbox called Close with Caption Close

The basic form is now in place. Finally, let's place some code behind the form by choosing the e-mail Trackit button, right-clicking on it, and selecting Build Event | Code Builder.

Support Code for Access 2000 Administration Tool

To add code to the Access form, click on the Code Icon on the MS Access toolbar. This will open up the Microsoft VBA editor. Alternately, you can right-click on form controls, select build event, and launch the VBA editor.

cmdEmailTrackit_Click()

This sub uses the Outlook and MAPI objects to create Outlook e-mail when the user clicks on the e-mail button on the SEND_E-MAIL form

```
Private Sub cmdEmailTrackit_Click()
'This sub will create and send e-mail tackit forms to each employee selected.
On Error GoTo Err_cmdEmailTrackit_Click

'MAPI variables used to access CDO
Dim mapiSession As MAPI.Session
Dim mapiFolder As MAPI.Folder
Dim mapiTrackit As MAPI.Message
Dim mapiRecipient As MAPI.Recipient
Dim mapiRecipientCollection As MAPI.Recipients

'Outlook variables
Dim olApp As Outlook.Application
Dim olNameSpace As Outlook.NameSpace
Dim olDefaultFolder As Outlook.mapiFolder
Dim olTrackit As Outlook.MailItem
Dim olRecipient As Outlook.Recipient

Dim intPeopleKey As Integer
Dim strEmailAddress As String
Dim lngRC As Long

    DoCmd.Hourglass True

    'Create a session using CDO to prompt user to correct unresolved addresses
    Set mapiSession = CreateObject("MAPI.Session")
```

> The original application (from which this study was derived) used a function to identify the user's profile from their LAN ID when creating a new Outlook object. Since we don't want to make any assumptions about profile naming conventions, we leave it here to the user to decide how to extract this information. For the purposes of testing, simply use your local profile name.
>
> To find your profile name, select the Mail icon in control panel, and click **Show Profiles**. If you don't have any profiles configured, you may disregard this step. CDO (Collaboration Data Objects) will simply create an Outlook object and ignore the **ProfileName** property.

```
    mapiSession.Logon profileName:="xxxxx", ShowDialog:=False
    'profile name of outlook mailbox
    Set mapiFolder = mapiSession.Inbox
    Set mapiTrackit = mapiFolder.Messages.Add(Type:="IPM.Note.TrackitForm2")
    Set mapiRecipientCollection = mapiTrackit.Recipients

    Set mapiRecipient = mapiTrackit.Recipients.Add(Field1.Column(0))
```

379

```
        On Error Resume Next
        'Prompt user to correct unresolved addresses
        mapiRecipientCollection.Resolve ShowDialog:=True
         If Err = 0 Then
             intPeopleKey = Field1.Column(1)
             strEmailAddress = mapiRecipient.Name
             On Error GoTo Err_cmdEmailTrackit_Click
        Else
             Err.Clear
             On Error GoTo Err_cmdEmailTrackit_Click
             mapiRecipientCollection(1).Delete
        End If

        'cleanup
        mapiSession.Logoff
        Set mapiSession = Nothing
        Set mapiFolder = Nothing
        Set mapiTrackit = Nothing
        Set mapiRecipient = Nothing
        Set mapiRecipientCollection = Nothing

        'Create a session using the Outlook object model
        'to allow easy reference to fields on the form.
        Set olApp = New Outlook.Application
        Set olNameSpace = olApp.GetNamespace("MAPI")
        Set olDefaultFolder = olNameSpace.GetDefaultFolder(olFolderInbox)
```

This code uses the `PopulateAndSentTrackit` procedure in our `basTrackitFunctions` to write data from the SQL server database into the Outlook 2000 form and send it to the identified recipient.

```
     Set olTrackit = olDefaultFolder.Items.Add("IPM.Note.TrackitForm2")
        Set olRecipient = olTrackit.Recipients.Add(strEmailAddress)
        'get the information from the EMPLOYEE_FULL_VIEW and populate the e-mail
        lngRC = PopulateAndSendTrackit(intPeopleKey, olTrackit)

        Set olTrackit = Nothing
        Set olApp = Nothing
        Set olNameSpace = Nothing
        Set olDefaultFolder = Nothing
        Set olTrackit = Nothing
        Set olRecipient = Nothing

Exit_cmdEmailTrackit_Click:
    DoCmd.Hourglass False
    Exit Sub

Err_cmdEmailTrackit_Click:
    MsgBox Err.Number & ": " & Err.Description
    GoTo Exit_cmdEmailTrackit_Click

End Sub
```

Form_Load()

This sub, called when the e-mail form is initialized, simply populates the combo box with the names of all the employees in the Asset Tracking (KAT) database.

```
Private Sub Form_Load()
Dim strSQL As String

    strSQL = "Select Name,People_Key from EMPLOYEE_FULLNAME_VIEW ORDER BY Name"
    Me!Field1.RowSource = strSQL

End Sub
```

Close_Click()

```
Private Sub Close_Click()
On Error GoTo Err_Close_Click

    DoCmd.Close

Exit_Close_Click:
    Exit Sub

Err_Close_Click:
    MsgBox Err.Description
    Resume Exit_Close_Click
End Sub
```

PopulateAndSendTrackit

This function, created in the `basTrackitFunctions` module, handles populating the Outlook 2000 form controls and fields.

```
Option Compare Database
Option Explicit
Function PopulateAndSendTrackit(intPeopleKey As Integer, _
                        olTrackit As Outlook.MailItem) As Long
On Error GoTo Err_PopulateAndSendTrackit

Dim db As Database
Dim qdfTrackitDetails As QueryDef
Dim rstTrackitDetails As Recordset

Dim olPageCollection As Object
Dim intCount As Integer
Dim objControl As Object
Dim objField As Object
Dim objQueryField As Object
Dim intCounter As Integer
Dim objTotalField As Object
Dim intIndex As Integer
Dim objNewField As Object
Const ForWriting = 2
Dim objFileSystemObject As Object
Dim objTextFile As Object
Dim rstComboList As Recordset, qdfComboList As QueryDef
Dim varDSN As Variant
```

This code passes the PeopleKey parameter into TrackitEMPLOYEE_FULL_VIEWQuery and opens the resultant recordset. It then populates each control on the form, writes Employee, Asset, Region, and Position information to a text file, attaches the file to the form e-mail, and sends it to the identified recipient.

```
DoCmd.Hourglass True

    Set db = CurrentDb
    Set qdfTrackitDetails = db.QueryDefs("TrackitEMPLOYEE_FULL_VIEWQuery")
    qdfTrackitDetails.Parameters("PeopleKey") = intPeopleKey
    Set rstTrackitDetails = qdfTrackitDetails.OpenRecordset

    If Not rstTrackitDetails.EOF Then
        Set olPageCollection = olTrackit.GetInspector.ModifiedFormPages

        'For each field in the query update a
        'control with the same name on the form.
        For Each objQueryField In rstTrackitDetails.Fields
            'if control not found
            If objQueryField.Name <> "Serial_Number" And _
                objQueryField.Name <> "MFG" And _
                objQueryField.Name <> "Model" And _
                objQueryField.Name <> "Asset_Type" And _
                objQueryField.Name <> "Lease_Number" Then
            Set objControl = olPageCollection("Employee Message") _
                                        .Controls(objQueryField.Name)
                objControl.Text = IIf(IsNull(objQueryField.Value), "", _
                                                objQueryField.Value)
            End If
        Next

        rstTrackitDetails.MoveLast
        Set objTotalField = olTrackit.UserProperties.Find("EquipmentTotal")
        objTotalField.Value = rstTrackitDetails.RecordCount
        Set objTotalField = Nothing
        rstTrackitDetails.MoveFirst
        intCounter = 0

        Set objFileSystemObject = CreateObject("Scripting.FileSystemObject")
        Set objTextFile = objFileSystemObject _
                    .createTextFile("c:\" & intPeopleKey & ".txt", True)

        'Add Database Information
        objTextFile.WriteLine "[Database]"
        objTextFile.WriteLine "KAT_SQL" 'DSN

        'Fill Combo List Information
        Set rstComboList = db.OpenRecordset("Position_Desc_Query", _
                                        dbOpenForwardOnly)
        objTextFile.WriteLine "[Position]"
        Do Until rstComboList.EOF
            objTextFile.WriteLine rstComboList!Position_Desc
            rstComboList.MoveNext
        Loop
```

```
        Set rstComboList = Nothing

        Set rstComboList = db.OpenRecordset("Region_Desc_Query", _
                                            dbOpenForwardOnly)
        objTextFile.WriteLine "[Region]"
        Do Until rstComboList.EOF
            objTextFile.WriteLine rstComboList!Region_Desc
            rstComboList.MoveNext
        Loop
        Set rstComboList = Nothing

        Set rstComboList = db.OpenRecordset("Asset_Desc_Query", dbOpenForwardOnly)
        objTextFile.WriteLine "[Asset]"
        Do Until rstComboList.EOF
            objTextFile.WriteLine rstComboList!Asset_Desc
            rstComboList.MoveNext
        Loop
        Set rstComboList = Nothing

        objTextFile.WriteLine "[Equipment]"
        Do Until rstTrackitDetails.EOF
            'Load data into file
            objTextFile.Write (IIf(IsNull(rstTrackitDetails!Serial_Number), "", _
                                   rstTrackitDetails!Serial_Number))
            objTextFile.Write ("," & IIf(IsNull(rstTrackitDetails!MFG), "", _
                                   rstTrackitDetails!MFG) _
            & " " & IIf(IsNull(rstTrackitDetails!Model), "", _
                        rstTrackitDetails!Model) & _
            " " & IIf(IsNull(rstTrackitDetails!Asset_Type), "", _
                        rstTrackitDetails!Asset_Type))
            objTextFile.Write ("," & IIf(IsNull(rstTrackitDetails!Lease_Number), _
                                   "", rstTrackitDetails!Lease_Number))
            objTextFile.WriteLine (", ,")
            intCounter = intCounter + 1
            rstTrackitDetails.MoveNext
        Loop
    
End If

objTextFile.Close

olTrackit.Attachments.Add "c:\" & intPeopleKey & ".txt"

If Forms!SEND_E-MAIL_FORM!fraEmailOptions = 1 Then
    olTrackit.DeleteAfterSubmit = True
    olTrackit.Send
    objFileSystemObject.DeleteFile "c:\" & intPeopleKey & ".txt"
Else
    olTrackit.DeleteAfterSubmit = False
    olTrackit.Close olSave
    olTrackit.Display
End If
```

```
        Set db = Nothing
        qdfTrackitDetails.Close
        Set qdfTrackitDetails = Nothing
        rstTrackitDetails.Close
        Set rstTrackitDetails = Nothing

        Set objTextFile = Nothing
        Set objFileSystemObject = Nothing

Exit_PopulateAndSendTrackit:
        Exit Function

Err_PopulateAndSendTrackit:
        MsgBox Err.Number & ": " & Err.Description
        GoTo Exit_PopulateAndSendTrackit

End Function
```

Deployment

There are a number of considerations to bear in mind when deploying this application across a large organization. Most importantly, you must decide how to deploy the Outlook form. You can either publish the form in the Organizational Forms Library or have users publish the form in their Personal Forms library – the former is usually the best solution. By placing the Outlook form in the Organizational library, you can upgrade it without manually transmitting the updated form to end-users and expecting them to re-publish their Asset Tracking form. However, there are some scenarios that necessitate using Personal Forms libraries:

❑ No Microsoft Exchange server exists for publishing

❑ Access to Organizational Folders is highly restricted

❑ You want to override a form in the Organizational library

You can see that we've made no specific references in the MS Access source code to "look" for the Outlook form. MS Outlook handles the search for forms by looking first in the Personal Forms Library and then in the Orgainzational Forms Library (if it exists). Other considerations include:

❑ Standard ODBC configuration for users and security setup. Our case study assumed that all Administrators would have a configured DSN. Moreover, we assumed that the userid and password for each user would be the same. This is probably not very secure and could encourage database hacking.

❑ Distribution of the Microsoft Data Access Components (MDAC 2.0). This component set is required for the case study and would probably be deployed to users in a large organization in a software rollout.

Case Study: Time and Billing Application

This chapter builds a case study for a Time and Billing application. It is limited in scope, serving mainly to illustrate an integrated application that combines a number of Outlook capabilities:

- ❑ Custom Outlook forms
- ❑ A COM add-in
- ❑ E-mail routing
- ❑ Interfacing output to a custom Word template
- ❑ Custom Outlook Bar group management
- ❑ Posting Office Document items to an Outlook folder

The COM add-in built in this chapter is built using the Microsoft Office 2000 Developer Edition (MOD), but VB 6 can be used with no code changes. The chapter concludes with some ideas for enhancing the application for various workflow requirements.

The following diagram shows the flow of the parts of the application. Use it as a reference as you read this section to help you understand how this application works.

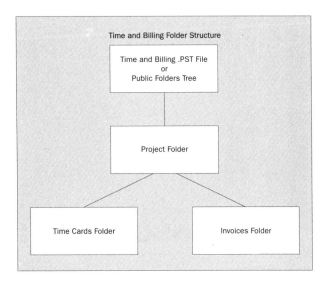

The application has a custom Outlook form, built on the Message form (IPM.Note) that serves as a weekly time card form (see Chapter 2 for information about Outlook form design). It is submitted by email to the user's manager. The manager is looked up in the GAL (Global Address List) of an Exchange Server installation. If there is no GAL, the manager is not resolved in the GAL, or there is no entry for the manager, an Address Book dialog box is presented to the user for selection of a manager.

> **The GAL in an Exchange Server installation has a Manager field for each entry that returns a Recipient object. If the GAL is set up so that each employee has a Manager, workflow applications such as this one are easy to configure.**

After the time card is filled in, and a project is selected, the Send button emails the time card to the manager. The manager can either approve or reject the time card. A text box is provided for the manager's comments. If the time card is rejected, it is returned to the user. If it is approved, it is routed to the time card folder.

> **The forms and folders for this application are supplied in a Time and Billing .PST (Personal Folders) file. This file can be opened in Outlook, and the application can be used as is. You can also copy the Projects folder and subsidiary Invoices and Time Cards folders to the Public Folders tree in an Exchange Server installation. If the application is run from the Public Folders tree, some of the code must be modified to look for the folders in that tree. The modifications are indicated where they are needed.**

If an approved time card is opened in the Time Cards folder a New Invoice toolbar button is created that generates an invoice using a custom Word template with the weekly time and project hourly rate. The invoice is automatically posted to the Invoices folder after it is generated. After an invoice is generated from a time card the New Invoice toolbar button is disabled so that no more than one invoice can be generated from an approved time card.

The following diagram shows the folder structure for the application.

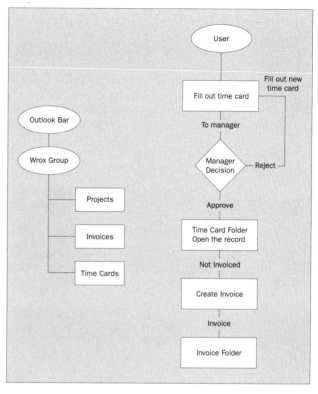

The other custom Outlook form used in this application is a Projects form. The Projects form is a customized Contact form (IPM.Contact) that has no code, just some custom fields and a modified layout. The project hourly rate and other customer information for a project is stored in the Projects form in the Projects folder. The information from the Projects forms in the Projects folder is used to fill a listbox in the time card with the names of projects. The project selected in the listbox is used to look up the project hourly rate when an invoice is generated.

The invoice is created in a document created from a custom Word template. The Outlook data is placed into Word Bookmarks in the document. After the invoice is generated, it is attached to an Office Document item and posted into the Invoices folder. Although the Office Document item shows an attachment of the Word document in the preview pane, when the it is opened the Word item itself opens.

The COM add-in is used to create and destroy a custom Outlook Bar group that has shortcuts to the folders for the application.

> The folders, forms and VBScript code behind the Time Card form are all available for download from the Wrox Web site. They are packaged in the `Time and Billing.pst` file. The custom Word template that is used in the application is also available for download on the Wrox Web site.

Time Card Forms and Dialog Boxes

The Address Book dialog box that appears if no manager can be resolved is the familiar Outlook dialog. It cannot be generated from the Outlook object model. It can only be generated by using the CDO object model. The `Manager` property is a property of the `AddressEntry` object, and in a bit of circular logic is an `AddressEntry` object itself. Although the property is present in all `AddressEntry` objects, accessing it from an Outlook Address Book or Personal Address Book returns an error. The property is only actually present in an entry in a GAL. The occurrence of an error after the attempt to access the `Manager` property is what is used to trigger the call to the Address Book dialog box. This enables the user to select a manager. The following screen shot shows an Address Book dialog box for Outlook installed in Internet only mode.

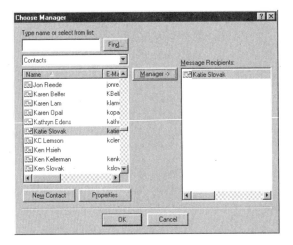

The following screen shot shows the **Message** tab of the TimeCard form in design mode. Although it is not necessary for this application, the message box has been removed, along with the Cc field and command button. This show the customizations that can be done on the first page of the Message form in Outlook 2000. The **Message** tab is hidden in the form that the user sees, the run mode form.

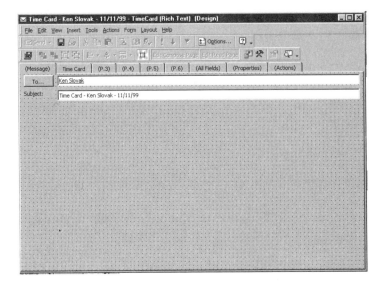

The following screen shot shows the Time card tab in design mode., This tab was renamed from the default name (P.2), and is the only tab that the user sees. It contains a date field that is automatically filled in when the time card is sent for approval, a combo box that enables the user to select a project for the time card, a field for the name of the person submitting the time card to be automatically filled in, and date and time controls for the days and hours worked.

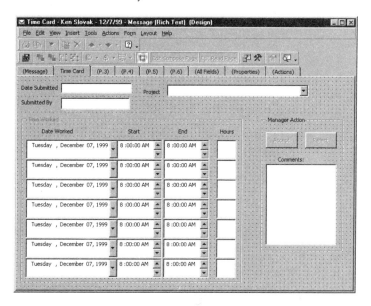

The date and time controls are 2 instances of the same ActiveX control, the DTPicker control. This control has properties that permit it to be a selector for dates or times. The disabled Accept and Reject buttons, and the Comments text box, are only visible and enabled in run mode to the manager that reviews the time card.

Instructions for building the forms used in this application are not given in this chapter because they are available for download from the Wrox Web site. See Chapter 2 for more information about Outlook form design. I will briefly describe setting the properties of the DTPicker control, because it has non-standard properties. Only the properties that are used in this application are described here. For more information about the DTPicker, see the Visual Basic 6.0 Controls Reference and the MSDN Library.

The only properties that affect the DTPicker are the second list of Properties in the context menu that appears when the DTPicker is right-clicked. A DTPicker can be set to be either used for time or date input. It does not honor the Enabled and Read-only properties that are in the standard Properties sheet. The following screen shot shows the DTPicker control's Properties sheet, with the format listbox open.

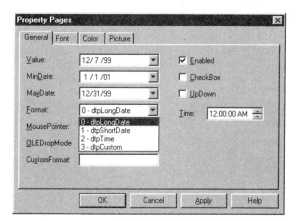

The All Fields tab of the form shows the user defined fields that are present in the form. The following screen shot shows the All Fields tab of the form in design mode.

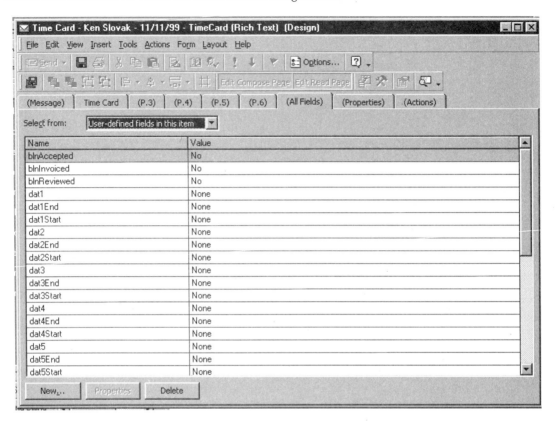

The following screen shot shows the Properties tab of the form in design mode. It is important to update the version of the form each time you publish it so that the forms cache is updated, and the user is presented with the latest version of the form. One practice that can cause version conflicts and even forms cache corruption is publishing a form in more than one place in the system. Before you publish a form decide where you want it to live. One other item of interest in this tab is that the form icons have been changed to the Document icon, rather than the default Post icon. The large and small icons for the form were changed by clicking the Change Large Icon and Change Small Icon buttons and changing the default Post icon for an IPM.Note form to the icon used for Documents. The icons are stored in the Forms subfolder, usually at C:\Program files\Microsoft Office\Office\Forms.

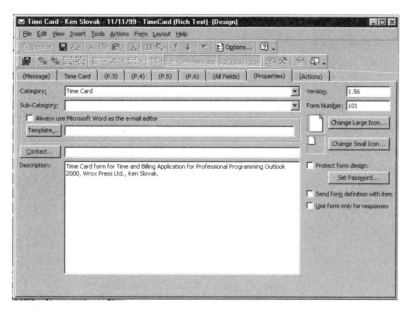

Time Card Routing

The following screen shot shows the form as it appears to the user when he fills it out. The Project combo box is filled dynamically when the form opens by searching for all the project names in the Projects forms in the Projects folder. You can see that the date and user name have been filled out automatically. The command buttons and the comments text box are invisible. In Outlook versions prior to Outlook 2000 hiding and showing controls was a major cause of one-offed forms. This has been fixed in Outlook 2000. This and one-offed forms are discussed in more detail in Chapter 2.

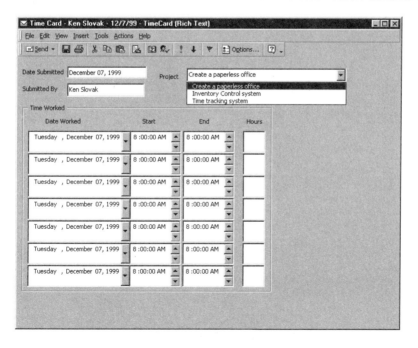

The following screen shot shows the form as it appears to the manager who is reviewing it for approval. Once it is reviewed he can either approve or reject it. If he approves it the form is moved to the Time Cards folder. If he rejects it the form is sent back to the user. These actions are automatic. Notice that the Forward, Reply, and Reply to All toolbar buttons are not available in this received form. Those Actions were disabled on the Actions tab of the form in design mode.

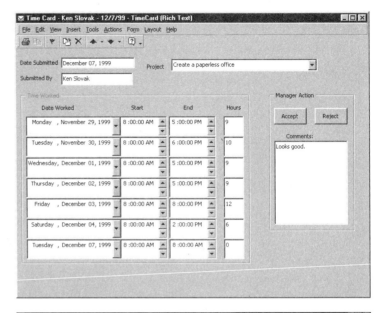

The following screen shot shows a received time card in the manager's Inbox. Because the form has VBScript code it cannot be displayed in the preview pane. It must be opened to be read. The Outlook Bar shows the custom group that was created by the COM add-in. The shortcuts to the folders provide quick navigation around the folders of the application. Notice that the icon for the time card is the Outlook Document icon.

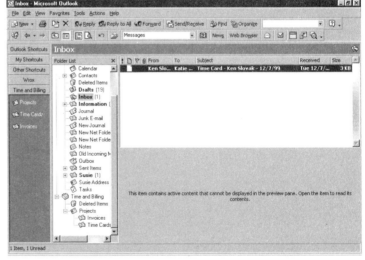

As already mentioned in Chapter 2, the time card is a custom form and should therefore be sent in RTF format. Make sure that any address that is being used as a manager's address is set to be sent to in RTF format. This is done in Corporate/Workgroup mode by right-clicking on the email address, selecting **Properties,** and checking the box labeled **Always send to this recipient in Microsoft Outlook rich text format.** You can do this either when composing a message or in an open contact record. The same is done in Internet Only mode by opening the contact record and unchecking the **Send using plain text** checkbox.

Time Card Form Code

The code for the TimeCard form uses global variables to hold folder objects for the Time Card, Invoices and Projects folders. These folders are referenced in many of the procedures in the code. A global variable is also declared for the path to the Time Card tab, a ModifiedFormPages object. Constants are declared for some of the constants that are implicit in VBA. The toolbar variable provides a global variable for the custom invoice generation toolbar button. The following code is VBScript code that is placed in the code page of the TimeCard form.

```
Option Explicit

'Global Boolean flag
Dim g_blnResolved

'Global objects
Dim g_oFormPages 'Item.GetInspector.ModifiedFormPages("Time Card")
Dim g_oParent 'Parent of the Time Card folder (Projects)
Dim g_oFolder 'Root folder (Time and Billing)
Dim g_oTimeCard 'Time Cards folder
Dim g_oInvoices 'Invoices folder

'Global declarations
Const olJournalItem = 4
Const msoControlButton = 1
Const msoButtonIconAndCaption = 3
Const wdFormatDocument = 0

'Invoice to Word toolbar
Dim g_oInvoiceToolbar
```

The Open event handler performs most of the work done by the code in the form. It initializes the global variables and establishes the current user of the form and whether the form is a new or previously created form. This is done by checking the EntryID property of the item that the open form is displaying to see if it is a null string. Until the form's item is saved for the first time the EntryID property is a null string. The DTPicker ActiveX controls must be resized to the desired size when the form opens. If you don't do this, the controls become tiny; too small to be used for date or time selection.

```
Function Item_Open()
    Dim oNS
    Dim oUser
    Dim oManager
    Dim oRecipient
    Dim oRecipients
    Dim oItem
    Dim oItems
    Dim sManager
    Dim sID

    On Error Resume Next
    g_blnResolved = False
    Set oNS = Application.GetNameSpace("MAPI")
```

```
Set oUser = oNS.CurrentUser

Set g_oInvoiceToolbar = Nothing

Call SetFolders() 'initialize the folder global variables.
Call SetDTPickers()'initialize the DTPicker control sizes.
```

If the form is a new form, the approval controls are disabled and made invisible. The Projects folder is searched, and every project (represented by a contact record) is listed in the project listbox on the time card form. The DTPickers that select dates are initialized to the current date in new forms also.

```
If Item.EntryID = "" Then 'new item.
    'Disable command buttons and frame
    g_oFormPages.Controls("frmManager").Visible = False
    g_oFormPages.Controls("frmManager").Enabled = False
    g_oFormPages.Controls("cmdAccept").Visible = False
    g_oFormPages.Controls("cmdAccept").Enabled = False
    g_oFormPages.Controls("cmdReject").Visible = False
    g_oFormPages.Controls("cmdReject").Enabled = False

    'Disable the comments box.
    g_oFormPages.Controls("txtBody").Visible = False
    Item.UserProperties("txtBody").Locked = False

    Item.UserProperties("blnAccepted").Value = False
    Item.UserProperties("blnReviewed").Value = False

    'Search the Parent folder, where Projects are stored,
    'and initialize the combobox with a list of all the
    'projects found.
    For Each oItem in g_oParent.Items
        g_oFormPages.Controls("cmbProject").AddItem _
            oItem.UserProperties("txtProject").Value
    Next

    Call SetDTPickerDates() 'initialize the DTPickers to today
```

The current user's name and the current date are stored, and a title line for the form is created from this data. The manager name is pulled from the GAL, and if no GAL is available, or the manager's name is not entered or does not resolve, the Address Book dialog is launched to enable the user to select a manager. After a manager is selected the Recipient object that the manager represents is checked to make sure that it resolves as an address in the address book.

```
'Store the user name.
Item.UserProperties("txtUser").Value = oUser.Name
'Store the current date.
Item.UserProperties("datSubmitted").Value = Date

'Set up a Subject line for the form.
sID = "Time Card - " & oUser.Name & " - " & _
    Item.UserProperties("datSubmitted").Value
```

```
        Item.Subject = sID

        'Try to find a Manager and his email address.
        'This method will only work with entries in the GAL.
        Set oManager = oUser.AddressEntry.Manager
        sManager = oManager.Name
        If sManager = "" Then
          'Either not in GAL, or no GAL.
          sManager = FindManager(sID) 'let the user pick one.
          If sID = "" Then
            MsgBox "No Manager Selected"
          Else
            'Get a recipient from the EntryID of the choice.
            Set oRecipient = oNS.GetRecipientFromID(sID)
            sManager = oRecipient.Name
          End If
        End If
        'Address the form and check for address resolution.
        Set oRecipient = Item.Recipients.Add(sManager)
        If Not oRecipient.Resolve Then
          Item.UserProperties("txtReviewer").Value = ""
          MsgBox "Manager not resolved"
        Else
          Item.UserProperties("txtReviewer").Value = sManager
          g_blnResolved = True
        End If
```

If the form is not a new form then logical tests are made to see if the form is being reviewed for approval, has already been approved, or has been rejected. Checks are also made to see if the current user is the manager or the original person who created the form. The current state of the form determines what actions may be performed on it, and what controls are available and whether they are locked.

```
      Else 'not a new form.
        'Restore the selected project.
        g_oFormPages.Controls("cmbProject").Value = _
          Item.UserProperties("txtProject").Value

        'Restore the times and dates.
        Call SetDTPickerValues()

        'Enable the frame control.
        g_oFormPages.Controls("frmManager").Visible = True
        g_oFormPages.Controls("frmManager").Enabled = True
```

If the current user is the manager that the time card is addressed to the form is checked to see if it has been reviewed already. If it has been reviewed, the New Invoice toolbar button is created if the form has not already been invoiced. The Accept and Reject command buttons and the Comments text box are made visible but not enabled.

```
        'If the current user is the Manager (reviewer).
        sManager = Item.UserProperties("txtReviewer").Value
        Set oRecipient = oNS.CreateRecipient(sManager)
        If oUser = oRecipient Then
```

```
    Call LockFields() 'lock the controls.
    'See if the form has been reviewed already
    If Item.UserProperties("blnReviewed").Value = True Then
      If Item.UserProperties("blnInvoiced").Value = False Then
        'Create the toolbar for invoicing.
        CommandBarCreate
      End If

      g_oFormPages.Controls("cmdAccept").Visible = True
      g_oFormPages.Controls("cmdAccept").Enabled = False
      g_oFormPages.Controls("cmdReject").Visible = True
      g_oFormPages.Controls("cmdReject").Enabled = False

      'Lock the comments box.
      g_oFormPages.Controls("txtBody").Visible = True
      Item.UserProperties("txtBody").Locked = True
```

If the form has not been reviewed yet by the manager, the Accept and Reject command buttons and the Comments text box are made visible and enabled.

```
    Else 'Not reviewed yet
      g_oFormPages.Controls("cmdAccept").Visible = True
      g_oFormPages.Controls("cmdAccept").Enabled = True
      g_oFormPages.Controls("cmdReject").Visible = True
      g_oFormPages.Controls("cmdReject").Enabled = True

      'Unlock the comments box.
      g_oFormPages.Controls("txtBody").Visible = True
      Item.UserProperties("txtBody").Locked = False
    End If
```

If the user is not the manager, the New Invoice toolbar button is created if the form has not already been invoiced. All the controls are locked to prevent any changes from being made to them.

```
    'Not the Manager (reviewer), accepted form.
    ElseIf Item.UserProperties("blnAccepted").Value = True Then
      If Item.UserProperties("blnInvoiced").Value = False Then
        'Create the toolbar for invoicing.
        CommandBarCreate
      End If

    Call LockFields() 'lock the controls.
    'Disable command buttons
    g_oFormPages.Controls("cmdAccept").Visible = False
    g_oFormPages.Controls("cmdAccept").Enabled = False
    g_oFormPages.Controls("cmdReject").Visible = False
    g_oFormPages.Controls("cmdReject").Enabled = False

    'Lock the comments box.
    g_oFormPages.Controls("txtBody").Visible = True
    Item.UserProperties("txtBody").Locked = True
```

398

If the form is a rejected form that has been opened, all the controls are locked unless the person opening the form is the person who originally submitted the time card.

```
      'Not the Manager (reviewer), rejected form.
      ElseIf Item.UserProperties("blnAccepted").Value = False Then
        'Disable command buttons
        g_oFormPages.Controls("cmdAccept").Visible = False
        g_oFormPages.Controls("cmdAccept").Enabled = False
        g_oFormPages.Controls("cmdReject").Visible = False
        g_oFormPages.Controls("cmdReject").Enabled = False

        'Lock the comments box.
        g_oFormPages.Controls("txtBody").Visible = True
        Item.UserProperties("txtBody").Locked = True

        'Now see if this is the time card submittor.
        If Item.UserProperties("txtUser").Value <> oUser.Name Then
          'Not the time card submittor.
          Call LockFields() 'lock the controls.
```

If the person opening the form is the person who originally submitted the time card, the manager is substituted for the time card recipient in the form's `Recipients` collection so that the form can be resubmitted.

```
        Else 'this is the time card submittor, rejected form.
          'Let him resubmit the form.
          Item.UserProperties("blnReviewed").Value = False
          'Remove the submittor as recipient and replace
          'with the saved Manager name.
          Set oRecipients = Item.Recipients
          oRecipients.Remove 1
          Set oRecipient = oRecipients. _
            Add(Item.UserProperties("txtReviewer").Value)
        End If
      End If
    End If

    'Clean up
    Set oNS = Nothing
    Set oUser = Nothing
    Set oManager = Nothing
    Set oRecipient = Nothing
    Set oRecipients = Nothing
    Set oItems = Nothing
    Set oItem = Nothing
  End Function
```

When the time card is approved the `Click` event for that button fires. This event handler calls procedures to calculate and store the required data and then saves the form and moves it to the Time Cards folder. After the form is moved, the `Item_Close` event won't fire, so the global objects are dereferenced here. An alternative approach is to call the `Item_Close` procedure directly.

```
Sub cmdAccept_Click()
   On Error Resume Next
   Item.UserProperties("blnAccepted").Value = True
   Item.UserProperties("blnReviewed").Value = True

   FindTotalTime 'save the total time worked.
   FindProjectInfo 'get the project information

   Item.Save 'save the changes, this invokes the Write event.
   Item.Move g_oTimeCard 'move to Time Cards folder.

   'Clean up globals, since Close event will not
   'fire after the item is moved.
   Set g_oFormPages = Nothing
   Set g_oParent = Nothing
   Set g_oFolder = Nothing
   Set g_oTimeCard = Nothing
   Set g_oInvoiceToolbar = Nothing
End Sub
```

The `FindTotalTime` procedure uses the `DateDiff` function to calculate the amount of time worked in minutes for each day in the time card. The default start and end times are 8:00 AM, so if no entry is made for a day the time difference for that day will be 0. The `UserProperties` collection of the `Item` is used to reference the individual user defined fields in the form. Remember that in Outlook VBScript the `Item` and `Application` objects are intrinsic and do not need to be instantiated. After the total time worked is calculated, it is converted into hours from minutes.

```
Sub FindTotalTime()
   Dim lTime
   Dim sStart
   Dim sEnd
   Dim i

   With Item
     lTime = 0
     For i = 1 To 7
       sStart = "dat" & CStr(i) & "Start"
       sEnd = "dat" & CStr(i) & "End"
       'use the DateDiff function to find the minutes worked
       'for each line item in the time card.
       lTime = lTime + DateDiff("n",.UserProperties(sStart).Value, _
         .UserProperties(sEnd).Value)
     Next
   End With

   'Save the total time. This is converted from minutes to hours first
   lTime = (lTime / 60)
   Item.UserProperties("txtTotalTime").Value = CStr(lTime)
End Sub
```

The `FindProjectInfo` procedure retrieves data from the Projects folder item that represents the selected project for the time card. The hierarchy of the Time and Billing folder tree makes the Projects folder the Parent folder of the Time Cards folder. The data retrieved from the Projects folder is stored in user defined fields in the time card form.

```
Sub FindProjectInfo()
    Dim lCharges
    Dim sAddress
    Dim sName
    Dim sCompany
    Dim oItem

    'Search the Parent folder, where Projects are stored,
    'and find the selected project and the billing rate for it.
    For Each oItem in g_oParent.Items
        If oItem.UserProperties("txtProject").Value = _
        Item.UserProperties("txtProject").Value Then
            lCharges = oItem.BillingInformation
            sName = oItem.FullName
            sAddress = oItem.MailingAddress
            sCompany = oItem.CompanyName
            Exit For
        End If
    Next

    Item.UserProperties("txtBillingCharges").Value = _
        CStr(lCharges * (Item.UserProperties("txtTotalTime").Value))

    Item.UserProperties("txtAddress").Value = sAddress
    Item.UserProperties("txtContact").Value = sName
    Item.UserProperties("txtCompanyName").Value = sCompany

    'Clean up
    Set oItem = Nothing
End Sub
```

The **Reject** command button `Click` event handler removes the original recipient of the form, the manager, and replaces that recipient with the person who originally sent the time card for approval. This is an example of one method of routing a form.

```
Sub cmdReject_Click()
    Dim oRecipient
    Dim oRecipients

    On Error Resume Next
    Item.UserProperties("blnAccepted").Value = False
    Item.UserProperties("blnReviewed").Value = True

    Item.UserProperties("txtTotalTime").Value = 0 'clear time total.

    'Remove the manager as recipient and replace with the saved
    'name of the person who submitted the form.
    Set oRecipients = Item.Recipients
```

```
    oRecipients.Remove 1
    Set oRecipient = oRecipients.Add(Item.UserProperties("txtUser").Value)
    If Not oRecipient.Resolve Then
      MsgBox "Recipient not resolved"
      g_blnResolved = False
    Else
      g_blnResolved = True
      Item.Send 'if the new recipient resolves, return card to sender.
    End If

    'Clean up
    Set oRecipient = Nothing
    Set oRecipients = Nothing
  End Sub
```

The SetFolders procedure has been written to work with either Personal Folders files or Public Folders locations. The code for the Public Folders locations is commented out. If your application will run in Public Folders locations change the commented lines as indicated. This procedure also drills down the folders hierarchy to instantiate the folder variables for the application.

```
Sub SetFolders()
  Dim oNS

  On Error Resume Next
  Set oNS = Application.GetNameSpace("MAPI")

  'If this folder set is under the Public Folders tree uncomment
  'the next statements and comment out the one after that.
  'Set g_oFolder = oNS.Folders("Public Folders")
  'Set g_oParent = g_oFolder.Folders("All Public Folders")
  'Set g_oFolder = g_oParent.Folders("Time and Billing")

  'Comment out if in Public Folders.
  Set g_oFolder = oNS.Folders("Time and Billing")

  Set g_oParent = g_oFolder.Folders("Projects")
  Set g_oTimeCard = g_oParent.Folders("Time Cards")
  Set g_oInvoices = g_oParent.Folders("Invoices")

  'Set this one since the reference is used often.
  set g_oFormPages = Item.GetInspector.ModifiedFormPages("Time Card")

  'Clean up
  Set oNS = Nothing
End Sub
```

The SetDTPickers procedure initializes the sizes of the DTPicker controls when it is called from the Item_Open event handler.

```
Sub SetDTPickers()
  Dim i
  Dim sControl

  'Initialize the DTPicker controls size, they will
```

```
    'be tiny if not, when the form is opened.
  On Error Resume Next
  With g_oFormPages
     For i = 1 To 21
        sControl = "DTPicker" & CStr(i)
        .Controls(sControl).Height = 29.25
     Next

     For i = 1 To 7
        sControl = "DTPicker" & CStr(i)
        .Controls(sControl).Width = 140
     Next

     For i = 8 To 21
        sControl = "DTPicker" & CStr(i)
        .Controls(sControl).Width = 70
     Next
  End With
End Sub
```

The SetDTPickerValues procedure refreshes the DTPicker controls from the user defined fields in the form when the form is reopened after being initially transmitted.

```
Sub SetDTPickerValues()
  Dim i
  Dim sControl
  Dim sDat

  'Initialize the DTPicker controls with the stored values.
  On Error Resume Next
  With g_oFormPages
     For i = 1 To 7
        sControl = "DTPicker" & CStr(i)
        sDat = "dat" & CStr(i)
        .Controls(sControl).Value = _
           Item.UserProperties(sDat).Value
     Next

     For i = 8 To 14
        sControl = "DTPicker" & CStr(i)
        sDat = "dat" & CStr(i - 7) & "Start"
        .Controls(sControl).Value = _
           Item.UserProperties(sDat).Value
     Next

     For i = 15 To 21
        sControl = "DTPicker" & CStr(i)
        sDat = "dat" & CStr(i - 14) & "End"
        .Controls(sControl).Value = _
           Item.UserProperties(sDat).Value
     Next
  End With
End Sub
```

The `SetDTPickerDates` procedure initializes the DTPicker date controls with the current date when the form is opened for the first time.

```
Sub SetDTPickerDates()
  Dim i
  Dim sControl

  'Set the date controls to today.
  With g_oFormPages
    For i = 1 To 7
      sControl = "DTPicker" & CStr(i)
      .Controls(sControl).Value = Date
    Next
  End With
End Sub
```

The `LockFields` procedure locks the controls when the form is being reviewed or after is has been approved. The `Locked` property does not prevent DTPicker controls from being changed, so all the DTPicker controls were placed in a frame control which is disabled to prevent the DTPicker controls from being changed. The `UnLockFields` procedure enables the frame control in which the DTPicker controls are placed, thereby enabling changes to the DTPicker controls.

```
Sub LockFields()
  'Lock the controls on the form. DTPicker controls
  'don't have a Locked or Enabled property, so they
  'are placed in a frame control that can be disabled.
  'This locks all the controls in the frame.
  On Error Resume Next
  g_oFormPages.Controls("frmTime").Enabled = False

Sub UnLockFields()
  'Unlock the DTPicker controls on the form.
  On Error Resume Next
  g_oFormPages.Controls("frmTime").Enabled = True
End Sub

End Sub
```

If the initial attempt to resolve a manager's name fails the `FindManager` CDO procedure is called. It performs an anonymous logon to a CDO session using the current Outlook session. It then uses the `AddressBook` method to start the Address Book dialog. The `EntryID` of the selected person is returned to the calling procedure. If no one is selected, a `Null` string is returned to the calling procedure. As described in Chapter 6 in the discussion about the `AddressBook` method the `OneAddress` argument is not used to prevent an error from occurring for Outlook Internet-only mode users.

```
Function FindManager(sName)
  'Use CDO to open the Address Book dialog box.
  Dim oSession
  Dim oRecips

  On Error Resume Next
  'Set an anonymous CDO logon piggybacked on the existing
```

```
   'Outlook session.
   Set oSession = Application.CreateObject("MAPI.Session")
   oSession.Logon "", "", False, False

   'Allow more than one choice so that the OneAddress named argument
   'will not cause an error if run in Internet only mode. Setting it
   'to True fires an error. We deal with more than 1 selection later.
   Set oRecips = oSession.AddressBook(,"Choose Manager",,,,"&Manager")

   'If Err is 0 then the user selected a name. If not, might be an
   'error or the user might have cancelled the selection.
   If Err = 0 Then
     sName = oRecips.Item(1).ID 'only use the first recipient ID.
   Else
     sName = ""
   End If

   'Log off the CDO session.
   oSession.Logoff

   'Clean up
   Set oSession = Nothing
   Set oRecips = Nothing
End Function
```

The `CommandBarCreate` procedure is called when the time card form is opened after it has been approved, and if it has not yet been invoiced. It creates a button on a custom toolbar that has a Word icon, and that calls the invoicing procedure when it is clicked.

```
Sub CommandBarCreate
  Dim oInvoiceButton

  On Error Resume Next
  'Add a new temporary toolbar for the Invoice button.
  Set g_oInvoiceToolbar = Item.GetInspector.CommandBars. _
    Add("Invoice", 1, False, True)
  g_oInvoiceToolbar.Visible = True
  'See if the button exists.
  Set oInvoiceButton = g_oInvoiceToolbar.FindControl(,,"WroxInvoice")
  If oInvoiceButton Is Nothing Then
    Set oInvoiceButton = g_oInvoiceToolbar.Controls.Add
    oInvoiceButton.FaceId = 2498 'Word icon
    oInvoiceButton.BeginGroup = True
        oInvoiceButton.Caption = "New Invoice"
        oInvoiceButton.Tag = "WroxInvoice" 'unique tag.
        oInvoiceButton.ToolTipText = "Create an Invoice for this Time Card"
        oInvoiceButton.Style = msoButtonIconAndCaption
        oInvoiceButton.OnAction = "cmdInvoice_Click" 'what the button does.
        oInvoiceButton.Visible = True
  End If

  'Clean up
  Set oInvoiceButton = Nothing
End Sub
```

When the New Invoice toolbar button is pressed, the cmdInvoice_Click event fires. The event handler calls the procedure that merges the data to the custom Word template.

```
Sub cmdInvoice_Click
  If Item.UserProperties("blnInvoiced").Value = False Then
    MergeToInvoice
  End If
End Sub
```

The SetItemPropsFromDTPicker procedure is called by the Item_Write event handler to store the data from the DTPicker controls in user defined fields in the form.

```
Sub SetItemPropsFromDTPicker()
  Dim i
  Dim sDat
  Dim sControl
  Dim sHours
  Dim sStart
  Dim sEnd
  Dim lTime

  'Save the values from the controls in UserProperties in the form.
  With g_oFormPages
    Item.UserProperties("txtProject").Value = _
      .Controls("cmbProject").Value

    For i = 1 To 7
      sDat = "dat" & CStr(i)
      sControl = "DTPicker" & CStr(i)
      Item.UserProperties(sDat).Value = _
        .Controls(sControl).Value
    Next

    For i = 8 To 14
      sDat = "dat" & CStr(i - 7) & "Start"
      sControl = "DTPicker" & CStr(i)
      Item.UserProperties(sDat).Value = _
        .Controls(sControl).Value
    Next

    For i = 15 To 21
      sDat = "dat" & CStr(i - 14) & "End"
      sControl = "DTPicker" & CStr(i)
      Item.UserProperties(sDat).Value = _
        .Controls(sControl).Value
    Next
  End With
```

The hours worked for each day entered in the time card form are calculated using the `DateDiff` function and are also stored in user defined fields in the form.

```
    'Save the hours worked
    With Item
      For i = 1 To 7
        sStart = "dat" & CStr(i) & "Start"
        sEnd = "dat" & CStr(i) & "End"
        sHours = "txtHours" & CStr(i)
        lTime = DateDiff("n",.UserProperties(sStart).Value, _
          .UserProperties(sEnd).Value)
        lTime = (lTime / 60)
        If lTime < 0 Then lTime = 0
        .UserProperties(sHours).Value = CStr(lTime)
      Next
    End With
End Sub
```

The `Item_Write` event handler calls the `SetItemPropsFromDTPicker` procedure to store data in user defined fields in the form.

```
Function Item_Write()
    'Save the global values in UserProperties.
    On Error Resume Next
    Call SetItemPropsFromDTPicker() 'store controls values.
End Function
```

The `Item_Send` event handler cancels the `Send` event if a recipient has not been properly resolved.

```
Function Item_Send()
    'Cancel the Send event if address not resolved.
    If g_blnResolved = False Then
      Item_Send = False
    End If
End Function
```

The `Item_Close` event handler deletes the custom toolbar if it exists and dereferences the global object variables.

```
Function Item_Close()
    'Close event will fire when the item is sent.
    'It will not fire if the item is approved and
    'moved to the Time Cards folder.
    If Not g_oInvoiceToolbar Is Nothing Then
      g_oInvoiceToolbar.Delete 'delete the custom toolbar.
    End If

    Set g_oFormPages = Nothing
    Set g_oParent = Nothing
    Set g_oFolder = Nothing
    Set g_oTimeCard = Nothing
    Set g_oInvoiceToolbar = Nothing
End Function
```

The `MergeToInvoice` procedure performs the merge of data from the form to the custom Word template. If you change the storage location of the template from the `C:\My Documents` folder be sure to change the template path variable. The method of merging to the document Bookmarks is identical to the procedure shown in Chapter 4.

```
Sub MergeToInvoice()
  Dim oWord
  Dim oDoc
  Dim oDocItem
  Dim sBkmName
  Dim blnFill
  Dim sWordTemplateName
  Dim sTempFile

  sWordTemplateName = "C:\My Documents\Time and Billing Invoice.dot"
  sTempFile = "C:\My Documents\WroxTempInvoice.doc"

  'Get a Word Application object
  On Error Resume Next
  Set oWord = GetObject(, "Word.Application")
  If oWord Is Nothing Then
      Set oWord = CreateObject("Word.Application")
    End If
    'Add a document based on our template.
    Set oDoc = oWord.Documents.Add(sWordTemplateName)

  'Fill each Bookmark in turn.
  sBkmName = "FullName"
     blnFill = FillBookmark(sBkmName, Item. _
   UserProperties("txtContact").Value, _
       oDoc)

  'Repeat the function call for each Bookmark.
     sBkmName = "CompanyName"
  blnFill = FillBookmark(sBkmName, Item. _
    UserProperties("txtCompanyName").Value, _
        oDoc)

     sBkmName = "MailingAddress"
  blnFill = FillBookmark(sBkmName, Item. _
    UserProperties("txtAddress").Value, _
        oDoc)

     sBkmName = "BillingDate"
  blnFill = FillBookmark(sBkmName, Date, _
    oDoc)

  sBkmName = "BillingTime"
     blnFill = FillBookmark(sBkmName, Item. _
   UserProperties("txtTotalTime").Value, _
     oDoc)
```

```
    sBkmName = "BillingCharges"
        blnFill = FillBookmark(sBkmName, Item. _
    UserProperties("txtBillingCharges").Value, _
            oDoc)
```

The following code is used to save the document to a temporary file in the file system and then attach it to a `DocumentItem` object. The `DocumentItem` object is created as a form with a `MessageClass` of `IPM.Document.Word.Document.8`. The attached document becomes an intrinsic part of the `DocumentItem` object.

```
    oDoc.SaveAs sTempFile, wdFormatDocument
        oDoc.Close
    Set oDocItem = g_oInvoices.Items.Add("IPM.Document.Word.Document.8")

    With oDocItem
        .Subject = Item.Subject
        .Attachments.Add(sTempFile)
        .Save
    End With
```

After the document is attached to the `DocumentItem` object the temporary Word document file that was stored in the file system is deleted and the user defined field that tracks whether the form has been invoiced is updated.

```
    If Err = 0 Then
        Item.UserProperties("blnInvoiced").Value = True
        If Not g_oInvoiceToolbar Is Nothing Then
            g_oInvoiceToolbar.Delete 'delete the custom toolbar.
        End If
        Set g_oInvoiceToolbar = Nothing
    End If

    Kill sTempFile

    'Clean up
    Set oWord = Nothing
    Set oDoc = Nothing
    Set oDocItem = Nothing
End Sub
```

The `FillBookmark` utility function is used to insert data into a Word Bookmark. This is the same function that was used for that purpose in Chapter 4.

```
Function FillBookmark(sBookmark, sValue, oDoc)
    On Error Resume Next
    With oDoc
    If .Bookmarks.Exists(sBookmark) Then
        .Bookmarks(sBookmark).Range.Text = sValue
        FillBookmark = True
```

```
      Else
         FillBookmark = False
      End If
      End With
End Function
```

Invoicing From a Time Card

The following screen shot shows a time card form that has been approved, with the custom New Invoice toolbar button in a custom toolbar below the Standard toolbar. This button creates the invoice for the time card.

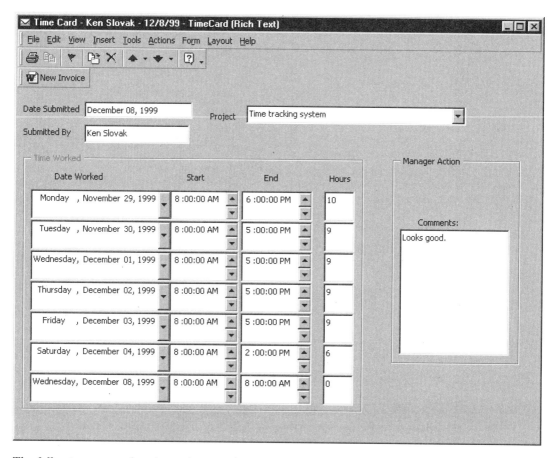

The following screen shot shows the posted invoice in the Invoices folder. It appears as an attachment to a posted document, but when the posted document is opened the attached document opens directly.

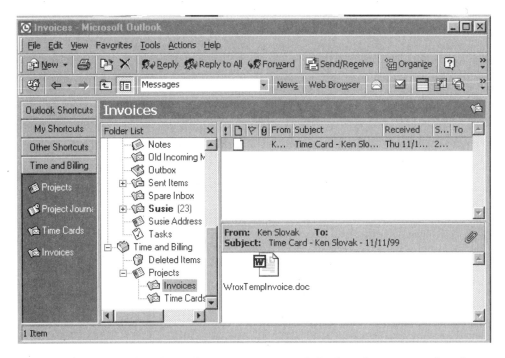

The following screen shot shows the security warning dialog box that appears when the posted invoice is opened. This warning appears whenever you open an item that has been attached to an Outlook form. The warning can be disabled from appearing, but that will open executable attachments with no warning or option to save them to disk.

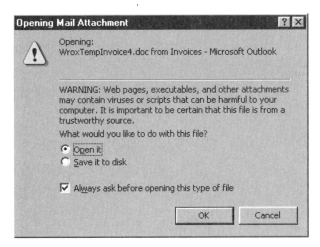

The Word Template

The Word invoicing template is available for downloading from the Wrox web site. It has Bookmarks named, in order, `FullName`, `CompanyName` and `MailingAddress`. The three Bookmarks in the table are named `BillingDate`, `BillingTime` and `BillingCharges`. The following screen shot shows the Word template for the invoices. It shows the placement of the Bookmarks and how the data for the billing information is placed in a Word table.

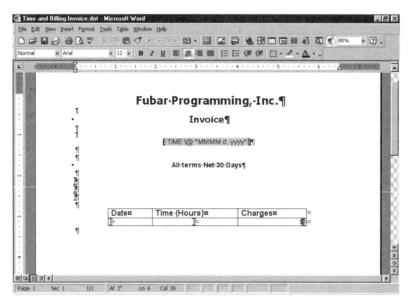

The following screen shot shows a completed invoice, with all the customer and billing information inserted.

Projects Form

The Projects form is modified from the standard Contacts form. The modifications consist of the addition of project name and number information. The hourly billing rate for the project is stored in the normally unused `BillingInformation` field that is present in all Outlook forms except for the StickyNote forms. The layout of the form is changed, and some fields are removed. This form is available for download in the `Time and Billing.pst` file on the Wrox Web site.

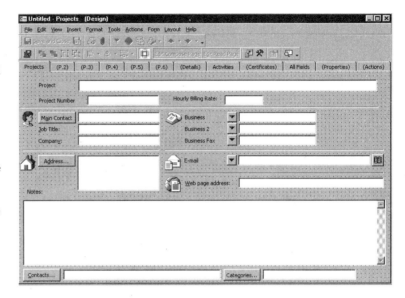

These forms and templates show how different types of Outlook items can be used to integrate with each other in your applications. Many other customized and standard Outlook forms can be added to an application to give you as much functionality as you need.

The COM Add-in

The COM add-in for this case study was created in Outlook VBA, with MOD (Microsoft Office 2000 Developer Edition) installed. This is in contrast with the COM add-in that was created in Chapter 7, which was created with VB 6. If you have VB 6 installed and do not have MOD, the code can be copied directly, with no modifications, to a VB 6 COM add-in project. See Chapter 7 for instructions on creating a COM add-in using VB 6.

To successfully compile this COM add-in, you have to set the required library references in the Tools | References menu. The required libraries for this add-in are:

- ❏ Microsoft Outlook 9.0 Object Library
- ❏ Microsoft Office 9.0 Object Library
- ❏ Visual Basic for Applications
- ❏ OLE Automation
- ❏ Microsoft Word 9.0 Object Library
- ❏ Microsoft Add-In Designer.

To open a blank COM add-in project, choose File | New Project | Add-In Project. The references to the Microsoft Add-In Designer library (IDTExtensibility2), Visual Basic for Applications, and OLE Automation should be automatically added to the references list. You will have to add the references to the Outlook, Office and Word libraries yourself. Set the properties sheet of the designer class module as shown in the following screen shot.

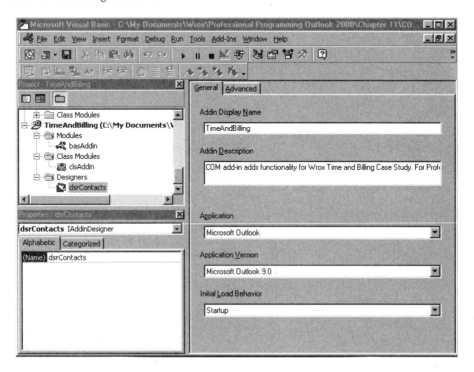

Give the designer module an appropriate name and insert one class module, and name it `clsAddin`. Insert one code module and name it `basAddin`. In this COM add-in we will use the class module as a container for most of the code that does the real work of the add-in (the implementation). The designer class module is used only to provide an object for the interface of the IDTExtensibility2 library and to instantiate the class module. In the COM add-in in Chapter 7 we put the class module's code in the designer module. In this one we will separate the implementation and interface sections into separate modules.

Every event procedure of the IDTExtensibility2 implementation must be present in the compiled program, so if you aren't using an event put a comment line in the event procedure to prevent the compiler from removing it. In this COM add-in we will only handle the `OnConnection` and `OnDisconnection` events of the IDTExtensibility2 implementation. More details of the other events provided by IDTExtensibility2 are presented in Chapter 7, with greater detail on the property sheet settings. Creating a COM add-in using MOD is the same as creating a COM add-in with VB 6, so the same information applies to both languages. The following code is placed in the code page of the designer module.

```
Option Explicit

' Implement extensibility library.
Implements IDTExtensibility2

' Private module-level variables.
Private gBaseClass As New clsAddin

Private Sub AddinInstance_Initialize()
'
End Sub

Private Sub AddinInstance_Terminate()
'
End Sub

Private Sub IDTExtensibility2_OnAddInsUpdate(custom() As Variant)
'
End Sub

Private Sub IDTExtensibility2_OnBeginShutdown(custom() As Variant)
'
End Sub

Private Sub IDTExtensibility2_OnStartupComplete(custom() As Variant)
'
End Sub
```

The OnConnection event handler calls the InitHandler method of the class module to instantiate the COM add-in. The Application and ProgId properties of the COM add-in are passed as arguments of the method.

```
Private Sub IDTExtensibility2_OnConnection(ByVal Application As Object, _
    ByVal ConnectMode As AddInDesignerObjects.ext_ConnectMode, _
    ByVal AddInInst As Object, custom() As Variant)

    gBaseClass.InitHandler Application, AddInInst.ProgId
End Sub
```

The OnDisconnection event handler first checks to see if the user disconnected the COM add-in. If so, the Time and Billing Outlook Bar group is removed. Then the UnInitHandler method of the class module is called to destroy the COM add-in's objects.

```
Private Sub IDTExtensibility2_OnDisconnection(ByVal RemoveMode As _
    AddInDesignerObjects.ext_DisconnectMode, custom() As Variant)

    On Error Resume Next

    'If UserClosed, then remove the added OutlookBar group
    If RemoveMode = ext_dm_UserClosed Then
      If GroupExist("Time and Billing") Then
        GroupDestroy "Time and Billing"
      End If
```

```
      End If

      'Tear down the class
      gBaseClass.UnInitHandler
      Set gBaseClass = Nothing
   End Sub
```

In this COM add-in the `InitHandler` method instantiates an `Application` object for handling any Outlook events that you want to handle. These can be any of the events that you can handle in the `ThisOutlookSession` module. In this case only the `Explorer_Close` event is being handled. The COM add-in is only being used to create and destroy a custom Outlook Bar group.

The COM add-in in Chapter 7 also used Explorer events to show a custom Property page for contacts folders. You can use Explorer events to show and hide menu and toolbar buttons, and you can do the same with an Inspector object by handling those events. Folder events are particularly useful. The advantage of a COM add-in over doing the same things in the `ThisOutlookSession` module is that a COM add-in can be distributed far more easily than the Outlook VBA project. The following code is placed in the `clsAddin` class module.

```
'Class: clsAddin
'***********************************************************************
'Object variables for Event procedures
Private WithEvents oOL As Outlook.Application
Private WithEvents oExplorer As Outlook.Explorer

'Use gsProgID to set the OnAction property of CB buttons
Private gsProgID As String

Friend Sub InitHandler(oApp As Outlook.Application, sProgID As String)
   On Error Resume Next
   'Declared WithEvents
   Set oOL = oApp
   Set oExplorer = oOL.ActiveExplorer
   'Instantiate a public module-level Outlook application variable
   Set goApp = oOL
   gsProgID = sProgID

   InitOLB
End Sub
```

The `UnInitHandler` method is used to destroy any objects that you have created that have not been dereferenced already.

```
Friend Sub UnInitHandler()
    'You must dereference all objects in this procedure
    'or Outlook will remain in memory
    On Error Resume Next
    Set oExplorer = Nothing
    Set goApp = Nothing
    Set oOL = Nothing
End Sub
```

In some cases Outlook may not fire the OnDisconnection event during shutdown. This is caused by various MAPI issues, such as starting Outlook from the Send to Mail action. In those cases the UnInitHandler is called when the last Explorer window is shut down. That ensures that all objects of the COM add-in are destroyed.

```
Private Sub oExplorer_Close()
    If oOL.Explorers.Count <= 1 Then
        Call UnInitHandler
    End If
End Sub
```

The InitOLB sub is a private sub of the class. It is specific to this COM add-in, but can be made a more general procedure to add Outlook Bar groups and folder shortcuts by changing the procedure declaration to InitOLB(sGroup As String, ParamArray oFolders() As Outlook.MAPIFolder) to pass the group name and an arbitrary array of folder arguments to the procedure. In that case, the UBound function would be used to set an upper limit to a loop that created new shortcuts.

The procedure as written uses a path in a Personal Folders file. The commented portion of the code provides a path in a Public Folders tree.

```
'*********************************************************
'Procedure: InitOLB
'*********************************************************
Private Sub InitOLB()
  Dim oParent As Outlook.MAPIFolder
  Dim oTimeCard As Outlook.MAPIFolder
  Dim oInvoices As Outlook.MAPIFolder
  Dim oNS As Outlook.NameSpace

  If Not GroupExist("Time and Billing") Then
    GroupCreate "Time and Billing"
    Set oOL = CreateObject("Outlook.Application")
    Set oNS = goApp.GetNamespace("MAPI")

    'If this folder set is under the Public Folders tree uncomment
    'the next statement and comment out the following statement.
    'Set oParent = oNS..Folders("Public Folders").Folders("All " _
    ' & "Public Folders").Folders("Time and Billing").Folders("Projects")
    Set oParent = oNS.Folders("Time and Billing").Folders("Projects")
    Set oTimeCard = oParent.Folders("Time Cards")
    Set oInvoices = oParent.Folders("Invoices")

    If Not ShortcutExist("Projects", "Time and Billing") Then
      FolderShortcutCreate "Time and Billing", oParent
    End If
    If Not ShortcutExist("Time Cards", "Time and Billing") Then
      FolderShortcutCreate "Time and Billing", oTimeCard
    End If
    If Not ShortcutExist("Invoices", "Time and Billing") Then
      FolderShortcutCreate "Time and Billing", oInvoices
    End If
```

```
        End If

    Set oParent = Nothing
    Set oTimeCard = Nothing
    Set oInvoices = Nothing
    Set oNS = Nothing
End Sub
```

The following functions are located in the code module `basAddin`, providing functions for checking for the existence of an Outlook Bar group or shortcut, for creating a group or folder shortcut, and for destroying a group. The path to get to a group is through the `Panes` collection of an Explorer or Inspector. The exact path is quite obscure, going from the `Panes` collection to the `Contents` object, which is an `OutlookBarStorage` object, to a `Groups` property, which contains an `OutlookBarGroups` collection.

The `GroupExist` function is used to check whether an Outlook Bar group already exists. It compares a group name passed to it as an argument with the list of current Outlook Bar groups.

```
Option Explicit

Public goApp As Outlook.Application

Public Function GroupExist(sGroup As String) As Boolean
    Dim oGroup As Outlook.OutlookBarGroup
    Dim oPane As Outlook.OutlookBarPane

    On Error Resume Next
    GroupExist = False
    'Get the Pane object
    Set oPane = goApp.ActiveExplorer.Panes.Item("OutlookBar")

    'See if any Group has the specified name in the Groups collection
    For Each oGroup In oPane.Contents.Groups
      If oGroup.Name = sGroup Then
        GroupExist = True
      End If
    Next oGroup

    Set oGroup = Nothing
    Set oPane = Nothing
End Function
```

The `GroupCreate` procedure creates a new Outlook Bar group. This group is placed last in the list of groups in the Outlook Bar.

```
Public Sub GroupCreate(sGroup As String)
    Dim oPane As Outlook.OutlookBarPane
    Dim oGroup As Outlook.OutlookBarGroup

    On Error Resume Next
    'Get the Pane object
    Set oPane = goApp.ActiveExplorer.Panes.Item("OutlookBar")
    'Add the new group using the Add method. The groups are stored
```

```
'in the Contents object. Use the Index argument to set the
'position of the new group to the top of the Outlook Bar
oPane.Contents.Groups.Add sGroup
Set oGroup = oPane.Contents.Groups.Item(sGroup)
'Set the group to use small icons
oGroup.ViewType = olSmallIcon

Set oPane = Nothing
Set oGroup = Nothing
End Sub
```

The `GroupDestroy` procedure is called when the COM add-in is disconnected from Outlook. It removes a named Outlook Bar group, in this case the Time and Billing group.

```
Public Sub GroupDestroy(sGroup As String)
   Dim oPane As Outlook.OutlookBarPane
   Dim oGroups As Outlook.OutlookBarGroups

   On Error Resume Next
   'Get the Pane object
   Set oPane = goApp.ActiveExplorer.Panes.Item("OutlookBar")
   'Get the Group object
   Set oGroups = oPane.Contents.Groups
   oGroups.Remove (sGroup)

   Set oPane = Nothing
   Set oGroups = Nothing
End Sub
```

The `ShortcutExist` function is called to check whether a specified shortcut exists in a specified Outlook Bar group.

```
Public Function ShortcutExist(sShortcut As String, sGroup As String) As Boolean
   Dim oShortcuts As Outlook.OutlookBarShortcuts
   Dim oShortcut As Outlook.OutlookBarShortcut
   Dim oGroup As Outlook.OutlookBarGroup
   Dim oPane As Outlook.OutlookBarPane

   On Error Resume Next
   ShortcutExist = False
   'First see if the group exists, if not, the shortcut cannot exist
   If GroupExist(sGroup) Then
      'Find the Shortcuts collection for that group
      Set oPane = goApp.ActiveExplorer.Panes.Item("OutlookBar")
      Set oGroup = oPane.Contents.Groups.Item(sGroup)
      Set oShortcuts = oGroup.Shortcuts

      'See if any shortcut has the specified name in the Shortcuts collection
      For Each oShortcut In oShortcuts
         If oShortcut.Name = sShortcut Then
            ShortcutExist = True
         End If
      Next oShortcut
```

```
      End If

   Set oShortcuts = Nothing
   Set oShortcut = Nothing
   Set oGroup = Nothing
   Set oPane = Nothing
End Function
```

The `FolderShortcutCreate` procedure creates an Outlook Bar shortcut to an Outlook folder.

```
Public Sub FolderShortcutCreate(sGroup As String, oFolder _
         As Outlook.MAPIFolder)
   Dim oShortcuts As Outlook.OutlookBarShortcuts
   Dim oPane As Outlook.OutlookBarPane
   Dim oGroup As Outlook.OutlookBarGroup

   On Error Resume Next
   'Find the Shortcuts collection for the group
   Set oPane = goApp.ActiveExplorer.Panes.Item("OutlookBar")
   Set oGroup = oPane.Contents.Groups.Item(sGroup)
   Set oShortcuts = oGroup.Shortcuts

   'Use the Add method to add the specified folder to the Shortcuts collection
   oShortcuts.Add oFolder, oFolder.Name

   Set oShortcuts = Nothing
   Set oPane = Nothing
   Set oGroup = Nothing
End Sub
```

The code in the designer, `clsAddin` and `basAddin` complete the COM add-in for the Time and Billing application. The COM add-in is now ready to be compiled. Compile and package the add-in the same way that the COM add-in in Chapter 7 was compiled and packaged. The result is the TimeAndBilling COM add-in.

Installing the Forms

The forms for this case study are contained in a `.PST` (Personal Folders) file named `Time and Billing.pst`. You can open this file from within Outlook 2000 after you install it on your hard drive or on a network hard drive. Once the Time and Billing folders are open in Outlook, you can work with the project in a few ways.

You can copy the Projects folder and its Invoices and Time Cards subfolders into your default Personal Folders or Public Folders tree. You can also choose to work with the Time and Billing Personal Folders file, and close it when you are finished with it.

To use the forms that are published in the Projects and Time Cards folders, you can publish them into the folders where you move the project or into the Organizational Forms Library (or Personal Forms Library). To publish the forms, choose Tools | Forms | Design a Form. Then select Outlook Folders in the Look In combobox and select Projects. Use the Browse command button and then navigate to the Projects folder and select the Projects form. Select Open to open the form in design mode. Then choose Tools | Forms | Publish Form As and publish the form in the selected location. Make sure to highlight the Projects form in the dialog box so that the MessageClass of the form is shown as IPM.Contact.Projects. Then close the form and choose not to save any changes.

Repeat the above process for the TimeCard form, selecting the Time Cards folder as the location of the form to open. Make sure that the form name is highlighted, and the MessageClass shows as IPM.Note.TimeCard.

> **The code in the Time/Card form defaults to a location in a Personal Folders file. If the form folders are installed under the Public Folders tree you must modify the VBScript code to look there for the folders. The instructions for modifying the code are located in comments in the code at the required locations.**

When you open the form, make sure to press and hold the Shift key when you press the Open command button. Otherwise, the code behind the form will execute when the form is opened, and you will be prompted for a manager or one will be selected from the GAL. Publish the form in the selected location, and make sure not to include the form definition with the form. Then close the form and choose not to save any changes.

After the forms are published in your Outlook installation, open both forms in turn to install the forms.

The TimeCard form contains instances of the DTPicker OCX control, from the MSCOMCT2.OCX file. If this control is not already installed in your system, it must be installed for the form to work without errors. This control set is available with the other parts of the case study, if you do not already have it installed. The version of the control used in the Outlook form is version 6.00.8418. After the control is installed, it must be registered in order to use it. See the MSDN Library or the Visual Basic 6.0 Controls Reference for more information on the DTPicker control and distributing and registering ActiveX controls.

Installing the COM Add-In

The COM add-in is written in VBA, and is compiled with the Microsoft Office 2000 Developer Edition (MOD). If you have MOD installed, you can load the Time and Billing.vba file into the VBE, and compile and make the COM add-in. This will automatically install the add-in in the Windows Registry, and in Outlook 2000.

If you do not have MOD installed, a Setup program is provided for a fully compiled version of the add-in. This installation consists of three files, the first of which, Setup.exe, installs and registers the COM add-in. The other two files are Setup.lst and Time and Billing.CAB. The CAB file is a compressed file that contains the COM add-in (a DLL), and the required support files. This installation package was created with the MOD Package and Deployment Wizard. All these files are available from the Wrox web site.

Once the COM add-in is installed in your system, it can be controlled from the Options | Other | Advanced Options | COM Add-Ins dialog box in the Outlook Tools menu. The following screen shot shows the COM Add-Ins dialog box, with the TimeAndBilling add-in checked.

To disable the add-in, uncheck the TimeAndBilling add-in. To remove it completely from Outlook, highlight it and choose the Remove command button. If the add-in is removed, it may be added to the list of available add-ins again by choosing the Add command button and browsing to the location of the add-in. If the COM add-in is unchecked, after the OK command button is pressed the Time and Billing Outlook Bar group is automatically removed.

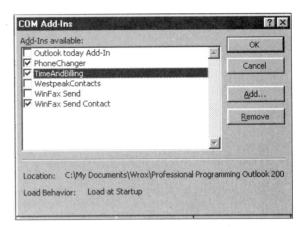

Extending the Case Study

This case study is an illustration of how to integrate custom forms and folders with an Outlook COM add-in. It is not intended to be a complete finished application. Extensive error handling is not present, and many ideas for extended functionality can be added to it. The following are some examples of features that can be added to the case study to extend its functionality.

- Add comprehensive error checking. For instance, you may want to ensure that there is only one entry per day and that the seven possible entries correspond to the seven days in one week.

- Enable the time card to be filled in on a daily basis and be submitted at the end of the week.

- Add code to create Journal entries for the Invoices that are created.

- Link the invoicing and time card information to a database, or use a database as the primary storage area and use automation code to pull or push the data between the database and Outlook.

- Add more custom forms to handle related Tasks and Appointments.

- Extend the COM add-in to provide custom menu and toolbar buttons.

- Use the analytical capabilities of Excel to analyze the collected data.

- Design custom Word templates to replicate the look of the Outlook forms and use Bookmarks to place the data from the forms in documents created from these templates. This provides **WYSIWYG** (what you see is what you get) printing capability.

- Add code to link the individual contacts and `DocumentItems` that contain the invoices to the Projects contacts forms.

Code to add linkages to the parent Projects form for a Time Card is added to the `Item_Write` event of the Time Card form. This code would place a link to the parent project (which is a contact item) in the `Links` collection of the current object. This code could look similar to the following code snippet.

```
If g_blnNewTimeCard Or Item.Links.Count = 0 Then
   Item.Links.Add(g_oParent)
End If
```

After code linking the parent item to the Time Card is added, the links can be made available in the Activities pages of the different Projects forms. To do this, right-click on the Projects folder in the Folder List or the Outlook Bar and choose **Properties**. Select the **Activities** tab and create a new Folder Group. In the Folder Group dialog box you can select which folders are searched when the Activities tab of the Projects form is selected. The Folder Group dialog box is shown in the following screen shot.

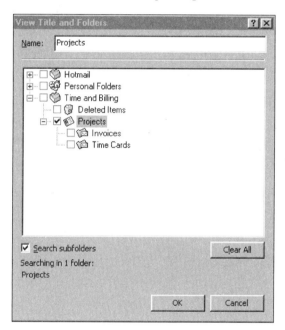

Summary

This case study covered a lot of ground. It integrated custom Outlook forms, a COM add-in, data transfer to a custom Word template, forms routing, Outlook Bar group management and Document item posting to Outlook folders. It can provide a beginning and basis for a complete workflow application. It also shows some of the power that is available to Outlook developers.

Case Study: Customer Service Application

At this point we have seen bits and pieces of code that accomplish a variety of things and they can be used on a regular basis in your day-to-day work. In this case study however, we will examine how you can use some of this code to make an entire application that goes beyond your typical Outlook desktop programming. In addition, you will also see how the Collaboration Data Objects (CDO) components that we have seen so far can be combined with other Microsoft technologies to create globally accessible applications complete with e-mail messaging.

Premise – The Acme Company

As a consultant to the Acme Company, you have been asked to develop a customer service application. The Acme Company offers different models of products and each product has one product manager. A customer should be able to submit their comments and questions on particular product model and receive an instant reply, based on their query, by e-mail. In addition, a log of these inquiries should be kept and copies of all customer inquiries should be directed to the individual product managers. Also, since Acme has customers all around the world, this application needs to be globally accessible.

In order to fulfill all of these requirements, we shall need to build the following components:

❑ An Access database to serve as a repository for e-mail information and maintain the log of the customer inquiries.

❑ A set of Active Server Pages (ASP) to serve as the customer interface. An ASP application can be deployed on both an intranet and the World Wide Web, which will fit the application requisite for being globally accessible.

❑ VBScript code calling the CDO library in order to handle all of the messaging transactions.

Since we are dealing with three distinct components, it is important to establish a base line server configuration to manage all of these programs. In order for these programs to function you will need:

❑ Windows NT Server (updated with the latest Service Pack) running Microsoft Internet Information Server 4.0. You can also use Windows 2000 with Internet Information Server 5.0 if it is available to you. This allows for the deployment of ASP 2.0 code, as well as the necessary CDO dynamic link libraries.

❑ Access 2000, along with the necessary ODBC drivers. Since the database we will be using is not very complex, Access 97 is a fine substitute although all of the ensuing screen shots and instructions will assume that you are using Access 2000. Since we are not using any code within Access, you will find that you will be able to follow along very easily if you are using Access 97.

> If you intend to use this sample application in practice and expect a lot of activity at your site, you will probably want to adapt it to use SQL Server, which is better suited to support high-traffic situations.

This chapter will assume a basic understanding of all these programs, but there will be more details on each of the program components as things get more complex, for the benefit of those that are not too familiar with them.

But I'm An Outlook Programmer!

It may be that you only develop desktop or network Outlook programs and never need to create globally accessible applications. However, this case study involves VBScript (which you have seen applied in Outlook forms) and covers more of the CDO (Collaboration Data Objects) model – the base for most messaging applications. You will find that with your current programming knowledge, you will be able to make quite an easy transition to Active Server Pages programming, taking your development skills up to a whole new level.

As such, this case study sets out to demonstrate how these now familiar elements of Outlook development can be used in their own right, to produce powerful (and highly scalable) applications on the Internet. At the very least, you will get a 'behind the scenes' look at how Internet applications are developed, as well as building on your understanding of the interaction between Internet programs and the desktop.

So, enough with the introductions – let's start building our application!

Access Database Component

The database for this application will serve as the foundation upon which all the other pages are built, and around which our ASP and CDO code will be written. An important point to remember is that we are building a web application, not an Access application. Therefore, if you have Access development experience, you may find you have the tendency to want to over-complicate the database process. Since the main interface with the database will be via Active Server Pages, our database will simply be a means of information storage, and probably one of the least complex databases you'll have ever worked with.

Let's start by examining the data that we need to store in generic terms. Our database design will be guided by the fact that the Acme Company offers widgets in different models and each model is assigned a product manager. Since most of Acme's customers own only one model of product, their e-mails will be directed to one product manager only. Therefore, a customer inquiry might take any of the following paths (including a model-specific response):

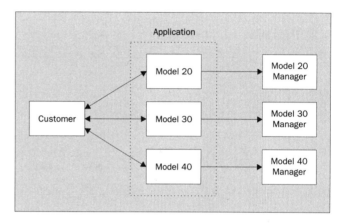

This relationship between a product and a product manager will become more important as we start tying together all of the separate components. For now, let's get started on creating the database tables that we are going to need.

Don't get intimidated by the Access 2000 interface. For this database we can disregard most of the other options and we will focus our efforts on working with tables. For this application, we will need the following tables:

Table Name	Description
tblManagers	To serve as the main administrative interface – used to designate product managers for all of the customer inquiries.
tblLog	To maintain a log of the customer inquiries.
tblLetters	To contain preset text for response to inquiries – sorted by model and keywords.

Since this database is fairly simple, we shouldn't spend that much time analyzing each table. However, you should notice that standard database normalization rules are used (even though they could be bypassed for these tables). Normalization rules center on the principle that all data should be stored in its most simple, compact format (for purposes of future expansion and optimized querying).

For example, if you had a list of contacts, and a notes field related to each, you would put the contact info in one table and the notes fields in a different table. You then use an ID (unique to each entry inside either table, but matched one-to-one *between* tables) to tie the data in the two tables together. You *could* put them in one table, but this would simply defeat the principle. Normalization can make the difference between a merely good database and a truly robust application.

Next we have to decide what fields should be contained within each table. Just by looking at the table names we can begin to make a good guess at what information should be contained within each one – a separate chart is provided for each.

tblManagers

Field Name	Data Type	Description
ID (Primary Key)	AutoNumber	This field assigns a unique identifier to each manager.
MFname	Text	The first name of the manager
MLname	Text	The last name of the manager
Email	Text	The internet e-mail address of the manager. (Make sure to enter an e-mail address for the default value in the field properties section This way, if a product is not assigned a manager, the e-mail will still arrive at the company and not get bounced back to the customer.)
Model	Text	The model of the product which the manager is assigned

tblLog

Field Name	Data Type	Description
ID (Primary Key)	AutoNumber	This field assigns a unique identifier to each message in the log.
Fname	Text	The first name of the customer sending the inquiry.
Lname	Text	The last name of the customer sending the inquiry.
Email	Text	The e-mail address of the customer sending the inquiry.
Model	Text	The model number of the product that the customer enters on the web form. This field is eventually used to determine the product manager for which the application generates an e-mail.
NOQ	Text	Nature Of Question. This gives a general indication of the users request. This field is later used to find the form letter that will be sent to the customer.
General	Memo	This is the free form section where a user can enter their specific questions and remarks.
TAD	Date/Time	Time and Date that the message was added the database log.

tblLetters

Field Name	Data Type	Description
ID (Primary Key)	AutoNumber	This field assigns a unique identifier to each pre-written letter.
Model	Text	This field associates a particular form letter with a model number of a product that is offered by the Acme company.
NOQ	Text	Nature Of Question. This field associates a particular form letter with a type of question on a product that is offered by the Acme company.
Letter	Memo	This contains the actual text of the letter that will be sent to customers.

Creating Tables in Access

In order to create these tables in Access, start by opening up a new database and naming it customers.mdb. Click on the Tables tab on the left-hand menu and then on the icon labeled Create table in Design view – this will open up a window like the one shown below:

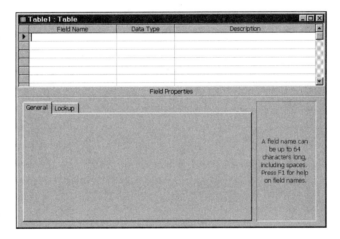

Fill in the Field Names and Data Types columns according to the field charts above. You should now designate one field as the primary key. The chosen field will then be used internally by Access to uniquely identify each entry, helping your queries run more efficiently and keeping your database in its most compact format.

To do this, you must first put the cursor in the Field Name that you want to be the primary key – for the purpose of this case study, use the ID field. In the middle of the top toolbar, click on the key icon (as shown in the figure below).

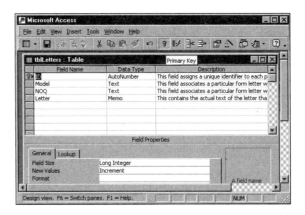

You will find that there is now a small key icon added to the left side of the Field Name, indicating that the primary key is now set. It is not essential to fill in the description, but it can help to have done so once you have worked with the database a bit and want to come back and modify it. Now save the tables appropriately.

We shall be dealing with five standard models and seven standard query types:

❑ Model 20	❑ General Question
❑ Model 30	❑ Warranty Question
❑ Model 40	❑ Product Return
❑ Model 50	❑ Service Options
❑ Model 60	❑ Accessory Options
	❑ Company Questions
	❑ Other

Initially, the only table that should be left blank is the `tblLog`. For `tblLetters`, you should provide an entry for each combination of model and query. (Don't worry about filling the letter field for all of these – entries for just a few will be quite adequate for testing purposes.) In `tblManagers`, you should assign a product manager to each model.

ODBC Connection

The last step in finishing up the Access component of this case study is to create a new ODBC DSN link to the database on the server that will run our application. This will make our database accessible to Internet Information Server and it will allow us to call the database from our Active Server Pages. If you have never worked with ODBC links before, you will find that the process quite easy.

You may be wondering why we use this method rather than the more up to date OLEDB for Jet. ODBC is still widely used, and is easier to set up and far more flexible than OLEDB. Therefore, to keep the focus of the chapter on the messaging side of the application, we are best served by ODBC.

Start by making sure that the customers.mdb database is closed. Then, open the Control Panel (when you implement the project, this must be done on the server) and click on the icon labeled **ODBC Data Sources**. This will open the window shown opposite:

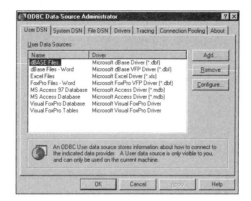

In this case, we want to create a System DSN, since we want the database to be accessible programmatically from within our application. Select the **System DSN** tab and click on the **Add** button – from the list now presented, you want to choose the `Microsoft Access Driver (*.mdb)`, as shown in the screenshot below:

Don't be too concerned with the version numbers shown in this box. Most of these drivers are current as long as the database program that you are using was installed properly.

This will then open up the setup window shown below:

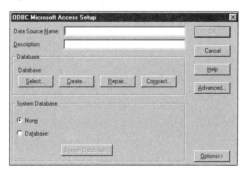

In the field **Data Source Name:** we need to name our ODBC connection. The selection of a connection name is very important, as we are going to call it from our code, and it should therefore have no spaces or funny characters (like ampersands). For this case study, we will name the connection `Acme`.

In the database box you should click on the button labeled **Select**. This will open up a file window, shown below, where you should choose the database that we were just working on, `customers.mdb`.

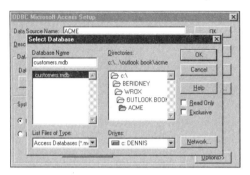

Once this has been selected, your DSN window should look like the screenshot below:

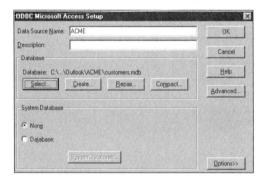

While there are many other options in this dialog box, the database selection and ODBC connection naming are sufficient. Click **OK** to return to the main ODBC window. The new Acme connection that we just created should be in the System DSN list, as shown below:

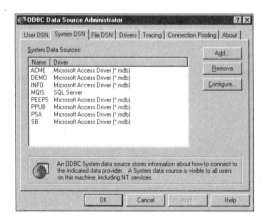

The database and ODBC connection are now both ready for some ASP code. At this point you should close the Access database (as we will not be able to open it with our ASP code if it is already open on the server).

Active Server Pages & CDO Component

Put simply, ASP is a Microsoft technology that allows you to create web pages with dynamic content, and permitting virtually endless development possibilities. One of the most popular ways to create dynamic pages is to tie the pages' contents to the contents of a database — as the database changes, so does the information displayed on the web page. This connection also allows developers to collect information much more easily than ever before possible.

> **For Internet developers, ASP has created a fundamental shift from creating *web pages* to creating *web applications*. ASP requires developers to look at application-wide (rather than minute page) issues.**

The upside of this is that it allows for more content on a web site, creating a new paradigm in site development and possible types of Internet applications. You can recognize ASP pages because they have the extension .asp (instead of the more common .htm or .html seen on the World Wide Web).

If you are familiar with web site development on UNIX boxes, you may already know about ColdFusion from Allaire. ColdFusion pages are similar to ASP in the sense that they can still create dynamic web pages that are tied to a database. While there are currently some ports of ASP that allow it to run on UNIX boxes, ColdFusion is mainly used for sites that are run on UNIX and ASP is used for pages that are hosted on a Windows NT server. While there is quite a bit of differing code and syntax between ASP and ColdFusion, you will find that the general concepts are the same for both languages.

The code presented for this application will probably look familiar to you, and you should be able to pick it up quite easily. The ASP code shown here is actually just VBScript, and this is embedded within the HTML of a web page, encased within <% %> tags — this is shown in the following example (file named first.asp). Comments are included to help you differentiate between the ASP and HTML code.

> **Note that this is ASP code and must therefore be accessed from a server in order to function properly.**

For further information on HTML, see 'Instant HTML Programmer's Reference, HTML 4.0 Edition', ISBN 1861001568, from Wrox Press

For further information on ASP, see Wrox's 'ASP Programmer's Reference', ISBN 1861002459.

```
<html>
<head>
<title>First ASP Page</title>
</head>

<body>
<!--The following is HTML Code -->
<font face="Arial">
<b>First ASP Example</b>
<hr>
The current time and date is:
<BR>

<%
'This is ASP code
Response.write now ()
%>

</font>
</body>
</html>
```

Notice that inside the `<% %>` tags, you are free to write the VBScript code as you wish, following the same conventions for comments that you use in VB or VBA. Also notice that we are calling the common VB function `now()` to display the time and date. This combination of HTML and VBScript should create the output shown below.

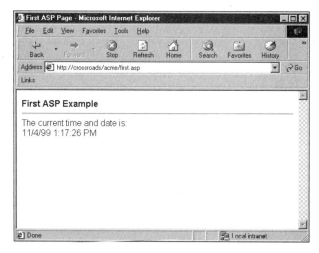

Another important thing to remember about ASP is that all code is executed at the server and *not on the browser* – users (or competitors) will therefore not be able to steal your ASP code, as the page displayed is all in HTML tags. To illustrate this point, take a look at the HTML code generated by `first.asp` (click on View | Source on the main menu bar).

```
<html>
<head>
<title>First ASP Page</title>
</head>

<body>
<!--The following is HTML Code -->
<font face="Arial">

<b>First ASP Example</b>
<hr>
The current time and date is:
<BR>
11/4/99 1:17:26 PM
</font>
</body>
</html>
```

Notice that all of the code that was within the `<% %>` tags is no longer there, but has been replaced by equivalent HTML code – only the result is displayed. This is obviously a very basic example. As we progress, you will see how to embed both HTML and VBScript code in order to create this customer service application.

Rather than using a converted Outlook form, we're going to create our Active Server Pages from scratch. You will find that this is not as difficult as you might think, and will put you in a better position to understand your own converted Outlook forms (as well as other converted Office forms).

There are currently many development products available for ASP code (such as Microsoft's Visual Interdev or Allaire's HomeSite). Rather than recommending one particular product and risking the chance that it is not readily available to you, all the following examples will be written in Windows Notepad. During your own development, feel free to use the tool of your choice.

Creating the Main Customer Interface

When a customer visits the Acme Company web site, they will be presented with a form – this should allow them to fill out their questions and comments, and then submit it for processing. Once it has been submitted, they should be given confirmation and be directed to their e-mail box, (where they will find an automatic response from the server).

First, we must create a form like the one shown below, which we shall name `customer.html`.

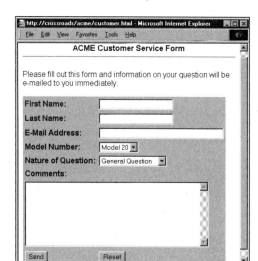

This form includes fields into which the customer can enter their e-mail address, the nature of their question and the product that they currently own. These last two use comboboxes, which will play a significant role in our code development.

The HTML code for this page is included in the following example. It is presented in full, because ASP coding is highly dependent on the HTML forms that customers are asked to fill out, and this will consequently affect our entire application.

```html
<html>
<head>
<title>ACME Customer Service Form</title>
</head>

<body>
<font face="Arial">
<p align=center><STRONG>ACME Customer Service Form </STRONG>
<HR>
</p>
<P align=left>Please fill out this form and information on your question will be
e-mailed to you immediately. </P>

<form action="process.asp" method="post">
<table bgcolor="#c0c0c0" cellspacing="2" cellpadding="2" border="0">
<tr>
    <td><STRONG>First Name:</STRONG> </td>
    <td><STRONG><input name="Fname"></STRONG></td></tr>
<tr>
    <td><STRONG>Last Name:</STRONG> </td>
    <td><STRONG><input name="LName"></STRONG></td></tr>
<tr>
    <td><STRONG>E-Mail Address:</STRONG> </td>
    <td><STRONG><input name="Email" size="35"></STRONG></td></tr>
```

```
<tr>
    <td><STRONG>Model Number:</STRONG> </td>
    <td><select name="Model">
    <option value="Model 20" selected>Model 20</option>
    <option value="Model 30">Model 30</option>
    <option value="Model 40">Model 40</option>
    <option value="Model 50">Model 50</option>
    <option value="Model 60">Model 60</option>
</select></td></tr>
<tr>
    <td><STRONG>Nature of Question:</STRONG>  </td>
    <td><select name="NOQ">
    <option value="General Question" selected>General Question</option>
    <option value="Warranty Question">Warranty Question</option>
    <option value="Product Return">Product Return</option>
    <option value="Service Options">Service Options</option>
    <option value="Accessory Options">Accessory Options</option>
    <option value="Company Question">Company Question</option>
    <option value="Other">Other</option></select></td>
</tr>
<tr><td><STRONG>Comments:</STRONG></td><td></td></tr>

<tr><td colspan=2><TEXTAREA cols=45 name="General" rows=8></TEXTAREA></td></tr>

<tr><td></td><td></td></tr>

<tr>
<td>
<input type="submit" value="Send"></td><td><input type="reset" value=Reset>
</td>
</tr>

</table>
</form>
</font>
</body>
</html>
```

Most of this web page is standard HTML code. We therefore highlight only the parts that will be important in the development of the ASP pages.

The first important part is the declaration of the form that is being used.

```
<form action="process.asp" method="post">
```

Here, we are sending the information to the file named process.asp by means of the post method. While ASP can also handle the get method, we use the post method because it is more convenient to send the form information in the HTTP headers than in an impossibly long URL (as would be the case using the get method).

437

Like most HTML forms, it is also important to use a naming convention for all fields presented on the form. This is demonstrated below:

```
<tr>
<td><STRONG>First Name:</STRONG> </td>
<td><STRONG><input name="Fname"></STRONG></td></tr>
<tr><td><STRONG>Last Name:</STRONG> </td>
<td><STRONG><input name="LName"></STRONG></td>
</tr>
<tr>
<td><STRONG>E-Mail Address:</STRONG> </td>
<td><STRONG><input name="Email" size="35"></STRONG></td>
</tr>
```

These names are matched to the database field names to which they will eventually correspond. In the long run, it is much easier to keep track of your fields if you use the same field names.

As for the two combo boxes, displayed and actual values for each option are the same. Again, it is important that these values match the database since we will use ASP code to create queries based on these values.

Note that in a real-world scenario, we would be best off acquiring these values dynamically from the database, as this would ensure a match no matter what values were used. However, this is not an ASP-oriented case study, so we can simplify matters considerably by hard-coding the values into our samples, then ensuring that the contents of our database match up.

```
<tr>
    <td><STRONG>Model Number:</STRONG> </td>
    <td><select name="Model">
     <option value="Model 20" selected>Model 20</option>
     <option value="Model 30">Model 30</option>
     <option value="Model 40">Model 40</option>
     <option value="Model 50">Model 50</option>
     <option value="Model 60">Model 60</option>
</select></td></tr>
<tr>
    <td><STRONG>Nature of Question:</STRONG>  </td>
    <td><select name="NOQ">
     <option value="General Question" selected>General Question</option>
     <option value="Warranty Question">Warranty Question</option>
     <option value="Product Return">Product Return</option>
     <option value="Service Options">Service Options</option>
     <option value="Accessory Options">Accessory Options</option>
     <option value="Company Question">Company Question</option>
     <option value="Other">Other</option></select></td>
</tr>
```

Creating the Processing Script

Our focus is now on the file process.asp, since this will handle all of the interfaces between our web page, the Access database and the CDO library. It's really the workhorse of this application so we will look at it in very distinct sections. Let's begin by looking at the entire text of the code.

```
<!--#include file="adovbs.inc"-->
<!--#include file="cdovbs.inc"-->
<%
FName=Request.Form("FName")
LName=Request.Form("LName")
EMail=Request.Form("EMail")
Model=Request.Form("Model")
NOQ=Request.Form("NOQ")
General=Request.Form("General")
TAD = now()

Set objConn = Server.CreateObject("ADODB.Connection")
objConn.Open "Acme"

Set objEmailRS = Server.Createobject("ADODB.Recordset")

strEMail = "SELECT EMail FROM tblManagers WHERE Model LIKE '"& Model &"'"
Set objEmailRS = objConn.Execute(strEMail)

Manager = objEmailRS.Fields("Email")
objEmailRS.Close
Set objEmailRS = Nothing

Set objMail = Server.CreateObject("CDONTS.Newmail")
objMail.From = EMail
objMail.To = Manager
objMail.Subject = "Customer Service Inquiry - " & Model
objMail.Body = General
objMail.Send
Set objMail = Nothing

strMessage = "SELECT Letter FROM tblLetters WHERE Model LIKE '"& Model _
          &"'     AND NOQ LIKE '"& NOQ &"'"

Set objLetter = Server.Createobject("ADODB.Recordset")
Set objLetter = objConn.Execute(strMessage)

Set objResponse = Server.CreateObject("CDONTS.Newmail")
objResponse.From = Manager
objResponse.To = EMail
objResponse.Subject = "ACME Inquiry - " & Model
objResponse.Body = objLetter.Fields("Letter")
objResponse.Send
Set objResponse = Nothing

Set objLog = Server.Createobject("ADODB.Recordset")
objLog.Open "tblLog", "Acme", adOpenKeySet, adLockPessimistic, adCmdTable
objLog.AddNew

objLog.Fields("FName") = FName
objLog.Fields("LName") = LName
objLog.Fields("Email") = EMail
objLog.Fields("Model") = Model
```

```
objLog.Fields("NOQ") = NOQ
objLog.Fields("General") = General
objLog.Fields("TAD") = TAD

objLog.Update

objLog.Close
Set objLog = Nothing

objConn.close
Set objConn = Nothing

Response.Redirect "confirm.html"
%>
```

The first thing you will notice about this code is the fact that there is no HTML whatsoever. The code essentially serves as a processing script that handles the information and passes the customer on to another page. It will carry out the following actions:

❑ declare the include files that we need for both the ASP and CDO code

❑ bring the variables from the form (that the customer filled out) to the script

❑ establish the connection to our ODBC data source, `customers.mdb`

❑ find the correct product manager to send the e-mail to

❑ send the e-mail to the manager

❑ find the correct reply letter to send to our customer

❑ send the e-mail to the customer

❑ add the customer inquiry to our log

❑ redirect the customer to a confirmation page, `confirm.html`

We can now start looking at the code in sections. The very first part calls the files we must `include` for the ASP code (`adovbs.inc`) and the CDO library (`cdovbs.inc`).

Both these files are very common (and most likely already exist on your server) allowing us to use conventional naming methods for properties in our code instead of having to use their numeric equivalents.

```
<!--#include file="adovbs.inc"-->
<!--#include file="cdovbs.inc"-->
```

The next part stores the user-entered form text as variables.

```
<%
FName=Request.Form("FName")
LName=Request.Form("LName")
EMail=Request.Form("EMail")
Model=Request.Form("Model")
```

```
NOQ=Request.Form("NOQ")
General=Request.Form("General")
TAD = now()
```

Notice again that these variables match the field names we established in the database. The only variable that we don't request from the form is TAD, using the now() function to establish its current value instead.

In this case, our form used the post method, so we now use the Form property of the Request object. If we had used the get method, we would use the Querystring property:
FName=Request.Querystring("FName")

The next set of code declares our ODBC connection and opens it, enabling us to call any of the tables in our database and manipulate the data in any way we want.

```
Set objConn = Server.CreateObject("ADODB.Connection")
objConn.Open "Acme"
```

We only need one ODBC connection, so we need only declare this once. Also, since this is an application that will be used over and over again, it is imperative that the connection gets closed out once the code has finished. (There are other pieces of code here that will demonstrate this.)

Next, we need to find the correct product manager to send our first e-mail to. The first part of this code declares the record set object that will hold the results of our query. The query is declared in the variable strEMail, and is in the form of an SQL statement using the variable Model as the search criteria.

```
strEMail = "SELECT EMail FROM tblManagers WHERE Model LIKE '"& Model &"'"
```

If we were to translate this SQL statement into everyday words, it would say "show me all the e-mail addresses of managers assigned to the model entered by the user". Since our database has only one product manager, this SQL statement will only return one e-mail address.

If you have used query statements in Access or other database programs, you will find that these SQL statements are slightly different to those you use with other databases. Their syntax can also change according to the server or database program that you are using – you may have to change your ASP code accordingly. If an error is generated when you first run an ASP application, the cause will usually be found in the SQL statement.

In order to execute our query, we call the connection object, objConn (that was previously established to carry it out) and store the result of the query (the product manager's e-mail address) in a new variable, Manager.

```
Set objEmailRS = objConn.Execute(strEMail)
Manager = objEmailRS.Fields("Email")
```

Next, we close out and discard the record set object objEmailRS.

```
objEmailRS.Close
Set objEmailRS = Nothing
```

441

These two lines are very important, because our application uses a variety of record sets and objects. It is imperative that we close out and discard each of these objects as soon as we finish with them. In a large-scale adaptation of this application, this will improve the speed considerably and ease the load on the server. Even when speed is not an issue (or the difference is negligible) this is always good practice.

Utilizing CDO Objects

We now look at how to use CDO code from within ASP pages and send the series of e-mails we need. (There are many white papers and other articles available on the CDO library and its evolution, so only a brief explanation of its history is included here.)

The full name of the library we'll be using is 'Collaboration Data Objects for NT Server' (CDONTS). It is the result of many refinements involving both Internet Information Server basic SMTP service and OLE ActiveX libraries. CDONTS allows us to send messages quickly and efficiently, all within the structure of well-defined and easy to use objects and methods. If you are unsure as to whether you have CDONTS, you can do a search for the dynamic link library, CDONTS.dll.

Using the CDO library is very straightforward, as long as a logical pattern is followed. When you think of the process you go through to send e-mail to a friend, you probably follow the same generic steps.

- ❑ Open the e-mail messaging program
- ❑ Designate the sender of the message (by default, this is the owner of the account)
- ❑ Choose a recipient for the message
- ❑ Write the body of the message
- ❑ Send the message

CDO follows the same generic steps to send a message programmatically. Let's start by taking a look at the actual CDO code.

```
Set objMail = Server.CreateObject("CDONTS.Newmail")
```

This first line simply declares objMail as a CDO object and it invokes a Newmail, the CDO equivalent of opening up the e-mail program – the CDO library is now loaded into server memory and is ready to start generating our first e-mail message.

```
objMail.From = EMail
objMail.To = Manager
objMail.Subject = "Customer Service Inquiry - " & Model
objMail.Body = General
```

These lines continue to build the actual e-mail message. In this case, we use the customer's e-mail address as the From address and the Manager variable (declared earlier) is being used as the To address.

The Subject of the e-mail message uses a combination of pre-determined text and the Model variable that we collected from the customer. The Body of the message simply consists of the contents of the General variable, in which the customer wrote their comments. It is important that the manager receives these comments, as they may include questions that the database cannot automatically answer.

The last two lines send the message and close out the `objMail` object to conserve server memory.

```
objMail.Send
Set objMail = Nothing
```

The end result is that the product manager will receive an e-mail like the one below:

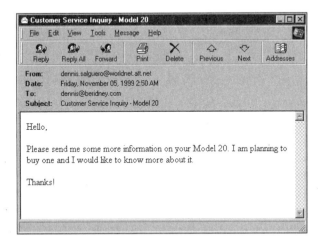

If you have skipped ahead, you will notice that we use almost exactly the same piece of code later on in the ASP page to send the e-mail to the customer. So why not use the same CDO object, `objMail`? We can't do this – once you send a message with the `Newmail` object, all existing `Newmail` objects (regardless of their assigned object name) are closed out and the `Send` property cannot be used again until you declare a brand new object. Therefore, this snippet of code is modified and re-declared in order to send out the second e-mail.

If you have had experience in setting up e-mail accounts you should notice that one important aspect of e-mail is missing from this code. There is no mention of an SMTP server! Furthermore, the `From` address could contain virtually anything – there doesn't need to be a valid e-mail address to send a message with CDO. If you check the detailed header of a message sent to you with CDO code, you will find that a generic Microsoft SMTP mailer (or your Exchange server) is used to send the message with the name of your server being the only identifying information contained within the header.

The next piece of our code will find the standard letter that needs to be sent to our customer according to their product model and question.

```
strMessage = "SELECT Letter FROM tblLetters WHERE Model LIKE '"& Model &"' _
                                      AND NOQ LIKE '"& NOQ &"'"

Set objLetter = Server.Createobject("ADODB.Recordset")
Set objLetter = objConn.Execute(strMessage)
```

Notice that we are using the same connection object (objConn) to execute the new SQL statement. This is perfectly acceptable, as we are using the same ODBC data source and have not closed it out yet.

The SQL statement in this section looks for the letter corresponding to both the product model and the nature of the question that our customer asked.

Next, we need to send the e-mail message to our customer, with the body of the message consisting of the information that we found in our database.

```
Set objResponse = Server.CreateObject("CDONTS.Newmail")
objResponse.From = Manager
objResponse.To = EMail
objResponse.Subject = "ACME Inquiry - " & Model
objResponse.Body = objLetter.Fields("Letter")
objResponse.Send
Set objResponse = Nothing
```

As mentioned earlier, this code is very similar to the one used to send the e-mail to the product manager. Naturally, we have reversed the From and To fields so that the letter is sent to the customer and shown as coming from the product manager. The Subject line is changed to remind the user of their inquiry and the Model variable that they designated earlier.

As for the Body of the message, we set its value using a field directly from the record set, as shown above. It will generate the following letter to your customer.

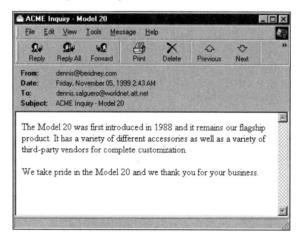

Once again, the last two lines send the e-mail message and close out the CDO object.

```
objResponse.Send
Set objResponse = Nothing
```

The last remaining step in our process is to write to the customer inquiry to our log. While we employ the same method that we used to declare the record set, this code shows a different way to open it:

```
Set objLog = Server.Createobject("ADODB.Recordset")
objLog.Open "tblLog", "Acme", adOpenKeySet, adLockPessimistic, adCmdTable
```

We open the table named `tblLog` from the ODBC data source named `Acme`. The parameters we include will open the record set as a key set (which lets us read and write to it), with pessimistic record locking. We also aid the ASP code, by letting it know that `tblLog` is a table. Fortunately, we can use the text equivalent of these parameters (since we declared the `adovbs.inc` file at the beginning of the code.)

You should also note the fact that this section is missing a SQL statement. In this example, we are adding a new record to our log, so we do not need to declare a SQL string. Instead, we declare each field and its value separately. The only exception is the AutoNumber field, since Access will fill this is automatically.

We must now add the information to each of the fields in the log. However, we first need to start a blank record with the `AddNew` property.

```
objLog.AddNew

objLog.Fields("FName") = FName
objLog.Fields("LName") = LName
objLog.Fields("Email") = EMail
objLog.Fields("Model") = Model
objLog.Fields("NOQ") = NOQ
objLog.Fields("General") = General
objLog.Fields("TAD") = TAD

objLog.Update
```

Notice that each field in our record set is declared individually and a variable assigned to the value of each field. This is where we see the benefits of making sure that our ASP variables match our field names — it definitely makes for easier coding! We finish updating the record set by declaring `objLog.Update`.

The last two lines of this section close out the record set and discard the object.

```
objLog.Close
Set objLog = Nothing
```

The final part of the script closes the ODBC data source and redirects the application to a confirmation page with the following code:

```
objConn.close
Set objConn = Nothing

Response.Redirect "confirm.html"
%>
```

By closing out the connection object, we free up
some more memory on the server and leave the
script ready for the next customer to use. Remember
that process.asp has no HTML code whatsoever.
Therefore, once the form is submitted the customer
immediately sees the file confirm.html shown
here.

confirm.html

```
<html>
<head>
<title> ACME: Confirmation </title>
</head>

<body>
<font face="Arial">
<P align=center>
<STRONG>
Thank you for your comments.
<br>
Please check your e-mail box in a few minutes to see our response.
<br>
<br>
</STRONG>
<A href="customer.html">
Click here to return to the customer service form
</P></A>

</font>
</body>
</html>
```

Note that the user doesn't ever see process.asp. The application just seems to jump from the form to
this confirmation page.

Expanding the Application

We currently have a good working model for our application, but it can still be expanded in several useful ways. Since the main purpose of this case study (and the book as a whole) is Outlook and Internet messaging, our expansion efforts will first focus on the e-mail parts of this application and then we can look at other sections.

If we return to the generic model of how to create and send e-mails, there are two more realms that we haven't explored. When composing an e-mail you can:

❑   Designate a priority level for a message

❑   Designate a blind carbon copy (bcc:) recipient (to receive a copy of the message, but go unlisted as a recipient in the message header)

Message Priority Level

On the main customer form we have a combo box where the customer designates the nature of their question. However, there is also the option of designating their question as Other. In this case, we can assume that the user's question will lie within their general comments. Therefore, these messages should be designated with a higher priority and it will let managers know that they need to read the message before all the others.

In order to accomplish this, we need to take a look at the piece of code where the product manager's e-mail is generated. We can set the priority level of the message once we have the address information entered. In order to find customer inquiries that were designated as Other in the NOQ variable, we test NOQ using an If statement.

```
Set objMail = Server.CreateObject("CDONTS.Newmail")
objMail.From = EMail
objMail.To = Manager

If NOQ = "Other" Then
objMail.Importance = cdoHigh
Else
objMail.Importance = cdoNormal
End If

objMail.Subject = "Customer Service Inquiry - " & Model
objMail.Body = General
```

You can see that this code utilizes the Importance property of our mail object.

We also use the conventional names for high and low priority. The fact that both of these begin with cdo *designate these variables as being located in the* cdovbs.inc *include file, declared at the top of the code.*

The addition of this code results in an e-mail just like the one shown.

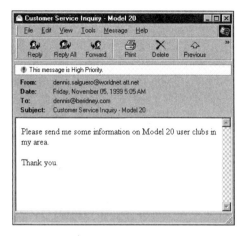

The message is now marked as being **High Priority** and the product manager can reply to the customer based on the e-mail's message contents. All other messages will be **Normal Priority** and can be handled by the product manager accordingly.

Additional Recipients

There may be times when you want to include additional recipients for your e-mail message. We use the next snippet of code as an example – we add the company manager as a Blind Carbon Copy (**bcc:**) on every message sent to the product managers. We must therefore add a line to the code that specifies the addressing information on messages sent to the product managers:

```
objMail.From = EMail
objMail.To = Manager
objMail.Bcc="manager@acme.com"
objMail.Subject = "Customer Service Inquiry - " & Model
```

> *By adding this just below the* To *address, we keep with the format of a standard e-mail message. If you want to make a standard carbon copy (*cc:*) then you can modify the code thus:*
> `objMail.CC="manager@acme.com"`

If you look at a diagram of the CDO object model (see Appendix B), you will see that we have bypassed the `Session` and `Folder` objects and jumped into the `Messages` object. This allows us to create faster code, as the `Session` object would require an SMTP server login and a `Folder` declaration for every transaction. Note though, that the `Session` object is required if you are interfacing with an Exchange Server.

Almost everything else in the `Messages` hierarchy should be familiar to you, since we have seen examples with this application – the one exception is the `Attachments` object. This application does not lend itself to attachments, as we wouldn't want to flood our customer's e-mail box with large messages.

Nevertheless, for the sake of completeness, we include some sample code for sending an attachment. We use the same object as for the message to the product manager.

```
Set objMail = Server.CreateObject("CDONTS.Newmail")
objMail.From = EMail
objMail.To = Manager
objMail.Subject = "Customer Service Inquiry - " & Model
objMail.Body = General
objMail.AttachFile ("c:\acme\logo.gif", "Company Logo")
objMail.Send
Set objMail = Nothing
```

As you can see, the `AttachFile` object in this example has two parameters. The first is the path of the file you want to attach. If you make a mistake with the file path, an error statement will be generated and the e-mail message will not be sent. The second parameter is the caption we want to use for the attached file, which will appear in the message header.

Expanding the Access Database

So far, we have used the Access database as a storage area and nothing else. However, with some knowledge of Access development, the Access database can become a control console of sorts for this application.

> *As this section is peripheral to the Case Study, we will not go into details regarding its implementation. All relevant files can be downloaded at www.wrox.com.*

We start by creating a form for the customer inquiry log. Until this point, we have taken the log's utility for granted, but we can now develop a form enabling us to view these entries in an organized fashion, as shown here:

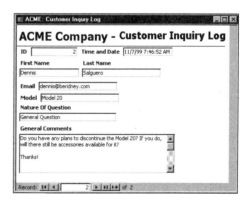

Notice that this has the same general layout as the web page filled out by the customer. This form sorts inquiries according to the date and time they were submitted (putting older inquiries first). The design view of the form is shown:

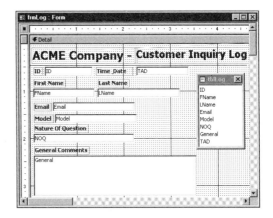

Here you can see the field list on the right-hand side and the organization behind the form. Note that the field names in the list match the conventions used throughout, but in the form, more descriptive names are used for the labels.

The next form we should look at is the one on which we can write response letters to be sent to our customers.

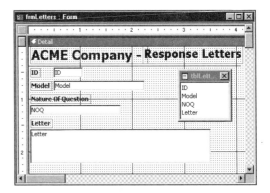

Again we see the field list with the more descriptive names being used for the actual form. This form is very plain and simple to use. It was designed with the premise that this form would be used primarily for data entry, so there shouldn't be any kind of trick to using it. This design results in this form:

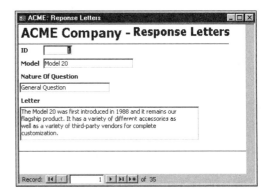

With only three fields to fill out (the ID field is an AutoNumber) this makes for a very efficient data entry form.

We also need a form for the product managers, to contain their e-mail address as shown here.

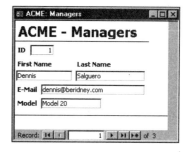

The key to this form is that the e-mail address must be accurate – otherwise the product mangers will never receive any customer inquiries. You may want to ensure this by assigning an aliased e-mail address to the form and adjusting the 'true' e-mail address accordingly. This way your customer will never receive their inquiry as undeliverable.

Finally, we need a menu form to control all the other forms. This will be the first form users see when opening the database. An example of this form is shown here.

Note that the buttons on this main menu can be created with either VBA code or macros, depending on your experience with Access. Either way, this menu goes a long way towards making the Access side of this application easy for anyone to use, whether they have experience of working with Access or not.

We now have an application on the customer side and an Access application on the server side. The Access forms will ensure that company users can keep the most up to date information for the customer service application. However, one very important factor must be kept in mind. If the database is opened on the server in Exclusive mode, it will shut off all other current sessions and reject any new sessions. The ODBC connection will therefore not be able to open it, and any attempt will result in a read-only error. You therefore have two options:

❑ Make sure that you only update the database when there are no customers accessing the application. This type of an update can take place along with other network maintenance at a time when server load is low or non-existent.

❑ Suspend the services on your web site while you make the updates. While this will generate a HTTP 404 error, you can always put up a temporary web page to alert users to your network status.

There is in fact a third option, which is to open the database in Shared mode, thus allowing multi-user access. However, this comes with its own particular brand of problems, and is not recommended for use with the application as it stands.

Other Expansion Possibilities

Naturally, there are many other possibilities when it comes to extending this application. Many of these go far beyond the scope of this book, while others can be accomplished by adapted use of the components established here. Examples include:

❑ Maintaining a customer registration database – a case history of customer inquiries to be maintained and utilized by managers. A case history would add more personalization to customer replies and provide internal information on trends in product usage.

❑ Implementing a message board – this is a popular way for customers to help each other with questions, easing some of the load on the company's staff. This application provides a solid foundation for a message board.

❑ Many companies offer web page components for customer service, many of which can easily be integrated into this web application. You could take this one step further, doing without the messaging and convert this into a fax-back application, the user receiving a faxed response at a chosen number.

Summary

If you have used other languages to program Internet applications before, you have probably noticed that this project resembles a form-mail script, common to Perl programming. However, we have also seen some of the flexibility offered by the CDO library, and how it can be integrated with existing tools such as databases and messaging clients.

We have demonstrated how you can tie customer interface forms and CDO commands to a database (something that wasn't always easy with Perl), and make it globally accessible with Active Server Pages. With this foundation, you can go on to create equally robust applications, building your development according to your own individual needs.

Outlook 2000 Object Summary

Collections

Name	Description
Actions	A collection of actions that can be executed on an item, and which can appear on the toolbar and the <u>A</u>ctions menu of the item's GUI.
AddressEntries	This collection holds all the names and the information about a group of contacts that is contained in the address book.
AddressLists	The holder of the AddressList objects. This can be thought of as the email equivalent of a bookshelf for phone books.
Attachments	A collection of the files inserted into the body of an item.
Exceptions	This collection contains objects which hold information about any exceptions to the RecurrencePattern of an AppointmentItem.
Explorers	The collection of Explorer objects currently open.
Folders	A collection of MAPIFolder objects.
Inspectors	The collection of Inspector objects currently open.
Items	A collection of Outlook items.
Links	A collection of items linked to an Outlook item. In Outlook 2000, only ContactItem objects can be linked to other items.
OutlookBarGroups	The collection of groups on the Outlook Bar.
OutlookBar Shortcuts	The collection of shortcuts in an Outlook Bar group.

Name	Description
Pages	The collection of pages for an `Inspector` object.
Panes	The collection of panes displayed by an `Explorer` object.
PropertyPages	The collection of custom pages which have been added to the Options or Properties dialog.
Recipients	A collection containing all of the `Recipient` objects for an Outlook item.
Selection	The collection of the Outlook items which are currently selected in the `Explorer`.
SyncObjects	A collection of synchronization profiles.
UserProperties	A collection of the user-defined properties for an Outlook item.

Collection Properties

The same five properties are shared by all the collection objects. These are:

Name	Returns	Description
Application	`Application` object	Returns the parent application of the collection. Read-only.
Class	`OlObject Class` constant	Returns a numeric value specifying the class the collection object belongs to. Read-only.
Count	Long	Returns the number of objects in the collection. Read-only.
Parent	Object	Returns the parent object of the collection. Read-only.
Session	`NameSpace`	Returns the `NameSpace` object. Read only

Actions Collection

Methods

Name	Returns	Description
Add	`Action` object	Adds a new `Action` object to the collection.

Name	Returns	Description
Item(Index)	Action object	Returns the Action object specified by the Index parameter.
Remove(Index)		Removes from the collection the object specified by the Index parameter.

AddressEntries Collection

Methods

Name	Returns	Description
Add(Type, [Name], [Address])	Address Entry object	Returns a newly created AddressEntry object which is added to the collection.
GetFirst()	Address Entry object	Returns the first object in the collection.
GetLast()	Address Entry object	Returns the last object in the collection.
GetNext()	Address Entry object	Returns the next object in the collection.
GetPrevious()	Address Entry object	Returns the previous object in the collection.
Item(Index)	Address Entry object	Returns the AddressEntry object specified by the Index parameter.
Sort ([Property], [Descending])		Sorts the collection. Property specifies the property to sort by. Descending is one of the OlSortOrder constants and specifies whether the sort order will be descending or ascending.

AddressLists Collection

Methods

Name	Returns	Description
Item(Index)	Address List object	Returns the AddressList object specified by the Index parameter.

Attachments Collection

Methods

Name	Returns	Description
Add(*Source*, [*Type*], [*Position*], [*Display Name*])	Attachment object	Creates and returns a new Attachment object. The parameter Source specifies the path and file name or the item for the attachment; Type is one of the OlAttachmentType constants and DisplayName specifies the display name for an attachment of type olByValue.
Item(Index)	Attachment object	Returns the Attachment object specified by the Index parameter.
Remove(Index)		Removes from the collection the object specified by the Index parameter.

Exceptions Collection

Methods

Name	Returns	Description
Item(Index)	Exception object	Returns the Exception object specified by the Index parameter.

Explorers Collection

Methods

Name	Returns	Description
Add(Folder, [Display Mode])	Explorer object	Returns a newly created Explorer object. The parameters specify the MAPIFolder to be displayed in the explorer and one of the OlFolderDisplayMode constants to indicate the display mode for the explorer.
Item(Index)	Explorer object	Returns the Explorer object specified by the Index parameter.

Events

Name	Description
NewExplorer	Occurs after a new explorer has been created, but before it is displayed.

Folders Collection

Methods

Name	Returns	Description
Add(Name, [Type])	MAPIFolder object	Creates a new MAPIFolder object.
GetFirst()	MAPIFolder object	Returns the first object in the collection.
GetLast()	MAPIFolder object	Returns the last object in the collection.
GetNext()	MAPIFolder object	Returns the next object in the collection.
GetPrevious()	MAPIFolder object	Returns the previous object in the collection.
Item(Index)	MAPIFolder object	Returns the MAPIFolder object specified by the Index parameter.
Remove(Index)		Removes from the collection the object specified by the Index parameter.

Events

Name	Description
FolderAdd	Raised when a new MAPIFolder is added.
FolderChange	Raised when a MAPIFolder changes.
FolderRemove	Raised when a MAPIFolder is deleted.

Inspectors Collection

Methods

Name	Returns	Description
Add(Item)	Inspector	Returns a newly created Inspector object for the object Item.

Table Continued on Following Page

Name	Returns	Description
Item(Index)	Inspector object	Returns the Inspector object specified by the Index parameter.

Events

Name	Description
NewInspector	Raised when a new Inspector object is opened.

Items Collection

Methods

Name	Returns	Description
Add(Type)	Item	Creates a new Outlook item of the given Type and returns it. Type may be any valid message class or one of the OlItemType constants.
Find(Filter)	Item	Applies the filter string specified in the Filter parameter and returns the first item in the collection matching the criterion. Property names included in the filter string must be placed in square brackets.
FindNext	Item	Returns the next item meeting the criterion set by the Find method.
GetFirst()	Item	Returns the first object in the collection.
GetLast()	Item	Returns the last object in the collection.
GetNext()	Item	Returns the next object in the collection.
GetPrevious()	Item	Returns the previous object in the collection.
Item(Index)	Item	Returns the Outlook item specified by the Index parameter.
Remove(Index)		Removes from the collection the object specified by the Index parameter.
ResetColumns		Resets the properties that have been cached by the SetColumns method.
Restrict (Filter)	Items collection	Returns a new collection of items which match the criterion specified in the Filter parameter.

Name	Returns	Description
SetColumns (Columns)		Sets certain properties (listed in the comma-delimited string Columns) to be cached in memory for faster access.
Sort(Property, [Descending])		Sorts the collection. Property specifies the property to sort by. Descending is a Boolean parameter which specifies whether the sort order will be descending (True) or ascending (False).

Properties

In addition to the five properties shared by all the collections and which are listed above, the Items collection has an extra property, IncludeRecurrences:

Name	Returns	Description
Include Recurrences	Boolean	Specifies whether the collection should include recurring AppointmentItem objects. Will always be False if the collection does not contain any appointment items. Read/write.

Events

Name	Description
ItemAdd	Occurs when a new item is created.
ItemChange	Occurs when anything about an item gets modified.
ItemRemove	Occurs when an item is deleted from the Items collection.

Links Collection

Methods

Name	Returns	Description
Add(Item)	Link object	Adds the specified Item to the collection. In Outlook 2000, this must be a ContactItem.
Item(Index)	Link object	Returns the Link object specified by the Index parameter.
Remove(Index)		Removes from the collection the object specified by the Index parameter.

OutlookBarGroups Collection

Methods

Name	Returns	Description
Add(Name, [Index])	OutlookBar Group object	Adds a new group to the Outlook Bar with the specified Name at the position Index on the bar (1 is the top), and returns that group.
Item(Index)	OutlookBar Group object	Returns the OutlookBarGroup object specified by the Index parameter.
Remove(Index)	.	Removes from the collection the object specified by the Index parameter.

Events

Name	Description
BeforeGroupAdd	Occurs before a group is added to the Outlook Bar.
BeforeGroupRemove	Occurs before a group is removed from the Outlook Bar.
GroupAdd	Occurs when a group is added to the Outlook Bar.

OutlookBarShortcuts Collection

Methods

Name	Returns	Description
Add(Target, Name, [Index])	OutlookBar Shortcut object	Adds a new shortcut to an OutlookBarGroup and returns it as an OutlookBarShortcut object. The parameters specify the Target of the shortcut, its Name and its position within the group. Index is zero-based.
Item(Index)	OutlookBar Shortcut object	Returns the OutlookBarShortcut object specified by the Index parameter.
Remove(Index)		Removes from the collection the object specified by the Index parameter.

Events

Name	Description
BeforeShortcutAdd	Occurs before a shortcut is added to a group.
BeforeShortcut Remove	Occurs before a shortcut is removed from a group.
ShortcutAdd	Occurs when a shortcut has been added to a group.

Pages Collection

Methods

Name	Returns	Description
Add(Name)	Page	Creates a new page with the specified Name and returns it.
Item(Index)	Page	Returns the page specified by the Index parameter.
Remove(Index)		Removes from the collection the object specified by the Index parameter.

Panes Collection

Methods

Name	Returns	Description
Item(Index)	Pane	Returns the pane specified by the Index parameter.

PropertyPages Collection

Methods

Name	Returns	Description
Add(Page, [Caption])	Property Page object	Adds a new property page to the Options or Properties dialog box with the specified Caption. The parameter Page may be either a PropertyPage object or the ProgID of the ActiveX control that implements the page.
Item(Index)	Property Page object	Returns the PropertyPage object specified by the Index parameter.

Table Continued on Following Page

Name	Returns	Description
Remove(Index)		Removes from the collection the object specified by the Index parameter.

Recipients Collection

Methods

Name	Returns	Description
Add(Name)	Recipient object	Creates a new Recipient object with the specified display name and returns it.
Item(Index)	Recipient object	Returns the Recipient object specified by the Index parameter.
Remove(Index)		Removes from the collection the object specified by the Index parameter.
ResolveAll	Boolean	Resolves each Recipient object in the collection against the Address Book. Returns True if the attempt succeeds, otherwise False.

Selection Collection

Methods

Name	Returns	Description
Item(Index)	Item	Returns the item specified by the Index parameter.

SyncObjects Collection

Methods

Name	Returns	Description
Item(Index)	SyncObject object	Returns the SyncObject specified by the Index parameter.

UserProperties Collection

Methods

Name	Returns	Description
Add(Name, Type, [AddToFolder Fields], [DisplayFormat])	UserProperty object	Creates and returns a new user property with the specified Name and of the specified Type (which may be one of the OlUserPropertyType constants). AddToFolderFields is a Boolean and specifies whether the property is to be added to the folder fields; DisplayType specifies the index of the format for the Type.
Find(Name, Custom)	UserProperty object	Finds and returns a UserProperty object with the specified Name, if it exists. The Custom parameter indicates whether the property to be found is a user property (True) or a system property (False).
Item(Index)	UserProperty object	Returns the UserProperty object specified by the Index parameter.
Remove(Index)		Removes from the collection the object specified by the Index parameter.

Objects

Name	Description
Action	An action which a recipient can execute on an item. The action's name may appear on the Actions menu and on the toolbar of the item's GUI. The actions already defined are Reply, Reply to All, Forward and Reply to Folder, although not all items support all these actions.
AddressEntry	This is the information about an individual or process to which you can send messages.

Table Continued on Following Page

Name	Description
AddressList	This is the phone book in the desk draw. If you want to find a person's address or phone number, you would look it up in the phone book. So this will be the Global Address Book, Personal Address book or the Contacts Folder if this is marked as a readable AddressList object.
Application	Represents the entire Outlook 2000 application.
Appointment Item	This is an appointment that you will find in a Calendar Folder. It can consist of a single appointment or a series of recurring appointments.
Attachment	Represents an attached file or object embedded in or linked to an Outlook item.
ContactItem	Holds the contact information that you will find in MAPIFolder objects that are of Class olFolderContacts.
DistListItem	This object allows us to group common recipients and contacts together in one object. This allows us to send mail to multiple recipients using only one Recipient entry.
DocumentItem	Represents any object other than an Outlook item – usually an Office document – in an Outlook folder.
Exception	Represents an exception to a recurring series of appointments.
Explorer	Represents the window in which the folder's content is displayed.
Form Description	Represents an Outlook form.
Inspector	This is the window that an Outlook item is displayed in.
JournalItem	The JounalItem represents a single entry for a transaction tracked by Outlook. This entry covers a given period of time.
Link	The Link object represents an Outlook item linked to another item. In Outlook 2000, only ContactItem objects can be linked to other items.
MailItem	The MailItem object represents an electronic mail message which resides in any MAPIFolder of type olFolderInbox.
MAPIFolder	This is an Outlook folder that is displayed in an explorer. This can contain items or other folders.

Name	Description
MeetingItem	This is the item that is located in the Inbox of the recipients of an AppointmentItem. The MeetingItem is always associated with an AppointmentItem.
NameSpace	This is an abstract root for any data source. The only valid namespace for Outlook is "MAPI".
NoteItem	The electronic equivalent of a yellow PostIt note. These can be used to write down facts to remember, and are not sent to other users.
OutlookBar Group	A group of shortcuts on the Outlook Bar.
OutlookBar Pane	The pane containing the Outlook Bar in an Explorer window.
OutlookBar Shortcut	A shortcut on the Outlook Bar.
OutlookBar Storage	Represents the contents of the Outlook Bar pane.
PostItem	Holds information which can be posted to public and private MAPIFolders. This object is similar to an item on a bulletin board.
PropertyPage	A custom property page which can be added to the Options or the Properties dialog box.
PropertyPage Site	The container for a PropertyPage object.
Recipient	A user or resource for Outlook. In almost all cases this will be an addressee for a mail message.
Recurrence Pattern	Holds the information about the entire collection of recurring meetings or appointments.
RemoteItem	The RemoteItem object is a smaller copy of an original message located on the server. The purpose of this object is to give you information on a message without having to download the entire message, and thus to allow much faster access.
ReportItem	The ReportItem object represents a system message, which is usually sent when a problem has occurred with a mail message sent by the user. This message will outline what the problem was.
SyncObject	Represents a synchronization profile for the user.

Table Continued on Following Page

Name	Description
TaskItem	The TaskItem object represents information about a job that needs to be completed.
TaskRequest AcceptItem	The TaskRequestAcceptItem object is created when the assigned recipient accepts a TaskRequestItem object.
TaskRequest DeclineItem	The TaskRequestDeclineItem object is created when the assigned recipient declines a TaskRequestItem object.
TaskRequest Item	The TaskRequestItem object is created in the recipient's Inbox when a TaskItem is delegated and the request is received by the recipient.
TaskRequest UpdateItem	The TaskRequestUpdateItem object is created when the assigned recipient makes a change to the status or the due date of the TaskItem object.
UserProperty	Represents a user-defined custom property added to an item.

Action Object

Methods

Name	Returns	Description
Delete		Deletes the current Action from the Actions collection.
Execute	Item	Executes the current Action and returns the item which this creates.

Properties

Name	Returns	Description
Application	Application object	Returns the parent application of the object. Read-only.
Class	OlObject Class constant	Returns a numeric value specifying the class the object belongs to. Read-only.
CopyLike	OlAction CopyLike constant	Specifies the inheritance style for the properties of the item created by the action. Read/write.
Enabled	Boolean	Specifies whether the action is to be available. Read/write.

Name	Returns	Description
MessageClass	String	A string specifying the form for the item which results from the execution of the action. Only valid for default actions. Read/write.
Name	String	The name of the Action, by which it can be referenced. Read/write.
Parent	Object	Returns the object's parent object. Read-only.
Prefix	String	A string (for example "Re") which is prefixed to the subject of the Action's parent item. Read/write.
ReplyStyle	OlAction ReplyStyle constant	A long integer indicating the style for including the original text in the new item. Read/write.
Response Style	OlAction Response Style constant	A long integer indicating whether the item created by the action should be opened or sent immediately. Read/write.
Session	NameSpace object	Returns the current NameSpace object. Read-only.
ShowOn	OlAction ShowOn constant	Specifies whether the action will be shown on the menu and/or toolbar of the item's GUI. Read/write.

AddressEntry Object

Methods

Name	Returns	Description
Delete		Deletes the current AddressEntry from the AddressEntries collection.
Details ([HWnd])		Displays a dialog box showing the properties of the AddressEntry, allowing the user to make changes to them. The optional parameter HWnd is a long integer which specifies the parent window handle. Default is zero.

Table Continued on Following Page

Name	Returns	Description
GetFreeBusy (StartDate, Interval, [Complete Format])	String	Returns a string representing the user's schedule for the next 30 days starting at the start date passed in, with each character representing a slot of Interval minutes. If CompleteFormat is False or omitted, free time is represented by a zero, busy time by a one. If CompleteFormat is True, the intervals are each represented by the appropriate OlBusyStatus constant.
Update([make Permanent], [refresh Object])		Posts the changes to the AddressEntry to the messaging system.

Properties

Name	Returns	Description
Address	String	The email address of the Recipient. Read/write.
Application	Application object	Returns the parent application of the object. Read-only.
Class	OlObject Class constant	Returns a numeric value specifying the class the object belongs to. Read-only.
DisplayType	OlDisplay Type constant	Returns the type of Recipient the AddressEntry refers to. Do not confuse this with the Type property. Read-only.
ID	String	Returns a string that uniquely identifies the object. Read-only.
Manager	AddressEntry object	Returns the AddressEntry for the manager of the user represented by the current AddressEntry. Read-only.
Members	Address Entries collection	If the AddressEntry is a distribution list, this returns a collection of AddressEntry objects for its members. Otherwise, it returns Nothing. Read-only.
Name	String	The display name for the AddressEntry. Read/write.

Name	Returns	Description
Parent	Object	Returns the object's parent object. Read-only.
Session	NameSpace object	Returns the current `NameSpace` object. Read-only.
Type	String	The type of email address (e.g. `"SMTP"`) that is stored in the `Address` property. Read/write.

AddressList Object

Properties

Name	Returns	Description
Address Entries	Address Entries collection	Returns the collection of `AddressEntry` objects that belong to the `AddressList`. Read-only.
Application	Application object	Returns the parent application of the object. Read-only.
Class	OlObject Class constant	Returns a numeric value specifying the class the object belongs to. Read-only.
ID	String	Returns a string that uniquely identifies the object. Read-only.
Index	Long	Returns the position of the `AddressList` in the `AddressLists` collection (starting from 1). Read-only.
IsReadOnly	Boolean	Specifies whether the `AddressList` object can be modified. Read-only.
Name	String	Returns the display name for the `AddressList`. Read-only.
Parent	Object	Returns the object's parent object. Read-only.
Session	NameSpace object	Returns the current `NameSpace` object. Read-only.

Application Object

Methods

Name	Returns	Description
ActiveExplorer	Explorer object	Returns the currently active Explorer object. If no explorer is active then Nothing is returned.
ActiveInspector	Inspector object	Returns the current Inspector object. If no inspector is active then Nothing is returned.
ActiveWindow	Explorer or Inspector object	Returns the topmost window for Outlook. This will either be an Explorer or Inspector object. If there is no active window then Nothing is returned.
CreateItem(Item Type)	Item	Generates a new item based on the value supplied in the parameter, which can be any of the OlItemType constants.
CreateItemFrom Template(Template Path, [Infolder])	Item	Will generate a new item in the Infolder folder, based on the template (.otf file) with the path and file name given in the TemplatePath parameter.
CreateObject (ObjectName)	Object	Creates a new automated object of the class specified in the ObjectName parameter.
GetNameSpace(Type)	NameSpace object	Gets a reference to the root object for any data source. The only Type supported is "MAPI" (though this is not case-sensitive).
Quit		Causes Outlook to close down and sign out of the messaging system.

Properties

Name	Returns	Description
Answer Wizard()	AnswerWizard object	Returns the AnswerWizard object for the Outlook application. Read-only.
Application	Application object	Returns another reference to the Application object itself. Read-only.
Assistant	Assistant object	Returns a reference to the Office Assistant. Read-only.
Class	OlObjectClass constant	Returns a numeric value specifying the class the object belongs to. Read-only.
COMAddIns	COMAddIns collection	Returns a collection that represents all of the COM add-ins loaded in Outlook. Read-only.
Explorers	Explorers collection	Returns the Explorers collection containing all loaded Explorer objects. Read-only.
Inspectors	Inspectors collection	Returns the Inspectors collection that contains all loaded Inspector objects. Read-only.
Language Settings()	Language Settings object	Returns a LanguageSettings object that represents all the language settings for Microsoft Office. Read-only.
Name	String	Returns the name of the application object. This will normally be "Outlook". Read-only.
Parent	Object	Returns the object which instantiated Outlook. If called from within an Outlook macro, this will return Nothing. Read-only.
ProductCode	String	Returns the GUID for Outlook.
Session	NameSpace object	Returns the current NameSpace object. Read-only.
Version	String	Returns the full version number for the application. Read-only.

Events

Name	Description
ItemSend	Occurs when an item is sent to the recipients.
NewMail	Occurs when a new item is received in the Inbox.
OptionsPagesAdd	Occurs before the Options dialog is shown.
Quit	Occurs when Outlook shuts down.
Reminder	Occurs before the Reminder dialog is shown.
Startup	Occurs after all the add-ins have been loaded when Outlook is starting up.

AppointmentItem Object

Methods

Name	Returns	Description
ClearRecurrence Pattern		Resets the item to a single occurrence.
Close(SaveMode)		Causes the Inspector object for the item to be closed. The SaveMode parameter specifies whether changes to the item will be saved or discarded, and may be one of the OlInspectorClose constants.
Copy	Appointment Item object	Creates and returns an identical AppointmentItem object.
Delete		Deletes the current item.
Display([Modal])		Causes the Inspector object for the item to be opened. The Modal parameter specifies whether the window is to be opened modally (True) or modelessly (False). The default is False.
ForwardAsVcal	MailItem object	Creates a new MailItem with the AppointmentItem attached as a virtual calendar item.
GetRecurrence Pattern	Recurrence Pattern object	Returns the RecurrencePattern object that contains the information about the recurrence of the appointment.

Name	Returns	Description
Move(Dest Fldr)		Moves the current `AppointmentItem` to the new `MAPIFolder`, `DestFldr`.
PrintOut		Prints the item using the printer's default settings.
Respond(IResponse, [fNoUI], [fAdditional TextDialog])	MeetingItem object	Allows the user to accept or decline the meeting. `IResponse` may be one of the `OlMeetingResponse` constants `olMeetingAccepted`, `olMeetingDecline` or `olMeetingTentative`. The `fNoUI` parameter is `True` if there is no User Interface, and `fAdditionalDialog` is `True` if the user is to be prompted to send or send with comments.
Save		Saves the item to the current folder for an existing item or to the default folder for a newly created item.
SaveAs(Path, [Type])		Saves the current item to the hard drive with the path and filename specified in the `Path` parameter. The type of file the item is to be saved as may be specified in the `Type` parameter, which may be one of the `OlSaveAsType` constants.
Send		Sends the item to the recipients defined in the `Recipients` property.

Properties

Name	Returns	Description
Actions	Actions collection	Returns an `Actions` collection of the available `Action` objects for the item. Read-only.
AllDayEvent	Boolean	Specifies whether the appointment is to occupy the whole day. Read/write.
Application	Application object	Returns the parent application of the object. Read-only.
Attachments	Attachments collection	Returns a collection of the attachments associated with the item. Read-only.

Table Continued on Following Page

Name	Returns	Description
Billing Information	String	Contains a free-form string that can be used to hold the billing information associated with the item. Read/write.
Body	String	A free-form string containing the body of the item. Setting this causes the EditorType of the item's Inspector object to revert to default. Read/write.
BusyStatus	OlBusyStatus constant	Indicates the busy status for the user for this appointment. Read/write.
Categories	String	Specifies the categories that are assigned to the item. Read/write.
Class	OlObject Class constant	Returns a numeric value specifying the class the object belongs to. Read-only.
Companies	String	A free form string containing the company names associated with the item. Read/write.
Conference ServerAllow External	Boolean	Reserved for future use.
Conference Server Password	String	Reserved for future use.
ConversationIndex	String	Returns the index representing the current conversation thread. Read-only.
ConversationTopic	String	Returns the topic for the conversation thread. Read-only.
CreationTime	Date	Returns the date and time at which the item was created. Read-only.
Duration	Long	Specifies the length of time that the appointment is due to last, in minutes. Read/write.
End	Date	Specifies the date and time at which the appointment is due to finish. Read/write.
EntryID	String	Returns a unique string identifier for the item. Read-only.

Name	Returns	Description
Form Description	Form Description object	Returns the FormDescription object for the item. Read-only.
GetInspector	Inspector object	Returns the Inspector object for displaying the current item. Read-only.
Importance	OlImportance constant	Specifies the importance level for the item. Read/write.
IsOnline Meeting	Boolean	Specifies whether the appointment is an on-line meeting or not. Read/write.
IsRecurring	Boolean	Indicates whether this is a recurring appointment or not. Read-only.
Last Modification Time	Date	Returns the date and time that the item was last changed. Read-only.
Links	Links collection	Returns a Links collection that represents the contacts with which this item is associated. Read-only.
Location	String	Contains information that identifies where the appointment is to occur. Read/write.
Meeting Status	OlMeeting Status constant	Specifies the status for the meeting. Read/write.
MessageClass	String	Specifies the message class of the item. This property maps you to the form that is associated with the item. Read/write.
Mileage	String	A free-form string which can be used to hold the mileage for the item. Read/write.
NetMeeting AutoStart	Boolean	Specifies whether an online meeting should be started automatically or not. Read/write.
NetMeeting DocPathName	String	Specifies the path for the Office document that is associated with the meeting. Read/write.
NetMeeting Organizer Alias	String	Specifies the email address for the organizer of the meeting. Read/write.

Table Continued on Following Page

Name	Returns	Description
NetMeeting Server	String	Specifies the name of the net server that will host the meeting. Read/write.
NetMeeting Type	OlNetMeeting Type constant	Specifies the type of meeting. Read/write
NetShowURL	String	Specifies the URL for a NetShow meeting. Read/write.
NoAging	Boolean	Specifies whether or not the item can be archived. Read/write.
Optional Attendees	String	Returns the string of names of the optional attendees. Read-only.
Organizer	String	Returns the name of the organizer. Read-only.
Outlook Internal Version	Long	Returns the build number of the Outlook version used to create the item. Read-only.
Outlook Version	String	Returns the major and minor version number for the Outlook Application used to create the item. For Outlook 2000, this is "9.0". Read-only.
Parent	Object	Returns the object's parent object. Read-only.
Recipients	Recipients collection	Returns the collection of Recipients that have been invited to the appointment. Read-only.
Recurrence State	OlRecurrence State constant	Returns the recurrence status of the appointment. Read-only.
Reminder Minutes BeforeStart	Long	Specifies the number of minutes the reminder should occur before the start of the appointment. Read/write.
Reminder Override Default	Boolean	Specifies whether the defaults for the reminder should be ignored. Read/write.
ReminderPlay Sound	Boolean	Specifies whether the reminder should play a sound or not. Read/write.
ReminderSet	Boolean	Specifies whether a reminder should be fired for this appointment. Read/write.

Name	Returns	Description
Reminder SoundFile	String	Specifies the path and filename for the sound file for the reminder. Read/write.
ReplyTime	Date	Specifies the date and time when the reply to the meeting request was sent. Read/write.
Required Attendees	String	A semicolon-delimited string of the names of the required attendees for the appointment. Read/write.
Resources	String	A semicolon-delimited string containing the names of resources (recipients who will be blind-CC'd) for this meeting. Read/write.
Response Requested	Boolean	Specifies whether the originator wants a response to the meeting request or not. Read/write.
Response Status	OlResponse Status constant	Specifies the status for the appointment. Read/write.
Saved	Boolean	Indicates whether the item has changed since it was last saved. Read-only.
Sensitivity	OlSensitivity constant	Specifies the level of sensitivity for the item. Read/write.
Session	NameSpace object	Returns the current NameSpace object. Read-only.
Size	Long	Returns the size of the item in bytes. Read-only.
Start	Date	Specifies the start date and time for the appointment. Read/write.
Subject	String	Contains the subject of the item. Read/write.
UnRead	Boolean	Indicates whether the item is to be marked as "Unread". Read/write.
User Properties	User Properties collection	Returns the UserProperties collection for the item. Read-only.

Events

Name	Description
AttachmentAdd	Occurs when a new attachment is added to the item.
AttachmentRead	Occurs when an attachment is opened.
BeforeAttachment Save	Occurs just before the attachment is saved.
BeforeCheckNames	Occurs just before Outlook resolves the recipients for the item.
Close	Occurs when the Inspector object is shut down.
CustomAction	Occurs when a custom action is executed.
CustomProperty Change	Occurs when one of the custom properties for the item is changed.
Forward	Occurs when the item is forwarded.
Open	Occurs when the item is opened in an Inspector.
PropertyChange	Occurs when one of the non-custom properties is changed.
Read	Occurs when the item is opened for editing.
Reply	Occurs when the Reply action is executed on the item.
ReplyAll	Occurs when the ReplyAll action is executed on the item.
Send	Occurs when the item is sent.
Write	Occurs when the Save or SaveAs method is executed on the item.

Attachment Object

Methods

Name	Returns	Description
Delete		Deletes the current Attachment from the Attachments collection.
SaveAsFile(Path)		Saves the attachment with the specified path and filename.

Properties

Name	Returns	Description
Application	Application object	Returns the parent application of the object. Read-only.
Class	OlObjectClass constant	Returns a numeric value specifying the class the object belongs to. Read-only.
DisplayName	String	The name displayed below the attachment icon (this does not have to be the attachment's filename.) Read/write.
FileName	String	The attachment's filename. Read-only.
Index	Long	Returns the position of the Attachment in the Attachments collection (starting from 1). Read-only.
Parent	Object	Returns the object's parent object. Read-only.
PathName	String	The attachment's full path (for a linked attachment). Read-only.
Position	Long	Specifies the position of the attachment within the body of the item. Read/write.
Session	NameSpace object	Returns the current NameSpace object. Read-only.
Type	OlAttachmentType constant	Returns the type of the attachment. Read-only.

ContactItem Object

Methods

Name	Returns	Description
Close (SaveMode)		Causes the Inspector object for the item to be closed. The SaveMode parameter specifies whether changes to the item will be saved or discarded, and may be one of the OlInspectorClose constants.

Table Continued on Following Page

Name	Returns	Description
Copy	Contact Item object	Creates and returns an identical ContactItem object.
Delete		Deletes the current contact item.
Display ([Modal])		Causes the Inspector object for the item to be opened. The Modal parameter specifies whether the window is to be opened modally (True) or modelessly (False). The default is False.
ForwardAs Vcard	MailItem object	Forwards the contact as an attachment to the returned MailItem.
Move (DestFldr)		Moves the current ContactItem to the new MAPIFolder, DestFldr.
PrintOut		Prints the item using the printer's default settings.
Save		Saves the item to the current folder for an existing item or to the default folder for a newly created item.
SaveAs(Path, [Type])		Saves the current item to the hard drive with the path and filename specified in the Path parameter. The type of file the item is to be saved as may be specified in the Type parameter, which may be one of the OlSaveAsType constants.

Properties

Name	Returns	Description
Account	String	Specifies the account information. Read/write.
Actions	Actions collection	Returns an Actions collection of the available Action objects for the item. Read-only.
Anniversary	Date	Specifies the date of the contact's anniversary. Read/write.
Application	Application object	Returns the parent application of the object. Read-only.

Name	Returns	Description
AssistantName	String	The name of the contact's assistant. Read/write.
Assistant Telephone Number	String	The telephone number for the contact's assistant. Read/write.
Attachments	Attachments collection	Returns a collection of the attachments associated with the item. Read-only.
Billing Information	String	Contains a free-form string that can be used to hold the billing information associated with the item. Read/write.
Birthday	Date	The date of the contact's birthday. Read/write
Body	String	A free-form string containing the body of the item. Setting this causes the EditorType of the item's Inspector object to revert to default. Read/write.
Business2 Telephone Number	String	The second business telephone number for the contact. Read/write.
Business Address	String	The entire unparsed business address for the contact. Read/write.
Business AddressCity	String	The city part of the contact's business address. Read/write.
Business AddressCountry	String	The country part of the contact's business address. Read/write.
Business AddressPostal Code	String	The postal code part of the contact's business address. Read/write.
Business AddressPost OfficeBox	String	The Post Office Box of the contact's business address. Read/write.
Business AddressState	String	The state code for the contact's business address. Read/write.

Table Continued on Following Page

Name	Returns	Description
Business AddressStreet	String	The street information for the contact's business address. Read/write.
BusinessFax Number	String	The contact's business fax number. Read/write.
BusinessHome Page	String	The URL of the home web page of the business. Read/write.
Business Telephone Number	String	The contact's business telephone number. Read/write.
Callback Telephone Number	String	The telephone number at which the contact may be called back. Read/write.
CarTelephone Number	String	The contact's car telephone number. Read/write.
Categories	String	Specifies the categories that are assigned to the item. Read/write.
Children	String	The names of the contact's children. Read/write.
Class	OlObject Class constant	Returns a numeric value specifying the class the object belongs to. Read-only.
Companies	String	A free form string containing the company names associated with the item. Read/write.
CompanyAndFull Name	String	A concatenation of the CompanyName and the contact's full name. Read-only.
CompanyLast FirstNoSpace	String	The CompanyName concatenated with the contact's LastName, FirstName and MiddleName, having no spaces between and the last and first names. Read-only.
CompanyLast FirstSpaceOnly	String	The CompanyName concatenated with the LastName, FirstName and MiddleName, with a space between and the last and first name. Read-only.

Name	Returns	Description
CompanyMain Telephone Number	String	The main telephone number for the contact's company. Read/write.
CompanyName	String	The name of the company that the contact works for. Read/write.
Computer NetworkName	String	The name of the contact's computer network. Read/write.
Conversation Index	String	Returns the index representing the current conversation thread. Read-only.
Conversation Topic	String	Returns the topic for the conversation thread. Read-only.
CreationTime	Date	Returns the date and time at which the item was created. Read-only.
CustomerID	String	The customer ID for the contact. Read/write.
Department	String	The name of the department the contact works in. Read/write.
Email1Address	String	The contact's first email address. Read/write.
Email1Address Type	String	The address type (e.g. "SMTP") of the contact's first email address. Read/write.
Email1Display Name	String	The display name for the contact's first email address. This is formed from the FullName property. Read-only.
Email1EntryID	String	The entry ID of the contact's first email address. Read-only.
Email2Address	String	The contact's second email address. Read/write.
Email2Address Type	String	The address type (e.g. "SMTP") of the contact's second email address. Read/write.
Email2Display Name	String	The display name for the contact's second email address. This is formed from the FullName property. Read-only.
Email2EntryID	String	The entry ID of the contact's second email address. Read-only.

Table Continued on Following Page

Name	Returns	Description
Email3Address	String	The contact's third email address. Read/write.
Email3Address Type	String	The address type (e.g. "SMTP") of the contact's third email address. Read/write.
Email3Display Name	String	The display name for the contact's third email address. This is formed from the FullName property. Read-only.
Email3EntryID	String	The entry ID of the contact's third email address. Read-only.
EntryID	String	Returns a unique string identifier for the item. Read-only.
FileAs	String	The keyword for the contact. Read/write.
FirstName	String	The contact's first name. Read/write.
Form Description	Form Description object	Returns the FormDescription object for the item. Read-only.
FTPSite	String	The contact's FTP site entry. Read/write.
FullName	String	The whole name of the contact. Read/write.
FullNameAnd Company	String	The full name and the company name concatenated together. Read-only.
Gender	OlGender constant	The gender of the contact. Read/write.
GetInspector	Inspector object	Returns the Inspector object for displaying the current item. Read-only.
GovernmentID Number	String	The government ID number for the contact. Read/write.
Hobby	String	The contact's hobby. Read/write.
Home2Telephone Number	String	The second home telephone number for the contact. Read/write.

Name	Returns	Description
HomeAddress	String	The entire unparsed home address of the contact. Read/write.
HomeAddress City	String	The city part of the home address. Read/write.
HomeAddress Country	String	The country part of the home address. Read/write.
HomeAddress PostalCode	String	The postal code part of the home address. Read/write.
HomeAddress PostOfficeBox	String	The Post Office Box of the home address. Read/write.
HomeAddress State	String	The state code for the home address. Read/write.
HomeAddress Street	String	The street information for the home address. Read/write.
HomeFaxNumber	String	The contact's home fax number. Read/write.
HomeTelephone Number	String	The home telephone number of the contact. Read/write.
Importance	OlImportance constant	Specifies the importance of this contact. Read/write.
Initials	String	The initials of the contact. These are extracted from the FullName. Read/write (but note that any changes to this property will be overridden by the FullName property).
InternetFree BusyAddress	String	The URL for the contact's free/busy information. Read/write.
ISDNNumber	String	The contact's ISDN number. Read/write.
JobTitle	String	The contact's job title. Read/write.
Journal	Boolean	Specifies whether all transactions are to be entered into the journal. Read/write.
Language	String	Specifies the language for the contact. Read/write.

Table Continued on Following Page

487

Name	Returns	Description
LastFirstAnd Suffix	String	Returns the `LastName`, `FirstName`, `MiddleName` and `Suffix` with a comma between the last and first names; all the other names have a space between them. Returns nothing if there is no suffix. Read-only.
LastFirstNo Space	String	Returns the `LastName`, `FirstName` and `MiddleName` with no space between the last and first names. Read-only.
LastFirstNo SpaceCompany	String	Returns the `LastName`, `FirstName` and `MiddleName` with no space between the last and first names, followed by the company name. Read-only.
LastFirstSpace Only	String	Returns the `LastName`, `FirstName` and `MiddleName` with a space between them. Read-only.
LastFirstSpace OnlyCompany	String	Returns the `LastName`, `FirstName` and `MiddleName` with a space between them, followed by the company name. Read-only.
Last Modification Time	Date	Returns the date and time that the item was last changed. Read-only.
LastName	String	Specifies the contact's last name. Read/write.
LastNameAnd FirstName	String	Returns the `LastName` and `FirstName`, separated by a comma. Read-only.
Links	Links collection	Returns a `Links` collection that represents the other contacts with which this contact is associated. Read-only.
MailingAddress	String	The entire unparsed mailing address of the contact. By default this is the address specified by the `SelectedMailingAddress` property. Read/write.
MailingAddress City	String	The city part of the mailing address. Read/write.
MailingAddress Country	String	The country part of the mailing address. Read/write.

Name	Returns	Description
MailingAddress PostalCode	String	The postal code part of the mailing address. Read/write.
MailingAddress PostOfficeBox	String	The Post Office Box of the mailing address. Read/write.
MailingAddress State	String	The state code for the mailing address. Read/write.
MailingAddress Street	String	The street information for the mailing address. Read/write.
ManagerName	String	The name of the manager of the contact. Read/write.
MessageClass	String	Specifies the message class of the item. This property maps you to the form that is associated with the item. Read/write.
MiddleName	String	The middle name of the contact. Read/write.
Mileage	String	A free-form string which can be used to hold the mileage for the item. Read/write.
Mobile Telephone Number	String	The contact's mobile phone number. Read/write.
NetMeeting Alias	String	The contact's ID or alias for Net Meetings. Read/write.
NetMeeting Server	String	The name of the server to host the Net Meeting. Read/write.
NickName	String	The contact's nickname. Read/write.
NoAging	Boolean	Specifies whether or not the item can be archived. Read/write.
OfficeLocation	String	The office location information for the contact. Read/write.
Organizational IDNumber	String	The organizational ID number for the contact. Read/write.
OtherAddress	String	The entire, unparsed form of another address for the contact. Read/write.
OtherAddress City	String	The city part of the other address. Read/write.

Name	Returns	Description
OtherAddress Country	String	The country part of the other address. Read/write.
OtherAddress PostalCode	String	The postal code part of the other address. Read/write.
OtherAddress PostOfficeBox	String	The Post Office Box part of the other address. Read/write.
OtherAddress State	String	The state code for the other address. Read/write.
OtherAddress Street	String	The street information for the other address. Read/write.
OtherFaxNumber	String	Another fax number for the contact. Read/write.
OtherTelephone Number	String	Another telephone number for the contact. Read/write.
Outlook Internal Version	Long	Returns the build number of the Outlook version used to create the item. Read-only.
Outlook Version	String	Returns the major and minor version number for the Outlook Application used to create the item. For Outlook 2000, this is "9.0". Read-only.
PagerNumber	String	The contact's pager number. Read/write.
Parent	Object	Returns the object's parent object. Read-only.
PersonalHome Page	String	The URL for the contact's personal web page. Read/write.
Primary Telephone Number	String	The primary phone number for the contact. Read/write.
Profession	String	The profession of the contact. Read/write.
RadioTelephone Number	String	The radio telephone number of the contact. Read/write.
ReferredBy	String	The name of the person that referred this contact to you. Read/write.
Saved	Boolean	Indicates whether the item has changed since it was last saved. Read-only.

Name	Returns	Description
Selected MailingAddress	OlMailing Address constant	Specifies which address is the mailing address: none, home, business or other. Read/write.
Sensitivity	OlSensitivity constant	Specifies the level of sensitivity for the item. Read/write.
Session	NameSpace object	Returns the current NameSpace object. Read-only.
Size	Long	Returns the size of the item in bytes. Read-only.
Spouse	String	The name of the contact's spouse. Read/write.
Subject	String	Contains the subject of the item. Read/write.
Suffix	String	The contact's suffix. Read/write.
TelexNumber	String	The contact's telex number. Read/write.
Title	String	The contact's title. Read/write.
TTYTDD Telephone Number	String	The TTY/TDD telephone number of the contact. Read/write.
UnRead	Boolean	Indicates whether the item is to be marked as "Unread". Read/write.
User1	String	The first MS Schedule+ user for the contact. Read/write.
User2	String	The second MS Schedule+ user for the contact. Read/write.
User3	String	The third MS Schedule+ user. for the contact. Read/write.
User4	String	The fourth MS Schedule+ user for the contact. Read/write.
User Certificate	String	The authentication certificate for the contact. Read/write.
UserProperties	User Properties collection	Returns the UserProperties collection for the item. Read-only.

Name	Returns	Description
WebPage	String	The URL for the contact's web page. Read/write.
YomiCompanyName	String	The Japanese phonetic rendering of the company name. Read/write.
YomiFirstName	String	The Japanese phonetic rendering of the contact's first name. Read/write.
YomiLastName	String	The Japanese phonetic rendering of the contact's last name. Read/write.

Events

Name	Description
AttachmentAdd	Occurs when a new attachment is added to the item.
AttachmentRead	Occurs when an attachment is opened.
BeforeAttachment Save	Occurs just before the attachment is saved.
BeforeCheckNames	Occurs just before Outlook resolves the recipients for the item.
Close	Occurs when the Inspector object is shut down.
CustomAction	Occurs when a custom action is executed.
CustomProperty Change	Occurs when one of the custom properties for the item is changed.
Forward	Occurs when the item is forwarded.
Open	Occurs when the item is opened in an Inspector.
PropertyChange	Occurs when one of the non-custom properties is changed.
Read	Occurs when the item is opened for editing.
Reply	Occurs when the Reply action is executed on the item.
ReplyAll	Occurs when the ReplyAll action is executed on the item.
Send	Occurs when the item is sent.
Write	Occurs when the Save or SaveAs method is executed on the item.

DistListItem Object

Methods

Name	Returns	Description
AddMembers (Recipients)		Adds to the distribution list all the Recipient objects that are part of the Recipients collection passed in as a parameter.
Close(Save Mode)		Causes the Inspector object for the item to be closed. The SaveMode parameter specifies whether changes to the item will be saved or discarded, and may be one of the OlInspectorClose constants.
Copy	DistList Item object	Creates and returns an identical DistListItem object.
Delete		Deletes the current item.
Display ([Modal])		Causes the Inspector object for the item to be opened. The Modal parameter specifies whether the window is to be opened modally (True) or modelessly (False). The default is False.
GetMember (Index)	Recipient object	Returns the member of the distribution list specified in the Index parameter as a Recipient object.
Move(Dest Fldr)		Moves the current item to the new MAPIFolder, DestFldr.
PrintOut		Prints the item using the printer's default settings.
Remove Members (Recipients)		Removes from the distribution list all the Recipient objects that are part of the Recipients collection passed in as a parameter.
Save		Saves the item to the current folder for an existing item or to the default folder for a newly created item.
SaveAs(Path , [Type])		Saves the current item to the hard drive with the path and filename specified in the Path parameter. The type of file the item is to be saved as may be specified in the Type parameter, which may be one of the OlSaveAsType constants.

Properties

Name	Returns	Description
Actions	Actions collection	Returns an Actions collection of the available Action objects for the item. Read-only.
Application	Application object	Returns the parent application of the object. Read-only.
Attachments	Attachments collection	Returns a collection of the attachments associated with the item. Read-only.
Billing Information	String	Contains a free-form string that can be used to hold the billing information associated with the item. Read/write.
Body	String	A free-form string containing the body of the item. Setting this causes the EditorType of the item's Inspector object to revert to default. Read/write.
Categories	String	Specifies the categories that are assigned to the item. Read/write.
Class	OlObject Class constant	Returns a numeric value specifying the class the object belongs to. Read-only.
Companies	String	A free form string containing the company names associated with the item. Read/write.
Conversation Index	String	Returns the index representing the current conversation thread. Read-only.
Conversation Topic	String	Returns the topic for the conversation thread. Read-only.
CreationTime	Date	Returns the date and time at which the item was created. Read-only.
DLName	String	Specifies the name of the distribution list. Read/write.
EntryID	String	Returns a unique string identifier for the item. Read-only.
Form Description	Form Description object	Returns the FormDescription object for the item. Read-only.

Name	Returns	Description
GetInspector	Inspector object	Returns the Inspector object for displaying the current item. Read-only.
Importance	OlImportance constant	Specifies the importance level for the item. Read/write.
Last Modification Time	Date	Returns the date and time that the item was last changed. Read-only.
Links	Links collection	Returns a Links collection that represents the contacts with which this item is associated. Read-only.
MemberCount	Long	Returns the number of members in the distribution list. Read-only.
MessageClass	String	Specifies the message class of the item. This property maps you to the form that is associated with the item. Read/write.
Mileage	String	A free-form string which can be used to hold the mileage for the item. Read/write.
NoAging	Boolean	Specifies whether or not the item can be archived. Read/write.
Outlook Internal Version	Long	Returns the build number of the Outlook version used to create the item. Read-only.
Outlook Version	String	Returns the major and minor version number for the Outlook Application used to create the item. For Outlook 2000, this is "9.0". Read-only.
Parent	Object	Returns the object's parent object. Read-only.
Saved	Boolean	Indicates whether the item has changed since it was last saved. Read-only.
Sensitivity	OlSensitivity constant	Specifies the level of sensitivity for the item. Read/write.

Table Continued on Following Page

Name	Returns	Description
Session	NameSpace object	Returns the current NameSpace object. Read-only.
Size	Long	Returns the size of the item in bytes. Read-only.
Subject	String	Contains the subject of the item. Read/write.
UnRead	Boolean	Indicates whether the item is to be marked as "Unread". Read/write.
User Properties	UserProperties collection	Returns the UserProperties collection for the item. Read-only.

Events

Name	Description
AttachmentAdd	Occurs when a new attachment is added to the item.
AttachmentRead	Occurs when an attachment is opened.
BeforeAttachment Save	Occurs just before the attachment is saved.
BeforeCheckNames	Occurs just before Outlook resolves the recipients for the item.
Close	Occurs when the Inspector object is shut down.
CustomAction	Occurs when a custom action is executed.
CustomProperty Change	Occurs when one of the custom properties for the item is changed.
Forward	Occurs when the item is forwarded.
Open	Occurs when the item is opened in an Inspector.
PropertyChange	Occurs when one of the non-custom properties is changed.
Read	Occurs when the item is opened for editing.
Reply	Occurs when the Reply action is executed on the item.
ReplyAll	Occurs when the ReplyAll action is executed on the item.
Send	Occurs when the item is sent.
Write	Occurs when the Save or SaveAs method is executed on the item.

DocumentItem Object

Methods

Name	Returns	Description
Close (SaveMode)		Causes the Inspector object for the item to be closed. The SaveMode parameter specifies whether changes to the item will be saved or discarded, and may be one of the OlInspectorClose constants.
Copy	DocumentItem object	Creates and returns an identical DocumentItem object.
Delete		Deletes the current item.
Display ([Modal])		Causes the Inspector object for the item to be opened. The Modal parameter specifies whether the window is to be opened modally (True) or modelessly (False). The default is False.
Move (DestFldr)		Moves the current item to the new MAPIFolder, DestFldr.
PrintOut		Prints the item using the printer's default settings.
Save		Saves the item to the current folder for an existing item or to the default folder for a newly created item.
SaveAs (Path, [Type])		Saves the current item to the hard drive with the path and filename specified in the Path parameter. The type of file the item is to be saved as may be specified in the Type parameter, which may be one of the OlSaveAsType constants.

Properties

Name	Returns	Description
Actions	Actions collection	Returns an Actions collection of the available Action objects for the item. Read-only.
Application	Application object	Returns the parent application of the object. Read-only.

Table Continued on Following Page

497

Name	Returns	Description
Attachments	Attachments collection	Returns a collection of the attachments associated with the item. Read-only.
Billing Information	String	Contains a free-form string that can be used to hold the billing information associated with the item. Read/write.
Body	String	A free-form string containing the body of the item. Setting this causes the EditorType of the item's Inspector object to revert to default. Read/write.
Categories	String	Specifies the categories that are assigned to the item. Read/write.
Class	OlObject Class constant	Returns a numeric value specifying the class the object belongs to. Read-only.
Companies	String	A free form string containing the company names associated with the item. Read/write.
Conversation Index	String	Returns the index representing the current conversation thread. Read-only.
Conversation Topic	String	Returns the topic for the conversation thread. Read-only.
CreationTime	Date	Returns the date and time at which the item was created. Read-only.
EntryID	String	Returns a unique string identifier for the item. Read-only.
Form Description	Form Description object	Returns the FormDescription object for the item. Read-only.
GetInspector	Inspector object	Returns the Inspector object for displaying the current item. Read-only.
Importance	OlImportance constant	Specifies the importance level for the item. Read/write.
Last Modification Time	Date	Returns the date and time that the item was last changed. Read-only.
Links	Links collection	Returns a Links collection that represents the contacts with which this item is associated. Read-only.

Name	Returns	Description
Message Class	String	Specifies the message class of the item. This property maps you to the form that is associated with the item. Read/write.
Mileage	String	A free-form string which can be used to hold the mileage for the item. Read/write.
NoAging	Boolean	Specifies whether or not the item can be archived. Read/write.
Outlook Internal Version	Long	Returns the build number of the Outlook version used to create the item. Read-only.
Outlook Version	String	Returns the major and minor version number for the Outlook Application used to create the item. For Outlook 2000, this is `"9.0"`. Read-only.
Parent	Object	Returns the object's parent object. Read-only.
Saved	Boolean	Indicates whether the item has changed since it was last saved. Read-only.
Sensitivity	OlSensitivity constant	Specifies the level of sensitivity for the item. Read/write.
Session	NameSpace object	Returns the current NameSpace object. Read-only.
Size	Long	Returns the size of the item in bytes. Read-only.
Subject	String	Contains the subject of the item. Read/write.
UnRead	Boolean	Indicates whether the item is to be marked as `"Unread"`. Read/write.
User Properties	User Properties collection	Returns the UserProperties collection for the item. Read-only.

Events

Name	Description
AttachmentAdd	Occurs when a new attachment is added to the item.
AttachmentRead	Occurs when an attachment is opened.
BeforeAttachment Save	Occurs just before the attachment is saved.
BeforeCheckNames	Occurs just before Outlook resolves the recipients for the item.
Close	Occurs when the Inspector object is shut down.
CustomAction	Occurs when a custom action is executed.
CustomProperty Change	Occurs when one of the custom properties for the item is changed.
Forward	Occurs when the item is forwarded.
Open	Occurs when the item is opened in an Inspector.
PropertyChange	Occurs when one of the non-custom properties is changed.
Read	Occurs when the item is opened for editing.
Reply	Occurs when the Reply action is executed on the item.
ReplyAll	Occurs when the ReplyAll action is executed on the item.
Send	Occurs when the item is sent.
Write	Occurs when the Save or SaveAs method is executed on the item.

Exception Object

Properties

Name	Returns	Description
Application	Application object	Returns the parent application of the object. Read-only.
AppointmentItem	Appointment Item object	Returns the instance of the AppointmentItem which is the exception to the recurrence pattern. Read-only.
Class	OlObjectClass constant	Returns a numeric value specifying the class the object belongs to. Read-only.

Name	Returns	Description
Deleted	Boolean	Indicates whether the AppointmentItem has been deleted from the recurrence pattern. Read-only.
OriginalDate	Date	Returns the original date and time of the AppointmentItem. Read-only.
Parent	Object	Returns the object's parent object. Read-only.
Session	NameSpace object	Returns the current NameSpace object. Read-only.

Explorer Object

Methods

Name	Returns	Description
Activate		Causes the Explorer window to move to the foreground.
Close		Closes the Explorer object.
Display		Opens the Explorer object (included for backward compatibility).
IsPaneVisible (Pane)	Boolean	Indicates whether a pane is visible in the explorer. The parameter Pane must be one of the OlPane constants.
ShowPane (Pane, Visible)		Displays or hides the pane specified in the Pane parameter, which should be one of the OlPane constants. Visible must be set to True to show the pane or False to hide it.

Properties

Name	Returns	Description
Application	Application object	Returns the parent application of the object. Read-only.
Caption	String	Returns the title of the explorer window. Read-only.

Table Continued on Following Page

501

Name	Returns	Description
Class	OlObject Class constant	Returns a numeric value specifying the class the object belongs to. Read-only.
CommandBars	CommandBars collection	Returns a collection representing all the toolbars and menus available for the explorer. Read-only.
Current Folder	MAPIFolder object	Specifies the currently displayed MAPIFolder. Read/write.
CurrentView	String	Specifies the current view for the explorer. Read/write.
Height	Long	Specifies the height of the explorer in pixels. Read/write.
Left	Long	Specifies the number of pixels the left edge of the explorer window is from the left edge of the screen. Read/write.
Panes	Panes collection	Returns the collection of panes currently displayed by the explorer. Read-only.
Parent	Object	Returns the object's parent object. Read-only.
Selection	Items collection	Returns a Selection collection of all the selected items in the Explorer object. Read-only.
Session	NameSpace object	Returns the current NameSpace object. Read-only.
Top	Long	Specifies the number of pixels the top edge of the explorer window is from the top edge of the screen. Read/write.
Width	Long	Specifies the width of the explorer window in pixels. Read/write.
WindowState	OlWindow State constant	Specifies whether the window is normal, maximized or minimized. Read/write.

Events

Name	Description
Activate	Occurs when the explorer window becomes the active window.

Name	Description
BeforeFolder Switch	Occurs before the active MAPIFolder is switched.
BeforeViewSwitch	Occurs before the active view is switched.
Deactivate	Occurs when the explorer window is deactivated and another window becomes active.
FolderSwitch	Occurs when a new MAPIFolder is activated.
SelectionChange	Occurs when the current collection of selected items is changed.
ViewSwitch	Occurs when the view is changed.

FormDescription Object

Method

Name	Description
PublishForm (Registry, [Folder])	Registers the FormDescription object in the form registry. Registry is one of the OlFormRegistry constants and defines the class of the form; Folder (used only with folder form registry) is a MAPIFolder object which specifies the folder from which the form must be accessed.

Properties

Name	Returns	Description
Application	Application object	Returns the parent application of the object. Read-only.
Category	String	The category assigned to the FormDescription. Read/write.
CategorySub	String	The sub-category assigned to the FormDescription. Read/write.
Class	OlObjectClass constant	Returns a numeric value specifying the class the object belongs to. Read-only.
Comment	String	A comment assigned to the FormDescription. Read/write.

Table Continued on Following Page

Name	Returns	Description
ContactName	String	The name of a person to contact about the FormDescription. Read/write.
DisplayName	String	The display name of the form. Read/write.
Hidden	Boolean	Specifies whether the form is hidden (whether it can be used only as the response from another custom form). Read/write.
Icon	String	The path and filename of the icon for the form. Read/write.
Locked	Boolean	Specifies whether the form can be modified. Read/write.
MessageClass	String	Specifies the message class of the item. This property maps you to the form that is associated with the item. Read-only.
MiniIcon	String	The path and filename of the mini-icon for the form. Read/write.
Name	String	The name of the FormDescription object and the caption for the form. Read/write.
Number	String	The number for the form. Read/write.
OneOff	Boolean	Specifies whether the form will be discarded after use. Read/write.
Parent	Object	Returns the object's parent object. Read-only.
Password	String	Specifies the password required to modify the form. Read/write.
ScriptText	String	A string containing all the VBScript for the form. Read-only.
Session	Name Space object	Returns the current NameSpace object. Read-only.
Template	String	The name of the form's template (.dot file). Read/write.
UseWordMail	Boolean	Specifies whether MS Word is to be used as the default editor for the form. Read/write.
Version	String	Specifies the version number. Read/write.

Inspector Object

Methods

Name	Returns	Description
Activate		Causes the Inspector move to the foreground.
Close (SaveMode)		Closes the Inspector object with the option of saving the changes (specified in the SaveMode parameter, which can be one of the OlInspectorClose constants).
Display ([Modal])		Opens the Inspector. The parameter specifies the modality of the inspector window: True for modal and False for modeless. Note that not all Inspector objects support modal display.
HideFormPage(PageName)		Causes the form page with the display name PageName to be hidden.
IsWordMail	Boolean	Specifies whether the item is actually shown in an Inspector object (False) or in Microsoft Word (True).
SetCurrentFormPage(PageName)		Displays the form page with the display name PageName and causes it to have the focus.
ShowFormPage(PageName)		Shows the form page with the display name PageName but does not set the focus to it.

Properties

Name	Returns	Description
Application	Application object	Returns the parent application of the object. Read-only.
Caption	String	Returns the title of the inspector window. Read-only.
Class	OlObject Class constant	Returns a numeric value specifying the class the object belongs to. Read-only.
CommandBars	CommandBars collection	Returns a collection representing all the toolbars and menus available for the inspector. Read-only.

Table Continued on Following Page

Name	Returns	Description
CurrentItem	Item	Returns the item being displayed by the inspector. Read-only.
EditorType	OlEditorType constant	Returns a constant that defines the type of editor that that will be used to display the item. Read-only.
Height	Long	Specifies the height of the inspector in pixels. Read/write.
HTMLEditor	HTML Document Object Model	Returns the HTML DOM of the message being displayed. Read-only.
Left	Long	Specifies the number of pixels the left edge of the inspector window is from the left edge of the screen. Read/write.
ModifiedFormPages	Pages collection	Returns the form pages that are available in the item, which can include up to five customizable pages. Read-only.
Parent	Object	Returns the object's parent object. Read-only.
Session	NameSpace object	Returns the current NameSpace object. Read-only.
Top	Long	Specifies the number of pixels the top edge of the inspector window is from the top edge of the screen. Read/write.
Width	Long	Specifies the width of the inspector window in pixels. Read/write.
WindowState	OlWindowState constant	Specifies whether the window is normal, maximized or minimized. Read/write.
WordEditor	Word Document Object Model	Returns the Word object model for the message being displayed. Read-only.

Events

Name	Description
Activate	Occurs when the inspector is activated.
Deactivate	Occurs when the inspector is deactivated and another window is activated.

JournalItem

Methods

Name	Returns	Description
Close (SaveMode)		Causes the `Inspector` object for the item to be closed. The `SaveMode` parameter specifies whether changes to the item will be saved or discarded, and may be one of the `OlInspectorClose` constants.
Copy	Journal Item object	Creates and returns an identical `JournalItem` object.
Delete		Deletes the current item.
Display ([Modal])		Causes the `Inspector` object for the item to be opened. The `Modal` parameter specifies whether the window is to be opened modally (`True`) or modelessly (`False`). The default is `False`.
Forward	MailItem object	Executes the **Forward** action on the item and returns the resulting `JournalItem`.
Move (DestFldr)		Moves the current item to the new `MAPIFolder`, `DestFldr`.
PrintOut		Prints the item using the printer's default settings.
Reply	MailItem object	Creates a `MailItem` addressed to the originator of the item.
ReplyAll	MailItem object	Creates a new `MailItem` addressed to the sender and all original recipients of the item.
Save		Saves the item to the current folder for an existing item or to the default folder for a newly created item.
SaveAs (Path, [Type])		Saves the current item to the hard drive with the path and filename specified in the `Path` parameter. The type of file the item is to be saved as may be specified in the `Type` parameter, which may be one of the `OlSaveAsType` constants.
StartTimer		Starts the timer for the journal item.
StopTimer		Stops the timer for the journal item.

Properties

Name	Returns	Description
Actions	Actions collection	Returns an Actions collection of the available Action objects for the item. Read-only.
Application	Application object	Returns the parent application of the object. Read-only.
Attachments	Attachments collection	Returns a collection of the attachments associated with the item. Read-only.
Billing Information	String	Contains a free-form string that can be used to hold the billing information associated with the item. Read/write.
Body	String	A free-form string containing the body of the item. Setting this causes the EditorType of the item's Inspector object to revert to default. Read/write.
Categories	String	Specifies the categories that are assigned to the item. Read/write.
Class	OlObject Class constant	Returns a numeric value specifying the class the object belongs to. Read-only.
Companies	String	A free form string containing the company names associated with the item. Read/write.
ContactNames	String	Returns a string containing the display names of the contacts associated with the item. Read-only.
Conversation Index	String	Returns the index representing the current conversation thread. Read-only.
Conversation Topic	String	Returns the topic for the conversation thread. Read-only.
CreationTime	Date	Returns the date and time at which the item was created. Read-only.
DocPosted	Boolean	Returns True if the journal item was posted as part of the journalized session. Read-only.
DocPrinted	Boolean	Returns True if the journal item was printed out as part of the journalized session. Read-only.
DocRouted	Boolean	Returns True if the journal item was routed as part of the journalized session. Read-only.

Name	Returns	Description
DocSaved	Boolean	Returns True if the journal item was saved as part of the journalized session. Read-only.
Duration	Long	Specifies the length of time that the item is due to last, in minutes. Read/write.
End	Date	Specifies the date and time at which the journal entry is due to finish. Read/write.
EntryID	String	Returns a unique string identifier for the item. Read-only.
Form Description	Form Description object	Returns the FormDescription object for the item. Read-only.
GetInspector	Inspector object	Returns the Inspector object for displaying the current item. Read-only.
Importance	OlImportance constant	Specifies the importance level for the item. Read/write.
Last Modification Time	Date	Returns the date and time that the item was last changed. Read-only.
Links	Links collection	Returns a Links collection that represents the contacts with which this item is associated. Read-only.
MessageClass	String	Specifies the message class of the item. This property maps you to the form that is associated with the item. Read/write.
Mileage	String	A free-form string which can be used to hold the mileage for the item. Read/write.
NoAging	Boolean	Specifies whether or not the item can be archived. Read/write.
Outlook Internal Version	Long	Returns the build number of the Outlook version used to create the item. Read-only.
Outlook Version	String	Returns the major and minor version number for the Outlook Application used to create the item. For Outlook 2000, this is "9.0". Read-only.

Table Continued on Following Page

Name	Returns	Description
Parent	Object	Returns the object's parent object. Read-only.
Recipients	Recipients collection	Returns a collection of the Recipient objects associated with the item. Read-only.
Saved	Boolean	Indicates whether the item has changed since it was last saved. Read-only.
Sensitivity	OlSensitivity constant	Specifies the level of sensitivity for the item. Read/write.
Session	NameSpace object	Returns the current NameSpace object. Read-only.
Size	Long	Returns the size of the item in bytes. Read-only.
Start	Date	Specifies the start date and time for the journal entry. Read/write.
Subject	String	Contains the subject of the item. Read/write.
Type	String	A free-form string that can be used to identify the type of the journal entry. Read/write.
UnRead	Boolean	Indicates whether the item is to be marked as "Unread". Read/write.
User Properties	User Properties collection	Returns the UserProperties collection for the item. Read-only.

Events

Name	Description
AttachmentAdd	Occurs when a new attachment is added to the item.
AttachmentRead	Occurs when an attachment is opened.
BeforeAttachmentSave	Occurs just before the attachment is saved.
BeforeCheckNames	Occurs just before Outlook resolves the recipients for the item.
Close	Occurs when the Inspector object is shut down.

Name	Description
CustomAction	Occurs when a custom action is executed.
CustomProperty Change	Occurs when one of the custom properties for the item is changed.
Forward	Occurs when the item is forwarded.
Open	Occurs when the item is opened in an Inspector.
PropertyChange	Occurs when one of the non-custom properties is changed.
Read	Occurs when the item is opened for editing.
Reply	Occurs when the Reply action is executed on the item.
ReplyAll	Occurs when the ReplyAll action is executed on the item.
Send	Occurs when the item is sent.
Write	Occurs when the Save or SaveAs method is executed on the item.

Link Object

Properties

Name	Returns	Description
Application	Application object	Returns the parent application of the object. Read-only.
Class	OlObject Class constant	Returns a numeric value specifying the class the object belongs to. Read-only.
Item	Item	Returns the item represented by the Link. Read-only.
Name	String	Returns the display name of the item represented by the Link. Read-only.
Parent	Object	Returns the object's parent object. Read-only.
Session	NameSpace object	Returns the current NameSpace object. Read-only.
Type	Long	Returns the OlObjectClass constant for the type of item the Link represents. Since in Outlook 2000, the item must always be a ContactItem, this will always return olContact, or 40. Read-only.

MailItem Object

Methods

Name	Returns	Description
ClearConversation Index		Clears the conversation index.
Close(SaveMode)		Causes the Inspector object for the item to be closed. The SaveMode parameter specifies whether changes to the item will be saved or discarded, and may be one of the OlInspectorClose constants.
Copy	MailItem object	Creates and returns an identical MailItem object.
Delete		Deletes the current item.
Display([Modal])		Causes the Inspector object for the item to be opened. The Modal parameter specifies whether the window is to be opened modally (True) or modelessly (False). The default is False.
Forward	MailItem object	Executes the **Forward** action on the item and returns the resulting MailItem.
Move(DestFldr)		Moves the current item to the new MAPIFolder, DestFldr.
PrintOut		Prints the item using the printer's default settings.
Reply	MailItem object	Creates a MailItem addressed to the originator of the item.
ReplyAll	MailItem object	Creates a new MailItem addressed to the sender and all original recipients of the item.
Save		Saves the item to the current folder for an existing item or to the default folder for a newly created item.

Name	Returns	Description
SaveAs(Path, [Type])		Saves the current item to the hard drive with the path and filename specified in the Path parameter. The type of file the item is to be saved as may be specified in the Type parameter, which may be one of the OlSaveAsType constants.
Send		Sends the item to the recipients defined in the Recipients property.

Properties

Name	Returns	Description
Actions	Actions collection	Returns an Actions collection of the available Action objects for the item. Read-only.
Alternate Recipient Allowed	Boolean	If set to True then the Recipient can forward the message. Read/write.
Application	Application object	Returns the parent application of the object. Read-only.
Attachments	Attachments collection	Returns a collection of the attachments associated with the item. Read-only.
Auto Forwarded	Boolean	Specifies whether the MailItem was automatically forwarded. Read/write.
BCC	String	Returns a string containing the display names of the Blind Carbon Copy recipients. Read/write.
Billing Information	String	Contains a free-form string that can be used to hold the billing information associated with the item. Read/write.
Body	String	A free-form string containing the body of the item. Setting this causes the EditorType of the item's Inspector object to revert to default. Read/write.
Categories	String	Specifies the categories that are assigned to the item. Read/write.
CC	String	Returns a string containing the display names of the Carbon Copy recipients. Read/write.

Table Continued on Following Page

Name	Returns	Description
Class	OlObject Class constant	Returns a numeric value specifying the class the object belongs to. Read-only.
Companies	String	A free form string containing the company names associated with the item. Read/write.
Conversation Index	String	Returns the index representing the current conversation thread. Read-only.
Conversation Topic	String	Returns the topic for the conversation thread. Read-only.
CreationTime	Date	Returns the date and time at which the item was created. Read-only.
Deferred DeliveryTime	Date	Specifies the date and time when the message is due to be sent. Read/write.
DeleteAfter Submit	Boolean	Specifies whether the message is to be deleted after being sent. Read/write.
EntryID	String	Returns a unique string identifier for the item. Read-only.
ExpiryTime	Date	Specifies the date and time when the item is to become invalid and can be deleted. Read/write.
FlagDueBy	Date	Specifies the date and time by which the FlagRequest is due. Read/write.
FlagRequest	String	A free-form string specifying the request to be flagged to the recipient. Read/write.
FlagStatus	OlFlagStatus constant	Specifies the flag status for the message. Read/write.
Form Description	Form Description object	Returns the FormDescription object for the item. Read-only.
GetInspector	Inspector object	Returns the Inspector object for displaying the current item. Read-only.
HTMLBody	String	Specifies the body of the MailItem in HTML format. Read/write.
Importance	OlImportance constant	Specifies the importance level for the item. Read/write.

Name	Returns	Description
Last Modification Time	Date	Returns the date and time that the item was last changed. Read-only.
Links	Links collection	Returns a Links collection that represents the contacts with which this item is associated. Read-only.
MessageClass	String	Specifies the message class of the item. This property maps you to the form that is associated with the item. Read/write.
Mileage	String	A free-form string which can be used to hold the mileage for the item. Read/write.
NoAging	Boolean	Specifies whether or not the item can be archived. Read/write.
Originator Delivery Report Requested	Boolean	Determines whether a delivery report is returned when a message is delivered. Read/write
Outlook Internal Version	Long	Returns the build number of the Outlook version used to create the item. Read-only.
Outlook Version	String	Returns the major and minor version number for the Outlook Application used to create the item. For Outlook 2000, this is "9.0". Read-only.
Parent	Object	Returns the object's parent object. Read-only.
ReadReceipt Requested	Boolean	Specifies whether a read report will be returned upon the message being read. Read/write.
ReceivedBy EntryID	String	Returns the Entry ID of the recipient who received the message. Read-only.
ReceivedBy Name	String	Returns the display name of the recipient who received the message. Read-only.
ReceivedOn BehalfOf EntryID	String	Returns the Entry ID of the delegated recipient. Read-only.
ReceivedOn BehalfOfName	String	Returns the display name of the delegated recipient. Read-only.

Table Continued on Following Page

Name	Returns	Description
ReceivedTime	Date	Returns the date and time when the MailItem was received. Read-only.
Recipient ReassignmentP rohibited	Boolean	Specifies whether the recipient can forward the message. Read/write.
Recipients	Recipients collection	Returns a collection of the Recipient objects associated with the item. Read-only.
Reminder Override Default	Boolean	Specifies whether the defaults for the reminder should be ignored. Read/write.
ReminderPlay Sound	Boolean	Specifies whether the reminder should play a sound or not. Read/write.
ReminderSet	Boolean	Specifies whether a reminder should be fired for this item. Read/write.
Reminder SoundFile	String	Specifies the path and filename for the sound file for the reminder. Read/write.
ReminderTime	Date	Specifies the date and time when the reminder is to be fired. Read/write.
RemoteStatus	OlRemote Status constant	Specifies the remote status of the item. Read/write.
Reply Recipient Names	String	Returns a semicolon-delimited string containing the display names of the reply recipients. Read-only.
Reply Recipients	Recipients collection	Returns a collection of the recipients to be included on the reply message if the recipient should reply to the message. Read-only.
Saved	Boolean	Indicates whether the item has changed since it was last saved. Read-only.
SaveSent Message Folder	MAPIFolder object	Specifies the MAPIFolder where the copy of the message will be saved after it has been sent. Read/write.
SenderName	String	Returns the display name of the sender. Read-only.

Name	Returns	Description
Sensitivity	OlSensitivity constant	Specifies the level of sensitivity for the item. Read/write.
Sent	Boolean	Returns True if the message has already been sent. Read-only.
SentOn	Date	Returns the date and time when the item was sent. Read-only.
SentOnBehalf OfName	String	Returns the display name of the intended sender. Read/write.
Session	NameSpace object	Returns the current NameSpace object. Read-only.
Size	Long	Returns the size of the item in bytes. Read-only.
Subject	String	Contains the subject of the item. Read/write.
Submitted	Boolean	Returns True if the item has been submitted. This informs you if the message is in the Outbox but has not yet been sent. Read-only.
To	String	Contains a semicolon-delimited string containing the display names of the recipients named in the To field. Read/write.
UnRead	Boolean	Indicates whether the item is to be marked as "Unread". Read/write.
User Properties	User Properties collection	Returns the UserProperties collection for the item. Read-only.
Voting Options	String	A semicolon-delimited string containing the options for the voter. Read/write.
Voting Response	String	A string containing the voting response of the sender. Read/write.

Events

Name	Description
AttachmentAdd	Occurs when a new attachment is added to the item.
AttachmentRead	Occurs when an attachment is opened.

Table Continued on Following Page

Name	Description
BeforeAttachment Save	Occurs just before the attachment is saved.
BeforeCheckNames	Occurs just before Outlook resolves the recipients for the item.
Close	Occurs when the Inspector object is shut down.
CustomAction	Occurs when a custom action is executed.
CustomProperty Change	Occurs when one of the custom properties for the item is changed.
Forward	Occurs when the item is forwarded.
Open	Occurs when the item is opened in an Inspector.
PropertyChange	Occurs when one of the non-custom properties is changed.
Read	Occurs when the item is opened for editing.
Reply	Occurs when the Reply action is executed on the item.
ReplyAll	Occurs when the ReplyAll action is executed on the item.
Send	Occurs when the item is sent.
Write	Occurs when the Save or SaveAs method is executed on the item.

MAPIFolder Object

Methods

Name	Returns	Description
CopyTo (DestFldr)	MAPIFolder object	Copies the current MAPIFolder object to the new folder DestFldr.
Delete		Deletes the current MAPIFolder from the Folders collection.
Display		Causes the Explorer object for the MAPIFolder to be opened.
GetExplorer	Explorer object	Returns an inactive Explorer object initialized to the current MAPIFolder.
MoveTo (DestFldr)		Moves the current MAPIFolder object to the new folder DestFldr.

Properties

Name	Returns	Description
Application	Application object	Returns the parent application of the object. Read-only.
Class	OlObject Class constant	Returns a numeric value specifying the class the object belongs to. Read-only.
Default ItemType	OlItemType constant	Returns the constant that represents the default item type for the folder. Read-only.
Default MessageClass	String	Returns the message class that represents the default item type for the folder. Read-only.
Description	String	Contains the description for the MAPIFolder. Read/write.
EntryID	String	Returns a unique string identifier for the folder. Read-only.
Folders	Folders collection	Returns a collection containing all the sub-folders of the MAPIFolder. Read-only.
Items	Items collection	Returns a collection of all the items in the MAPIFolder. Read-only.
Name	String	The display name of the MAPIfolder. Read/write.
Parent	Object	Returns the object's parent object. Read-only.
Session	NameSpace object	Returns the current NameSpace object. Read-only.
StoreID	String	A unique identifier that is generated when the MAPIFolder is created. Read-only.
Type	String	The type of folder. The only type currently supported is "MAPI". Read-only.
UnReadItem Count	Long	The number of items in the folder that have not yet been read. Read-only.
WebViewAllow Navigation	Boolean	Specifies whether the Back and Forward buttons on the toolbar are enabled. Read/write.

Table Continued on Following Page

Name	Returns	Description
WebViewOn	Boolean	Specifies whether the web paged specified by the WebViewURL property is displayed. Read/write.
WebViewURL	String	Specifies the web page to be shown if WebViewOn is set to True. Read/write.

MeetingItem Object

Methods

Name	Returns	Description
Close (SaveMode)		Causes the Inspector object for the item to be closed. The SaveMode parameter specifies whether changes to the item will be saved or discarded, and may be one of the OlInspectorClose constants.
Copy	MeetingItem object	Creates and returns an identical MeetingItem object.
Delete		Deletes the current item.
Display ([Modal])		Causes the Inspector object for the item to be opened. The Modal parameter specifies whether the window is to be opened modally (True) or modelessly (False). The default is False.
Forward	MeetingItem object	Executes the Forward action on the item and returns the resulting MeetingItem.
GetAssociated Appointment (AddTo Calendar)	Appointment Item object	Returns the associated AppointmentItem object. The Boolean AddToCalendar parameter specifies whether the appointment should be added to the default calendar folder.
Move (DestFldr)		Moves the current item to the new MAPIFolder, DestFldr.
PrintOut		Prints the item using the printer's default settings.

Name	Returns	Description
Reply	MailItem object	Creates a `MailItem` addressed to the originator of the item.
ReplyAll	MailItem object	Creates a new `MailItem` addressed to the sender and all original recipients of the item.
Save		Saves the item to the current folder for an existing item or to the default folder for a newly created item.
SaveAs(Path , [Type])		Saves the current item to the hard drive with the path and filename specified in the `Path` parameter. The type of file the item is to be saved as may be specified in the `Type` parameter, which may be one of the `OlSaveAsType` constants.
Send		Sends the item to the recipients defined in the `Recipients` property.

Properties

Name	Returns	Description
Actions	Actions collection	Returns an `Actions` collection of the available `Action` objects for the item. Read-only.
Application	Application object	Returns the parent application of the object. Read-only.
Attachments	Attachments collection	Returns a collection of the attachments associated with the item. Read-only.
Auto Forwarded	Boolean	Specifies whether the `MeetingItem` was automatically forwarded. Read/write.
Billing Information	String	Contains a free-form string that can be used to hold the billing information associated with the item. Read/write.
Body	String	A free-form string containing the body of the item. Setting this causes the `EditorType` of the item's `Inspector` object to revert to default. Read/write.
Categories	String	Specifies the categories that are assigned to the item. Read/write.

Table Continued on Following Page

521

Name	Returns	Description
Class	OlObject Class constant	Returns a numeric value specifying the class the object belongs to. Read-only.
Companies	String	A free-form string containing the company names associated with the item. Read/write.
Conversation Index	String	Returns the index representing the current conversation thread. Read-only.
Conversation Topic	String	Returns the topic for the conversation thread. Read-only.
CreationTime	Date	Returns the date and time at which the item was created. Read-only.
Deferred DeliveryTime	Date	Specifies the date and time when the message is due to be sent. Read/write.
DeleteAfter Submit	Boolean	Specifies whether the message is to be deleted after being sent. Read/write.
EntryID	String	Returns a unique string identifier for the item. Read-only.
ExpiryTime	Date	Specifies the date and time when the item is to become invalid and can be deleted. Read/write.
FlagDueBy	Date	Specifies the date and time by which the FlagRequest is due. Read/write.
FlagRequest	String	A free-form string specifying the request to be flagged to the recipient. Read/write.
FlagStatus	OlFlagStatus constant	Specifies the flag status for the message. Read/write.
Form Description	Form Description object	Returns the FormDescription object for the item. Read-only.
GetInspector	Inspector object	Returns the Inspector object for displaying the current item. Read-only.
Importance	OlImportance constant	Specifies the importance level for the item. Read/write.
Last Modification Time	Date	Returns the date and time that the item was last changed. Read-only.

Name	Returns	Description
Links	Links collection	Returns a Links collection that represents the contacts with which this item is associated. Read-only.
MessageClass	String	Specifies the message class of the item. This property maps you to the form that is associated with the item. Read/write.
Mileage	String	A free-form string which can be used to hold the mileage for the item. Read/write.
NoAging	Boolean	Specifies whether or not the item can be archived. Read/write.
Originator Delivery Report Requested	Boolean	Specifies whether the originator of the meeting will receive a delivery report. Read/write.
Outlook Internal Version	Long	Returns the build number of the Outlook version used to create the item. Read-only.
Outlook Version	String	Returns the major and minor version number for the Outlook Application used to create the item. For Outlook 2000, this is "9.0". Read-only.
Parent	Object	Returns the object's parent object. Read-only.
ReceivedTime	Date	Returns the date and time when the MeetingItem was received. Read-only.
Recipients	Recipients collection	Returns a collection of the Recipient objects associated with the item. Read-only.
ReminderSet	Boolean	Specifies whether a reminder has been set for the MeetingItem. Read/write.
ReminderTime	Date	Specifies the date and time when the reminder is to be fired. Read/write.
Reply Recipients	Recipients collection	Returns a collection of the Recipients who will receive a message should one of the recipients reply to the message. Read-only.
Saved	Boolean	Indicates whether the item has changed since it was last saved. Read-only.

Table Continued on Following Page

Name	Returns	Description
SaveSent Message Folder	MAPIFolder object	Specifies the MAPIFolder where the copy of the item will be saved after it has been sent. Read/write.
SenderName	String	Returns the display name of the sender. Read-only.
Sensitivity	OlSensitivity constant	Specifies the level of sensitivity for the item. Read/write.
Sent	Boolean	Returns True if the item has already been sent. Read-only.
SentOn	Date	Returns the date and time when the item was sent. Read-only.
Session	NameSpace object	Returns the current NameSpace object. Read-only.
Size	Long	Returns the size of the item in bytes. Read-only.
Subject	String	Contains the subject of the item. Read/write.
Submitted	Boolean	Returns True if the item has been submitted. This informs you if the message is in the Outbox but has not yet been sent. Read-only.
UnRead	Boolean	Indicates whether the item is to be marked as "Unread". Read/write.
User Properties	User Properties collection	Returns the UserProperties collection for the item. Read-only.

Events

Name	Description
AttachmentAdd	Occurs when a new attachment is added to the item.
AttachmentRead	Occurs when an attachment is opened.
BeforeAttachment Save	Occurs just before the attachment is saved.
BeforeCheckNames	Occurs just before Outlook resolves the recipients for the item.
Close	Occurs when the Inspector object is shut down.

Name	Description
CustomAction	Occurs when a custom action is executed.
CustomProperty Change	Occurs when one of the custom properties for the item is changed.
Forward	Occurs when the item is forwarded.
Open	Occurs when the item is opened in an Inspector.
PropertyChange	Occurs when one of the non-custom properties is changed.
Read	Occurs when the item is opened for editing.
Reply	Occurs when the Reply action is executed on the item.
ReplyAll	Occurs when the ReplyAll action is executed on the item.
Send	Occurs when the item is sent.
Write	Occurs when the Save or SaveAs method is executed on the item.

NameSpace Object

Methods

Name	Returns	Description
AddStore(Store)		Creates a new personal profile folder. The Store parameter contains the path of the profile folder (.pst file).
CreateRecipient (RecipientName)	Recipient object	Used mostly with GetSharedDefaultFolder, but it can also be used to verify a name in the address book.
GetDefaultFolder (FolderTypeEnum)	MAPIFolder object	Returns the default MAPIFolder object for the item type specified in the FolderTypeEnum parameter, which can be one of the OlDefaultFolder constants.

Table Continued on Following Page

Name	Returns	Description
GetFolderFromID (EntryID, [StoreID])	MAPIFolder object	Returns the `MAPIFolder` object based on its Entry ID. Its Store ID may also be given as a parameter.
GetItemFromID (EntryID, [StoreID])	Item	Returns the item that is specified by the Entry ID.
GetRecipientFrom ID(EntryID)	Recipient object	Will return the Recipient based on its Entry ID.
GetSharedDefault Folder(Recipient , Object, FolderTypeEnum)	MAPIFolder object	Returns the specified default `MAPIFolder` for the specified recipient. `FolderTypeEnum` may be any of the `OlDefaultFolders` constants.
Logoff		Logs the user off from the current MAPI session.
Logon		Logs the user onto a MAPI session.
PickFolder	MAPIFolder object	Presents the user with a list of available folders to select from. If **Cancel** is selected instead of a folder then `Nothing` is returned.

Properties

Name	Returns	Description
AddressLists	Address Lists collection	Returns an `AddressLists` collection representing the root of the Address Book. Read-only.
Application	Application object	Returns the parent application of the object. Read-only.
Class	OlObject Class constant	Returns a numeric value specifying the class the object belongs to. Read-only.
CurrentUser	Recipient object	Returns a `Recipient` object representing the current user. Read-only.
Folders	Folders collection	Returns a collection containing all the `MAPIFolder` objects in the `NameSpace`. Read-only.

Name	Returns	Description
Parent	Object	Returns the object's parent object. Read-only.
Session	NameSpace object	Returns the current NameSpace object. Read-only.
SyncObjects	SyncObjects collection	Returns a collection of all the synchronization profiles. Read-only.
Type	String	The type of namespace. The only type currently supported is "MAPI". Read-only.

Events

Name	Description
OptionsPagesAdd	Occurs when a **Properties** dialog is opened.

NoteItem Object

Methods

Name	Returns	Description
Close(Save Mode)		Causes the Inspector object for the item to be closed. The SaveMode parameter specifies whether changes to the item will be saved or discarded, and may be one of the OlInspectorClose constants.
Copy	NoteItem object	Creates and returns an identical NoteItem object.
Delete		Deletes the current item.
Display ([Modal])		Causes the Inspector object for the item to be opened. The Modal parameter specifies whether the window is to be opened modally (True) or modelessly (False). The default is False.
Move (DestFldr)		Moves the current item to the new MAPIFolder, DestFldr.
PrintOut		Prints the item using the printer's default settings.

Table Continued on Following Page

Name	Returns	Description
Save		Saves the item to the current folder for an existing item or to the default folder for a newly created item.
SaveAs(Path, [Type])		Saves the current item to the hard drive with the path and filename specified in the Path parameter. The type of file the item is to be saved as may be specified in the Type parameter, which may be one of the OlSaveAsType constants.

Properties

Name	Returns	Description
Application	Application object	Returns the parent application of the object. Read-only.
Body	String	A free-form string containing the body of the item. Setting this causes the EditorType of the item's Inspector object to revert to default. Read/write.
Categories	String	Specifies the categories which are assigned to the item. Read/write.
Class	OlObject Class constant	Returns a numeric value specifying the class the object belongs to. Read-only.
Color	OlNote Color constant	Specifies the color in which the note is to be displayed. Read/write.
CreationTime	Date	Returns the date and time at which the item was created. Read-only.
EntryID	String	Returns a unique string identifier for the item. Read-only.
GetInspector	Inspector object	Returns the Inspector object for displaying the current item. Read-only.
Height	Long	Specifies the height of the note in pixels. Read/write.
Last Modification Time	Date	Returns the date and time that the item was last changed. Read-only.

Name	Returns	Description
Left	Long	Specifies the number of pixels the left edge of the `NoteItem` window is from the left edge of the screen. Read/write.
Links	Links collection	Returns a `Links` collection that represents the contacts with which this item is associated. Read-only.
MessageClass	String	Specifies the message class of the item. This property maps you to the form that is associated with the item. Read/write.
Parent	Object	Returns the object's parent object. Read-only.
Saved	Boolean	Indicates whether the item has changed since it was last saved. Read-only.
Session	NameSpace object	Returns the current `NameSpace` object. Read-only.
Size	Long	Returns the size of the item in bytes. Read-only.
Subject	String	Returns the subject of the item, calculated from the body of the note. Read-only.
Top	Long	Specifies the number of pixels the top edge of the note window is from the top edge of the screen. Read/write.
Width	Long	Specifies the width of the note window in pixels. Read/write.

OutlookBarGroup Object

Properties

Name	Returns	Description
Application	Application object	Returns the parent application of the object. Read-only.
Class	OlObject Class constant	Returns a numeric value specifying the class the object belongs to. Read-only.

Table Continued on Following Page

Name	Returns	Description
Name	String	The display name for the object. Read-only.
Parent	Object	Returns the object's parent object. Read-only.
Session	NameSpace object	Returns the current NameSpace object. Read-only.
Shortcuts	OutlookBar Shortcuts collection	Returns the collection of OutlookBarShortcut objects within the OutlookBarGroup. Read-only.
ViewType	OlOutlookBar ViewType constant	Specifies the size of the icons for the OutlookBarGroup. Read/write.

OutlookBarPane Object

Properties

Name	Returns	Description
Application	Application object	Returns the parent application of the object. Read-only.
Class	OlObject Class constant	Returns a numeric value specifying the class the object belongs to. Read-only.
Contents	OutlookBar Storage object	Returns the OutlookBarStorage object for the OutlookBarPane. Read-only.
CurrentGroup	OutlookBar Group object	Specifies the OutlookBarGroup currently open in the OutlookBarPane. Read/write.
Name	String	The display name for the object. Read-only.
Parent	Object	Returns the object's parent object. Read-only.
Session	NameSpace object	Returns the current NameSpace object. Read-only.
Visible	Boolean	Specifies whether the OutlookBarPane is currently visible (True) or hidden (False). Read/write.

Events

Name	Description
BeforeGroupSwitch	Occurs before the active group is switched and a new OutlookBarGroup is opened.
BeforeNavigate	Occurs before the user navigates to another pane.

OutlookBarShortcut Object

Properties

Name	Returns	Description
Application	Application object	Returns the parent application of the object. Read-only.
Class	OlObjectClass constant	Returns a numeric value specifying the class the object belongs to. Read-only.
Name	String	The display name for the object. Read-only.
Parent	Object	Returns the object's parent object. Read-only.
Session	NameSpace object	Returns the current NameSpace object. Read-only.
Target	Variant	Specifies the target of the shortcut. This may be a MAPIFolder, a file-system folder, a file-system path or a URL. Read-only.

OutlookBarStorage Object

Properties

Name	Returns	Description
Application	Application object	Returns the parent application of the object. Read-only.
Class	OlObjectClass constant	Returns a numeric value specifying the class the object belongs to. Read-only.
Groups	OutlookBar Groups collection	Returns a collection of the OutlookBarGroup objects in the OutlookBarStorage object. Read-only.

Table Continued on Following Page

Name	Returns	Description
Parent	Object	Returns the object's parent object. Read-only.
Session	NameSpace object	Returns the current NameSpace object. Read-only.

PostItem Object

Methods

Name	Returns	Description
Clear Conversation Index		Clears the conversation index.
Close (SaveMode)		Causes the Inspector object for the item to be closed. The SaveMode parameter specifies whether changes to the item will be saved or discarded, and may be one of the OlInspectorClose constants.
Copy	PostItem object	Creates and returns an identical PostItem object.
Delete		Deletes the current item.
Display ([Modal])		Causes the Inspector object for the item to be opened. The Modal parameter specifies whether the window is to be opened modally (True) or modelessly (False). The default is False.
Forward	PostItem object	Executes the Forward action on the item and returns the resulting PostItem.
Move (DestFldr)		Moves the current item to the new MAPIFolder, DestFldr.
Post		Submits the PostItem to the target public folder. This is equivalent to sending a MailItem.
PrintOut		Prints the item using the printer's default settings.
Reply	MailItem object	Creates a MailItem addressed to the originator of the item.

Name	Returns	Description
Save		Saves the item to the current folder for an existing item or to the default folder for a newly created item.
SaveAs(Path, [Type])		Saves the current item to the hard drive with the path and filename specified in the Path parameter. The type of file the item is to be saved as may be specified in the Type parameter, which may be one of the OlSaveAsType constants.

Properties

Name	Returns	Description
Actions	Actions collection	Returns an Actions collection of the available Action objects for the item. Read-only.
Application	Application object	Returns the parent application of the object. Read-only.
Attachments	Attachments collection	Returns a collection of the attachments associated with the item. Read-only.
Billing Information	String	Contains a free-form string that can be used to hold the billing information associated with the item. Read/write.
Body	String	A free-form string containing the body of the item. Setting this causes the EditorType of the item's Inspector object to revert to default. Read/write.
Categories	String	Specifies the categories that are assigned to the item. Read/write.
Class	OlObject Class constant	Returns a numeric value specifying the class the object belongs to. Read-only.
Companies	String	A free form string containing the company names associated with the item. Read/write.
Conversation Index	String	Returns the index representing the current conversation thread. Read-only.
Conversation Topic	String	Returns the topic for the conversation thread. Read-only.

Table Continued on Following Page

Name	Returns	Description
CreationTime	Date	Returns the date and time at which the item was created. Read-only.
EntryID	String	Returns a unique string identifier for the item. Read-only.
ExpiryTime	Date	Specifies the date and time when the item is to become invalid and can be deleted. Read/write.
Form Description	Form Description object	Returns the FormDescription object for the item. Read-only.
GetInspector	Inspector object	Returns the Inspector object for displaying the current item. Read-only.
HTMLBody	String	Specifies the body of the PostItem in HTML format. Read/write.
Importance	OlImportance constant	Specifies the importance level for the item. Read/write.
Last Modification Time	Date	Returns the date and time that the item was last changed. Read-only.
Links	Links collection	Returns a Links collection that represents the contacts with which this item is associated. Read-only.
MessageClass	String	Specifies the message class of the item. This property maps you to the form that is associated with the item. Read/write.
Mileage	String	A free-form string which can be used to hold the mileage for the item. Read/write.
NoAging	Boolean	Specifies whether or not the item can be archived. Read/write.
Outlook Internal Version	Long	Returns the build number of the Outlook version used to create the item. Read-only.
Outlook Version	String	Returns the major and minor version number for the Outlook Application used to create the item. For Outlook 2000, this is "9.0". Read-only.

Name	Returns	Description
Parent	Object	Returns the object's parent object. Read-only.
ReceivedTime	Date	Returns the date and time when the post was received. Read-only.
Saved	Boolean	Indicates whether the item has changed since it was last saved. Read-only.
SenderName	String	Returns the display name of the sender. Read-only.
Sensitivity	OlSensitivity constant	Specifies the level of sensitivity for the item. Read/write.
SentOn	Date	Returns the date and time when the item was sent. Read-only.
Session	NameSpace object	Returns the current NameSpace object. Read-only.
Size	Long	Returns the size of the item in bytes. Read-only.
Subject	String	Contains the subject of the item. Read/write.
UnRead	Boolean	Indicates whether the item is to be marked as "Unread". Read/write.
User Properties	User Properties collection	Returns the UserProperties collection for the item. Read-only.

Events

Name	Description
Attachment Add	Occurs when a new attachment is added to the item.
Attachment Read	Occurs when an attachment is opened.
Before Attachment Save	Occurs just before the attachment is saved.
BeforeCheck Names	Occurs just before Outlook resolves the recipients for the item.

Table Continued on Following Page

Name	Description
Close	Occurs when the Inspector object is shut down.
CustomAction	Occurs when a custom action is executed.
Custom Property Change	Occurs when one of the custom properties for the item is changed.
Forward	Occurs when the item is forwarded.
Open	Occurs when the item is opened in an Inspector.
Property Change	Occurs when one of the non-custom properties is changed.
Read	Occurs when the item is opened for editing.
Reply	Occurs when the Reply action is executed on the item.
ReplyAll	Occurs when the ReplyAll action is executed on the item.
Send	Occurs when the item is sent.
Write	Occurs when the Save or SaveAs method is executed on the item.

PropertyPage Object

Methods

Name	Description
Apply	Applies any changes that have been made to the PropertyPage.
GetPageInfo (HelpFile, HelpContext)	Returns information about the PropertyPage. The parameters specify the path of the help file for the page and the context ID for the help topic associated with the page.

Property

Name	Returns	Description
Dirty	Boolean	Specifies whether the contents of the PropertyPage have been modified.

PropertyPageSite Object

Method

Name	Description
OnStatus Change	Notifies Outlook that a `PropertyPage` has been altered.

Properties

Name	Returns	Description
Application	Application object	Returns the parent application of the object. Read-only.
Class	OlObject Class constant	Returns a numeric value specifying the class the object belongs to. Read-only.
Parent	Object	Returns the object's parent object. Read-only.
Session	NameSpace object	Returns the current `NameSpace` object. Read-only.

Recipient Object

Methods

Name	Returns	Description
Delete		Deletes the current `Recipient` from the `Recipients` collection.
FreeBusy (Start, MinPerChar, [Complete Format])	String	Returns a string representing the `Recipient`'s schedule for the next 30 days starting at the start date passed in, with each character representing a slot of `MinPerChar` minutes. If `CompleteFormat` is `False` or omitted, free time is represented by a zero, busy time by a one. If `CompleteFormat` is `True`, the intervals are each represented by the appropriate `OlBusyStatus` constant.
Resolve	Boolean	Resolves the current recipient against the Address Book. Returns `True` if the attempt succeeds, `False` if it fails.

Properties

Name	Returns	Description
Address	String	Specifies the email address for the current Recipient. Read/write.
AddressEntry	AddressEntry object	Returns the AddressEntry object for the recipient. If the recipient has not yet been resolved, the Resolve method for the recipient will be called. Read-only.
Application	Application object	Returns the parent application of the object. Read-only.
AutoReponse	String	Contains the text of the automatic response for the current recipient. Read/write.
Class	OlObjectClass constant	Returns a numeric value specifying the class the object belongs to. Read-only.
DisplayType	OlDisplayType constant	Returns the type of Recipient this is. Do not confuse this with the Type property. Read-only.
EntryID	String	Returns a unique string identifier for the item. Read-only.
Index	Long	Returns the position of the Recipient in the Recipients collection (starting from 1). Read-only.
Meeting Response Status	OlResponse Status constant	Returns the status of the recipient's response to a meeting request. Read-only.
Name	String	The display name for the object. Read-only.
Parent	Object	Returns the object's parent object. Read-only.
Resolved	Boolean	Indicates whether the recipient has been validated against the address book. Read-only.
Session	NameSpace object	Returns the current NameSpace object. Read-only.
Tracking Status	OlTracking Status constant	Specifies the tracking status for the recipient. Read/write.

Name	Returns	Description
Tracking StatusTime	Date	Specifies the tracking status date and time. Read/write.
Type	OlJournal RecipientType, OlMailRecipient Type, OlMeeting RecipientType or OlTaskRecipient Type constant.	Specifies the type of the recipient depending on the type of item the recipient belongs to. Read/write.

RecurrencePattern Object

Method

Name	Returns	Description
GetOccurrence (Date_Time)	AppointmentItem object	Returns the AppointmentItem object for the specified date and time.

Properties

Name	Returns	Description
Application	Application object	Returns the parent application of the object. Read-only.
Class	OlObjectClass constant	Returns a numeric value specifying the class the object belongs to. Read-only.
DayOfMonth	Long	Specifies the day of the month on which the recurring appointment or task will occur. Read/write.
DayOfWeekMask	olDaysOfWeek constant	Specifies the mask for the day of the week on which the appointment or task occurs. Read/write.
Duration	Long	Specifies the length of time that the item is due to last, in minutes. Valid only for recurring appointments. Read/write.

Table Continued on Following Page

Name	Returns	Description
EndTime	Date	Specifies the date and time at which the appointment is due to end. Read/write.
Exceptions	Exceptions collection	Returns the collection of exceptions to the recurrence pattern. Read-only.
Instance	Long	Specifies the recurrence pattern for recurrences of the type olRecursMonthNth or olRecursYearNth. Read/write.
Interval	Long	Specifies the number of units (weeks, months etc.) between one occurrence and the next. Read/write.
MonthOfYear	Long	Specifies the month on which the recurrence pattern is to occur. Read/write.
NoEndDate	Boolean	Specifies whether the recurrence pattern recurs indefinitely or has an end date. Read/write.
Occurrences	Long	Specifies how many times the recurrence will occur. Read/write.
Parent	Object	Returns the object's parent object. Read-only.
PatternEndDate	Date	Specifies the date on which the recurrence pattern is due to end. Read/write.
PatternStart Date	Date	Specifies the date on which the recurrence pattern is to start. Read/write.
RecurrenceType	OlRecurrence Type constant	Specifies the frequency of the recurrence pattern. Read/write.
Regenerate	Boolean	Specifies whether the recurrence pattern should be regenerated after it has been passed through. Read/write.
Session	NameSpace object	Returns the current NameSpace object. Read-only.
StartTime	Date	Specifies the start date and time for this occurrence. Read/write.

RemoteItem Object

Methods

Name	Returns	Description
Close (SaveMode)		Closes the item. The `SaveMode` parameter specifies whether changes to the item will be saved or discarded, and may be one of the `OlInspectorClose` constants. However, note that a `RemoteItem` cannot be displayed.
Copy		This method does not work for the `RemoteItem` object.
Delete		Deletes the current item.
Display ([Modal])		Causes a message box to be displayed prompting the user to select what action will be carried out on the item on the server the next time a connection is made.
Move (DestFldr)		This does not work for the `RemoteItem` object.
PrintOut		Prints the item using the printer's default settings.
Save		Saves the `RemoteItem` object to the current `MAPIFolder`.
SaveAs(Path , [Type])		Saves the current item to the hard drive with the path and filename specified in the `Path` parameter. The type of file the item is to be saved as may be specified in the `Type` parameter, which may be one of the `OlSaveAsType` constants.

Properties

Name	Returns	Description
Actions	Actions collection	Returns an `Actions` collection of the available `Action` objects for the item. Read-only.
Application	Application object	Returns the parent application of the object. Read-only.
Attachments	Attachments collection	Returns a collection of the attachments associated with the item. Read-only.

Table Continued on Following Page

Name	Returns	Description
Billing Information	String	Contains a free-form string that can be used to hold the billing information associated with the item. Note that this property is not inherited from the original item. Read/write.
Body	String	Specifies the body for the RemoteItem object, although it is not displayed and is not inherited from the original item. Read/write.
Categories	String	Specifies the categories that are assigned to the item. Note that this property is not inherited from the original item. Read/write.
Class	OlObject Class constant	Returns a numeric value specifying the class the object belongs to. Read-only.
Companies	String	A free-form string containing the company names associated with the item. Note that this property is not inherited from the original item. Read/write.
Conversation Index	String	Returns the index representing the current conversation thread. Read-only.
Conversation Topic	String	Returns the topic for the conversation thread. Read-only.
CreationTime	Date	Returns the date and time at which the item was created. Read-only.
EntryID	String	Returns a unique string identifier for the item. Read-only.
Form Description	Form Description object	This does not work for the RemoteItem object.
GetInspector	Inspector object	This does not work for the RemoteItem object.
Has Attachment	Boolean	Returns True if there are attachments associated with the RemoteItem. Read-only.
Importance	OlImportance constant	Specifies the importance level for the item. Read/write.

Name	Returns	Description
Last Modification Time	Date	Returns the date and time that the item was last changed. Read-only.
Links	Links collection	Returns a Links collection that represents the contacts with which this item is associated. Read-only.
MessageClass	String	Specifies the message class of the item. This property maps you to the form that is associated with the item. Read/write.
Mileage	String	A free-form string which can be used to hold the mileage for the item. Note that this property is not inherited from the original item. Read/write.
NoAging	Boolean	Specifies whether or not the item can be archived. Read/write.
Outlook Internal Version	Long	Returns the build number of the Outlook version used to create the item. For the RemoteItem, this always returns zero. Read-only.
Outlook Version	String	Returns the major and minor version number for the Outlook Application used to create the item. For the RemoteItem, this always returns an empty string. Read-only.
Parent	Object	Returns the object's parent object. Read-only.
Remote MessageClass	String	Returns the message class of the remote item represented by the RemoteItem object. Read-only.
Saved	Boolean	Indicates whether the item has changed since it was last saved. Read-only.
Sensitivity	OlSensitivity constant	Specifies the level of sensitivity for the item. Read-only.
Session	NameSpace object	Returns the current NameSpace object. Read-only.
Size	Long	Returns the size of the item in bytes. Read-only.

Table Continued on Following Page

Name	Returns	Description
Subject	String	Contains the subject of the item. Read/write.
TransferSize	Long	Returns the transfer size of the remote item in bytes. Read-only.
TransferTime	Long	Returns the estimated transfer time in seconds for the remote item. Read-only.
UnRead	Boolean	Indicates whether the item is to be marked as "Unread". Read/write.
User Properties	User Properties collection	Returns the UserProperties collection for the item. Read-only.

Events

Name	Description
AttachmentAdd	Occurs when a new attachment is added to the item.
AttachmentRead	Occurs when an attachment is opened.
BeforeAttachment Save	Occurs just before the attachment is saved.
BeforeCheckNames	Occurs just before Outlook resolves the recipients for the item.
Close	This event does not work for the RemoteItem object.
CustomAction	Occurs when a custom action is executed.
CustomProperty Change	Occurs when one of the custom properties for the item is changed.
Forward	This event does not work for the RemoteItem object.
Open	This event does not work for the RemoteItem object.
PropertyChange	Occurs when one of the non-custom properties is changed.
Read	Occurs when the item is opened for editing.
Reply	This event does not work for the RemoteItem object.
ReplyAll	This event does not work for the RemoteItem object.
Send	This event does not work for the RemoteItem object.
Write	Occurs when the Save or SaveAs method is executed on the item.

ReportItem

Methods

Name	Returns	Description
Close (SaveMode)		Causes the `Inspector` object for the item to be closed. The `SaveMode` parameter specifies whether changes to the item will be saved or discarded, and may be one of the `OlInspectorClose` constants.
Copy	ReportItem object	Creates and returns an identical `ReportItem` object.
Delete		Deletes the current item.
Display ([Modal])		Causes the `Inspector` object for the item to be opened. The `Modal` parameter specifies whether the window is to be opened modally (`True`) or modelessly (`False`). The default is `False`.
Move (DestFldr)		Moves the current item to the new `MAPIFolder`, `DestFldr`.
PrintOut		Prints the item using the printer's default settings.
Save		Saves the item to the current folder for an existing item or to the default folder for a newly created item.
SaveAs(Path , [Type])		Saves the current item to the hard drive with the path and filename specified in the `Path` parameter. The type of file the item is to be saved as may be specified in the `Type` parameter, which may be one of the `OlSaveAsType` constants.

Properties

Name	Returns	Description
Actions	Actions collection	Returns an `Actions` collection of the available `Action` objects for the item. Read-only.
Application	Application object	Returns the parent application of the object. Read-only.

Table Continued on Following Page

Name	Returns	Description
Attachments	Attachments collection	Returns a collection of the attachments associated with the item. Read-only.
Billing Information	String	Contains a free-form string that can be used to hold the billing information associated with the item. Read/write.
Body	String	A free-form string containing the body of the item. Setting this causes the EditorType of the item's Inspector object to revert to default. Read/write.
Categories	String	Specifies the categories that are assigned to the item. Read/write.
Class	OlObject Class constant	Returns a numeric value specifying the class the object belongs to. Read-only.
Companies	String	A free-form string containing the company names associated with the item. Read/write.
Conversation Index	String	Returns the index representing the current conversation thread. Read-only.
Conversation Topic	String	Returns the topic for the conversation thread. Read-only.
CreationTime	Date	Returns the date and time at which the item was created. Read-only.
EntryID	String	Returns a unique string identifier for the item. Read-only.
Form Description	Form Description object	Returns the FormDescription object for the item. Read-only.
GetInspector	Inspector object	Returns the Inspector object for displaying the current item. Read-only.
Importance	OlImportance constant	Specifies the importance level for the item. Read/write.
Last Modification Time	Date	Returns the date and time that the item was last changed. Read-only.
Links	Links collection	Returns a Links collection that represents the contacts with which this item is associated. Read-only.

Name	Returns	Description
MessageClass	String	Specifies the message class of the item. This property maps you to the form that is associated with the item. Read/write.
Mileage	String	A free-form string which can be used to hold the mileage for the item. Read/write.
NoAging	Boolean	Specifies whether or not the item can be archived. Read/write.
Outlook Internal Version	Long	Returns the build number of the Outlook version used to create the item. Read-only.
Outlook Version	String	Returns the major and minor version number for the Outlook Application used to create the item. For Outlook 2000, this is "9.0". Read-only.
Parent	Object	Returns the object's parent object. Read-only.
Saved	Boolean	Indicates whether the item has changed since it was last saved. Read-only.
Sensitivity	OlSensitivity constant	Specifies the level of sensitivity for the item. Read-only.
Session	NameSpace object	Returns the current NameSpace object. Read-only.
Size	Long	Returns the size of the item in bytes. Read-only.
Subject	String	Contains the subject of the item. Read/write.
UnRead	Boolean	Indicates whether the item is to be marked as "Unread". Read/write.
User Properties	User Properties collection	Returns the UserProperties collection for the item. Read-only.

Events

Name	Description
AttachmentAdd	Occurs when a new attachment is added to the item.
AttachmentRead	Occurs when an attachment is opened.
BeforeAttachment Save	Occurs just before the attachment is saved.
BeforeCheckNames	Occurs just before Outlook resolves the recipients for the item.
Close	Occurs when the Inspector object is shut down.
CustomAction	Occurs when a custom action is executed.
CustomProperty Change	Occurs when one of the custom properties for the item is changed.
Forward	Occurs when the item is forwarded.
Open	Occurs when the item is opened in an Inspector.
PropertyChange	Occurs when one of the non-custom properties is changed.
Read	Occurs when the item is opened for editing.
Reply	Occurs when the Reply action is executed on the item.
ReplyAll	Occurs when the ReplyAll action is executed on the item.
Send	Occurs when the item is sent.
Write	Occurs when the Save or SaveAs method is executed on the item.

SyncObject Object

Methods

Name	Description
Start	Begins the synchronization process.
Stop	Ends the synchronization process.

Properties

Name	Returns	Description
Application	Application object	Returns the parent application of the object. Read-only.
Class	OlObjectClass constant	Returns a numeric value specifying the class the object belongs to. Read-only.
Name	String	The display name for the object. Read-only.
Parent	Object	Returns the object's parent object. Read-only.
Session	NameSpace object	Returns the current NameSpace object. Read-only.

Events

Name	Description
OnError	Raised when an error occurs during synchronization.
Progress	Raised periodically during synchronization.
SyncEnd	Raised when synchronization ends.
SyncStart	Raised when synchronization begins.

TaskItem Object

Methods

Name	Returns	Description
Assign		Prepares the TaskItem to be delegated to another recipient. This method must be run before the task can be sent.
Cancel Response State		Resets an unsent response to a task request back to its state before the response.
Clear Recurrence Pattern		Resets the item to a single occurrence.

Table Continued on Following Page

Name	Returns	Description
Close (SaveMode)		Causes the Inspector object for the item to be closed. The SaveMode parameter spccifies whether changes to the item will be saved or discarded, and may be one of the OlInspectorClose constants.
Copy	TaskItem object	Creates and returns an identical TaskItem object.
Delete		Deletes the current item.
Display ([Modal])		Causes the Inspector object for the item to be opened. The Modal parameter specifies whether the window is to be opened modally (True) or modelessly (False). The default is False.
Get Recurrence Pattern	Recurrence Pattern object	Returns the RecurrencePattern object that contains the information about the recurrence of the task.
Mark Complete		Marks the task as completed.
Move (DestFldr)		Moves the current item to the new MAPIFolder, DestFldr.
PrintOut		Prints the item using the printer's default settings.
Respond (IResponse, fNoUI, fAdditional TextDialog)		Allows the user to accept or decline the task. IResponse may be one of the OlTaskResponse constants olTaskAccept or olTaskDecline. The fNoUI parameter is True if there is no User Interface, and fAdditionalDialog is True if the user is to be prompted to send or send with comments.
Save		Saves the item to the current folder for an existing item or to the default folder for a newly created item.
SaveAs(Path, [Type])		Saves the current item to the hard drive with the path and filename specified in the Path parameter. The type of file the item is to be saved as may be specified in the Type parameter, which may be one of the OlSaveAsType constants.

Name	Returns	Description
Send		Sends the item to the recipients defined in the Recipients property.
Skip Recurrence		Skips the current instance of the recurring task and sets you to the next instance.
StatusReport	MailItem object	Creates a status report for the task addressed to the recipients specified in the StatusUpdateRecipients property.

Properties

Name	Returns	Description
Actions	Actions collection	Returns an Actions collection of the available Action objects for the item. Read-only.
ActualWork	Long	Specifies the actual amount of time in minutes spent on the task. Read/write.
Application	Application object	Returns the parent application of the object. Read-only.
Attachments	Attachments collection	Returns a collection of the attachments associated with the item. Read-only.
Billing Information	String	Contains a free-form string that can be used to hold the billing information associated with the item. Read/write.
Body	String	A free-form string containing the body of the item. Setting this causes the EditorType of the item's Inspector object to revert to default. Read/write.
CardData	String	Specifies the text for the card data. Read/write.
Categories	String	Specifies the categories that are assigned to the item. Read/write.
Class	OlObject Class constant	Returns a numeric value specifying the class the object belongs to. Read-only.
Companies	String	A free-form string containing the company names associated with the item. Read/write.

Table Continued on Following Page

551

Name	Returns	Description
Complete	Boolean	Indicates whether the task has been completed. Read/write.
ContactNames	String	Returns a string containing the display names of the recipients associated with the item. Read-only.
Contacts	String	Returns a string containing the display names of the Link objects associated with the task. Read/write.
Conversation Index	String	Returns the index representing the current conversation thread. Read/write.
Conversation Topic	String	Returns the topic for the conversation thread. Read-only.
CreationTime	Date	Returns the date and time at which the item was created. Read-only.
Date Completed	Date	Specifies the date and time when the task was completed. Read/write.
Delegation State	OlTask Delegation Status constant	Returns the delegation state for the task. Read-only.
Delegator	String	Returns the display name of the delegator. Read-only.
DueDate	Date	Specifies the date and time by which the task is due to be completed. Read/write.
EntryID	String	Returns a unique string identifier for the item. Read-only.
Form Description	Form Description object	Returns the FormDescription object for the item. Read-only.
GetInspector	Inspector object	Returns the Inspector object for displaying the current item. Read-only.
Importance	OlImportance constant	Specifies the importance level for the item. Read/write.
IsRecurring	Boolean	Indicates whether this is a recurring task or not. Read-only.

Name	Returns	Description
Last ModificationDate	Date	Returns the date and time when the item was last changed. Read-only.
Links	Links collection	Returns a Links collection that represents the contacts with which this item is associated. Read-only.
MessageClass	String	Specifies the message class of the item. This property maps you to the form that is associated with the item. Read/write.
Mileage	String	A free-form string which can be used to hold the mileage for the item. Read/write.
NoAging	Boolean	Specifies whether or not the item can be archived. Read/write.
Ordinal	Long	Specifies the position in the view for the task. Read/write.
Outlook Internal Version	Long	Returns the build number of the Outlook version used to create the item. Read-only.
Outlook Version	String	Returns the major and minor version number for the Outlook Application used to create the item. For Outlook 2000, this is "9.0". Read-only.
Owner	String	Specifies the display name of the owner for the task. Setting this does not affect the ownership of the task. Read/write.
Ownership	OlTask Ownership constant	Indicates the ownership state of the task. Read-only.
Parent	Object	Returns the object's parent object. Read-only.
Percent Complete	Long	Indicates the percentage of the task that has been completed. Read/write.
Recipients	Recipients collection	Returns a collection of the Recipient objects associated with the item. Read-only.

Table Continued on Following Page

Name	Returns	Description
Reminder Override Default	Boolean	Specifies whether the defaults for the reminder should be ignored. Read/write.
ReminderPlay Sound	Boolean	Specifies whether the reminder should play a sound or not. Read/write.
ReminderSet	Boolean	Specifies whether a reminder should be fired for this task. Read/write.
Reminder SoundFile	String	Specifies the path and filename for the sound file for the reminder. Read/write.
ReminderTime	Date	Specifies the date and time when the reminder is to be fired. Read/write.
Response State	OlTask Response constant	Returns the overall status of the response for the task. Read-only.
Role	String	A free-form string which specifies the role that the owner has to the task. Read/write.
Saved	Boolean	Indicates whether the item has changed since it was last saved. Read-only.
SchedulePlus Priority	String	Indicates the Schedule+ priority for the task. Read/write.
Sensitivity	OlSensitivity constant	Specifies the level of sensitivity for the item. Read/write.
Session	NameSpace object	Returns the current NameSpace object. Read-only.
Size	Long	Returns the size of the item in bytes. Read-only.
StartDate	Date	Specifies the start date and time for the task. Read/write.
Status	OlTaskStatus constant	Indicates the progress of work on the task. Read/write.

Name	Returns	Description
StatusOn Completion Recipients	String	Returns a semicolon-delimited string of the display names of recipients which are to receive a completion report for this task. The recipients that appear here will be assigned a BCC type. Read-only.
StatusUpdate Recipients	String	Returns a semicolon-delimited string of the display names of recipients which are to receive update reports for this task. The recipients that appear here will be assigned a CC type. Read-only.
Subject	String	Contains the subject of the item. Read/write.
TeamTask	Boolean	Indicates whether this is a team task. Read/write.
TotalWork	Long	Specifies the total work for the task. Read/write.
UnRead	Boolean	Indicates whether the item is to be marked as "Unread". Read/write.
User Properties	User Properties collection	Returns the UserProperties collection for the item. Read-only.

Events

Name	Description
AttachmentAdd	Occurs when a new attachment is added to the item.
AttachmentRead	Occurs when an attachment is opened.
BeforeAttachment Save	Occurs just before the attachment is saved.
BeforeCheckNames	Occurs just before Outlook resolves the recipients for the item.
Close	Occurs when the Inspector object is shut down.
CustomAction	Occurs when a custom action is executed.
CustomProperty Change	Occurs when one of the custom properties for the item is changed.
Forward	Occurs when the item is forwarded.
Open	Occurs when the item is opened in an Inspector.

Table Continued on Following Page

Name	Description
PropertyChange	Occurs when one of the non-custom properties is changed.
Read	Occurs when the item is opened for editing.
Reply	Occurs when the Reply action is executed on the item.
ReplyAll	Occurs when the ReplyAll action is executed on the item.
Send	Occurs when the item is sent.
Write	Occurs when the Save or SaveAs method is executed on the item.

TaskRequestAcceptItem Object

Methods

Name	Returns	Description
Close (SaveMode)		Causes the Inspector object for the item to be closed. The SaveMode parameter specifies whether changes to the item will be saved or discarded, and may be one of the OlInspectorClose constants.
Copy	TaskRequest AcceptItem object	Creates and returns an identical TaskRequestAcceptItem object.
Delete		Deletes the current item.
Display ([Modal])		Causes the Inspector object for the item to be opened. The Modal parameter specifies whether the window is to be opened modally (True) or modelessly (False). The default is False.
GetAssociated Task (AddTo TaskList)	TaskItem object	Returns a reference to the associated TaskItem. The parameter indicates whether the item is to added to default tasks folder.
Move(DestFldr)		Moves the current item to the new MAPIFolder, DestFldr.

Name	Returns	Description
PrintOut		Prints the item using the printer's default settings.
Save		Saves the item to the current folder for an existing item or to the default folder for a newly created item.
SaveAs(Path, [Type])		Saves the current item to the hard drive with the path and filename specified in the Path parameter. The type of file the item is to be saved as may be specified in the Type parameter, which may be one of the OlSaveAsType constants.

Properties

Name	Returns	Description
Actions	Actions collection	Returns an Actions collection of the available Action objects for the item. Read-only.
Application	Application object	Returns the parent application of the object. Read-only.
Attachments	Attachments collection	Returns a collection of the attachments associated with the item. Read-only.
Billing Information	String	Contains a free-form string that can be used to hold the billing information associated with the item. Read/write.
Body	String	A free-form string containing the body of the item. Setting this causes the EditorType of the item's Inspector object to revert to default. Read/write.
Categories	String	Specifies the categories that are assigned to the item. Read/write.
Class	OlObject Class constant	Returns a numeric value specifying the class the object belongs to. Read-only.
Companies	String	A free form string containing the company names associated with the item. Read/write.
Conversation Index	String	Returns the index representing the current conversation thread. Read-only.

Table Continued on Following Page

Name	Returns	Description
Conversation Topic	String	Returns the topic for the conversation thread. Read-only.
CreationTime	Date	Returns the date and time at which the item was created. Read-only.
EntryID	String	Returns a unique string identifier for the item. Read-only.
Form Description	Form Description object	Returns the FormDescription object for the item. Read-only.
GetInspector	Inspector object	Returns the Inspector object for displaying the current item. Read-only.
Importance	OlImportance constant	Specifies the importance level for the item. Read/write.
Last Modification Time	Date	Returns the date and time that the item was last changed. Read-only.
Links	Links collection	Returns a Links collection that represents the contacts with which this item is associated. Read-only.
MessageClass	String	Specifies the message class of the item. This property maps you to the form that is associated with the item. Read/write.
Mileage	String	A free-form string which can be used to hold the mileage for the item. Read/write.
NoAging	Boolean	Specifies whether or not the item can be archived. Read/write.
Outlook Internal Version	Long	Returns the build number of the Outlook version used to create the item. Read-only.
Outlook Version	String	Returns the major and minor version number for the Outlook Application used to create the item. For Outlook 2000, this is "9.0". Read-only.
Parent	Object	Returns the object's parent object. Read-only.

Name	Returns	Description
Saved	Boolean	Indicates whether the item has changed since it was last saved. Read-only.
Sensitivity	OlSensitivity constant	Specifies the level of sensitivity for the item. Read/write.
Session	NameSpace object	Returns the current NameSpace object. Read-only.
Size	Long	Returns the size of the item in bytes. Read-only.
Subject	String	Contains the subject of the item. Read/write.
UnRead	Boolean	Indicates whether the item is to be marked as "Unread". Read/write.
User Properties	UserProperties collection	Returns the UserProperties collection for the item. Read-only.

Events

Name	Description
AttachmentAdd	Occurs when a new attachment is added to the item.
AttachmentRead	Occurs when an attachment is opened.
BeforeAttachment Save	Occurs just before the attachment is saved.
BeforeCheckNames	Occurs just before Outlook resolves the recipients for the item.
Close	Occurs when the Inspector object is shut down.
CustomAction	Occurs when a custom action is executed.
CustomProperty Change	Occurs when one of the custom properties for the item is changed.
Forward	Occurs when the item is forwarded.
Open	Occurs when the item is opened in an Inspector.
PropertyChange	Occurs when one of the non-custom properties is changed.
Read	Occurs when the item is opened for editing.

Table Continued on Following Page

Name	Description
Reply	Occurs when the Reply action is executed on the item.
ReplyAll	Occurs when the ReplyAll action is executed on the item.
Send	Occurs when the item is sent.
Write	Occurs when the Save or SaveAs method is executed on the item.

TaskRequestDeclineItem Object

Methods

Name	Returns	Description
Close(SaveMode)		Causes the Inspector object for the item to be closed. The SaveMode parameter specifies whether changes to the item will be saved or discarded, and may be one of the OlInspectorClose constants.
Copy	TaskRequest DeclineItem object	Creates and returns an identical TaskRequestDeclineItem object.
Delete		Deletes the current item.
Display([Modal])		Causes the Inspector object for the item to be opened. The Modal parameter specifies whether the window is to be opened modally (True) or modelessly (False). The default is False.
GetAssociated Task (AddTo TaskList)	TaskItem object	Returns a reference to the associated TaskItem. The parameter indicates whether the item is to added to default tasks folder.
Move(DestFldr)		Moves the current item to the new MAPIFolder, DestFldr.
PrintOut		Prints the item using the printer's default settings.

Name	Returns	Description
Save		Saves the item to the current folder for an existing item or to the default folder for a newly created item.
SaveAs(Path, [Type])		Saves the current item to the hard drive with the path and filename specified in the Path parameter. The type of file the item is to be saved as may be specified in the Type parameter, which may be one of the OlSaveAsType constants.

Properties

Name	Returns	Description
Actions	Actions collection	Returns an Actions collection of the available Action objects for the item. Read-only.
Application	Application object	Returns the parent application of the object. Read-only.
Attachments	Attachments collection	Returns a collection of the attachments associated with the item. Read-only.
Billing Information	String	Contains a free-form string that can be used to hold the billing information associated with the item. Read/write.
Body	String	A free-form string containing the body of the item. Setting this causes the EditorType of the item's Inspector object to revert to default. Read/write.
Categories	String	Specifies the categories that are assigned to the item. Read/write.
Class	OlObject Class constant	Returns a numeric value specifying the class the object belongs to. Read-only.
Companies	String	A free form string containing the company names associated with the item. Read/write.
Conversation nIndex	String	Returns the index representing the current conversation thread. Read-only.

Name	Returns	Description
Conversation Topic	String	Returns the topic for the conversation thread. Read-only.
CreationTime	Date	Returns the date and time at which the item was created. Read-only.
EntryID	String	Returns a unique string identifier for the item. Read-only.
Form Description	Form Description object	Returns the FormDescription object for the item. Read-only.
GetInspector	Inspector object	Returns the Inspector object for displaying the current item. Read-only.
Importance	OlImportance constant	Specifies the importance level for the item. Read/write.
Last Modification Time	Date	Returns the date and time that the item was last changed. Read-only.
Links	Links collection	Returns a Links collection that represents the contacts with which this item is associated. Read-only.
MessageClass	String	Specifies the message class of the item. This property maps you to the form that is associated with the item. Read/write.
Mileage	String	A free-form string which can be used to hold the mileage for the item. Read/write.
NoAging	Boolean	Specifies whether or not the item can be archived. Read/write.
Outlook Internal Version	Long	Returns the build number of the Outlook version used to create the item. Read-only.
Outlook Version	String	Returns the major and minor version number for the Outlook Application used to create the item. For Outlook 2000, this is "9.0". Read-only.
Parent	Object	Returns the object's parent object. Read-only.

Name	Returns	Description
Saved	Boolean	Indicates whether the item has changed since it was last saved. Read-only.
Sensitivity	OlSensitivity constant	Specifies the level of sensitivity for the item. Read/write.
Session	NameSpace object	Returns the current NameSpace object. Read-only.
Size	Long	Returns the size of the item in bytes. Read-only.
Subject	String	Contains the subject of the item. Read/write.
UnRead	Boolean	Indicates whether the item is to be marked as "Unread". Read/write.
User Properties	User Properties collection	Returns the UserProperties collection for the item. Read-only.

Events

Name	Description
AttachmentAdd	Occurs when a new attachment is added to the item.
AttachmentRead	Occurs when an attachment is opened.
BeforeAttachment Save	Occurs just before the attachment is saved.
BeforeCheckNames	Occurs just before Outlook resolves the recipients for the item.
Close	Occurs when the Inspector object is shut down.
CustomAction	Occurs when a custom action is executed.
CustomProperty Change	Occurs when one of the custom properties for the item is changed.
Forward	Occurs when the item is forwarded.
Open	Occurs when the item is opened in an Inspector.
PropertyChange	Occurs when one of the non-custom properties is changed.
Read	Occurs when the item is opened for editing.

Table Continued on Following Page

Name	Description
Reply	Occurs when the Reply action is executed on the item.
ReplyAll	Occurs when the ReplyAll action is executed on the item.
Send	Occurs when the item is sent.
Write	Occurs when the Save or SaveAs method is executed on the item.

TaskRequestItem Object

Methods

Name	Returns	Description
Close(SaveMode)		Causes the Inspector object for the item to be closed. The SaveMode parameter specifies whether changes to the item will be saved or discarded, and may be one of the OlInspectorClose constants.
Copy	TaskRequest Item object	Creates and returns an identical TaskRequestItem object.
Delete		Deletes the current item.
Display ([Modal])		Causes the Inspector object for the item to be opened. The Modal parameter specifies whether the window is to be opened modally (True) or modelessly (False). The default is False.
GetAssociated Task (AddTo TaskList)	TaskItem object	Returns a reference to the associated TaskItem. The parameter indicates whether the item is to added to default tasks folder.
Move(DestFldr)		Moves the current item to the new MAPIFolder, DestFldr.
PrintOut		Prints the item using the printer's default settings.
Save		Saves the item to the current folder for an existing item or to the default folder for a newly created item.

Name	Returns	Description
SaveAs(Path, [Type])		Saves the current item to the hard drive with the path and filename specified in the Path parameter. The type of file the item is to be saved as may be specified in the Type parameter, which may be one of the OlSaveAsType constants.

Properties

Name	Returns	Description
Actions	Actions collection	Returns an Actions collection of the available Action objects for the item. Read-only.
Application	Application object	Returns the parent application of the object. Read-only.
Attachments	Attachments collection	Returns a collection of the attachments associated with the item. Read-only.
Billing Information	String	Contains a free-form string that can be used to hold the billing information associated with the item. Read/write.
Body	String	A free-form string containing the body of the item. Setting this causes the EditorType of the item's Inspector object to revert to default. Read/write.
Categories	String	Specifies the categories that are assigned to the item. Read/write.
Class	OlObjectClass constant	Returns a numeric value specifying the class the object belongs to. Read-only.
Companies	String	A free form string containing the company names associated with the item. Read/write.
Conversation Index	String	Returns the index representing the current conversation thread. Read-only.

Table Continued on Following Page

Name	Returns	Description
Conversation Topic	String	Returns the topic for the conversation thread. Read-only.
CreationTime	Date	Returns the date and time at which the item was created. Read-only.
EntryID	String	Returns a unique string identifier for the item. Read-only.
Form Description	Form Description object	Returns the FormDescription object for the item. Read-only.
GetInspector	Inspector object	Returns the Inspector object for displaying the current item. Read-only.
Importance	OlImportance constant	Specifies the importance level for the item. Read/write.
Last Modification Time	Date	Returns the date and time that the item was last changed. Read-only.
Links	Links collection	Returns a Links collection that represents the contacts with which this item is associated. Read-only.
MessageClass	String	Specifies the message class of the item. This property maps you to the form that is associated with the item. Read/write.
Mileage	String	A free-form string which can be used to hold the mileage for the item. Read/write.
NoAging	Boolean	Specifies whether or not the item can be archived. Read/write.
Outlook Internal Version	Long	Returns the build number of the Outlook version used to create the item. Read-only.
Outlook Version	String	Returns the major and minor version number for the Outlook Application used to create the item. For Outlook 2000, this is "9.0". Read-only.
Parent	Object	Returns the object's parent object. Read-only.

Name	Returns	Description
Saved	Boolean	Indicates whether the item has changed since it was last saved. Read-only.
Sensitivity	OlSensitivity constant	Specifies the level of sensitivity for the item. Read/write.
Session	NameSpace object	Returns the current NameSpace object. Read-only.
Size	Long	Returns the size of the item in bytes. Read-only.
Subject	String	Contains the subject of the item. Read/write.
UnRead	Boolean	Indicates whether the item is to be marked as "Unread". Read/write.
User Properties	UserProperties collection	Returns the UserProperties collection for the item. Read-only.

Events

Name	Description
AttachmentAdd	Occurs when a new attachment is added to the item.
AttachmentRead	Occurs when an attachment is opened.
BeforeAttachmentSave	Occurs just before the attachment is saved.
BeforeCheckNames	Occurs just before Outlook resolves the recipients for the item.
Close	Occurs when the Inspector object is shut down.
CustomAction	Occurs when a custom action is executed.
CustomPropertyChange	Occurs when one of the custom properties for the item is changed.
Forward	Occurs when the item is forwarded.
Open	Occurs when the item is opened in an Inspector.
PropertyChange	Occurs when one of the non-custom properties is changed.
Read	Occurs when the item is opened for editing.

Table Continued on Following Page

Name	Description
Reply	Occurs when the Reply action is executed on the item.
ReplyAll	Occurs when the ReplyAll action is executed on the item.
Send	Occurs when the item is sent.
Write	Occurs when the Save or SaveAs method is executed on the item.

TaskRequestUpdateItem

Methods

Name	Returns	Description
Close(SaveMode)		Causes the Inspector object for the item to be closed. The SaveMode parameter specifies whether changes to the item will be saved or discarded, and may be one of the OlInspectorClose constants.
Copy	TaskRequest UpdateItem object	Creates and returns an identical TaskRequestUpdateItem object.
Delete		Deletes the current item.
Display ([Modal])		Causes the Inspector object for the item to be opened. The Modal parameter specifies whether the window is to be opened modally (True) or modelessly (False). The default is False.
GetAssociated Task (AddToTask List)	TaskItem object	Returns a reference to the associated TaskItem. The parameter indicates whether the item is to added to default tasks folder.
Move(DestFldr)		Moves the current item to the new MAPIFolder, DestFldr.
PrintOut		Prints the item using the printer's default settings.
Save		Saves the item to the current folder for an existing item or to the default folder for a newly created item.

Name	Returns	Description
SaveAs(Path, [Type])		Saves the current item to the hard drive with the path and filename specified in the Path parameter. The type of file the item is to be saved as may be specified in the Type parameter, which may be one of the OlSaveAsType constants.

Properties

Name	Returns	Description
Actions	Actions collection	Returns an Actions collection of the available Action objects for the item. Read-only.
Application	Application object	Returns the parent application of the object. Read-only.
Attachments	Attachments collection	Returns a collection of the attachments associated with the item. Read-only.
Billing Information	String	Contains a free-form string that can be used to hold the billing information associated with the item. Read/write.
Body	String	A free-form string containing the body of the item. Setting this causes the EditorType of the item's Inspector object to revert to default. Read/write.
Categories	String	Specifies the categories that are assigned to the item. Read/write.
Class	OlObject Class constant	Returns a numeric value specifying the class the object belongs to. Read-only.
Companies	String	A free form string containing the company names associated with the item. Read/write.
Conversation Index	String	Returns the index representing the current conversation thread. Read-only.
Conversation Topic	String	Returns the topic for the conversation thread. Read-only.
CreationTime	Date	Returns the date and time at which the item was created. Read-only.
EntryID	String	Returns a unique string identifier for the item. Read-only.

Table Continued on Following Page

Name	Returns	Description
Form Description	Form Description object	Returns the FormDescription object for the item. Read-only.
GetInspector	Inspector object	Returns the Inspector object for displaying the current item. Read-only.
Importance	OlImportance constant	Specifies the importance level for the item. Read/write.
Last Modification Time	Date	Returns the date and time that the item was last changed. Read-only.
Links	Links collection	Returns a Links collection that represents the contacts with which this item is associated. Read-only.
MessageClass	String	Specifies the message class of the item. This property maps you to the form that is associated with the item. Read/write.
Mileage	String	A free-form string which can be used to hold the mileage for the item. Read/write.
NoAging	Boolean	Specifies whether or not the item can be archived. Read/write.
Outlook Internal Version	Long	Returns the build number of the Outlook version used to create the item. Read-only.
Outlook Version	String	Returns the major and minor version number for the Outlook Application used to create the item. For Outlook 2000, this is "9.0". Read-only.
Parent	Object	Returns the object's parent object. Read-only.
Saved	Boolean	Indicates whether the item has changed since it was last saved. Read-only.
Sensitivity	OlSensitivity constant	Specifies the level of sensitivity for the item. Read/write.
Session	NameSpace object	Returns the current NameSpace object. Read-only.

Name	Returns	Description
Size	Long	Returns the size of the item in bytes. Read-only.
Subject	String	Contains the subject of the item. Read/write.
UnRead	Boolean	Indicates whether the item is to be marked as "Unread". Read/write.
User Properties	UserProperties collection	Returns the UserProperties collection for the item. Read-only.

Events

Name	Description
AttachmentAdd	Occurs when a new attachment is added to the item.
AttachmentRead	Occurs when an attachment is opened.
BeforeAttachment Save	Occurs just before the attachment is saved.
BeforeCheckNames	Occurs just before Outlook resolves the recipients for the item.
Close	Occurs when the Inspector object is shut down.
CustomAction	Occurs when a custom action is executed.
CustomProperty Change	Occurs when one of the custom properties for the item is changed.
Forward	Occurs when the item is forwarded.
Open	Occurs when the item is opened in an Inspector.
PropertyChange	Occurs when one of the non-custom properties is changed.
Read	Occurs when the item is opened for editing.
Reply	Occurs when the Reply action is executed on the item.
ReplyAll	Occurs when the ReplyAll action is executed on the item.
Send	Occurs when the item is sent.
Write	Occurs when the Save or SaveAs method is executed on the item.

UserProperty Object

Method

Name	Returns	Description
Delete		Deletes the current `UserProperty` object from the `UserProperties` collection.

Properties

Name	Returns	Description
Application	Application object	Returns the parent application of the object. Read-only.
Class	OlObjectClass constant	Returns a numeric value specifying the class the object belongs to. Read-only.
Formula	String	Specifies the formula for the property. Read/write.
Name	String	The display name for the object. Read-only.
Parent	Object	Returns the object's parent object. Read-only.
Session	NameSpace object	Returns the current `NameSpace` object. Read-only.
Type	OlUser PropertyType constant	Indicates the data type that the property can hold. Read-only.
Validation Formula	String	A free-form string containing the validation formula for the property. Read/write.
ValidationText	String	The validation text for the property. Read/write.
Value	Variant	Specifies the value for the property. Read/write.

CDO 1.21 Object Model Reference

In this Appendix, you'll find a complete list of the objects, methods and properties in the CDO 1.21 object model. Note that any parameters in square brackets are optional arguments to a method.

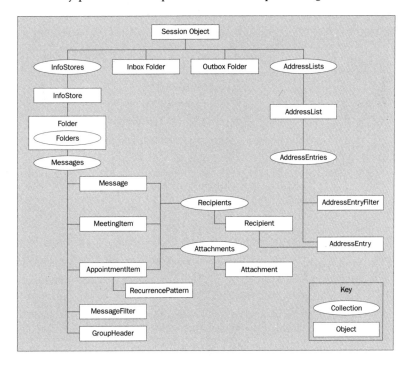

Objects

Object	Description
AddressEntries	Collection containing a number of AddressEntry objects.
AddressEntry	Defines addressing information valid for a given messaging system. An address usually represents a person or process to which the messaging system can deliver messages.
AddressEntryFilter	The AddressEntryFilter object specifies criteria for a search on an AddressEntries collection.
AddressList	The AddressList object supplies a (distribution) list of address entries to which a messaging system can deliver messages.
AddressLists	Collection containing a number of AddressList objects.
AppointmentItem	The AppointmentItem object represents an appointment in a calendar folder.
Attachment	The Attachment object represents a document that is an attachment of a message.
Attachments	Collection containing a number of Attachment objects.
Field	A Field object represents a MAPI property on a CDO Library object.
Fields	Collection containing a number of Field objects.
Folder	The Folder object represents a folder or container within the MAPI system. A folder can contain subfolders and messages.
Folders	Collection containing a number of Folder objects.
GroupHeader	The GroupHeader object represents the header for a grouping of messages within a table view.
InfoStore	The InfoStore object provides access to the folder hierarchy of a message store.
InfoStores	Collection containing a number of InfoStore objects.
MeetingItem	The MeetingItem object represents a meeting in a folder.
Message	The Message object represents a single message, item, document, or form in a folder.
MessageFilter	The MessageFilter object specifies criteria for restricting a search on a Messages collection.
Messages	Collection containing a number of AppointmentItem, GroupHeader, MeetingItem and Message objects.
Recipient	The Recipient object represents a recipient of a message.
Recipients	Collection containing a number of Recipient objects.
RecurrencePattern	The RecurrencePattern object describes the recurrence pattern for an AppointmentItem object.
Session	The Session object contains session-wide settings and options. It also contains properties that return top-level objects, such as CurrentUser.

AddressEntries Collection

This object represents a **large** collection of `AddressEntry` objects.

Methods

Name	Returns	Description
Add (*addresstype* [, *name*] [, *address*])	AddressEntry	The `Add` method creates and returns a new `AddressEntry` object in the `AddressEntries` collection containing the *addresstype* (CdoPR_ADDRTYPE) and optionally the display *name* and *address* for the entry.
Delete()	None	The `Delete` method deletes all the address entries in the `AddressEntries` collection.
GetFirst()	AddressEntry	The `GetFirst` method returns the first `AddressEntry` object in the `AddressEntries` collection. It returns `Nothing` if there is no address entry in the collection.
GetLast()	AddressEntry	The `GetLast` method returns the last `AddressEntry` object in the `AddressEntries` collection. It returns `Nothing` if there is no address entry in the collection.
GetNext()	AddressEntry	The `GetNext` method returns the next `AddressEntry` object in the `AddressEntries` collection. It returns `Nothing` if no next object exists, for example if already positioned at the end of the collection.
GetPrevious()	AddressEntry	The `GetPrevious` method returns the previous `AddressEntry` object in the `AddressEntries` collection. It returns `Nothing` if no previous object exists, for example if already positioned at the beginning of the collection.
Sort ([*SortOrder*] [, *PropTag*]) Sort ([*SortOrder*] [, *name*])	None	The `Sort` method sorts the address entries in the collection on the specified property – either a named *CdoPropTag* constant or a tag *name* – according to the specified *sort order* (a constant of type `CdoSortOrder`). The default order is ascending if none is given. If no proptag or name is specified, a repeat is made of the last sort performed.

Properties

Name	Returns	Description
Application	String	The string 'Collaboration Data Objects'.
Class	CdoObjectClass	The class of the CDO object. In this case, CdoAddressEntries (21)
Count	Long	The number of AddressEntry objects in the collection or if this is not possible, returns &H7FFFFFFF.
Filter	AddressEntryFilter	The AddressEntryFilter object for the AddressEntries collection.
Item(*index*) Item(*search*)	AddressEntry	Returns a single AddressEntry object from the collection identified by either its *index* in the collection or some *search* criteria.
Parent	AddressList	The parent AddressList object.
RawTable	IUnknown	An IUnknown pointer to the MAPI table that underlies the AddressEntries collection.
Session	Session	The current CDO Session object.

AddressEntry Object

Represents the address of a user or distribution list. Also contains information related to address owner's availability.

Methods

Name	Returns	Description
Delete()	None	Deletes the AddressEntry object.
Details ([*parentWindow*])	None	Displays a dialog containing detailed (at least the display name and address) information about an AddressEntry object. Optionally, the method can take a long integer reference to the *parent window* where the call originated.
GetFreeBusy (*StartTime*, *EndTime*, *Interval*)	String	Returns a string indicating the free/busy status of the user for each time interval specified in minutes between the start and end times given. The string contains one character (0, 1, 2 or 3) per interval corresponding to the CdoBusyStatus constants.

Name	Returns	Description
IsSameAs (*AEObject2*)	Boolean	`True` if the `AddressEntry` object is the same as *AEObject2*.
Update ([*makePermanent*] [, *refreshObject*])	None	Saves any changes made to the `AddressEntry` object. `Update` takes two boolean parameters. *makePermanent* commits all changes to the object and *refreshObject* loses all changes not yet made permanent. The default call is `Update` (*True, False*) .

Properties

Name	Returns	Description
Address	String	Specifies the messaging address of an address entry or message recipient. (e.g. an email address)
Application	String	The string 'Collaboration Data Objects'.
Class	CdoObjectClass	The class of the CDO object. In this case, `CdoAddressEntry` (8)
DisplayType	CdoDisplayType	A `CdoDisplayType` constant representing the display type of the address entry (User, Distribution List, Forum, etc)
Fields Fields (*index*) Fields (*proptag*) Fields (*name*)	Object (Field or Fields)	Returns the specified field attached to the `AddressEntry` object based on either *index* value (integer), *cdoPropTag* (long) or *name*. Returns `Fields` collection if no parameter is specified.
ID	String	The unique identifier of the `AddressEntry` object.
Manager	AddressEntry	The `AddressEntry` object corresponding to the manager of the user whose `AddressEntry` object this is.
MAPIOBJECT	IUnknown	An IUnknown pointer to this object.
Members	AddressEntries	Returns an `AddressEntries` collection containing the `AddressEntry` objects for those users in this distribution list.
Name	String	The display name or alias for the object.
Parent	AddressEntries, Recipient	The parent `AddressEntries` collection or `Recipient` object.

Name	Returns	Description
Session	Session	The current CDO `Session` object.
Type	String	The `Type` property specifies the address type, such as SMTP, fax, or X.400.

AddressEntryFilter Object

The `AddressEntryFilter` object specifies the criteria for a search on an `AddressEntries` collection.

Methods

Name	Returns	Description
IsSameAs (*AEFObject2*)	Boolean	`True` if the `AddressEntryFilter` object is the same as *AEFObject2*.

Properties

Name	Returns	Description
Address	String	The *full* address for the `AddressEntry` object being filtered.
Application	String	The string 'Collaboration Data Objects'.
Class	CdoObjectClass	The class of the CDO object. In this case, `CdoAddressEntryFilter` (9)
Fields Fields (*index*) Fields (*proptag*) Fields (*name*)	Object (Field or Fields)	Returns the specified field attached to the `AddressEntryFilter` object based on either *index* value (integer), *cdoPropTag* (long) or *name*. Returns `Fields` collection if no parameter is specified.
Name	String	Specifies a value for the default filter property. This value will be used in an ambiguous name resolution search. e.g 'tom' would find 'Tom', 'Tomas', 'Tomkinson' etc.
Not	Boolean	`True` if values should be negated before being ANDed or ORed to the filter.
Or	Boolean	`True` if the values in the filter should be ORed together rather than ANDed, which is the default.
Parent	AddressEntries	The parent `AddressEntries` collection.
Session	Session	The current CDO `Session` object.

AddressList Object

Methods

Name	Returns	Description
IsSameAs (*ALObject2*)	Boolean	True if the AddressList object is the same as *ALObject2*.

Properties

Name	Returns	Description
AddressEntries AddressEntries (*index*)	AddressEntry, AddressEntries	Returns either the collection of AddressEntry objects in the AddressList, or AddressEntry number *index*. Note that using *index* is only safe if the collection's count property returns a value other than &H7FFFFFFF.
Application	String	The string 'Collaboration Data Objects'.
Class	CdoObjectClass	The class of the CDO object. In this case, CdoAddressList (7)
Fields Fields (*index*) Fields (*proptag*) Fields (*name*)	Field, Fields	Returns the specified field attached to the AddressList object based on either *index* value (integer), *cdoPropTag* (long) or *name*. Returns Fields collection if no parameter is specified.
ID	String	The unique identifier of the AddressList object.
Index	Long	The index value of this AddressList object within its parent AddressLists collection.
IsReadOnly	Boolean	True if the current AddressList is read-only. Note this does not apply to the AddressEntry objects in the list.
Name	String	The name of the AddressList as a string.
Parent	AddressLists	The parent AddressLists collection.
Session	Session	The current CDO Session object.

AddressLists Collection

A collection of one or more `AddressList` objects. Note that `AddressLists` is regarded as a small collection for which the `Count` property is reliable. This object has no methods.

Properties

Name	Returns	Description
Application	String	The string 'Collaboration Data Objects'.
Class	CdoObjectClass	The class of the CDO Object. In this case, `CdoAddressLists` (20).
Count	Long	The exact number of `AddressList` objects in the collection.
Item(*index*) Item(*name*)	AddressList	Returns a single `AddressList` object from the collection identified by either its *index* in the collection or by being the first object in the collection whose name property matches *name*.
Parent	Session	The current CDO `Session` object.
Session	Session	The current CDO `Session` object.

AppointmentItem Object

The `AppointmentItem` object represents an appointment in a calendar folder. Only the properties and methods unique to the `AppointmentItem` object are listed here. It also inherits all the properties and some of the methods (`CopyTo`, `Delete`, `IsSameAs`, `MoveTo`, `Options`, `Send` and `Update`) defined in the `Message` object.

Methods

Name	Returns	Description
ClearRecurrenceP attern()	None	Removes any recurrence settings from this appointment.
GetRecurrence Pattern()	RecurrencePattern	Returns a `RecurrencePattern` object defining the recurrence settings for this appointment.
Respond (*RespondType*)	MeetingItem	Returns a `MeetingItem` object for responding to a meeting request for an appointment.

Properties

Name	Returns	Description
AllDayEvent	Boolean	Indicates whether this appointment is an all-day event.
BusyStatus	CdoBusyStatus	The busy flag for this user with respect to this appointment.
Class	CdoObjectClass	The class of the CDO Object. In this case, CdoAppointment (26).
Duration	Long	The duration of this appointment.
EndTime	Variant (vbDate)	The end date/time of this appointment.
IsRecurring	Boolean	True if this appointment is recurring.
Location	String	Returns or sets the location of this appointment.
MeetingResponse Status	CdoResponseStatus	The user's response status (Accepted, Declined, etc) to this AppointmentItem.
MeetingStatus	CdoMeetingStatusType	The current meeting status for this AppointmentItem.
Organizer	AddressEntry	The user who called the meeting.
ReminderMinutes BeforeStart	Long	How many minutes before the start of this appointment a reminder should be issued.
ReminderSet	Boolean	True if the user will be reminded of this appointment.
ReplyTime	Variant (vbDate)	The date/time a recipient replied to the meeting request for this appointment.
ResponseRequested	Boolean	True if a response is required to the meeting request for this appointment.
StartTime	Variant (vbDate)	The start date/time of this appointment.

Attachment Object

The `Attachment` object represents a document that is an attachment of a message.

Methods

Name	Returns	Description
Delete	None	Deletes the `Attachment` object.
IsSameAs (*AttObject2*)	Boolean	`True` if the `Attachment` object is the same as *AttObject2*.
ReadFromFile (*FileName*)	None	Loads the contents of an attachment from a file or OLE docfile source.
WriteToFile (*FileName*)	None	Saves the attachment to a file or OLE docfile in the file system. Note this overwrites any previous contents of the file without warning.

Properties

Name	Returns	Description
Application	String	The string 'Collaboration Data Objects'.
Class	CdoObjectClass	The class of the CDO Object. In this case, `CdoAttachment(5)`
Fields Fields (*index*) Fields (*proptag*) Fields (*name*)	Object (Field or Fields)	Returns the specified field attached to the `AddressList` object based on either *index* value (integer), *cdoPropTag* (long) or *name*. Returns `Fields` collection if no parameter is specified.
Index	Long	The index number for the `Attachment` object within its parent `Attachments` collection.
MAPIOBJECT	IUnknown	An `IUnknown` pointer to the `Attachment` object.
Name	String	The display name of the `Attachment` object
Parent	Attachments	The parent `Attachments` collection.
Position	Long	The position of the attachment within the text of the message.
Session	Session	The current CDO `Session` object.

Name	Returns	Description
Source	Variant (String or Message object)	The full path and file name, OLE class name, or unique message identifier for the attachment.
Type	CdoAttachmentType	The attachment type with one of the CdoAttachmentType constant values.

Attachments Collection

The Attachments collection object contains zero or more Attachment objects. Note that Attachments is regarded as a small collection for which the Count property is reliable.

Methods

Name	Returns	Description
Add([*Name*] [, *Position*] [, *Type*] [, *Source*])	Attachment	Creates and returns a new Attachment object in the Attachments collection. Allows you to specify a display *name*, *position* in message, *type* and *source* for the attachment.
Delete()	None	Deletes all the attachments in the Attachments collection.

Properties

Name	Returns	Description
Application	String	The string 'Collaboration Data Objects'.
Class	CdoObjectClass	The class of the CDO Object. In this case, CdoAttachments(18)
Count	Long	The exact number of Attachment objects in the collection.
Item(*index*) Item(*recordKey*)	Attachment	Returns either Attachment number *index* from the collection or the first Attachment whose MAPI *recordKey* matches that one given as a parameter.
Parent	Message	The parent Message object.
Session	Session	The current CDO Session object.

Field Object

A `Field` object represents a MAPI property that is defined on a CDO object. A full list of MAPI properties can be found in Appendix B under the heading `CdoPropTags`.

Methods

Name	Returns	Description
Delete()	None	Deletes the user-defined or optional `Field` object from the `Fields` collection.
ReadFromFile (*FileName*)	None	Loads the value of a string or binary field from a file.
WriteToFile (*FileName*)	None	Saves the field value to a file in the file system.

Properties

Name	Returns	Description
Application	String	The string 'Collaboration Data Objects'.
Class	CdoObjectClass	The class of the CDO Object. In this case, `CdoField(6)`
ID	Long	The long integer value corresponding to the MAPI property value. See the CdoPropTag section of Appendix B for a complete list.
Index	Long	The index of the current `Field` object in the `Fields` collection.
Name Name(*PropsetID*)	String	The name of the current `Field` object.
Parent	Fields	The parent `Fields` collection.
Session	Session	The current CDO `Session`.
Type	Integer	The type of the value stored in the current `Field` object. (vbArray, vbBoolean, vbLong. etc)
Value	Variant	The value of the `Field` object.

Fields Collection

The Fields collection object contains zero or more Field objects. Note that Fields is regarded as a small collection for which the Count property is reliable.

Methods

Name	Returns	Description

Add (*Name,*
    Type
[, *Value*]
[, *PropsetID*])
 	
Add (*PropTag,*
    value)
	Field	Creates and returns a new Field object in the Fields collection. For a custom field, you must specify its *name* and the *type* of value it holds. Optionally, you can also give it a *value* and specify the *property set* it belongs to. For predefined MAPI properties, you must specify the *property tag* and its new *value*.

Delete()	None	Deletes all user-defined and optional fields in the Fields collection object.
SetNamespace (*PropsetID*)	None	Selects the property set that is to be used for accessing named properties in the Fields collection.

Properties

Name	Returns	Description
Application	String	The string 'Collaboration Data Objects'.
Class	CdoObjectClass	The class of the CDO Object. In this case, CdoFields (19)
Count	Long	The exact number of Field objects in the collection.
Item (*index*) Item (*Proptag*) Item (*name* [, *PropsetID*])	Field	Returns a single Field from the collection based on its *index* number, the MAPI *property tag* it has a value for, or its custom *name* and *property set* if necessary.
Parent	Object	This collection's immediate parent.
Session	Session	The current CDO Session.

Folder Object

The Folder object represents a folder or container within the MAPI system. As in client programs, a Folder object can contain other folders and messages.

Methods

Name	Returns	Description
CopyTo (*folderID* [, *storeID*] [, *name*] [, *copySubfolders*])	Folder	Makes and returns a copy of the Folder object at another folder hierarchy location (and InfoStore if need be). You can also specify a new name for the copy of the folder and whether or not to copy its subfolders.
Delete()	None	Deletes the Folder object from its parent Folders collection or InfoStore object.
IsSameAs (*FolObject2*)	Boolean	True if the Attachment object is the same as *FolObject2*.
MoveTo (*folderID* [, *storied*])	Folder	Relocates the Folder object to another folder hierarchy location.
Update([*makePermanent*] [, *refreshObject*])	None	The Update method saves changes to the Folder object. Update takes two boolean parameters. *makePermanent* commits all changes to the object and *refreshObject* loses all changes not yet made permanent. The default call is Update(*True, False*)

Properties

Name	Returns	Description
Application	String	The string 'Collaboration Data Objects'.
Class	CdoObjectClass	The class of the CDO Object. In this case, CdoFolder(2)
FolderID	String	The unique ID of this object's parent folder.
Folders	Folders	The Folders collection of subfolders in the current folder.
HiddenMessages	Messages	A collection of hidden messages in the current folder.
ID	String	The unique identifier of the current folder.
MAPIOBJECT	IUnknown	An IUnknown pointer to the current folder.
Messages	Messages	A collection of messages in the current folder.

Name	Returns	Description
Name	String	The name of the current folder.
Parent	Folders	The parent Folders collection.
Session	Session	The current CDO Session.
StoreID	String	The ID of the parent information store.

Folders Collection

This object represents a **large** collection of Folder objects.

Methods

Name	Returns	Description
Add (*Name*)	Folder	Creates and returns a new Folder object in the Folders collection.
Delete()	None	Deletes all the folders in the Folders collection.
GetFirst()	Folder	Returns the first Folder object in this Folders collection or Nothing there is no folder in the collection.
GetLast()	Folder	Returns the last Folder object in the Folders collection or Nothing if there is no folder in the collection.
GetNext()	Folder	Returns the next Folder object in the Folders collection or Nothing if no next object exists, for example if already positioned at the end of the collection.
GetPrevious()	Folder	Returns the previous Folder object in the Folders collection or Nothing if no previous object exists, for example if already positioned at the beginning of the collection.
Sort([*SortOrder*] [, *PropTag*]) Sort([*SortOrder*] [, *name*])	None	The Sort method sorts the address entries in the collection on the specified property – either a named *CdoPropTag* constant or a tag *name* – according to the specified *sort order* (a constant of type CdoSortOrder). The default order is ascending if none is given. If no proptag or name is specified, a repeat is made of the last sort performed.

Properties

Name	Returns	Description
Application	String	The string 'Collaboration Data Objects'.
Class	CdoObjectClass	The class of the CDO Object. In this case, CdoFolders(15)
Count	Long	The number of Folder objects in this collection or if this is not possible, returns &H7FFFFFFF.
Parent	Folder	The Parent Folder object.
RAWTABLE	IUnknown	An IUnknown pointer to current folder table.
Session	Session	The current CDO Session object.

GroupHeader Object

The GroupHeader object represents the header for a group of messages within a table view. This group has been brought into existence by defining which categories messages should be grouped by.

Properties

Name	Returns	Description
Application	String	The string 'Collaboration Data Objects'.
Class	CdoObjectClass	The class of the CDO Object. In this case, CdoGroupHeader(25)
Count	Long	The number of messages in the group or if this is not possible, returns &H7FFFFFFF.
Level	Long	The indentation level of the group header within the table view. Takes a value between 1 and 4.
Name	String	The display name for the grouping of message objects. Generally describes the category.
Unread	Long	The number of unread messages in the group or if this is not possible, returns &H7FFFFFFF.
Parent	Messages	The Parent Messages collection.
Session	Session	The current CDO Session object.

InfoStore Object

The `InfoStore` object provides access to the folder hierarchy of a message store.

Methods

Name	Returns	Description
IsSameAs (*ISObject2*)	Boolean	`True` if the `InfoStore` object is the same as *ISObject2*.

Properties

Name	Returns	Description
Application	String	The string 'Collaboration Data Objects'.
Class	CdoObjectClass	The class of the CDO Object. In this case, `CdoInfoStore(1)`
Fields Fields (*index*) Fields (*proptag*) Fields (*name*)	Object (Field or Fields)	Returns the specified field attached to the `InfoStore` object based on either *index* value (integer), *cdoPropTag* (long) or *name*. Returns the `Fields` collection if no parameter is specified.
ID	String	The unique identifier of the current store.
MAPIOBJECT	IUnknown	An IUnknown pointer to the current store.
Name	String	The display name of the current store.
ProviderName	String	The name of the `InfoStore`'s message store provider.
RootFolder	Folder	The root of the IPM subtree for the `InfoStore` object.
Parent	InfoStores	The Parent `InfoStores` collection.
Session	Session	The current CDO `Session` object.

InfoStores Collection

The `Infostores` collection object contains zero or more `Infostore` objects. Note that `Infostores` is regarded as a small collection for which the `Count` property is reliable. This object has no methods.

Properties

Name	Returns	Description
Application	String	The string 'Collaboration Data Objects'.
Class	CdoObjectClass	The class of the CDO Object. In this case, `CdoInfoStores(14)`

Table Continued on Following Page

Name	Returns	Description
Count	Long	Returns the exact number of InfoStore objects in the collection.
Item(*Index*) Item(*StoreName*)	InfoStore	Returns an InfoStore object from the collection specified either by *index* or by its *name*.
Parent	Session	The current CDO Session object.
Session	Session	The current CDO Session object.

MeetingItem Object

The MeetingItem object represents a meeting in a folder. It has all properties and most methods defined in the Messages object. Only the properties and methods unique to the MeetingItem object are listed here. It also inherits all the properties and some of the methods (CopyTo, Delete, Forward, IsSameAs, MoveTo, Options, Reply, ReplyAll, Send and Update) defined in the Message object.

Methods

Name	Returns	Description
GetAssociated Appointment()	AppointmentItem	Returns the AppointmentItem object associated with this meeting.
Respond(*RespType*)	MeetingItem	Returns a MeetingItem object for responding to this meeting request.

Properties

Name	Returns	Description
Class	CdoObjectClass	The class of the CDO Object. In this case, CdoMeetingItem(27)
MeetingType	String	The type of this meeting item with one of the CdoMeetingType constant values.

Message Object

The Message object represents a single message, item, document, or form in a folder.

Methods

Name	Returns	Description
CopyTo (*folderID* [, *storeID*])	Message	Makes and returns a copy of the Message object in another folder, located in a different InfoStore if needed.

Name	Returns	Description
Delete (*DeletedItems*)	None	Deletes the Message object. Boolean parameter determines whether object is moved to the Deleted Items folder or deleted permanently.
Forward()	Message	Returns a new Message object with which to forward the current Message object.
IsSameAs (*MsgObject2*)	Boolean	True if the Attachment object is the same as *MsgObject2*.
MoveTo (*folderID* [, *storeID*])	Message	Moves the Message object to another folder (in a different InfoStore if necessary).
Options ([*parentWindow*])	None	Displays a modal dialog box where the user can change the submission options for a message.
Reply()	Message	Returns a new Message object that can be used to reply to the sender of the current message.
ReplyAll()	Message	Returns a new Message object that that can be used to reply to the sender and all recipients of the current message.
Send ([*saveCopy*] [, *showDialog*] [, *parentWindow*])	None	Sends the message to the recipients through the messaging system.
Update ([*makePermanent*] [, *refreshObject*])	None	Saves the message in the messaging system.

Properties

Name	Returns	Description
Application	String	The string 'Collaboration Data Objects'.
Attachments Attachments (*index*)	Object (Attachments or Attachment)	Either Attachment object number *index* or the entire Attachments collection for the message if *index* is not specified.
Categories	String Array	An array of the categories (up to 4) assigned to the message.
Conversation	Do not use	**The Conversation property is obsolete**. Use the ConversationIndex and ConversationTopic properties instead.

Table Continued on Following Page

Name	Returns	Description
ConversationIndex	String	Specifies the message's index number in the conversation thread.
ConversationTopic	String	Specifies the subject of the conversation thread of the message.
Class	CdoObjectClass	The class of the CDO Object. In this case, CdoMsg(3)
DeliveryReceipt	Boolean	True if a user requires an acknowledgement of the message being delivered.
Encrypted	Boolean	True if a message has been encrypted or encryption has been requested for this message.
Fields Fields (*index*) Fields (*proptag*) Fields (*name*)	Object (Field or)Fields	Returns the specified field attached to the Message object based on either *index* value (integer), *cdoPropTag* (long) or *name*. Returns all fields if no parameter is specified.
FolderID	String	The unique identifier of the Folder containing the message.
ID	String	The unique identifier of the current message.
Importance	CdoImportance	The importance of the message as CdoNormal (the default), CdoLow, or CdoHigh.
MAPIOBJECT	IUnknown	An IUnknown pointer to the current message.
Parent	Messages	The Messages collection containing this Message.
ReadReceipt	Boolean	True if a user requires an acknowledgement of the message being read.
Recipients Recipients (*index*)	Recipients	Returns one or all of the recipients to receive this Message object.
Sender	AddressEntry	Returns the sender of a message as an AddressEntry.
Sensitivity	CdoSensitivity	The sensitivity of the message. Takes one of the CdoSensitivity constants.
Sent	Boolean	True if the message has been sent through the messaging system.

Name	Returns	Description
Session	Session	The current CDO Session.
Signed	Boolean	True if the message has been tagged with a digital signature.
Size	Long	The approximate size in bytes of the message.
StoreID	String	The ID for the InfoStore holding the Message object.
Subject	String	The subject of the message.
Submitted	Boolean	True when the message has been submitted.
Text	String	The text of the message.
TimeCreated	Variant (vbDate)	The date/time the message was first saved.
TimeExpired	Variant (vbDate)	The date/time the message will expire.
TimeCreated	Variant (vbDate)	The date/time the message was first saved.
TimeLastModified	Variant (vbDate)	The date/time the message was most recently saved.
TimeReceived	Variant (vbDate)	The date/time the message was received.
TimeSent	Variant (vbDate)	The date/time the message was sent.
Type	String	The message class for the message.
Unread	Boolean	True if the message has not been read by the current user.

MessageFilter Object

Represents the criteria used to search for specific Message objects in a Messages collection.

Methods

Name	Returns	Description
IsSameAs (*MsgFObject2*)	Boolean	True if the MessageFilter object is the same as *MsgFObject2*.

Properties

Name	Returns	Description
Application	String	The string 'Collaboration Data Objects'.
Class	CdoObjectClass	The class of the CDO Object. In this case, CdoMessageFilter(10)

Name	Returns	Description
Conversation	String	Sets a filter to match only messages with the conversation topic given.
Fields Fields (*index*) Fields (*proptag*) Fields (*name*)	Object (Field or Fields)	Returns the specified field attached to the Message object based on either *index* value (integer), *cdoPropTag* (long) or *name*. Returns all fields if no parameter is specified.
Importance	CdoImportance	Sets a filter to match only messages with the same importance value.
Not	Boolean	True if all search criteria are to be negated before being ANDed or ORed to the filter.
Or	Boolean	True if the restriction values are to be ORed instead of ANDed to search criteria.
Parent	Messages	The Messages collection holding this MessageFilter.
Recipients	Recipients	Sets a filter to match only messages with a specific Recipient object. Note this matches the *name* of the Recipient, not the address.
Sender	String	Sets a filter to match only messages with a specific sender. Note this matches the *name* of the sender, not the address.
Sent	Boolean	Sets a filter to match only messages that have been sent through the messaging system.
Session	Session	The current CDO Session object.
Size	Long	Sets a filter to match only messages that have a *greater* total size than the value given
Subject	String	Sets a filter to match only messages whose subject contains this value as a substring.
Text	String	Sets a filter to match only messages whose main text contains this value as a substring.
TimeFirst	Variant (vbDate)	Sets a filter to match only messages received at or after the specified time/date.
TimeLast	Variant(vbDate)	Sets a filter to match only messages received at or before the specified time/date.
Type	String	Sets a filter to match only messages with the same MAPI message class.
Unread	Boolean	Sets a filter to match only messages that haven't been read.

Messages Collection

This object represents a **large** collection of one or more `AppointmentItem`, `GroupHeader`, `MeetingItem`, and `Message` objects.

Methods

Name	Returns	Description
Add([*subject*] [, *text*] [, *type*] [, *importance*])	Object (AppointmentItem or Message)	Creates and returns a new `Message` or `AppointmentItem` object in the `Messages` collection. Optionally, you can specify the *subject*, body *text*, *type* and *importance* level of the message.
Delete()	None	Deletes all the objects in the `Messages` collection.
GetFirst ([*type*])	Nothing or Object (AppointmentItem, GroupHeader, MeetingItem or Message)	Returns the first object in the `Messages` collection or first object with specific `type` property (`IPM.Note`, etc) if specified. It returns `Nothing` if there is no messages in the collection.
GetLast ([*type*])	Nothing or Object (AppointmentItem, GroupHeader, MeetingItem or Message)	Returns the last object in the `Messages` collection or last object with specific `type` property (`IPM.Note`, etc) if specified. It returns `Nothing` if there is no messages in the collection.
GetNext()	Nothing or Object (AppointmentItem, GroupHeader, MeetingItem or Message)	Returns the next object in the `Messages` collection. It returns Nothing if no next object exists, for example if already positioned at the end of the collection.
GetPrevious()	Nothing or Object (AppointmentItem, GroupHeader, MeetingItem or Message)	Returns the previous object in the `Messages` collection. It returns Nothing if no previous object exists, for example if already positioned at the beginning of the collection.
Sort([*SortOrder*] [, *PropTag*]) Sort([*SortOrder*] [, *name*])	None	The `Sort` method sorts the address entries in the collection on the specified property – either a named *CdoPropTag* constant or a tag *name* – according to the specified *sort order* (a constant of type `CdoSortOrder`). The default order is ascending if none is given. If no proptag or name is specified, a repeat is made of the last sort performed.

Properties

Name	Returns	Description
Application	String	The string 'Collaboration Data Objects'.
Class	CdoObjectClass	The class of the CDO Object. In this case, CdoMessages (16)
Count	Long	The number of AppointmentItem, MeetingItem, or GroupHeader and Message objects in the collection, or if this is not possible, &H7FFFFFFF.
Filter	MessageFilter	The MessageFilter object for the Messages collection.
Item (*index*) Item (*search*)	Object (AppointmentItem, GroupHeader, MeetingItem or Message)	Returns a single object from the Messages collection identified by either its *index* in the collection or some *search* criteria.
Parent	Folder	The Folder object containing this collection.
RAWTABLE	IUnknown	An IUnknown pointer to current message table.
Session	Session	The current CDO Session object.

Recipient Object

The Recipient object represents a recipient of a message.

Methods

Name	Returns	Description
Delete()	None	Deletes the Recipient object from its parent Recipients collection.
GetFreeBusy (*StartTime, EndTime, Interval*)	String	A string indicating the free/busy status of the user for each *Interval* (in minutes) between *StartTime* and *EndTime*.
IsSameAs (*RecObject2*)	Boolean	True if the Recipient object is the same as *RecObject2*.
Resolve ([*ShowDialog*])	None	Assembles the recipient's address entry information into a full messaging address. Optionally, if ambiguities occur, *ShowDialog* can be set to true to prompt the user for clarification.

Properties

Name	Returns	Description
Address	String	The full address for the recipient.
AddressEntry	AddressEntry	The AddressEntry object representing the recipient.
AmbiguousNames	AddressEntries	The AddressEntries collection of suggestions that might resolve the ambiguity in an AddressEntry object.
Application	String	The string 'Collaboration Data Objects'.
Class	CdoObjectClass	The class of the CDO Object. In this case, CdoRecipient(4)
DisplayType	CdoDisplayType	The display type of the recipient (User, Distribution List, etc)
ID	String	The unique identifier of the current Recipient object.
Index	Long	The index number of the Recipient object within the Recipients collection.
MeetingResponse Status	CdoResponseStatus	The status of this recipient's response to a meeting request.
Name	String	The name of the Recipient object.
Parent	Recipients	The Recipients collection containing this object.
Session	Session	The current CDO Session object.
Type	CdoRecipientType	The type of the Recipient object, either To, Cc, or Bcc.

Recipients Collection

The Recipients collection object contains zero or more Recipient objects. Note that Recipents is regarded as a small collection for which the count property is reliable.

Methods

Name	Returns	Description
Add([name] [, address] [, type] [, entryID])	Recipient	Adds and returns a new Recipient object to the Recipients collection. Optionally you can specify the recipient's display name, full address, recipient type and unique ID for the corresponding AddressEntry object if appropriate.

Table Continued on Following Page

Name	Returns	Description
AddMultiple (*names* [, *type*])	None	Adds zero or more new Recipient objects in the Recipients collection as specified by a list of display *names* or addresses. You can also specify what *type* of recipient they are.
Delete()	None	Deletes all the recipients in the Recipients collection.
GetFirstUnresolved ()	Recipient	Returns the first unresolved Recipient in the collection or Nothing if there aren't any.
GetFreeBusy (*StartTime*, *EndTime*, *Interval*)	String	Returns a string indicating the combined free/busy status of all the recipients for each *Interval* (in minutes) between *StartTime* and *EndTime*.
GetNextUnresolved ()	Recipient	Returns the next unresolved Recipient in the collection or Nothing if there aren't any.
Resolve ([*ShowDialog*])	None	Assembles in turn each of the recipients' address entry information into a full messaging address. Optionally, if ambiguities occur, *ShowDialog* can be set to true to prompt the user for clarification.

Properties

Name	Returns	Description
Application	String	The string 'Collaboration Data Objects'.
Class	CdoObjectClass	The class of the CDO Object. In this case, CdoRecipients(17)
Count	Long	The exact number of Recipient objects in the collection.
Item (*Index*)	Recipient	Returns Recipient object number *index* from the collection.
RAWTABLE	IUnknown	An **IUnknown** pointer to the current Recipient table.
Parent	Message	The Message collection holding this collection.

Name	Returns	Description
Resolved	Boolean	True if all of the recipients in the collection have had their address information resolved.
Session	Session	The current CDO Session object.

RecurrencePattern Object

The RecurrencePattern object describes the recurrence pattern for an AppointmentItem object. This object has no methods.

Properties

Name	Returns	Description
Application	String	The string 'Collaboration Data Objects'.
Class	CdoObjectClass	The class of the CDO Object. In this case, CdoRecurrencePattern(28)
DayOfMonth	Long	The day of the month on which the appointment recurs.
DayOfWeekMask	Long	The mask for the days of the week on which the appointment recurs.
Duration	Long	The duration of the recurring appointment in minutes.
EndTime	Variant (vbDate)	The finish time for each recurrence of the appointment.
Instance	Long	The specific day of the month on which an appointment occurs when described as 'First Wednesday of the month'.
Interval	Long	The number of recurrence units between each appointment. See RecurrenceType property.
MonthOfYear	Long	The month of the year in which the appointment recurs.
NoEndDate	Boolean	True if the recurrence pattern has no end date.
Occurrences	Long	The number of times the appointment reoccurs.
Parent	AppointmentItem	The Parent AppointmentItem object.

Name	Returns	Description
PatternEndDate	Variant (vbDate)	The last possible date for the last appointment to occur.
PatternStartDate	Variant (vbDate)	The first possible date that the appointment may reoccur.
RecurrenceType	CdoRecurTypes	The recurrence unit and the frequency with which the appointment recurs. (Daily, Weekly, etc).
Session	Session	The current CDO Session object.
StartTime	Variant (vbDate)	The starting time for each recurrence of the appointment.

Session Object

The Session object is CDO's topmost object, offering access to a CDO application's mail and collaboration objects.

Methods

Name	Returns	Description
AddressBook ([*recipients*] [, *caption*] [, *oneAddress*] [, *forceResolution*] [, *recipLists*] [, *toLabel*] [, *ccLabel*] [, *bccLabel*] [, *parentWindow*])	Recipients	Displays the users address book in a dialog box. Addresses then selected are returned in a Recipients collection. Optionally, you can specify the *recipients* collection to add addresses to, a *caption* for the book, whether users must select *one address* at a time, whether the addresses selected must be resolved, which of the To, Cc and Bcc list boxes to display, their display labels, and finally a handle to the *parentWindow*.
CompareIDs (*ID1*, *ID2*)	Boolean	Returns True if *ID1* and *ID2* represent the same CDO object, or False if not.
CreateConversation Index ([*ParentIndex*])	String	Creates or updates a new conversation index or a child conversation index based on a parent conversation index.
DeliverNow()	None	Requests the immediate delivery of all undelivered messages submitted in the current session.
GetAddressEntry (*ID*)	AddressEntry	Returns the AddressEntry object with the ID specified.

Name	Returns	Description
GetAddressList (*ALType*)	AddressList	Returns either the default global or personal address list as specified by *ALType*.
GetArticle (*ArticleID*, *FolderID* [, *StoreID*])	Message	Returns a `Message` object with ID *ArticleID* from the folder (and infostore) as specified.
GetDefaultFolder (*Type* [, *mailbox*])	Folder	Returns the default folder of the specified *type* (from the specified *mailbox* if needed).
GetFolder (*folderID* [, *storeID*])	Folder	Returns a `Folder` object with ID *folderID* (from a certain message store if needed).
GetInfoStore (*storeID*)	InfoStore	Returns an `InfoStore` object with the given ID.
GetMessage (*messageID* [, *storeID*])	Object	Returns a `Message` object with ID *messageID* (from a certain message store if needed).
GetOption (*OptType*)	Variant	Returns the user preference for displaying the calendar.
Logoff()	None	Logs off and ends the session.
Logon ([*profileName*] [, *profilePassword*] [, *showDialog*] [, *newSession*] [, *parentWindow*] [, *NoMail*] [, *ProfileInfo*])	None	Logs on to the messaging system, optionally supplying the *profile name* and *password* to use, whether to display the Show Profile dialog box, if the application should start a new CDO session, the handle to the *parentWindow*, if mail should be disabled and the info needed to create a new profile for the session.
SetLocaleIDs (*LocaleID*, *CodePageID*)	None	Sets the Locale and Codepage IDs for the current session.
SetOption (*OptType*, *OptValue*)	None	Sets the user preference for displaying the calendar either by *name* or by *value*.

Properties

Name	Returns	Description
AddressLists AddressLists(*index*) AddressLists(*name*)	Object (AddressLists or AddressList)	Returns an AddressList as specified by its *index* in the AddressLists collection or its *name*. If neither is specified, returns the entire AddressLists collection.
Application	String	The string 'Collaboration Data Objects'.
Class	CdoObjectClass	The class of the CDO Object. In this case, CdoSession(0)
CurrentUser	AddressEntry	The AddressEntry object for the user currently using the application.
Inbox	Folder	The current user's Inbox folder.
InfoStores InfoStores (*index*) InfoStores (*name*)	InfoStores	Returns an InfoStores as specified by its *index* in the InfoStores collection or its *name*. If neither is specified, returns the entire InfoStores collection.
MAPIOBJECT	IUnknown	An IUnknown pointer to the session object.
Name	String	The display name of the profile logged on to this session.
OperatingSystem	String	The Name and version number of the current operating system.
Outbox	Folder	The current user's Outbox folder
OutOfOffice	Boolean	True if the user is currently considered out of the office.
OutOfOfficeText	String	The text of the message others receive if they send mail to this user while the user is out of the office.
Parent	Nothing	Nothing.
Session	Session	The current CDO Session object.
Version	String	The version number of CDO as a string, for example "1.2.1".

C

Resources

Outlook

Microsoft Knowledge Base articles about Outlook development, technical White Papers and Resource Kits:
http://www.microeye.com/outtech.html

CDO

A web site with many samples of CDO code and a CDO questions forum:
http://www.cdolive.com/start.htm

Downloadable CDO help file at:
http://www.microsoft.com/outlookdev/freestuff/CDOhlpdl.htm

ADO

Primary information source for ADO:
http://www.microsoft.com/data/ado/

A very good ADO FAQ web site:
http://www.able-consulting.com/ADO_Faq.htm

ADSI

Reference information about ADSI:
http://msdn.microsoft.com/library/psdk/adsi/ds2_ref_2x45.htm

General

Main reference page for all development technologies:
http://msdn.microsoft.com/default.asp

Microsoft MSDN Office developer web site:
http://msdn.microsoft.com/officedev/

Information and articles about ASP, CDO and ADSI:
http://www.asptoday.com/

Support and Errata

One of the most irritating things about any programming book is when you find that bit of code you've just spent an hour typing simply doesn't work. You check it a hundred times to see if you've set it up correctly and then you notice the spelling mistake in the variable name on the book page. Of course, you can blame the authors for not taking enough care and testing the code, the editors for not doing their job properly, or the proofreaders for not being eagle-eyed enough, but this doesn't get around the fact that mistakes do happen.

We try hard to ensure no mistakes sneak out into the real world, but we can't promise that this book is 100% error free. What we can do is offer the next best thing by providing you with immediate support and feedback from experts who have worked on the book and try to ensure that future editions eliminate these gremlins. The following section will take you step by step through the process of posting errata to our web site to get that help. The sections that follow, therefore, are:

- ❑ Wrox Developers Membership
- ❑ Finding a list of existing errata on the web site
- ❑ Adding your own errata to the existing list
- ❑ What happens to your errata once you've posted it (why doesn't it appear immediately)?

There is also a section covering how to e-mail a question for technical support. This comprises:

- ❑ What your e-mail should include
- ❑ What happens to your e-mail once it has been received by us

So that you only need view information relevant to yourself, we ask that you register as a Wrox Developer Member. This is a quick and easy process, that will save you time in the long-run. If you are already a member, just update membership to include this book.

Wrox Developer's Membership

To get your FREE Wrox Developer's Membership click on Membership in the top navigation bar of our home site – http://www.wrox.com. This is shown in the following screenshot:

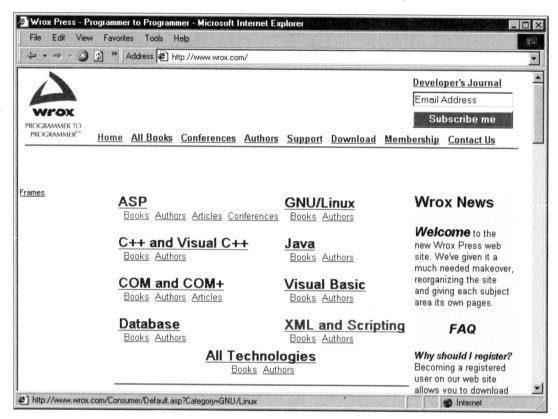

Then, on the next screen (not shown), click on **New User**. This will display a form. Fill in the details on the form and submit the details using the **Register** button at the bottom. Before you can say 'The best read books come in Wrox Red' you will get the following screen:

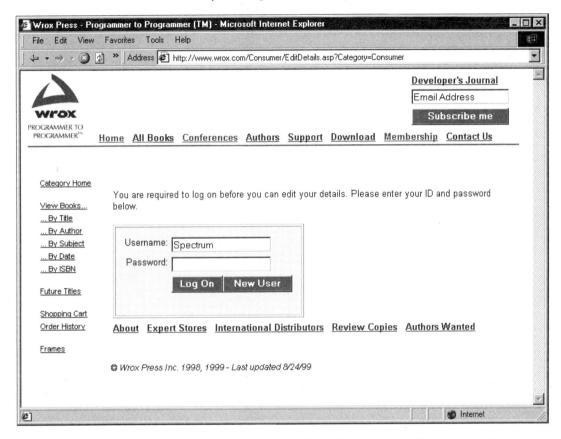

Type in your password once again and click **Log On**. The following page allows you to change your details if you need to, but now you're logged on, you have access to all the source code downloads and errata for the entire Wrox range of books.

Finding an Errata on the Web Site

Before you send in a query, you might be able to save time by finding the answer to your problem on our web site – http:\\www.wrox.com.

Each book we publish has its own page and its own errata sheet. You can get to any book's page by clicking on **Support** from the top navigation bar.

Halfway down the main support page is a drop down box called **Title Support**. Simply scroll down the list until you see **Professional JavaScript**. select it and then hit **Errata**.

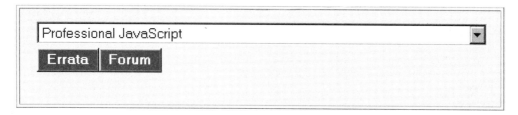

This will take you to the errata page for the book. Select the criteria by which you want to view the errata, and click the **Apply criteria** button. This will provide you with links to specific errata. For an initial search, you are advised to view the errata by page numbers. If you have looked for an error previously, then you may wish to limit your search using dates. We update these pages daily to ensure that you have the latest information on bugs and errors.

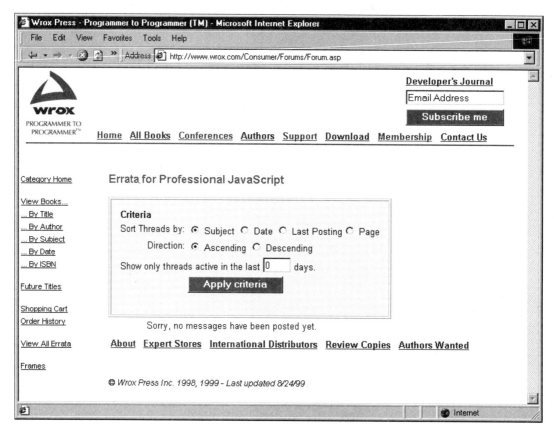

Add an Errata : E-mail Support

If you wish to point out an errata to put up on the website or directly query a problem in the book page with an expert who knows the book in detail then e-mail support@wrox.com, with the title of the book and the last four numbers of the ISBN in the subject field of the e-mail. A typical email should include the following things:

- ❏ The **name, last four digits of the ISBN** and **page number** of the problem in the Subject field.
- ❏ Your **name, contact info** and the **problem** in the body of the message.

We won't send you junk mail. We need the details to save your time and ours. If we need to replace a disk or CD we'll be able to get it to you straight away. When you send an e-mail it will go through the following chain of support:

Customer Support

Your message is delivered to one of our customer support staff who are the first people to read it. They have files on most frequently asked questions and will answer anything general immediately. They answer general questions about the book and the web site.

Editorial

Deeper queries are forwarded to the technical editor responsible for that book. They have experience with the programming language or particular product and are able to answer detailed technical questions on the subject. Once an issue has been resolved, the editor can post the errata to the web site.

The Authors

Finally, in the unlikely event that the editor can't answer your problem, s/he will forward the request to the author. We try to protect the author from any distractions from writing. However, we are quite happy to forward specific requests to them. All Wrox authors help with the support on their books. They'll mail the customer and the editor with their response, and again all readers should benefit.

What We Can't Answer

Obviously with an ever-growing range of books and an ever-changing technology base, there is an increasing volume of data requiring support. While we endeavor to answer all questions about the book, we can't answer bugs in your own programs that you've adapted from our code. So, while you might have loved the online music store in Chapter 14, don't expect too much sympathy if you cripple your company with a live adaptation you customized from Chapter 14. But do tell us if you're especially pleased with the routine you developed with our help.

How to Tell Us Exactly What You Think

We understand that errors can destroy the enjoyment of a book and can cause many wasted and frustrated hours, so we seek to minimize the distress that they can cause.

You might just wish to tell us how much you liked or loathed the book in question. Or you might have ideas about how this whole process could be improved. In which case you should e-mail feedback@wrox.com. You'll always find a sympathetic ear, no matter what the problem is. Above all you should remember that we do care about what you have to say and we will do our utmost to act upon it.

Index

Index

Index

E

X

WROX
PROGRAMMER TO PROGRAMMER™

Wrox writes books for you. Any suggestions, or ideas about how you want information given in your ideal book will be studied by our team.
Your comments are always valued at Wrox.

Free phone in USA 800-USE-WROX
Fax (312) 893 8001

UK Tel. (0121) 687 4100   Fax (0121) 687 4101

Professional Outlook 2000 Development - Registration Card

Name _____

Address _____

_____

_____

City _____ State/Region _____

Country _____ Postcode/Zip _____

E-mail _____

Occupation _____

How did you hear about this book? _____

☐ Book review (name) _____

☐ Advertisement (name) _____

☐ Recommendation _____

☐ Catalog _____

☐ Other _____

Where did you buy this book? _____

☐ Bookstore (name) _____ City _____

☐ Computer Store (name) _____

☐ Mail Order _____

☐ Other _____

What influenced you in the purchase of this book?

☐ Cover Design

☐ Contents

☐ Other (please specify) _____

How did you rate the overall contents of this book?

☐ Excellent   ☐ Good

☐ Average   ☐ Poor

What did you find most useful about this book? _____

_____

What did you find least useful about this book? _____

Please add any additional comments. _____

_____

What other subjects will you buy a computer book on soon? _____

What is the best computer book you have used this year?

_____

Note: This information will only be used to keep you updated about new Wrox Press titles and will not be used for any other purpose or passed to any other third party.

3315   *Check here if you DO NOT want to receive support for this book* ☐   3315

wrox

PROGRAMMER TO PROGRAMMER™

NB. If you post the bounce back card below in the UK, please send it to:

Wrox Press Ltd., Arden House, 1102 Warwick Road,
Acocks Green, Birmingham B27 6BH. UK.

Computer Book Publishers